Childhood and Adolescence

Childhood and Adolescence

CROSS-CULTURAL PERSPECTIVES AND APPLICATIONS

Second Edition

Uwe P. Gielen and Jaipaul L. Roopnarine, Editors

An Imprint of ABC-CLIO, LLC
Santa Barbara, California • Denver, Colorado

Library of Congress Cataloging-in-Publication Data

Names: Gielen, Uwe P. (Uwe Peter), 1940– editor. | Roopnarine, Jaipaul L., editor.
Title: Childhood and adolescence : cross-cultural perspectives and applications / Uwe P. Gielen and Jaipaul L. Roopnarine, editors.
Other titles: Childhood and adolescence (Praeger)
Description: Second edition. | Santa Barbara, California : Praeger, [2016] | Earlier edition held in conjunction with the Workshop on Childhood and Adolescence in Cross-Cultural Perspective (2000 : New York Academy of Sciences). | Includes bibliographical references and index.
Identifiers: LCCN 2015035184 | ISBN 9781440832239 (alk. paper) | ISBN 9781440832246 (ebook) | ISBN 9781440836817 (pbk. : alk. paper)
Subjects: LCSH: Child psychology—Cross-cultural studies. | Adolescent psychology—Cross-cultural studies. | Ethnopsychology.
Classification: LCC BF721 .W67 2016 | DDC 155.4—dc23
LC record available at http://lccn.loc.gov/2015035184

ISBN: 978-1-4408-3223-9
EISBN: 978-1-4408-3224-6
Paperback ISBN: 978-1-4408-3681-7

20 19 18 17 16 1 2 3 4 5

This book is also available on the World Wide Web as an eBook.
Visit www.abc-clio.com for details.

Praeger
An Imprint of ABC-CLIO, LLC

ABC-CLIO, LLC
130 Cremona Drive, P.O. Box 1911
Santa Barbara, California 93116-1911

This book is printed on acid-free paper ∞

Manufactured in the United States of America

Contents

Part V Difficult Circumstances and Adjustments

Preface

Since the 1970s there has been a rapidly growing research interest in child and adolescent development across cultures. It is the purpose of this volume to present an overview of some of the most recent and challenging work in this area. It includes the contributions of a prominent international group of psychologists and cultural anthropologists who share the conviction that a comprehensive understanding of human development requires a contextual approach in which ecological and cultural factors play a prominent role. Their contributions describe and analyze the socioemotional, sociocognitive, and behavioral development of children and adolescents in a wide variety of sociocultural settings spread throughout the world. The volume is about the lives of the more than 2.2 billion children and teenagers who, in just a few years, will grow into young women and men ready to shape the future for us all.

This volume is intended to be read by psychologists, cultural and psychological anthropologists, sociologists, psychologists counseling young people from a broad variety of cultural backgrounds, educators teaching students from numerous countries, and advanced undergraduate and graduate students interested in cross-cultural contributions to the study of childhood and adolescence. The book should be of equal interest to teachers, researchers, persons working in a variety of mental health fields, and all those who wish to know what life is like for girls and boys growing up in a wide range of economic and sociocultural settings.

Many of the chapters included in this volume are of an integrative nature, while others focus on applied issues. The contributors were asked to analyze an area of cross-cultural research falling within the purview of their expertise, while reflecting on their own research programs in the wider context of related studies conducted by other authors. Thus, the reader will gain an overview of specific cross-cultural research topics which include, for instance, worldwide changes in children's lives, cultural models of stages in human development, parent-child relationships, and family systems in areas as diverse as the Arab world, the West Indies, and Japan as well as South Korea, sibling relationships, gender roles and gender differences together with their manifold implications including violence directed at girls, adolescence in the developing majority world, growing up internationally, the adjustment of bicultural children from immigrant families, the difficult lives of street and war-traumatized children in low-income countries (LICs), and children suffering from various internalizing and externalizing disorders, all as refracted through the eyes of leading contributors to the scientific literature. In contrast, the chapters are less centered on broad disciplinary and well-known debates such as those between cultural and cross-cultural psychologists, cultural and psychological anthropologists, or anthropologists and psychologists. The volume's predominant focus is on substantive contributions in the context of medium-range theories and hypotheses rather than on arcane epistemological, theoretical, or methodological debates.

The contributors include many leading scholars who are well known for their creative work in cross-cultural developmental psychology and anthropology. Between them they have lived in and/or conducted research in just about every corner of the world. In addition, we are pleased to include chapters from several promising younger scholars whose work is bound to shape emerging trends in basic and applied cross-cultural research on children, adolescents, and emerging adults.

Throughout the book, the reader will encounter children and adolescents from diverse sociocultural backgrounds: Mayan elementary school children teaching their younger siblings the ins and outs of their culture, boys and girls soaking up the gender roles of their traditional societies in an almost osmosis-like fashion (but also beginning to question them), Chinese American boys and girls making successful school and peer adjustments but also experiencing considerable stress in their bicultural lives, teenagers in developing countries becoming increasingly savvy about the steadily spreading and changing global teenage culture, transnational children being shuttled back and forth between different societies, and child soldiers attempting to survive in a murderous world. Reading about such a diversity of lives, the reader cannot but arrive at a more global, holistic, differentiated, down-to-earth, and culturally informed conception of human development than may be found in mainstream textbooks.

Preparing this volume has been a pleasure because so many people supported our efforts. Amy Chen, Laudia Joseph, Luke Kluisza, and others contributed their considerable typing, proofreading, and computer skills while helping to prepare the book manuscript. Richard Relkin reviewed several chapters and made excellent suggestions for improving them. St. Francis College, through the Institute for International and Cross-Cultural Psychology, provided much-appreciated institutional support. And above all, we as editors would like to extend our sincere thanks to each of the authors without whose contributions this volume would not exist.

We also express appreciation to the University Seminars at Columbia University for assistance in the preparation of the manuscript for publication. Material drawn from this work was presented to the University Seminar on Moral Education.

We dedicate this globally oriented book to the children of this world.

Uwe P. Gielen and Jaipaul L. Roopnarine
St. Francis College, Syracuse University

Introduction

Uwe P. Gielen

> In Brazil childhood is a privilege of the rich and practically nonexistent for the poor.
>
> D. M. Goldstein, 1998

> I am those 66 million girls who are out of school.
>
> Malala Yousafzai, 2014

The systematic cross-cultural study of childhood and adolescence is a relatively recent endeavor, sponsored by two originally rather reluctant parents, namely developmental psychology and cultural anthropology. During the first 90 years of its existence, from about 1880–1970, developmental psychologists showed only limited interest in the systematic cross-cultural study of human development. Instead, they attempted to delineate what they claimed were universal trajectories of development as well as a variety of general mechanisms of learning and information processing. The overwhelming majority of their research studies were conducted in the United States, Canada, and Europe, with a few studies from non-Western cultures thrown in to make the intellectual meal appear a bit more spicy and exotic. Culture as a crucial shaping influence on development was largely overlooked. Cultural and social anthropologists, in turn, spent their time attempting to understand a wide variety of mostly non-Western cultures. As part of their efforts, they were eager to grasp the "natives' point of view," but employed adults rather than children as informants because it seemed obvious to them that adults were better informed about their own culture than children. Over the years anthropologists collected a considerable amount of information on children in nonindustrial societies (Grove & Lancy, this volume); however, this information was available in scattered form only until very recently. Neither developmental psychologists nor anthropologists saw human development as a transformative process in which sociocultural forces constantly interact with biological and psychological forces to create a rich diversity of "biopsychosociocultural" entities.

The scarcity of systematic cross-cultural research on children and adolescents came under critical scrutiny in the 1980s and 1990s when public opinion in the United States and Western Europe began to be swayed by multiculturalism, and at the same time, the forces of globalization were making themselves felt in a pervasive manner. This led an increasing number of social scientists to conceptualize diverse developmental trajectories for minority group members, immigrants, and representatives of the mainstream culture. Others began to pay increasing attention to the development of children and adolescents in non-Western societies, including postindustrial countries such as Japan as well as many countries located in the developing or "majority" world. In addition, numerous social scientists in the non-Western world have begun to study human development as it takes place in their own cultures, finding that Western approaches and research results can at times be quite misleading. As a result, some of them increasingly favor indigenous, more emically oriented theoretical frameworks, methods, and research goals.

In the face of ever-accelerating global change, the developmental scenarios proposed by the early founders of the field of developmental psychology such as Preyer, Freud, Gesell, Hall, Piaget, and others now appear too static, too homogeneous, too Euro-American, too middle-class, too male, and too monocultural. In response to these developments, a variety of research projects on culturally diverse groups of children and adolescents have been initiated, with some of them being widely regarded as constituting the cutting edge of research on socioemotional development. This volume takes stock of some of these innovative research efforts and hopes to provide the reader with a map for related future endeavors.

In addition to the academicians, a broad variety of action-oriented international organizations have sprung up in recent decades that aim to improve the lives of children. Of special importance in this regard is UNESCO, a United Nations Organization that publishes a yearly review of "The State of the World's Children." This publication contains essential and up-to-date global statistics about children that have been used by several authors in this volume (see, for instance, chapters 3, 4, 8, 10, 14). Moreover, two prominent advocates for children shared the 2014 Nobel Peace Prize: Kailash Satyarthi from India and Malala Yousafzai from Pakistan. Satyarthi, a 60-year-old Hindu, has for decades struggled to free child laborers from bondage so that they may have a childhood. The Pakistani teenager Yousafzai was shot in the head at age 15 by the Taliban because of her advocacy for girls' education. She somehow survived this ordeal and two years later became the youngest Nobel Prize winner in history. She received the award for "her courageous and dangerous fight for girls' right to education," a fight that will be with us for some time to come.

The message propagated not only by these two powerful advocates for children but also by many chapter authors in this volume is crystal clear: Far too many children around the world suffer because they are malnourished, are caught up in violent conflicts, are recruited or used by armed forces and groups, become refugees, suffer physical and sexual assault, endure sexual slavery, trafficking, or forced marriage, or are sold to the highest bidder who then puts them to work. Too often, children are among the primary victims as violent conflicts worsen especially in the Middle East and Africa. The three chapters contained in Part V of this volume are specifically focused on children and adolescents that live in difficult circumstances or experience some form of psychopathology. In addition, this chapter contains a concluding section briefly describing 10 organizations dedicated to improving the lives of families and children especially in the LICs.

CONTRIBUTIONS

It is the purpose of the present volume to present an overview of selected areas of research in the field of cross-cultural human development together with specific examples of such research. The chapters have been prepared by some of the main contributors to the scientific literature in the belief that productive researchers are best able to convey to the reader the intellectual background, purposes, scope, intricacies, and main findings of their own ongoing research projects. The volume is divided into an introduction, five sections, an epilogue, and a concluding section. Each of the five sections contains several chapters revolving around related questions, topics, and issues of concern. At the same time, the respective authors have adopted a broad variety of theoretical perspectives and methodological approaches. Taken together, these represent much of the richness, complexity, and intellectual fervor and tensions of the newly emerging field that at its core favors a much more contextual approach than can be found in mainstream developmental psychology.

Part I: Worldwide Perspectives on Childhood and Adolescence

The first part of the book contains four broadly conceived chapters that set the stage for the contributions to follow.

How did the cross-cultural study of human development evolve, and what are some of the main assumptions that have guided the field in recent years? These two questions are posed by *Uwe P. Gielen* in his chapter, "The Cross-Cultural Study of Human Development: A Skeptical Yet Optimistic Historical Introduction." The author points out that the field has traditionally adopted a double identity: On the one hand, cross-cultural comparisons have been used to test the general validity of leading developmental theories such as those proposed by G. Stanley Hall, Jean Piaget, Lev S. Vygotsky, Lawrence Kohlberg, John Bowlby, Erik H. Erikson, and Ronald Rohner. On the other hand, cross-cultural developmental psychology has evolved into a field with its very own problems and methodological concerns revolving around the study of the cultural nature of behavior and the evolving mind. Gielen reviews the history of the field by focusing on some early and highly speculative evolutionary theorizing, Margaret Mead's contrasting emphasis on cultural relativism, the lasting legacies left by the contributions of Piaget, Kohlberg, and Vygotsky, the comparative studies of John and Beatrice Whiting as well as their students, the return of neo-evolutionary approaches including those proposed by John Bowlby and his student Mary D. S. Ainsworth, and the recent rise of more layered, contextual, culturally aware, and multidisciplinary approaches that attempt to explain the complex lives led by children in an increasingly multicultural and continuously changing world.

Guided by a synthetic approach, Gielen then introduces 10 assumptions that can be said to structure modern cross-cultural inquiries into the nature of human development. These assumptions favor the multidisciplinary study of socioemotional and cognitive development with the help of a whole array of methodologies mostly created by psychologists and anthropologists. These two fields, in turn, have favored rather different ways of studying human development across cultures.

Gielen concludes that only a combination of anthropological and psychological approaches, together with additional contributions from fields such as demography, sociology, and biology, can create a comprehensive, balanced, and valid picture of human development in all its complexities around the world. In contrast to this project, mainstream developmental psychology is said to remain in many ways myopic and ethnocentric.

For many years psychologists have proposed that children and adults are expected to go through a variety of cognitive and socioemotional stages. Many of these stage theories rely predominantly on research evidence collected in Western and other postmodern societies where children live in small families, go to school for many years, experience a prolonged adolescence, and assume full adult responsibilities only in their mid-to-late 20s—or even later. By way of contrast, *M. Annette Grove* and *David F. Lancy*, in their chapter entitled "Cultural Models of Stages in Child Development," introduce an anthropologically and globally oriented approach to the comparative study of life cycle changes in childhood and adolescence.

Based on David Lancy's unique collection of close to 1,000 ethnographies and anthropologically oriented articles, the authors propose a sequence of six life stages that can be found in traditional foraging societies, among nomadic pastoralists, and in traditional, village-based horticultural and agricultural societies. The stages trace a person's trajectory through life beginning with the "birth and external womb" phase, and proceeding to the young child's "social birth" when he or she joins the community, to be followed by a "stage of separation" and weaning, a stage of "getting noticed" and assuming more responsibilities, to a highly variable adolescent phase, named "youth in limbo," and finally to the "adulthood" stage when a person settles down, marries, has children, and is involved in mature activities contributing to the survival of society. Driven by functional requirements as well as biological, cognitive, and social processes of maturation and development, these stages are said to be universal in character throughout history and across a rich diversity of sociocultural conditions.

In the following chapter entitled, "The Changing Lives of 2.2 Billion Children: Global Demographic Trends and Economic Disparities," *Uwe P. Gielen* provides us with an overview of the world's children below the age of 18 by examining worldwide economic and demographic trends. His analysis points to striking differences in children's environments between the poorer and the richer countries as manifested by divergent fertility and mortality data, rapid declines in family size, changing gender roles, the emergence of prolonged schooling, a period of extended adolescence and "emerging adulthood" in the wealthier nations, and the contrasting importance of child labor in the poor countries. After analyzing pertinent information about 10 representative nations located around the globe, the author introduces us to 20 worldwide trends that, in his opinion, will continue to shape global childrearing conditions in the foreseeable future. Throughout his chapter he stresses the pervasive and long-term impact of material conditions on children's well-being and life chances, in contrast to more "culturologically" oriented approaches that emphasize the importance of different cultural belief systems. The thrust of his chapter is to discuss some central aspects of children's lives rather than to arrive at a theory designed to trace children's development through a series of stages.

In their chapter, "Literacy Development: Global Research and Policy Perspectives," *Daniel A. Wagner* and his graduate students, *Fatima Tuz Zahra* and *Jinsol Lee* present a broad overview of literacy acquisition. Whereas in the past, literacy was often transmitted in families and religious institutions, today the development and maintenance of a nationwide schooling system is the universal ambition of nations located around the world.

For 91% of all younger children in today's world, going to school and achieving literacy constitutes a central task. Whereas in industrialized countries, formal schooling is almost universal and begins around the age of 6, in the low-income and developing nations the acquisition of literacy may also take place in adolescence and even adulthood. Moreover, close to one billion youths remain illiterate to various degrees, living largely in the poorer nations.

Wagner et al. review the past and present contexts of literacy; discuss various controversies revolving around the question of how best to define literacy; outline global policies and policy debates centering on literacy learning in children, youth, and adults; survey the literature on literacy acquisition from a developmental point of view; and examine questions of literacy instruction for various age groups. Throughout their chapter, the authors emphasize the practical and policy-oriented aspects of research on learning and literacy acquisition. Especially in the LICs, an increasing number of children are now going to school although many of them fail to become literate because of overcrowding in the schools, lack of school books, poorly trained and paid teachers, and so on. In the modern world, being literate is a must for everybody, and those youngsters kept out of school for economic, political, or gender related reasons will see their chances for a satisfactory future life sharply diminished. It should be added that the drive to increase global literacy levels—as described by Wagner and his team—will be central to the globally oriented set of ambitious goals that the United Nations (including UNESCO) have recently accepted (Fall 2015). Moreover, these goals are expected to guide many efforts by the United Nations for the next 15 years.

Taken together, the four chapters contained in Part I paint a broad picture of some of the main theoretical approaches, substantive and methodological assumptions, worldwide findings, and selected applications that can be found in historical and modern cross-cultural research on childhood and adolescence. The interplay between material conditions, culture, and human development is examined from a variety of perspectives, most of which emphasize a socio-ecological framework for the study of children's concrete circumstances together with their socioemotional and identity development, family interactions, peer relationships, educational adjustment, and successes and failures in the light of sometimes very difficult social and environmental circumstances. Because worldwide data on children have become increasingly available and because systematic cross-cultural research has multiplied in recent years, it is now becoming possible for the first time in history to sketch a globally constructed and reasonably realistic picture of how children and adolescents develop, learn, adjust, thrive, and suffer in their increasingly multicultural environments.

Part II: Childcare, Parenting, and Family Systems

The three contributions to Part II are united by a shared focus on childcare and parent-child relationships. These are investigated within the context of specific empirical studies conducted by the respective chapter authors as well as other researchers in three important but geographically and culturally quite diverse areas that represent a broad variety of cultural and ecological settings. Indeed, the center of attention in this section shifts from an initial focus on children and parents in the Arab world to a consideration of families residing in English-speaking Caribbean countries and in Caribbean immigrant communities in North America, to an overview of family life and childcare in the post-Confucian societies of South Korea and Japan.

Are there any similarities in the way perceived interpersonal behavior exerts its influence on children and adolescents' personality dispositions across a wide variety of societies? Yes, says Ronald Rohner, whose theory on the psychological effects of interpersonal and parental acceptance and rejection has by now been widely tested and validated across the globe including in the Arab world. In their chapter "Interpersonal Acceptance and Rejection in the Arab World: How Do They Influence Children's Development?", *Ramadan A. Ahmed, Ronald P. Rohner, Abdul Khaleque*, and *Uwe P. Gielen* summarize the results of more than 120 empirical studies that have used Rohner's theoretical approach as well as his measures in countries such as Bahrain, Egypt, Kuwait, Lebanon, Qatar, Saudi Arabia, Sudan, and Yemen. Because most of these studies have been written up in Arabic either in the form of dissertations and master's theses or else as articles in Arab journals, they remain largely unknown to psychologists outside the Middle East. Indeed, Western psychologists frequently underestimate the amount of empirical work that has already been done in the non-Western world because they cannot read non-Western languages, do not have ready access to the widely scattered scientific literature, or simply don't care about becoming familiar with it (Draguns, 2001).

Taken together the research results provide strong support for Rohner's Interpersonal Acceptance-Rejection Theory as well as his measures: Arab children of various ages who feel accepted rather than rejected or neglected by their parents (and others) are consistently more likely to report higher levels of self-esteem and self-acceptance, scholastic achievement, altruistic behavior, reflectivity rather than impulsivity, social responsibility, achievement of a stable identity, and other positive personality traits. Moreover, they feel less anxious, lonely, and depressed, experience fewer hostile impulses, and engage in fewer delinquent actions. The authors suggest that given the consistency of the results reported, the time has arrived for Arab psychologists and others to guide the public about how to best raise and educate children while improving overall levels of mental health among Arab children, adolescents, and ultimately, adults. In this way, Arab psychologists should be able to make a long-term contribution to the private and public welfare of more than 340 million people living in an often strife-torn world. This would indeed be a worthwhile ambition!

In their chapter entitled "Family Structure and Socialization Patterns in Caribbean and Caribbean Immigrant Families: Developmental Outcomes," *Jaipaul L. Roopnarine* and *Elif Dede Yildirim* focus on family structures, socialization patterns, and their developmental impact on children in English-speaking Caribbean families living at home or in the United States and Canada. The families include mostly African Caribbean families, Indo Caribbean families, and those of mixed ethnic backgrounds. Because in past years, colonialism, slavery, and indentureship had severely disrupted the long-term stability of far too many families, modern Caribbean mating and family systems continue to include more or less stable visiting unions, common law families, married families, single-parent families, blended families, sibling families, and so on. At the same time the prevailing gender roles exhibit many traditional aspects. Although parents frequently exhibit considerable warmth toward their children, they also punish them physically and attempt to exert tight control over them. This pattern tends to continue when Caribbean families migrate to North America. Indeed the conclusions of Roopnarine and Yildirim's chapter are relevant to two sections in this volume: the section on childcare, parenting, and families and the later section focusing on immigrant and transnational children.

The authors review a variety of parent-child relationships and adjustment patterns together with parental childrearing styles and patterns of parental support for their children's education. In this context, one may ask whether there exists a mismatch between the rather strict and authoritarian, homework-oriented childrearing styles favored by so many Caribbean immigrant parents and the more liberal, child-centered approaches favored by most American and Canadian primary school teachers and developmental psychologists.

During the past few decades, a considerable number of empirical studies have explored the nature of family life, child care and parental childrearing styles, the role of grandparents, gender roles, schooling systems, and other institutional and sociocultural conditions shaping the lives of children in post-Confucian societies such as Taiwan, Hong Kong, China, Japan, South Korea, and Singapore. These studies can be of special theoretical interest because they allow us to assess the effects of modernization on societies whose cultural past has been quite different from that of the postmodern societies located in North America and Europe. Tracing such effects enables us to explore the question whether the overall impact of economically driven modernization processes on family life and child development tends to outweigh the impact of the historically quite pronounced cultural differences between the "collectivistic" East and the "individualistic" West.

Jung-Hwan Hyun, Jun Nakazawa, David W. Shwalb, and *Barbara J. Shwalb*'s chapter, "Parents and Childcare in South Korean and Japanese Families," explores some recent demographic, sociocultural, educational, and psychological changes as they impact the nature of family life and childcare in these post-Confucian societies. The authors observe that in both societies the respective family roles of fathers, mothers, and grandparents have evolved in rather similar ways. Given that modern women marry later than their mothers and grandmothers did, have far fewer children, are better educated, and have been joining the labor force in large numbers, Korean and Japanese fathers are now increasingly expected to participate in childcare and housework—yet a good many of them are dubious about their skills in these areas. Furthermore, many mothers find it difficult to arrive at a satisfactory balance between work and family life. They often look to their own parents to play an important role in raising their grandchildren. The children, in turn, are worked to their bones by the highly competitive educational systems. Moreover, the men in particular are expected by companies to work long hours. It is therefore no surprise that basic tensions exist between the conflicting demands of the profit-driven and highly competitive private sector, the many time-consuming family tasks that mothers and increasingly fathers are expected to fulfill, and the recent pressures on institutions and governments to create more family-friendly communities and work places so that fertility rates will not sink even further in these rapidly aging societies.

The tensions and society-wide problems that Hyun et al. describe can, in various permutations, also be found in Western societies, although some societies such as those in Norway and Denmark have been more successful in establishing family-friendly policies than South Korea, Japan or, for that matter, the United States. The Big Message here is: In those societies where economic competition is relentlessly emphasized, family life tends to take a backseat to the needs of the workplace. In consequence, gender roles change, fewer children are conceived, the average family size declines, immigration from abroad increases, and the societies age rapidly. These factors have already led to a population decrease in some societies. What a contrast to the poor but highly fertile and rapidly expanding societies that predominate in much of sub-Saharan Africa and South Asia!

Part III: Three Themes in Children's Lives: Gender Roles, Siblings, and Becoming an Adolescent

The contributions to Part III of the book revolve around three fundamental themes in children's lives: the significance of gender roles for children and adolescents, the importance of sibling relationships, and the arrival of puberty and with it, adolescence. In all known societies, children are socialized into different gender roles that, in turn, shape their identity and opportunities throughout the life cycle. Furthermore, in traditional societies at least, the large majority of children grow up together with siblings with whom they are expected to maintain lifelong bonds and alliances. In addition, some form of adolescence can be found in a broad variety of societies, although the nature and length of this developmental period varies considerably across the globe.

Together with her former mentor and coworker, John E. Williams, *Deborah L. Best* has been known for her worldwide investigations of gender-linked stereotypes and self-perceptions (e.g., Williams & Best, 1990a, 1990b). It does not come as a surprise, therefore, that in the wide-ranging chapter by Deborah L. Best and her coauthor, *Caitlin D. Bush* on "Gender Roles in Childhood and Adolescence," the authors arrive at the conclusion that pancultural similarities in sex and gender greatly outweigh the cultural differences that are found. This conclusion stands in stark contrast to Margaret

Mead's earlier claims that gender roles and gender differences can vary dramatically across cultures.

Best and Bush review a variety of prominent perspectives structuring the worldwide study of gender roles and gender differences. Some of these emphasize biological aspects beginning with the fact that in all human societies modal sex differences in physical characteristics can be found. Other approaches concern themselves with the "psycho-socio-cultural" aspects of gender such as gender identity, gender roles, gender-role ideology, gender stereotypes, and gender differences. In addition, the authors discuss cross-cultural socialization practices regarding girls and boys, cultural practices that influence the behavior of females and males, sociocultural change in gender roles, and so on. These topics are the special foci of Best and Bush's wide-ranging chapter.

A variety of theories have been advanced to explain the ubiquitous presence of gender roles and gender differences around the world as well as cross-cultural variations in gender-linked cultural practices. These include various versions of evolutionary theory, social role theory, social learning theory, cognitive stage theories, and gender schema theories. As is so often the case in psychology, each of these theories is able to account for some of the findings contained in the cross-cultural literature, but no single theory can provide a convincing and comprehensive account of all the findings.

In her chapter entitled "Sibling Interactions," the cultural psychologist *Ashley E. Maynard* emphasizes that the study of sibling relationships in non-Western cultures has added to our understanding of the role that siblings play as guides for each other in internalizing cultural practices. Frequently, they provide critical social support and help to shape the social and emotional development, cognitive development, language socialization, and play activities of their brothers and sisters. In her account, Maynard emphasizes the usefulness of the ecocultural approach that sees childrearing and development as a cultural project in the context of a society's surrounding ecology.

A considerable number of studies have suggested that siblings may play an important role in the younger child's understanding and sociocognitive appropriation of the adult world. In play, for instance, and guided by their siblings, young children frequently reproduce selected features of the adult world and anticipate some of their future roles in that world. Many socially useful skills and behaviors such as social perspective taking, linguistic and listening skills, understanding and sympathizing with others' emotional states, taking care of others, and understanding complex, hierarchically ordered social roles inside and outside the family are promoted in the context of sibling interactions.

In many societies of the past and the present—but not in the postmodern societies—large families have been and continue to be the norm. In sub-Saharan Africa, for instance, popular pronatalist ideologies emphasize that large numbers of children are a blessing, since they will contribute to a family's economic strength, political power, and spiritual continuity across generations. In such societies, older siblings play an essential role in the upbringing of children and adolescents. While the parents are involved in economic and other activities to ensure the survival of the family, children especially young girls are expected to care for their younger siblings, socialize them, and guide them on their developmental path toward becoming a responsible member of society.

In the following chapter, *Katelyn E. Poelker* and *Judith L. Gibbons* present a broadly conceived synthesis of research on "Adolescents in the Majority World." These adolescents experience different economic and sociocultural circumstances depending on their country of residence, gender, rural versus urban home, access to or lack of formal schooling, family responsibilities, and so on. Whereas in many traditional societies—and especially so in the case of poor and uneducated girls—adolescence used to constitute a brief intermediary period between childhood and adulthood, in modern "information societies" this period has grown in length and frequently merges almost imperceptibly into a diffuse new stage of life, "emerging adulthood."

A central focus of the chapter concerns the adolescents' daily activities, their well-being, and their social relations with family members, peers, and friends. Compared to their peers in the industrialized world, adolescents in the developing world are especially likely to fulfill family responsibilities such as performing household chores and caring for siblings. At the same time, they are less likely to receive a secondary level school education—if any education at all. This is especially true for girls who are likely to be socialized into a way of life that makes the early assumption of family responsibilities and hard work the norm. Given this situation, it is not surprising that adolescents in the poorer nations receive lower scores on scales of psychological well-being than their counterparts in more affluent countries. They are, however, more likely to develop a sense of shared identity and interconnectedness with their immediate social world in contrast to that sense of independence and individuality so highly regarded in much of the West. In addition, as children develop into adolescents and then young adults, their life perspectives are bound to become more future-oriented. This certainly holds true for youths in the developing nations who must choose from a very limited—and limiting—array of economic and social alternatives.

However, during the past 30 years, rapid technological, economic, social, and cultural changes have reached even the most remote geographic areas. In response, a global teenage culture is now attracting youngsters living in nations or areas as distant from each other as Papua New Guinea, Egypt, and Chile. This teenage culture is important because youth worldwide must increasingly prepare themselves for a future in which rapid sociocultural change will be the norm rather than the exception.

Part IV: Transnational and Immigrant Children

The three contributions included in Part IV focus on the psychosocial and linguistic adaptation and acculturation of immigrant, Third Culture, and transnational children and adolescents in a variety of multicultural societies. In this context and for convenience sake, a distinction may be drawn between the respective concerns of "multicultural psychology" and "cross-cultural psychology." Multicultural psychology is interested in group differences of a predominantly domestic nature. Questions of bicultural identity, majority-minority relationships, identity politics, political struggles for power, and the integration of immigrants into mainstream society are typical issues raised by multicultural psychologists. In contrast, cross-cultural psychologists frequently wish to compare the nature of psychological processes between members of different cultural groups and nations located around the world. However, the study of transnational and immigrant children is ideally suited to unite the divergent research interests and political concerns of these two groups of social scientists. Moreover, international migration is forcing an increasing number of individuals to struggle with the question of how best to reconcile multiple and potentially competing cultural identities. Psychologically speaking, this is a difficult task, but it nevertheless can prepare the youths to deal more effectively with the complexities of the modern world. In contrast, those nostalgic—and at times resentful—natives who prefer to live in the more isolated and restricted monocultural worlds of yesterday will likely be left behind by the sweeping forces of globalization.

Today, people are increasingly migrating across national borders and from continent to continent. In mid-2013, the United Nations Population Division (UNPD) counted 231.5 million persons around the world whom they designated as "immigrant stock." These included settlers, refugees and asylum seekers, professionals working overseas, contract workers, and unauthorized workers, all of whom live permanently or at least for considerable periods of time outside their country of birth. In addition, there are those "Third Culture Kids" that the American language teacher *Gene H. Bell-Villada* discusses in his chapter, "Growing Up Internationally, and How It Shapes a Child." These are children who spend significant portions of their childhood years overseas but who subsequently return to their passport countries where a good number of them will regard themselves as outsiders in their own country. Most Third Culture Kids grow up and go to school abroad because their parents work abroad as missionaries, diplomats, soldiers, international educators, at multinational companies, or perhaps at one of the many nongovernmental organizations. Still other children—sometimes called transnational children—are forced by various family circumstances to shuttle back and forth between their country of origin and their immigration country.

In his chapter, Bell-Villada uses his own multinational childhood as a biracial *gringo* in Puerto Rico, Havana, and Caracas to demonstrate that growing up as a "Third Culture Kid" or global nomad can be confusing and may isolate the child from his or her later surroundings once the child—or later on as a young adult—returns to his or her passport country. Much of his chapter focuses on the positive and negative psychological meanings and the impact that the experience of being a global nomad tends to exert on the lives of the boys and girls growing up in this fashion.

During the past few decades, the Canadian psychologist *John W. Berry* has developed an influential theory stating that different immigrants tend to endorse one of four immigration strategies that he calls, respectively: assimilation, integration, marginalization, and separation. He and his distinguished Dutch colleague, *Paul Vedder* discuss these strategies and their psychosocial and societal consequences in their chapter, "Adaptation of Immigrant Children, Adolescents, and Their Families." The authors suggest that under most circumstances a strategy of "integration" is optimally suited not only for the successful adaptation of immigrants but also because it can serve as a guideline for forging successful multicultural societies. Integration refers here to a situation where immigrants are interested in maintaining their original heritage while at the same time interacting positively with other groups in the new society. In contrast, an attitude of assimilation emphasizes that the immigrant wants above all to fit into the new society while downplaying the importance of his or her original cultural heritage. The alternative strategy of separation attempts to minimize meaningful interactions with other groups while at the same time, the individual is attempting to hold on to his or her original culture. Finally, marginalized individuals are said to be those who are interested neither in maintaining their old culture nor in having sustained relations with other cultural groups. This strategy tends to isolate those who pursue it and is frequently accompanied by poor psychosocial adjustment. In their chapter, Berry and Vedder analyze the positive and negative impacts of these four acculturation strategies both at the individual and societal levels while underlining the psychosocial and ethical strengths of truly multicultural societies such as Canada. The theory may also help us understand better why some societies such as France experience problems in integrating Muslim immigrants from North Africa and elsewhere.

In recent decades, New York City has grown into the largest "Chinese city" outside of Asia. In their chapter entitled "Chinese American Adolescents and Emerging Adults in New York City: Striving for a Place in the

Sun," *Jennifer Ho* and *Uwe P. Gielen* report the results of a psychosocial study of young first- and second-generation immigrants of Han (i.e., ethnic Chinese) descent who have spent much or all of their lives in the Big Apple. Unlike many second-generation Chinese immigrants living in the country's wealthier suburbs, Chinatown's immigrant families are frequently led by working-class parents who lead modest lives, work very long hours, and speak little or no English. Economically, culturally, and linguistically most of these parents continue to live in a predominantly Chinese world, but at the same time they fervently hope that their children will succeed in climbing the steep ladder of educational success, with the long-term goal of joining America's mainstream society as successful accountants, lawyers, businessmen, teachers, professors, or medical doctors.

Based on detailed interviews and autobiographical essays, Ho and Gielen explore the family relationships, self-conceptions, gender roles, and educational and professional aspirations of immigrant adolescents. Many of them must struggle with serious issues related to poverty, linguistic handicaps, cultural and psychosocial tensions between the Chinese world of their demanding parents and the more individualistic American world of their high schools and colleges, as well as the ensuing difficulties that occur when they are trying to establish an integrated bicultural identity. Too often, the ironic outcome of such struggles is that while the student is highly successful in educational terms, she also experiences feelings of social anxiety and depression together with episodes of self-doubt. This research finding holds true above all for Chinese American girls who tend to be more educationally successful but also more emotionally troubled than the boys. The boys, in turn, are more likely to drop out of college and perhaps become a disappointment both to themselves and to their parents.

The three contributions contained in this part demonstrate the complexity of the study of children and adolescents from immigrant and transnational backgrounds. Many factors influence the children's identity development, school performance, and psychosocial and cultural adjustment including: age of arrival in the new country, linguistic proficiency, adaptation to new school environments, family factors, the interaction between one's family and the larger society, the response of the host society to immigrant families and their children, the cultural distance between the original society and the new society. Given that global rates of migration have increased in recent years, it is imperative that the sociocultural context of immigrant and transitional children be investigated, not only in the United States but also from a comparative and worldwide point of view. To the culturally aware psychologist, such studies can exert a special kind of fascination because they repeatedly remind him or her just how intricately intertwined psychosocial, cultural, societal, and biological processes really are.

Part V: Difficult Circumstances and Adjustments

In many parts of the world, a large number of children are forced to live in difficult circumstances detrimental to their physical well-being and mental health. The circumstances include being surrounded by civil war, being subjected to extreme poverty, malnutrition, excessive labor, destructive family circumstances including having to endure severe physical punishment, being forced into prostitution, sexual trafficking (especially of young girls), being orphaned through disease and wars, and living in the streets. Indeed, UNICEF has declared 2014 a devastating year for children, with as many as 15 million children being caught up in violent conflicts especially in the Middle East and Africa (UNICEF, December 8, 2014).

In their chapter "Violence against Girls," *Janet A. Sigal, Carrol S. Perrino, Florence L. Denmark, Emily A.A. Dow, Renata Strashnaya, Talia Zarbiv,* and *Felicia Wright* examine several forms of globally or regionally prevalent forms of violence against girls including protracted physical punishment and abuse, child marriages, sexual abuse and sexual trafficking, and crimes such as honor killings. Inspired by Bronfenbrenner's bioecological model as well as related contextual and systems-oriented approaches, the chapter authors review the literature and conclude that culturally sensitive approaches are especially important in areas such as child abuse that cannot always be easily distinguished from culturally normative forms of corporal punishment. They also point out that whereas the United Nations Convention on the Rights of the Child defines a child as anyone less than 18 years old, it has been a common practice throughout the ages to pressure or force girls well below that age to get married. Today, child marriages remain common in many of the poorer regions of Africa and South Asia, a cultural practice that can lead to much physical and mental suffering for these very young wives and mothers.

Even more serious than child marriages are the many cases of international and internal sex trafficking and, especially in the Middle East, the custom of honor killings of young females which are carried out because of actual or merely perceived "misconduct," being the victim of rape, or refusing to marry a much older but economically successful man. Because the honor killings are frequently hushed up it is impossible to find reliable statistical estimates of their prevalence. In addition, the spread of globalization has facilitated the rise of international criminal organizations that derive huge profits from the sexual trafficking of young girls. In their chapter, Sigal et al. analyze these and other global patterns of violence directed against girls and then review selected interventions that appear to have been successful in mitigating several gender-specific forms of violence.

In their chapter, "Cultural Nuances and Other Particulars That Impact Street Children and War-Traumatized Adolescents," *Lewis Aptekar* and

Lisa Oliver introduce us to a provocative review of the pertinent research literature. Indeed, some of the findings analyzed by them may come as a surprise to the reader. A study of street children in Guatemala and Colombia, for instance, concluded that male street children were often better off than their siblings who remained at home. However, there are far fewer girls on the streets than boys, and they tend to have difficult relationships with their families of origin, whereas their male counterparts often do not.

In the first part of their review, Aptekar and Oliver discuss developmental and gender differences among street children, differences between street children living in the developing and the developed world, children and adolescents traumatized by war, and differences between war-traumatized boys and girls. Subsequently, the authors shift their focus to those problems that arise when researchers are collecting data about street children and war-traumatized adolescents. Additional topics discussed by them include difficulties in supplying mental health services to such children and the frequent necessity of having to make excruciating moral choices when working with them. Aptekar and Oliver's chapter is bound to challenge some preconceived notions we, as readers, might have about the nature and situation of street and war-traumatized children and adolescents. At the same time, their chapter includes vivid examples that will stay in the attentive reader's mind for a long time.

Cross-cultural psychologists and, even more so, cultural anthropologists frequently emphasize differences in cultural meanings and behavior patterns—after all, if these did not exist, cross-cultural researchers would be out of a job! In contrast to this pattern, *Thomas M. Achenbach*, in his chapter entitled "Developmental Psychopathology: Multicultural Challenges, Findings, and Applications," focuses on a variety of cross-culturally *similar* psychopathological syndromes. Children around the world share a variety of "internalizing" problems such as being withdrawn, presenting with various somatic complaints, being anxious and depressed, experiencing severe self-doubts, suffering from phobias. Others—and especially boys—are more likely to exhibit "externalizing" symptoms such as staying away from school, being involved in a variety of delinquent behaviors, displaying a variety of aggressive behaviors, and/or finding it difficult to focus their attention.

Achenbach's "Empirically Based Paradigm for Assessment and Taxonomy" has generated assessment instruments that have already been translated into 61 languages (and counting), and it has inspired more than 4,000 published studies. A broad variety of developmental assessment instruments is now available for completion by parents, teachers, caregivers, direct observers, psychometricians, clinical interviewers, and the children themselves. Cross-culturally similar syndromes appear when these instruments are factor analyzed. In his chapter, the author introduces some examples of such instruments and subsequently reviews a number of representative cross-cultural findings based on them. For instance, longitudinal studies spanning recent decades have shown that American children suffer increasingly from some of the problems delineated earlier, whereas Dutch children showed only small increases in the same time frame. It appears that some small European nations such as Denmark, Norway, Switzerland, and the Netherlands are more successful than the United States in creating benign sociocultural environments for their nation's children. One reason for this cross-cultural difference is that about 20% of all American children grow up in poverty, whereas in the aforementioned countries this holds true for only about 6%–8% of all children.

Achenbach's approach suggests that children's psychopathology can be assessed in reliable and valid ways in a great diversity of cultural settings. Not surprisingly, this paradigm has already been found useful for a variety of practical purposes such as epidemiological research, longitudinal studies, training mental health workers, evaluating treatment outcomes, and assessing immigrants and refugees in numerous cultures. At the same time, the author's research center is now in the possession of an incomparable databank that enables researchers to compare the results of new studies against a vast array of already available cross-cultural data on children's and adults' psychopathology.

Epilogue

One of the most experienced cross-cultural human development authors and researchers is *Harry W. Gardiner* (Gardiner & Kosmitzki, 2011) who has participated in the creation of developmental cross-cultural psychology since its beginnings in the early 1970s. In his concluding epilogue, "Cross-Cultural Human Development: Following the Yellow Brick Road in Search of New Approaches for the 21st Century," he comments briefly on the origins of research on cross-cultural development, points to its relationships with other social sciences, summarizes some present trends in the field, and considers its possible future.

He emphasizes the advantages of an ecocultural, thoroughly contextual, and interdisciplinary approach, and suggests that the time has come to "give cross-cultural psychology and anthropology away" by applying it to pressing social policy issues. Surely, this is an appropriate conclusion for the many contributions contained in this volume emphasizing throughout that the cross-cultural study of human development has coalesced into a vital field of scientific study incorporating important suggestions and implications for improving the lives of children and adolescents around the globe. Not only does it represent an inherently fascinating field of study but, within a few decades, this branch of knowledge has grown into an interdisciplinary field that, by focusing on children, adolescents, and soon-to-be adults, can help us comprehend some important aspects of humanity's troubled march toward the future.

POSTLUDE: IMPROVING LIVES AROUND THE WORLD

In recent decades, innovative efforts by organizations and individuals have helped save and improve the lives of millions around the world. Relatively small amounts of money can make a powerful difference in the lives of children, women, and men who struggle against diseases, for economic survival, and for the chance to be educated against great odds. For example, if you send a donation to *The Smile Train*, an operation can be performed to remove a disfiguring cleft lip and palate on a little child's face; your contribution will change the life for that child forever! Alternatively, you can go to *Kiva's* website and select someone for a microloan, thereby helping a poor person—not rarely a single woman with children—gain some economic independence. And then there is the *SOS Children's Village* organization, which is active on five continents and has improved the lives of innumerable children including refugees and orphans.

Under "Suggested Readings," you will find the reference for Nicholas D. Kristof and Sheryl WuDunn's important book, *A Path Appears: Transforming Lives, Creating Opportunities,* which you may want to read. Also listed is the website for idealist.org, which contains information about internships and jobs in not-for-profit organizations.

In addition, you will see the web addresses of 10 organizations that have dedicated themselves to improving the lives of those in need, and moreover have a good track record in doing so. You do not need to command the resources of a Bill Gates to make a meaningful difference in the lives of others—even small amounts of money can have an important impact on the life of a child in countries such as Bangladesh, Ethiopia, Haiti, Mali, Nepal, or other impoverished and developing nations. Finally, you may wish to keep in mind an important research finding: People who are generous and give to others are actually happier than those miserly souls that prefer to keep their resources entirely to themselves (Aknin et al., 2013). This finding holds true in rich and poor countries alike: Being supportive of others improves people's well-being in a broad range of circumstances and cultural settings.

FOUNDATIONS

UNICEF (http://unicef.org). UNICEF is mandated by the UN General Assembly to advocate for the protection of children's rights, help meet their basic needs, and expand their opportunities to reach their full potential.

SOS Children's Village (http://www.sos-childrensvillages.org/). SOS Children's Village, an organization active in 134 countries, is focused on building families for children in need and helping them to develop their futures and their communities.

The Smile Train (http://www.cmiletrain.org/site/PageServer). The Smile Train is focused on solving a single problem: cleft lip and palate. In many of the developing countries, millions of children are suffering with unrepaired clefts.

Half the Sky Foundation (http://www.halfthesky.org/). Thousands of children are enrolled in Half the Sky's five programs that provide care and hope for children living in China's orphanages. For the children, many of whom will never be adopted, these programs are the closest thing they will ever receive to the love and support of a birth family.

Doctors without Borders (http://doctorswithoutborders.org/). This international medical humanitarian organization provides aid in some 60 countries to people whose survival is threatened by violence, neglect, or catastrophes. It supports the work of medical volunteers many of whom elect to work in difficult and dangerous conditions.

Grameen Bank (http://www.grameen-info.org/). This bank provides credit to the poorest of the poor in rural Bangladesh, without any collateral. It uses credit as a cost-effective weapon to fight poverty.

Heifer International (http://www.heifer.org/). The simple idea of giving families a source of food rather than short-term relief caught on and has continued for over 60 years. Families in 130 countries have been given the gifts of self-reliance and hope.

Kiva (http://www.kiva.org). Kiva is the world's first person-to-person micro-lending website, empowering individuals to lend to unique entrepreneurs around the globe. You can choose someone to lend to, thereby supporting economic independence for the person and helping his or her family and community.

Oxfam (http://www.oxfam.org/). Working with more than 3,000 local partner organizations, Oxfam helps people living in poverty to assert their dignity as full citizens and take full control of their lives.

The Global Fund to Fight AIDS, Tuberculosis, and Malaria (http://www.theglobalgund.org). This international financing institution invests the world's money to save lives. To date, it has committed billions of dollars in 140 countries to support large-scale prevention, treatment and care programs against the three diseases that endanger the lives of children and their guardians.

SUGGESTED READINGS

Books and Articles

Gardiner, H.W., & Kosmitzki, C. (2011). *Lives across cultures: Cross-cultural human development* (5th ed.). Boston, MA: Allyn & Bacon. (An easy-to-read and cross-culturally informed summary of what psychologists know about the human life cycle.)

Kristof, N.D., & WuDunn, S. (2014). *A path appears: Transforming lives, creating opportunity.* New York: Knopf. (A Pulitzer Prize–winning couple with extensive overseas experience tells the reader how to make the world a better place for children—and for everybody else. The book provides good websites for those who want to get involved.)

UNICEF. (Nov. 2014). *The state of the world's children: Reimagine the future: Innovation for every child.* New York: UNICEF. (Every year UNICEF publishes this important survey which contains updated, worldwide demographic data as well as a different special focus for each year. The volume can be bought or downloaded from the web.)

Websites

Idealist.org: Looking to improve the world? For internships, volunteer opportunities, jobs in not-for-profit organizations, go to: http:///www.idealist.org.

United Nations General Assembly (1989). *Convention on the Rights of the Child.* http://www.ohchr.org/EN/ProfessionalInterest/Pages/CRC.aspx. (This United Nations Convention is the first international, legally binding, and comprehensive legal document protecting the rights of children. It was adopted in 1989 and as of 2015, it has been ratified by all states represented in the UN except for the new country of South Sudan and the United States. The reader is invited to ask: Why does the United States not wish to ratify this important convention?)

REFERENCES

Aknin, L. B., Barrington-Leigh, C. P., Dunn, E. W., Helliwell, J. F., Burns, J., Biswas-Diener, R., . . . Norton, M. I. (2013). Prosocial spending and well-being: Cross-cultural evidence for a psychological universal. *Journal of Personality and Social Psychology, 104*(4), 635–652.

Draguns, J. G. (2001). Toward a truly international psychology: Beyond English only. *American Psychologist, 56,* 1019–1030.

Gardiner, H. W., & Kosmitzki, C. (2011). *Lives across cultures: Cross-cultural human development* (5th ed.). Boston, MA: Allyn & Bacon.

UNICEF (8 December 2014). *Press release: With 15 million children caught up in major conflicts, UNICEF declares 2014 a devastating year for children.* Downloaded on December 9, 2014, from http://www.unicef.org/media/media_78058.html?p=printme.

Williams, J. E., & Best, D. L. (1990a). *Measuring sex stereotypes: A multi-nation study.* Newbury Park, CA: Sage Publications.

Williams, J. E., & Best, D. L. (1990b). *Sex and psyche: Gender and self viewed cross-culturally.* Newbury Park, CA: Sage Publications.

Part I

WORLDWIDE PERSPECTIVES ON CHILDHOOD AND ADOLESCENCE

1

The Cross-Cultural Study of Human Development: A Skeptical Yet Optimistic Historical Introduction

Uwe P. Gielen

Our new global society requires a new global science of human development.

Pema ("Lotus Blossom") is an 11-year-old girl living in Stok Village, located high up in the Western Himalayas in the Indian district of Ladakh. It is the year 1992, and like most inhabitants of the village, her family follows the tenets of Tibetan Buddhism, which give significance and meaning to their lives. The family includes herself, her younger brother, her mother, her "older father" and "younger father" (two brothers married to the same wife), as well as her paternal grandparents. The family is poor and owns a few small fields planted with barley together with some goats, sheep, and *dzo* (the offspring of a yak and a cow). While Pema loves skipping down to the small village school in the morning, on some days her parents tell her that she must instead guard some of the family's animals that are grazing in the meadows glittering in the sunshine high above the village. She feels lonely up there in the mountains and at times scared, too, although she otherwise lives in a very peaceful society. Pema feels that her parents care deeply for her, but family survival comes first, and so she remains separated from her classmates on too many days. While only limited psychological and anthropological research has been carried out on children in Ladakh, the few existing studies do suggest that Pema is likely to grow up into a mild-mannered and caring young woman (Gielen, 2001; Norberg-Hodge & Russel, 1994).

At the same time, however, Ladakh's society has been changing steadily during the past few decades, with many local students now attending colleges and universities in faraway Delhi. Indeed, Ladakh has come under the influence of economic, political, military, religious, social, and cultural forces emanating both from the big cities in India and abroad. As in other areas of the world, these influences are having both a positive and a negative impact on the identity concerns of adolescents and emerging adults who until the 1970s and 1980s would have lived in a much more isolated, culturally unique, and relatively cohesive society. Fraternal polyandry, for instance, is disappearing fast. Consequently, Pema's evolving outlook on life is likely to differ substantially from that of her parents; indeed, recent research evidence suggests that the many ongoing changes in Ladakh are contributing to a rise in psychopathology among the young people (Ozer, 2012). Exposed to Indian and foreign media images as well as Western tourists pursuing a visibly more opulent life style, Ladakh's adolescents may experience disturbing feelings of "relative deprivation" when they reflect on the modest lives they and their families lead especially in the rural areas (cf. Jensen & Arnett, 2012). Based on their largely indirect exposure to Indian and foreign cultural influences, they are experiencing a form of "remote acculturation" (cf. Roopnarine & Yildirim, chapter 6, this volume).

Many thousands of miles away, in the middle-sized German town of Giessen, 16-year-old Holger is living together with his older brother, his mother, and his well-paid father, who has been drifting away from the family after an extended series of marital squabbles. The boy tries to isolate himself from the tensions in his home by getting lost in cyberspace, playing endless games on his computer, and fanatically following the ups and downs of his favorite soccer team, Eintracht Frankfurt. His school performance has recently taken a downward course for reasons he does not fully understand, although his godfather tries to give him good advice and protect him from the impact of his father's verbal attacks. The father fears for the future of his son, but also feels guilty because he suspects that his own behavior lies behind some of the psychological problems Holger is experiencing. Holger has a good relationship with his brother, Peter—but Peter is preoccupied with his upcoming *Abitur Prüfungen* (baccalaureate examinations), the results of which will determine which university, if any, he will be allowed to attend.

It is not too difficult for most of us to appreciate and understand Holger's family situation, his preoccupations, his inner tensions, and his ways of dealing with them. But Pema's life presents a puzzle to us: After all, we do not send 11-year-old girls up the mountains to take care of goats and sheep; we do not know families where two brothers are married to the same wife; and we are unfamiliar with the many invisible *lha* (deities, spirits) whose protective yet sometimes dangerous powers Pema and her family sense all around them. There are so many questions we might ask about her development as it unfolds within the context of her village society:

- What effects do her responsibilities have on her social, emotional, and cognitive development?
- In what ways do her parents' Buddhist beliefs influence their childrearing practices, and how do these practices in turn influence Pema's psychosocial adjustment?
- What might gender roles be like in a society that until recently practiced fraternal polyandry (Gielen, 1993)?
- Do her parents periodically remove her from school because she is a girl rather than a boy?
- Would it be sensible to ask Pema to respond to some of Kohlberg's moral dilemmas, or would they have to be reshaped completely?
- Are there any children in Ladakh who suffer from attention deficit disorders or the various other psychological problems commonly encountered in Western societies such as Germany?
- What is adolescence like in a society where some children are expected to work from an early age?
- Could it be true that there is hardly any "adolescence" at all for poor girls who marry early?
- How will the ongoing social changes in Ladakh's society influence Pema's development?
- Are the prevailing psychosocial conditions in Ladakh in any way similar to those in other parts of India, other agricultural societies, preindustrial Europe, or other Buddhist societies?
- If by accident, Pema and Holger meet (this is not impossible, since quite a few German tourists visit Ladakh each year), what would they see in each other, either in their first encounter or after a more extended series of interactions?

Cultural and psychological anthropologists have for many years asserted that humankind shares a fundamental psychic unity while simultaneously endorsing the notion of cultural relativism, with its claim that belief systems, attitudes, perceptions, feelings, and behaviors tend to differ radically from one society to the next. Following a related train of thought, a prominent team of psychological anthropologists and cultural psychologists has titled its theoretical review chapter as follows: "The Cultural Psychology of Development: One Mind, Many Mentalities" (Shweder et al., 1998). However, such seemingly contradictory statements mean little unless they are redeemed by convincing evidence demonstrating how the abstraction "one mind" can be reconciled with the more concrete evidence for "many mentalities," and how the vague idea of "psychic unity" fits together with the apparently contradictory idea of "cultural relativism." Applied to the developmental changes that Pema and Holger are undergoing, this means that psychological anthropologists would have to demonstrate that, whereas their radically different lives are unfolding in two highly divergent socioecologies, similar psychological processes and developmental principles are at work in both cases. To demonstrate such similarities and to unveil general developmental principles at work in different cultures may turn out to be the ultimate challenge for cross-cultural developmental research, rather than the much simpler demonstration that developmental trajectories vary from one cultural context to the next (for an example, see Grove & Lancy, chapter 2, this volume).

To see the lives of children and adolescents such as Pema and Holger in comparative perspective, to search for similarities and differences in their life trajectories, to understand holistically their development-in-ecological-and-sociocultural-context, to investigate how proximate and distal causes—as mediated by the nested developmental niches (Super & Harkness, 1986) within which human growth takes place—shape the unfolding of their lives, this is the complex but fascinating task cross-cultural developmental psychologists and psychological anthropologists have set for themselves. In this endeavor, they are helped by representatives from many other disciplines, including demographers who summarize human life cycles with the aid of dry but powerful statistics (e.g., see Gielen, chapter 3, this volume), sociologists who are apt to conceptualize human development as occurring within the framework of social structures, historians who inform us that in former times, Western childhood was of a quite different nature than it is now, epidemiologists who provide data useful for a better understanding of physical and psychosocial mal-developments, ethologists who emphasize adaptive, biologically based response systems, evolutionary psychologists and anthropologists who see human development from a cross-species as well as cross-cultural point of view, and so many others.

Traditionally, cross-cultural developmental psychology has adopted a double identity. On the one hand, cross-cultural comparisons represent a useful and necessary methodological tool to test the general validity of just about any developmental theory, whether it be the cognitive-developmental theories of Kohlberg and Piaget, the sociohistorical approach of Vygotsky, theories of socioemotional development such as those proposed by Freud, Erikson, and Rohner (e.g., Ahmed, Khaleque, Rohner & Gielen, chapter 5, this volume), evolutionary theories such as Bowlby's attachment theory, developmental theories of psychopathology including that depicted by Achenbach in this volume (chapter 16), or theories on gender roles such as those analyzed by Best and Bush in chapter 8. On the other hand, cross-cultural developmental psychology constitutes a field with its very own problems and questions: How does the nature of childhood change when a society modernizes (Gielen, chapter 3, this volume)? Are the major syndromes of child psychopathology similar or dissimilar around the world (Achenbach, chapter 16, this volume)? Is adolescence a universal phenomenon, or is it relative to time and place? What kinds of immigrant children and adolescents are most likely to adapt well to their new cultural environments (Berry & Vedder, chapter 12, this volume)? Why are Chinese immigrant adolescents from working-class and lower middle-class backgrounds so educationally successful in New York City (Ho & Gielen, chapter 13, this volume)? What are some of the prevalent forms of violence against girls, and why do they exist (Sigal et al., chapter 14, this volume)? What are some of the culture-specific forms of childrearing that can be found in Japan and Korea (Hyun, Nakazawa, Shwalb, & Shwalb, chapter 7, this volume)? What lives do street children in the majority (i.e., developing) world lead (Aptekar & Oliver, chapter 15, this volume)? Is it true that culture and mind make each other up? The attempts to answer these and many other questions of a related kind constitute the field of cross-cultural human development.

A BRIEF HISTORY OF CROSS-CULTURAL HUMAN DEVELOPMENT STUDIES

The cross-cultural study of human development as a recognized field of study with its own definite identity is no more than 40 years old. By 1975–1982, a critical mass of studies investigating the psychological development of children and adolescents in a variety of non-Western and Western societies had accumulated. Quite a few of these were reviewed in R.H. Munroe, R.L. Munroe, and B.B. Whiting's *Handbook of Cross-Cultural Development* (1981), the first comprehensive survey of the field. In addition, the six-volume *Handbook of Cross-Cultural Development* included a volume titled *Developmental Psychology* (1981), coedited by Triandis and Heron. Together with two brief introductory textbooks written, respectively, by Munroe and Munroe (1975) and by Werner (1979), these handbook volumes announced to the social sciences community that a comprehensive developmental psychology could not be built merely on the study of North American and European "mainstream" children and adolescents, but that instead a thorough understanding of human development in a rich diversity of socioecological conditions was needed for this purpose.

It would take at least another decade, however, before this message began to sink in, so that today, for instance, publishers systematically encourage authors of mainstream developmental psychology textbooks to include in their accounts research conducted in non-Western societies. One suspects that the main impetus for this evolution did not merely derive from developments within the field (e.g., Stevens & Gielen, 2007), but also from a growing awareness that Western societies, and together with them our students, are becoming ever more multicultural and globally oriented in character. In addition, colleagues in countries as far apart as India, Mexico, China, and Cameroon have been complaining loudly that

American children and adolescents are hardly representative of the world's children and adolescents, but that instead they merely constitute a small and in many ways unrepresentative minority (Henrich, Heine, & Norenzayan, 2010). After all, more than 85% of all children and adolescents live in the so-called developing world, and more of them live in India alone than in Western Europe and the United States combined (Gielen, chapter 3, this volume).

It may be useful in this context to recapitulate briefly how cross-cultural human development studies evolved during the 20th century (Thompson, Hogan, & Clark, 2012). In the late 19th and early 20th centuries, Darwin's evolutionary theory dominated Anglo-Saxon scientific thinking in both anthropology and psychology. Spurred by the dubious pronouncements of Social Darwinism, these immature disciplines were seduced by evolutionary considerations and a kind of rough analogical thinking to postulate close parallels between phylogenetic and ontogenetic development (Jahoda, 2000; Jahoda & Lewis, 1988/1989). While anthropologists developed evolutionary schemes tracing the development of humanity from a stage of "savagery" to the stage of "barbarism" and then on to the stage of "civilization," psychologists such as G. S. Hall claimed that in their development, children in civilized society recapitulate the evolution of humankind from its primitive protohuman origins to the complexities of contemporary English and American society (Hall, 1904). Children and adolescents in non-Western societies, in turn, were studied only occasionally. However, it was widely assumed that adolescents in many African and other "primitive" societies suffered from "arrested development"—due, perhaps, to the debilitating influence of sexual preoccupations, as well as racial differences (e.g., Kidd, 1906/1969). Ethnocentric beliefs in the moral and racial superiority of one's own society went hand in hand with unbridled speculation and a general paucity of detailed observational studies. While the more extreme forms of this approach had become discredited by the 1930s, milder versions of it have left distinct traces in the works of Freud, Jung, and Vygotsky, to cite but a few prominent psychologists still influential today.

Margaret Mead (1901–1978), the Culture and Personality School, and Cultural Relativism

While few systematic studies of children and adolescents were conducted among nonliterate people during the 1920s and 1930s, these years saw the rising influence of German American anthropologist Franz Boas (a former student of Wilhelm Wundt!), together with his students Margaret Mead and Ruth Benedict. They argued that "the growing child is systematically patterned [by his culture] in every detail, in posture as well as in gesture, in tempo as well as in speech, in his way of thinking, in his capacity to feel as well as in the forms which his feeling takes and that only by an understanding of the extent and internal relationships of any of these systems of socialization can the psychologist operate usefully with 'the Zuñi child' or 'the Arapesh child'" (Mead, 1954, p. 737). Mead's views, in particular, exerted not only an enormous influence on American anthropology and the educated American public, but she was also viewed by psychologists as the foremost expert on the "psychology of primitive children." In this context, she was invited to write survey chapters on this topic in several editions of the leading handbook of child psychology of the day (Mead, 1931, 1954). In the chapters, she saw it as her mission to convince psychologists that they must assimilate "the more recent findings of ethnologists which stress that a fully acculturated member of a living culture differs in *every respect,* and *systematically,* from members of any other culture" (Mead, 1954, p. 737, emphases by Gielen).

Mead first achieved scientific and public fame through the publication of her book *Coming of Age in Samoa* (1928). To this day, it remains one of her most frequently read but also most controversial books (Freeman, 1983). Written in a convincing literary style, she reports in it the results of her six-month investigation of 67 girls living in several villages in Western Samoa. For the first time, a professionally trained anthropologist (though still a graduate student) was systematically testing a major psychological hypothesis about the very nature of adolescence among a group of non-Western young girls, and did so for comparative purposes. Mead wished to know whether adolescence is "naturally" (i.e., mainly because of biological reasons) a period of *Sturm und Drang* ("Storm and Stress"), or whether the turmoil of adolescence results mainly from cultural influences. Both explicitly and implicitly, she was pitting culture against biology, sexual repression against sexual freedom, the power of instincts against the power of learning, competitive American society against easygoing Polynesian society, and fast-moving, modern civilization against more slowly moving, traditional village society. Based on her observations, she concluded that Samoan girls live in a casual society supporting diffuse socioemotional bonds, where premarital sexual relationships are widely accepted and sexual jealousies are uncommon. In her view, adolescence in Samoa lacked the typically Western qualities of rebelliousness, emotional conflict, restlessness, confusion, and inner and interpersonal uproar. Consequently, adolescence must be a product of culture much more than a product of biology.

Many years later, Australian anthropologist Freeman (1983) would launch a strident attack on her observations regarding Samoan society and the teenage girls living in it. In contrast to Mead, he emphasized the importance of virginity for the girls, the frequency of rape, suicides, other aggressive or self-destructive behavior especially among young men, and many other phenomena indicating that adolescence in Samoa is, and presumably was in prior decades, quite stressful. Mead, he asserted, had been misled by her inexperience, the brevity of her stay in Samoa, her limited command of the Samoan language, her credulity, and above all by her belief in the doctrine of cultural determinism to see what she expected and wanted to see.

While some of Freeman's assertions and criticisms were too sweeping, there is little doubt that Mead's observations do not constitute decisive evidence in favor of her theoretical ideas. She did, however, ask precisely the right kind of questions about how to test Hall's theory and more generally, any other developmental theory. (For recent and better-balanced assessments of the Storm and Stress theory of adolescence, see Arnett, 1999, 2012.)

While Mead and her friend Benedict were not completely consistent adherents to the doctrine of cultural relativism, they did more than anybody else to popularize it among American cultural anthropologists and the public at large. Mead, for instance, followed up her study in Samoa with studies of young children among the Manus of the Admiralty Islands north of New Guinea (Mead, 1930), claiming that contrary to Piaget's universalistic theory of cognitive development, the children displayed little if any animistic thinking. Furthermore, after having investigated sex roles and temperamental differences between the sexes among three contrasting societies in New Guinea, she concluded that "many, if not all, of the personality traits which we have called masculine or feminine are as lightly linked to sex as are the clothing, the manners, and the form of head-dress that a society at a given period assigns to either sex" (Mead, 1935/1963, p. 280). Later she would argue that her book had been misunderstood and that in it, she did not postulate a complete absence of innate sex differences in regards to temperament and personality. Many passages in her book, however, would seem to imply just that—and this is how her often feminist readers understood her.

Subsequent studies of Mead's contrasting three societies, the Arapesh, Mundugumor, and Tschambuli have led the investigators to sharply contrasting conclusions. Mead's supposedly gentle and nurturing Arapesh men, for instance, were actually involved in many homicides (Tuzin, 1977), and those supposedly emotional, fickle, gossipy, artsy, somewhat effeminate Tschambuli men were in fact "unemployed head hunters" who, contrary to Mead's description, dominated their wives (Gewertz, 1981). Some of Mead's relativistic conclusions have proven just too pat, and her interpretations of her field observations are sometimes surprisingly far off the mark. Nevertheless, her influence on American cultural anthropology and the public was enormous during her lifetime, in part because she preached what her educated and liberal followers wanted to hear.

Under the influence of Benedict and Mead, cultural relativism became the reigning doctrine of American cultural anthropology. As such, it entered into an alliance with the environmentalism that formed the center of the academically predominant learning theories of the psychologists Hull, Spence, Tolman, Guthrie, Miller, Dollard, and Skinner. Miller and Dollard (1941), for instance, claimed that it was the job of psychologists to study the *mechanisms* on which all learning is based, whereas anthropologists should investigate the culturally variable *content* that a child is expected to learn. In other words, the learning theorist can tell us *how* we learn and the cultural anthropologist *what* we learn. This statement implies that the major learning mechanisms such as classical conditioning, operant conditioning, and observational learning are universal in character, whereas the norms, values, beliefs, and behaviors children are expected to acquire are relative to their respective cultures.

The long-term result of this suggested professional division of labor was indeed ironic: American psychology soon became a monocultural enterprise paying lip service to the importance of culture while ignoring it in practice (Gielen, 1994). Miller and Dollard's suggestion had become a handy recipe for professional compartmentalization that most American psychologists were very happy to follow. This trend was strengthened in the years after World War II, when American psychologists began to see themselves as the undisputed leaders of international psychology. Most of them ignored the resurrection of psychology in central Europe, its alternative visions, and the progress that it was making elsewhere around the globe. Even today, far too few American psychologists consult foreign professional journals on a regular basis even when these journals are published in English (Arnett, 2008; Draguns, 2001). This holds true although American psychologists probably make up less than 25% of the world's more than one million psychologists (Zoma & Gielen, 2015).

In the 1970s and 1980s, the Culture and Personality school of thought began to lose influence in American academic circles for a number of reasons. Grand theories in general, and Freudian theory in particular, seemingly had not fulfilled their promise and began to be considered as premature. For instance, many representatives of the Culture and Personality school had claimed that they could discern "modal personalities" or "national characters" among the peoples they studied. But empirical data tended to show otherwise: Even in relatively small-scale societies a considerable variety of personalities could be found. Likewise, many attempts to link specific early childrearing practices such as length of breast-feeding, weaning procedures, swaddling, and strictness of toilet training to adult character structures proved inconclusive (e.g., Orlansky, 1949), although Freudian theorists had predicted just such links. Finally, psychoanalytically inclined anthropologists seemed unable to develop reliable and reasonably objective methods of measurement and interpretation. In hindsight and in spite of its achievements (Barnouw, 1985), the Culture and Personality approach must be considered a magnificent failure. The rising skepticism about the methodological adequacy of the approach, in particular, would lead John W. M. Whiting, Irvin Child, William Lambert, and Beatrice B. Whiting to adopt a much more behavioristic approach, which culminated in the Six Cultures and Adolescence in a Changing World projects.

John Whiting (1908–1999), Beatrice B. Whiting (1914–2003), and Their Innovative Research Projects

In the early 1950s, several scholars began to plan a systematic series of childrearing studies in several carefully selected societies based on a unified handbook for fieldworkers by Whiting, Child, and Lambert (1966). The handbook emphasized the importance of structured behavioral observations and interviews while the more "Freudian" and projective Child Thematic Apperception Test was only occasionally used. Six field research teams applied this approach to systematically chosen samples of mothers and 3–10-year-old children among the Gusii (Kenya), Okinawans (Japan), Mixtecan Indians (Mexico), Rajputs (India), inhabitants of Tarong (Philippines), and New Englanders (United States). A central focus of these studies comprised nine behavior systems: succorance, nurturance, self-reliance, achievement, responsibility, obedience, dominance, sociability, and aggression. The results of these studies were published and analyzed in a series of influential volumes, including those by B. B. Whiting (1963), Minturn and Lambert (1964), B. B. Whiting and J. W. M. Whiting (1975), and B. B. Whiting and Edwards (1988).

The Six Cultures project represents a major step forward in the comparative study of human development. For the first time, it became possible to compare, in a quantitative fashion, systematically structured behavioral observations of carefully selected samples of children across a number of predominantly non-Western cultures rather than engaging in ad hoc and post facto comparisons. The Whitings and their students analyzed and compared mothers' caretaking practices as well as children's age trends, gender differences, and behavior patterns among children living in different family arrangements and socioecological settings. To this day, their findings rank among the more solidly established in the comparative literature on human development. At the same time, the Whitings trained a generation of students who have made, and continue to make, numerous contributions to the field. They typically kept their respect for empirical observations and generalizations at a time when many American cultural anthropologists were becoming increasingly enthralled by the much more subjectivist, relativistic, non-quantitative, and politicized perspectives of postmodernism (d'Andrade, 2000).

Beginning in the early 1980s, Beatrice and John Whiting initiated and coordinated a project titled "Adolescence in a Changing World." The project originally included seven teams of anthropologists who, based on a shared methodological approach, returned to their field sites to investigate adolescence as part of several rapidly changing societies. Reasonably detailed reports about adolescence in five cultural groups have resulted from this effort together with a special issue of *Ethos* (Schlegel, 1995; for summaries and analyses of the results of this project, see Dasen, 2000; Whiting & Whiting, 1991; Poelker & Gibbons, chapter 10, this volume).

The joint project included studies of adolescents in an Australian Aboriginal community (Burbank, 1988), two Ijo communities in Nigeria (Hollos & Leis, 1989), a settlement of Inuits in Canada (Condon, 1988), a peri-urban Kikuyu community in Kenya (Worthman & Whiting, 1987), and a small town in Morocco (Davis & Davis, 1989). Taken together, these studies have provided us with a rich picture of the emergence of adolescence in five widely separated communities undergoing rapid social change. A broad variety of issues are discussed in the various reports. These include adolescent sexuality, mate selection, the balance between adolescent autonomy and relatedness, circumcision, gender differences, generation gaps, parental influences and control, sociocultural continuities and discontinuities, the effects of introducing modern schooling and mass media produced outside the community on the adolescents and their parents, and many other issues. Seen as a whole, the studies represented a major step forward in our understanding of the nature of adolescence in developing societies. Methodologically speaking, they suggest that striking a flexible balance between following standardized investigative procedures and providing a complex, sensitive, but less standardized ethnographic account of community practices can produce rich results (for a broad international survey of adolescence, see Arnett, 2012).

Jean Piaget's (1896–1980) Cognitive-Developmental Approach

While the Whitings were attempting to move psychological anthropology away from its excessive emphasis on poorly specified Freudian theories and interpretive methods in favor of a more objective, measurement-oriented behavioristic approach, another kind of revolution was under way in American developmental psychology. Influenced by Chomsky's devastating critique (1959) of Skinner's *Verbal Behavior* (1957), the growth of psycholinguistics, and new approaches to the study of memory, perception, and thinking, American psychology was becoming more cognitivist in nature. A crucial role in this process was played by the American psychologists' rediscovery of the works, respectively, of Swiss epistemologist Piaget (1986–1980) and Soviet psychologist and educator Vygotsky (1896–1934), both of whom had rejected behaviorism and its conditioning paradigms in favor of a more interactional view emphasizing the intricacies of mental development. An important role in this historical rediscovery process was played by the work of Lawrence Kohlberg (1927–1987), who—taking into account J. Baldwin, Cooley, and G.H. Mead's theories about the social origins of the self as a consequence of social role-taking—extended Piaget's stage model to the study of perspective- and social role-taking, moral reasoning, and gender identity development.

Piaget's central contribution to developmental psychology is his detailed model of cognitive transformations that are said to arise out of the child's active engagement with his or her environment. These transformations follow an inner developmental logic of differentiation and hierarchical integration quite different in character from the piecemeal acquisition of behavior emphasized by behavioristic learning theories.

According to cognitive-developmental theory, mental structures arise out of the interaction between the maturing organism and the physical and social environment. In this view, the structures are neither simply "wired" into the organism nor are they "hammered" into it through mechanistic learning processes or through cultural indoctrination. Rather, the growing child constructs step by step a picture of reality that reflects, simultaneously, universal properties of the world as well as emerging (Kantian) "categories of experience" such as quantity, substantiality, causality, space, time, and logical relations of inclusion, implication (Kohlberg, 1969/1984, pp. 8–18). Both Piaget and Kohlberg were cognitive constructivists although they eschewed the more extreme and relativistic assertions of social constructivism that serve as the underpinning of postmodern thinking.

Piaget had originally created his universalistic four-stage model of cognitive development without much regard for cross-cultural considerations. Influenced in part by Mead's insistence on the cultural specificity of mental functioning, he somewhat reluctantly supported in his later years the effort to test his model cross-culturally (Piaget, 1966). In spite of these inauspicious beginnings, many hundreds of studies have in recent decades been conducted in a broad range of cultures to support, or throw into doubt, the validity of his epistemological approach (for summaries of this research, see Dasen & Heron, 1981; Segall, Dasen, Berry, & Poortinga, 1999). Although cognitive development is almost certainly not as stage-like as Piaget had originally postulated, modified versions of his theory have in general survived the cross-cultural testing process fairly well: Many aspects of the first three stages of development, usually evolving in the same sequence though at varying ages, can be found in a wide range of cultures. In contrast, the last stage of formal operations is much more culturally and individually variable. At the same time, the mostly nonsocial type of intelligence assessed by Piagetian tests may not be appreciated in some nontechnological cultures.

The Baoulé of the Ivory Coast, for instance, value instead a form of social intelligence and wisdom that is not easily measured by existing psychological tests, but is somehow recognized by them (Dasen et al., 1985). In this context, one may speculate that in contrast to Baoulé society, modern industrial societies place a special emphasis on cognitive sophistication, because this emphasis helps them to reproduce themselves and thrive in the midst of a highly competitive and technologically oriented global environment. An adequate understanding of the inner logic of modern science and its ubiquitous applications demands that a person has reached Piaget's fourth stage, that of formal operations. It is also likely that advanced forms of education facilitate the kind of abstract and hypothetical thinking required by the stage of formal operations.

Lawrence Kohlberg (1927–1987): Sociomoral Reasoning Follows a Universal Trajectory

By the 1950s and early 1960s, cultural relativism had conquered American anthropology and sociology at a time when various versions of behavioristic and social learning theories predominated in American (though not in European) academic psychology. Applied to the cross-cultural study of human development, this historical evolution meant that processes of enculturation and socialization were seen as the central phenomena needing explanation. By enculturation, anthropologists such as Herskovitz (1948, pp. 39–42) meant that children and adolescents learn—often non-consciously—the values, norms, and contents of their culture and make them their own. In a related fashion, most American psychologists were convinced that through the process of socialization, children and adolescents acquire the set of values, norms, and behavior patterns that are customary and prescribed in their respective cultures and subcultures. The growing individual was believed to internalize group norms because of positive and negative sanctions by others, learning by reinforcement, imitation, and observation, and perhaps also through a more "Freudian" process of identification with authority figures such as parents and teachers. While society was seen as molding most children and adolescents into whatever shape it deems desirable, psychopaths and other deviants were considered examples of a failed socialization and enculturation process.

In contrast to these theories, Piaget and his follower Kohlberg insisted that children live in worlds of their own that differ qualitatively from those of adults. Furthermore, their theories postulate that children's worlds are repeatedly transformed in a process of cognitive growth that follows its own inherent logic of differentiation and integration rather than being structured by the learning mechanisms emphasized by behaviorists and social learning theorists. By applying this way of thinking to the process of moral reasoning development, Kohlberg (1969/1984) undermined the implicit and explicit consensus of American psychologists and anthropologists about the very nature of socialization and enculturation. He opposed both cultural relativism (i.e., the empirical claim that morality does *in fact* differ radically from society to society) and moral relativism (i.e., the normative belief that given the cultural specificity of moral norms, social scientists *should not* judge other societies by the culturally arbitrary standards of their own society). Instead, he postulated that moral reasoning everywhere follows a sequence of stages that culminates in principled forms of moral reasoning about universal problems of justice. As in Piaget's theory, the sequence of stages is said to be universal although the speed of development and the final stage of attainment may vary from society to society and from individual to individual.

Kohlberg assumes that universal categories of social experience evolve as the growing child interacts with others based on the process of social role-taking. In all societies, social interaction and communication are said to be based on the growing awareness "that the other is in some way like the self and that the other knows or is responsive to the self in a system of complementary expectations" (Kohlberg, 1969/1984, p. 9). Complementary expectations, in turn, are conceptualized through universal mental operations such as approving, blaming, assigning rights, duties, and obligations, making "should" statements, and making references to values, ideals, and norms. With increasing experience, the growing child and adolescent learns to coordinate these mental operations in an ever more differentiated and integrated fashion. This process, in turn, is assumed to give rise to developmentally ordered stages of moral reasoning whose general structures do not directly derive from cultural indoctrination, but rather from the child and adolescent's efforts to make sense out of his or her social experience. Nevertheless, culture and individual experience are both expected to shape much of the specific content of moral judgments. They also provide facilitating or constraining conditions for the developmental process.

In response to Kohlberg's theory, various critics of his theory (e.g., Dien, 1982; Gilligan, 1982; Vine, 1986) soon began to argue that Kohlberg's stages of moral reasoning, and above all the more advanced stages of principled reasoning, incorporate fundamental Western, male, and social-class biases. In the critics' view, Kohlberg's emphasis on moral autonomy as the endpoint of development reflects an ideological, male-oriented preoccupation with the modern Western themes of autonomy and individualism, thus making his theory ethnocentric and sexist in nature.

Following the rather casual publication of Kohlberg's initially collected cross-cultural data as part of a theoretical chapter in 1969, well over 150 studies have investigated whether the development of moral reasoning does indeed follow the sequence suggested by him. The studies have been conducted in a broad variety of cultures and have employed a variety of methods including his own interview method, Rest's Defining Issues Test (1986), Lind's Moralisches Urteil Test (1986), Gibbs' Sociomoral Reflection Measure for Kohlberg's initial four stages, and others. The studies have generally validated the existence and developmental properties of the preconventional (stages 1 and 2) and conventional (stages 3 and 4) levels of moral reasoning, but the cross-cultural evidence for the postconventional, principled forms of moral reasoning has been weaker (e.g., Eckensberger & Zimba, 1997; Gibbs, 2013; Gielen, 1996; Rest, Narvaez, Bebeau, & Thoma, 1999; Snarey, 1985). However, after surveying a series of studies applying the Defining Issues Test mostly to high school and university students in 14 countries, Gielen and Markoulis (2001) concluded that postconventional forms of moral reasoning are both recognized and preferred by many older East Asian students, and that postconventional forms of moral reasoning and moral autonomy were already present in the classical philosophical traditions of China, Greece, and India some 2,500 years ago. Criticizing Kohlberg's critics, they draw a clear dividing line between the notion of moral autonomy (which the studies indicate exists just as much in collectivistic societies such as Taiwan or Israeli kibbutzim as in Western individualistic societies such as the United States) and rugged individualism (which constitutes a culturally variable ideology). In addition, their survey revealed few systematic gender differences. Their conclusions are directly at variance with many of the criticisms of Kohlberg's theory noted earlier.

Although there exists considerable cross-cultural support for Kohlberg's structural stage theory (Gielen, 1996; Snarey, 1985) and it is regularly cited in developmental psychology textbooks, he has remained an outsider to much of cross-cultural psychology. This is hardly surprising, since deep down most cross-cultural researchers remain convinced that cross-cultural variations in moral norms outweigh whatever developmental similarities there might exist—if any. In contrast to this situation, Vygotsky's much more speculative and loosely argued theory has found many Western followers in recent decades.

Lev S. Vygotsky (1896–1934): A Marxist Cultural-Historical Theory of Development

There are few stories as strange in the history of Western (and especially American) psychology as the resurrection of the ideas of Vygotsky, which began in the 1960s and continues to this day. Vygotsky, who began his life in the same year as Piaget (1896) but died 46 years before him, became a significant force in Soviet psychology following his move to Moscow in 1924. There, he formed a group of talented psychologists around him, including Luria, Leontiev, Bozhovich, Zaporoshets, and others. When Stalin began to impose an increasingly orthodox Marxist-Leninist ideology in the early 1930s, he became a kind of persona non grata for some of his Marxist colleagues and died in political isolation in 1934.

Vygotsky argued that the development of all higher cognitive processes and functions is by nature social and all social development has a cognitive basis. The social basis of higher cognitive processes, in turn, is intertwined with the economic conditions and schooling systems prevailing in a given society. In this context, Vygotsky and Luria (1930/1993) developed a threefold Marxist vision bringing together phylogenetic, sociohistorical, and ontogenetic development. Internalized symbolic signs are said to mediate between environment and behavior, so that these "psychological tools" structure all higher mental processes including attention, memory, intentional behavior, self-control, developmentally appropriate learning, and so on. A fundamental part of this process is the "interiorization" of speech, which occurs in the context of social communication. According to the theory, children's development is shaped through a process of social guidance whereby parents, teachers, older siblings, and others help them accomplish new and relatively difficult actions that they will later be able to complete by themselves. Culture plays a central role in this developmental process since it provides the symbolic means by which it takes place.

Endorsing the Marxist theory of societal evolution, Vygotsky prepared and, in 1931 and 1932, his student Luria organized two psychological expeditions to Soviet Central Asia. They hoped to validate Vygotsky's hypothesis that the political-economic-educational and social-cognitive dimensions of human existence are intertwined, with educational factors providing the lead for subsequent psychological transformation. Comparing traditional, mostly illiterate Muslim peasants and agropastoralists with better-educated members of collectivistic *kolkhozes,* Luria's interviews seemed to show, for instance, that the illiterate traditionalists were unable (or merely unwilling?) to solve simple syllogisms or to engage in counter-factual thinking. However, because Vygotsky and Luria were sharply criticized in the Soviet Union for their cross-cultural and "cross-historical" interpretations of the expeditions' results, their conclusions were in the main published only in 1974 (Luria, 1974, 1976). During the 1930s, comrade Stalin determined the truth of social scientific assertions in the USSR, and those finding themselves on the wrong side of ideological debates were frequently killed or deported to *gulags* in Siberia and elsewhere.

Vygotsky's ideas have played a central role in the recent flowering of cultural psychology in the West. Western' psychologists such as Bruner, Cole (a personal student of Luria), Greenfield, Rogoff, Valsiner, van der Veer, Wertsch, and many others have appropriated and elaborated on Vygotsky's central insights by (re)introducing his paradigm into developmental psychology and by providing considerable cross-cultural evidence for notions such as zone of proximal development, guided learning, social co-construction, mediated learning, scaffolding (see, e.g., Cole, 1996; Rogoff, 1990; in addition, Maynard, chapter 9, this volume, provides examples of guided learning processes among siblings). It is not exaggerated to say that Vygotsky's sociocognitive vision of cultural learning and development has generated more excitement among modern American cultural psychologists than most other theoretical paradigms.

When American psychologists began to appropriate Vygotsky's ideas beginning in the 1960s, they conveniently shoved aside the Marxist basis of his theorizing. One could never guess from most American textbook discussions, for instance, that Marxist educator Vygotsky developed and used his notion of a zone of proximal development in order to lend support to the proclaimed goal of Soviet education: to create the new Soviet Man. Similarly, Luria's expedition to Central Asia occurred in the context of Russian-Soviet expansionism accompanied by mass starvation, mass murder, and an utterly brutal process of forcing hapless peasants and pastoralists to join collectivistic *kolkhozes*—or to starve and die (Obayan, 2013). Luria, however, convinced himself that these bloody political developments meant above all social, political, and cognitive progress (Gielen & Jeshmaridian, 2015; Luria, 1979).

The highly selective appropriation of Vygotsky's ideas by American developmental psychologists has frequently denuded them of their historical, political, and cross-cultural context. His Marxist ideas in general, and his tendency to perceive distinct parallels between historical and ontogenetic development in particular, have been widely ignored, in part because they are dubious and in part because they are incompatible with the ahistorical, individualistic ideological framework implicitly or explicitly favored by most American developmental psychologists. There hangs a fine mist of irony over this process of appropriation, since the very same psychologists have also insisted on the crucial importance of sociocultural context in one's understanding of the development of children, adolescents, and everybody else (Gardiner & Kosmitzki, 2010; see also Gardiner's concluding chapter [Epilogue] in this volume). Yet, what could be more noncontextual and politically motivated than the highly selective reception of Vygotsky's Marxist ideas among too many Western developmental psychologists?

It is instructive to compare the respective roles of Piaget, Kohlberg, and Vygotsky in the evolution of cross-cultural developmental psychology. Piaget's central image of the child was that of an autonomous small scientist who, through his or her physical and mental actions upon the physical and social world and the feedback he or she receives from it, gradually develops an increasingly complex, differentiated, structured, and integrated way of interpreting the world. Accordingly, the impact of cultural belief systems on this developmental process is just this: they are influences speeding it up or slowing it down rather than being a constituent part of it. Kohlberg added to this theory his conception of an evolving, increasingly coordinated process of social role-taking together with a co-evolving self. However, cultural belief systems played only a limited role in his account, since it represents a social rather than a cultural theory. Unlike Kohlberg, however, few cross-cultural psychologists seem to be aware that evolving processes of social role-taking, although constituting a necessary and fundamental basis of *all* human societies, cannot be reduced to the internalization of cultural norms. They do not understand that a hole yawns at the center of their theories of social development.

While cross-cultural investigations have played an important role in exploring the general validity of Piaget's and Kohlberg's theories, they have done little to redefine them in an essential way. In this sense, one may argue that many of these cross-cultural investigations exhibit a certain kind of theoretical sterility: they are icing on the cake, but not the cake itself. In comparison to these scientific endeavors, the followers of Vygotsky have introduced greater theoretical innovation and added more flesh to his theories. I suspect that this is true because of two reasons. On the one hand, culture plays a more central role in Vygotsky's theory than it does in Piaget's or Kohlberg's theories. On the other hand, Vygotsky wrote his major works in a mere 10 years, which, as a consequence, tend to be of a sketchy and preliminary nature. Consequently, in order to arrive at a more detailed picture of sociocognitive development, Vygotsky's followers have had to tease out and further develop the implications of his overall approach—a creative task that continues to engage their attention to this day.

Together, Piaget, Kohlberg, and Vygotsky helped to move American developmental psychology away from its excessive reliance on mechanistic learning theories that had created the misleading image of the newborn infant as a largely "empty organism." Instead of perceiving children as being molded, in a one-directional way, by society and its socialization agents, theorists such as Kohlberg and Bronfenbrenner (1995) view children as active co-constructors of their own development. Equipped with a specific temperament, a range of incipient competencies, evolving modules of the mind, and a repertoire of proximity-seeking behaviors, young children, according to some newer theories, actively elicit from their caretakers a variety of caretaking behaviors in tune with evolutionary demands, which are then executed according to various culturally and personally shaped scripts.

Together with the linguist Noam Chomsky, Piaget, Kohlberg, and Vygotsky, each in his own way, were descendants of the Enlightenment period. As such, they assigned in their theories primary importance to cognition, rationality, active information processing, and conscious, goal-directed behavior. This placed them in direct opposition to the irrational accounts of Freud, the learning theorists, and evolutionary social scientists. Freud, in particular, emphasized unconscious motivation and the emotions in his stark portrayal of human nature. While Freud and his followers have steadily lost ground in academic psychology because of the serious methodological shortcomings of their approach, a new family of irrational theories has emerged in the recent cross-cultural literature on human development. These are the neo-evolutionary theories, which claim that humans, like other animals, are the mostly unwitting "servants" of their genes. The genes program them to pursue inclusive fitness as the ultimate goal in life—or else face extinction in the next generation.

The Return of Evolutionary Theory and the Rise of Neo-Evolutionary Approaches

As noted previously, Darwinian theories have exerted an enormous influence on the development of Anglo-Saxon psychology, sociology, anthropology, and comparative research. At the same time, they have also evoked considerable resistance. Mead's cultural relativism, for instance, largely ignores the forces of biological evolution and differentiation. Her insistence that gender roles and gender differences derive overwhelmingly from culture rather than from biology provides a good example. It places her in direct contradiction to Darwinian and neo-Darwinian theories of sexual selection and to the extensive cross-cultural evidence on gender differences and gender roles that has accumulated after her earlier research was published (Best & Bush, chapter 8, this volume).

The resistance against evolutionary theories was in part fueled by liberal scholars' repugnance against the pronouncements of Social Darwinism, which favored conservative ideologies supporting Western imperialism, racialism, capitalist exploitation, opposition to social welfare legislation, and the general notion that the progress of humankind should not be held up by misguided compassion for the weak, the poor, those thought to be backward, and those who fall by the wayside in the struggle for survival. Social Darwinism offered far too many pseudoscientific moral rationalizations justifying why the powerful should rule and exploit the powerless, and why the big fish should be allowed to eat the little fish, preferably without the useless and "progress-inhibiting" pangs of guilt. Many American robber barons, for instance, embraced this account because it helped them to feel better about their dark deeds: not only was God (supposedly) on their side, but sociocultural evolution was as well. How wonderful!

Throughout the 20th century, however, scientific evolutionary theory progressed greatly and, in the 1960s and 1970s, began to be applied to human development in more subtle and convincing ways than it had been true before. These changes were initially fueled by important advances in evolutionary biology such as those made by Maynard Smith (1964), Hamilton (1964), Trivers (1972), Wilson (1975, 1978), and Dawkins (1976). In addition, European ethologists such as Lorenz (1981), Tinbergen (1951), and Eibl-Eibesfeldt (1989) together with more eclectic primatologists such as Goodall (1986), de Waal (2006), Boesch (2009), and Tomasello (2010) have emphasized the value of naturalistic field observations of animal and human behavior as well as the importance of cross-species comparisons for a biologically and evolutionary theory-oriented understanding of human adaptation. In addition, evolutionary psychologists such as Buss (1989, 1995) and Daly and Wilson (1988), researchers working in the area of evolutionary ecology including Konner (1982) and Blurton-Jones (1993) have shown how neo-evolutionary theory can throw light on many aspects of human development in a variety of socioecological conditions.

As a relatively early example of this new kind of evolutionary theorizing, we may cite Bowlby's (1907–1990) influential attachment theory (1982). Influenced by psychoanalytic considerations, studies pointing to the detrimental effects of infant care in some orphanages, Lorenz's demonstration of the phenomenon of "imprinting" among various birds, and Harlow's classic research (e.g., Harlow & Zimmerman, 1959) on the effects of early social deprivation on rhesus monkeys, Bowlby proposed that over the long course of human evolution, children must have evolved powerful attachment behaviors so that they would stay close to their caretakers and be protected from predators and other sources of harm. This notion meant, among other things, that we can understand behavior only by considering its "environment of adaptedness," which, in the case of humans, refers mostly to the environment they encountered during the course of many thousands of years as hunters and gatherers.

The child's attachment behaviors include all those gestures and signals serving to maintain proximity to their caretaker(s): smiling, babbling, grasping, following, sucking, crying, and so on. After an initial phase of indiscriminate responsiveness to a variety of humans, the child's attachment behaviors become increasingly focused on a particular person—most often, the baby's mother. When separated from her, the baby displays signs of separation anxiety and, in the presence of strangers, stranger anxiety.

Bowlby's theory was taken up by his research assistant, Mary D. S. Ainsworth (1927–2013), who in the early 1950s made careful naturalistic observations of attachment behaviors among young children living in several villages in the vicinity of Kampala, Uganda (Ainsworth, 1967). Furthermore, she also explored the possibility that babies may develop specific attachment styles while using the mother as a secure base from which to explore. In later studies in the United States, she developed a specific behavioral test to study children's attachment behavior, the Strange Situation (Ainsworth, Bell, & Stanton, 1971).

Bowlby's evolutionary theorizing and Ainsworth's cross-cultural and methodological explorations have stimulated a great amount of subsequent research (Cassidy & Shaver, 2010). Later cross-cultural research, for instance, has demonstrated considerable cross-cultural variation in the frequency and nature of children's attachment reactions (IJzendoorn & Kroonenburg, 1988; IJzendoorn & Sagi, 1999). These appear to result, in part, from differing ecological conditions that favor certain cultural values. These, in turn, are translated into different parental childrearing practices, which may be expected to lead to different reactions of children in the Strange Situation. In addition, the Strange Situation has different meanings in dissimilar cultures, thus making cross-cultural differences difficult to interpret.

Although Bowlby's original formulations had been more or less culture-blind (LeVine et al., 1994), evolutionary theorizing and cross-cultural research on human development can be natural allies: for several decades now, researchers inspired by evolutionary theory have conducted cross-cultural investigations of infant behavior, childrearing practices of mothers and fathers, birth spacing and weaning, parental investment in children, child abuse and infanticide, gender differences (e.g., Best & Bush, chapter 8, this volume), sexual jealousies, adolescent preferences for mates, adolescent behavior, relationships between kin, altruism, murder, and numerous other topics in a broad variety of cultures. In this context, neo-evolutionary theorists have already proposed hundreds of specific hypotheses that have been, or should be, tested cross-culturally.

Many of the investigations instigated by evolutionary theory are based on a paradigm that differs significantly from the alternative paradigms adopted by many cross-cultural developmental psychologists (Bjorklund & Pellegrini, 2002). For instance, evolutionary theorists usually take the general validity of the principles of natural selection, inclusive fitness, and so on, for granted, whereas most psychologists know only too well that their preferred paradigm is merely one among several equally plausible paradigms. While evolutionary theorists emphasize the lasting influence of distal but powerful (and frequently nonobvious) causes working themselves out over thousands of generations, psychologists tend to focus on more obvious proximate causes. It should be added that according to evolutionary theory, natural selection functions as the final, long-term arbiter of behavioral tendencies and evolved behavioral adaptations, but these functions may be fulfilled through a variety of proximate mechanisms.

Whereas many evolutionary theorists favor "hard" observational methods and data focused on concrete behaviors in their functional contexts, cross-cultural psychologists more often employ questionnaires designed to elicit culturally meaningful descriptions and self-descriptions of thoughts, feelings, and behaviors. Additionally, evolutionary theorists believe that there is a general human nature that manifests itself in all cultures and includes many selfish tendencies. From the point of view of evolutionary theory, infanticide, murder, rape, male competition for status, constantly shifting balances between agonistic and cooperative behaviors, conflicts between parents and their offspring, "politically incorrect" behavioral sex differences, and many other "evolved behaviors" may be expected to occur under certain circumstances in all societies. In contrast, cultural anthropologists and psychologists (together with their more ideologically inclined allies, the feminists and Marxists) tend to believe that humans are above all shaped by sociocultural conditions that, in principle, can be ameliorated in the service of societal progress. In the view of some evolutionary theorists (and others), however, cultural anthropologists and psychologists have tended to overlook some of the harsher aspects of life in non-Western societies because they do not wish to be accused of the mortal academic sin of ethnocentrism (Edgerton, 1992). From the point of view of neo-Darwinian theorists, many postmodern studies, in particular, intermingle fact and interpretation to such an extent that their scientific validity must remain in doubt.

Neo-evolutionary theorists have a very long way to go before they can be said to provide a comprehensive and convincing account of ontogenetic development in the context of gene-culture coevolution. Nevertheless, it seems likely to me that a successful and general future theory of cross-cultural human development will need to take into account evolutionary considerations. Such an integration of seemingly contradictory perspectives will be made easier by the fact that some of the newer evolutionary theories are increasingly paying attention to the nature of cultural transmission (e.g., Blackmore, 1999) and to interactions between ecological conditions, biological mechanisms, and cultural mechanisms. There is much room in neo-Darwinian theories of human development for behavioral plasticity together with both inter-individual and cross-cultural diversity, as long as it is understood that such diversity is ultimately grounded in past and present evolutionary adaptations to frequently shifting ecological conditions. In the encounter between evolutionary theory and culture theory, both approaches are bound to reemerge in substantially altered forms.

There is, nevertheless, something surrealistic about the recent debates surrounding neo-Darwinian theories. Just when women's fertility levels in almost all industrialized societies have declined to extremely low levels never before seen in history (Gielen, chapter 3, this volume), we are told that as humans we are genetically programmed to maximize our "inclusive fitness." It is difficult to see how the increasing number of childless and "child-poor" couples and singles practicing their modern lifestyles can be said to pursue such strategies. Instead, it appears that the enticements of rich industrialized societies, long-term attendance at educational institutions, women's improved access to effective birth control methods, and women's deepening involvement in the world of work (Hyun, et. al chapter 7, this volume) act at cross-purposes with the "evolutionary imperative" emphasized by neo-Darwinian theories.

Be that as it may, our long-term goal as cross-cultural developmentalists should be to create an overall, vertically integrated theory that simultaneously takes into account several levels of biological distal and proximate causes, psychological processes, sociocultural forces, ecological conditions, and their mutual interactions. At present, however, we are far from understanding what such a comprehensive and integrated theory might look like.

Additional Historical Contributions and Developments

The foregoing review of some highlights in the history of cross-cultural human development research has neglected numerous creative contributions to the field. Because of space constraints, we can mention here only a few of them. These include Erikson's suggestive and cross-culturally fruitful formulation (1963) of ego-identity development throughout the human lifecycle, Rohner's investigations (cf. Ahmed, Khaleque, Rohner, & Gielen, chapter 5, this volume) of interpersonal/parental acceptance and rejection across a broad variety of cultures together with his varied research methods, LeVine's broadly integrative approach (1970; LeVine et al., 1994) to the study of childcare, personality, and culture, Arnett's (2012) theory of "emerging adulthood" as a new post-adolescent stage in modern societies, Super and Harkness's cross-culturally fruitful notion (1986) of a "developmental niche," Pinker's (1994) extensive work on cross-linguistic comparisons and language universals, Stevenson, Stigler, and Lee's widely cited cross-national comparisons (e.g., Stevenson & Lee, 1990; Stevenson & Stigler, 1992) of children's performance on mathematics and other tests in East Asia and the United States, Hofstede's (2001) and Triandis's delineations (1995) of cross-culturally universal dimensions of values such as collectivism-individualism, together with the idea that these notions can be applied to cross-culturally shaped developmental scripts (e.g., Greenfield & Cocking, 1994), Kağitçibaşi's effort (2007) to conceptualize family systems and human development in an integrative way, and so many other efforts.

Recent decades have seen the rise of several contextually oriented theories including Bronfenbrenner's (1979, 1995) bio ecological systems theory of human development and socialization. His theory postulates four interacting and concentric systems that together define environmental contexts for lifelong development. In addition, Bronfenbrenner later on added a time-related fifth system, the chronosystem.

In this context, Bronfenbrenner postulated that the growing child is first of all interacting face to face with members of its microsystems, such as family members, peers, classmates, and neighbors. To this should be added the mesosystem, which consists of those interconnections between the various microsystems that are influencing the life of a child in an indirect fashion, for instance, interactions between parents and teachers. The exosystem refers to relationships between those social settings in which the child does not play an active role and the child's immediate context, the microsystems. Finally, the macrosystem refers to the broader sociocultural contexts in which a person's development occurs. These may consist of socioeconomic conditions, prevailing norms and value systems, a society's shared identity and heritage, and so on. Without necessarily applying Bronfenbrenner's theory in detail, many of the following chapters in this volume are contextually oriented and emphasize the impact that various macrosystems and exosystems exert on children's development in the context of their microsystems.

In recent decades, the field of cross-cultural human development has profited from the rise of psychology in many non-Western countries. In Asia, for instance, there exists now a critical mass of psychologists in India (e.g., Saraswathi, 1999), Indonesia, Japan and South Korea (e.g., Gielen & Naito, 1999; Shwalb & Shwalb, 1996, see also Hyun et al., chapter 7, this volume), and China/Hong Kong/Taiwan (e.g., Bond, 2010; Chen & Wang, 2010). Other important areas include Argentina, Brazil, Mexico, South Africa, and to some extent the Arab countries (Ahmed et al., chapter 5, this volume). Moreover, a considerable amount of global research on family functioning has recently been published (e.g., Roopnarine & Gielen, 2005; Shwalb, Shwalb, & Lamb, 2013).

Although developmental research in non-Western and semi-Western countries is not necessarily comparative in nature, indigenous psychologists are, implicitly or explicitly, confronted with the question of whether the theoretical principles and findings of mainstream Western developmental psychology are applicable in their respective countries. Although the present volume does not focus on the international scene in developmental psychology, a few pioneering works containing significant material about child and adolescent development in non-Western cultures may be cited. These include Shwalb and Shwalb (1996) for Japan, Lau (1997) for Chinese societies, Kakar (1978/1981), Saraswathi (1999), and Saraswathi and Kaur (1993) for India, Suvannathat, Bhanthumnavin, Bhuapirom, and Keats (1985) for Thailand, Nsamenang (1992) for sub-Saharan Africa, and Ahmed and Gielen (1998) for the Arab world. For more recent summaries, the reader may wish to consult various contributions to Bornstein's (2010) edited handbook.

Today, the cross-cultural and multicultural study of human development is a thriving enterprise in which no single discipline, theoretical approach, or methodology predominates (Bornstein, 2010; Jensen, 2015). Rather, the field may be compared to a multicolored blanket that has been stitched together by a crew of scientific artists, but not always in a very coherent fashion or planned manner. Furthermore, there exists now an international community of developmental researchers located on several continents that can more easily cooperate in comparative investigations than ever before, thanks to modern means of communication.

In addition, a group of psychologists and other social scientists such as Berry, Foner, Fuligni, Neto, Ogbu, Phinney, Portes, Roopnarine, Rumbaut, Silbereisen, Schmitz, Suárez-Orozco, Vedder, and Waters have shown a special research interest in the psychological development of immigrant children, adolescents, and young adults, together with a preference for cross-cultural comparisons (see in this context the respective contributions by Berry & Vedder, Ho & Gielen, and Roopnarine & Yildirim, chapter 12, chapter 13, and chapter 6, respectively, in this volume). One important research question asks whether and how immigrant adolescents attempt to reconcile and integrate competing cultural frameworks and identities. Moreover, one can find now a growing number of global nomads or "Third Culture Kids" (TCKs). As described and analyzed by Bell-Villada in this volume, such children grow up in several countries and then, like President Barack H. Obama, they return or move to their passport countries. However, their cosmopolitan experiences make them stand out from their native peers who tend to have a more limited understanding of international and global matters. In one sense, TCKs are quite unlike immigrant children since they return to their own country and are likely to speak its main language fluently. Yet in another way, TCKs, immigrant children, and transnational children do tend to resemble each other because they all are faced with the task of integrating quite varied and potentially contradictory multicultural experiences and value systems into their identity and behavioral repertoires.

In a somewhat similar way, the growing interconnectivity of cultures around the world exposes more and more children and adolescents—such as Pema in Ladakh—to multiple cultural frameworks even if they do not migrate to another country. After all, the culturally isolated societies that anthropologists used to study in the past hardly exist anymore. Nigerian teenage boys, for instance, may be seen to text each other about such varied topics as American Rappers, the exploits of West African football stars in the English Premier League, international movie stars, attractive girls they ogled in their church, and tentative plans to move to the exploding megacity of Lagos in the hope of "making it."

TEN GENERAL ASSUMPTIONS STRUCTURING PRESENT-DAY CROSS-CULTURAL INVESTIGATIONS OF HUMAN DEVELOPMENT

As the field of cross-cultural human development studies matured and a growing number of researchers and theoreticians began to introduce empirical evidence derived from a large variety of societies, many members of the scientific community began to share a number of general assumptions about the nature of the field. Because these assumptions form the tacit background for many contributions to the present book, a brief summary of them may prove helpful:

1. Human development is the outcome of a continuous interaction between long-term evolutionary forces, evolved general and individual biological predispositions, complex psychological processes, changing physical environments increasingly shaped by technological innovations, conflicting and evolving social forces, and intricate cultural belief systems. Biological evolution and sociocultural evolution proceed in an intertwined fashion and provide the general conditions under which individual lives evolve over time. Development results from multiple causes, operating through multiple, highly complex processes, at multiple levels, and these are frequently connected to each other through feedback loops. Consequently, no single sovereign theory is likely to be able to explain cross-cultural human development in all of its intricacies. Instead, human development must be analyzed in multiple ways at different levels of complexity.
2. Cultural forces are ubiquitous, complex, evolving, intertwined with economic, technological, and ecological conditions, and not rarely contradictory in nature. In order to understand their ongoing role in the process of human development, the "variable" of culture must be broken up. However, culture is not simply an external variable influencing the functioning of the mind and the expression of behavior, but rather, culture, mind, and behavior "make each other up." Such a perspective is especially favored by cultural psychologists (e.g., Shweder et al., 1998).
3. In light of the foregoing, cultural determinism and cultural relativism as well as biological determinism constitute outdated points of view that do not adequately take into account the interaction between biological predispositions, mental processes, behavioral tendencies, (physical) environmental forces, and evolving sociocultural conditions. Similarly, the *analytic* distinction between nature and nurture should not be reified (taken to be a real phenomenon), since all behavior is performed by biological organisms acting and developing in some kind of physical and sociocultural environment. Best and Bush, for instance, outline in their chapter on gender roles how the interaction between biological and sociocultural factors has been conceived in cross-cultural theories and empirical studies of gender differences and gender roles.
4. Human development in all its variety can be understood only in cross-cultural perspective, if representatives of different disciplines contribute their special

perspectives and methodologies to the joint enterprise. The more problem-centered a research project, the more likely it is that multidisciplinary cooperation does in fact take place rather than remaining only a theoretical ideal. However, at present, no comprehensive graduate program exists that trains its students systematically and simultaneously in the different disciplines, viewpoints, and methodologies needed to give an adequate account of cross-cultural human development. The establishment of such programs is long overdue and will probably require the cooperation between researchers from different institutions.

5. In a general way, conclusions reached by researchers about the nature of cross-cultural human adaptation and development should be compatible with evolutionary theory. This does not mean, however, that all or even most specific evolutionary hypotheses are necessarily true, since human development is influenced by numerous, and often contradictory, biological, psychological, and sociocultural factors. The balance between enabling and constraining forces is not easily summarized by a ready set of theoretical generalizations derived from evolutionary theory—or from any other theory for that matter. Moreover, evolutionary theorists frequently advance highly speculative hypotheses about processes said to have taken place in the distant past while evolving over very long periods of time. Some of these hypotheses and so-so stories should be approached with considerable skepticism.

   There exist at present three groups of modern evolutionary theorists, each of which has tended to approach human development from a different angle (Smith, 2000). For instance, a number of scholars have conducted quantitative behavioral studies of infants, children, and childcare among foragers, pastoralists, and horticulturalists (e.g., Hewlett & Lamb, 2005). A second group of researchers, identifying themselves as evolutionary psychologists, have attempted to identify universal "modules" or "mental organs" of the mind, such as a module for language (Pinker, 1994). These are thought to have evolved during Bowlby's "environment of evolutionary adaptation" (1969). Finally, a group of evolutionary cultural anthropologists have focused on the evolutionary nature of culture and cultural diversity together with an attempt to try to apply the notion of "selection mechanisms" to cultural inheritance systems (e.g., Blackmore, 1999). These three groups have already made valuable if sometimes controversial contributions to the cross-cultural study of human development, each in their own way.

6. Cross-cultural development researchers should not depend on a single methodology. In many research situations, a multimethod approach sometimes called triangulation (e.g., Cournoyer, 2000; Holtzman, Diaz-Guerrero, & Swartz, 1975; Rohner, 1986) is optimal, since it can tell us to what extent a phenomenon is "created" by a specific method, and to what extent a phenomenon can be considered robust in nature by manifesting itself across a variety of methods. Although from a theoretical point of view, most researchers favor a multimethod approach, for practical reasons this often remains an ideal rather than becoming a routine aspect of the research process. In this context,

multidisciplinary teams and approaches may be considered especially fruitful since members of different disciplines naturally tend to favor, and are competent in applying, a variety of methods and techniques.

7. Anthropologists and psychologists sometimes distinguish between "emic" and "etic" perspectives in the study of behavior. The emic viewpoint emphasizes the understanding of behavior within a given cultural framework of meanings, whereas the etic viewpoint interprets behavior within a framework of scientific concepts that frequently originate outside a given culture. Explicitly or implicitly, researchers guided by evolutionary approaches as well as mainstream psychologists have tended to favor etic forms of theorizing. In contrast, many cultural anthropologists, cultural psychologists, and researchers favoring indigenous approaches emphasize the advantages of an emic perspective. It should be added, however, that the traditional focus of many cultural anthropologists on unique, deterministic, self-existing cultural configurations not anchored in psychological processes is largely incompatible with the viewpoint adopted by most contributors to this volume.

   Like many other analytic distinctions in the social sciences, the dichotomy between "emic" and "etic" viewpoints can be misleading. While investigating development within a given culture, all researchers must pay at least some attention to an (emic) understanding of the point of view of their respondents. At the same time, all scientific cross-cultural comparisons must by necessity rely on observations and responses that can be classified according to some scientific system of meaning more or less external to the respondents (Triandis, 2000). Although sometimes advocated, a consistently emic approach is neither possible nor desirable since it would imprison the researcher in a unique, never-to-be-repeated framework of meanings relative to time and place. Similarly, an exclusive emphasis on "indigenous psychologies" would soon prove self-defeating: Since there exist thousands of different cultures and subcultures as well as at least 7,000 languages in this world, such an effort would result in thousands of separate psychologies united by little more than the term "psychology." The outcome of the effort would be an epistemological nightmare.

8. Much has been made of the fact that the social sciences in general, and cross-cultural theories and research on human development in particular, originated in the West, where to this day one can find the majority of active researchers and theoreticians. Emphasizing this, Canadian cross-cultural psychologist Berry found the discipline of mainstream psychology "so culture-bound and culture-blind that . . . it should not be employed as it is" (1983, p. 449). Such an observation is not entirely wrong but it is also not that helpful. The fact that a given scientific theory originated in a particular cultural context cannot tell us how valid or scientifically useful it is. To accuse, for instance, psychology of a Western bias is of limited value since Western psychologists have produced a rich variety of contradictory theories none of which can be said to represent "the" Western outlook. Indeed, there may be no such thing as a "Western" theory, nor have non-Western social scientists been able to develop truly different theories from those created by American and European researchers. Instead,

disciplinary boundaries have often proven more difficult to cross than cultural boundaries between investigators who, though coming from different cultural backgrounds, are pursuing shared research goals. Professional tunnel vision, excessive attachment to one's favorite scientific theory in the face of contradictory evidence, a restrictive methodological outlook, and unwillingness to face the ostracism consequent to one's contradicting basic ideas and assumptions fashionable in one's academic-political milieu tend to create much greater impediments to scientific progress in the social sciences than cross-cultural differences between investigators.

From a more pragmatic perspective, however, the increasing importance of non-Western researchers in the social sciences can only be welcomed. Often, they have access to culturally varied research populations as well as bringing with them a different set of research priorities. Many of them function in a bicultural or multicultural mode on a daily basis, since they are surrounded by their local culture while also participating in the larger, mostly English-speaking community of international scientists. Having been trained at Western universities—or, alternatively, at local universities following the Western model of scientific training—they experience in themselves those cultural tensions that both liberate and alienate them from their local sociocultural contexts. This process can serve as a powerful catalyst for cultural insights that may be hidden from Western researchers who may be too embedded in their own culture to see it, or other cultures, clearly.

Concerning the cross-cultural study of human development, then, the field will do well to follow Mao Tse-Tung's slogan (though not his violent execution of it): "Let a Thousand Flowers Bloom."

9. It is widely understood by modern cross-cultural researchers that intragroup differences in psychological functioning are frequently more pronounced than intergroup differences. In other words, even if a psychological researcher finds clear statistical differences between the means of two contrasting cultural samples, the overlap between the two groups may nevertheless be large. This holds especially true in complex, steadily changing modern societies that typically include numerous subcultures whose members live in different subjective worlds yet who are also exposed to the same mainstream culture(s).

In contrast to this understanding, earlier representatives of the Personality and Culture school such as Mead tended to overemphasize the homogeneity of the (mostly small) cultures they studied, thereby consistently underestimating psychological variation among its members. For Mead and for Benedict, the concept of culture had almost assumed the characteristics of an ideal Platonic form, and they considered as "deviants" those (supposedly) few members not living up to its ideals (as they understood them). At the same time, Mead also asserted that (as previously discussed) all members of a given culture are fundamentally different from all members of all other cultures. In a somewhat similar vein, many proponents of national character and modal personality studies, whether implicitly or explicitly, have mistakenly assumed that most members of a given society are molded by it into a single—or perhaps a very few—predominant personality type(s). This assumption, it may be added, also entails important implications for the question of whether the study of cross-cultural differences or similarities is more important: Whereas theorists and researchers interested in cross-cultural differences tend to "level" within-group differences and "sharpen" between-group differences, those interested in similarities between cultural groups tend to downplay between-group differences in their search for common human proclivities.

10. A considerable (though not unlimited) variety of childrearing strategies is appropriate for rearing competent children, adolescents, and adults who are able to function successfully in the ecological conditions both surrounding, and being created by, their societies. Furthermore, as societies change, formerly adaptive childrearing strategies may grow maladaptive. In such a situation, parents must increasingly educate children and adolescents for a world that does not yet exist and that they cannot fully anticipate or comprehend. The children and adolescents, in turn, need to internalize knowledge and ways of behaving that increasingly derive from peer group contact, schools, the mass media, and other institutions outside the home. Consequently, the "developmental niches" of adolescents living in traditional agricultural societies and those residing in modern information societies tend to be of a quite different nature (Gielen, chapter 3, this volume). Traditional societies tend to convey relatively unitary worldviews and forms of knowledge to their youngsters, whereas rapidly changing modern societies can transmit only preliminary, fragmentary, and sometimes-contradictory ideals, messages, forms of knowledge, and skills to their future generations.

    The appropriateness of specific childrearing strategies needs to be evaluated in the context of the socioecological conditions to which a group must adapt. For instance, the authoritative, child-centered, self-esteem–promoting childrearing strategies favored by most American developmental textbook writers are probably much more adaptive for a fast-changing, individualistic, postmodern society with small families than for a traditional, agricultural society based on large, polygynous families that necessitate more authority-oriented value systems emphasizing a child's responsibilities and duties in a situation of economic scarcity. Similarly, a societal emphasis on childrearing strategies promoting the development of interpersonal sensitivity, emotional warmth, tender-minded concern for outgroup members, and responsive obedience would be ill suited for the many horticultural, nomadic, and agricultural societies of the past (and sometimes present) that had to survive under conditions of permanent warfare and intertribal or intercity hostility (e.g., many Amazonian Indians, American Plains Indians, nomads inhabiting the Arabian Peninsula, the Pakhtun/Pathan of Afghanistan and Pakistan, precolonial New Guinea, neighbors of the Aztec Empire, classical Greek city-states). Unfortunately, childrearing methods and personality development have been insufficiently studied in those societies in which interpersonal and intertribal forms of violence are (or were) quite common (for a drastic example, see Lindholm, 1998).

CROSS-CULTURAL PSYCHOLOGISTS AND PSYCHOLOGICAL AND CULTURAL ANTHROPOLOGISTS

We have seen that the cross-cultural study of human development prospers when an interdisciplinary team of researchers applies a variety of theoretical approaches and methods to systematically selected and culturally varied samples of respondents. While this ideal is rarely realized in full, it may be useful in the context of this volume to take a look at the two disciplines that in recent decades have contributed the most to the cross-cultural study of human development: cross-cultural psychology and cultural/psychological anthropology. Historically, the anthropologists came first, but in recent years, the number of cross-culturally active psychologists has easily surpassed the number of cultural/psychological anthropologists active in the field. This situation is, for instance, reflected among the membership of the Society for Cross-Cultural Research: whereas psychological anthropologists—especially those associated with the perspective of Beatrice and John Whiting—were once dominant in this association, nowadays psychologists make up the majority of its membership. In contrast, a shrinking and aging group of quantitatively oriented cross-cultural anthropologists feels increasingly marginalized in their profession by those anthropologists advocating more qualitative and ideologically inspired postmodern perspectives (d'Andrade, 2000). In contrast to this situation, cross-cultural and multicultural psychologists have increased their numbers while intensifying their impact on mainstream psychology, especially during the last three decades.

Table 1.1 presents an ideal-type comparison between the respective approaches of cross-cultural psychologists and cultural/psychological anthropologists. It should be understood that the contrasting comparisons do not point to absolute differences between the two disciplines but rather to tendencies underlying many but by no means all investigations. Furthermore, this chapter tends to downplay differences between psychological and cultural anthropologists, between cultural psychologists and cross-cultural psychologists, and between cross-cultural psychologists and anthropologists, in the interest of arriving at a synthetic overview of the cross-cultural study of ontogenetic development.

American psychologists have traditionally emphasized experimentation as the royal road to knowledge followed by quantifiable observations and questionnaire responses. In their view, it should be the central purpose of scientific investigation to understand relationships between variables as specified by specific hypotheses. The hypotheses typically center on questions designed to elucidate the nature of major psychological processes designated as learning, memory, cognition, perception, emotion, development, personality dimensions, personality dynamics, and so on. To test the

Table 1.1 Some Idealized Differences between Cultural Anthropologists and Cross-Cultural Psychologists

	Cross-Cultural Psychologists	**Cultural/Psychological Anthropologists**
Purpose of the investigation	To understand relationships between variables	To understand small-scale cultures, subcultures, or major institutions; some quantitative investigations
Range of problems investigated	Psychological processes suggested by current theories of perception, memory, cognitive development, personality dimensions and dynamics, etc.	Broad range of everyday behaviors held together by cultural worldviews, values, societal institutions, ecological conditions
Most frequently studied populations	Captive populations in schools, colleges, universities, etc., that are part of large-scale literate societies	Villagers, foragers, people living in neighborhoods or members of organizations
Main focus of professional training	Experimental procedures and statistical techniques, survey techniques, quantitative observation methods based on category systems	Creation of holistic ethnographies, interview schedules, disciplined observations of common behaviors
Nature of data	Quantitative, supplanted by some qualitative observations and interviews	Qualitative observations together with some quantitative supportive data; observations of everyday behaviors and events
Time framework for data collection	Often only 30–90 minutes per respondent	9–24 months
Sampling procedures	Large, systematically selected samples categorized by age, gender, SES, cultural membership, etc.	Small number of (sometimes psychologically marginal) informants, small and underspecified selection of respondents, household survey data
Concern for cultural context of investigation	Low to moderate	Central to investigation
Concern for economic context of investigation	Frequently lacking or tangential to investigation	Models of production, economic basis of group under investigation are part of the "big picture"

Table 1.1 Continued

	Cross-Cultural Psychologists	**Cultural/Psychological Anthropologists**
Common methodological criticisms of field	Behaviors torn out of cultural context; trivial conclusions because they are based on small range of investigated problems and responses; too much reliance on formal questionnaires and verbal reports rather than observations of day-to-day behaviors; methodologies too artificial and supporting false sense of precision; need more longitudinal studies	Insufficient delineation of underlying psychological processes; poor sampling procedures; lack of quantitative data; interpretations too subjective and based on non-repeatable data collection procedures; postmodern studies marred by subjective perspectives

hypotheses, specific samples of research participants are drawn, participants who, for the sake of convenience rather than for theoretical reasons, are most often selected from captive populations such as nurseries and preschools, schools, colleges and universities, and inmates of old-age homes. Research participants are most often characterized according to general categories such as age, gender, ethnic or cultural group, and social class background of their family.

In practice, a major proportion of the available cross-cultural psychological literature has compared "Western" samples (especially Americans) with "non-Western" samples, with the latter frequently including students from East Asian countries. These are often said to represent a "collectivistic" culture whereas, in contrast, American students are meant to represent the mind-set of persons living in individualistic cultures. The Americans are frequently—and falsely—designated as representatives of "the" West, whereas East Asian students are often—and falsely—considered to be typical representatives of (the whole of) Asia. In this context, little attention tends to be paid to the fact that a broad variety of ways of life can be found in Asia, ranging from that of Muslim peasants in Central Asia to the contrasting lifeways of Siberian nomads, Tibetan hermits in the Himalayas, Chinese internal migrants reading self-empowerment literature, gun-wielding tribesmen from Afghanistan, Indian computer experts, Balinese temple dancers, and playful coeds from Tokyo dressing up as their favorite *manga* (cartoon) characters. Similarly, "the" West includes, in reality, quite varied cultural traditions and populations such as Portuguese small-town businessmen, conservative churchgoing wives of Greek farmers, Swedish reindeer herders, Dutch prostitutes, young adherents of French right-wing parties opposing the presence and cultural practices of Muslim immigrants from North Africa, Swiss bankers, combative English "soccer hooligans" from working-class backgrounds, and many others who may little resemble American students in their opinions, behaviors, feelings, and identities. In addition, some Latin American societies such as Argentina and Chile are just as "Western" as Canada or the United States. The implicit or explicit tendency of many American and non-American social scientists to treat American society as "the" model Western society reflects its hegemony in the military, economic, linguistic, mass media, and social science areas, but it nevertheless constitutes poor scientific practice that encourages stereotypical thinking among social scientists and their readers.

Nonliterate populations, lower-class respondents, villagers depending on agriculture, representatives of foraging cultures, mature working adults, aging housewives, and so on, are much less frequently selected for cross-cultural investigation. While recent investigators have tended to show an increased concern for the respondents' cultural context, only a limited number of investigations report observations of daily behavior in natural settings. Instead, much of cross-cultural psychology has become a kind of comparative-study-of-responses-to-questionnaires-by-university-students-from-various-nations. *The field relies too much on students' reports about their own and other people's behavior rather than studying the behavior itself.* In Lewis Aptekar and Lisa Oliver's chapter in this volume (chapter 15), the reader will encounter a lucid discussion of why questionnaire-oriented methodologies are, for instance, inappropriate for the study of street children. Many street children are masters at presenting themselves in different ways to different researchers in an attempt to solicit their material support. Could it not be true that many other children and adolescents are similarly concerned with presenting themselves in the "right" light to those researchers pursuing them with questionnaires?

In contrast to the analytic and quantitative research paradigm underlying most investigations by cross-cultural psychologists, cultural and psychological anthropologists have tended to emphasize a more contextual, qualitative approach to the study of culturally defined groups and the psychological processes occurring in those individuals making them up (see the respective chapters by Grove & Lancy and Ho & Gielen, chapters 2 and 13, respectively, in this volume). The participant observation of everyday behaviors based on empathic role-taking as well as the drawing of inferences about underlying worldviews and other culturally constituted meaning systems remains at the center of many anthropological investigations. Anthropologists are also far more likely to study villagers, foragers, pastoralists, and nonliterate or semiliterate populations than most psychologists, whose continued preference for questionnaire-based methodologies rules out the employment of nonliterate and semiliterate populations in their studies, anyway.

My comparison of "the" cultural anthropology approach with "the" cross-cultural psychology approach suggests that a combination of the two ways of doing social science should prove productive, especially since the respective strengths of the two approaches might compensate for some of their corresponding weaknesses. There has, indeed, been some mutual recognition of this possibility. However, a comparison between recent articles published in two typical journals—*Ethos* as the house journal of the Society for Psychological Anthropology, and the *International Journal of Behavioral Development* as the official publication of the psychology oriented International Society for the Study of Behavioral Development—demonstrates that the two disciplines continue to favor distinctive methodological approaches. Nevertheless, increased cross-disciplinary collaboration and integration would almost certainly make it more likely that a more balanced, complex, and realistic understanding of human development emerges from our investigations. We hope that this volume will contribute toward this goal. It contains mostly contributions by cross-cultural psychologists who, however, are often well aware of parallel developments in psychological anthropology.

CONCLUSION

In this chapter I have reviewed some of the tasks of cross-cultural developmental psychologists and anthropologists. In addition, I have discussed the history of cross-cultural developmental research, identified some of its underlying assumptions and methodological principles, and compared methodological approaches, respectively, taken by anthropologists and by psychologists.

While cross-cultural human development is a relatively new field of scientific study, it is remarkable that the contributions in this volume arrive at a good many sound conclusions opposed to those expressed in many developmental psychology textbooks, by professional psychologists, or by the general public. For instance, conventional wisdom tells us that parents are the main socializing agents of children, an assumed "fact" that, indeed, forms the taken-for-granted cornerstone of orthodox psychoanalysis with its emphasis on the Oedipus complex. Yet this premise cannot be accurate, states Maynard in her chapter on sibling interactions, since in many cultures siblings are more important socialization agents than parents. There are many more examples discussed in the following chapters that demonstrate that cross-cultural developmental psychology can free us from ethnocentric blinders, throw into doubt theories at variance with the prevailing psychocultural conditions in many non-Western societies, redefine what is important in human development, and ultimately help us gain a more comprehensive and less biased understanding of the human condition. This is certainly an appropriate goal for the new century in which cross-cultural misunderstandings are likely to have serious, even deadly consequences for children, adolescents, and adults alike.

Although the field of cross-cultural developmental research can boast only of a short history, it is becoming increasingly clear that it will be long-lasting. In the past, American and European researchers argued that the study of (mostly mainstream) children and adolescents in their respective countries will one day result in a comprehensive and universally valid theory of human development—such notions have been debunked. Rather, in order to develop such a theory, it is necessary to trace and compare the developmental trajectories of children, adolescents, and adults in a broad spectrum of ecological and sociocultural settings around the globe. Such a path has been taken by the contributors to this volume, as is demonstrated in the following chapters.

REFLECTIVE QUESTIONS

1. What main approaches have influenced the cross-cultural study of human development during the beginnings of the newly emerging field?
2. How did the "Six Cultures Project" and the "Adolescence in a Changing World Project" of Beatrice Whiting, John Whiting, and their students advance the comparative investigation of cultural childrearing conditions?
3. Both Margaret Mead and the traditional American learning theories postulated that human beings are largely shaped by their social environments, although they did so in different ways. In what ways have the theories of Piaget, Kohlberg, and Vygotsky helped to move American psychology away from that earlier, one-sided emphasis on nurture rather than nature?
4. The chapter delineates 10 general assumptions structuring many recent, cross-cultural investigations of human development. Is there a main theme underlying these assumptions?
5. How do cross-cultural psychologists and cultural anthropologists differ in the way they tend to approach the comparative study of human development? What are some of the methodological strengths and weaknesses of the two fields?
6. How does globalization influence the lives of adolescents residing in the majority world?

SUGGESTED READINGS

Books and Articles

Beckwith, C., & Fisher A. (1999). *African ceremonies* (vols.1–2). New York: Harry N. Abrams. (Two beautiful photography volumes depicting African coming-of-age and other ceremonies that were at the center of traditional societies but are now fading rapidly.)

Henrich, J., Heine, S.J., & Norenzayan, A. (2010). The weirdest people in the world? *Behavioral and Brain Sciences, 33,* 61–135. (Argues that Americans and other Westerners are not at all representative of the world.)

Jensen, L.A., & Arnett, J.J. (2012). Going global: New pathways for adolescents and emerging adults in a changing world. *Journal of Social Issues, 68*(3), 473–492. (Globalization alters the nature of adolescence in most parts of the world.)

Snarey, J. (1985). Cross-cultural universality of socio-moral development: A review of Kohlbergian research. *Psychological Bulletin, 97,* 202–232. (Snarey's main conclusions are probably still valid 30 years later.)

Whiting, B.B., & Edwards, C.P. (1988). *Children of different worlds: The formation of social behavior.* Cambridge, MA: Harvard University Press. (A classic culture-comparative study.)

REFERENCES

Ahmed, R.A., & Gielen, U.P. (Eds.). (1998). *Psychology in the Arab countries.* Menoufia, Egypt: Menoufia University Press.

Ainsworth, M.D.S. (1967). *Infancy in Uganda: Infant care and the growth of love.* Baltimore, MD: Johns Hopkins University Press.

Ainsworth, M.D.S., Bell, S.M.V., & Stanton, D.J. (1971). Individual differences in Strange-Situation behaviour of one-year-olds. In H.R. Schaffer (Ed.), *The origins of human social relations* (pp. 17–57). New York: Academic Press.

Arnett, J.J. (1999). Adolescent storm and stress reconsidered. *American Psychologist, 54,* 317–326.

Arnett, J.J. (2008). The neglected 95%: Why American psychology needs to become less American. *American Psychologist, 63*(7), 602–614.

Arnett, J.J. (2012). *Adolescence and emerging adulthood: A cultural approach* (5th ed.). Upper Saddle River, NJ: Prentice-Hall.

Barnouw, V. (1985). *Culture and personality* (4th ed.). Homewood, IL: Dorsey Press.

Bjorklund, D.F., & Pellegrini, A. D. (2002). *The origins of human nature: Evolutionary developmental psychology.* Washington, DC: American Psychological Association.

Blackmore, S. (1999). *The meme machine.* Oxford, UK: Oxford University Press.

Blurton-Jones, N. (1993). The lives of hunter-gather children: Effects of parental behavior and parental reproductive strategy. In M.E. Pereira & L.A. Fairbanks (Eds.), *Juvenile primates* (pp. 309–326). New York: Oxford University Press.

Boesch, C. (2009). *The real chimpanzee: Sex strategies in the forest.* Cambridge, UK: Cambridge University Press.

Bond, M. (Ed.). (2010). *The Oxford handbook of Chinese psychology.* Oxford, UK: Oxford University Press.

Bornstein, M.H. (Ed.).(2010). *Handbook of cultural developmental science.* New York: Psychology Press.

Bowlby, J. (1969). *Attachment and loss.* Vol. 1, *Attachment.* New York: Basic Books.

Bowlby, J. (1982). *Attachment and loss.* Vol. 1, *Attachment* (2nd ed.). New York: Basic Books.

Bronfenbrenner, U. (1979). *The ecology of human development: Experiments by nature and design.* Cambridge, MA: Harvard University Press.

Bronfenbrenner, U. (1995). Developmental ecology through space and time: A future perspective. In P. Moen, G.H. Elder, Jr., & K. Luscher (Eds.), *Examining lives in context: Perspectives on the ecology of human development* (pp. 619–647). Washington, DC: American Psychological Association.

Burbank, V. (1988). *Aboriginal adolescence: Maidenhood in an Australian Aboriginal community.* New Brunswick, NJ: Rutgers University Press.

Buss, D. M. (1989). Sex differences in human mate preferences: Evolutionary hypothesis tested in thirty-seven cultures. *Behavioral and Brain Sciences, 12,* 1–49.

Buss, D. M. (1995). *The evolution of desire: Strategies of human mating.* New York: Basic Books.

Cassidy, J., & Shaver, P. R. (Eds.). (2010). *Handbook of attachment: Theory, research, and clinical applications* (2nd ed.). New York: Guilford Press.

Chen, X., & Wang, L. (2010). China. In M. J. Bornstein (Ed.), *Handbook of cultural developmental science* (pp. 429–444). New York: Psychology Press.

Chomsky, N. (1959). [Review of *Verbal Behavior* by B. F. Skinner]. *Language, 35,* 26–58.

Cole, M. (1996). *Cultural psychology: A once and future discipline.* Cambridge, MA: Belknap Press.

Condon, R. G. (1988). *Inuit youths: Growth and change in the Canadian Artic.* New Brunswick, NJ: Rutgers University Press.

Cournoyer, D. E. (2000). Universalist research: Examples drawn from the methods and findings of Parental Acceptance/Rejection Theory. In A. L. Comunian & U. P. Gielen (Eds.), *International perspectives on human development* (pp. 213–232). Lengerich, Germany: Pabst Science.

Daly, M., & Wilson, M. (1988). *Homicide.* New York: Aldine de Gruyter.

d'Andrade, R. (2000). The sad story of anthropology, 1950–1999. *Cross-Cultural Research, 34* (3), 219–232.

Dasen, P. R. (2000). Rapid social change and the turmoil of adolescence: A cross-cultural perspective. In J. L. Gibbons & U. P. Gielen (Eds.), Adolescence in international and cross-cultural perspective, Special issue, *International Journal of Group Tensions, 29* (1–2), 17–49.

Dasen, P. R., Dembele, B., Ettien, K., Kabran, K., Kamagate, D., Koffi, D. A., & N'Guessan, A. (1985). Ngoulèlê: L'intelligence chez les Baoulé [N'goulèlê: Intelligence among the Baoulé]. *Archives de Psychologie, 53,* 293–324.

Dasen, P. R., & Heron, A. (1981). Cross-cultural tests of Piaget's theory. In H. C. Triandis & A. Heron (Eds.), *Handbook of cross-cultural psychology,* Vol. 4, *Developmental psychology* (pp. 295–342). Boston, MA: Allyn & Bacon.

Davis, S. S., & Davis, D. A. (1989). *Adolescence in a Moroccan town: Making social sense.* New Brunswick, NJ: Rutgers University Press.

Dawkins, R. (1976). *The selfish gene.* Oxford, UK: Oxford University Press.

de Waal, F. (2006). *The inner ape: A leading primatologist explains why we are who we are.* New York: Riverhead Track.

Dien, D. S. (1982). A Chinese perspective on Kohlberg's theory of moral development. *Developmental Review, 2,* 331–341.

Draguns, J. G. (2001). Toward a truly international psychology: Beyond English only. *American Psychologist, 56,* 1019–1030.

Eckensberger, L. H., & Zimba, R. (1997). The development of moral judgment. In J. W. Berry, P. R. Dasen, & T. S. Saraswathi (Eds.), *Handbook of cross-cultural psychology,* Vol. 2, *Basic processes and human development* (pp. 299–338). Needham Heights, MA: Allyn & Bacon.

Edgerton, R. B. (1992). *Sick societies: Challenging the myth of primitive harmony.* New York: Free Press.

Eibl-Eibesfeldt, I. (1989). *Human ethology.* New York: Aldine de Gruyter.

Erikson, E. H. (1963). *Childhood and society* (2nd ed.). New York: Norton.
Freeman, D. (1983). *Margaret Mead and Samoa: The making and unmaking of an anthropological myth.* Cambridge, MA: Harvard University Press.
Gardiner, H. W., & Kozmitzki, C. (2010). *Lives across cultures: Cross-cultural human development* (5th ed.). Boston, MA: Allyn & Bacon.
Gewertz, D. (1981). A historical reconsideration of female dominance among the Chambri of Papua New Guinea. *American Ethnologist, 8,* 94–106.
Gibbs, J. C. (2013). *Moral development and reality: Beyond the theories of Kohlberg, Hoffman, and Haidt* (3rd ed.). Oxford, UK: Oxford University Press.
Gielen, U. P. (1993). Gender roles in traditional Tibetan cultures. In L. L. Adler (Ed.), *International handbook on gender roles* (pp. 413–437). Westport, CT: Greenwood.
Gielen, U. P. (1994). American mainstream psychology and its relationship to international and cross-cultural psychology. In A. L. Comunian & U. P. Gielen (Eds.), *Advancing psychology and its applications: International perspectives* (pp. 26–40). Milan, Italy: FrancoAngeli.
Gielen, U. P. (1996). Moral reasoning in cross-cultural perspective: A review of Kohlbergian research. *World Psychology, 2* (3–4), i–viii, 265–496.
Gielen, U. P. (2001). Some themes in the ethos of Buddhist Ladakh. In P. Kaplanian (Ed.), *Ladakh Himalaya Occidental ethnologie, écologie* (pp. 115–126). Paris: Author.
Gielen, U. P., & Jeshmaridian, S. S. (2015). Lev S. Vygotsky: A Hamletian spirit with Marxist dispositions. In G. Rich & U. P. Gielen (Eds.), *Pathfinders in international psychology* (pp. 93–104). Charlotte, NC: Information Age Publishing.
Gielen, U. P., & Markoulis, D.C. (2001). Preference for principled moral reasoning: A developmental and cross-cultural perspective. In L. L. Adler & U. P. Gielen (Eds.), *Cross-cultural topics in psychology* (2nd ed., pp. 81–101). Westport, CT: Praeger.
Gielen, U. P., & Naito, T. (1999). Teaching perspectives on cross-cultural psychology and Japanese society. *International Journal of Group Tensions, 28*(3–4), 319–344.
Gilligan, C. (1982). *In a different voice: Psychology theory and women's development.* Cambridge, MA: Harvard University Press.
Goodall, J. (1986). *The chimpanzees of Gombe: Patterns of behavior.* Cambridge, MA: The Belknap Press of Harvard University Press.
Greenfield, P.M., & Cocking, R. R. (Eds.). (1994). *Cross-cultural roots of minority child development.* Hillsdale, NJ: Erlbaum.
Hall, G. S. (1904). *Adolescence.* New York: Appleton.
Hamilton, W. D. (1964). The genetical evolution of social behavior. *Journal of Theoretical Behavior, 7,* 1–52.
Harlow, H. W., & Zimmerman, R. (1959). Affectional responses in the infant monkey. *Science, 130,* 421–432.
Henrich, J., Heine, S. J., & Norenzayan, A. (2010). The weirdest people in the world? *Behavioral and Brain Sciences, 33,* 61–135.
Herskovitz, M. J. (1948). *Man and his works: The science of cultural anthropology.* New York: Knopf.
Hewlett, B. S. (1991). *Intimate fathers: The nature and context of Aka pygmy paternal infant care.* Ann Arbor, MI: University of Michigan Press.
Hewlett, B. S., & Lamb, M. E. (Eds.). (2005). *Hunter-gatherer childhoods: Evolutionary, developmental, and cultural perspectives.* New Brunswick, NJ: Transaction/Aldine.
Hofstede, G. (2001). *Culture's consequences: Comparing values, behaviors, institutions, and organizations across nations* (2nd ed.). Thousand Oaks, CA: Sage.

Hollos, M., & Leis, P.E. (1989). *Becoming Nigerian in Ijo society.* New Brunswick, NJ: Rutgers University Press.

Holtzman, W.H., Diaz-Guerrero, R., & Swartz, J.D. (1975). *Personality development in two cultures: A cross-cultural longitudinal study of school children in Mexico and the United States.* Austin, TX: University of Texas Press.

IJzendoorn, M.H., & Kroonenberg, P.M. (1988). Cross-cultural patterns of attachment: A meta-analysis of the Strange Situation. *Child Development, 59,* 147–156.

IJzendoorn, M.H., & Sagi, A. (1999). Cross-cultural patterns of attachment. In J. Cassidy & P.R. Shaver (Eds.), *Handbook of attachment: Theory, research, and clinical applications* (pp. 713–734). New York: Guilford.

Jahoda, G. (2000). On the prehistory of cross-cultured development research. In A.L. Comunian & U.P. Gielen (Eds.), *International perspectives on human development* (pp. 5–17). Lengerich, Germany: Pabst Science.

Jahoda, G., & Lewis, I.M. (1988/1989). Introduction: Child development in psychology and anthropology. In G. Jahoda & I.M. Lewis (Eds.), *Acquiring culture: Cross cultural studies in child development* (pp. 1–34). London, UK: Routledge.

Jensen, L.A. (Ed.). (2015). *The Oxford handbook of human development and culture: An interdisciplinary perspective.* New York: Oxford University Press.

Jensen, L.A., & Arnett, J.J. (2012). Going global: New pathways for adolescents and emerging adults in a changing world. *Journal of Social Issues, 68*(3), 473–492.

Kağitçibaşi, Ç. (2007). *Family, self, and human development across cultures: Theory and applications* (2nd ed.). New York: Routledge.

Kakar, S. (1978/1981). *The inner world: A psychoanalytic study of childhood and society in India.* New Delhi, India: Oxford University Press.

Kidd, D. (1906/1969). *Savage childhood.* New York: Negro Universities Press.

Kohlberg, L. (1969/1984). Stage and sequence. In L. Kohlberg, *The psychology of moral development: The nature and validity of moral stages* (pp. 7–169). Cambridge, MA: Harper.

Konner, M. (1982). *The tangled wing: Biological constraints on the human spirit.* New York: Holt, Rinehart, & Winston.

Lau, S. (Ed.). (1997). *Growing up the Chinese way: Chinese child and adolescent development* (2nd ed.). Hong Kong: Chinese University Press.

LeVine, R.A. (1970). Cross-cultural study in child psychology. In P. Mussen (Ed.), *Carmichael's manual of child psychology* (3rd ed., Vol. 2, pp. 559–612). New York: Wiley.

LeVine, R.A., Dixon, S., LeVine, S., Richman, A., Leiderman, P.H., Keefer, C.H., & Brazelton, T.B. (1994). *Child care and culture: Lessons from Africa.* Cambridge, UK: Cambridge University Press.

Lind, G. (1986). Cultural differences in moral judgment competence? A study of West and East European university students. *Behavior Science Research, 20* (1–4), 208–225.

Lindholm, C. (1998). The Swat Pukhtun family as a political training ground. In R.J. Castillo (Ed.), *Meanings of madness* (pp. 40–44). Pacific Grove, CA: Brooks/Cole.

Lorenz, K. (1981). *The foundations of ethology.* New York: Touchstone Book (Simon & Schuster).

Luria, A.R. (1974). *Ob istoricheskom razvitii poznavatel'nykh protssesov* [Historical development of cognitive processes]. Moscow, Russia: Nanka.

Luria, A.R. (1976). *Cognitive and development: Its cultural and social foundations.* Cambridge, MA: Harvard University Press.

Luria, A.R. (1979). *The making of a mind: A personal account of Soviet psychology.* Cambridge, MA: Harvard University Press.

Maynard Smith, J. (1964). Group selection and kin selection. *Nature, 201,* 1145–1147.
Mead, M. (1928). *Coming of age in Samoa.* New York: Morrow.
Mead, M. (1930). *Growing up in New Guinea: A comparative study of primitive education.* New York: William Morrow.
Mead, M. (1931). The primitive child. In C. Murchison (Ed.), *A handbook of child psychology* (pp. 669–687). Worcester, MA: Clark University Press.
Mead, M. (1935/1963). *Sex and temperament in three primitive societies.* New York: Morrow Quill.
Mead, M. (1954). Research on primitive children. In L. Carmichael (Ed.), *Manual of child psychology* (2nd ed., pp. 735–780). New York: Wiley.
Miller, N.E., & Dollard, J. (1941). *Social learning and imitation.* New Haven, CT: Yale University Press.
Minturn, L., & Lambert, W. (1964). *Mothers of six cultures: Antecedents of child rearing.* New York: Wiley.
Munroe, R.L., & Munroe, R.H. (1975). *Cross-cultural human development.* Prospect Heights, IL: Waveland Press.
Munroe, R.H., Munroe, R.L., & Whiting, B.B. (1981). *Handbook of cross-cultural human development.* New York: Garland STPM Press.
Norberg-Hodge, H., with Russell, H. (1994). Birth and childrearing in Zangskar. In J. Crook & H. Osmaston (Eds.), *Himalayan Buddhist villages: Environment, resources, society, and religious life in Zangskar, Ladakh* (pp. 519–532). Bristol, UK: University of Bristol.
Nsamenang, A.B. (1992). *Human development in cultural context: A Third World perspective.* Newbury Park, CA: Sage.
Obayon, I. (2013). The Kazakh famine: The beginnings of sedentarization. *Online encyclopedia of mass violence.* Retrieved from http://www.massviolence.org/The-Kazakh-Famine-The-Beginnings
Orlansky, H. (1949). Infant care and personality. *Psychological Bulletin, 46,* 1–48.
Ozer, S. (2012). Perceptions of psychopathology in relation to socio-cultural changes among Ladakhi youth. *Psychological Studies* (India), *57*(3), 310–319.
Pereira, M.E., & Fairbanks, L.A. (Eds.). (1993). *Juvenile primates.* New York: Oxford University Press.
Piaget, J. (1966). Nécessité et signification des recherches comparatives en psychologie génétique [Need and significance of cross-cultural studies in genetic psychologie]. *International Journal of Psychology, 1,* 3–13.
Pinker, S. (1994). *The language instinct.* New York: Harper/Perennial.
Rest, J. (1986). *Manual for the Defining Issues Test: An objective test of moral development* (3rd ed.). Minneapolis, MN: Center for the study of Ethical Development, University of Minnesota.
Rest, J., Narvaez, D., Bebeau, M.J., & Thoma, S.J. (1999). *Postconventional moral thinking: A neo-Kohlbergian approach.* Mahwah, NJ: Erlbaum.
Rogoff, B. (1990). *Apprenticeship in thinking: Cognitive development in social context.* New York: Oxford University Press.
Rohner, R. P. (1986). *The warmth dimension.* Beverly Hills, CA: Sage.
Roopnarine, J.L., & Gielen, U.P. (Eds.). (2005). *Families in global perspective.* Boston, MA: Pearson Education/Allyn & Bacon.
Saraswathi, T.S. (Ed.). (1999). *Culture, socialization, and human development: Theory, research, and applications in India.* New Delhi, India: Sage.
Saraswathi, T.S. (2003). *Cross-cultural perspectives in human development: Theory, research, and practice.* New Delhi, India: Sage.

Saraswathi, T.S., & Kaur, B. (Eds.). (1993). *Human development and family studies in India.* New Delhi, India: Sage.

Schlegel, A. (1995). Introduction. Special issue on adolescence, *Ethos, 23,* 3–14.

Segall, M.H., Dasen, P.R., Berry, J.W., & Poortinga, Y.H. (1999). *Human behavior in global perspective* (2nd ed.). Boston, MA: Allyn & Bacon.

Shwalb, D.W., & Shwalb, B. (Eds.). (1996). *Japanese childrearing: Two generations of scholarship.* New York: Guilford.

Shwalb, D.W., Shwalb, B.J., & Lamb, M.E. (Eds.). (2013). *Fathers in cultural context.* New York: Routledge.

Shweder, R.A., Goodnow, J., Hatano, G., LeVine, R.A., Markus, H., & Miller, P. (1998). The cultural psychology of development: One mind, many mentalities. In W. Damon (Ed.), *Handbook of child psychology* (5th ed.), Vol. 1 (R.M. Lerner, Ed.), *Theoretical models of human development* (pp. 865–937). New York: Wiley.

Skinner, B.F. (1957). *Verbal behavior.* New York: Appleton.

Smith, E.A. (2000). Three styles in the evolutionary study of human behavior. In L. Cronk, N. Chagnon, & W. Irons (Eds.), *Adaptation and human behavior* (pp. 27–46). New York: Aldine.

Snarey, J. (1985). Cross-cultural universality of socio-moral development: A critical review of Kohlbergian research. *Psychological Bulletin, 97,* 202–232.

Stevens, M.J., & Gielen, U.P. (Eds.). (2007). *Toward a global psychology: Theory, research, intervention, and pedagogy.* Mahwah, NJ: Erlbaum.

Stevenson, H.W., & Lee, S.Y. (1990). Contexts of achievement: A study of American, Chinese, and Japanese children. *Monographs of the Society for Research in Child Development,* 55.

Stevenson, H.W., & Stigler, J. (1992). *The learning gap: Why our schools are failing and what we can learn from Japanese and Chinese education.* New York: Summit Books.

Super, C., & Harkness, S. (1986). The developmental niche: A conceptualization of the interface of child and culture. *International Journal of Behavioral Development, 9,* 545–570.

Suvannathat, C., Bhanthumnavin, D., Bhuapirom, L., & Keats, D.M. (Eds.). (1985). *Handbook of Asian child development and child rearing practices.* Bangkok, Thailand: Burapasilpa Press.

Thompson, D., Hogan, J.D., & Clark, P.M. (2012). *Developmental psychology in historical perspective.* Hoboken, NJ: Wiley-Blackwell.

Tinbergen, N. (1951). *The study of instinct.* Oxford, UK: Clarendon Press.

Tomasello, M. (2010). *Origins of human communication* (Jean Nicod Lectures). Cambridge, MA: A Bradfort Book.

Triandis, H.C. (1995). *Individualism and collectivism.* Boulder, CO: Westview.

Triandis, H.C. (2000). Cross-cultural versus cultural psychology: A synthesis. In A.L. Comunian & U.P. Gielen (Eds.), *International perspectives on human development* (pp. 81–95). Lengerich, Germany: Pabst Science.

Triandis, H.C., & Heron, A. (1981). *Handbook of cross-cultural psychology.* Vol. 4, *Developmental psychology.* Boston, MA: Allyn & Bacon.

Trivers, R.L. (1972). Parental investment and sexual selection. In B. Campbell (Ed.), *Sexual selection and the descent of man* (pp. 136–179). Chicago, ILL: Aldine de Gruyter.

Tuzin, D.F. (1977). *The Ilahita Arapesh.* Berkeley, CA: University of California Press.

Vine, I. (1986). Moral maturity in socio-cultural perspective: Are Kohlberg's stages universal? In S. Mogdil & C. Mogdil (Eds.), *Lawrence Kohlberg: Consensus and controversy* (pp. 431–450). London, UK: Falmer Press.

Vygotsky, L. S., & Luria, A. R. (1930/1993). *Studies on the history of behavior: Ape, primitive, and child.* (Victor I. Golod & Jane E. Knox, Eds. and Trans.). Hillsdale, NJ: Erlbaum.

Werner, E. E. (1979). *Cross-cultural child development: A view from Planet Earth.* Monterey, CA. Brooks/Cole.

Whiting, B. B. (Ed.). (1963). *Six cultures: Studies of childrearing.* New York: Wiley.

Whiting, B. B., & Edwards, C. P. (1988). *Children of different worlds: The formation of social behavior.* Cambridge, MA: Harvard University Press.

Whiting, B. B., & Whiting, J. W. M. (1975). *Children of six cultures: A psycho-cultural analysis.* Cambridge, MA: Harvard University Press.

Whiting, B. B., & Whiting, J. W. M. (1991). Preindustrial world, Adolescence in. In R. A. Lerner & A. C. Petersen (Eds.), *Encyclopedia of adolescence,* 2 vols. (pp. 814–829). New York: Garland.

Whiting, J. W. M., Child, I. L., & Lambert, W. W. (1966). *Field guide for a study of socialization.* New York: Wiley.

Wilson, E. O. (1975). *Sociobiology: The new synthesis.* Cambridge, MA: Belknap Press.

Wilson, E. O. (1978). *On human nature.* Cambridge, MA: Belknap Press.

Worthman, C. M., & Whiting, J. W. M. (1987). Social change in adolescent sexual behavior, mate selection, and pre-marital pregnancy rates in a Kikuyu community. *Ethos, 15,* 145–165.

Zoma, M., & Gielen, U. P. (2015). How many psychologists are there in the world? *International Psychology Bulletin, 19*(1), 47–50.

2

Cultural Models of Stages in Child Development

M. Annette Grove and David F. Lancy

INTRODUCTION

Societies vary with respect to their locally constructed or cultural or "folk" models (Strauss, 1992) of the life course. However, predictable transitions can be found as children progress through naturally occurring stages (walking, talking, gaining sense, puberty). Societies draw on these biologically based transitions to construct models of development. Ethnographic and historic records provide evidence of the behavioral changes in children that may be marked by a shift in the child's status. Drawing on these data, we construct a broadly applicable cultural model of child development. This model coalesces around six life cycle stages, which correspond to evolutionary biologists' analyses of human development (e.g., Bogin & Smith, 2012, p. 521). This report draws on a long-term project designed to develop an anthropological perspective on human development (Lancy, 1996, 2007, 2010, 2012, 2014, 2015; Lancy & Grove, 2011; Lancy, Gaskin, & Bock, 2010). Our database consists largely of ethnographic accounts of childhood from nearly 1,000 societies, ranging from the Paleolithic to the present and from every area of the world.

Ethnographers, as participant observers, become immersed in the societies they study. In writing about the lives of their subjects or informants, they weave together strands of information gathered from participant observation, interviews, and personal experience into a detailed account. We collate and analyze these accounts from a wide range of societies across time. Ideally, each ethnography provides at least some description of childhood in the society under study. We then draw on these descriptions to detect consistent patterns in the organization of prominent life stages and the transitions between them.

STAGES IN DEVELOPMENT

Our survey of the ethnographic record indicates that life stages are rarely formalized; instead we must tease out the existence of stages from descriptions of children's behavior and the behavior of others toward the child (Mead, 1947, p. 234). For example, Weisner and Gallimore refer to a widespread but unnamed phenomenon they call "toddler rejection" (1977, p. 177), which captures how many societies view children during the post-weaning period. Anthropologists consistently note a shift in the status and treatment of the child between the ages 2 and 3, but this stage is rarely labeled as such in the vernacular.

Stage One: Birth and the External Womb

The child's birth may be cloaked in secrecy. Pregnancy is rarely acknowledged publicly as many factors can have a harmful effect on the outcome. The mother may adopt a wait-and-see attitude as she may not be able to carry the fetus to full term due to poor health. Lack of support from the family or the community may force her to choose to terminate the pregnancy. This attitude continues through a post-partum period of seclusion where mother and infant may be hidden behind a curtain of privacy. This allows for the disposal of an unhealthy or unwanted infant. After birth an infant is often perceived as still intimately linked with its mother. "[The Somali] conception is that the newborn child for a certain time after birth is still . . . part of the flesh and blood of the mother" (Cerulli, 1959, p. 25). The "Ovimbundu infant is 'born pink' and gradually becomes a person [*omunu*]" (Childs, 1949, pp. 120–121). The Lepcha infant in Nepal is considered to be "still in the womb. . . . It is not even referred to as a human child; it is called a rat–child" (Gorer, 1938, p. 289).

The idea of the post-partum womb is a key concept affecting how the infant is perceived and cared for. Mother and infant are considered as inseparable after birth as when the infant was in the womb. Among the Wari of Amazonia, "mother and infant are treated as a unit; for about six weeks after birth they remain secluded together inside their house . . . babies of both sexes are called *arawet*, which translates literally as 'still being made'" (Conklin & Morgan, 1996, p. 672). The use of swaddling, wrapping an infant tightly in layers of cloth, and severely confining cradles or cradleboards is widespread. Nurzay women explained that "the newborn baby's flesh is *oma* [lit. unripe] like uncooked meat, and that only by swaddling will it become strong [*chakahosi*] and solid like cooked [*pokh*] meat" (Casimir, 2010, p. 16).

An even more common practice is that of re-creating the womb externally, by attaching the baby to its mother with a piece of material such as the manta pouch (high Andes; Tronick, Thomas, & Daltabuit, 1994, pp. 1009–1010). Nursing occurs largely unnoted by others. The baby remains invisible (Lancy & Grove, 2011, p. 283) thereby protecting it from any threats including witchcraft and the supernatural. Swaddling prevents the infant from becoming agitated or moving its limbs vigorously (Lancy, 2014; Nicholaisen, 1988). Navajo babies are kept "in a cradleboard to make them straight and strong. Some women let their children lie on sheepskins and roll about, but they are weak, sick children" (Leighton & Kluckhohn, 1948, p. 23).

Another common notion (Razy, 2007) is that the infant is in a liminal state, dangling precariously between the human and spirit worlds. There is the idea that the infant's spirit and body are quite loosely connected and that, if the infant is not kept quiet and secluded, it may choose to return to the world of spirits (Arden, 2011; Leavitt, 1989). Each of these ideas may be rooted in the fact that an infant may not survive long. Data from a range of societies suggest that from one-fifth to one-half of newborns don't survive to five years (Dentan, 1978, p. 111; Dunn, 1974, p. 385; Kramer & Greaves, 2007, p. 720; Le Mort, 2008, p. 25).

Stage Two: Joining the Community

In Stage One, the infant isn't yet considered a fully human, distinct entity. The threat of death or infanticide is so great that the infant's passing frequently goes unnoticed; there is no formal funeral, burial, or mourning (Becker, 2007, p. 282; Gorer, 1938, p. 209). Gestation continues after birth. The infant must exit from this socially constructed womb and pass through a second birth. This second or social birth (Fabian, 1990; Lepowsky, 1987) may be marked by a rite of passage such as naming or the first haircut (Masters, 1953). Among the Azande, when the survival of the infant seems likely, the whole community participates in the ceremony in which he or she is removed from the birthing hut and passed through the smoke of a greenwood fire (Baxter & Butt, 1953, p. 72). After the infant has survived its first year, the Kurds of Rawanduz give him or her the first haircut (Masters, 1953, p. 159). The Balinese undertake a similar rite at about the same age. Before the first haircut the infant is not allowed to touch the ground and must be carried at all times (Geertz, 1961, p. 104). The child is now viewed as human or at least as almost human. An important element in the construction of personhood is the child's acquisition of kin and linkages to his or her father, clan, and extended family (Blanchy, 2007). "Many Hubeer . . . post-natal practices [involve the] shedding of the symbols for maternal ties [and establishment of] agnatic links" (Helander, 1988, p. 150). The transition from crawling (which is animal-like) to walking (human) may be highlighted. The child is now acknowledged as human or at least as potentially human.

Another aspect of the baby's "coming out" is the increased involvement of alloparents. Many individuals may act as supplementary caretakers. Humans are cooperative breeders. The infant who survives to enjoy a second birth is placed under the care of the grandmother and/or older siblings (Hrdy, 2006, p. 25) freeing the mother to return to her several duties. Mothers, eager to attract the assistance of allomothers, may "market" their babies to neighbors and kin (Ochs & Schiefflin, 1984, p. 279; see also Gottlieb, 2004) because a thriving infant will attract the caring attention of many. Of course, the healthy infant may also attract threats from those who might be envious of the fertile mother so steps must be taken to protect the now very public baby from malevolence (Einarsdottir, 2008, pp. 116–117; Friedl, 1997, p. 88; Jenkins, Orr-Ewing, & Heywood, 1985, p. 43). The nursling enjoys a kind of honeymoon of affection and care from all sides but as weaning approaches, a change is evident.

Stage Three: Separation

This stage corresponds to the modern Western "early childhood" stage. A prominent feature of this stage is "toddler rejection" (Weisner & Gallimore, 1977, p. 176). Abrupt and severe weaning, sometimes well before the child might wean itself, is widely reported, usually when the mother again becomes pregnant. Bofi mothers living in Central Africa cover "their nipples with red fingernail polish, and/or a bandage to resemble a wound" (Fouts, 2004, p. 138), thus initiating the weaning process, which may be completed by 18 months (Fouts, 2005, p. 356). Extended nursing may be seen as prolonging infancy and creating a "weak, simpering" adult (Turner, 1987, p. 107). The mother, eager to wean the child from her back and return to her labors, may, yet again, be faced with the same tearful resistance that occurred during weaning from the breast (Maretzki, Maretzki, & Whiting, 1963, p. 447). The Nso of Cameroon believe that "a standing baby . . . makes less work for the mother" (Keller, 2007, p. 124). Yoruba "mothers and grandmothers [prefer] wiry and agile babies who learn to walk early" (Zeitlin, 1996, p. 412).

Aside from the attentions of allomothers, the lure of the neighborhood playgroup provides a welcome diversion during this period of separation from the mother. Among the Mandinka, once a new sibling arrives "*dénanola* (infancy) is over." The child gains access to the social group of peers, which aids in his or her "forgetting of the breast" (Whittemore, 1989,

p. 92). The Kpelle call the area where children play together the "mother ground," as it is usually located next to a few working, but watchful adults (Lancy, 1996, p. 85). Alloparents and the playgroup not only free up the mother, but playmates and sibling caretakers actively socialize the growing child. Through imitation of their caretakers "toddlers learn to feed and dress themselves, go outside to urinate and defecate and help with household chores" (Martini & Kirkpatrick, 1992, p. 124). Marquesan mothers see toddlers as developing skills because they *want* to hang out with and emulate their older siblings. In rural Bengal, "little girls accompany older girls in gathering, and they gradually learn the needed skills" (Rohner & Chaki-Sircar, 1988, p. 33).

The rejected toddler, better able to control his or her emotions, is readmitted into the family circle where he or she observes the behaviors and conversations of older children and family members. This creates a kind of classroom atmosphere in which the child rapidly learns its culture. Matsigenka "children are embedded in the middle of quotidian activities where they are positioned to quietly observe and learn what others are doing" (Ochs & Izquierdo, 2009, p. 395). A three-year-old Wolof child will choose his own place at the family meal where he is "encouraged to acquire and participate in social norms" (Zempleni-Rabain, 1973, p. 222). In addition to learning social graces, the child is slowly folded into the family economy (Lancy, 2012). In Samoa, Margaret Mead offered one of the earliest descriptions of the phenomenon: "The tiniest little staggerer has tasks to perform—to carry water, to borrow fire brands, to fetch leaves to stuff the pig. . . . Learning to run errands tactfully is one of the first lessons of childhood" (Mead, 1928, p. 633). Among the Giriama of Kenya, a child who falls between two and three years of age is a *kahoho kuhuma madzi* or "water carrier" (Wenger, 1989, p. 98). Often the child is overeager to emulate those older then him or her, and they will be reined in. In Botswana, toddlers may be prevented from handling grain for fear they'll let it spill on the ground (Bock & Johnson, 2004). Bamana children are prevented from messing up planted rows in the garden (Polak, 2003, p. 126) and little Inuit boys are kept some distance from the prey during a hunt so they won't scare it off (Matthiasson, 1979, p. 74). Around the ages 5–7, a shift in expectations occurs. Tolerance for the child's helpful but clumsy and inconsistent contributions wanes.

Stage Four: Getting Noticed

At around five- to seven years old, children are said to "gain sense"; they become "useful." They are worthy of adults' attention (Lancy & Grove, 2011). Although children may participate in household chores from an early age, they may not be trusted with more serious responsibilities until they reach a certain level of maturity (Bugos & McCarthy, 1984, p. 510;

Grindal, 1972, p. 28). "Among the Gamo in southern Ethiopia, the social status of the child is closely connected with the economic tasks that he or she performs. Children up to the age of about five are called *Gesho Noyta*; they are not yet given any tasks. Children between the ages of 5 and 10 are called *Não*; at this age, the children begin to assist their fathers and mothers with their work. In the following age group, called *Wet'te Não*, girls and boys already assume full responsibility in domestic and agricultural activities" (Leibel, 2004, p. 80). Until this time, the child's lack of sense was excused and the child spared the criticism an older child might receive (Maretzki et al., 1963, p. 481; Read, 1960, p. 89). At the 5–7 stage, however, adult patience wears thin and a six-year-old Parakanã child must uncomplainingly and without supervision look after a crèche of younger children (Gosso, 2010). Pakistani Pashtun girls in middle childhood are sent by their mothers to discreetly collect local gossip and provide detailed reports on the latest events in the village (Lindholm, 1982, p. 181). The workload and responsibility grows in proportion to the child's size, strength, and competency. Javanese and Nepalese children work about 4 hours a day as six- to eight-year-olds, but by age 15 this rises to 10 or more hours a day (Nag, White, & Peet, 1978). Twelve-year-old Aka and Hadza children are already self-sufficient foragers (Hewlett & Cavalli-Sforza, 1986, p. 930; Hill & Hurtado, 1996, p. 223), and a 12-year-old Bakgalagadi girl is expected to be able to run an entire household (Lancaster, 1984, p. 86).

Gender differentiation increases at this time as well. Girls become more closely tied to the domestic sphere. In contrast, boys gain more freedom (Edwards, 2005, p. 87), especially if they relocate to all-male housing (Morton, 1996, p. 112). Limits are placed on interactions between boys and girls. Heightened modesty requirements are reflected in a change in clothing (Lawton, 2007, p. 46). On Ulithi atoll children of both sexes are given scratchy plant-based skirts at about five or six. Children frequently attempt to remove these new garments, which "results in scoldings, warnings, and rewards to keep [children] from discarding them" (Lessa, 1966, p. 98): The Dusun call boys "without loincloth" and girls "without a skirt" until about five-years old when nomenclature changes. Boys are called "child man"; girls are called "virgin" (Williams, 1969, p. 86). Girls are expected to help with childcare and running the household (Nerlove et al., 1974, p. 275): their workload increases whereas boys, no longer under the control of their mothers, may have even more freedom to roam (Nag et al., 1978). Boys in Iran are "turned out in the morning like cows," coming home only for food and sleep (Friedl, 1997, p. 148; Watson-Franke, 1976, p. 194).

Stage Five: Youth in Limbo

Adolescence is the most variable stage cross-culturally (Crawford, 1991, p. 17). Schlegel and Barry, in a thorough review of the ethnographic literature, assert that adolescence exists in all societies (1991, p. 18). However, puberty (in girls) may begin as early as 12 years (11½ for U.S. girls) of age in well-nourished societies or as late as 17 in societies where proteins and calories are scarce (Eveleth & Tanner, 1990, p. 170). The end of adolescence occurs when a couple creates an independently functioning household and begins bearing children. For example, in the traditional fishing village of Kau Sai, China, marriage and household formation may begin as early as 16, immediately following first menses (Ward, 1970, p. 115), while Maasai males were expected to wait until they are in their 30s to marry (Spencer, 1970, p. 137). In the first example, development from adolescent to adult proceeds without difficulty as children readily learn the gender-appropriate skills of adults and are ready to assume adult-level responsibilities at an early age. In the second example, a rigid male hierarchy prevents pubertal males from marrying and, instead, assigns them to warrior status. The *moran* role requires them to avoid women by living on the margins of the group's territory. Pubescent girls marry into the polygynous households of older men of high status (Spencer, 1970).

In most traditional societies, adolescence lasting longer than a year or two becomes problematic primarily due to the challenge of adolescent sexuality. Youths are likely to be interested in sex well before society thinks they are capable of taking on the responsibility of a family. The initiation rite is, therefore, one means to enforce emotional maturity and deference to one's elders. Another tactic is seclusion. Guajiro (Venezuela) girls are secluded for up to five years in a dimly lit hut. "If the girl cries she will be severely criticized for her childish attitude and reminded of her new status as an adult woman who must exercise self-control" (Watson-Franke, 1976, p. 197). Among the Makiritare of the Orinoco basin in South America, initiation and seclusion begin at the first signs of menstruation (Guss, 1982, p. 264). The primary purpose of seclusion seems to be to preserve the girl's virtue to ensure a successful marriage, while the secondary purpose may be to shape the girl's outlook to more closely match that of the older women. A high-ranking Tlingit girl in the region of Southeast Alaska and Western Canada spends two years in seclusion during which she is provided with homilies and more forceful reminders to maintain behavior consonant with her rank, such as avoiding gossip (Markstrom, 2008, p. 145). Following seclusion, the Tlingit girl was considered marriageable and "prudent . . . parents took pains to marry her off promptly" (De Laguna, 1965, p. 21). Even in the absence of seclusion or initiation, pubertal girls are sheltered by the distaff side of the household. Their association with and close ties to the mother begin quite early as they assist with their younger sibs and with work in the house, garden, and with livestock and craft production. So while adolescent males enjoy a wider compass for their activities, adolescent girls rarely leave their mother's orbit.

The parallel process for boys is removal to a men's house or dormitory. Igbo boys in Nigeria move out of their natal homes into the bachelor's house (Ottenberg, 2006, p. 118). The proximity to men provides the young men a chance to observe and replicate male behaviors (Wagley, 1977, p. 149). This sequestration erases the taint of femininity acquired during years of association with their mothers and other women. Many societies extend this process of gender socialization via an initiation period. Among the Sambia of New Guinea, the first stage in this initiation includes days of hazing, fasting, beating, sleeplessness, and sudden surprises, followed by forced nose bleeding to remove female contaminants (Herdt, 1990, p. 376). Traditionally, war-like societies tended to hypermasculinize youth through initiation rites, segregation of males, and thought control. Alternately, adolescent males may be conscripted to serve in work "gangs" that benefit the society as a whole. Young Rotuman males, for example, "form the nucleus of communal labor in every village" (Howard, 1970, pp. 66–67). During their tenure as workers they are often reminded of their subservient status by the village elite. This is a principal theme and objective of adolescent initiation rites. "When [a Chaga] adolescent flouts parental authority and has become a cause of public annoyance, father and mother agree that he should be curbed by the *kisusa* rite" (Raum, 1940, p. 303).

Even after serving their time as warriors or members of a work gang, adolescents must still acquire the requisite property necessary to establish a household. This may include payment of a bride-price or dowry, doing bride-service for one's future in-laws, the construction of a home for the new couple, or acquiring critical resources such as tools or livestock.

Stage Six: Adulthood

Outside contemporary industrial society, most societies were and are organized as a gerontocracy where status is governed by fertility and age (Lancy, 1996, p. 13, 2015, pp. 2–3). Marriage may carry little weight. A Bagisu bride is given a "woman's" skirt, but is not allowed to wear it until after the birth of her first child (La Fontaine, 1959, p. 47). In Sumatra, there is no difference between a married Malay woman and her unmarried sisters—until she gives birth to her first child (Swift, 1965, p. 124). The same criterion is often applied to young men (Leavitt, 1998 p. 186). A Tzeltal Maya villager is not considered a full-fledged community member until he marries and has a child (Hunt, 1962, p. 96). In most societies, children of 10 years of age may already be capable of the full range of "adult" subsistence tasks (Lancy, 2012). So, like marriage, competence is not a reliable marker of adult status either.

Viewing the adolescent stage through a cultural lens reveals wide variability in onset and termination. Among foragers, adolescence is prolonged relative to agrarian societies because of the relative challenges of becoming a productive forager versus the ease with which children can herd or work in the fields (Hames & Draper, 2004). However, successful child-bearing is often cited by anthropologists as the most significant aspect of the passage to full adulthood for males as well as females.

SUMMARY

Models of human development (Strauss, 1992) vary cross-culturally; however, our survey of the ethnographic record reveals broad commonalities presumably organized by predictable biological markers of change and development. This regularity has allowed us to construct a generally applicable model with six broadly defined stages in development. In Stage One, the newborn, yet to be acknowledged by society and still seen as part of the mother, is kept tucked away in some form of an external womb, until its survival is sure. Stage Two proceeds when the infant's survival becomes clear and he or she is introduced to and integrated into the community. Stage Three finds the child unhappily weaned from the breast and back, and left mostly under the care of sibling caretakers and allomothers. The unhappy state of the toddler is soothed by the lure of the playgroup. In Stage Four children become useful. As they gain common sense they are entrusted with ever more difficult tasks. Gender differentiation increases as girls become more closely tied to the domestic sphere, whereas boys are allowed more freedom. Stage Five or adolescence varies widely across cultures. Adolescence may be long or short, but controlling budding interest in sex and subservience and obedience among the young is a major focus of socialization practices such as seclusion and initiation. Stage Six begins with marriage, but it is the successful bearing and raising of children that earns one adult status.

REFLECTIVE QUESTIONS

1. As we continue to press Western ideas and definitions of childhood and parenting on the rest of the world, what can we gain from looking at childhood through an anthropological lens?
2. As issues of street children, child labor, education, attachment, identity, parental control/free range childhoods, and more continue at the forefront of research on childhood, what kind of knowledge can we gain from looking at childhood through an anthropological lens?

SUGGESTED READINGS

Books and Articles

DeLoache, J., & Gottlieb, A. (Eds.). (2000). *A world of babies: Imagined childcare guides for seven societies.* Cambridge, UK: Cambridge University Press.

Einarsdottir, J. (2004). *Tired of weeping: Mother love, child death, and poverty in Guinea-Bissau.* Madison, WI: University of Wisconsin Press.

Friedl, E. (1997). *Children of Deh Koh: Young life in an Iranian village.* Syracuse, NY: Syracuse University Press.
Greenfield, P. M. (2004). *Weaving generations together: Evolving creativity in the Maya of Chiapas.* Santa Fe, NM: School of American Research (SAR).
Herdt, G. A. (2005). *The Sambia: Ritual, sexuality, and change in Papua New Guinea.* Independence, KY: Wadsworth.
Hewlett, B. S., & Lamb, M. E. (Eds.). (2005). *Hunter-gatherer childhoods: Evolutionary, developmental, and cultural perspectives.* New Brunswick, NJ: Transaction/ Aldine.
Hill, K., & Hurtado, A. M. (1996). *Ache life history: The ecology and demography of a foraging people.* New Brunswick, NJ: Aldine Transaction.
Keller, H. (2007). *Cultures of infancy.* Mahwah, NJ: Erlbaum.
Kramer, K. L. (2005). *Maya children: Helpers on the farm.* Cambridge, MA: Harvard University Press.
Lancy, D. F., Bock, J., & Gaskins, S. (Eds). (2010). *The anthropology of learning in childhood.* Lanham, MD: AltaMira Press.
LeVine, R. A., & New, R. (2008). *Anthropology and child development: A Cross-Cultural Reader.* New York: Wiley-Blackwell.
Mabilia, M. (2005). *Breast feeding and sexuality: Beliefs and taboos among the Gogo mothers in Tanzania.* Oxford, UK: Berghahn Books.
Markstrom, C. A. (2008). *Empowerment of North American Indian girls: Ritual expressions at puberty.* Lincoln, NE: University of Nebraska Press.
Marlowe, F. W. (2010). *The Hadza: Hunter-gatherers of Tanzania.* Berkeley, CA: University of California Press.
Morton, H. (1996). *Becoming Tongan: An ethnography of childhood.* Honolulu, HI: University of Hawai'i Press.

Website

ACYIG: (http://www.aaanet.org/sections/acyig/newsletter/newsletter-archive/)

REFERENCES

Arden, T. (2011). Empowered children in classic Maya sacrificial rites. *Childhood in the Past, 4,* 133–145.
Baxter, P. T. W., & Butt, A. (1953). *The Azande, and related peoples of the Anglo-Egyptian Sudan and Belgian Congo.* London, UK: International African Institute.
Becker, M. J. (2007). Childhood among the Etruscans: Mortuary programs at Tarquinia as indicators of the transition to adult status. In A. Cohen & J. B. Rutter (Eds.), *Constructions of childhood in ancient Greece and Italy* (pp. 281–292). Athens, Greece: American School of Classical Studies at Athens, Hesperia Supplement 410.
Blanchy, S. (2007). Le tambavy des bébés à Madagascar: Du soin au ritual d'ancestralité [The "tambavy" of babies in Madagascar: From care to the ritual of ancestrality]. In D. Bonnet & L. Pourchez (Eds.), *Du soin au rite dans l'enfance* [From care to ritual in childhood] (pp. 146–166). Paris, France: IRD.
Bock, J., & Johnson, S. E. (2004). Subsistence ecology and play among the Okavango Delta peoples of Botswana. *Human Nature, 15*(1), 63–82.

Bogin, B., & Smith, B.H. (2012). Evolution of the human life cycle. In S. Stinson, B. Bogin, & D. O'Rourke (Eds.), *Human biology: An evolutionary and biocultural perspective* (2nd ed., pp. 515–586). New York: John Wiley.

Bugos, P.E., Jr., & McCarthy, L.M. (1984). Ayoreo infanticide: A case study. In G. Hausfater & S.B. Hrdy (Eds.), *Infanticide: Comparative and evolutionary perspectives* (pp. 503–520). New York: Aldine.

Casimir, M.J. (2010). *Growing up in a pastoral society: Socialization among Pashtu nomads*. Köln, Germany: Kölner Ethnologische Beiträge.

Cerulli, E. (1959). *How a Hawiye tribe used to live*. Rome, Italy: A Cura dell'Amministrazione Fiduciaria Italiana della Somalia Instituto poligrafico dello Stato P.V.

Childs, G.M. (1949). *Umbundu kinship and character: Being a description of social structure and individual development of the Ovimbundu of Angola*. London, UK: Oxford University Press.

Conklin, B.A., & Morgan, L.M. (1996). Babies, bodies, and the production of personhood in North America and a native Amazonian society. *Ethos, 24*(4), 657–694.

Crawford, S. (1991). When do Anglo-Saxon children count? *Journal of Theoretical Archeology, 2*, 17–24.

de Laguna, F. (1965). Childhood among the Yakutat Tlingit. In E.M. Spiro (Ed.), *Context and meaning in cultural anthropology* (pp. 3–23). New York: Free Press.

Dentan, F. K. (1978). Notes on childhood in a non-violent context: The Semai case. In A. Montagu (Ed.), *Learning nonaggression the experience of non-literate societies* (pp. 94–143). London, UK: Oxford University Press.

Dunn, P. (1974). That enemy is the baby: Childhood in imperial Russia. In L. de Mause (Ed.), *The history of childhood* (pp. 383–405). New York: Harper and Row.

Edwards, C.P. (2005). Children's play in cross-cultural perspective: A new look at the six culture study. In F.F. McMahon, D.E. Lytle, & B. Sutton-Smith (Eds.), *Play: An interdisciplinary synthesis* (pp. 81–96). Lanham, MD: University Press of America.

Einarsdóttir, J. (2008). The classification of newborn children: Consequences for survival. In L. Clements & J. Read (Eds.), *Disabled people and the right to life* (pp. 406–432). London, UK: Routledge.

Eveleth, P.B., & Tanner, J.M. (1990). *Worldwide variation in human growth*. New York: Cambridge University Press.

Fabian, S.M. (1990). *Space-time of the Bororo of Brazil*. Gainesville, FL: University Press of Florida.

Fouts, H.N. (2004). Social contexts of weaning: The importance of cross-cultural studies. In U.P. Gielen & J.L. Roopnarine (Eds.), *Childhood and adolescence: Cross-cultural perspectives and applications* (pp. 133–148). Westport, CT: Praeger.

Fouts, H. N. (2005). Families in Central Africa: A comparison of Bofi farmer and forager families. In J.L. Roopnarine & U.P. Gielen (Eds.), *Families in global perspective* (pp. 347–363). Boston, MA: Pearson.

Friedl, E. (1997). *Children of Deh Koh: Young life in an Iranian village*. Syracuse, NY: Syracuse University Press.

Geertz, H. (1961). *The Javanese family: A study of kinship and socialization*. New York: Free Press.

Gorer, G. (1968). *Himalayan village: An account of the Lepchas of Sikkim*. New York: Basic Books.

Gosso, Y. (2010). Play in different cultures. In P.K. Smith (Ed.), *Children and play* (pp. 80–98). Chichester, UK: Wiley/Blackwell.

Gottlieb, A. (2004). *The afterlife is where we come from: The culture of infancy in West Africa*. Chicago, IL: University of Chicago Press.

Grindal, B.T. (1972). *Growing up in two worlds: Education and transition among the Sisala of Northern Ghana*. New York: Holt, Rinehart, and Winston.

Guss, D.M. (1982). The enculturation of Makiritare women. *Ethnology, 21*(3), 259–269.

Hames, R., & Draper, P. (2004). Women's work, childcare, and helpers at-the-nest in a hunter-gatherer society. *Human Nature, 15*(4), 319–334.

Helander, B. (1988). *Slaughtered camel: Coping with fictitious descent among the Hubeer of Southern Somalia*. Uppsala, Sweden: University of Uppsala, Department of Anthropology.

Hewlett, B.S., & Cavalli-Sforza, L.L. (1986). Cultural transmission among Aka pygmies. *American Anthropologist, 88*, 922–934.

Hill, K., & Hurtado, A. M. (1996). *Ache life history: The ecology and demography of a foraging people*. New York: Aldine de Gruyter.

Howard, A. (1970). *Learning to be Rotuman: Enculturation in the South Pacific*. New York: Teachers College Press.

Hrdy, S.B. (2006). Evolutionary context of human development: The cooperative breeding model. In C.S. Carter, L. Ahnert, K.E. Grossmann, S.B. Hrdy, M.E. Lamb, S.W. Porges, & N. Sachser, (Eds.), *Attachment and bonding: A new synthesis* (pp. 9–32). Cambridge, MA: MIT Press.

Hunt, M.E.V. (1962). *The dynamics of the domestic group in two Tzeltal Villages: A contrastive comparison*. Chicago, IL: University of Chicago Library.

Jenkins, C.L., Orr-Ewing, A.K., & Heywood, P.F. (1985). Cultural aspects of early childhood growth and nutrition among the Amele of Lowland Papua New Guinea. In L.B. Marshall (Ed.), *Infant care and feeding in the South Pacific* (pp. 29–50). New York: Gordon and Breach.

Keller, H. (2007). *Cultures of infancy*. Mahwah, NJ: Lawrence Erlbaum.

Kramer, K. L., & Greaves, R. D. (2007). Changing patterns of infant mortality and maternal fertility among Pum'e foragers and horticulturalists. *American Anthropologist, 109*(4), 713–725.

La Fontaine, J. S. (1959). *The Gisu of Uganda*. London: International African Institute.

Lancaster, J.B. (1984). Evolutionary perspectives on sex differences in the higher primates. In A.S. Rossi (Ed.), *Gender and the life course* (pp. 3–28). New York: Aldine.

Lancy, D.F. (1996). *Playing on the mother ground: Cultural routines for children's development*. New York: Guilford.

Lancy, D.F. (2007). Accounting for the presence/absence of mother-child play. *American Anthropologist, 109*(2), 273–284.

Lancy, D.F. (2010). When nurture becomes nature: Ethnocentrism in studies of human development. *Behavioral and Brain Sciences, 33*, 39–40.

Lancy, D.F. (2012). The chore curriculum. In G. Spittler & M. Bourdillion (Eds.), *African children at work: Working and learning in growing up* (pp. 23–57). Berlin, Germany: Lit Verlag.

Lancy, D.F. (2014). "Babies aren't persons": A survey of delayed personhood. In H. Otto & H. Keller (Eds.), *Different faces of attachment: Cultural variations of a universal human need* (pp. 66–109). Cambridge, UK: Cambridge University Press.

Lancy, D.F. (2015). *The anthropology of childhood: Cherubs, chattel, and changelings* (2nd ed.). Cambridge, UK: Cambridge University Press.

Lancy, D. F., Gaskins, S., & Bock, J. (Eds.). (2010). *The anthropology of learning in childhood.* Lanham, MD: AltaMira Press.

Lancy, D. F., & Grove, M. A. (2010). Learning guided by others. In D. F. Lancy, S. Gaskins, & J. Bock (Eds.), *The anthropology of learning in childhood* (pp. 145–179). Lanham, MD: AltaMira Press.

Lancy, D. F., & Grove, M. A. (2011). "Getting noticed": Middle childhood in cross-cultural perspective. *Human Nature, 22,* 281–302.

Lawton, C. (2007). Children in classical attic votive reliefs. In A. Cohen & J. B. Rutter (Eds.), *Constructions of childhood in ancient Greece and Italy* (pp. 41–60). Princeton, NJ: The American School of Classical Study at Athens.

Le Mort, F. (2008). Infant burials in pre-pottery Neolithic Cyprus: Evidence from Khiroitia. In K. Bacvarov (Ed.), *Babies Reborn: Infant/Child Burials in Pre- and Protohistory* (pp. 23–32). BAR International Series 1832. Oxford: Archaeopress.

Leavitt, S. C. (1998). The Bikhet mystique. In G. Herdt & S. C. Leavitt (Eds.), *Adolescence in Pacific Island societies* (pp. 173–194). Pittsburgh, PA: University of Pittsburgh Press.

Leibel, M. (2004). *A will of their own: Cross-cultural perspectives on working children.* London, UK: Zed.

Leighton, D., & Kluckhohn, C. C. (1948). *Children of the people.* Cambridge, MA: Harvard University Press.

Lepowsky, M. (1998). Coming of age on Vanatinai: Gender sexuality, and power. In G. Herdt & S. C. Leavitt (Eds.), *Adolescence in Pacific Island societies* (pp. 123–147). Pittsburgh, PA: University of Pittsburgh Press.

Lessa, W. A. (1966). *Ulithi: A Micronesian design for living.* New York: Holt, Rinehart & Winston.

Lindholm, C. (1982). *Generosity and jealousy: The Swat Pukhtun of northern Pakistan.* New York: Columbia University Press.

Maretzki, T. W., Maretzki, H., & Whiting, B. B. (1963). Taira: An Okinawan village. In B. B. Whiting (Ed.), *Six cultures: Studies of child rearing* (pp. 363–539). New York: John Wiley and Sons.

Markstrom, C. A. (2008). *Empowerment of North American Indian girls: Ritual expressions at puberty.* Lincoln, NE: University of Nebraska Press.

Martini, M., & Kirkpatrick, J. (1992). Parenting in Polynesia: A view from the Marquesas. In J. L. Roopnarine & J. D. Carter (Eds.), *Parent-child socialization in diverse cultures* (pp. 199–222). Norwood, NJ: Ablex.

Masters, W. M. (1953). *Rowanduz: A Kurdish administrative and mercantile center.* New Haven, CT: HRAF Computer File.

Matthiasson, J. S. (1979). But teacher, why can't I be a hunter: Inuit adolescence as a double-blind situation. In I. Karigoudar (Ed.), *Childhood and adolescence in Canada* (pp. 72–82). Toronto, Canada: McGraw-Hill Ryerson.

Mead, M. (1928). Samoan children at work and play. *Natural History, 28,* 626–636.

Mead, M. (1947). Age patterning in personality development. *American Journal of Orthopsychiatry, 17*(2), 231–240.

Morton, H. (1996). *Becoming Tongan: An ethnography of childhood.* Honolulu, HI: University of Hawai'i Press.

Nag, M., White, B., & Peet, R. C. (1978). An anthropological approach to the study of the economic value of children in Java and Nepal. *Current Anthropology, 19*(2), 293–306.

Nerlove, S.B., Roberts, J.M., Klein, R.E., Yarbrough, C., & Habicht, J.-P. (1974). Natural indicators of cognitive development: An observational study of rural Guatemalan children. *Ethos, 2*(3): 265–295.

Nicholaisen, I. (1988). Concepts and learning among the Punan Bah of Sarawak. Acquiring culture. In G. Johoda & I.M. Lewis (Eds.), *Acquiring culture: Cross-Cultural studies of child development* (pp. 193–221). London, UK: Taylor & Francis.

Ochs, E., & Izquierdo, C. (2009). Responsibility in childhood: Three developmental trajectories. *Ethos, 37*, 391–413.

Ochs, E., & Schieffelin, B.B. (1984). Language acquisition and socialization: Three developmental stories and their implications. In R.A. Shweder & R.A. LeVine (Eds.), *Culture theory: Essays on mind, self and society* (pp. 276–320). New York: Cambridge University Press.

Ottenberg, S. (2006). Emulation in boy's masquerades: The Afikpo case. In Ottenberg, S., & Binkley, D. A. (Eds.), *Playful Performers: African Children's Masquerades.* (pp. 117–127). London: Transaction Publishers.

Polak, B. (2003). Little peasants: On the importance of reliability in child labour. In H. d'Almeida-Topor, M. Lakroum, & G. Spittler (Eds.), *Le travail en Afrique noire: Représentations et pratiques époque contemporaine* (pp. 125–136). Paris, France: Karthala.

Raum, O.F. (1940). *Chaga childhood.* London, UK: Oxford University Press.

Razy, É. (2007). *Naître et devenir: Anthropologie de la petite enfance en pays Soninké, Mali* [Birth and becoming: The anthropology of infancy in Soninké, Mali]. Nanterre, France: Société D'ethnologie,

Read, M. (1960). *Children of their fathers.* New Haven, CT: Yale University Press.

Rohner, R.P., & Chaki-Sircar, M. (1988). *Women and children in a Bengali Village.* Hanover, NH: University Press of New England.

Schlegel, A., & Barry H.L., III (1991). *Adolescence: An anthropological inquiry.* New York: The Free Press.

Spencer, P. (1970). The function of ritual in the socialization of the Samburu Moran. In P. Mayer (Ed.), *Socialization: The approach from social anthropology* (pp. 127–157). London, UK: Tavistock.

Strauss, C. (1992). Models and motives. In R. d'Andrade & C. Strauss (Eds.), *Human motives and cultural models* (pp. 1–20). Cambridge, UK: Cambridge University Press.

Swift, M. G. (1965). *Malay Peasant Society in Jelebu.* New York: Athlone Press.

Tronick, E.Z., Thomas, R.B., & Daltabuit, M. (1994). The Quechua manta pouch: A caretaking practice for buffering the Peruvian infant against the multiple stressors of high altitude. *Child Development, 65*, 1005–1013.

Turner, D.M. (1987). What happened when my daughter became a Fijan. In B. Butler & D.M. Turner (Eds.), *Children and anthropological research* (pp. 92–114). New York: Plenum Press.

Wagley, C. (1977). *Welcome of tears: The Tapirapé Indians of central Brazil.* New York: Oxford University Press.

Ward, B.E. (1970). Temper tantrums in Kau Sai: Some speculations upon their effects. In P. Mayer (Ed.), *Socialization: The approach from social anthropology* (pp. 107–125). London, UK: Tavistock.

Watson-Franke, M.B. (1976). To learn for tomorrow: Enculturation of girls and its social importance among the Guajiro of Venezuela. In J. Wilbert (Ed.), *Enculturation in*

Latin America (pp. 191–211). Los Angeles, CA: UCLA Latin American Center Publications.

Weisner, T. S., & Gallimore, R. (1977). My brother's keeper: Child and sibling caretaking. *Current Anthropology, 18*, 169–190.

Wenger, M. (1989). Work, play and social relationships among children in a Giriama community. In D. Belle (Ed.), *Children's social networks and social supports* (pp. 91–115). New York: Wiley.

Whittemore, R. D. (1989). *Child caregiving and socialization to the Mandinka way: Toward an ethnography of childhood.* Unpublished Ph.D. dissertation. Los Angeles: University of California-Los Angeles.

Williams, T. R. (1969). *A Borneo childhood: Enculturation in Dusun society.* New York: Holt, Reinhart, and Winston.

Zeitlin, M. (1996). My child is my crown: Yoruba parental theories and practices in early childhood. In S. Harkness & C. M. Super (Eds.), *Parents' cultural belief systems: Their origins, expressions, and consequences* (pp. 407–427). New York: Guilford.

Zempleni-Rabain, J. (1973). Food and strategy involved in learning fraternal exchange among Wolof children. In P. Alexandre (Ed.), *French perspectives in African studies* (pp. 220–233). London, UK: Oxford University Press for the International African Institute.

3

The Changing Lives of 2.2 Billion Children: Global Demographic Trends and Economic Disparities

Uwe P. Gielen

> Children are the wealth of a family.
>
> Nigerian Proverb
>
> By 2050, the median age in Europe is expected to rise to 52.3 years.
>
> Demographer William Frey

Eleven-year-old Fatima[1,2] has been sitting in front of a carpet-loom for much of the day. Performing a series of well-rehearsed hand movements she snips away at the short threads emerging from the carpet's knots just a few inches from her face. Like some of the other young girls sitting close by, she has performed this work for several years and, in consequence, has grown near-sighted. She can only vaguely make out the green rice shoots glittering in Kashmir's afternoon sun outside the factory.

With puberty approaching, Fatima knows that her carpet-weaving days will soon come to an end. Her family will also need to find a husband for her, a prospect that evokes a mixture of conflicting emotions in her. Some years ago her family's fate took a turn for the worse when two of her older brothers were killed by soldiers "sweeping" her village near the outskirts of Kashmir's capital, Srinagar. Although she has only a vague understanding of the larger world outside her family home, she senses that her future is precarious and that the life looming ahead of her will likely be a difficult one. Because she is barely literate, and given the precarious economic situations of her family, her chances of joining an educated family in marriage are slim.

Many miles to the east of her, Takashi is sitting in front of a computer to gather information for an essay he has been asked to write for one of his school classes. Living in a small apartment in Hiroshima, Takashi's parents have given him a room so that he can concentrate better on his all-important studies. Like many of his peers he is visiting a tutorial after-school program (*juko*) in order to prepare himself for a series of demanding entrance examinations whose outcome will shape his future.

Takashi's small room is filled with electronic gadgets and, for years, he has been a consumer of *manga* (cartoons) and TV programs directed at teenagers like himself. Over the years he has been exposed—through his teachers, parents, the mass media, and the web—to a steady stream of information about the outside world. His ambition is to become a "salaryman," hopefully at the big car company where his uncle works. It is a sensible ambition and Takashi's mind is already filled with some pretty clear notions about the steps he will have to undertake in order to fulfill his dream.

The two fictional youngsters, Fatima and Takashi live in highly divergent worlds shaped by the different socioeconomic structures of their respective societies, by contrasting demographic structures and trends, religious beliefs and customs, patterns of family life, gender-related ideologies, and the intermittent strife that has devastated too many families in the Valley of Kashmir but that finds only a dim echo in Japan's daily news. Whereas Fatima's childhood and emerging adulthood is likely to follow a pattern shared by many other poor girls in low-income Muslim societies, Takashi is pursuing a path that, in its outlines, is shaped by Japan's increasingly global and secular "information society." In this chapter, we are mostly concerned with the economic and demographic trends and forces that help determine the divergent developmental pathways of youths such as Fatima and Takashi. In addition, the reader may wish to consult the chapter by Poelker and Gibbons in this volume (chapter 10), which focuses on adolescents in low- and medium-income countries.

When we take into account the differences in children's social networks, we can observe two contrasting forms of social life emerge in the postindustrial countries and in the low-income countries of Asia, Africa, and Latin America. Many children in the developing world live in semi-traditional yet steadily changing societies that place much emphasis on intricate family relationships, collectivistic patterns of living, early responsibility training for children, traditional gender roles, favoritism toward males, obedience and respect for elders, and the obligation of adolescents and young adults to marry early, be fruitful and contribute to the common good. Since families tend to be large, children are shaped in the image of comforting and caring siblings as part of a framework of intricate family relationships. The children are expected to learn values, norms, and social roles through task assignment, observation, admonition, and a kind of nonverbal and semi-verbal osmosis rather than through elaborate explanations by their parents.

In contrast, many children in the postindustrial countries in East Asia, Europe, and North America live in small families or single-parent households, may have divorced parents, interact with few or no siblings, occupy their own rooms, spend many years in educational institutions, are continuously exposed to consumerism and the mass media, are increasingly encouraged to pursue a path of individualistic self-actualization, and grow up in a world of contested and changing gender roles (for South Korean and Japanese families, see the chapter by Hyun, Nakazawa, D. W. Shwalb, & B. Shwalb, chapter 7, in this volume). Because these youngsters are living in societies placing a premium on innovation and change, they spend many years in school surrounded by peers who strive to create their own teenage culture, a culture that will nevertheless be outdated in the not-so-distant future.

Traditionally, American and European textbooks on childhood and adolescence have based their theories and findings on the study of mostly Western youths in the postindustrial countries. This holds true although the great majority of children live in the non-Western and developing countries, a trend that is bound to intensify in the future. In addition, the textbooks pay insufficient attention to the economic, demographic, and cultural forces that shape the lives of children. In contrast to this scenario, I present here a picture of global childhood as shaped by changing childhood mortality rates, varying fertility patterns, increasing life expectancies, and drastic differences in life chances between the poor, the in-between, and the rich countries. Some of these cross-national differences can be readily observed in the lives of Fatima and Takashi, since in one way or the other such differences manifest themselves on a daily basis all around the world.

The recognition of childhood as the basis of all later human development has led to new ways of studying the situation of children on a global scale. Despite some encouraging efforts to increase the access of children and their parents to a stable food supply, safe water, health and educational services, while simultaneously reducing the spread of preventable diseases and protecting those in danger of exploitation, surviving the first years of life remains a challenge especially for the 900 million children who live in the world's least-developed countries. As societies are beginning to evolve in the new millennium, accelerated sociocultural change and increasing complexity in an integrated panorama of ecological, demographic, socioeconomic, and technological forces call for a greater investment in the world's next generation.

Drawing on data provided by UNESCO, the World Bank, the Population Reference Bureau, Save the Children, and other sources, the goal of this chapter is to provide an overview of the current state of the world's children by focusing on worldwide economic and demographic disparities and trends. Ten countries representing major regions of the world have been selected on the basis of high population density. Comparing these countries in the context of global statistics, I trace selected trends regarding their economic performance, population increases, fertility and mortality rates, societal age structures, and the prevalence of child labor in many of the poor nations. Delineating these trends sets the stage for a better understanding of children's lives in a broad variety of sociocultural circumstances.

The quality of the data analyzed in this chapter varies considerably depending on the studied nations. When comparing various demographic statistics, estimates and projections, I observed some discrepancies between various sources and dealt with them according to my best judgment. On the whole, demographic and economic information proves most reliable for the industrialized countries but is sometimes subject to conflicting interpretations and doubt for the poorer countries. This holds especially true for information on children's literacy rates, enrollment figures in educational institutions, and illegal activities such as exposing young child laborers to hazardous conditions.

TEN COUNTRIES AND THEIR CHILDREN

Understanding the situation of the children in the early stages of the 21st century must begin with a systematic analysis of the global tapestry. The disparities across world regions are evident with the combined population of the world's rich countries constituting only a quarter of that of the poor countries. According to projections by the United Nations, during the next few decades, the world is anticipated to witness rapid population growth so that its projected population will reach 9–11 billion around the year 2050. Ninety-seven percent of the population increase is expected to take place in the developing countries of Asia, Africa, and Latin America, whose populations are rising by more than 70 million annually. During the same time period, many European nations are expected to experience a population decline in spite of considerable immigration from the Middle East, North Africa, and elsewhere.

In 2012 an estimated 2.2 billion children under the age of 18 lived in the world. Of these 1,152 million could be found in Asia, 477 million in Africa, 196 million in Latin America and the Caribbean, 203 million in industrialized countries, 153 million in the Middle East and North Africa, and 96 million in Central and Eastern Europe and the Commonwealth of Independent States (CEE/CIS Region). Strikingly, well over 85% of all children and adolescents are part of the largely non-European, nonwhite majority population in the Majority World (also called Third World or low- and medium-income countries), and that proportion has been steadily increasing. It is projected that India, China, Pakistan, Indonesia, and Nigeria (and then the United States) will contribute the most to population growth in the coming half-century. The United States is, indeed, among the very few fully industrialized countries whose population is projected to grow steadily during the next 50 years, due both to immigration and a higher (though declining) fertility rate than is found in most other postmodern societies.

Figure 3.1 depicts child populations for the year 2012 for the following 10 countries: India, China, Indonesia, Nigeria, United States, Brazil, Egypt, Russia, Japan, and Germany. Taken together, these nations mirror not only much of the diversity of humanity but they are also the most populous countries in their respective regions. The following section briefly describes these representative countries, which are ordered from most to least populous with respect to the number of children living in them together with some pressing issues faced by each nation.

The world's largest democracy, India, is expected to become the world's most populous nation around the year 2045. Despite India's uneven economic growth since it gained its independence in 1947, its gross domestic product (GDP) per capita and its school enrollment rates remain low. India's total population increased by 126% between 1975 and 2013. This high population growth rate is too fast for the country's expanding infrastructure to accommodate people's needs and ensure adequate living standards. Moreover, a third of the total population cannot afford regular meals. Shortages of adequate drinking water breed intestinal ailments and other diseases, which in turn contribute to rather high infant mortality rates. India's average life expectancy rate of 66 years remains below the world's average. The ratios for the ages 0–14, 15–64, and 65-over are 28%, 66%, and 6% of the total population, respectively (Central Intelligence Agency, 2014).

China, the world's third-largest country and its most populous nation, is located in East Asia. According to most estimates, it has the world's second-largest GDP. (Some recent estimates place China first as long as the respective GDPs of China and the United States are adjusted for unrealistic currency exchange rates and discrepancies in purchasing power.) Over the past 35 years, China's economy has moved from a Soviet-style collectivistic system toward more decentralized economic decision making. And although the more liberal economic policies, which were introduced in the 1980s, have greatly strengthened the nation's economy, its GDP per capita remains fairly low for the region. This trend is characterized in part by the fact that despite the country's industrial expansion and urbanization, close to half of the Chinese population still lives in villages and small towns with a limited food supply for the numerous inhabitants. Marked by an average life expectancy of 75 years, China's youths are those under 18 years of age who make up close to one-third of the total population. During 1975–2013, and despite its (only partially) realized one-child-per-family policy, China's total population increased by 70%. The ratios for the ages 0–14, 15–64, and

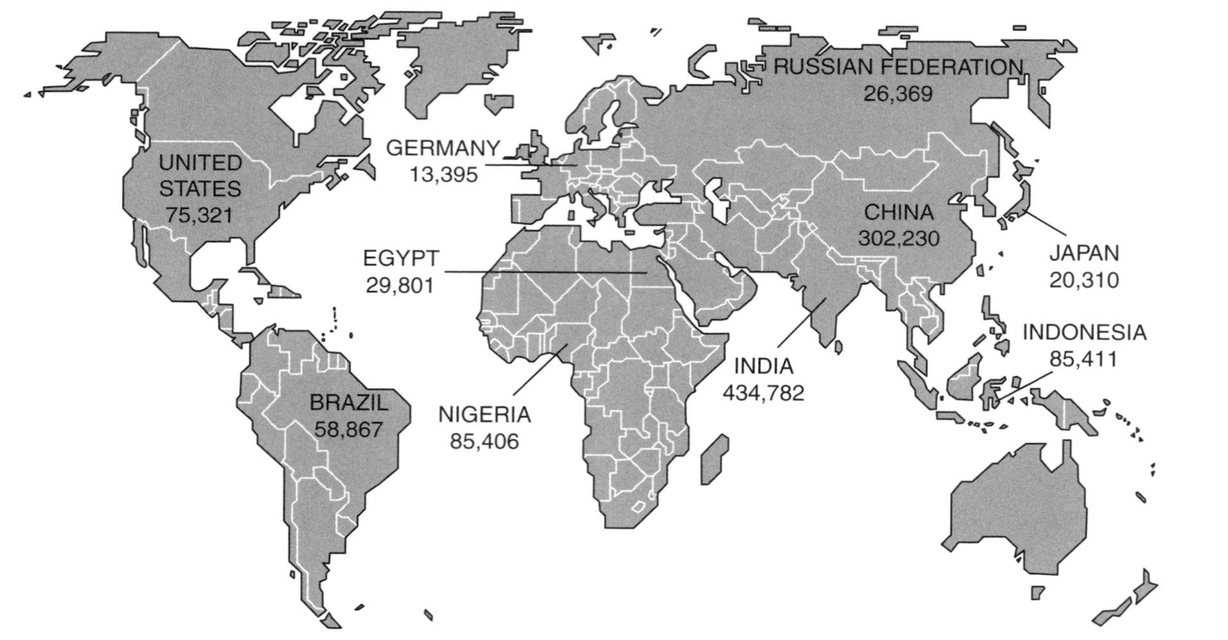

Figure 3.1 Population (in Thousands) under 18* in 10 Representative Countries (2012)

Notes: World population under 18 in 2012: 2,213,677,000.

*A child who celebrates his or her 18th birthday is considered to be an adult by UNICEF.

Source: UNICEF (2014).

65-over are 17%, 73%, and 9% of the total population, respectively (Central Intelligence Agency, 2014).

Indonesia is by far the largest country lying off the Southeast Asian coast. Eighty-seven percent of its predominantly Muslim population resides in overpopulated Java, the most habitable of Indonesia's over 13,600 islands. In response to improved health care and living conditions, a moderately high rate of population growth since 1960s has been affected by an increase in the average life expectancy and a corresponding decline in infant mortality rates. Nonetheless, fertility rates are also declining due to the diffusion of family planning services, birth control, and later marriages. Between 1975 and 2013, Indonesia's total population increased by 111%. The ratios for the ages 0–14, 15–64, and 65-over are 26%, 67%, and 6% of the total population, respectively (Central Intelligence Agency, 2014).

Nigeria is Africa's most populous nation with one of the world's highest natural population growth rates that is fueled by a very high fertility rate (6.0 children per woman). The country's demographic trends reflect those of a developing nation. Nigeria's total population mushroomed between 1975 and 2013 and increased by 202%. The ratios for the ages 0–14, 15–64, and 65-over are 43%, 54%, and 3% of the total population, respectively (Central Intelligence Agency, 2014). Nigeria's life expectancy (52 years) is much lower than the world's average. One of the fundamental issues in Nigeria concerns the scarcity of adequate health services: Significant numbers of people die from preventable diseases such as malaria and tuberculosis. In addition, there are more than 1.5 million of AIDS orphans in the country. The nation's low GDP per capita leaves a large percentage of the Nigerian population in poverty. Unfortunately, frequent violent altercations over access to water and valuable resources, religious tensions, and the high levels of political corruption contribute to the country's overall socioeconomic and political instability.

Rapid advancement in technology and steady market growth became the symbols of the world's foremost industrial power, the United States, which occupies the middle of the North American continent. The country's total population with its highly diverse ethnic origins increased by 53% between 1975 and 2013. A largely free-enterprise market economy contributes to the country's GDP per capita, which is among the highest among the world's major countries. The nation's excellent health services maintain high life expectancy, although they do not necessarily reach every person, especially among the urban and rural poor. The ratios for the ages 0–14, 15–64, and 65-over are 19%, 66%, and 14% of the total population, respectively (Central Intelligence Agency, 2014).

By far the largest and most populous country in South America, with a population of approximately 199 million, Brazil occupies a greater landmass than the combined whole of the rest of the continent. Its substantial migration from rural to urban areas exerts a direct influence on the nation's declining birth rate. This holds particularly true for the cities given that urban people constitute more than three-fourths of Brazil's total population. There has been a 109% increase in Brazil's total population between 1975 and 2013. Rapid population growth, however, is to some degree affected by moderately high mortality rates due to AIDS, malnutrition, and inadequate health care services, which vary according to the average income and remoteness of regions. As a consequence, Brazil's life expectancy (74 years) is slightly lower than that of China (75 years), Argentina (76 years) or Mexico (77 years) (UNICEF, 2014). The ratios for the ages 0–14, 15–64, and 65-over are 24%, 69%, and 8% of the total population, respectively (Central Intelligence Agency, 2014). The country's prospects for dynamic economic advancement are undermined by foreign debts, political corruption, tax evasion, enormous economic disparities between the rich and the poor, and widespread poverty. Nevertheless, the nation's developing market economy, which is based primarily on manufacture, financial services, agriculture, and trade, contributes to one of the highest GDP per capita among South American countries. Furthermore, Latin American countries such as Brazil and Mexico have in recent years made important advances toward improving children's health and education levels.

Since Egypt acquired full sovereignty in 1953, it has played a leading role in the Arab affairs of the Middle East. Egypt with its Nile-dependent agricultural sector and industrial foundation has the largest population in the Arab World and also in Northern Africa. Close to half of the Egyptians reside in rural areas and contribute to the country's high annual population growth. A closer look at the nation's religious structure provides a lucid explanation for a large and rapidly growing nation, which increases by more than one million every eight months (UNICEF, 2014): It is estimated that more than 90% of the population are Muslims (Ahmed, 2005). The ratios for the ages 0–14, 15–64, and 65-over are 32%, 63%, and 5% of the total population, respectively (Central Intelligence Agency, 2014). A 129% increase occurred in the country's total population between 1975 and 2013. A 1999 survey indicated that 50 percent of the young people between 20 and 25 years of age had never been married because of economic difficulties (Ahmed, 2005). The educational background of women has been identified as a major determinant in decisions made by these young people (Ahmed, 1991). Overall, life expectancy has been improving since the 1990s and fertility rates have been declining (Ahmed, 2005). Egypt's comparatively high (by world standards) infant mortality rate is complemented by a sharp increase in the number of people emigrating in their search for employment elsewhere. The country's GDP per capita remains low in comparison with most non-African countries and the oil-rich Arab nations to its east.

Russia is the world's largest country and the ninth most populous nation. A striking demographic feature since the 1940s is the decline in birth rates. Russia's total population increased by only 10% between 1975 and 2013. Nonetheless, the country's GDP per capita fails to sustain its population. The ratios for the ages 0–14, 15–64, and 65-over are 16%, 70%, and 13% of the total population, respectively (Central Intelligence Agency, 2014). The average life expectancy (68 years) is lower than the world's average. As a result of fundamental political changes including the conversion of its former centrally planned economic system into a market economy, a noticeable deterioration in living standards was experienced by many members of the Russian population in the late 20th and early 21st centuries. As a direct consequence, individuals seek out opportunities for higher salaries and professional advancement elsewhere, thus triggering the exodus of the younger population from the motherland. Although migration rates have been gradually falling since 1995, the decline does not counterbalance the natural population decrease due to low birth rates.

As the world's third most powerful economy, Japan until the early 1990s experienced a dynamic post–World War II economic growth rate but has since experienced periods of economic stagnation. Characterized by high population density, Japan has a very high GDP per capita, very high living standards, and an advanced health care system. Indeed, Japan's average life expectancy of 83 years is the highest of any of the world's major countries. The country's demographic trends are similar to those of other technologically advanced nations: There was a 23% increase in Japan's total population between 1975 and 2013. A dramatic decline in birth and death rates is reflected in the ratios for the ages 0–14, 15–64, and 65-over, which are 13%, 61%, and 25% of the total population, respectively (Central Intelligence Agency, 2014). The decline reflects the effects of the Japanese family's transformation (Naito & Gielen, 2005) and makes Japan one of the "oldest" societies on earth.

Germany, a major country of Central Europe, has one of the world's most technologically powerful and export-oriented economies. As the most populous and one of the richest nations of Western Europe, Germany's GDP per capita is among the world's highest. The country's total population has increased by 6% between 1975 and 2013. More than 85% of all Germans live in urban settings. Germany's population has a long life expectancy, a negative annual population growth, and a very low birth rate when compared to the rest of the world. The ratios for the ages 0–14, 15–64, and 65-over are 13%, 66%, and 21% of the total population, respectively (Central Intelligence Agency, 2014). At the current rate of growth, one of the many challenges faced by the German society today concerns a disproportionate aging to young population ratio—as it holds true for most European societies.

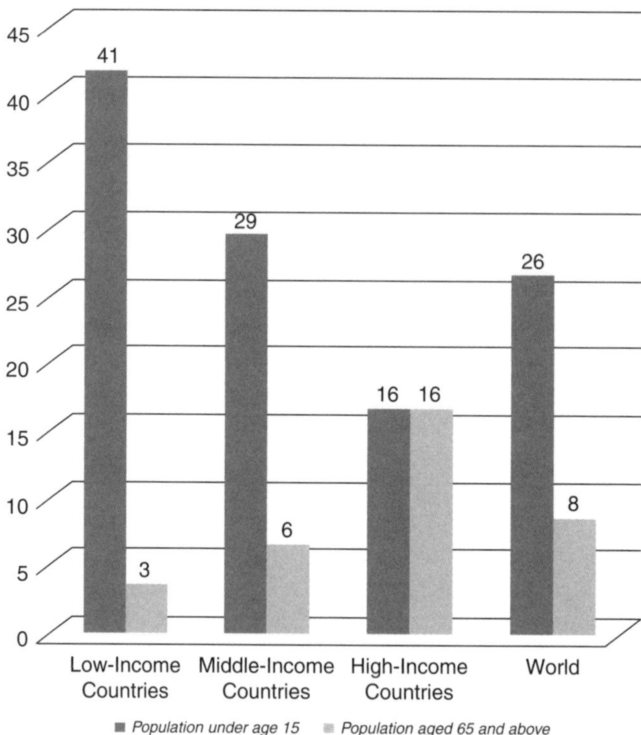

Figure 3.2 Percentage of Children (<15 Years) and Aged (65+ Years) in Low-, Middle-, High-Income Countries, and the World in 2010

Source: Population Reference Bureau (2012, p. 10). *2012 World population data sheet.*

Table 3.1 Economic and Demographic Indicators of 10 Selected Countries in 2012

	Total Population (in millions)	**GDP per Capita (PPP US$)[a]**	**GDP per Capita (US$)**	**Life Expectancy (in years)**	**Fertility Rates (per woman)**
USA	317.5	50,610	50,120	79	2.0
Japan	127.3	36,320	47,870	83	1.4
Germany	82.8	41,370	44,010	81	1.4
Russia[b]	143.2	22,760	12,700	68	1.5
Brazil	198.7	11,720	11,630	74	1.8
China	1,377.1	9,210	5,740	75	1.7
Egypt	80.7	6,640	3,000	71	2.8
Indonesia	246.9	4,810	3,420	71	2.4
India	1,236.7	3,840	1,530	66	2.5
Nigeria	168.8	2,420	1,430	52	6.0

[a]PPP (purchasing power parity): A rate of exchange that accounts for price differences across countries, allowing international comparisons of real output and incomes: PPP US$1 has the same purchasing power in the domestic economy as $1 has in the United States.

[b]Russian Federation.

Source: Adopted from *The State of the World 2014 in Numbers: Every Child Counts* (2014).

As has already been mentioned, close to 99% of the world population growth takes place in the developing nations, whereas Europe and several East Asian countries are characterized by fewer births than deaths each year. The rich nations are also older with a much smaller percentage of children under 15 as opposed to the poor countries (Figure 3.2). Such dramatic changes in the composition of the world population place heavy demands on adequate health care, social support systems, and public education in the poorer nations. Increases in life expectancy have been driven by technological advances in medicine, thus augmenting a palpable gap between the industrialized world and various poor countries such as Nigeria (Table 3.1). Data provided in Figure 3.3 show that in 2010, the overall under-five mortality rate in high income countries was only 5.5% of that in the low-income countries although the rates have been declining worldwide.

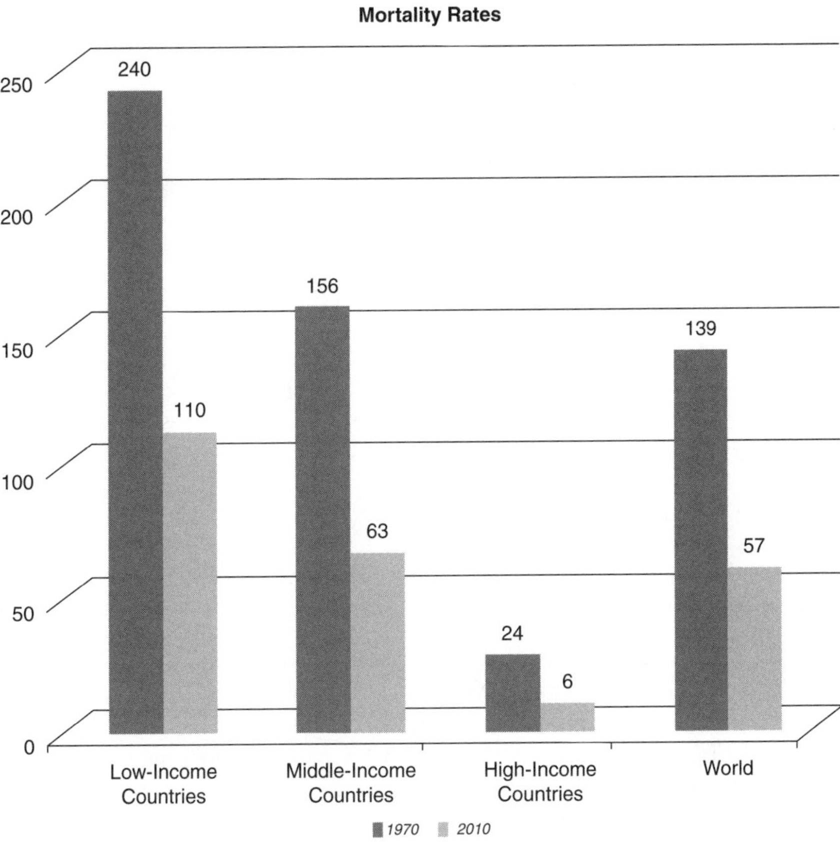

Figure 3.3 Under-Five Mortality Rates (per 1,000 Live Births) in 1970 and 2010: Low-, Middle-, High-Income Countries, and the World

Source: UNICEF (2012, p. 83). *The state of the world's children.*

SOCIO-DEMOGRAPHIC FACTORS AND CHILDREN'S LIVES

Economic Indicators

The demographics of the world are closely related to the countries' overall economic status (Table 3.1). Given the dramatic impact of socioeconomic status on children's welfare, it is important to focus on the economic conditions prevailing in a particular country rather than its geographic location. Although all communities follow certain guidelines for childrearing practices, children's well-being depends to an important degree on their residence in a wealthy or a poor community. The United Nations classifies the world's countries into four categories: low-income countries (GNI per capita is $1,035 or less), lower-middle-income countries (GNI per capita is $1,036 to $4,085), upper-middle-income countries (GNI per capita is $4,086 to $12, 615), and high-income countries (GNI per capita is at least $12,616) (UNICEF, 2014). However, due to the different exchange rates and the variety of native currencies, it seems preferable to refer to the "gross domestic product per capita" (GDP) indicator when adjusted for purchasing power (see Table 3.1).

Table 3.1 shows the economic patterns for the 10 countries ranging from the highest GDP per capita (USA: US$ 50,610) to the lowest GDP per capita (Nigeria: US$ 2,420). With this background, it is possible to contrast different nations against one another for the purpose of shedding light on some of the main factors affecting children's well-being. For example, by taking India's and Japan's GDPs into account, we can predict that Japanese children have concrete chances of survival and productive adulthood as opposed to India's many undernourished children who are also much less likely to attend school. In addition, child labor remains a common practice in India. Thus, allocation of resources and their variations from country to country are fundamental to the newborn's well-being. Essentially, parental investment of time, energy, and resources determines the child's chances for a healthy future.

Fertility Rates

Birth rates and their trends provide the most useful indicators for offering insights into the future levels of population (Table 3.1). Fertility rates vary tremendously across countries and world regions (Figure 3.4). In 2013, the total lifetime number of children born per woman ranged from 1.1 children per woman in wealthy Taiwan to 7.6 children in desperately poor Niger (Africa) (Population Reference Bureau, 2014). Thus, as fertility rates steadily decline in both middle-income and high-income countries, poor countries, particularly in the sub-Saharan region, contribute the most to the world population growth. This is true although a rampant AIDS epidemic tends to reduce population increases especially in southern Africa.

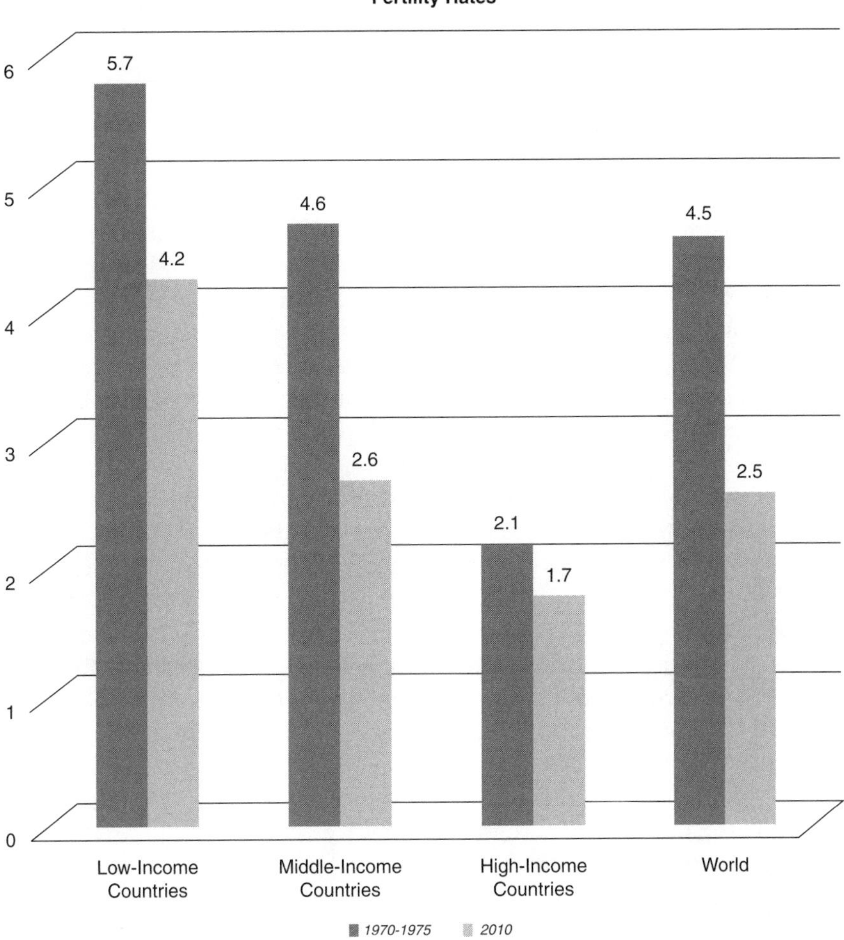

Figure 3.4 Total Fertility Rates in 1970–1975 and 2010 in Low-, Middle-, High-Income Countries, and the World

Source: UNDP (2002, p. 165) and UNICEF (2014, p. 111). *The state of the world's children.*

The foregoing suggests that children born in industrialized nations with much smaller family sizes are likely to experience different family influences, types of threats to their physical health, developmental changes, and cultural- and gender-related pressures when compared to children born in developing countries. Therefore, approaching the topic of female fertility through a multidisciplinary perspective including considerations derived from evolutionary theory promotes understanding of the evolved mechanisms of parents' investments into their reproductive patterns that strongly influence differences in fertility (Blurton-Jones, 1989).

Between 1970 and 2010, both children's under-five mortality rates and women's fertility rates declined steadily in most countries around the world. As indicated in Figure 3.3, the reduction in children's deaths before the age of 5 was especially dramatic in the developing middle-income countries but also quite substantial in the very poor nations. Moreover, as shown in Figure 3.4, the decline in women's fertility rates was most dramatic in the middle-income countries but less substantial in the low-income countries. In almost all high-income countries, fertility rates have dropped below the so-called "replacement rate" of 2.1 children per woman per lifetime.

Various sociocultural forces play an important role in determining the average number of children a woman can bear in an age-specific group (United Nations Development Programme, 2002). Many cultures, for example, hold a traditional view that the number of children (and especially boys) determines the value of a woman—that is, her social status and her contribution to the welfare of the group. Such pronatalist ideologies are especially prevalent in many African and Muslim societies. It is believed that having large numbers of children will increase the likelihood that one's family will succeed in the search for economic and social stability as well as social status. In contrast, the vast majority of young people in the industrialized countries delay getting married and having children since they believe that receiving college and university degrees will strongly improve one's chance of securing a well-paid and intrinsically rewarding professional position. In many postmodern countries, the number and percentage of adults living in one-person households has dramatically increased over the past few decades (Klinenberg, 2013). For instance, in Japan, the young generation has been postponing the actual creation of a family in contradiction to long-standing societal norms emphasizing family life. Recent reports by the Japanese Ministry of Health, Labor, and Welfare document a clear increase in the median age of first marriage for women (from 25 in 1975 to 29 in 2012). Another example in this category is Germany where the average woman gets married at age 30.5. To counteract such trends, and after the number of births had fallen to a 14-year low in 2002, the government of wealthy Singapore initiated a national campaign to encourage people to fall in love, tie the knot, and have babies. Singapore's fertility rate, however, stubbornly remains at a very low level, namely, below 1.3 children per woman per lifetime (UNICEF, 2014).

When we travel to almost any low-income country, the picture is reversed. Here socioeconomic insecurity is translated into both early marriages and the early onset of reproduction. As Table 3.1 indicates, the correlation between poverty and high fertility rates across the world's nations is pronounced. In Nigeria, for instance, the total fertility rate is 6.0 and the gross national income per capita is US$ 1,430. Conversely, Western Europe has a total fertility rate of 1.7 with a GNI per capita of US$ 42,220 (Population Reference Bureau, 2014).

Various authors have analyzed fertility patterns within the framework of various cultural barriers, such as social customs and taboos. A number of intriguing findings originate in the analysis of birth intervals. Given that the physiological cost of having a boy is greater to the mother than the cost of having a girl, Blanchard and Bogaert (1997) report that birth intervals are longer following a male child rather than a female child. A study by Nath, Leonetti, and Steele (1999) demonstrates that the estimated relative risks of shorter birth intervals are increased for an Indian mother belonging to middle, poor, and very poor income groups, when compared to the upper-income group mothers. Furthermore, it was also found that higher fertility was associated with compensating effects of having older relatives, especially grandmothers, in the households.

In China, after decades of encouraging reproduction under the rule of Chairman Mao Tse-Tung (Zedong) (1893–1976), the government informed its people about the importance of family planning due to an expected population increase to 1.5–1.6 billion by the year 2050. The (partial) implementation of the One-Child Policy has become a controversial topic despite its major goals of fighting the widespread poverty that existed and ensuring the overall quality of life. According to this plan, most families should have only one child, although in many rural areas, the average number of babies born per woman is closer to two. Moreover, China's government is now reconsidering its One-Child Policy because the country's population has been aging steadily.

Generally, a second child born without a paid permission hardly exists in the legal sense and, therefore, faces numerous obstacles in seeking ways to advance in life. It is illegal for unmarried Chinese women to bear children (Bureau of Democracy, Human Rights, and Labor, 2000). Furthermore, Chinese women are reportedly sterilized or forced to abort a pregnancy (USCR, 2002). Many critics of the One-Child Policy believe that the long-standing preference for boys has made female infanticide more common. Although the Maternal and Child Health Care Law forbids the use of ultrasound to identify female fetuses and terminate pregnancies, many families, especially in the rural areas, resort to this procedure to meet the demands of labor and of traditional cultural expectations (Bureau of Democracy, Human Rights, and Labor, 2000). Similar preferences for boys over girls have been reported for various Southeast Asian countries such as Bangladesh where, as a consequence, a disproportionate number of male babies are allowed to enter world. In contrast, many female babies are aborted. Other female children are omitted from national census figures because families try to hide them from authority figures or because they are considered unimportant.

Mortality Rates

In areas characterized by high infant mortality rates (e.g., Nigeria: 78 infant deaths per thousand below 1 year of age), individuals tend to produce more offspring than individuals in areas with low infant mortality rates (e.g., Germany: 3 infant deaths/below 1 year of age) (UNICEF, 2014). Despite an impressive record of reduced infant mortality rates throughout the world due to increasingly widespread immunization for preventable diseases, malnutrition, unsanitary conditions, HIV/AIDS, and violent conflicts continue to have a detrimental impact on lower-income countries especially in sub-Saharan Africa. One consequence of the pervasive HIV/AIDS crisis in African countries such as Botswana, Zimbabwe, Swaziland, and Lesotho is a very high number of orphaned children. Most of them will face an exceedingly difficult future. For instance, an estimated 15 million children in sub-Saharan Africa had lost at least one parent due to AIDS by 2000–2001. Consequently, average life expectancy hovers around 50 years in some African countries such as Lesotho, South Africa, and Swaziland, thereby reversing decades of improvement in health services.

On a more positive note, the world's under-five infant mortality rate (Figure 3.3) declined dramatically between 1990 and 2012 (from 90 to 48 deaths per thousand births), with corresponding changes occurring in every region of the world (Save the Children, 2015; UNICEF, 2014). One of the major factors contributing to such an effect appears to be education, especially that of mothers (Singh & Gielen, 1995). Generally, it is assumed that high rates of low birth weight result from mothers' low educational achievement and inadequate nutritional and prenatal care, which usually go hand-in-hand with various socioeconomic pressures.

Literacy

Current indicators provide somewhat conflicting evidence on the number of children enrolled in primary and secondary institutions (see United Nations Development Programme, 2014; Wagner, Zahra, & Lee, chapter 4, this volume). There are, however, indications of a steady rise in school enrollment rates; at present approximately 91% of the world's younger children go to school. Overall, literacy rates in industrialized countries such as Japan and Germany are much higher than in lower-income nations such as Nigeria and India. While the majority of developed countries are very close to achieving universal school enrollment, too many children in the low-income nations, especially girls, are still deprived of access to education. The majority of out-of-school youths can be found in sub-Saharan Africa, South Asia, and Southeast Asia, regions where gender disparities in schooling are also likely to be most pronounced (Wagner, Zahra, & Lee, chapter 4, in this volume). Nevertheless, most countries have reduced gender gaps in education although in some Islamic countries and regions such as Afghanistan, Pakistan, and northern Nigeria, violent opposition against girls' education has increased substantially. In contrast, in many of the industrialized countries girls are less likely to drop out of high school and college than boys. For the first time in history, women in the younger generations now tend to be better educated than men in various industrialized countries such as the United States.

The significant differences in fertility rates that have been found between urban and rural women are often a consequence of corresponding differences in levels of female education. Furthermore, children born to women with prenatal care have a greater chance of surviving the first year of life. Unfortunately, too often the social setting dictates whether or not children receive adequate education. In India, for example, many girls internalize the expectations imposed upon them by a patriarchally oriented society, learn to master household tasks, and become child caretakers (Saraswathi, 2000). In this scenario, boys enjoy the privilege of being a male child with tangible opportunities for academic achievement as opposed to girls. Similarly, in Mali, West Africa, children are generally cared for by their older siblings, while girls around the age of 7 already take on the majority of household chores (Dettwyler, 1994). According to KIDS COUNT (Population Reference Bureau, 2000), the birth rate for mothers who have not completed high school is four times higher in the poorest communities than in the wealthiest countries.

The 2014 World Population Data Sheet identifies India as the world's second most populous nation and it is expected to become a leader in this category by 2045. Although India had originally been a pioneer in implementing a family planning program (1952), the country's annual population growth had reached 15.5 million by the late 1990s. In response, the Indian Government devised the National Population Policy to gain control over the country's population growth consistent with its socioeconomic development goals. The policy aims at reaching the replacement-level fertility rate and achieving universal standards of public health, sanitation, civil and social services, immunization, and education. Since many Indian women do not regulate their reproductive behavior, the policy also captures the importance of educating both women and men about effective family planning. However, recent indications are that fertility rates even among the poorer women have been rapidly declining in some southern states like Kerala and Tamil Nadu. In contrast, the decline has been less in the already overpopulated and desperately poor northern states such as Uttar Pradesh and Bihar.

Going to school and becoming fully literate has numerous and mostly positive consequences for children's life chances and their ways of thinking and being. By way of contrast, illiteracy and semi-literacy in today's world condemns a youngster to a life of physical toil, economic hardship, exploitation by others, lower life expectancy, ignorance about family planning, and exclusion from numerous sources of information. Whereas informal education is embedded in family life and the child's round of daily activities, formal education is set apart from the context of his or her everyday life and takes place under the impersonal guidance of experts who are expected to impart superior knowledge and skills (Greenfield & Lave, 1982). Formal education makes the child aware of faraway worlds and new ways of thinking, thereby implicitly supporting challenges to traditional values and lifeways. Most adolescents know that education is their ticket for a more prosperous, exciting, and satisfying future. It allows them to participate in the creation of a new and increasingly globalized world, however strife-torn it may turn out to be. Child labor, in contrast, enmeshes them in self-perpetuating cycles of poverty.

CHILD LABOR

An Overview

Many reports illustrate a clear relationship between low socioeconomic status and school dropout rates both within and across countries (UNICEF, 2014). In societies where people depend on economic subsistence, many children provide an extra set of helpful hands for the most part of the day, thus failing to enjoy the immediate fruits of primary education, which provides the fundamentals of literacy and other skills for a productive future. If successful integration into the developing economy and having an educated citizenry are essential goals of almost all the nations around the world, then a new workforce must be fully equipped with the applicable reading and writing as well as social and vocational skills.

For instance, following Indonesia's economic crisis in the late 1990s, it became very difficult for farming families to survive without children's assistance. According to a UNICEF report, multiple threats to basic socioeconomic conditions of the world's fourth-most populous nation began to present a state of dire emergency. Millions of children dropped out of school in those years to earn a living on the streets (United Nations Children Fund, 2000). Apparently, the number of teenage prostitutes also increased during those years. More recently, however, Indonesia has resumed economic growth and is again sending an increasing percentage of its children to school.

Child Labor: A Global Picture

The International Labour Office (2013) and UNICEF (2015) have estimated that in 2012–2014, an estimated 150–168 million children between the ages of 5 and 17 were engaged in some form of full-time labor, including some 50 million children between the ages of 5 and 14. These numbers amount to 10%–11% of the world's child population. In sub-Saharan Africa, an estimated 21% of all children are engaged in child labor. Approximately 53% of the world's child laborers are exposed to hazardous conditions compromising their physical, mental, social, and educational development. Most of these children take part in various activities related to intensive manual labor.

Knowledge of the selective forces that have been related to child labor can help clarify their catalytic traits within the framework of a particular socioeconomic milieu. In agricultural societies, for instance, even young children are expected to contribute to the welfare of the family and the community. The evidence for certain factors leading to child exploitation has been abundantly discussed in the literature (International Labour Office, 2013; Kannan, 2014; Seabrook, 2001). However, although many thousands of cases have been recorded and analyzed, they represent a controversial matter—controversial in terms of the opposing views held by the families, NGOs, and the child workers themselves.

In its search for socioemotional stability, the young generation often identifies itself by the way it contributes to the socioeconomic productivity of their community. Many societies view child labor as a common social obligation and in some instances, children do not define what they do as work since their family's poverty does not leave them with much choice. A good number of the children, however, end up in bondage to ruthless employers, in outright slavery, or as teenage prostitutes; others are abducted by force or else are being enticed through promises of food and clothes (Faleiro, 2011; Onishi, 2001; see also the respective chapters by Sigal et al. and Aptekar & Oliver, chapters 14 and 15, respectively, in this volume). HIV infection is a constant threat to child-prostitutes, and many of them will die young.

Child labor can be a delicate issue and as such it must be examined within the normative frameworks and economic realities of the respective societies in which it occurs. Scheper-Hughes (1992), for instance, describes a poverty-stricken region of northeastern Brazil, where children are most often raised in single-parent families. Their mothers are low-paid laborers on sugar plantations or serve as maids or as other domestics, but are themselves unable to pay for caretakers. Consequently, older children must assume major responsibilities at an earlier age and learn how to watch their younger siblings or start earning money for the family. A similar situation prevails in many other poor regions of the world including many regions in sub-Saharan Africa and on the Indian subcontinent.

The fact that many products and services produced by the children in the developing nations are being consumed in the market economies of wealthy nations has important implications. Essentially, living in a competitive environment requires a great deal of physical energy and a quick ability to resist the harsh and callous surroundings. In view of the many children who need to work in hazardous conditions in order to increase their and their family's chances of physical and economic survival, it is necessary to understand that although many domestic employers profit more than their vulnerable workers, they themselves are nonetheless governed by the frequently whimsical forces of the global market.

Employers, of course, have always been interested in pursuing wealth that could be acquired in a rapid and cost-effective way. Seabrook (2001) identifies several characteristics of international child employment including being paid by completed piece, fulfilling the duties of a domestic servant, or serving as an apprentice free of charge. It is implied that in exchange for their labor, children receive priceless practical experience and moral education. However, in reality, children form a major portion of the labor force that is engaged in hazardous activities including handling chemicals and other toxins, working in factories, glass manufacturing, stone quarries, construction, mines, dumps, and mills (Seabrook, 2001). As children, furthermore, they are least likely to be able to resist exploitation, sexual advances by employers without a conscience, and exposure to toxic environments. In far too many cases, children's working conditions in the poorer countries resemble the exploitative conditions described by Charles Dickens and others for 19th-century England. Indeed, historical accounts of the nature of childhood in the Western countries prior to World War I (e.g., Hiner, 1991) suggest many parallels to the childhood conditions depicted in this chapter for the present-day low-income and developing countries.

Although much of their time is spent in the deceptively firm and hazardous working environments, the children's lives are also defined by societal values and family obligations. Those nations that are both poor and embrace collectivistic values are likely to have the largest number of child workers. In terms of regional incidence, the child-to-work ratio is the highest in sub-Saharan Africa and in the poorer regions of South Asia.

The failure to promptly educate the youth can only be partially attributed to families' lack of financial resources necessary to compensate for the absence of their school-going children and the additional expenses for the "students." Yet there is another side to the issue in question. The conspicuous remarks of the employers, the families, and the children themselves indicate their mutual reluctance to give up valuable labor time in favor of education. Their argument appears to be even more pertinent in light of a high unemployment rate among school graduates in many parts of the world (Seabrook, 2001). In fact, a frequently voiced argument states that when daily work occupies millions of "less-fortunate" children, it keeps their minds focused on something "constructive" rather than "deviant." It is common for many tourists, local police, and ordinary citizens, who regularly pass by the clusters of fragile bodies forming the contours of the city's pavements, to view street children as "antisocial" or criminal elements (Aptekar & Oliver, chapter 15, this volume). In and around Rio de Janeiro's violent *favelas* (slums), for instance, it is not uncommon for police and members of unofficial militias to shoot street children on some pretext or other (*The Economist*, March 20, 2014).

Furthermore, most families wish to provide their children with certain skills essential to their survival in the immediate environment. Thus, a farmer would teach his children how to cultivate the land, distinguish good seeds from the bad ones, harness the power of domestic animals, and interpret the weather (Seabrook, 2001). An opposed view would be that educational attainment initiates socioeconomic advancement. However, cultural norms dictate specific guidelines for one's contribution to the welfare of the social group and thus monitor the citizens' personal development.

Although the realization and optimization of basic human rights such as the right to education evolves according to a historical process, instant "solutions" proposed by outsiders to the problem of child labor can prove ineffective and impractical when compared to steady improvements in a society's economic performance and the growth of shared cultural understandings about how precious children and their education are. The basic dilemma involved in child labor has been stated as follows: If you stop child labor, you stop the most important human right of all—the right to survive. If, however, you ensure decent wages for adults and/or provide financial support to poor families, they will not need to send their children to work (Bhuiyan, as cited in Seabrook, 2001).

In recent decades, considerable efforts have been undertaken in various countries to reduce the number of children forced to engage in full-time child labor by enrolling them instead in school. In Brazil, for instance, the large-scale and effective Bolsa Familia social welfare program covered 26% of the country's population in the year 2011. The program stipulates that in exchange for conditional cash transfers, poor families participating in it must ensure that their young children are vaccinated and attend school on a regular basis rather than working full time. Similar programs have also been instituted in other Latin American countries.

In India, Kailash Satyarthi, the co-winner of the 2014 Nobel Peace Prize, and his Bachpan Bachao Andolan ("Save the Childhood Movement") have been attacking the "scourge of child labor" (his words) since 1980—and with considerable success. Declaring in his acceptance speech for the Nobel Prize that he represented "the sound of silence, the cry of innocence, and the face of invisibility," he has freed more than 80,000 children from the bondage of child labor (Doherty, 2014). The Brazilian and Indian examples suggest that sustained organizational efforts can be quite successful in reducing the incidence of heavy child labor; indeed, the worldwide downward trend of child labor in recent years has been quite encouraging in this respect (International Labour Office, 2013). However, in the three countries of Bangladesh, India, and Pakistan an estimated 22 million primary school children—including a disproportionate number of girls—still are not attending school (Doherty, 2014). In addition, these countries are centers of national and international human trafficking that includes the abduction of numerous children for purposes of child labor and child prostitution—as it also holds true for various countries in Africa and the Middle East (Batstone, 2010; United Nations Office on Drugs and Crime, 2014).

ARRIVING AT THE BIG PICTURE

In the foregoing we have seen that the dramatic demographic and economic changes of the past 30–40 years have led to divergent physical and social environments for children and adolescents living, respectively, in the poor, the intermediate, and the wealthy nations. Inevitably, these changes are intertwined with dramatic cultural shifts redefining what childhood, adolescence, and parenthood are, can be, and should be. Basic family structures, gender roles, parental ethnotheories and childrearing ideologies, sibling relationships, educational expectations by both parents and children, child labor, consumption patterns, dating practices (if any), adolescents' thoughts about their identities and their possible futures, youths' exposure to both local and global mass media are all undergoing economically induced but culturally structured shifts and redefinitions.

To illustrate such changes let us focus for a moment on the most basic question underlying parenthood: Why do parents wish to have children at all, and why do they want either many or only a few children (Kağitçibaşi, 2007)? In traditional agricultural and urban settings, parents tend to see children as an insurance that somebody will take care of them in their old age. Given the absence of acceptable social security systems in most of these societies, and given the high mortality rates of both children and adults, being parent to a large number of children is likely to protect one against the possibility of economic destitution and a life of isolation and loneliness. At the same time, children, from early on, can contribute their labor as babysitters for their younger siblings, as water carriers, as workers in the fields, in commercial enterprises, as shoe polishers or small-scale traders in the streets, or as maids in other families' homes. In such a situation, to be the parent of many children is truly seen as a blessing. When, for instance, poor Somali Muslim mothers were asked how many children they wished to have, several answered: As many as possible—and their actions matched their sentiments (Dybdahl & Hundeide, 1998).

In contrast, middle-class parents in postindustrial societies frequently state that they value their children because they provide emotional companionship rather than economic support. Indeed, in the modern world, bringing up children and sending them to school for many years is quite expensive, and most families can afford only a few children if they wish to protect their own living standards. Given the widespread introduction of pension and old-age insurance systems, and unlike in many of the poor countries, adult children are in most cases not asked to support their parents financially, although middle-aged persons (especially women) are increasingly confronted with the task of taking care of parents suffering from Alzheimer's disease, senility, and other debilitating diseases. In addition, numerous females who have been entering higher educational institutions are postponing childbearing. Others remain single or choose not to have any children (Klinenberg, 2013). We find, consequently, that the higher the percentage of females enrolled in primary, secondary, and tertiary educational institutions and the greater their orientation toward pursuing a career, the lower a country's birthrate. Indeed, the fertility rates for almost all East Asian and European societies are well below the so-called replacement rate (an average of 2.1 children per woman per lifetime in industrialized societies).

Drastic redefinitions of gender roles, the desirability of motherhood, redefinitions of fatherhood, and gender-related authority patterns typically accompany the declining birthrates (Hyun et al., chapter 7, this volume). Feminist ideologies have sprung up among the elite women of the West, are now readily endorsed by otherwise conventional college women, and are increasingly spreading to well-educated, Westernized women in the developing world. In contrast, such ideologies have found only a weak echo among the poor and uneducated women in nonwestern countries who, instead, are involved in a harsh struggle for survival.

Based on the foregoing discussions, Table 3.2 compares, in summary form, worldwide differences in children's environments between the poor and the wealthy countries.

These differences are presented in ideal-type form; that is, worldwide trends are condensed into a snapshot emphasizing contrasting economic conditions, fertility and mortality patterns, family structures, childrearing goals, gender roles, schooling and labor practices, relationships between the generations, the role of peer groups, and other relevant factors influencing the development of children. It is postulated that economic and demographic forces have a powerful impact on the differences depicted in Table 3.2. Without denying the importance of religious, secular, and culture-specific belief systems for the upbringing of children, it is further assumed that the belief systems are themselves highly responsive to economic and demographic conditions and changes, although there is often a lag between evolving economic conditions and subsequent cultural transformations. In addition, the forces of globalization as well as rapid changes in technology are now exerting a major influence on the lives, attitudes, and preferences of adolescents in the majority world.

Table 3.2 Comparison of Children's Environments in Traditional Low- and Postmodern High-Income Countries

	Poor Traditional Countries	Postmodern Wealthy Countries
Societies		
Economic basis of society	Agriculture; subsistence farming; trade; some manufacturing; the few nomadic and isolated foraging societies are now fading away; extensive migration to the cities and their slums accelerates socioeconomic change	Information and service industries; extensive manufacturing; small agricultural sector; global trade
Division of labor	Limited division of labor, rather homogenous society	Extreme sociocultural heterogeneity: more than 200,000 different job titles in United States
Societal complexity; rural vs. urban areas	Lower complexity especially in rural areas	High complexity especially in the numerous urban areas
Life expectancy and mortality rates	High but declining child mortality rates; low life expectancy	Very low child mortality rates; very high life expectancy
Impact of external/ global influences	Increasing, often indirect	Powerful and direct
Speed of societal change	Slow but steadily increasing	Very rapid
Balance between tradition and innovation	Tradition emphasized but increasing exposure to innovation often introduced from abroad	High rate of cultural change favors innovation over tradition; in many Islamic countries struggle between tradition, modernity, and religious "truth"
Gender roles	Gender roles sharply distinguished and seen as part of the natural and sacred order; patriarchal and hierarchical conceptions	Contested and less differentiated gender roles; gender roles perceived as changeable and human made; increasing egalitarianism
Ferdinand *Tönnies* (1853–1936)	*Gemeinschaft*	*Gesellschaft*
Family		
Family size and fertility rates	High fertility rates; large families; pronatalist ideologies	Very low, below replacement fertility rates (2.1); small nuclear families

Table 3.2 Continued

	Poor Traditional Countries	Postmodern Wealthy Countries
Family structures and stability	Low divorce rates; fewer single-parent families; extended families especially among the well-to-do; polygamy in African societies; family instability in many sub-Saharan countries	High divorce rates; many single-parent and childless families; increase in variety of family types; many young adult singles
Economic functions of family	Wide range of functions especially in subsistence economies; peasants rather than farmers	Family is shedding many economic functions
Socialization/teaching functions of family	Pervasive but teaching functions now shifting toward schools	Many functions transferred to schools, preschools, daycare centers
Parental reasons for having children	It is traditional; economic utility; they add to families' political influence; emotional companionship; a spiritual goal; children manifest God's blessing; they validate adult status and social identity	Children provide emotional companionship but are expensive; having children is an individual preference competing with other preferences
Children		
Child labor	Many teenagers and some younger children in the labor force; lower school enrollment for females; exploitative child labor is common	Little pre-teen child labor; part-time jobs for teenagers
Number and influence of siblings	Many siblings; especially girls often involved in childrearing duties; early responsibility training	Few siblings; more limited sibling influence; individualistic childrearing approaches
Schooling and literacy	Illiteracy and semi-literacy still fairly common but declining	Universal schooling for both boys and girls; most teenagers enrolled in school; tertiary education expanding
Social relations	Long-term relations with kin and known ingroup members	Numerous short-term and medium-term interactions with non-kin strangers and semi-strangers

(*Continued*)

Table 3.2 Continued

	Poor Traditional Countries	Postmodern Wealthy Countries
Children's exposure to civil war, guerrillas	Fairly common: children may be abducted and forced to become soldiers and "war brides" (especially in some African countries)	Rare
Impact of HIV/AIDS on families and children	Powerful threat especially in southern and eastern Africa responsible for numerous orphans; less prevalent in Muslim societies; both female and male victims	Limited except among drug users, homosexuals, prostitutes; victims mostly male
Adolescents		
Length of adolescent period	Brief or barely existent for many girls; brief for boys but more prolonged in African polygamous and age-graded ethnic groups	Prolonged period; now often followed by "emerging adulthood" period (18–26 years)
Age of marriage for girls	Often very low (13–20 years) but now increasing due to schooling	Increasing (mean = 25–30 years); increasing ambivalence about marriage
Are marriages arranged or semi-arranged?	Mostly yes	Mostly no
Value of premarital chastity for girls	Very high in Middle Eastern, Muslim, Hindu societies; high in Confucian-heritage societies, less so in some sub-Saharan societies, low in foraging societies	Rapidly declining in most Western societies (e.g., Scandinavia) and increasingly so in some East Asian societies
Age of marriage for boys	Variable but increasing; high in many polygamous societies	Increasing; more ambivalence about marriage
Knowledge and value differences between generations	Limited but increasing due to modernization and global influences	Pervasive especially in the knowledge area, less so for basic values
Peer group influence	Moderate (although strong for males in some age-graded African societies)	Pervasive for both males and females
Adolescents' exposure to mass media	Limited (especially for girls) but steadily increasing	Pervasive

Table 3.2 Continued

	Poor Traditional Countries	Postmodern Wealthy Countries
Adolescent subcultures	Emerging especially in the big cities	Well developed; increasingly influenced by social and other media
Impact of global teenage culture(s)	Growing via media influence	Powerful: many adolescents are becoming semi-bicultural
Impact of consumerism on adolescent lifestyle	Struggle for survival sharply limits consumerism	Strong impact of consumerism on lifestyle identity, wellbeing
Self	Collectivistic self embedded in kin and other face-to-face social networks	Individualistic, emphasizing personal preferences and life styles; changeable self-constructions

Given the ideal-type nature of the comparisons, it should not come as a surprise that some societies cannot be placed on a smooth continuum between the poorest and the wealthiest societies. Saudi Arabia and some of the oil-producing Arab states in the Gulf region, for instance, are newly wealthy societies whose characteristics fail to match several of the generalizations contained in Table 3.2. Indeed, it may be argued that the religious history of those countries can supply better explanations for some of the gender roles and childrearing conditions to be found there than the kind of global analysis presented in this chapter. Nevertheless, a broadly conceived global analysis is the only way to arrive at the "Big Picture" and to understand, at least in rough outline, what main factors are governing children's lives over the long run.

The comparisons contained in Table 3.2 can be translated and elaborated into a series of 20 trends that characterize the global transformation of childhood in our times. These trends are certainly not of a linear, uninterrupted, irreversible nature, but they are nevertheless part and parcel of the ongoing formation of a dynamic if strife-torn world community. Driven by technological advances and their pervasive effects, worldwide economic and demographic forces, and global political-economic-cultural influences and competition between societies, these broad trends may be summarized as follows:

Societies, their families, and their children are transformed over time:

- From agriculture and herding-based subsistence-level societies to postmodern information societies.
- From societies emphasizing tradition and time-honored sacred archetypes to those emphasizing innovation and constant change.

- From societies with traditional hierarchically ordered gender roles anchored in predominantly patriarchal sacred traditions to societies emphasizing changeable gender roles perceived as human-made and expected to be egalitarian in nature.
- From families fighting for economic and physical survival to families participating in consumerism.
- From families involved in subsistence economy to families shedding many economic functions.
- From families fulfilling numerous economic functions to families emphasizing socioemotional functions.
- From big families to small families.
- From societies with numerous children to societies with numerous aged persons.
- From more stable to more unstable families.
- From a few to highly diverse family types.
- From child labor inside and outside the family to children's long-term enrollment in educational institutions.
- From societies emphasizing informal education to societies emphasizing formal ways of extended schooling.
- From families educating and training their children to children who are mostly educated in schools.
- From a collectivistic emphasis on children's obedience, respectfulness, manners, and responsibility toward an emphasis on children's independence, individuality, and self-actualization.
- From authoritative parents expected to be knowledgeable and in control to more fallible parents who may need to learn new skills and ideas from their technology-savvy adolescent children.
- From brief adolescence to prolonged adolescence followed by a period of emerging adulthood that may, or may not, lead to marriage.
- From adolescents' orientation toward learning from the community toward adolescents' fascination with the mass media as well as the ubiquitous information found on the web.
- From adolescents' orientation toward authoritative adults to adolescents' involvement in constantly changing adolescent subcultures shaped by both local and global forces.
- From preparing adolescents for known social roles and life in a known future society to preparing adolescents for unknown social roles created by a society in constant flux.
- From children who as adults will be expected to ensure the long-term economic survival and welfare of their parents to children who are expected to enrich the socioemotional lives of their parents.

As societies transform themselves, they often display a challenging mixture of traditional and modern features. In India, for instance, we may observe all of the following: ancient Hindu rituals, tribal societies in the northeastern regions pursuing their traditional yet changing ways of life, a mixture of traditional and modern skirmishes between guerillas and government troops in Kashmir, including the latent threat of nuclear bombs, Mumbai's impressive modern skyline but also the building of roads with the help of extensive manual labor and ancient tools, a thriving movie industry depicting ancient gods engaged in laser-beam warfare, seemingly traditional villages deeply affected by the "green revolution" and the national mass media, families that follow both traditional and nontraditional customs, poor villagers glued to communal TV screens depicting soap operas taking place in the households of rich city dwellers, and so on. Not surprisingly, India's childrearing systems often display the same dazzling mixture of ancient and modern features (Sharma, 2003). "Timeless" India is finally on the move although economic and cultural changes in this country have so far not matched the pace of changes found in countries such as South Korea, Taiwan, and China.

We may inquire in this context how the lives of Fatima and Takashi, whom we encountered in the very beginning of this chapter, fit into the rough picture sketched earlier. Fatima's work as a carpet weaver, together with her family surroundings, marginal literacy, poor economic prospects, possible exposure to civil unrest, and likely future as a traditional mother with quite a few children—preferably boys if Allah wills it—mirror, in individual form, many of the characteristics we have attributed to poor traditional societies. In a corresponding fashion, Takashi's present (and future) existence is mostly shaped by the features of a prosperous information society, including small family size, long years of schooling, extensive exposure to peer group and media influence, consumerism, and the prospects for a long healthy life.

We should not forget, however, that there are many more Fatimas than Takashis in this world although most developmental psychology textbooks fail to reflect this basic fact. Most of them do not have much to say about the lives of poor Muslim girls such as Fatima, and as a consequence they remain mostly invisible to the reader.

CONCLUSION

I have sketched a picture of global childhood that emphasizes economic and demographic influences rather than foregrounding contrasts between collectivistic and individualistic cultural scripts or the at times bloody competition between alternative religious, nationalist, and secular ideologies that dominates today's newspaper headlines.

I believe that in the long run, technological changes and the ensuing transformation of the material basis of societies will prove of central importance in shaping the lives of children everywhere. At the same time let us hope that American life cycle psychology will continue to grow less ethnocentric in nature and pay more attention to the "Big Picture" rather than taking as normative the life trajectories of children growing up in Western postindustrial societies. Even the recent spate of comparisons between American or European children and those residing in East Asian countries does not lead to a satisfactory understanding of global childhood, in part because the comparisons leave out too many children in the poorer and less technologically advanced countries.

Let's expand our own horizons and those of our students by teaching developmental psychology from a truly global perspective, with due consideration for the long-term impact of material factors and the lives of otherwise mostly invisible children in the poor countries. It is both scientifically desirable and morally appropriate to do so.

REFLECTIVE QUESTIONS

1. Why are the childhoods of Fatima and Takashi so different in nature?
2. In what ways are children around the world doing both better and worse than several decades ago?
3. Why do people have children? Are there any differences in this respect between low- and high-income countries?
4. Why can child labor in low-income countries be considered a delicate issue from both an economic and cultural point of view? Why have countries such as India failed to stop child labor?
5. How is adolescence changing in the low- to medium-income countries?
6. Discuss three major trends influencing global changes in childhood.

NOTES

1. The fictional lives of Fatima and Takashi are based on those of several youngsters the author has met respectively in Kashmir and Japan.

2. This chapter is a major revision of Gielen and Chumachenko's chapter contained in the first edition of this volume.

SUGGESTED READINGS

Books and Articles

Carpenter, E. A. (2014). *Precious children of India: Giving voice to destitute children of the world.* Abbotsford, WI: Life Sentence Publishing.

Greenfield, P. M. (2009). Linking social change and developmental change: Shifting pathways of human development. *Developmental Psychology, 45*(2), 401–418.

Websites

International Labor Organization (ILO). (2013). *Marking progress against child labour: Global estimates on child labor 2000–2012.* Geneva, Switzerland: International Labour Office. http://www.ilo.org/wcmsp5/groups/public/—-ed_norm/—-ipec/documents/publication/wcms_221513.pdf

Save the Children (2015). *The urban disadvantage: State of the world's children 2015.* Retrieved on May 5, 2015, from http://www.savethechildren.org.za/sites/savethechildren.org.za/files/resources/SOWM%202015.pdf

United Nations Children's Fund (UNICEF). (2014). *The state of the world's children 2014 in numbers: Every child counts.* Retrieved on February 3, 2015, from www.unicef.org/sowc2014/numbers. New York: Oxford University Press.

REFERENCES

Ahmed, R.A. (1991). Women in Egypt and the Sudan. In L.L. Adler (Ed.), *Women in cross-cultural perspective* (pp. 107–133). New York: Praeger.

Ahmed, R.A. (2005). Egyptian families. In J.L. Roopnarine & U.P. Gielen (Eds.), *Families in global perspective* (pp. 151–168). Boston, MA: Allyn & Bacon.

Batstone, D. (2010). *Not for sale: The return of the global slave trade—and how we can fight it* (rev. ed.). New York: HarperOne.

Blanchard, R., & Bogaert, A.F. (1997). The relation of closed birth intervals to the sex of the preceding child and the sexual orientation of the succeeding child. *Journal of Biosocial Science, 29,* 111–118.

Blurton-Jones, N.J. (1989). The cost of children and the adaptive scheduling of births: Toward a sociobiological perspective on demography. In A. Rosa, C. Vogel, & E. Voland (Eds.), *The sociobiology of sexual and reproductive strategies* (pp. 265–282). London, UK: Chapman & Hall.

Bureau of Democracy, Human Rights, and Labor. (2000). *Country reports on human rights.* Retrieved from http:/www.usis.usemb.se/human/2000/

Central Intelligence Agency. (2014). *The world factbook 2014.* Retrieved from https://www.cia.gov/library/publications/the-world-factbook/

Dettwyler, K.A. (1994). *Dancing skeletons: Life and death in West Africa.* Prospect Heights, IL: Waveland Press.

Doherty, B. (2014). Kailash Satyarthi: The tireless, unlikely and accessible Nobel peace prize winner. *The Guardian*, October 12, 2014.

Dybdhal, R., & Hundeide, K. (1998). Childhood in the Somali context: Mothers' and children's ideas about childhood and parenthood. *Psychology and Developing Societies, 10*(2), 131–145.

The Economist (2014). Police violence in Brazil: Serial killing. March 20, 2014 (by H.J.).

Faleiro, S. (2011). The other India: Where are the children? *The New York Times,* October 12, 2011.

Greenfield, P.M., & Lave, J. (1982). Cognitive aspects of informal education. In D.A. Wagner & H.W. Stevenson (Eds.), *Cultural perspectives on child development* (pp. 181–207). San Francisco, CA: W. Freeman.

Hiner, R. (1991). Introduction. In J. Hawes & R. Hiner (Eds.), *Children in historical and comparative perspective* (pp. 1–12). New York: Greenwood Press.

International Labor Office (ILO). (2013). *Marking progress against child labour: Global estimates on child labor 2000–2012.* Geneva, Switzerland: International Labour

Office. Retrieved from http://www.ilo.org/wcmsp5/groups/public/—-ed_norm/—-ipec/documents/publication/wcms_221513.pdf

Kağitçibaşi, Ç. (2007). *Family, self, and human development across cultures: Theory and applications* (2nd ed.). New York: Psychology Press.

Kannan, S. (2014, February 5). Child labour: India's hidden shame. BBC News, Delhi. Retrieved from http://www.bbc.com/news/business-25947984

Klinenberg, E. (2013). *Going solo: The extraordinary rise and surprising appeal of living alone.* New York: Penguin.

Naito, T., & Gielen, U.P. (2005). The changing Japanese family: A psychological portrait. In J.L. Roopnarine & U.P. Gielen (Eds.), *Families in global perspective* (pp. 63–84). Boston, MA: Allyn & Bacon.

Nath, D.C., Leonetti, D.L., & Steele, M.S. (1999). *Analysis of birth intervals in a non-contracepting Indian population: An evolutionary ecology approach.* Seattle, WA: Center for Studies in Demography and Ecology. (CSDE Working Paper No. 99–03).

Onishi, N. (2001). The bondage of poverty that produces chocolate. *New York Times,* July 29, pp. A1, A6.

Population Reference Bureau. (2000). *KIDS COUNT international data sheet.* Retrieved from http:/www.prb.org or http:/www.childtrends.org

Population Reference Bureau. (2014). *2014 World population data sheet.* Retrieved from http:/www.prb.org

Saraswathi, T.S. (2000). Adult-child continuity in India: Is adolescence a myth or an emerging reality? In A.L. Comunian & U.P. Gielen (Eds.), *International perspectives on human development* (pp. 431–448). Lengerich, Germany: Pabst Science Publishers.

Save the Children (2015). *The urban disadvantage: State of the world's children 2015.* Retrieved on from http://www.savethechildren.org.za/sites/savethechildren.org.za/files/resources/SOWM%202015.pdf

Scheper-Hughes, N. (1992). *Death without weeping: The violence of everyday life in Brazil.* Berkeley, CA: University of California Press.

Seabrook, J. (2001). *Children of other worlds.* Sterling, VA: Pluto Press.

Sharma, D. (Ed.). (2003). *Childhood, family and sociopolitical change in India: Reinterpreting the inner world.* New Delhi, India: Sage.

Singh, A., & Gielen, U.P. (1995). *Mothers' education, prevalence of contraceptives, and birth attendance by professional health personnel predict under-five mortality rate across 145 countries.* Unpublished paper, St. Francis College, New York City.

United Nations Children's Fund (UNICEF). (1989). *The Convention on the Rights of the Child.* Retrieved from http:/www.unicef.org/crc/convention.htm

United Nations Children's Fund (UNICEF). (2000). *The state of the world's children 2000.* Retrieved on April 28, 2015, from http://www.unicef.org/sowc/archive/ENGLISH/The%20State%20of%20the%20World%27s%20Children%202000.pdf. New York: UNICEF.

United Nations Children's Fund (UNICEF). (2012). *The state of the world's children 2012: Children in the urban world.* Retrieved on April 28, 2015, from http://www.unicef.org/sowc2012/pdfs/SOWC%202012-Main%20Report_EN_13Mar2012.pdf. New York: UNICEF.

United Nations Children's Fund (UNICEF). (2014). *The state of the world's children 2014 in numbers: Every child counts.* Retrieved on February 3, 2015, from www.unicef.org/sowc2014/numbers. New York: UNICEF.

United Nations Children's Fund (UNICEF). (2015). *An estimated 150 million children worldwide are engaged in child labor.* Retrieved on February 4, 2015, from http://data.unicef.org/child-protection/child-labour.

United Nations Development Programme. (2002). *Human development report.* New York: UNICEF.

United Nations Development Programme. (2014). *Human development report.* New York: UNICEF.

United Nations Office on Drugs and Crime. (2014). *The 2014 global report on trafficking in persons.* New York: United Nations.

United States Committee for Refugees (USCR). (2002). *China's one-child policy.* Retrieved from http://www.refugees.org/world/articles/women_rr99_8.htm

4

Literacy Development: Global Research and Policy Perspectives

Daniel A. Wagner, Fatima Tuz Zahra, and Jinsol Lee

A nine-year-old boy named Matin lives in a crowded working-class neighborhood in Dhaka, Bangladesh. On Monday at 8 A.M., Matin is sitting in his third-grade classroom by large windows overlooking a narrow street bustling with local taxis and rickshaws. It is easy to get distracted by the noise coming from the outside. His teacher is teaching a poem about a child who wakes up early in the morning and plans to conquer the world. She asks her students to read the poem aloud after her. The students then make sentences with the new words they have just learned. In the meantime, his teacher goes around the class asking children to pay attention and focus on their task.

Salma, a 10-year-old girl, lives with her single mother who is a domestic worker for a rich family a few kilometers away from their apartment. Salma is happy sitting in a small fourth-grade classroom, decorated with letters and pictures by the students themselves. Salma likes how her teacher teaches, and expresses her ambition to become a teacher one day. However, she misses school the next day, and eventually for a week. Her teacher learns from one of Salma's peers that she is not returning to school—her mother has decided that Salma should help out with her domestic job so that Salma could learn a real trade, and help the family cover some debts owed to their landlord.

Matin and Salma live in the same neighborhood. Salma carries her language textbook to work every day but finds no time to practice the new vocabulary words she studied in school. Matin continues to learn new words and make new sentences. One might ask why Matin's mother decided to keep him in school and Salma's mother chose a working path for her daughter. Since literacy development is a lifelong process, it is important to understand how literacy learning can impact on people's lives. How does knowing how to read, write, or count numbers affect the lives of children like Salma, Matin, and their parents? How does one measure the impact of literacy on human development across different age groups and cultures?

In this review, we provide a brief introduction to and definition of literacy development and its importance at various stages of human lives in differing cultural contexts. Several case studies are provided, along with a description of how literacy has been measured and its impact studied in recent years. Future directions for research and development follow, along with a number of questions for reflection and further inquiry.

Literacy development is a complex and dynamic phenomenon that varies across time, language, and geography. The origins of literacy can be traced back thousands of years, initially invented as a tool for communication to be shared among only a small portion of "educated" human society. However, within the past few centuries, many societies have experienced transitions from mostly illiterate to predominantly literate populations through a variety of means involving both formal and informal learning.

Today, United Nations Educational, Scientific, and Cultural Organization (UNESCO) estimates that about 80% of adults worldwide can read or write to some extent (UIS, 2011). Nonetheless, the transition to widespread literacy has not been uniform across societies. Contexts vary greatly across the globe, and these have played a significant role in the motivation and support for acquiring literacy, or not. For example, in Sweden, reading ability reportedly rose to above 90% by the mid-18th century as a result of the pressure from church and state on families to teach Bible reading at home (Johansson, 1982; Wagner, 1995). Among the Vai people of West Africa, literacy in the form of an indigenous script was developed and used for economic and personal written communication since the 19th century (Scribner & Cole, 1981). This tradition was transferred from one generation to another outside the structure of formal schooling. From these and other examples, it is clear that a historical examination of social context and literacy development is essential for understanding how literacy functions as a historical and cultural phenomenon.

The advent of modern public education, the increasing use of technology, and globalization are among the many factors that have contributed to changes in literacy over the years. At a macro-level, the expansion of literacy work reflects the increased social complexities of our rapidly changing societies in the 21st century. At a micro-level, changes take place at different stages of a child's life through the learning of basic cognitive skills in and out of school, while also serving the child's needs of everyday life. On the international policy stage, literacy is a core component of the United Nations development goals in the Education for All (EFA) initiative, as well as in the United Nations Millennium Development Goals (MDGs).

Despite the target among international agencies to achieve the MDGs by 2015, there are some major challenges that have prevented many countries from achieving such goals, including universal basic education and literacy. The United Nations Development Group Report (2014) highlights six areas of improvement based on lessons learnt from these challenges. They recommend localizing the agenda, improving institutional capacities to support these agenda, increasing participation of individuals to ensure monitoring and accountability of the programs, providing culturally sensitive approaches to development, and creating new opportunities for partnership with various civil societies and the private sector. In the world of literacy development, a focus on these recommendations may significantly improve and sustain culturally relevant literacy practices across people from different socio-ethnic backgrounds, age groups, and professions.

DEFINING LITERACY

With the multitude of experts and published works on the topic, one would suppose that there would be a fair amount of agreement on how to define the term "literacy." On the one hand, most specialists would agree that the term connotes aspects of reading and writing; on the other hand, major debates continue to revolve around issues such as what specific abilities or knowledge counts as literacy, and what levels can and should be defined for measurement. This section attempts to define literacy following the shifts in the global trends.

The UNESCO initially adopted a "functional" approach to define literacy:

> A person is functionally literate when he has acquired the knowledge and skills in reading and writing which enable him to engage effectively in all those activities in which literacy is normally assumed in his culture or group. (Gray, 1956, p. 19)

Continuing the trend of defining literacy in terms of functionality, the Global Monitoring Report of 2006 referred to literacy as "a context-bound *continuum* of reading, writing, and numeracy skills [italics added]" that is acquired and developed in and outside of schools through training and application. One should note that it took UNESCO nearly a half-century to shed itself of the dichotomy between "literates" and "illiterates" in favor of a continuum of literacy skills that can be measured. This movement was influenced by the International Adult Literacy Survey (IALS), where literacy was defined as "the ability to understand and employ printed information in daily activities, at home, at work and in the community—to achieve one's goals, and to develop one's knowledge and potential" (Organisation for Economic Co-operation and Development [OECD] & Statistics Canada, 2000). Similarly, the OECD's Programme for the International Assessment of Adult Competencies (PIAAC) defines literacy as "a range of skills from the decoding of written words and sentences to the comprehension, interpretation, and evaluation of complex texts" (OECD, 2013). Small-scale (and small sample) hybrid assessments (Wagner, 2011a), such as the Early Grade Reading Assessment (EGRA; Gove & Wetterberg, 2011), can be used in more localized (e.g., local language) contexts; EGRA defines literacy in young children through a set of measurable component skills, such as reading fluency and comprehension.

The preceding definitions of literacy were largely created by policy makers and educational psychologists. By contrast, anthropologists see literacy through ethnographic accounts of literacy practices, woven into the cultural life of distinct communities (Street, 1999). A sociocultural view of literacy focuses on uses of literacy in specific cultural contexts and literacy programs that become subject of ethnographic context-based inquiry (Street, 2005). Researchers have studied issues of power, hierarchy, and contextual implications for defining and understanding the outcomes of literacy (Cope & Kalanztis, 2000; Kress & Van Leeuwen, 2001).

In this review, we refer to literacy as a set of basic skills and knowledge in reading, writing, and numeracy used for a multiplicity of purposes in diverse contexts. Our understanding of literacy, therefore, is both flexible and multidimensional, and whose measurement must be empirically tested with sensitivity to cultural context.

EVOLUTION OF GLOBAL LITERACY POLICIES

An individual's literacy development will necessarily vary across his or her lifespan due to education, diverse life experiences, and demographic characteristics such as gender and ethno-linguistic variation. For example, gender disparities in literacy around the world remain a major concern for national and international policy makers in low-income countries (LICs). EFA Goal #5 aimed to eliminate gender disparities in primary and secondary education by 2005, and achieve broader gender equality in education by 2015. Despite significant progress globally, gender parity in primary and secondary education has not been achieved, especially in poor countries where large disparities remain (UNDG, 2015; UNESCO, 2013; see Figure 4.1).

Many LICs were formed out of multiple linguistic and ethnic groups, and recent processes of migration have increased the proximity of children from linguistically varied populations (Wagner, Murphy, & de Korne,

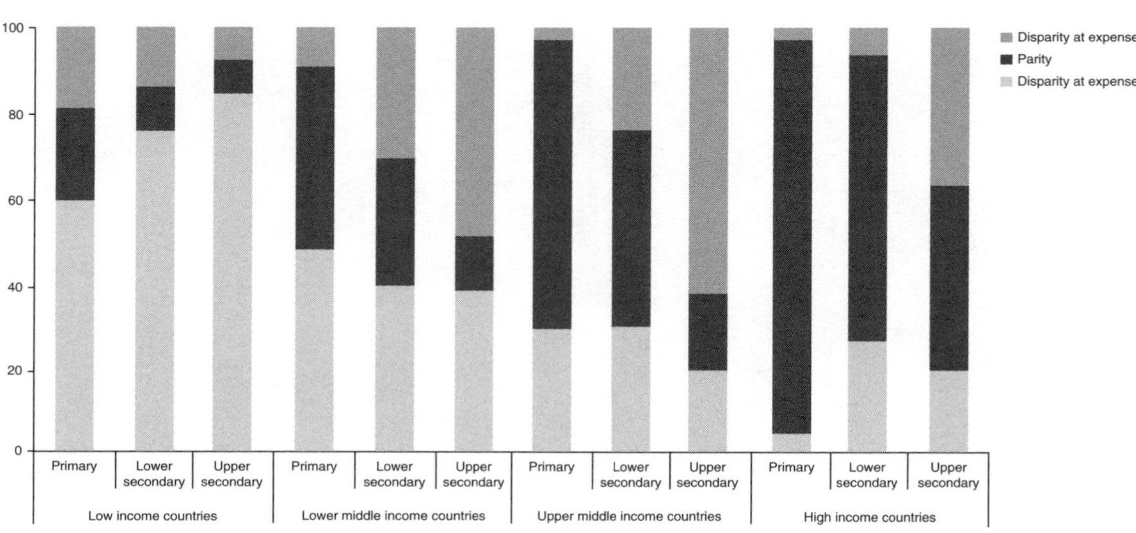

Figure 4.1 Gender Disparity in Low-Income Countries

Source: UNESCO (2013, p.11).

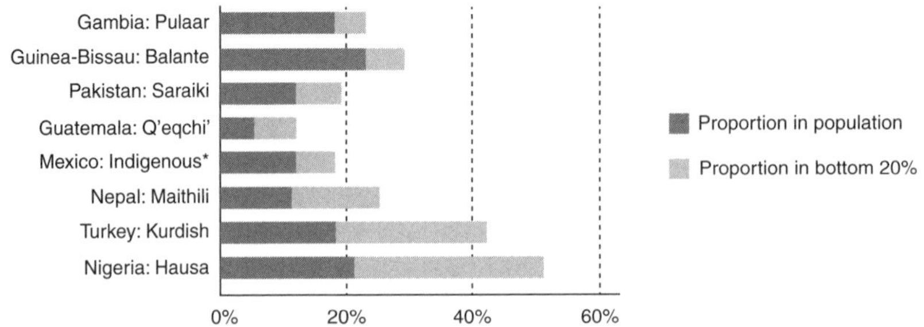

Figure 4.2 Percentage of Selected Language Groups in the Bottom 20% of the Education Distribution, in Selected Countries

Notes: The "bottom 20%" is the 20% of 17- to 22-year-olds with the fewest years of education.

* The indigenous language category in Mexico consists of those who speak indigenous languages only and do not speak Spanish.

Source: Adapted from UNESCO (2010, p. 152).

2012). This remains true even in countries with a single or focal national language policy. In such countries, poor enrollment, retention, and educational attainment of marginalized ethno-linguistic groups (see Figure 4.2) are particularly evident, where implicit policies (of language, ethnicity, economic or social status, gender, etc.) lead inexorably to the fewest years of formal schooling and lowest achievement outcomes.

Demographic characteristics, such as gender and language, help to explain large variations in literacy across and within countries. However, in terms of policy implementation and lifespan experiences, a closer look at age-related differences in literacy development is necessary. More often than not, an individual's age indicates his or her exposure to literacy education and related life experiences. As we shall see later in this chapter, the learning processes and needs for different age groups vary in substantial ways, and require particular attention when formulating literacy policies and programs.

LITERACY IN EARLY CHILDHOOD

In the first few years of life, early language and literacy development influences a child's potential for future success. Studies have shown that skills developed during these years can affect future acquisition of other proficiencies, and findings on brain development suggest that learning is a hierarchical and integrated process (Kuhl, 2010). As a result, there is a major movement toward support of early childhood development (ECD) programs to provide children with basic cognitive, social, and emotional skills that set the foundation for learning literacy and numeracy skills at later ages (Ball, Paris, & Govinda, 2014). Conversely, a lack of learning opportunities during the early stages can cumulatively hinder progress in the acquisition of higher order skills and future educational outcomes (Engle et al., 2007).

Empirical research of comprehensive, large-scale ECD programs in the United States has demonstrated that children who participate in these programs can avoid developmental delay in cognitive, social, and family outcomes (Anderson et al., 2003; Puma, Bell, Cook, Heid, & Lopez, 2005). Even though the research base in developing countries is less robust, evaluations of ECD programs in those contexts are beginning to show similar positive outcomes (Nores & Barnett, 2010). Children who attended preschool had higher scores in various measures of child development and learning outcomes, including literacy, vocabulary, and enhanced school readiness, than those who did not attend.

Informal literacy learning at home is also important for literacy development in young children, particularly through the parents. Studies have shown the importance of family engagement and home characteristics as they affect early language skills (Anders et al., 2012; Forget-Dubois, et al., 2009). Research has demonstrated significant relationships between parental support at home and gains in primary school writing and math scores, in addition to improved attendance (Epstein, Clark, Salinas, & Sanders, 1997). Nonetheless, in many disadvantaged families in LICs, the necessary parental support for learning to read is often very limited (Ball et al., 2014). Furthermore, when the language of instruction at school differs from the home language, the consequences can be lower literacy levels and higher dropout rates (Smits, Huisman, & Kruijff, 2008). These findings, taken together, reflect the importance of family engagement and parental involvement in promoting literacy policies during the early years for children around the world.

LITERACY IN SCHOOL

With the global growth of mass public education, primary schooling is the most common starting place for formal literacy learning, typically beginning with children between the ages 5 and 7 (Wagner, 2004). Despite widely varying differences in primary schools across the world, the importance of literacy remains central to the curriculum in nearly all schools. The minimal cognitive learning standard for all children is to read, write, and calculate by the end of five grades of primary schooling. This consensus among educational policy makers places literacy skills at the top of the international development agenda.

Most governments in LICs have implemented policies that align with the second MDG goal—to achieve universal primary education for all boys and girls by 2015, and this has led to a steadily reduced number of children out of school (Figure 4.3). Compulsory education laws now exist in 95% of 203 countries and territories. And, 23 countries that previously lacked such legal provisions have established them since 2000 (UNESCO, 2008). However, early school dropout remains persistent at a global rate of 25% since 2000, as 34 out of 137 million children who started first grade in 2011 are likely to leave before reaching the last grade of primary school. Furthermore, nearly 250 million children cannot read and write even after four years of primary education (UN Fact Sheet, 2013). Even though much progress has been made in promoting school access through governmental policies, there is a great need to improve the quality of primary education (Wagner et al., 2012).

Increasing efforts are being made to assess literacy levels among primary and secondary school students internationally. At the global level, OECD's influential Programme for International Student Assessment (PISA) has provided, since 2000, a series of triennial assessments that tests 15-year-old students from selected schools worldwide in key subjects including reading. Students representing more than 70 countries have participated in PISA, which assesses reading skills including text understanding, reflection, and evaluation of situations beyond the classroom. However, it is important to note that a number of problems must be considered regarding international assessments, including their comparability across countries (Wagner, 2010b, 2011a), especially since assessments like PISA have not

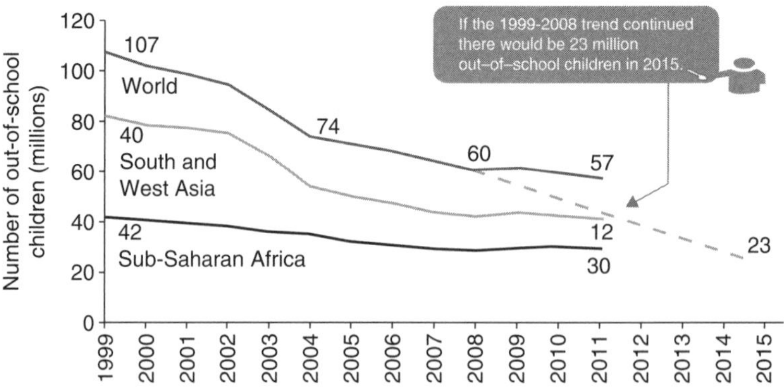

Figure 4.3 Number of Primary School Age Children Out of School, by Region, 1999–2011

Source: UNESCO (2013, p. 53).

as yet been sufficiently adapted to LICs. As mentioned, EGRA and other hybrid (smaller, quicker, cheaper or SQC) assessment instruments have been growing rapidly in both South Asia and Africa (Wagner, 2011a).

Overall, the rapid expansion of access to primary schooling over the past few decades has resulted in a steady increase in literacy rates across the globe, but has not been able to address serious problems of low literacy in the poorest countries. Many of these children are still unable to read at the end of the fifth grade. This not only poses a serious challenge to their future education but will also have an impact on their potential for economic growth.

YOUTH LITERACY

Among youth (aged 15–24 years), literacy rates have been improving over the past two decades due to an increased level of investment (USAID, 2012). The global literacy rate for youth, according to the UNESCO Institute of Statistics (UIS, 2011), increased from 83% in 1990 to 90% in 2011, which varies by region (Table 4.1). Youth literacy rates were highest among the regions in Central Asia, Central and Eastern Europe, East Asia and the Pacific, and Latin America and the Caribbean. Furthermore, in all eight regions, the literacy rates for youth were higher than the rates for adults in 2011 (UIS, 2011). These literacy trends reflect increased access to primary and secondary education for younger generations and suggest that adult literacy rates will climb as youth replace older cohorts in the future.

However, according to the data report by UIS (2011), 123 million youths still lacked basic literacy skills in 2011, with a majority of such youth concentrated in the two regions of South and West Asia (62 million persons)

Table 4.1 Historical Trends in Youth Literacy Rate

EFA Region	1990 (1985–1994 Census decade) in Percentage	2000 (1995–2004 Census decade) in Percentage	2011 (2005–2014 Census decade) in Percentage
Arab States	74	83	90
Central and Eastern Europe	98	99	99
Central Asia	100	100	100
East Asia and the Pacific	95	98	99
Latin America and the Caribbean	93	96	97
South and West Asia	60	74	81
Sub-Saharan Africa	66	68	70

Source: UIS (2013, p. 18).

and sub-Saharan Africa (48 million persons). These literacy rates are still lower among rural youth and girls, with a particularly large gender disparity in three regions: Arab States, South and West Asia, and sub-Saharan Africa. A major part of this problem results from young people who have never attended school or left school before acquiring strong literacy skills. Estimates suggest that 266 million adolescents from both lower and upper secondary education are out of school (G8 Education Experts, 2009), especially in rural areas (Fawcett, Hartwell, & Israel, 2010).

Further empirical research on youth populations is needed. Although youth and adult literacy is often considered within the same scope in many policy papers and discussions, the landscape of motivations, values, and behaviors of youth is often different and seems to be changing rapidly with increased globalization.

ADULT LITERACY

The fourth EFA Goal targets a 50% decrease in the level of adult illiteracy by 2015 through equitable access to basic and continuing education for adults, especially for women. Adult literacy has improved somewhat for a majority of countries in the world over the past two decades (see Table 4.2). As part of this effort, the United Nations Literacy Decade (2003–2012) pushed forward several initiatives to advance adult literacy and lifelong learning in LICs.

In UNESCO's *Belem Framework for Action*, literacy is treated as a human right that requires lifelong learning with "multidimensional objectives," such as economic, political, environmental, and vocational, to be fulfilled

Table 4.2 Historical Trends in Adult Literacy Rate

EFA region	1990 (1985–1994 Census decade) in Percentage	2000 (1995–2004 Census Decade) in Percentage	2011 (2005–2014 Census Decade) in Percentage
Arab States	55	68	77
Central and Eastern Europe	96	97	99
Central Asia	98	99	100
East Asia and the Pacific	82	92	95
Latin America and the Caribbean	86	90	92
South and West Asia	47	59	63
Sub-Saharan Africa	53	57	59

Source: UIS (2013, p. 10).

Table 4.3 Progress toward EFA Goal 4 by Region

	Likely to reach EFA 4	Additional effort needed to reach EFA 4	Unlikely to reach EFA 4 by 2015	No. of Countries Providing data
Africa	3	6	18	27
Arab States	6	6	4	16
Asia and the Pacific	11	12	5	28
Europe and North America	12	13	0	25
Latin America and the Caribbean	3	17	2	22
Total	35	54	29	118

Source: UIL (2013, p.19).

in one's lifetime (UIL, 2013). Low levels of adult literacy have persisted for decades in LICs mainly due to poorly financed programs in adult education. In some countries (e.g., Gambia, Kenya, or Botswana) adult education is considered a part of the national education system, while in others (e.g., Morocco, Namibia, the Philippines) adult literacy policies are promoted in independent agencies (UIL, 2010). In a few cases campaigns have been promoted to support adult literacy, such as in South Africa.

Overall, despite decades of efforts to reduce illiteracy, only 35 out of 118 countries are likely to reach EFA Goal 4 of a 50% reduction in adult illiteracy (UIL, 2013; see Table 4.3). This poor result is at least partly a reflection of the limited national and international investments made, but also of the complexity of motivating adults to take part in such programs. Demographic changes, including the increase in access to primary and secondary schooling, will no doubt continue to improve adult literacy rates, but low literacy and illiteracy will likely persist well into the future.

CASE STUDIES OF LITERACY PROGRAMS

Official statistics can provide a helpful sense of the educational policy environment, but they often leave one feeling uninformed about what happens "on the ground." Here we provide a more in-depth sense of how programs operate—in four case examples, one from each of the age groups discussed earlier.

Case study 1: Early Literacy Project in Mozambique. Fewer than half of the children in Mozambique complete the seven years of compulsory primary education (UNESCO, 2008). To address this problem, Save the Children and ELMA philanthropies began an Early Literacy Project in Mozambique in 2008 that provided teacher training, community mobilization, and reading promotion activities to support school readiness and literacy development for children (Mungoi et al., 2010). An experimental evaluation framework was used to study its impact on preschool-age children (Martinez, Naudeau, & Pereira, 2012). The baseline study involved a pre- and posttest design that drew a sample of 816 children between the ages 3 and 5. The findings showed that exposure to the preschool intervention program helped children, when compared with a non-intervention control group, develop improved concepts of print mastery, emergent writing skills, and *Shangana* language vocabulary skills (Mungoi et al., 2012). Further, all 10 of the intervention schools found an increase in performance among first-grade children on early literacy skills assessed when compared to control groups (see Figure 4.4). The findings demonstrate greater school readiness and significant increases in primary school enrollment rates among the intervention condition, and also resulted in significant improvements in cognitive and problem-solving abilities, fine-motor skills, and behavioral outcomes (Martinez et al., 2012).

Clearly, investing in young children can be effective in supporting literacy skills and school readiness even in poor LICs like Mozambique, but this necessitates better teacher training, improved community mobilization, and the encouragement of reading activities in early childhood programs.

Case study 2: Pratham Balsakhi Program in Indian Primary Schools. *Balsakhi,* (supported by Pratham, a major Indian educational NGO, and initiated in Mumbai in 1998), is a remedial program targeting children in primary grade levels who have low reading skills (Banerjee, Cole, Duflo, & Linden, 2007). The *Balsakhi* program is an example of an initiative utilizing

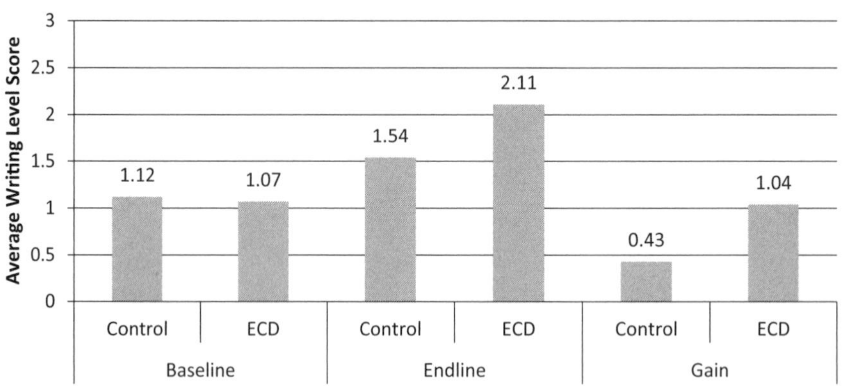

Figure 4.4 Performance on Writing Skills at Baseline, Endline, and Gain

Source: Adapted from Mungoi et al. (2011, p.7).

local community members as supplemental teachers. To support children's literacy skills development, the program recruited from the local community young women with a secondary education certification. These teachers are called *Balsakhis* (meaning child's friends) and were trained for two weeks, and also received feedback throughout the year. Each *Balsakhi* instructed a total of 15–20 children on basic reading and numeracy skills for two hours every day in school. They were required to follow a standardized curriculum developed by Pratham, and used available spaces such as classrooms, playgrounds, and hallways in school for instruction. The impact of the program was measured in Mumbai and Vadodara in 2002 and 2003 using an experimental design. Results showed that *Balsakhis* had helped to significantly improve the basic comprehension and math skills of children over two years (Banerjee et al., 2007).

The *Balsakhi* program demonstrates how learning gaps of children attending public primary schools in India can be reduced, especially in cases where government teachers often are absent or poorly motivated (Ramachandran, Pal, Jain, Shekar, & Sharma, 2005). Also, since *Balsakhis* were hired for a fraction of the regular pay of government teachers, the intervention was considered to be quite cost-effective (Banerjee et al., 2007, p.12).

Case study 3: Youth Literacy Program in Peru. *Programas de Alfabetización Educación Básica de Personas Adultas en Iberoamérica* (PAEBA) is a regional youth and adult literacy project introduced in Peru in 2003 (Di Pierro, 2008). As a program supported and financed through a public-private partnership, the module-based literacy and vocational training program targets illiterate Peruvians, who make up about 12.1% of the adult population. The program teaches basic literacy and numeracy along with communication and other work-related skills at three different levels (basic, intermediate, and advanced levels). PAEBA-Peru also makes use of mobile phones and e-learning to train youth and adults living in remote areas.

The project functions using two different approaches: *Aula Mentor* system and *Aulas Móviles* system (UNESCO, 2013). The *Aula Mentor* system requires students to pay a modest tuition fee, of which 50% is refundable for those who successfully complete the program. Trained tutors provide lessons on business entrepreneurship, technology skills, education, and health, while computers and online learning materials are made accessible to any interested adult learners in the community. The *Aulas Móviles* system functions with mobile classrooms, specially developed for training youth and adults in regards to community development, water and sanitation, hairdressing, and early childhood education. The trainers travel to remote areas and conduct workshops teaching skills and boosting positive attitudes and confidence among the learners.

A significant limitation of PAEBA is that the design of the curriculum focused on urban populations rather than the rural areas, where the very poor mainly reside. Further, the program did not seem to assess the literacy acquisition progress of learners.

Case study 4: Kha Ri Gude (Let Us Learn) Adult Literacy Program (KGALP). In South Africa, about one in four adults are considered to be functionally illiterate (UIS, 2011). Initiated by the government of South Africa, KGALP is run by the Department of Basic Education (DoBE) as a mass literacy program (or campaign) that delivers basic literacy education in 11 different languages (http://www.kharigude.co.za). Approximately 620,000 women (80%), young people (25%), and people with disabilities (8%) have participated in this program. The DoBE recruited over 75,000 community-based volunteers and trained them on teaching techniques, managing classrooms, using teaching modules, and conducting assessment. They were given a desk calendar with 35 literacy, 35 numeracy, and 10 general English lessons. Each volunteer instructor was paid a modest monthly salary and was assigned about 15–18 learners. Teachers' payment was contingent upon submitting Learner Assessment Portfolios (LAPs).

The instructors taught reading by systematically introducing higher to lower frequency phonemes and graphemes, and following linguistic typologies for the different languages of instruction. Lessons were based on contextual discussions on topics of learners' interest such as family, communities, health, HIV, nutrition, environment, and country-related subject matters.

KGALP employed an action research-based monitoring and evaluation system to improve the teaching quality and support the learners. Program supervisors consulted with the coordinators on a regular basis to address pressing issues or needs concerning the volunteer teachers or the learners.

By 2012, KGALP reported having assisted 3.5 million adult learners somewhat more than five years (SADOE, 2013; UIL, 2008), gaining basic literacy and numeracy skills to accomplish everyday tasks such as shopping, paying bills, and traveling. KGALP is considered to be a well thought-out and comprehensive program–with special provisions for learning in local languages while also empowering women and vulnerable adults with special needs. These features are important to establish credibility and accountability of both the learning and teaching processes in an adult educational program. Nevertheless, some challenges in the program were identified: lack of timely distribution of learning materials, learner absenteeism, and a fast-paced learning module that some adults are unable to follow (Dichaba & Dhlamini, 2013). Furthermore, while a monitoring and evaluation system has been put in place through the LAPs, the overall impact on learning has not yet been studied sufficiently. Even so, KGALP is one of the few recent, and highly developed, adult literacy programs implemented among poor and multilingual populations.

CONTEMPORARY CHALLENGES TO IMPROVING LITERACY

In spite of the considerable efforts of governments, school systems, and other agencies over many decades, efforts at achieving the improvement of, and equity in, literacy development have faced many challenges, including those described next.

Quality and Access. Both *access* (e.g., student enrolment and retention) and *quality* (of instruction and student learning) are critical. Many barriers to student enrollment and quality education exist, particularly for LICs. In early childhood, children's language and cognitive developmental needs are crucial, and in poor and rural areas, appropriate support has often not been available. In primary and secondary education, challenges exist regarding poor quality schooling, including with underpaid and/or unmotivated teachers. There are some innovative ways to overcome these challenges, such as in the *Balsakhi* program in India described earlier. In youth and adult literacy programs, a major challenge is to meet the diverse needs of learners who are no longer in formal school programs. Motivation continues to be a major barrier. The example of KGALP in South Africa provides a helpful example of how advanced planning and substantial financial resources can lead to substantial increases in access.

Assessment and Evaluation. Assessment usually refers to individual-level data that are collected to record the performance of a learner on a particular set of skills (e.g., reading skills). Evaluation refers to a summative process of measuring the major outcomes of a program in relation to stated programmatic objectives of the program (e.g., the degree of success of an adult literacy program in completing a planned curriculum). Assessments of learners' skills and program evaluations are crucial in determining the overall impact of any learning and education initiative. All assessments seek comparability, but these may vary in a number of key ways (Wagner, 2010b). Large-scale international and regional assessments (e.g., PISA) are aimed at cross-national comparability, while hybrid assessments are more focused on local contexts and increased validity. Hybrid assessments offer some kinds of comparability that large-scale assessments do not, such as comparing assessments among marginalized populations or younger children. Which types of comparability are most important depends on the policy goals desired, as well as timing and cost considerations. As in comparative education more generally, cultural context will determine whether and when empirical interpretations are deemed credible. Overall, hybrid assessments put a premium on local validity over international comparability (Wagner, 2011a).

In LICs and elsewhere, educational specialists and statisticians are often the primary guardians of learning assessment results. This restricted access to knowledge about learning achievement is due, at least in part, to the complexities of carrying out the technical aspects of assessments, but also perhaps to a reticence among policy makers who may worry about the public relations aspects of empirical differences between achievement levels of children by region, ethno-linguistic groups, private and public schools, and so forth. Hybrid (SQC) assessments have the potential of breaking new ground in accountability and local ownership, largely through the clear policy goal of providing information that matters to specific groups in a timely manner, such that change is possible, negotiable, and expected.

Technological Change. Information and communications technologies (ICTs) provide a major new set of contexts for literacy that is changing and expanding. One of the key distinctions is between learning how to read and reading to learn. With a smartphone reading or composing text message might look like similar actions, but could have quite different impacts on learning. For example, when a child holds a book or a smartphone with the purpose of reading, this common "practice" could help to improve reading instruction. Composing a text message could naturally help the writing process, but also have implications for language and communication skills. In other words, specific technological tools may be utilized differently depending on the user's intent and the device's design and capability (Wagner, 2014a).

There is growing evidence that the ways in which ICTs are utilized are also changing the nature of learning processes themselves. Observational studies indicate that young learners in wealthier communities actively use websites, message boards, social media, and so on. If given a choice, they often prefer social interaction on the Internet or mobiles in contrast to listening passively to an instructor or reading a textbook (Hinostroza, Isaacs, & Bougroum, 2014; Tolani-Brown, McCormac, & Zimmermann, 2009). Others have found that reading skills are significantly impacted by continuous interaction with web-based reading (Leu, O'Byrne, Zawilinski, McVerry, & Everett-Cacopardo, 2009).

In other words, ICTs are changing the ways that learning takes place, what gets learned, and not just standard reading outcomes. With the advent of e-books and social media, it is clear that young children with access to mobile devices have many new opportunities and ways to learn to be literate. In addition, given that such ICTs provide a "lower barrier for entry" for children to create texts themselves, they can write them rather than simply consuming them. In the age of new ICTs and their expansion across the globe (including the poorest communities), literacy learning is no longer restricted to the use of pencil, paper, or textbooks; rather our understanding of literacy necessitates a deep and adaptable understanding of technology for learning and instruction.

FUTURE DIRECTIONS

Since the first Education for All conference in Jomtien in 1990, and up through the current efforts to produce a new set of UN Development Goals for Post-2015, we have seen the frequent setting of ambitious goals to improve literacy (Wagner, 2014b). About a decade ago, we wrote that improving literacy will require "a set of strategies that incorporate and appeal to the developmental, cultural, linguistic, and cognitive domains of individuals in each society—to promote avenues of literacy development that fit with developmental as well as social and cultural dimensions of everyday life" (Wagner, 2004, p. 128). Since that time, we have learned more about the various ways that literacy is changing, how to better utilize assessment tools, and how to improve literacy from early childhood through adulthood.

The challenges are many. We have chosen to highlight three of these—access and quality, assessment and evaluation, and technological change—because we think that these are among the most tractable for future innovation and impact. The importance and significance of literacy to both individuals and societies necessitate looking at these challenges as resources to inform current practices and improve the future ones. Progress can be made only with the public and personal conviction that literacy—and improved learning more generally—is at the core of human and economic development.

REFLECTIVE QUESTIONS

1. What are several different ways that literacy has been defined?
2. Given the progress that has been made in literacy development, what are some of the major obstacles in order to achieve universal literacy? In what ways can policy makers and educators most effectively address these challenges?
3. Based on the evidence provided in several case studies, what are some of the best strategies to inform parents and local administrators to effectively implement literacy learning in low-income countries?
4. In what ways does cultural context determine effectiveness in youth and adult literacy programs?
5. How can the current research on the assessment of literacy contribute to a more effective way to improve educational outcomes in developing countries?

SUGGESTED READINGS

Books and Articles

Leu, D. J., O'Byrne, W. I., Zawilinski, L., McVerry, J. G., & Everett-Cacopardo, H. (2009). Expanding the new literacies conversation. *Educational Researcher, 38*(4), 264–269.

Street, B.V. (1999). The meanings of literacy. In D.A. Wagner, R.L. Venezky, & B.V. Street (Eds.), *Literacy: An international handbook* (pp. 34–38). Boulder, CO: Westview Press.

Wagner, D.A. (2011). What happened to literacy? Historical and conceptual perspectives on literacy in UNESCO. *International Journal of Educational Development*, 31, 319–323.

Wagner, D. A. (2014). *Learning and education in developing countries: Research and policy for the post-2015 UN development goals.* New York: Palgrave Pivot.

Websites

International Literacy Institute (ILI). http://www.literacy.org/

Save the Children. http://www.savethechildren.org/site/c.8rKLIXMGIpI4E/b.7084483/k.8F5A/Literacy_Boost.htm

UNESCO. http://en.unesco.org

UNESCO Institute for Statistics. http://www.uis.unesco.org/literacy/Pages/default.aspx

REFERENCES

Anders, Y., Rossbach, H.G., Weinert, S., Ebert, S., Kuger, S., Lehrl, S., & von Maurice, J. (2012). Home and preschool learning environments and their relations to the development of early numeracy skills. *Early Childhood Research Quarterly, 27*, 231–244.

Anderson, L.M., Shinn, C., Fullilove, M.T., Scrimshaw, S.C., Fielding, J.E., Normand, J., & Carande-Kulis, V.G. (2003). The effectiveness of early childhood development programs: A systematic review. *American Journal of Preventive Medicine, 24*, 32–46.

Ball, J., Paris, S.G., & Govinda, R. (2014). Literacy, numeracy, and higher order skills among children in developing countries. In D.A. Wagner (Ed.), *Learning and education in developing countries: Research and policy for the post-2015 UN development goals* (pp. 26–41). New York: Palgrave Macmillan.

Banerjee, A.S., Cole, S., Duflo, E., & Linden, L. (2007). Remedying education: Evidence from two randomized experiments in India. *The Quarterly Journal of Economics, 122*(3), 1235–1264.

Cope, B., & Kalanztis, M. (2000). *Multiliteracies: Literacy learning and the design of social futures* (pp. 60–92). London, UK: Routledge.

Dichaba, M.M., & Dhlamini, J.P. (2013). The value of critical pedagogy in mass-education for reducing illiteracy in South Africa: Kha Ri Gude current realities and prospects. *Mediterranean Journal of Social Sciences, 4*(3), 401–408.

Di Pierro, M.C. (2008). Youth and adult education in Latin America and the Caribbean: The recent trajectory. Retrieved on May 1, 2014, from http://www.scielo.br/pdf/cp/v38n134/en_a0638134.pdf

Engle, P.L., Black, M.M., Behrman, J.R., de Mello, M.C., Gertler, P.J., Kapiriri, L.M., & International Child Development Steering Group. (2007). Child development in developing countries 3: Strategies to avoid the loss of developmental potential in more than 200 million children in the developing world. *The Lancet, 369*, 229–242.

Epstein, J.L., Clark, L., Salinas, K.C., & Sanders, M.G. (1997). *Scaling up school-family-community connections in Baltimore: Effects on student achievement and attendance.* Baltimore, MD: CRESPAR and the Center on School, Family and Community Partnerships, Johns Hopkins University.

Fawcett, C., Hartwell, A., & Israel, R. (2010). Out-of-school youth in developing countries: What the data do (and do not) tell us. *United States Agency for International Development*. Retrieved from http://www.equip123.net/docs/e3-OSY.pdf

Forget-Dubois, N., Dionne, G., Lemelin, J. P., Perusse, D., Tremblay, R. E., & Boivin, M. (2009). Early child language mediates the relation between home environment and school readiness. *Child Development, 80*, 736–749.

G8 Education Experts. (2009). *G8 Education Experts Report 2009: Sharing Responsibilities to Advance Education for All. G8 Summit 2009.* Retrieved from http://ow.ly/JQxAq

Gove, A., & A. Wetterberg. (2011). *The early grade reading assessment: Applications and interventions to improve basic literacy*. Research Triangle Park, NC: RTI.

Gray, W. (1956). *The teaching of reading and writing.* Chicago, IL: UNESCO and Scott Foresman.

Hinostroza, J. E., Isaacs, S. & Bougroum, M. (2014). Information and communications technologies for improving students' learning opportunities and outcomes in developing countries. In D. A. Wagner (Ed.), *Learning and education in developing countries: Research and policy for the post-2015 UN development goals* (pp. 42–57). New York: Palgrave Macmillan.

Johansson, E. (1982). The history of literacy in Sweden. In H. J. Graff (Ed.), *Literacy and social development in the West: A reader* (pp. 151–182). Cambridge, UK: Cambridge University Press.

Kha Ri Gude (Let us learn) Adult Literacy Program (KGALP). (n.d.). Retrieved on May 21, 2014 from http://www.kharigude.co.za/

Kress, G., & van Leeuwen, T. (2001). *Multimodal discourse*. London, UK: Arnold.

Kuhl, P. K. (2010). Brain mechanisms underlying the critical period for language: Linking theory and practice. *Human Neuroplasticity and Education, 27*, 33–59.

Leu, D. J., O'Byrne, W. I., Zawilinski, L., McVerry, J. G., & Everett-Cacopardo, H. (2009). Expanding the new literacies conversation. *Educational Researcher, 38*(4), 264–269.

Martinez, S., Naudeau, S., & Pereira, V. (2012). *The promise of preschool in Africa: A randomized impact evaluation of early childhood development in rural Mozambique.* Washington, DC: The World Bank and Save the Children.

Mungoi, D., Mandlante, N., Nhatuve, I., Mahangue, D., Fonseca, J., & Dowd, A. J. (2012). *Endline report of early literacy among pre-school and primary school children in elma-supported schools Gaza province, Mozambique*. Maputo, Mozambique: Save the Children.

Nores, M., & Barnett, S. (2010). Benefits of early childhood interventions across the world: (Under)investing in the very young. *Economics of Education Review, 29*, 271–282.

OECD. (2013). Skills outlook: First results from the survey of adult skills. Retrieved on June 17, 2014, from http://www.oecd.org/site/piaac/Skills%20volume%201%20(eng)—full%20v12—eBook%20(04%2011%202013).pdf; http://www.scielo.br/pdf/cp/v38n134/en_a0638134.pdf

OECD and Statistics Canada (2000). *Literacy in the information age.* Retrieved on June 17, 2014, from http://www.oecd.org/education/skills-beyond-school/41529765.pdf

Puma, M., Bell, S., Cook, R., Heid, C., & Lopez, M. (2005). *Head Start impact study: First year findings*. Washington, DC: Author.

Ramachandran, V., Pal, M., Jain, S., Shekar, S., & Sharma, J. (2005). *Teacher motivation in India.* Discussion Paper, Azim Premji Foundation, Bangalore, India.

SADOE (South African Department of Education). (2013). *SADOE Ministerial Report*, http://peuoffice.com/wp-content/uploads/2013/12/Speech-ANA-5-December-2013-Final.pdf

Scribner, S., & Cole, M. (1981). *The psychology of literacy*. Cambridge, MA: Harvard University Press.

Smits, J., Huisman, J., & Kruijff, K. (2008). Home language and education in the developing world. *Background paper prepared for the Education for All Global Monitoring Report 2009*. Paris: UNESCO.

Street, B.V. (1999). The meanings of literacy. In D.A. Wagner, R.L. Venezky, & B.V. Street (Eds.), *Literacy: An international handbook* (pp. 34–38). Boulder, CO: Westview Press.

Street, B.V. (2005). *Understanding and defining literacy*. Background Paper for EFA Global Monitoring Report 2006. Retrieved on May 20, 2014, from http://unesdoc.unesco.org/images/0014/001461/146186e.pdf

Tolani-Brown, N., McCormac, M., & Zimmermann, R. (2009). An analysis of the research and impact of ICT in education in developing country contexts. *Journal of Education for International Development, 4*(2), 1–12.

UIL. (2008). *Kha Ri Gude (let us learn) adult literacy programme (KGALP)*. Effective literacy programmes. Retrieved on September 15, 2015, from http://www.unesco.org/uil/litbase/?menu=4&programme=69

UIL. (2010). *Global report of adult learning and education*. Retrieved on May 2, 2014, from http://uil.unesco.org/fileadmin/keydocuments/AdultEducation/en/GRALE_en.pdf

UIL. (2013). *Second global report of adult learning and education*. Retrieved March 24, 2015, from http://unesdoc.unesco.org/images/0022/002224/222407E.pdf

UIS. (2011). *Literacy assessment and monitoring programme (LAMP)*, Update No. 4. Retrieved on February 23, 2014, from http://www.uis.unesco.org/literacy/Documents/lamp-update-oct2011-v1-en.pdfa

UNESCO. (2008). *EFA global monitoring report 2008. Education for all by 2015: Will we make it?* Paris, France: UNESCO. Retrieved from http://unesdoc.unesco.org/images/0015/001548/154820e.pdf

UNESCO. (2010). *EFA global monitoring report 2010. Education for all: Reaching the marginalized*. Paris, France: UNESCO. Retrieved from http://unesdoc.unesco.org/images/0018/001866/186606E.pdf

UNESCO. (2013). *Global monitoring report*. Teaching and learning: Achieving quality for all. Gender Summary. Retrieved on May 28, 2014, from http://unesdoc.unesco.org/images/0022/002266/226662e.pdf

UNESCO Institute for Lifelong Learning (UIL). (2013). *Annual report*. Retrieved on May 2, 2014, from http://unesdoc.unesco.org/images/0022/002269/226992e.pdf

UNESCO Institute of Statistics (UIS). (2010). *Out-of-school adolescents*. Retrieved from http://www.uis.unesco.org/Library/Documents/out%20of%20school%20adol_en.pdf

UNESCO Institute of Statistics (UIS). (2013). *Adult and youth literacy, 1990–2015: Analysis of data for 41 selected countries*. Retrieved from http://www.uis.unesco.org/Education/Documents/literacy-statistics-trends-1985–2015.pdf

United Nations Development Group Report (UNDG). (2014). Delivering the post-2015 development agenda. Retrieved on February 17, 2015, from http://issuu.com/undevelopmentgroup/docs/delivering_the_post-2015_developmen/0

United Nations Development Group Report (UNDG). (2015). The Millennium Development Group Report 2015. Retrieved on September 15, 2015, from http://

www.un.org/millenniumgoals/2015_MDG_Report/pdf/MDG%202015%20 rev%20(July%201).pdf

United Nations (UN) Fact Sheet. (2013). *We can end poverty: Millennium development goals and beyond 2015.* UN Department of Public Information. Retrieved from http://www.un.org/millenniumgoals/pdf/Goal_2_fs.pdf

USAID. (2012). *Youth in development: Realizing the demographic opportunity.* Washington, DC: USAID Policy Youth.

Wagner, D. A. (1995). Literacy and development: Rationales, myths, innovations, and future directions. *International Journal of Educational Development, 15,* 341–362.

Wagner, D. A. (2004). Literacy development in global perspective: A research and policy approach. In U. P. Gielen & J. L. Roopnarine (Eds.), *Childhood and adolescence in cross-cultural perspective* (pp. 110–130). Westport, CT: Greenwood Press.

Wagner, D. A. (2010a). Literacy. In M. Bornstein (Ed.)., *Handbook of cultural developmental science* (pp. 161–173). New York: Taylor and Francis.

Wagner, D. A. (2010b). Quality of education, comparability, and assessment choice in developing countries. *COMPARE: A Journal of Comparative and International Education, 40*(6), 741–760.

Wagner, D. A. (2011a). *Smaller, quicker, cheaper: Improving learning assessments for developing countries.* Paris/Washington: UNESCO-IIEP & Fast Track Initiative/ GPE. http://unesdoc.unesco.org/images/0021/002136/213663e.pdf

Wagner, D. A. (2014a). *Mobiles for reading: A landscape research review.* Technical Report. Washington, DC: USAID/JBS. http://www.meducationalliance.org/ sites/default/files/usaid_wagner_report_finalforweb_14jun25_1.pdf

Wagner, D. A. (2014b). *Learning and education in developing countries: Research and policy for the post-2015 UN development goals.* New York: Palgrave Pivot.

Wagner, D. A., Murphy, K. M., & de Korne, H. (2012). *Learning first: A research agenda for improving learning in low-income countries.* Center for Universal Education Working Paper. Washington, DC: Brookings Institution. Retrieved from http:// www.brookings.edu/~/media/research/files/papers/2012/12/learning%20 first%20wagner%20murphy%20de%20korne/12%20learning%20first%20wagner%20murphy%20de%20korne.pdf

Part II

CHILDCARE, PARENTING, AND FAMILY SYSTEMS

5

Interpersonal Acceptance and Rejection in the Arab World: How Do They Influence Children's Development?

Ramadan A. Ahmed, Ronald P. Rohner, Abdul Khaleque, and Uwe P. Gielen

In an intermediate school in Cairo, Egypt, there were two 15-year-old male students: Ahmed and Saied. Ahmed was distinguished by both his excellent performance and his positive conduct in school, whereas Saied performed poorly in school and was known among his teachers and classmates for his aggressive/hostile and antisocial behavior. When researchers administered Rohner's Parental Acceptance-Rejection Questionnaire (PARQ) and Personality Assessment Questionnaire (PAQ) to Ahmed and Said, Ahmed's answers revealed that he perceived his parents as more accepting, less aggressive, less neglecting, and less rejecting than Said. Moreover, he also exhibited higher levels of positive psychological adjustment than his classmate.

The purpose of this chapter is to outline Ronald Rohner's interpersonal acceptance-rejection theory (IPARTheory, formerly known as parental acceptance-rejection theory, or PARTheory). We then summarize the rich and growing body of research that draws from IPARTheory and associated measures as used throughout much of the Arab world. This body of work includes more than 120 studies that explore the reliability and validity of Arabic adaptations of several measures of parental and interpersonal acceptance-rejection, antecedents of acceptance-rejection, and mental

---

Some of the research discussed in this chapter has also been reviewed in: Ahmed, R.A., Rohner, R.P., Khaleque, A., & Gielen, U.P. (2011). Parental Acceptance and Rejection: Theory, Measures, and Research in the Arab World. *ERIC Document Reproduction Service No. Ed 514028.*

health and educational consequences of perceived acceptance-rejection in the Arab world. Rohner has suggested that his theory can predict children's personality development because it is influenced by their perceptions of how their parents feel about them and how they are being treated. The chapter begins by outlining IPARTheory and then reviews a considerable amount of research that has been conducted in the past few decades to test the theory in the Arab world.

INTERPERSONAL ACCEPTANCE-REJECTION THEORY

Interpersonal acceptance-rejection theory (IPARTheory) is an evidence-based theory of socialization and lifespan development. The theory attempts to predict and explain the pancultural causes, consequences, and other correlates of interpersonal acceptance and rejection within the United States and worldwide (Rohner, 1986, 2004; Rohner, Khaleque, & Cournoyer, 2012; Rohner & Rohner, 1980). It attempts to answer five classes of questions with the help of three subtheories: personality subtheory, coping subtheory, and sociocultural systems subtheory.

Personality subtheory, described at greater length later, poses two general questions. First, it asks: Is it true, as the subtheory postulates, that children everywhere—regardless of differences in culture, language, race, ethnicity, gender, or other defining conditions—respond in the same way when they perceive themselves to be accepted or rejected by their parents or other major caregivers? Second, it asks: To what degree do the effects of childhood rejection extend into adulthood and old age?

Coping subtheory poses one basic question: What gives some children and adults the resilience to emotionally cope more effectively than most with the experiences of childhood rejection? Finally, sociocultural systems subtheory asks two very different classes of questions. First, it queries: Why are some parents warm and loving and others cold, aggressive, neglecting and/or rejecting? Is it true—as IPARTheory predicts—that certain psychological, familial, community, and societal factors tend to be reliably associated with specific variations in parental acceptance-rejection? Second, in what way is the total fabric of a given society as well as the behavior and beliefs of individuals within that society shaped by the tendency of most parents to either accept or reject their children? For example, is it true, as IPARTheory predicts, that a person's religious beliefs, artistic preferences, and other expressive beliefs and behaviors tend to be universally associated with their childhood experiences of parental love and love withdrawal?

The vast majority of empirical studies testing the major postulates of IPARTheory fall within the realm of personality subtheory. The majority of these deal with the effects of *parental* acceptance-rejection. This holds true for most studies in the Arab world too, as it does elsewhere (Ahmed, 2007b,

2008; Ahmed, Rohner, Khaleque, & Gielen, 2011). Accordingly, we focus heavily in this chapter on those studies. Before reviewing details of this subtheory—especially as they relate to parenting—and of the Arab studies that pertain to these details, however, we must define the concepts of parental acceptance and rejection (i.e., the warmth dimension of parenting).

The Warmth Dimension of Parenting

As construed in IPARTheory, the warmth dimension of parenting has to do with the quality of the affectional bond between parents and their children, and with the physical, verbal, and symbolic behaviors parents use to express these feelings. One end of the dimension is marked by parental acceptance, which refers to the warmth, affection, care, comfort, concern, nurturance, support, or simply love that children can experience from their parents and other caregivers. The other end of the dimension is marked by parental rejection, which refers to the absence or significant withdrawal of these feelings and behaviors, and by the presence of a variety of physically and psychologically hurtful behaviors and affects. All humans can be placed somewhere along the warmth dimension because as children they have experienced various degrees of love at the hands of their parents or other major caregivers.

Extensive cross-cultural research over the course of many decades has shown that parental rejection can be experienced by any one or a combination of four principal expressions: (a) cold and unaffectionate behavior and affect (the opposite of being warm and affectionate), (b) hostile and aggressive behavior and affect, (c) indifferent and neglecting behavior and affect, and (d) undifferentiated rejection. Undifferentiated rejection refers to individuals' beliefs that their parents or other attachment figures do not really care about them or love them, even though there might not be clear behavioral indicators that the parents or other caregivers are neglecting, unaffectionate, or aggressive toward them.

IPARTheory's Personality Subtheory

As we said earlier, IPARTheory's personality subtheory attempts to predict and explain major personality or psychological—especially mental health-related—consequences of perceived interpersonal acceptance and rejection. The subtheory is driven by the assumption that humans have an enduring and biologically based emotional need for positive response from the people that are most important to them (Baumeister & Leary, 1995; Bjorklund & Pellegrini, 2002; Leary, 1999). The need for positive response includes an emotional wish, desire, or yearning (whether consciously recognized or not) for comfort, support, care, concern, nurturance, and the like. In adulthood, the need becomes more complex and differentiated to satisfy the recognized or unrecognized wish for positive regard from people with whom one has an affectional bond of attachment. People who can best satisfy this need are most frequently parents for infants and children, but include significant others and non-parental attachment figures for adolescents and adults.

Additionally, IPARTheory's personality subtheory postulates that when children's need for positive response remains unsatisfied, they are predisposed to be anxious and insecure. In an attempt to allay these feelings and to satisfy their psychosocial needs, persons who feel rejected often increase their bids for positive response, but only up to a point. That is, they tend to become more dependent.

Parental rejection—as well as rejection by other attachment figures throughout life—may also lead to other negative personality outcomes. These include hostility, aggression, passive aggression, or problems with the management of hostility and aggression such as aggressive day dreams and aggressive fantasies; emotional unresponsiveness; immature dependence or defensive independence depending on the form, frequency, timing, duration, and intensity of perceived rejection; impaired self-esteem; impaired self-adequacy; emotional instability; and negative worldview. The theoretical rationale for these expectations is laid out in Rohner et al. (2012) and elsewhere (e.g., Rohner, 1986).

Negative worldview, negative self-esteem, negative self-adequacy, and some of the other personality dispositions just mentioned are important elements in the social-cognitive or mental representations of rejected persons. Thus, along with one's emotional state, mental representations tend to shape the way in which individuals perceive, construe, and react to new experiences, including interpersonal relationships. Mental representations also influence what and how individuals store and remember experiences (Baldwin, 1992; Clausen, 1972; Crick & Dodge, 1994; Epstein, 1994). Once created, individuals' mental representations of self, of significant others, and of the world around them tend to induce them to seek or to avoid certain situations and kinds of people. In effect, according to IPARTheory, the way individuals think about themselves and their world shapes the way they live their lives. This is notably true of rejected children and adults. For example, many rejected persons have a tendency to perceive hostility where none is intended, to see deliberate rejection in unintended acts of significant others, or to devalue their sense of personal worth in the face of strong counter-information. Moreover, rejected persons are likely to seek, create, interpret, or perceive experiences, situations, and relationships in ways that are consistent with their distorted mental representations. And they often tend to avoid or mentally reinterpret situations that are inconsistent with these representations.

Additionally, people who feel rejected by significant others often construct mental images of personal relationships as being unpredictable, untrustworthy, and perhaps hurtful.

According to IPARTheory, these negative mental representations are often carried forward into new relationships where rejected individuals may find it difficult to trust others emotionally (fear of intimacy) or where they may become hypervigilant and hypersensitive to any slights or signs of emotional undependability (rejection sensitivity). Because of all this selective attention, selective perception, faulty styles of causal attribution, and distorted cognitive information-processing, rejected individuals are expected to self-propel along qualitatively different developmental pathways from accepted or loved people.

Methods in IPARTheory Research

Even though five discrete methods or types of studies—described in Rohner, Parmar, and Ibrahim (2010)—have been used internationally to test core aspects of IPARTheory, the overwhelming majority of studies in the Arab world and elsewhere have used self-report questionnaires. The most often used questionnaires are the Parental Acceptance-Rejection Questionnaire (PARQ) (Rohner, 2005a), the Parental Acceptance-Rejection/Control Questionnaire (PARQ/Control) (Rohner, 2005b), and the Personality Assessment Questionnaire (PAQ) (Rohner & Khaleque, 2005). These and the other self-report questionnaires used in IPARTheory research are described at length in the *Handbook for the Study of Parental Acceptance and Rejection* (Rohner & Khaleque, 2005).

Three versions of the PARQ and PARQ/Control have been used in Arab research. The first version is used to assess *children's* perceptions of the degree of acceptance or rejection (and behavioral control) they receive at the hands of their mothers, fathers, or other caregivers. Another assesses *adults'* recollections of their childhood experiences of maternal or paternal acceptance-rejection (and behavioral control). The third version asks *parents* to reflect on their own accepting-rejecting and controlling behaviors. The PAQ, on the other hand, assesses individuals' (adults' and children's) self-perceptions of overall psychological adjustment as defined by seven of the personality dispositions central to personality subtheory that was described earlier.

PARENTAL ACCEPTANCE-REJECTION RESEARCH IN THE ARAB WORLD: AN OVERVIEW

The Arab world consists of 22 countries in which more than 330 million people reside. This world stretches from the Atlantic Ocean (e.g., Morocco) to Central Asia (e.g., Iraq), and from the Mediterranean Sea (e.g., Egypt) to the Horn of Africa (e.g., Somalia). This territory encompasses a vast realm of historical and cultural complexity. Throughout history, its influence has radiated across the continents of Asia, Africa, and Europe—and to practically every other part of the world as well. The earliest civilizations arose on the Mesopotamian plain between the Tigris and Euphrates Rivers in the country that now includes Iraq, as well as on the banks of the Egyptian Nile. Prophets whose religious teachings are followed by hundreds of millions of people have walked in this territory. On the following pages we provide a concise overview of research on parental acceptance-rejection conducted mostly by Arab researchers in this region during the past few decades.

Recent reviews of Arab literature related to children's perceptions of parents' behavior (Ahmed, 2007b, 2008; Ahmed & Gielen, 2006b; Ahmed et al., 2011) point out that Arab psychologists such as Nagaty showed an early interest in investigating parental behavior as perceived by children in Egypt, Iraq, Syria, Jordan, and the United States. Since the early 1960s, more than 500 Arab studies have been completed on children's perceptions of parental behavior. At least 120 of these studies (mostly master's theses and doctoral dissertations) employed Rohner's Parental Acceptance-Rejection Questionnaire (PARQ). Rohner's PARQ (and the PAQ as well) was first translated into Arabic by Salama (1986a, 1986b) in 1986. It was widely used in Egypt by her and her students (1987a, 1987b, 1987c, 1990a, 1990b). Her translation was also used in other Arab countries such as Saudi Arabia, Kuwait, Bahrain, Qatar, and Yemen. At the same time another Arabic translation of the PARQ was made by Ahmed (1985) in Sudan. This translation was used in several later studies (e.g., Ahmed, Gielen, & Avellani, 1987; Ahmed & Khalil, 1999; Gielen, Ahmed, & Avellani, 1992).

Most Arab studies using the PARQ have employed the adult form with adolescents. Other Arab studies administered the adult version to youth, mainly university students (e.g., Ahmed, 2007a; Almousa, 2007; Al-Theifairy, 1996; Faied, 2000, 2005; Rasmi, 2008; Zaidan, 1995). A third group of Arab researchers employed samples of adolescents and youth. Among them are Ahmed (2013a), Ahmed and Gielen (2006a), Ahmed and Ibrahim (in press, in prep.), and Al-Otaibi (2005). Only a few Arab researchers have used the Child PARQ to assess children's perceptions of parental acceptance-rejection (e.g., Abdalla, 2001; Abdel-Sadek, 1994; E. M. Ahmed, 1998; Al-Bery, 2007; Ali, 2000; Askar, 1996a; Bader, 2008; M. E. I. Mansour, 2011; Rohner et al., 2010; Salama, 1987a, 1987b). The majority of Arab studies using the PARQ have included both male and female respondents while employing the standard 60-item version of the PARQ for mothers, fathers, adults, and children. However, some recent Arab studies have used the short PARQ form (24 items, as was translated into Arabic by R. A. Ahmed [2007a] in Kuwait).

Additionally, the majority of Arab studies on the relationship between the perception of parental acceptance-rejection (as measured by the PARQ) and personality traits have used several personality questionnaires to assess personality traits in children, adolescents, and youths in relation to perceptions of parental acceptance-rejection. Pertinent examples include Gielen et al. (1992) and Taher (2005). Some of these studies employed both the PARQ and/or PAQ to assess this relationship (e.g., Abdel-Razek, 2005; Abou-el-Kheir, 1999; Ahmed, 2013a, 2013b; Ahmed & Ibrahim, in press, in prep.); Ahmed, Rohner, & Carrasco, 2012; Al-Azemy, 2012; Al-Sabah, 2010; Salama, 1987a; Shehata, 2006). The results of these studies have consistently suggested that the PAQ enjoys high levels of empirical validity. For instance, Althuwaikh's (2015) study investigated the efficiency/effectiveness of a group of personality and intelligence tests (among them the PAQ) in predicting successful performance among new students admitted to the Kuwait Police Academy. Results revealed strong associations between PAQ scores indicating healthier psychological adjustment and various measures used to assess problem solving, achievement motivation, commitment, social skills, psychological hardiness, and Raven's Progressive Matrices Test.

Many Arab researchers have shown a great interest in investigating children's perception of parental acceptance-rejection by using the PARQ. Among the 10 major research centers, 6 are located at Egyptian universities, 2 at Kuwaiti institutions, and 1 each at institutions located, respectively, in Qatar and Saudi Arabia. Altogether, a disproportionate amount of research has been conducted by Egyptian scholars.

Reliability of the Arabic Version of the PARQ

A large number of Arab studies, using either the standard adult form or short form of the PARQ, included an item analysis of the respondents' responses. Correlations of each item within a given scale with the total score of the scale were computed as were correlations of the total score of each scale with the total PARQ score. Typically all items were found to be significantly correlated (p less than 0.01), and no item was rejected. Correlations of items with the total score were reasonably higher. Typical examples include Ahmed (2007a), Ahmed and Gielen (2006a, 2008), Al-Sabah (2010), Rasmi (2008), Salama (1987a, 1987b, 1987c), and Taher (2005). A single Arab study (Helewa, 1997) used the test-retest method on the basis of a small sample of deaf adolescents, and reported very high correlation coefficients ranging between 0.94 and 0.98.

Salama (1991) adapted and translated into Arabic the Parenting Pattern Questionnaire (36 items), which is—as noted earlier—based on Rohner's PARQ. The scale was used in her study as well as in later ones. These include six Egyptian studies: Abdel-Razek (2000), Abou-el-Kheir (1995, 1998), Hamaza (2002), Zaeter (1998), and Zaeter and Abou-el-Kheir (1999). The results of these studies revealed fairly high alpha coefficients.

Several Arab studies have assessed PARQ reliability estimates by using the split-half method. For example, Bader (2001) in Saudi Arabia reported an overall correlation coefficient between PARQ odd and even items of $r = 0.91$ after being corrected by the Spearman-Brown formula. Virtually all of these studies show the PARQ and measures derived from it to be reliable for use in the Arab world.

Validity of the Arabic Version of the PARQ

Several Arab studies have sought to establish the validity of the PARQ by using a variety of methods. Bader (2001) in Saudi Arabia and El-Sayed (2000) in Egypt, for example, correlated item scores with the total score of related subscales. Results revealed high correlation coefficients for the four PARQ subscales.

Abou-el-Kheir (1989) assessed the concurrent validity of the PARQ by administering Arabic versions of Schaefer's CRPBI and Rohner's PARQ to 40 university students in Egypt, and reported the following significant correlations: 0.33 between CRPBI's and PARQ's acceptance subscales, and 0.38 between CRPBI's and PARQ's rejection subscales. Moreover, Mekhemer and Abdel-Razek (1999) found a strong positive correlation between children's scores on the PARQ's three subscales of rejection: (i.e., Hostility/Aggression, Indifference/ Neglect, and Undifferentiated/Rejection) and the children's score on a questionnaire used to assess childhood abuse experiences.

Factorial Validity. Several Arab studies have investigated the PARQ's factorial validity by using samples of children. Such validity studies seek to establish whether the PARQ measures a small number of internally consistent and meaningful patterns or factors representing fundamental aspects of perceived parental acceptance and rejection. A perceived parental rejection factor and a perceived parental acceptance factor emerged in all of these studies (Al-Sabah, 2010; Askar, 1996a; Bader, 2001; El-Sayed, 2000; Salama, 1987a, 1987b). Virtually all studies in the Arab world that have attempted to assess the validity of the PARQ have concluded that the measure is valid for use throughout the region (e.g., Ahmed, 2007a, 2008; Ahmed & Gielen, 2008; Ahmed et al., 2011).

Contextual Factors Associated with Parental Acceptance-Rejection

Demographic Variables. Several Arab studies have focused on the association between demographic variables (e.g., socioeconomic status, family size, birth order, mother's employment, economic hardship, place of residence, and children's sex and age) and children's perceptions of their parents' acceptance-rejection. Examples of these studies include Abdel-Razek (1996), Abou-el-Kheir (1999), Faried (1990), Helewa (1997), Salama (1987b, 1990a), and Taher (2005). Results of these studies generally show that children of higher socioeconomic status families, those living in small families, children of nonworking mothers, and rural children tend to perceive their parents to be more accepting, less aggressive, less neglecting, and less overall rejecting when compared to other children. Additionally, Taher (2005) found that nomadic or semi-nomadic Bedouin children in Kuwait tended to perceive their parents as being less accepting than did urban Kuwaiti children.

The majority of Arab studies (e.g., El-Sayed, 2000; Ibrahim, 1988; Salama, 1987b) have reported no significant differences between boys and girls in their perceptions of maternal and paternal acceptance. Helewa (1997), however, found that deaf male Egyptian adolescents perceived their parents to be significantly less accepting, more aggressive, more neglecting, and more rejecting, than did their female counterparts. A more recent study by Ahmed and Gielen (2008) reviewed age and sex differences in the perceptions of parental behavior among Arab children. In general, results revealed that female and older children, compared with their male and younger counterparts, tended to perceive their parents (especially fathers) as more accepting. Additionally, Ibrahim (1988) reported that Egyptian college men perceived their fathers to be less accepting than their mothers. It is interesting to note in this context that although Arab societies tend to grant greater power to men than to women, girls are more likely than boys to feel accepted by their parents—especially by their fathers.

Poverty. A single Arab study (Abdel-Razek, 1996) dealt with the relationship between economic hardship and perceptions of parental acceptance-rejection in children. The author found a positive correlation between families' economic hardship and their children's perceptions of parental rejection. This finding is consistent with results of other studies mentioned earlier which found that children of lower socioeconomic status families perceive their parents as more neglecting and rejecting, and less overall accepting.

Cross-National and Cross-Cultural Comparisons

A few Arab studies have investigated perceptions of parental acceptance-rejection cross-nationally, and especially between rural and urban children and between more or less nomadic Bedouin children and urban children (e.g., Hassab-Allah & El-Aqad, 2000; Taher, 2005). Askar (1996a), for example, focused on differences between Egyptian and Yemeni primary school children's perceptions of parental acceptance. No national differences were found between parental warmth or aggression, but Yemeni children perceived their parents to be more neglecting than did Egyptian children. Beyond this, both Egyptian and Yemeni boys perceived significantly more parental aggression than did girls. Additionally, Egyptian boys perceived their parents to be more neglecting and rejecting than did Egyptian girls. In a second study, Al-Theifairy (1996) compared Saudi and Egyptian male and female adolescents by using the PARQ (mother form) and PAQ. Parental rejection correlated significantly and positively with all PAQ subscales (except dependency) in both nations. Both Saudi and Egyptian males tended to perceive their mothers as less accepting than did their female counterparts. Finally, results showed that Egyptian males and females tended to perceive their mother as less accepting than did their Saudi peers.

A study by Al-Ragieeb (1996) investigated perceptions of parental acceptance-rejection and its relation with linguistic creativity and personal and social adjustment in samples of Kuwaiti and Egyptian adolescents. Results showed significant positive correlations between Kuwaiti's and Egyptian's adolescents' perception of parental acceptance and the levels of verbal and ideational creativity, and personal and social adjustment. Moreover, while Kuwaiti adolescent boys perceived their parents as being more rejecting, adolescent Egyptian boys tended to perceive their parents as more accepting. But adolescent Egyptian girls perceived their parents—especially their mothers—as more rejecting. In contrast, Kuwaiti adolescent girls tended to perceive their parents, especially mothers, as more accepting. The overall differences between Kuwaiti males and Egyptian males, and between Kuwaiti females and Egyptian females, were significant.

Recently, Rasmi (2008) examined the relationship between perceived parental rejection in childhood and three types of adjustment in young adulthood: positive (life satisfaction), negative (risky behavior), and acculturative (sociocultural difficulties). Subjects were 407 male and female university students from three ethnocultural groups: European Canadians (n = 147), Arab Canadians (n = 129), and Arabs in Egypt and Lebanon (n = 131). All respondents were between the ages of 18 and 25 years. Results showed that individuals who felt rejected in childhood were consistently less likely to enjoy a high level of psychological well-being, more likely to engage in risky behavior, less likely to be satisfied with their lives, and more likely to encounter sociocultural difficulties in young adulthood. Moreover, psychological well-being mediated negatively the relationships between perceived parental rejection and both risky behavior and life dissatisfaction. Finally, results showed that European Canadians reported the lowest scores on the scales measuring overall parental rejection, hostility/aggression, indifference/neglect, undifferentiated rejection, and negative self-construal. Arab Canadians and Arabs of the

Middle East (Egypt and Lebanon) were second and third, respectively, in this ranking. In line with these findings, the European Canadians perceived their parents as displaying the most warmth/affection, and they also reported higher scores on life satisfaction than did the other two ethnic groups. Arab Canadians and Arabs from the Middle East (Egypt and Lebanon) followed European Canadians in this ranking. No differences, however, were found between the three ethnocultural groups concerning their performance on the two scales used for assessing their psychological well-being and risky behavior.

Only two cross-cultural Arab studies have investigated psychological dispositions using the PAQ. Those studies included samples of Egyptian and Yemeni young adults (Askar, 1996b), and samples of Egyptian and Italian youth and adults (Abdel-Razek, 2005). Askar's study showed that Yemeni participants (especially females) were significantly more hostile/aggressive, dependent, and emotionally unstable than their Egyptian counterparts. Additionally, Yemeni participants reported significantly lower self-adequacy than did Egyptian respondents. The second study revealed that Egyptian males were significantly higher on all PAQ subscales except dependency than were their Italian counterparts. Moreover, Egyptian females, compared with their Italian peers, scored higher on the following PAQ subscales: negative self-adequacy, emotional unresponsiveness, emotional instability, and negative worldview. However, Italian males and females scored higher than the Egyptians on dependency. Taken together the two studies suggest that Yemeni youth and young adults tend to perceive relatively high levels of parental rejection; Egyptian young adults occupy a middle position, and Italian adolescents and young adults feel most accepted by their parents.

Relations between Corporal Punishment and Perceived Parental Acceptance-Rejection

Four Arab studies were carried out to investigate possible relationships between children's perceptions of parental acceptance-rejection and corporal punishment. These studies were conducted by Mohammed (1996) and by Abou-el-Kheir (1995, 1998) in Egypt, and by Ahmed and Gielen (2006a) in Kuwait. The studies employed Rohner's PARQ, PAQ, and the youth form of his Physical Punishment Questionnaire (PPQ; Rohner, Ripoll-Núñez, Moodie, & Ruan, 2005). Results of these studies generally indicate that children's and adolescents' perceptions of the severity and harshness of physical punishment are positively linked to their perceptions of parental rejection. It seems that in the Arab world as elsewhere, children who interpret being severely physically punished by their parents also tend to experience significant parental rejection.

Psychological Consequences of Perceived Parental Acceptance-Rejection

On the following pages we selectively review some of the major Arab studies pointing to the psychological consequences of perceived parental acceptance-rejection. Studies examining these consequences have focused on a broad variety of personality dispositions, including the formation of ego-identity; internalizing problems such as anxiety, depression, and phobias; externalizing problems and behaviors such as aggression, hostility, and delinquency; and a variety of positive feelings, behaviors, and personality traits including school achievement, altruistic behavior, and aesthetic feelings. Arab researchers have made significant contributions to the international research literature by examining such a broad range of personality-linked psychological phenomena in the context of IPARTheory.

Personality Dispositions. A broad variety of personality-related studies have investigated relationships between acceptance-rejection and self-esteem (Abou-el-Kheir, 1998; Salama, 1991); self-assertiveness (Elyan, 1992); personality traits/dispositions (Ahmed, 1998; Al-Azemy, 2012; Al-Baghadady, 2001; El-Sayed, 2000; Ibrahim, Parmar, & Rohner, 2006, Mohammed, 1996); locus of control (Al-Nafie, 1997; Ibrahim, 1988); psychological hardiness (Mekhemer, 1996); irrational beliefs, dogmatism, and flexibility-rigidity (Hassab-Allah & El-Aqad, 2000); loneliness (Mekhemer, 2003); dependency and self-criticism (Faied, 2000; Mohammed, 1994); feelings of shame (Faied, 2005); self-esteem and self-concept (Abou-el-Kheir, 1998; Ali, 1997; Bader, 2001, 2008, in Saudi Arabia; Salama, 1991, 1998, in Egypt); overall psychological adjustment (Abdel-Wahab, 1999; El-Shamy, 2004, in Egypt; and Gaber, 1998, in Algeria); level of aspiration (Ali, 2000, in Egypt); feelings of psychological security (Al-Bery, 2007; El-Sayed, 1994); positive emotions of female kindergartners' teachers (Ibrahim et al., 2006); and ego-strength and single-mindedness (Al-Otaibi, 2005). Results of these studies are largely consistent with results found in Western studies. All, for instance, have shown positive correlations between perceived parental acceptance and positive personality traits. Moreover, Ismaeel (2001) found in a study of child abuse and personality dispositions (using Rohner's PAQ) that those Saudi intermediate-school deaf children who experienced abuse (by fathers only) tended to self-report all the negative personality dispositions assessed on the PAQ. Moreover, he found that Saudi deaf males perceived significantly more abuse than did their female counterparts.

Ego-Identity, Identity Formation, and Identity Disorders. Four Arab studies (Abdel-Moety, 1991; Al-Beheray, 1990; Al-Otaibi, 2005; Ahmed, 2013a) focused on the relationship between perceptions of parental acceptance-rejection and ego identity, identity formation, and identity disorders in children, adolescents, and youth—all in light of Erikson's identity theory. In general, results of these studies are consistent with results of previous Western studies. For example, Al-Otaibi (2005) found a positive correlation between children's perceptions of their parents' rejection and higher scores on identity statuses such as moratorium, foreclosure, and diffusion. Similar to Al-Otaibi's (2005) findings, Ahmed's (2013a) study revealed strong positive correlations between perceptions of parental acceptance and healthier psychological adjustment on one hand and the mature identity status of achievement on the other.

Internalizing Problems: Depression, Anxiety, and Neuroticism. Several Arab studies have assessed relationships between children's perceptions of parental acceptance-rejection and their respective levels of depression, anxiety, and neuroticism. Examples include Ahmed and Khalil (1999), El-Sayed (2000), Faied (2000), Saied (1995), and Salama (1990a). In general, results of these studies show that children's perceptions of parental rejection are correlated with high levels of depression, anxiety, and neuroticism. In addition, El-Sayed (2000) showed that children who perceived their parents as more accepting also tended to exhibit higher levels of (self-reported) emotional stability and social adjustment, together with lower levels of anxiety. Recently, Almousa (2007) investigated the relationship between perfectionism (normality vs. neuroticism) and university students' perceptions of parental socialization styles by using Rohner's PARQ. Results revealed that normal students tended to perceive their parents as accepting and warm, whereas neurotic students tended to perceive their parents as more aggressive (hostile), more neglecting, more controlling, and more rejecting.

Internalizing Problems: Phobias in Children and Adolescents. Three Arab studies (Al-Shayji, 2003; Salama, 1987a; Salem, 2005) focused on the relationship between perceptions of parental acceptance-rejection and phobias in samples of children and adolescents. Findings reveal that respondents who perceived their parents as more rejecting tended to show higher rates of phobias, especially social phobias, than did respondents who felt accepted.

Children's Behavioral Problems. Several Arab psychologists have studied the relationship between perceptions of parental acceptance-rejection and children's behavioral and psychological problems such as exhibiting violence/aggression, bullying behavior, school truancy, and poor school performance. Examples include Abdel-Rahman (2003), Abdel-Razek (1996), Al-Azemy (2012), Khalifa (2003), and Mansour (2011). Results of their works indicate that children who perceive their parents as more rejecting tend to suffer from more psychological problems than those children who feel more accepted by their parents. For instance, Mansour's (2011) study focused on Bahraini children between the ages 10 and 13. It employed the child version of Rohner's PARQ as well as a locally devised measure to assess ADHD. Results showed that perceiving the father as rejecting predicted aggressive and impulsive behavior, ADHD, anxiety, and fear in children. Moreover, perceiving the mother as rejecting predicted ADHD, anxiety, fear, withdrawal behavior, and social isolation. Taken together these studies suggest that perceptions of parental rejection are associated with a variety of both internalizing and externalizing adjustment problems and behavior patterns among children, adolescents, and young adults.

Psychopathology. Only one Egyptian study (Abou-el-Kheir, 1989) has investigated perceptions of parental acceptance-rejection in samples of schizophrenic and normal subjects. Schizophrenics—compared with normal individuals—perceived their parents as less accepting, more aggressive, more neglecting, and more overall rejecting.

Chronically Ill and Handicapped versus Normal School-Aged Children. A single Arab study investigated the relationship between perceptions of parental acceptance-rejection among chronically ill versus normal school-aged children (Kamal, 1985). Results of this study showed that the chronically ill—compared with normal school-aged children—tended to perceive their parents as less accepting, more aggressive, more neglecting, and more rejecting in its undifferentiated form than did normal children. Moreover, results revealed the positive implications of parental acceptance for both chronically ill and normal children.

Helewa (1997) investigated parental acceptance-rejection in a sample of deaf male and female intermediate and secondary school students in Egypt. Males perceived their parents to be significantly less accepting, more aggressive, more neglecting, and more rejecting than did females. Similar results have been found by Abdalla (2001) in Egypt.

Finally, an Egyptian study by El-Sayed (1994) focused on the relationships between feelings of psychological security and perceptions of parental acceptance in samples of blind and sighted students. Her work showed that feelings of psychological security correlated significantly with perceived parental acceptance. A more recent Egyptian study (Al-Bery, 2007) investigated the relations between perceptions of parental acceptance-rejection and psychological security among 9- to-12-year-old male, primary school, normal children compared with delinquent children of similar age. The findings of Al-Bery's (2007) study were consistent with El-Sayed's (1994) results.

Children's Social Interaction Styles. Only a few Arab studies have investigated the relationship between perceptions of parental behavior and children's and adolescents' social interaction styles. Research topics in this grouping include peer rejection and loneliness among adolescents (Mekhemer, 2003), as well as children's prejudicial attitudes (Abou-Ghali, 1999). Results of these studies reveal positive correlations between children's perception of parental rejection and children's and adolescents' high levels of peer rejection, loneliness, and prejudicial attitudes.

Externalizing Problems and Maladaptive Behavior Patterns

Children's Aggression/Hostility and Violent Behavior. Several Arab studies focused on the relationship between children's perceptions of their parents' acceptance-rejection and children's aggressive and violent behavior. Examples include Alhanati (1990), Bader (2008), Elyan (1992), Helewa (1997), Mansour (2011), Salama (1991), and Taher (2005). Results of these studies reveal significant positive correlations between children's perceptions of parental rejection and children's and adolescents' high levels of aggression, hostility, and violent behavior. Additionally, Al-Otaibi et al. (unpublished) investigated the effectiveness of Rohner's PARQ in predicting attitudes toward extremity/extreme behavior among Kuwaiti male and female adolescents. The results agreed with the results of previous Arab and non-Arab studies showing that PARQ subscales such as neglect/indifference and undifferentiated rejection positively predict inclinations toward extremity/extreme behavior.

Juvenile Delinquency and Other Forms of Deviant Behavior. A few Arab studies have focused on the relationship between youth's perceptions of parental acceptance-rejection and juvenile delinquency (Al-Falaij, 1991; Zaeter, 1998; Zaeter & Abou-el-Kheir, 1999). The studies by Al-Bery (2007) and Zaeter (1998), for example, found that juvenile delinquents tended to perceive their parents to be less accepting than did nondelinquents. In addition, Zaeter and Abou-el-Kheir (1999) assessed the relationship between perceptions of parental acceptance-rejection and children's dependent personality and attitudes toward drug addiction among secondary school students. Comparable to previous Western studies, the results of several Arab studies revealed that those children who perceived their parents (especially fathers) as more accepting tended to be less delinquent, to be less dependent, and to endorse more negative attitudes toward drug addiction.

Recently, one study (Al-Azemy, 2012) investigated the relationships between perceptions of parental acceptance-rejection, bullying behavior, and psychological adjustment in Kuwaiti male and female children and adolescents. Her results revealed that those participants who perceived their parents (especially fathers) as rejecting tended to report a high incidence of bullying behavior and unhealthy psychological adjustment, whereas those participants who perceived their parents as accepting tended to engage in less bullying behavior while displaying healthier psychological adjustment. Finally, Al-Azemy (2012) found that those participants who perceived their parents (especially fathers) as neglecting tended to describe themselves as bullying victims. Finally, Al-Otaibi et al.'s unpublished study showed that perceptions of neglect/indifference and undifferentiated rejection successfully predicted positive attitudes toward extreme behavior among male and female Kuwaiti adolescents.

Cognitive Styles. The relationship between perceptions of parental acceptance-rejection and cognitive styles, especially impulsivity/reflectivity, has attracted the attention of a few Arab psychologists. One of these studies was conducted by Ramadan (1989). She investigated relationships among perceptions of parental acceptance-rejection and impulsivity/reflectivity in samples of gifted and normal students. Results revealed a positive correlation between perceptions of parental rejection and impulsivity, as well as a significant positive correlation between perceptions of parental acceptance and reflectivity.

Positive Psychological Consequences of Parental Acceptance

Cognitive Aspects. Several Arab studies have dealt with the relationship between perceptions of parental acceptance-rejection and cognition, such as cognitive distortion (Salama, 1990b), creative thinking in deaf-mute children (Abdalla, 2001), creative thinking (Al-Ragieeb, 1996), and critical thinking (Ahmed, unpublished). Results indicate positive correlations between parental rejection and children's cognitive distortions, as well as positive correlations between perceived acceptance and various components of critical thinking in children. One recent Arab study (Ahmed, 2013b, February) revealed strong positive associations between levels of emotional intelligence and perceptions of maternal and paternal acceptance (measured by the PARQ) and better psychological adjustment (measured by PAQ) among Kuwaiti adolescents and youth.

Children's Achievement Motivation and Academic Achievement. Very few Arab studies have explored the relationship between parental acceptance-rejection and achievement motivation. However, Mussellem (1997) and Zaidan (1995) did report positive correlations between parental acceptance and achievement motivation. Additionally, Bader (2001) studied the relationship between parental acceptance-rejection, self-concept, and scholastic achievement in a sample of Saudi primary school children. She found a strong correlation between parental acceptance and scholastic achievement. Results of a recent Saudi study by Bader (2008) support her earlier results.

Gifted versus Normal Students. Only one Arab study (Ramadan, 1989) has compared perceptions of parental acceptance-rejection of gifted students with those of their non-gifted peers. Results indicate that gifted students, especially those students in higher academic levels, tended to perceive their fathers (but not necessarily their mothers) as accepting.

Altruistic Behavior. A single Egyptian study (Abdel-Razek, 2000) investigated the perception of parental acceptance-rejection (as measured by the Parenting Pattern Questionnaire) and personality dispositions (as measured by Rohner's PAQ) as predictors of children's altruistic behavior. Both measures predicted altruistic behavior in children in theoretically meaningful ways.

Development of Moral Judgment. Two Arab studies investigated the relationship between perceived parental acceptance (measured by Rohner's PARQ) and the development of moral judgment (as measured by Rest's Defining Issues Test) (Ahmed et al., 1987; Gielen et al., 1992). Results showed a modest correlation between perceived parental acceptance and the development of moral judgment/reasoning abilities. In addition, an Egyptian study (Abdel-Sadek, 1994) investigated the development of moral judgment (as measured by Piaget's stories and a locally developed scale based on Kohlberg's theory), and its relation to intelligence and the perception of parental acceptance-rejection (as measured by the child version of Rohner's PARQ) in samples of rural and urban children and young adolescents. Results showed a positive correlation between children's and young adolescents' perceptions of parental acceptance, and the development of moral judgment and intellectual levels.

Aesthetic Feelings. Only one Arab study has dealt with the relationship between perceptions of parental acceptance-rejection and aesthetic feelings. This study by Ahmed and Khalil (1999) drew from a sample of intermediate and secondary-school male and female students in Egypt. The authors found that students who perceived their parents as being more accepting tended to express more aesthetic feelings, compared with students who perceived their parents as being more rejecting.

Social Responsibility. Mansour's study (2006) focused on the relationship between perceived parental acceptance-rejection and social responsibility among secondary school male and female students in Egypt. Results showed a positive relationship between perceived parental acceptance and self-reported social responsibility.

Similarities in Children's Perceptions of Acceptance-Rejection among Different Attachment Figures

A recent study (Ahmed et al., 2012) explored the respective contributions of acceptance by mothers, fathers, siblings, best friends, and teachers to psychological adjustment among 249 Kuwaiti male and female adolescents. Results showed that while perceived acceptance by siblings, best friends, and fathers (in that order) accounted for independent portions of variance in male adolescents' psychological adjustment, the most important influence on girls' psychological adjustment was the father's acceptance, followed by perceived acceptance by siblings and teachers. Moreover, the findings revealed similarities between children's perceptions of fathers and perceptions of various other attachment figures.

Arab Research on Perceived Parental Power and Prestige in Relation to Perceived Parental Acceptance-Rejection, Psychological Adjustment, and Other Variables

Recently, some attempts have been made to investigate Arab children's perceptions of parental power and prestige in relation to perceptions of maternal and paternal acceptance-rejection, psychological adjustment, and various psychological and demographic variables. So far, three relevant studies have been conducted in Kuwait (Ahmed & Ibrahim, in press, in prep.; Ibrahim, 2010). Ibrahim (2010) assessed one hundred and fifty-one 10- and 11-year-old children's perceptions of paternal versus maternal power and prestige, as related to children's psychological adjustment and conduct problems. Her results showed that 52% of Kuwaiti girls saw their mothers as more powerful than their fathers, but 60% of boys saw their fathers as more powerful. In addition, 61% of boys and 53% of girls believed their fathers were more prestigious than their mothers. Those children who believed the father had more power than the mother tended to self-report better psychological adjustment than children who believed their mothers had more power. Ibrahim's research and analysis of family dynamics suggested that while some Arab fathers may be powerful authorities in the family, about half of children perceived the mother as the more prestigious and powerful figure. At the same time, the children's psychological adjustment was associated with the father's role to a greater extent than to the mother's role.

The second study (Ahmed & Ibrahim, in press) investigated the relationship between perceived parental power and prestige, parental acceptance-rejection, and psychological adjustment among 768 Kuwaiti male and female adolescents, youths, and young adults. Arabic versions of four questionnaires were used: (a) the Parental Power-Prestige Questionnaire (3PQ), (b) the Youth and Adult Short version of the Parental Acceptance-Rejection Questionnaire (PARQ), (c) the Personality Assessment Questionnaire (PAQ), and (d) a Gender Inequality Scale (GIS). Results showed that while no significant difference was found between males' and females' perceptions of paternal acceptance-rejection, the females perceived lesser maternal acceptance than the males. Compared with their female counterparts, males reported slightly healthier psychological adjustment, while attributing more power and prestige to their parents than did females. Additionally, adolescents perceived both maternal and paternal acceptance as being significantly lower than did young adults. Young adults reported better psychological adjustment than did adolescents, and they reported higher levels of parental power (but not prestige). Perceived maternal and paternal acceptance correlated positively with healthier psychological adjustment. Perceived paternal rejection (but not maternal rejection) correlated negatively with perceived parental power and prestige. Finally, the mean score of the gender inequality scale indicated a tendency toward greater gender inequality than equality in Kuwait.

An as-yet unpublished study by Ahmed and Ibrahim (in prep.) explored associations between perceived parental power/prestige, perceived parental acceptance-rejection, feelings of alienation, tendency toward political participation and psychological adjustment in samples of male and female adolescents and young adults. Results indicated that perceived parental power correlated positively with the perceived parental acceptance (especially paternal acceptance), and healthier psychological adjustment. Moreover, perceived parental power (and perceived parental acceptance and healthier psychological adjustment) correlated negatively with feelings of alienation, and positively with political participation.

CONCLUSIONS AND SUGGESTIONS FOR FUTURE RESEARCH

In this chapter we have reviewed major features of IPARTheory and its associated measures. We also reviewed research conducted in Arab countries that tested a variety of hypotheses and research questions derived from the theory. On the whole, evidence from more than 120 Arab studies provides strong support for the theory, while also being consistent with research being conducted in many other nations worldwide. We find, for instance, that Arab children living in poverty, in rural areas, in difficult circumstances, and those lacking in education are more likely to feel rejected than do children who live in more favorable conditions. Additional evidence suggests that chronically ill children and those with disabilities are more likely to feel rejected than healthy children. Further evidence also suggests that boys in the Arab world often feel less accepted by parents than do girls—a finding that may surprise some Westerners.

Moreover, evidence suggests that perceived parental rejection often leads to such internalizing problems as depression, neuroticism, various forms of anxiety, feelings of loneliness, phobias, low self-esteem, and feelings of impaired self-adequacy. Other Arab children, however, react to feelings of rejection by developing externalizing behavior patterns and emotional syndromes such as acting out, experiencing aggressive and hostile impulses, engaging in delinquent actions, exhibiting impulsivity, and experiencing feelings of emotional numbness together with a lack of emotional expressiveness (for the distinction between internalizing and externalizing problems in adaptation, see Achenbach, chapter 16, this volume). When children are physically punished, they tend to see their parents as more rejecting while also developing a variety of maladaptive personality dispositions. On the positive side, however, research in Arab countries also supports the idea that children who feel accepted by their parents are more likely than rejected children to achieve a stable identity, excel in school, be gifted, engage in altruistic behavior, develop a rich inner world of aesthetic feelings, report feelings of positive self-esteem and positive self-adequacy, and self-report more social responsibility.

From a methodological point of view, it should be pointed out that Arab researchers have typically employed questionnaires in their studies, while neglecting ethnographic, holocultural, and other approaches that have been used by other IPARTheory researchers. Thus, the conclusions of Arab researchers tend not to be based on a triangulation of methodologies. Future research would profit from a greater use of the ethnographic method in order to add cultural specificity and culturally structured behavioral observations to the already-available evidence. For an example of this kind of approach researchers may profit from consulting Rohner and Chaki-Sircar's (1988) study of *Women and Children in a Bengali Village* that combines ethnographic description and analysis with interview results as well as data from the PARQ and the PAQ.

Overall, Arab research provides strong support for the pan-Arab applicability of IPARTheory and the research measures derived from it. Evidence provided in this review tends to be so robust and so consistent that we believe educators, psychologists, and other professionals should feel confident developing policies and practice-applications based on IPARTheory and its associated measures in the Arab world. For instance, Arab psychologists and educators might consider preparing written and visual materials for parents and other members of the general public that would provide advice and guidance for them about how to best bring up and educate children. A sustained effort along those lines might help parents and others foresee the deleterious consequences of rejection, and thereby help to improve the mental health of children in the Arab world. Such efforts might also be conducive to convincing the Arab public that psychologists can contribute useful and relevant ideas for the betterment of society, thereby lifting the status of the field in the eyes of laypersons.

In recent years, IPARTheory has taken a new turn. It is now believed that similar psychological reactions to feeling either accepted or rejected and neglected by parents occurs in a broad range of social relationships that include but also go beyond parent-child relationships. Several completed and ongoing Arab studies (e.g., Ahmed et al, 2012; Al-Otaibi, 2005; Al-Sabah, 2010; El-Sayed, 2000; El-Shamy, 2004; Ibrahim et al., 2006; Mansour, 2011) have explored or are exploring the possibility of relationships among perceptions of parental rejection, perceptions of rejection by teachers, and personality dispositions and emotions in children and adolescents. These studies, although less numerous and comprehensive than the studies focusing specifically on parental acceptance and rejection, nevertheless provide preliminary support for the idea that in the Arab world as elsewhere, perceived interpersonal acceptance and rejection in the larger social world tends to lead to similar psychological consequences as those that were found in studies of parental acceptance and rejection. Such studies have paved the way for a more comprehensive understanding of how humans generally react to experiences, perceptions, and feelings of either being accepted or rejected by others such as teachers, siblings, peers, friends, intimate partners, spouses, and other attachment figures. One successful attempt in this direction was made by Ahmed et al. (2012) who demonstrated similarities between perceptions of parents', siblings', best friends', and teachers' acceptance-rejection. We hope that Arab researchers will play an important role in demonstrating the theoretical propositions, empirical support, and practical applicability of such an expanded version of IPARTheory.

REFLECTIVE QUESTIONS

Some of the following questions encourage readers to go beyond the research evidence presented earlier and to consider potential applications to Arab (and other) societies.

1. How do (perceived) parental acceptance and rejection influence the personality characteristics of Arab children?
2. What kinds of intervention programs might improve parental childrearing styles by increasing parents' kindness and acceptance, and reduce their rejection?
3. What might be some similarities and differences in the perception of acceptance-rejection across generations (e.g., between children, their parents, and their grandparents)?
4. Are there any relationships between perceptions of parental acceptance-rejection and issues related to family life and marriage, such as mate selection and marital adjustment?
5. What role could official/nonofficial education, media, and mass communication play in increasing parents' acceptance and decreasing their rejection?
6. How might increasing the overall level of parental acceptance improve the public life of Arab societies?

SUGGESTED READINGS

Books and Articles

Ahmed, R. A. (2010). Middle East and North Africa. In Marc H. Bornstein (Ed.), *Handbook of cultural developmental science* (pp. 359–381). New York: Francis and Taylor.

Ahmed, R.A. (2013). The father's role in the Arab world: Cultural perspectives. In D.W. Shwalb, B.J. Shwalb, & M.E. Lamb (Eds.), *Fathers in cultural context* (pp. 122–147). New York: Routledge.

Rohner, R.P., & Britner, P.A. (2002). Worldwide mental health correlates of parental acceptance-rejection: Review of cross-cultural and intracultural evidence. *Cross-Cultural Research, 36*(1), 16–47.

Rohner, R.P., & Khaleque, A. (Eds.). (2005). *Handbook for the study of parental acceptance and rejection* (4th ed.). Storrs, CT: Rohner Research Publications.

Website

The Ronald and Nancy Rohner Center for the Study of Interpersonal Acceptance and Rejection: http://csiar.uconn.edu/.

REFERENCES

Abdalla, M.A.A. (2001). *Parental acceptance-rejection and its relation with creative thinking in a sample of deaf-mute children.* Unpublished master's thesis, Ain Shams University, Egypt (in Arabic).

Abdel-Moety, H.M. (1991). Family socialization and its influence (impact) on identity formation among university students. *Journal of the Faculty of Education, Tanta University* (Egypt), *14*(3), 233–277 (in Arabic).

Abdel-Rahman, M.A. (2003). *Parental acceptance-rejection as perceived by hearing handicapped, and its relation with children's psychological problems.* Unpublished doctoral dissertation, Ain Shams University, Egypt (in Arabic).

Abdel-Razek, E.A.M. (1996). *Economic hardship, parental controls and their relationship with children's psychological and behavioral problems.* Unpublished doctoral dissertation, Zagazig University, Egypt (in Arabic).

Abdel-Razek, E.A.M. (2000). Parenthood type and predicting personality variables for children's altruistic behavior. *Proceedings of the 7th International Conference on Counseling "Developing Man for a Better Society (Future orientation for a new century and new millennium)," Centre of Counseling, Ain Shams University* (pp. 105–156), November 5–7, 2000, Cairo, Egypt (in Arabic).

Abdel-Razek, E.A.M. (2005). A cross-cultural study of psychological dispositions between Egyptians and Italians. *Psychological Studies* (Egypt), *15*(1), 55–98 (in Arabic).

Abdel-Sadek, J.M.A. (1994). *The development of moral judgment in children and its relation with some psychological and demographic variables.* Unpublished doctoral dissertation, South Valley University, Egypt (in Arabic).

Abdel-Wahab, A.A. (1999). Parental acceptance-rejection and its relation with psychological adjustment in a sample of rural areas children. *Proceedings of the Annual Convention "Toward Better Care for Rural Area Children"* (pp. 135–165). Institute for Higher Studies on Childhood, Ain Shams University, Cairo, Egypt (in Arabic).

Abou-el-Kheir, M.M.S. (1989). *Parental socialization and its relation to schizophrenia.* Unpublished master's thesis, Zagazig University, Egypt (in Arabic).

Abou-el-Kheir, M.M.S. (1995). *Corporal (physical) punishment, styles of parental control, and their relation to children's psychological dispositions/characteristics.* Unpublished doctoral dissertation, Zagazig University, Egypt (in Arabic).

Abou-el-Kheir, M. M. S. (1998). Perception of father's image and self-esteem in university students. *Psychological Studies* (Egypt), *8*(3/4), 419–453 (in Arabic).

Abou-el-Kheir, M. M. S. (1999). Birth order and its relation to maternal acceptance/rejection and personality variables (traits) in a sample of adolescents. *Psychological Studies* (Egypt), *9*(3), 445–473 (in Arabic).

Abou-Ghali, A.M. (1999). *The relationships between prejudicial attitudes and parental treatment practices as perceived by children (university students).* Unpublished master's thesis, Al-Azhar University in Gaza, Palestine (in Arabic).

Ahmed, E. M. (1998). *Parental acceptance-rejection and its relation with anxiety in intermediate school students.* Unpublished master's thesis, Ain Shams University, Egypt (in Arabic).

Ahmed, R. A. (1985). *Rohner's Parental Acceptance-Rejection Questionnaire.* Khartoum, Sudan: The Press of Cairo University, Khartoum Branch (in Arabic).

Ahmed, R. A. (2007a). *PARQ Long and Short Forms in Kuwait: A correlation study.* Paper presented at the 36th annual meeting of the Society for Cross-Cultural Research, San Antonio, Texas, USA, February 21–24.

Ahmed, R. A. (2007b). Arab studies on parental acceptance-rejection. *Interpersonal Acceptance* (International Society for Interpersonal Acceptance and Rejection), *1*(3), 4, 8–10.

Ahmed, R. A. (2008). Review of Arab research on parental acceptance-rejection. In F. Erkman (Ed.), *Selected papers from the First International Congress on Interpersonal Acceptance and Rejection* (pp. 201–224), Istanbul, Turkey, June 22–24, 2006, Istanbul, Turkey: The Turkish Psychology Society (Istanbul Branch).

Ahmed, R. A. (2013a). The relations between identity statuses, perceptions of parental acceptance-rejection, and psychological adjustment in samples of Kuwaiti adolescents and youth. Paper presented at the *5th Seminar of the College of Social Science, Kuwait University,* Kuwait, February 11–13, 2013 (in Arabic).

Ahmed, R. A. (2013b). Emotional intelligence, parental acceptance-rejection, and psychological adjustment in Kuwait. Paper presented at the *42nd Annual Meeting of the Society for Cross-Cultural Research (SCCR),* Mobile, Alabama, USA, February 20–23, 2013.

Ahmed, R. A. (unpublished.). *Perception of parental acceptance-rejection and critical thinking in Kuwaiti students.* Kuwait University, Kuwait.

Ahmed, R. A., & Gielen, U. P. (2006a). *The relationship between perceived parental acceptance-rejection, perceived corporal (physical) punishment and personality dispositions in intermediate and secondary school male and female students in Kuwait.* Paper presented at the 35th annual meeting of the Society for Cross-Cultural Research. Savannah, GA, USA, February 22–25, 2006.

Ahmed, R. A., & Gielen, U. P. (2006b). *A critical review of Arab studies on parental acceptance-rejection.* Paper presented at the 1st International Congress on Interpersonal Acceptance and Rejection. Istanbul, Turkey, June 22–24, 2006.

Ahmed, R. A., & Gielen, U. P. (2008). *Age and sex differences as appeared in Arab research studies using Rohner's PARQ.* Paper presented at the 2nd International Congress on Interpersonal Acceptance and Rejection, Crete, Greece, July 3–6, 2008.

Ahmed, R. A., & Gielen, U. P., & Avellani, J. (1987). Perceptions of parental behavior and the development of moral reasoning in Sudanese students. In Ç. Kağitçibaşi (Ed.), *Growth and progress in cross-cultural psychology: Selected papers from the Eighth International Conference of the International Association of Cross-Cultural Psychology* (pp. 196–206). Amsterdam (The Netherlands): Swets & Zeitlinger.

Ahmed, R. A., & Ibrahim, M. A. (in press). Kuwaiti adolescents' and young adults' perceptions of parental power/prestige, parental acceptance-rejection, and psychological adjustment. To appear in *Proceedings of the 4th International Conference of the International Society for Interpersonal Acceptance and Rejection,* Changardahar, India, January 10–13, 2013.

Ahmed, R. A., & Ibrahim, M. A. (in prep.). *Relations between perceptions of parental acceptance-rejection, alienation feelings, political participation, and psychological adjustment among Kuwaiti adolescents and youth.*

Ahmed, R. A., & Khalil, E. A. (1999). Relationships between perceived parental behavior and neuroticism, self-confidence, and aesthetic feelings in a sample of Egyptian intermediate and secondary school students. In R. Roth (Ed.). *Psychologists facing the challenge of a globalization with human rights and mental health. Proceedings of the 55th Annual Convention of the International Council of Psychologists, ICP,* July 14–18, 1997 (pp. 51–61). Lengerich, Germany: Pabst Science Publishers.

Ahmed, R. A., Rohner, R. P., & Carrasco, M. E. (2012). Relationships between psychological adjustment and perceived parental, sibling, best friend, and teacher acceptance among Kuwaiti adolescents. In K. Ripoll-Nunez, A. L. Comunian, & C. M. Brown (Eds,). *Expanding horizons: Current research on interpersonal acceptance and rejection* (pp. 1–10). Boca Raton, FL.: Brown Walker Press.

Ahmed, R. A., Rohner, R. P., Khaleque, A., & Gielen, U. P. (2011). Parental acceptance and rejection: Theory, measures, and research in the Arab World. *ERIC Document Reproduction Service No. Ed 514028.*

Al-Azemy, A. T. M. (2012). *A study of bullying behavior and its relation to some demographic and psychological variables in samples of intermediate and secondary school male and female students in the State of Kuwait.* Unpublished master's thesis, Kuwait University, Kuwait (in Arabic).

Al-Baghadady, N. M. (2001). *Parental acceptance-rejection as perceived by children and its relation with some personality traits in male and female adolescents.* Unpublished master's thesis, Ain Shams University, Egypt (in Arabic).

Al-Beheray, A. (1990). Ego-identity and its relation to anxiety, self-esteem and parental behavior in university students: A study in the light of Erikson's theory. *Journal of the Faculty of Education, Zagazig University* (Egypt), *12*(21), 165–211 (in Arabic).

Al-Bery, M. A. (2007). Relations between socialization styles and psychological security as perceived by delinquent and non-delinquent children. Proceedings of the *1st Regional Conference on Psychology, Egyptian Psychologists Association (EPA)* (pp. 919–945). Cairo, Egypt, November 18–20, 2007 (in Arabic).

Al-Falaij, A. (1991). *Family conditions, ego development, and socio-moral development in juvenile delinquency: A study of Bahraini adolescents.* Unpublished doctoral dissertation, University of Pittsburg, PA, USA.

Alhanati, S. (1990). *Predictors of deficits in reality testing and object relationships: A comparative study of separations, perceived emotional neglect, and perceived aggression.* Dissertation Abstract International, *50* (10-B), 760.

Ali, E. E. (1997). *Parental acceptance-rejection as perceived by the blind child, and its relation with the child's self-concept.* Unpublished master's thesis, Ain Shams University, Egypt (in Arabic).

Ali, E. E. (2000). *Styles of parental treatment and their relation with level of aspiration in a sample of deaf-mute children.* Unpublished master's thesis, Zagazig University, Egypt (in Arabic).

Almousa, N.M. (2007). *Perfectionism (normality/neuroticism) and its relation with styles of parental socialization among male and female students at King Saud University.* Unpublished master's thesis, King Saud University, Saudi Arabia (in Arabic).

Al-Nafie, A.A. (1997). The relationship between styles of parental treatment and locus of control in a sample of male and female students at Umm el-Qura University, Mecca, Saudi Arabia. *Journal of the Faculty of Education, Al-Azhar University* (Egypt), *66*, 281–314 (in Arabic).

Al-Otaibi, D.R. (2005). *Perception of parental and its relation to identity disorder, ego-strength, and single-mindedness in samples of Kuwaiti adolescents and youth.* Unpublished master's thesis, Kuwait University, Kuwait (in Arabic).

Al-Otaibi, Gh., Al-Theifairy, A., & Al-Gazzar, J. *Styles of parental treatment and personality dispositions which predict attitudes toward extremeness/extreme behavior among secondary school students.* Unpublished master's thesis, Kuwait University, Kuwait (in Arabic).

Al-Ragieeb, Y.A.F. (1996). *Parental warmth and its relation with personality traits and creativity in a sample of primary school children in Kuwait and Egypt: A cross-cultural and comparative study.* Unpublished doctoral dissertation, Menia University, Egypt (in Arabic).

Al-Sabah, A.O.M.. (2010). *Parental acceptance-rejection, teacher's acceptance-rejection and personality dispositions in Kuwaiti intermediate and secondary school male and female students.* Unpublished master's thesis, Kuwait University, Kuwait (in Arabic).

Al-Shayji, M.S. (2003). *The relationship between perceptions of parental acceptance—rejection behavior and phobias in samples of secondary school male and female students in Kuwait.* Unpublished master's thesis, Kuwait University, Kuwait (in Arabic).

Al-Theifairy, A.B. (1996). *Perception of parental treatment and its relation with psychological dispositions in adolescents: A comparative and cross-cultural study on Saudi and Egyptian adolescents.* Unpublished master's thesis, Ain Shams University, Egypt (in Arabic).

Althuwaikh, A.F. (2015). *The efficiency of a psychological tests battery in predicting successful performance of Kuwait Police Academy new students.* Unpublished master's thesis, Kuwait University, Kuwait (in Arabic).

Askar, A.E. (1996a). Differences between Egyptian and Yemeni children in parental acceptance–rejection: A cross-cultural study. *Psychological Studies* (Egypt), *6*(2), 231–252 (in Arabic).

Askar, A.E. (1996b). Differences in personality assessment between Egyptian and Yemeni students: A cross-cultural study. *Psychological Studies* (Egypt), *6*(3), 411–435 (in Arabic).

Bader, F.M. (2001). Parental acceptance-rejection and its relation with self-concept and its influence (impact) on scholastic achievement in a sample of primary school female students in Jeddah City. *Resilat el-Khalif al-Arabi* (Saudi Arabia) *81*, 53–76 (in Arabic).

Bader, F.M. (2008). Style of parental treatment and self-concept and their relation with aggressive behavior. In S.S. Majeed (Ed.), *Violence and childhood: Psychological studies* (pp. 123–154). Amman, Jordan: Dar Safa (in Arabic).

Baldwin, M.W. (1992). Relational schemas and the processing of societal information. *Psychological Bulletin, 112*, 461–484.

Baumeister, R.F., & Leary, M.R. (1995). The need to belong: Desire for interpersonal attachments as a fundamental human motivation. *Psychological Bulletin, 117,* 497–529.

Bjorklund, D.F., & Pellegrini, A.D. (2002). *The origins of human nature: Evolutionary developmental psychology.* Washington, DC: APA Books.

Clausen, J.A. (1972). The life course of individuals. In M.W. Riley, M. Johnson, & A. Foner (Eds.), *Aging and society* (vol. 3, pp. 457–514). New York: Russell Sage Foundation.

Crick, N.R., & Dodge, K.A. (1994). A review and reformulation of social information-processing mechanisms in children's social adjustment. *Psychological Bulletin, 115,* 74–101.

El-Sayed, M.M. (2000). Children's perceptions of parental acceptance-rejection behavior and its relation with some personality traits in children: An empirical and clinical study. *Journal of the Faculty of Education, Assuit University* (Egypt), *16*(2), 365–403 (in Arabic).

El-Sayed, N.A.A. (1994). Feelings of psychological security and its relation to perceptions of parental acceptance-rejection in blind and normal children. *Journal of Children's Disabilities Center, Al-Azhar University* (Egypt), *3*(1), 73–115 (in Arabic).

El-Shamy, A. (2004). *Kindergarten female teachers' negative and positive emotions and their relation to the teachers' perception of parental acceptance-rejection.* Unpublished master's thesis, Mansoura University, Egypt (in Arabic).

Elyan, I.A.E. (1992). *A study on the relationship between parental acceptance-rejection and self-assertiveness and aggression/hostility among adolescents.* Unpublished master's thesis, Ain Shams University, Egypt (in Arabic).

Epstein, S. (1994). Integration of the cognitive and the psychodynamic unconscious. *American Psychologist, 49,* 709–724.

Faied, H.A.M. (2000). Dependency and self-criticism, and their relationship with perception of parental acceptance-rejection and depression. *Egyptian Journal of Psychological Studies* (Egypt), *10*(25), 163–213 (in Arabic).

Faied, H.A.M. (2005). Shame as mediator variable between depressive symptoms and both childhood emotional abuse and problem irresolvability of female college students. *Psychological Studies* (Egypt), *15*(3), 457–510 (in Arabic).

Faried, F.H.H. (1990). Perceptions of parental acceptance-rejection in rural and urban students of the second phase of basic education. *Journal of the Faculty of Education, Zagazig University* (Egypt), *11,* 451–507 (in Arabic).

Gaber, N. (1998). The impact of parental acceptance-rejection style on children's adjustment in adolescence. *Journal of the University of Costntine for Humanities* (Algeria), *9,* 37–52 (in Arabic).

Gielen, U.P., Ahmed, R.A., & Avellani, J. (1992). The development of moral reasoning and perceptions of parental behavior in students from Kuwait. *Moral Education Forum, 17*(3), 20–37.

Hamaza, J.M. (2002). Father's image and self-esteem among secondary school students: A psychological view. *Journal of Psychology* (Egypt), *16*(61), 172–189 (in Arabic).

Hassab-Allah, A.M.A., & El-Aqad, E.A. (2000). Irrational ideas and their relationship with dogmatism, flexibility-rigidity and parental rejection in students from Universities of Zagazig and South Valley. *Egyptian Journal of Psychological Studies* (Egypt), *10*(25), 79–119 (in Arabic).

Helewa, M.A.M. (1997). *The relationship between parental acceptance-rejection and aggressive behavior in boys and girls aged between 14 and 18 years.* Unpublished master's thesis, Ain Shams University, Egypt (in Arabic).

Ibrahim, A. S. (1988). Children's perception of parental acceptance-rejection behavior and its relation with their locus of control. *Journal of the Faculty of Education, Zagazig University* (Egypt), *3*(6), 169–200 (in Arabic).

Ibrahim, M. A. (2010). *Effects of parental power and prestige on children's psychological adjustment.* Paper presented at the *3rd* International Congress on Interpersonal Acceptance and Rejection, Padua, Italy, July, 2010.

Ibrahim, M. A., Parmar, P., & Rohner, R. P. (2006). *Relations between teachers' and parents' warmth and control, and youths' psychological adjustment, school conduct and academic performance in Kuwait.* Paper presented at the 1st International Congress on Interpersonal Acceptance and Rejection: "Acceptance: Essence of Peace," Istanbul, Turkey, June 22–24, 2006.

Ismaeel, A. E. (2001). Differences between family deprived and non-deprived children in child abuse and personality variables in a sample of Saudi intermediate school students. *Psychological Studies* (Egypt), *11*(2), 266–297 (in Arabic).

Kamal, F. A.-H. (1985). Relationships between perceived parental acceptance, parental rejection and personality characteristics of chronically ill school-aged children as compared to well school-aged children. *Dissertation Abstracts International, 46*(5B), 1512.

Khalifa, B. M. (2003). Children's perception of parental acceptance-rejection and its relation to late childhood problems in a sample of primary school male and female students in the State of Qatar. *Proceedings of the 10th International Conference on Counseling "Counseling and the Challenges of Development: The Population Problem," Centre of Counseling, Ain Shams University* (Vol. 1, pp. 69–130). December 13–15, 2003. Cairo, Egypt: Zahraa el-Sharek Bookshop (in Arabic).

Leary, M. R. (1999). Making sense of self-esteem. *Current Directions in Psychological Science, 8*, 32–35.

Mansour, M. E. I. (2011). Parental styles as predictors of behavioral problems among Bahraini children. *Psychological Studies* (Egypt), *21*(1), 99–135 (in Arabic).

Mansour, S. B. (2006). *Parental treatment as perceived by children and its relation with bearing social responsibility in secondary school male and female students.* Unpublished doctoral dissertation, Ain Shams University, Egypt (in Arabic).

Mekhemer, E. M. A. (1996). Perceived parental acceptance-rejection behavior and psychological hardiness among college students. *Psychological Studies* (Egypt), *6*(2), 275–299 (in Arabic).

Mekhemer, E. M. A. (2003). Perceived parental rejection, peers' rejection and loneliness among adolescents. *Psychological Studies* (Egypt), *13*(1), 59–105 (in Arabic).

Mekhemer, E. M. A., & Abdel-Razek, E. A.M. (1999). Childhood abuse experiences and their relation with personality dispositions: A comparison between juvenile delinquents and non-delinquents. *Proceedings of the annual conference of the Center of Counseling, Ain Shams University "Quality of Life"* (pp. 315–371). Cairo, Egypt (in Arabic).

Mohammed, M. T. A. (1994). *The relationship between types (styles) of parental treatment and dependency in a school situation.* Unpublished master's thesis, Ain Shams University, Egypt (in Arabic).

Mohammed, S. A.-K. (1996). *Physical punishment, perceived parental warmth, and children's personality dispositions.* Unpublished doctoral dissertation, Zagazig University, Egypt (in Arabic).

Mussallem, A. S. A. (1997). *Parental behavior and its relation with achievement motivation in boys and girls aged between 14 and 17 years.* Unpublished master's thesis, Ain Shams University, Egypt (in Arabic).

Ramadan, R.A. (1989). *The relationship between perceptions of parental acceptance-rejection behavior and impulsivity/reflectivity behavior in gifted and normal students.* Unpublished doctoral dissertation, Zagazig University, Egypt (in Arabic).

Rasmi, S. (2008). *"Spare the rod and spoil the child": A comparison of parental warmth and adolescent adjustment across culture.* Unpublished master's thesis, University of Guelph, Canada.

Rohner, R.P. (1986). *The warmth dimension: Foundations of parental acceptance-rejection theory.* Beverly Hills, CA: Sage. (Available from Rohner Research Publications, Storrs, CT).

Rohner, R.P. (2004). The parental "acceptance-rejection syndrome": Universal correlates of perceived rejection. *American Psychologist, 59,* 830–840.

Rohner, R.P. (2005a). Parental Acceptance-Rejection Questionnaire (PARQ): Test manual. In R.P. Rohner & A. Khaleque (Eds.), *Handbook for the study of parental acceptance and rejection* (4th ed., pp. 43–106). Storrs, CT: Rohner Research Publications.

Rohner, R.P. (2005b). Parental Acceptance-Rejection/Control Questionnaire (PARQ/Control): Test manual. In R.P. Rohner & A. Khaleque (Eds.), *Handbook for the study of parental acceptance and rejection* (4th ed., pp. 137–186). Storrs, CT: Rohner Research Publications.

Rohner, R.P., & Chaki-Sircar, M. (1988). *Women and children in a Bengali village.* Hanover, NH: University Press of New England.

Rohner, R.P., & Khaleque, A. (2005). Personality assessment questionnaire (PAQ): Test manual. In R.P. Rohner & A. Khaleque (Eds.), *Handbook for the study of parental acceptance and rejection* (4th ed., pp. 187–226). Storrs, CT: Rohner Research Publications.

Rohner, R.P., Khaleque, A., & Cournoyer, D.E. (2012). *Introduction to Parental Acceptance–Rejection Theory.* Retrieved on April 28, 2015, from http://csiar.uconn.edu/wp-content/uploads/sites/494/2014/02/INTRODUCTION-TO-PARENTAL-ACCEPTANCE-3–27–12.pdf

Rohner, R.P., Parmar, P., & Ibrahim, M.A. (2010). Perceived teachers' acceptance, parental acceptance, behavioral control, school conduct and psychological adjustment among school-age children in Kuwait. *Cross-Cultural Research, 46*(3), 269–282.

Rohner, R.P., Ripoll-Núñez, K.J., Moodie, N., & Ruan, C.-C. (2005). Physical Punishment Questionnaire Test Manual. In R.P. Rohner & A. Khaleque (Eds.), *Handbook for the study of parental acceptance and rejection* (4th ed., pp. 251–317). Storrs, CT: Rohner Research Publications.

Rohner, R.P., & Rohner, E.C. (1980). Worldwide tests of parental acceptance-rejection theory [Special issue], *Behavior Science Research, 15,* 1–21.

Saied, E.A. (1995). *Perception of parental acceptance-rejection and its relation to symptoms of depression in adolescents.* Unpublished master's thesis, Ains Shams University, Egypt (in Arabic).

Salama, M.M. (1986a). *Adult PARQ test manual.* Cairo, Egypt: The Anglo-Egyptian Bookshop (in Arabic).

Salama, M.M. (1986b). *Personality Assessment Questionnaire "PAQ".* Cairo, Egypt: The Anglo-Egyptian Bookshop (in Arabic).

Salama, M.M. (1987a). Children's phobias and their perceptions of parental acceptance-rejection behavior. *Journal of Psychology* (Egypt), *1*(2), 54–61 (in Arabic).

Salama, M.M. (1987b). Mother's employment, family size, and socioeconomic status as determinants of the children's perception of parental acceptance-rejection. *Journal* of *Psychology* (Egypt), *1*(4), 58–67 (in Arabic).

Salama, M.M. (1987c). Perceived parental acceptance-rejection and personality dispositions among college students in Egypt. In Ç. Kağitçibaşi (Ed.), *Growth and progress in cross-cultural psychology: Selected Papers from the Eighth International Conference of the International Association for Cross-Cultural Psychology* (pp. 181–188). Amsterdam, Netherlands: Swets & Zeitlinger.

Salama, M.M. (1990a). *The relationship between family size and children's dependency and aggression: Controlling for the effects of perceived acceptance-rejection in Zagazig, Egypt.* Paper presented at the IACCP Regional Meeting, Seoul, South Korea.

Salama, M.M. (1990b). Perceived parental rejection and cognitive distortions: Risk factors for depression. *The Egyptian Journal of Mental Health* (Egypt), *31*, 1–17.

Salama, M.M. (1991). Self-esteem and parental control in children at the end of adolescence and early adulthood. *Psychological Studies* (Egypt), *1*(4), 679–702 (in Arabic).

Salem, A.F. (2005). *Parental acceptance-rejection and its relation to children's phobias.* Unpublished doctoral dissertation, Ain Shams University, Egypt (in Arabic).

Shehata, A.M. (2006). *Styles of parental treatment as perceived by children and their relation with personality assessment in a sample of blind children.* Unpublished master's thesis, Ain Shams University, Egypt (in Arabic).

Taher, N.S.M. (2005). Perception of mother's practice in socialization and aggressive behavior in a sample of intermediate school male and female students in Kuwait. *Egyptian Journal of Psychological Studies* (Egypt), *15*(46), 393–438 (in Arabic).

Zaeter, M.A. (1998). Parental rejection and personality disorders in juvenile delinquents and non-delinquents. *Journal of the Faculty of Arts, Zagazig University* (Egypt), *22*, 313–370 (in Arabic).

Zaeter, M.A., & Abou-el-Khair, M.M.S. (1999). Dependent personality disorder and its relation to perception of parental control and the attitude toward drug addiction among secondary school students. *Proceedings of the 6th International Conference on Counseling "Quality of Life," Centre of Counseling, Ain Shams University* (pp. 545–615). Cairo, Egypt (in Arabic).

Zaidan, A.A.A. (1995). Students' perceptions of parental acceptance—rejection and its relation with achievement motivation in Teachers College male students in Al-Gof, Saudi Arabia. *The Educational Journal* (Kuwait), *10*(47), 103–125 (in Arabic).

6

Family Structure and Socialization Patterns in Caribbean and Caribbean Immigrant Families: Developmental Outcomes

Jaipaul L. Roopnarine and Elif Dede Yildirim

> The video of a [Trinidadian] mother beating her 12-year-old daughter featured on Facebook has raised the specter once again of the unresolved issue of the use of corporal punishment to discipline children who misbehave. Many persons have weighed in on the issue including the Prime Minister who has reportedly said she will examine the possibility of banning corporal punishment in the home in the same way it is now prohibited in schools. The question that naturally arises is whether this is in fact desirable and how far can and should such a prohibition, if put in place, go.
>
> Dana Seetahal, *Trinidad Express*, April 24, 2014.

The preceding quote captures some of the issues facing Caribbean parents who straddle traditional and contemporary methods of childrearing in an increasingly globalized world. Along with the residual effects of a brutal and oppressive history, a combination of interrelated factors such as ancestral traditions tied to Africa and Asia, fluctuating economic conditions, complex living arrangements and belief systems, interethnic unions and marriages, within region and international migration, and remote acculturation all define the outlines of contemporary family relationships and childrearing in Caribbean Community (CARICOM) countries. After briefly discussing some theoretical considerations and providing a basic sociodemographic profile of Caribbean families, we consider in this chapter four major issues pertaining to childrearing in the Caribbean: (a) family structural arrangements; (b) parental investment, styles, and practices; (c) remote acculturation, and (d) family practices and functioning and developmental outcomes in children. The primary focus of this chapter is on families in the English-speaking Caribbean; thus research conducted in countries such as Cuba, the Dominican Republic, and Haiti will not be reviewed.

THEORETICAL CONSIDERATIONS

A range of theoretical and conceptual frameworks have been employed to examine Caribbean family structural organization; interpersonal relationships; socialization processes; and overall economic, sociocultural, and psychological investment in children. These include, but are not limited to, cultural-ecological models (Whiting & Whiting, 1975); the biosocial perspective (Flinn, 1992); anti-colonial theory (Escayg, 2014); structural functional frameworks (Smith, 1957); social learning theory (Bandura, 1986); the bio-ecological model (Bronfenbrenner & Morris, 2006); immigrant adjustment, transnationalism, and remote acculturation (Berry, 1997; Ferguson, in press); and parenting styles and practices frameworks (Baumrind, 1967; Darling & Steinberg, 1993; Khaleque & Rohner, 2012a, 2012b; see also chapter 5 by Ahmed, Rohner, Khaleque, & Gielen in this volume). The utility of these frameworks for understanding psychological issues within Caribbean families has not gone unquestioned. A major criticism is their lack of consideration of the impact of the colonial experience on human development—that is, the destructive power of domination on the psyche of Caribbean peoples.

Of the aforementioned frameworks, the cultural ecological and the bio-ecological models have been used widely to examine socialization practices in the Caribbean. Their appeal may lie in the focus on distal and proximal family processes tied to contextual issues such as economic conditions, physical settings, and ideological beliefs. Despite their strengths, some researchers (e.g., Escayg, 2014) have proposed that human development in the formerly colonized countries should be assessed and viewed through an anticolonial theoretical lens or from a decolonized perspective. Essentially, it is argued that colonization and its inherent power hierarchy led to changes in patterns of family organization and possibly to childrearing practices that were originally present in the ancestral cultures. Some of the changes occurred as a result of the unequal power structures that existed in economic activities and family and gender relationships during periods of domination. Other changes emerged as adaptations of the resistance strategies that were used by the colonized to combat domination and oppression. Quite often, color and class played a significant role in defining the nature of relationships between the colonizer and the colonized, and so too did the blending of cultural practices among individuals who share a common cultural space. Interethnic marriages would further enhance the latter. As is the case with the use of newer theoretical perspectives such as colorism and critical race theory to guide work on human development processes of historically oppressed groups in the United States (Burton, Bonilla-Salvia, Ray, Buckelew, & Freeman, 2010), researchers who focus on Caribbean family socialization patterns are beginning to integrate anticolonial conceptualizations in their work on families and children.

SOCIODEMOGRAPHIC CHARACTERISTICS

Over the last two decades the English-speaking Caribbean has made progress on the economic and health fronts. Most Caribbean countries fall in the middle range on Human Development Indices (see Table 6.1). However, large pockets of poverty remain in countries such as Guyana, Jamaica, and Haiti, and paradoxes exist regarding economic development and health indicators in some countries. For example, the oil-rich nation of Trinidad and Tobago has higher infant and child mortality rates than other Caribbean nations with less per capita income. Most Caribbean nations have also placed a good deal of stock on early childhood education and schooling as one panacea to poverty reduction and improvements to human capital development in disenfranchised groups and challenging urban environments (Logie & Roopnarine, 2013). At the same time, crime and citizen insecurity constitute a major concern in the region as youth violence, human and drug trafficking, and interpersonal violence are on the increase (UNDP, 2012).

The Caribbean presents a diverse ethnic tapestry. African Caribbeans, the predominant group in most English-speaking countries, have ancestral ties to Africa and were mainly brought as slaves to the region. Other ethnic groups include Indo Caribbeans who were brought as indentured servants after slavery was abolished and are largely found in Trinidad and Tobago, Guyana, and Suriname; individuals of European ancestry; Syrians; Black Caribs who have both African and native Caribbean ancestry and reside in countries such as Dominica and Belize; Amerindians who are indigenous to certain geographic locations such as Guyana; individuals of Mixed-ethnic ancestry who are the offspring of interethnic marriages; Chinese Caribbean; and smaller numbers of recent migrants (e.g., Chinese and Indians). Table 6.1 presents some salient sociodemographic characteristics of families in the English-speaking Caribbean.

Table 6.1 Sociodemographic Characteristics of Caribbean Community (CARICOM) Countries

Country	Human Development Index	Life Expectancy	Early Childhood Education Enrollment Rate	Infant Mortality	Ethnicity
Barbados	0.776	74.9 M: 72.64 F: 77.37	71.94	10.93	African 92.4%, white 2.7%, Mixed 3.1%, East Indian 1.3%, other 0.2%, unspecified 0.2%
Belize	0.731	68.49 M: 66.88 F: 70.17	45.23	20.31	Mestizo 48.7%, Creole 24.9%, Maya 10.6%, Garifuna 6.1%, other 9.7%
Dominica	0.716	76.59 M: 73.63 F: 79.7	76.71	11.61	African 86.8%, Mixed 8.9%, Carib Amerindian 2.9%, white 0.8%, other 0.7%
Grenada	0.743	73.8 M: 71.24 F: 76.62	93.94	10.5	African 82%, Mixed African and European 13%, European and East Indian 5%, and trace of Arawak/Carib Amerindian
Guyana	0.635	67.81 M: 64.82 F: 70.96	56.81	33.56	East Indian 43.5%, African 30.2%, Mixed 16.7%, Amerindian 9.1%, other 0.5%
Haiti	0.469	63.18 M: 61.77 F: 64.6	NA	49.43	Black 95%, mulatto and white 5%
Jamaica	0.715	73.48 M: 71.87 F: 75.17	68.78	13.69	African 92.1%, Mixed 6.1%, East Indian 0.8%, other 0.4%, unspecified 0.7%

Montserrat	NA	73.9 M: 75.48 F: 72.24	72.66	13.66	African 88.4%, Mixed 3.7%, Hispanic/Spanish 3%, Caucasian/white 2.7%, East Indian/Indian 1.5%, other 0.7%
St. Kitts and Nevis	0.749	75.29 M: 72.88 F: 77.75	77.90	8.98	Predominantly African; some British, Portuguese, and Lebanese
St. Lucia	0.715	77.4 M: 74.69 F: 80.28	44.49	11.75	African descent 85.3%, Mixed 10.9%, East Indian 2.2%, other 1.6%, unspecified 0.1%
St. Vincent and Grenadines	0.717	74.86 M: 72.9 F: 76.88	79.51	13.07	African 66%, Mixed 19%, East Indian 6%, European 4%, Carib Amerindian 2%, other 3%
Trinidad and Tobago	0.769	72.29 M: 69.42 F: 75.24	66.85	24.82	East Indian 35.4%, African 34.2%, Mixed—other 15.3%, Mixed African/East Indian 7.7%, other 1.3%, unspecified 6.2%

Source: CIA: The Word Factbook.

FAMILY STRUCTURAL ARRANGEMENTS AND CHILDREARING

Because the diverse family structural arrangements for childrearing and the socialization of children in Caribbean cultural communities have been described in great detail in previous papers (Anderson, 2007; Chevannes, 2001; Roopnarine, 2013; Roopnarine, Evans, & Pant, 2011; Roopnarine & Jin, 2016), they are mentioned only briefly here. Although on the increase in a number of developed societies (e.g., United States, Norway), multiple-partner/fertility living arrangements have characterized Caribbean families for several generations and are likely present among Caribbean immigrant families in North America and Europe as well. The early work of anthropologists (Clarke, 1957; Smith, 1957) and sociologists (Simey, 1946) has identified several key characteristics that reflect the social-structural organization of families in Jamaica and Guyana. These are matrifocal organization, emphasis on conjugal ties, nonlegal unions entered into by low-income women, relationships that cannot easily be placed within the framework of a "household" system, and gendered roles that permit greater flexibility for women to seek employment activities (Anderson, 2007). Smith (1957) and others (e.g., Simey, 1946) recognized early on that a significant number of African Caribbean families did not resemble the nuclear family structure that was based on marriage. Instead, childbearing and childrearing occurred in a variety of unions: nonresidential visiting unions and co-residential unions entered into on the basis of marriage or common-law relationships.

Viewed within the parameters of union and residential status, Leo-Rhynie and Brown (2013) indicate that Caribbean family structural and organizational patterns include such diverse arrangements as the single-parent family, same-sex family, the extended family, the absent parent family, the guardian family, the sibling family, the blended family, the common-law family, the nuclear family, and the child-alone family. Whereas some of these family arrangements may be more common among particular ethnic groups than others, some forms of extendedness and alloparenting, a system in which many individuals act as caregivers, seem to be present among all ethnic groups across Caribbean nations. In short, emotional extensiveness, the warmth and care offered by women in the yard or compound, characterizes childrearing alliances among female caregivers in the Caribbean (Brodber, 1975; Flinn, 1992). Thus, it is often difficult to draw clear lines of demarcation between different family structural arrangements in Caribbean countries. For example, functional and/or emotional extendedness may be visible among families who are ordinarily considered nuclear in structure but have strong ties to kinship networks. That is, a couple with children may live in a separate household but maintain strong ties with and depend on relatives for childcare assistance and financial support.

Likewise, single-parent and multiple fertility families may also have strong ties to both kinship and non-kinship members and rely on them for different forms of support. Accordingly, the structural elements of families may not reflect the intimate social and psychological processes that are inherent in adult relationships in the Caribbean. Three common family living arrangements in the Caribbean are considered next.

Visiting Unions

As several Caribbean researchers (Anderson, 2007; Roopnarine, Krishnakumar, Narine, Logie, & Lape, 2013; Samms-Vaughan, 2005) have catalogued in Jamaica and Trinidad and Tobago, progressive mating is characteristic of African Caribbean families wherein men and women begin relationships in temporary, visiting unions. The mating pair usually has children in these relationships before moving on to common-law relationships. In her work on men (N = 1,142) in four communities in Jamaica, Anderson (2007) found that only 20.5% of fathers below 35 years of age were married. In separate studies, estimates of visiting relationships/regular girlfriend across Caribbean countries range from 7.4% to 33.4% (Anderson, 2007; Roopnarine et al., 2011; Samms-Vaughan, 2005). In these unions, the woman is usually younger and may reside with her parents or relatives while bearing children. Financial and emotional support from her mating partner is nebulous and any financial support may be sporadic.

Common-Law Families

After having children in visiting unions, men and women move on to other partners and establish common-law relationships wherein they reside together and share household resources. The power dynamics in these relationships favor males; they tend to hold on to and display traditional views about male-female roles and feel encumbered if their partners question their whereabouts (Anderson, 2007). With their new partners, couples have more children. Between 19% and 42% of couples in four communities in Jamaica, and in a national representative sample in Trinidad and Tobago, 28% of African Caribbean, 23% of Indo Caribbean, and 32% of individuals of Mixed-ethnic ancestry were in common-law relationships (Roopnarine et al., 2014). The complexity of these mating unions can be seen in the number of offspring with different partners. In Anderson's study, 53.9% of men had fathered children with one woman, 25.8% had children with two women, and 19% had children with three or more women. Jealousy and lack of economic support by male partners can interfere with the stability of these relationships (Flinn, 1992).

Married Families

Marriage is more synonymous with nuclear families but variations do exist. Two-parent nuclear families are present in all ethnic groups but are more prevalent in Indo Caribbean families in Trinidad and Tobago and Guyana (Roopnarine, Wang, Krishnakumar, & Davidson, 2013). As African Caribbean men age and attain better economic standing, they may marry. In Anderson's (2007) work in Jamaica, about 44.8% of men over 35 years were married and in a national representative sample of families in Trinidad and Tobago, 22% of African Caribbean men, 62% of Indo Caribbeans, and 27% of individuals of Mixed-ethnic ancestry were married reflecting the emphasis placed on marriage for entry into parenthood among Indo Caribbeans. Husband-wife relationships and the division of household and childcare responsibilities have remained traditional in a large number of these families. Although on the increase, divorce rates remain comparatively low among Caribbean families in general.

Childrearing: Investment, Beliefs, and Practices

As noted earlier, childrearing practices in Caribbean cultural communities are likely influenced by sociohistorical experiences such as slavery, indentured servitude, and colonialism. The extent to which the invasion of cultural space, transplantation, and creolization (blending of cultural practices) continue to influence current childrearing practices remains unclear. Different analyses and interpretation of these issues have been offered: from the maintenance of ancestral cultural traditions that are seen in different aspects of everyday family socialization practices (e.g., head shaving ceremony, Janeau, among Indo Caribbeans), to identity confusion (Escayg, 2014), and expressions of violence (Mason & Satchell, 2016). Moreover, it is often argued that matrifocality emerged out of the harsh treatment of families during slavery wherein males were marginalized (Brunod & Cook-Darzens, 2002).

For the current discussion it would be challenging to bridge exactly how the oppressive and inhumane conditions under slavery, indentured servitude, and the colonial experience are associated with existing patterns of childrearing and developmental sequelae. Following eco-cultural models and cultural theories (Greenfield, Keller, Fuligni, & Maynard, 2003), we acknowledge that these sociohistorical experiences by Caribbean peoples have had differing impacts on dimensions of family organization and social processes. But, harsh economic conditions and educational attainment may play significant roles in determining family structural organization patterns, childrearing styles, and investment in children today (Anderson, 2007; Samms-Vaughan, 2005). With this in mind, our goal is to discuss a few aspects of childrearing that have received increasing research attention and have long-term developmental implications for children: parental investment, parental beliefs about childrearing and development; parenting styles and practices; and academic, religious, and cultural (ethnic-racial) socialization.

Parental Investment

It has long been established that Caribbean women are the primary caregivers to children and that they invest more time in childrearing and household activities than men (Roopnarine et al., 1995). It is no secret that Caribbean women rear children with the assistance of multiple female caregivers sometimes in the absence of residential fathers or male caregivers. A national survey (Ricketts & Anderson, 2008) of parents in Jamaica offers newer insights into the daily activities between mothers and children. Unlike previous reports about the low levels of emotional investment among Caribbean parents (e.g., Leo-Rhynie, 1997), a majority of mothers talked with their young children regularly about their feelings and interests, praised, and hugged and kissed them; significant numbers engaged in recreational activities with children. A large-scale study in Trinidad and Tobago also indicated that caregivers across Indo, African, and Mixed-ethnic groups reported moderately high levels of positive parenting and material rewarding (Roopnarine et al., 2013). Similarly, high levels of warmth were reported among Indo Guyanese mothers and in a diverse sample of families in Trinidad and Tobago (Roopnarine et al., 2013, 2014). However, concerns remain about taking children's points of view and their worries into consideration during parent-child discourses in Jamaica and elsewhere. Many Caribbean parents are worried about relinquishing control over their children (Brown & Johnson, 2008).

In the area of cognitive investment in children, the data are equally as inconsistent. It is true that parents and teachers believe in the early academic training of children but they appear uncertain about the need for early stimulation (Charles & Williams, 2006). Parents are regularly faced with the challenge of providing shelter, food, and educational materials while attempting to meet the social and cognitive needs of children. Jamaican mothers and fathers reported engaging in play activities with children that are comparable to those in cultural settings around the world (Roopnarine, 2013). In a laboratory study comparing low birth weight and appropriate birth weight Jamaican infants, observations revealed that there were low levels of social and symbolic play between mothers and infants; vocalizations and object stimulation were also low. Mothers with higher levels of verbal intelligence provided more support for play during interactions than did mothers with lower verbal intelligence. Children spent most of their time away from objects or engaging in simple object manipulations despite significant differences in developmental quotient (as measured by the Griffiths Mental Developmental Scales) between the low and appropriate birth weight infants (Wachs, Chang, Walker, & Gardner, 2007). In another observational study that focused on early stimulation activities in high-risk families in St. Lucia, parents engaged in parallel activities or activities independent of children (Spijk, Rosenberg, & Jansenns 2008).

In short, from this meager body of work, the affectional distance that has been discussed in prior research may be changing wherein with greater educational attainment and economic ascendancy parents increasingly recognize the need to invest in positive stimulation activities with children. While some of this may be attributed to economic issues, men remain steadfast in their beliefs about biological fatherhood and traditional gender roles. Mate-shifting and migration continue to undermine men's cognitive and emotional investment in their offspring from current and previous mating unions. As will be seen in the next section, it is difficult to frame mothers' and fathers' parenting styles and practices within existing theories of socialization.

Parenting Styles and Practices

In a series of studies on parenting practices and styles, Roopnarine and his colleagues (Roopnarine et al., 2013; Roopnarine et al., 2014a, 2014b) examined parental warmth and control among samples of families in Trinidad and Tobago and Guyana. Guided by Baumrind's (1967) parenting typologies and Rohner's interpersonal acceptance-rejection theory (Rohner & Khaleque, 2005; see also chapter 5 in this volume) that emphasize the universal importance of parental warmth and the negative impact of controlling and rejecting parenting practices on childhood development, the aims of these studies were twofold: (a) to document the prevalence of different parental practices among diverse ethnic groups from different socioeconomic backgrounds and (b) to establish associations between warmth and control and childhood competence.

Overall, Caribbean families believe in obedience, unilateral respect, early academic training and competence, neatness, and control (Leo-Rhynie & Brown, 2013). Behavioral transgressions can be met with harsh treatment and denigration (e.g., labeling, demeaning the child). In some ethnic groups such as Indo Caribbeans in Trinidad, Guyana, and Suriname there is a tendency to be more indulgent during early childrearing than other ethnic groups in the region. The Javenese in Suriname believe in *rukun* (harmony), a prolonged period of relaxed childrearing during the first five years of life (Marshall & Van Der Wolf, 2013). As will become apparent, families in Caribbean cultural communities present a paradox in their childrearing strategies; they display high levels of warmth as well as high levels of control during early socialization practices.

Data indicate that families in both Guyana and Trinidad and Tobago used multiple forms of physical control as the predominant mode of disciplining preschool-aged children. For example, in a rural sample, 60% of Indo Guyanese mothers spanked their children, 30% slapped them, 30% shook them, 19% made children stand for a long period of time, and 14% shoved the child (Roopnarine et al., 2014a). A similar distribution of the use of different types of physical punishment was determined for Indo Trinidadian families (Roopnarine et al., 2013). High levels of endorsement and the use of physical punishment have been recorded in Barbados, Jamaica, Belize, and Suriname as well (Anderson & Payne, 1994; Brown & Johnson, 2008; Cappa & Khan, 2011). Socioeconomic status or geographical residence (rural or urban) did not influence the use of physical punishment, and the findings on the greater use of physical punishment with sons compared to daughters are equivocal (Roopnarine et al., 2014a). This does not necessarily mean that there is a change in the socialization of boys compared to girls because there is evidence to suggest that parents in Trinidad, Dominica, and Grenada hold on to traditional gendered views about childrearing (Barrow & Ince, 2008).

Not surprisingly, accompanying these harsh methods of discipline is the use of more authoritarian styles of parenting. By parenting style, we mean the emotive qualities that cut across parenting practices (Darling & Steinberg, 1993). Among Indo Caribbean families in Guyana and families from diverse ethnic groups in Trinidad and Tobago mothers displayed high levels of warmth that were comparable to those observed in other groups around the world (e.g., United States, Colombia, Italy, Jordan, Kenya, the Philippines, Thailand; Putnick et al., 2012). However, they also used high levels of control during parenting (Roopnarine et al., 2013). In these studies there were two clusters of families: one group was high in warmth and low in control, and the other was high in warmth and high in control. Trinidadian fathers' parenting practices were identical to the clusters found for the two groups of mothers. In a subsequent study conducted on a national representative sample of families in Trinidad and Tobago, again it was found that physical control was high among Indo, African, and individuals of Mixed-ethnic ancestry. But higher levels of control were found in African and Mixed-ethnic compared to Indo Caribbean families (Roopnarine et al., 2014b). This may be related to differences in beliefs about indulgence during early childhood among these ethnic groups.

In comparing parenting styles among families in Jamaica, the Bahamas, St. Kitts and Nevis, and St. Vincent, Lipps et al. (2012) found that the most prevalent parenting styles were authoritative (32.6%) and neglectful (28.4%). About 20.3% of children across countries experienced an authoritarian, and 18.7% experienced a permissive parenting style. A different pattern was found in St. Vincent where the predominant parenting style was neglectful (Lipps et al., 2012). By contrast, in a multiethnic Surinamese sample (East Indians, African Surinamese, Javanese, and Mixed-ethnic ancestry) there were no significant differences in parenting styles by ethnicity (Marshall et al., 2013), and in a rare study on children's perceptions of parenting styles, Ramkissoon (2002) reported that most Jamaican secondary school students saw their fathers in an authoritative light.

Our surmise is that significant numbers of Caribbean parents use parenting styles that would be considered less optimal for childrearing in developed societies. The combination of warmth and control does not fit neatly into well-formulated parenting frameworks and typologies (e.g., Baumrind's authoritarian, permissive, and authoritative styles). These attributes resemble the practices of some cultural groups in Asia where control is used as a child guidance technique or to show concern over children (Saraswathi & Dutta, 2010). Nonetheless, the meaning of different dimensions of control and their implications for childhood development in the Caribbean context need further attention.

Academic, Religious, and Ethnic Socialization

There are three other parenting practices that cut to the heart of childrearing in the Caribbean; academic, religious, and ethnic socialization. As introduced earlier, Caribbean parents place strong emphasis on early academic training that can sometimes be unrealistic and developmentally inappropriate. In a comparative analysis of parents' and teachers' beliefs about what children should learn in preschool in Jamaica, Guyana, St. Vincent, and the Grenadines, Leo-Rhynie, Minott, Gift, McBean, Scott, and Wilson (2009) found that parents overwhelmingly endorsed learning basic academic skills such as the alphabet and numbers. Likewise, assessments of parents' knowledge of basic developmental milestones among preschool-aged children in Trinidad and Tobago suggested that although a majority of parents understood when children acquire common cognitive and social skills, they had earlier developmental expectations of children in the academic domain (Roopnarine, Logie, Krishnakumar, Narine, & Davidson, 2015). Furthermore, parents in Trinidad and Tobago reported engaging in high levels of reading, writing, and working with number activities and in literacy-based activities such as reading and telling stories to children. Mothers engaged in higher levels of academic socialization than fathers across ethnic groups, which is possibly a result of mothers' greater involvement with children in general. Mixed-ethnic couples engaged in higher levels of academic socialization than Indo or African Caribbean groups.

How these beliefs and engagement in early academic activities translate into the acquisition of cognitive and social competence in children is largely unknown. Whether they are intended to assist children to break out of the cycle of poverty or to get a head start in life, beliefs and practices about early academic training are pervasive in Caribbean cultural communities and can add undue pressures on children to achieve beyond age-appropriate levels. Hothousing (i.e., involving children in the intense study of a topic to stimulate their minds) has been shown to create anxiety in children in other cultures (Burts, Hart, Charlesworth, & Kirk, 1990) and can negatively affect the treatment of children deemed delayed, "slow" or "stubborn." This may be particularly true for children who live in stressful economic and social environments.

In conjunction with academic socialization, Caribbean parents engage in a good deal of religious and ethnic or cultural socialization. While religious and spiritual socialization have common properties and focus on faith and related issues (Oser, Scarlett, & Bucher, 2006), ethnic-racial or cultural socialization involves imbuing children with ethnic pride, arming them with skills to deal with bias and discrimination, and exposing them to knowledge of their family's history and the accomplishments of their ethnic group (Hughes et al., 2006). Both types of socialization have been shown to serve a protective function against the effects of harsh home and neighborhood environments in multicultural societies (e.g., Caughy, Nettles, O'Campo, & Lohrfink, 2006; Letiecq, 2007). For example, harsh parenting influenced children's behavioral difficulties through ethnic socialization in Trinidad and Tobago (Roopnarine et al., 2014b) and church attendance was associated with greater family stability in terms of having a resident father in Jamaican families (Anderson, 2007).

Over two-thirds of families in Trindad and Tobago regularly attended places of worship; 84% prayed at home; and roughly 75% taught children religious beliefs. Furthermore, they engaged in high levels of ethnic socialization. There were ethnic differences in both religious and ethnic socialization among the three major groups in Trinidad and Tobago: Indo Caribbean caregivers engaged in more religious and ethnic socialization than African Caribbean and Mixed-ethnic caregivers. Interestingly, families with daughters engaged in more religious socialization than families with sons and caregivers in married families engaged in more religious socialization than those in unmarried families, as did families with better economic resources compared with those with limited economic resources. In short, across ethnic groups, caregivers in married families and those who had better economic resources regard spirituality as a key aspect of family and community life and accept the principles and doctrines of their religious faith as central to childrearing.

Immigrant Families, Parenting Practices, and Remote Acculturation

As can be seen in Table 6.2, migration from the Caribbean to the United States has increased steadily over the last two decades. Adults use diverse migration patterns: stair-step in which individuals from the poorer countries move to economically better-off countries (e.g., from Guyana to Trinidad and Tobago and Barbados) within the Caribbean and Latin America and then to the United States; serial migration in which one individual migrates first and then sends for others later on after attaining a measure of economic stability; persons migrate for schooling, business ventures, and seasonal work (e.g., farm laborers); entire families migrate as per U.S. immigration policies; and some individuals live transnational lives that transcend borders. Caribbean families/individuals in North America maintain strong ties to kinship members and friends in the home country. They send remittances to relatives via direct cash (individuals making trips) and more indirect means (wiring money, bank transfers), send material goods and clothing in "barrels" to children and relatives, make temporary trips to visit or vacation, find marital partners, and use Skype and Facebook to stay in touch with relatives and acquaintances.

Adjustment patterns to a new country vary tremendously depending on educational attainment, economic resources, family composition, length of separation from family members, familiarity with the new culture broadly speaking and in a more intimate sense through remote acculturation

Table 6.2 Caribbean Immigrant Population in the United States

Country	1990	2000	2010	2013
Barbados	43,015	52,170	52,829	52,499
Belize	29,957	40,150	47,197	50,296
Dominica	19,529	15,640	28,540	31,222
Grenada	17,730	29,270	29,110	32,820
Guyana	120,698	211,190	265,271	259,815
Haiti	225,393	419,315	587,149	593,980
Jamaica	334,140	553,825	659,771	714,743
Montserrat	3,493	3,905	NA	NA
St. Kitts and Nevis	7,447	11,055	5,910	NA
St. Lucia	6,959	13,525	NA	NA
St. Vincent and Grenadines	12,824	NA	23,088	23,868
Trinidad and Tobago	115,710	197,400	229,926	232,026

Sources: U.S. Census Bureau, Decennial Census 1990, 2000, and American Community Survey 2009–2013.

(Ferguson, in press), and the perceptions, attitudes, and behaviors of members of the new cultural community. Berry (1997; see also Berry & Vedder's chapter 12, this volume) has proposed four major adjustment scenarios among immigrants: separation (preference for natal culture practices), integration (combining elements of both cultures), marginalization (neither an orientation for natal nor new cultural practices), and assimilation (strong orientation to new culture). Individuals who combine elements of their ancestral culture with those of the new culture are presumed to have better educational and mental health outcomes (Berry, 1997), although some studies on immigrant families do not support this contention. Instead, they have found that a more insular approach whereby first-generation immigrant parents strongly emphasize natal culture values can have positive influences on children's educational achievement (e.g., Sanghavi, 2010). There are also transnationals who move from one cultural community to the next seemingly with relative ease and cosmopolitans who identify with their own culture but remain open to other cultural ways of thinking and knowing (Glick Schiller, Bach, & Blanc-Szanton, 1992; Glick Schiller, Darieva, & Gruner-Domic, 2011).

Until recently there has been little consideration of the concept of remote acculturation, "introduced as a modern form of non-migrant acculturation prompted by indirect and/or intermittent intercultural contact via newer forms of globalization such as information and communication technologies (ICT including cell phones, cable television, and internet) and multinational fast food companies" (Ferguson & Bornstein, 2012). However brief, social contacts through tourism, travel, and the exchange of material goods have transformed the lives of innumerable individuals around the world (Jensen, Arnett, & McKenzie, 2011). Because of the high levels of personal and media contacts between Caribbean parents and children and the diverse ethnic groups in the United States and Canada, the likelihood exists that such exposure may lead some Caribbean families to develop an orientation toward the behaviors and values of groups in the United States. Recent research on Caribbean youth illustrates such a movement.

To assess remote acculturation, Ferguson and Bornstein (2012) measured acculturation behaviors (orientation toward different cultures through social participation in entertainment activities, friendships, use of language, etc.), identity (degree of identification with different cultural groups), and values (obligations that children should have toward parents and family, and the rights of children in the family) in Jamaican families. Cluster analyses revealed two groups of adolescents; those with a bicultural profile or "Americanized Jamaicans" (33% of sample) who were high in orientation to Jamaican culture and high in orientation to European American culture reported lower family obligations, higher discrepancies among generations regarding intergenerational obligations, and higher parent-adolescent conflict as compared to a second cluster of "traditional Jamaicans" (67% of sample). The latter group was high in orientation to Jamaican culture and low in orientation to European American culture, reported stronger family obligations, lower intergenerational obligations discrepancies, and low parent-adolescent conflict. Interestingly, the orientation of Americanized Jamaicans to European American culture was similar to those of Jamaican immigrant adolescents residing in the United States. However, "traditional Jamaicans" and "Americanized Jamaican" adolescents had similar orientations toward African American culture (e.g., enjoy entertainment/TV shows). A small number of Jamaican mothers (11%) displayed a bicultural profile. These findings have implications for parent-child relationships in the Caribbean and among Caribbean immigrants in North America where parents must contend with the cultural orientation of their adolescents and their own childrearing practices and beliefs in a globalized world. Intergenerational discrepancies in family obligations and expectations have been shown to contribute to adjustment difficulties in both Caribbean and Caribbean immigrant children (Arnold, 1997; Sharpe & Schafie, in press).

Research on childrearing patterns among Caribbean immigrants in North America indicates that certain parenting practices that are observed in the Caribbean remain with families, at least during the initial period of adjustment to a new cultural community. Two studies (DeYoung & Zigler, 1994; Roopnarine, Krishnakumar, & Li, 2009) conducted in North America revealed that Caribbean immigrants living in New York City and northern New Jersey held on to traditional beliefs about the division of household and childcare responsibilities and employed more authoritarian parenting practices, and that Caribbean immigrants in Canada were dogmatic about maintaining physical methods of disciplining children (Hassan, Rosseau, Measham, & Lashley, 2008). Over time, these rigid views about parent-child relationships and parenting styles are likely to become modified as Caribbean immigrant families increasingly come into contact with the demands of democratic modes of childrearing practices in North America.

Family Socialization Practices and Cognitive and Social Childhood Outcomes

In view of the diverse mating patterns, family structural arrangements, and sometimes harsh parental treatment, there have been more attempts to link proximal and distal family processes in Caribbean families to childhood outcomes. Data on the associations between family stability, parenting style and parenting practices, and children's behavioral skills and cognitive performance are still sparse. Nonetheless, the findings of a few studies are instructive. In the Preschool Profiles Project in Jamaica, Samms-Vaughan (2005) found that child-shifting and multiple father figures were associated with behavioral difficulties in Jamaican children (e.g., social withdrawal) and positive family functioning was associated with lower health risks (e.g., suicides and emotional distress) in older children across Caribbean countries (Halcon et al., 2003). In related work on preschool-aged children, harsh parental treatment in the form of physical punishment was directly related to behavioral difficulties in children from Indo Guyanese as well as in Indo, African, and Mixed-ethnic families in Trinidad and Tobago (Roopnarine et al., 2013, 2014b). The last set of findings seems to contradict the hypothesis proposed by researchers in North America that the impact of physical punishment may be mediated via other parental processes in cultural settings in which physical punishment is normative (see Lansford, 2010, for a discussion of these issues).

In the cross-country comparisons of parenting styles in the Bahamas, St. Kitts and Nevis, Jamaica, and St. Vincent discussed earlier, Lipps and his colleagues found that perceived authoritarian and neglectful parenting styles were associated with more depressive symptoms in adolescents. Parallel findings were obtained for Indo-Guyanese families in which higher levels of behavioral control were related to poorer behavioral outcomes in children (Roopnarine et al., 2013); moreover, among Caribbean immigrants living in the New York City area, authoritarian parenting was negatively related to children's social skills (Roopnarine, Krishnakumar, Metindogan, & Evans, 2006). These associations are in line with propositions included in Baumrind's parenting styles framework (1967, 1996) as well as in Rohner's (Rohner & Khaleque, 2005) interpersonal acceptance-rejection theory that less warm and more controlling parenting undermines optimal childrearing outcomes. In most cultural settings, the authoritative parenting style appears to be associated with positive behavioral outcomes in young children. In other words, parental warmth and sensitivity promote the development of intellectual and social skills (as was shown in a meta-analysis by Khaleque & Rohner, 2012a), whereas high levels of parental physical (e.g., physical punishment, physically restricting child), psychological (e.g., making the child feel guilty, worthless), and behavioral (e.g., restriction, too much structure) control are associated with both internalizing and externalizing behaviors in children (see meta-analyses by Gershoff, 2002; Khaleque & Rohner, 2012b).

Predictably, poor economic resources, crowded living conditions, and instability in living arrangements were all associated with lower cognitive performance in Jamaican preschool-aged children. Children in married households performed better academically and had better cognitive scores than children in other family arrangements. Children who lived with biological fathers and surrogate mothers also had academic difficulties which could be attributed to a lack of emotional connection with temporary caregiving figures. As in several other studies, mothers' and fathers' educational levels were positively associated with children's cognitive performance (Samms-Vaughan, 2005). Additional research in this area indicates that preschoolers in Indo-Guyanese families who received high levels of parental warmth and low levels of control performed better academically than those who received high levels of warmth and moderately high levels of behavioral control (Roopnarine et al., 2013). Moreover, authoritarian parenting negatively affected the development of children's language skills among Caribbean immigrants in the United States (Roopnarine et al., 2006). Surprisingly, paternal warmth and affection did not show a significant association with children's cognitive skills in a diverse sample of Trinidadian families (Roopnarine et al., 2013). Furthermore, in Indo, African, Mixed-ethnic families in Trinidad and Tobago, other factors such as neighborhood characteristics, conduct problems, family income, and education were better predictors of children's early cognitive skills than parenting practices per se (Roopnarine, Logie, Krishnakumar, Narine, & Davidson, 2015). Whereas appropriate and adequate parenting practices are important for laying the foundation for children's early cognitive and social competence, in harsh ecological niches processes external to the family may assuage the best laid parental approaches to childrearing.

It is safe to say that certain parental styles and practices, poor economic conditions, childhood characteristics, and family structural arrangements are important predictors of children's cognitive and social skills in Caribbean families. Within a preventative science approach, several reviews (e.g., Maharaj, Nunes, & Renwick, 2009) have identified risk and resilience factors within families and communities that may guard against or at the very least attenuate the developmental risks associated with living in difficult family and neighborhood environments (Holmes et al., 2010). It was proposed that ethnic socialization and religiosity may mediate the associations between harsh parenting and childhood outcomes in difficult ecological niches. As in other cultural communities, ethnic socialization did mediate the association between maternal parenting practices and children's prosocial behaviors and behavioral difficulties but somewhat differently in ethnic groups in Trinidad and Tobago. For Indo and Mixed-ethnic Caribbean families, the association between positive parenting and prosocial behaviors was partially mediated via ethnic socialization; for African Caribbean families, positive parenting had a more direct association with children's prosocial behaviors. Comparable research on the mediating or moderating role of religiosity on the association between parenting practices and childhood outcomes in Caribbean countries was difficult to find. A Jamaican study did show that religiosity, as measured by church membership and church attendance, was related to greater commitment to fathering and less stereotyped views about masculinity among Jamaican men (Anderson, 2007) which augers well for paternal investment in children and partner-relationships. The nature of the relationship between partners appears crucial to men's investment in young children in other societies (Cabrera, Ryan, Mitchell, Shannon, & Tamis-LeMonda, 2008).

CONCLUDING COMMENTS

In English-speaking Caribbean societies, entry into parenthood occurs in diverse mating unions in which fathers may not reside with their children. Marriage and father co-residence is more commonly associated with Indo Caribbean than African Caribbean families. Irrespective of mating unions, male and female roles remain largely traditional. Parenting practices within the different mating systems are characterized by high levels of warmth and control. With continued large-scale population movement and increased cultural contact between Caribbean peoples and North Americans, some Caribbean youths and parents develop an orientation toward North American behaviors and values. Not unlike other cultural groups, unstable adult relationships, poor material resources, and harsh parental treatment have negative consequences on children's intellectual and social development. Ethnic-racial or cultural socialization seems to serve a protective function against harsh parenting practices and poor neighborhood conditions.

Like other developing societies, Caribbean nations have made significant strides in the health care and early childhood education areas. Yet these small nation-states have not adequately addressed such issues as harsh parenting, multiple mating patterns, escalating crime, domestic violence, and other risk factors that predispose young children to behavioral and emotional difficulties and lower educational achievement. To be fair, attempts have been made to improve parenting quality through early intervention programs (e.g., the Roving Caregivers Programme in Jamaica and SERVOL in Trinidad and Tobago). However, much more needs to be done at the policy level to systematically implement programs using different media (smartphones, webinars, etc.) and community approaches to improve parenting quality and increase men's economic and emotional investment in their families. On the research front, there should be an increased focus on identifying neighborhood and family factors that insulate children from harsh economic and social conditions at the individual, community, and societal levels.

REFLECTIVE QUESTIONS

1. How are parenting practices in Caribbean different from those in other cultural settings?
2. Does parental endorsement of physical punishment influence its association with childhood development?

3. How does mateshifting influence childhood development?
4. Do family protective factors attenuate the impact of harsh home and neighborhood environments on children's cognitive and social development?

SUGGESTED READINGS

Books and Articles

Chevannes, B. (2001). *Learning to be a man: Culture, socialization and gender identity in five Caribbean countries.* Kingston, Jamaica: University of the West Indies Press.

Logie, C., & Roopnarine, J. L. (2013). *Issues and perspectives in early childhood development and education in Caribbean Countries.* La Romaine, Trinidad: Caribbean Publishers.

Roopnarine, J. L., & Chadee, D. (2016). (Eds.). *Caribbean psychology: Indigenous contributions to a global discipline.* Washington, DC: American Psychological Association.

Singh, P., & Izarali, M. R. (2013). *The contemporary Caribbean: Issues and challenges.* New Delhi, India: Shipra Publications.

Websites

http://sta.uwi.edu/fhe/fdcrc/
Contains resources on research activities on and programs for children and families in Caribbean cultural communities.

http://www.unicef.org/easterncaribbean/resources.html
Provides profiles of Caribbean families and children, care, and a variety of other issues concerning human development.

REFERENCES

Anderson, P. (2007). *The changing roles of fathers in the context of Jamaican family life.* Kingston, Jamaica: Planning Institute of Jamaica and the University of the West Indies.

Anderson, S., & Payne, M. (1994). Corporal punishment in elementary education: Views of Barbadian school children. *Child Abuse and Neglect, 18,* 377–386.

Arnold, E. (1997). Issues in re-unification of migrant West Indian children in the United Kingdom. In J. L. Roopnarine & J. Brown (Eds.), *Caribbean families: Diversity among ethnic groups* (pp. 243–258). Norwood, NJ: Ablex.

Bandura, A. (1986). *Social foundations of thought and action: A social cognitive theory.* Englewood Cliffs, NJ: Prentice Hall.

Barrow, C., & Ince, M. (2008). *Early childhood in the Caribbean.* Working Papers in Early Childhood Development. The Hague, Netherlands: Bernard van Leer Foundation.

Baumrind, D. (1967). Child care practices anteceding three patterns of preschool behavior. *Genetic Psychology Monographs, 75,* 43–88.

Baumrind, D. (1996). Parenting: The discipline controversy revisited. *Family Relations, 45,* 405–414.

Berry, J. W. (1997). Immigration, acculturation, and adaptation. *Applied Psychology, 46*(1), 5–34. doi: 10.1111/j.1464–0597.1997.tb01087.x

Brodber, E. (1975). *A study of yards in the city of Kingston*. Mona, Jamaica: Institute for Social and Economic Research: Mona, Jamaica: University of the West Indies.

Bronfenbrenner, U., & Morris, P. A. (2006). The bioecological model of human development. In R. Lerner (Ed.), *Handbook of child psychology* (6th ed., pp. 793–828). Hoboken, NJ: Wiley.

Brown, J., & Johnson, S. (2008). Child rearing and child participation in Jamaican families. *International Journal of Early Years Education, 16*, 31–41.

Brunod, R., & Cook-Darzens, S. (2002). Men's role and fatherhood in French Caribbean families: A multi-systemic resource approach. *Clinical Child Psychology & Psychiatry, 7*, 559–569.

Burton, L. M., Bonilla-Silva, E., Ray V., Buckelew, R., & Freeman, E. H. (2010). Critical race theories, colorism, and the decade's research on families of color. *Journal of Marriage and the Family, 72*, 440–459.

Burts, D. C., Hart, C. H., Charlesworth, R., & Kirk, L. (1990). A comparison of frequencies of stress behaviors observed in kindergarten children in classrooms with developmentally appropriate versus developmentally inappropriate instructional practices. *Early Childhood Research Quarterly, 5*(3), 407–423.

Cabrera, N. J., Ryan, R. M., Mitchell, S. J., Shannon, J. D., Tamis-LeMonda, C. S. (2008). Low-income nonresident father involvement with their toddlers: Variation by fathers' race and ethnicity. *Journal of Family Psychology, 22*, 643–647.

Cabrera, N., & Tamis-LeMonda, C. (Eds.). (2013). *Handbook of father involvement*. New York: Routledge Press.

Cappa, C., & Kahn, S. M. (2011). Understanding caregivers' attitudes towards physical punishment of children: Evidence from 34 low- and middle-income countries. *Child Abuse and Neglect, 35*, 1009–1021.

Caughy, M. O. B., Nettles, S. M., O'Campo, P. J., & Lohrfink, K. F. (2006). Neighborhood matters: Racial socialization of African American children. *Child Development, 77*, 1220–1236.

Central Intelligence Agency. (2014). Central America and Caribbean. In *The world factbook*. Retrieved from https://www.cia.gov/library/publications/the-world-factbook/wfbExt/region_cam.html

Charles, L., & Williams, S. (2006). *Early childhood care and education in the Caribbean Region (CARICOM States)*. Background Paper for the Education for All: Global Monitoring Report 2007. Paris: UNESCO.

Chevannes, B. (2001). *Learning to be a man: Culture, socialisation and gender identity in five Caribbean communities*. Kingston, Jamaica: The University of the West Indies Press.

Clarke, E. (1957). *My mother who fathered me: A study of family in three selected communities in Jamaica*. London: George Allen & Unwin.

Darling, N., & Steinberg, L. (1993). Parenting style as context: An integrative model. *Psychological Bulletin, 113*, 487–496.

DeYoung, Y., & Zigler, E. (1994). Machismo in two cultures: Relations to childrearing practice. *American Journal of Orthopsychiatry, 64*, 386–395.

Escayg, K.-A. (2014). *Parenting and pedagogical practices: The racial socialization and racial identity of preschool Trinidadian children*. Unpublished doctoral dissertation, University of Toronto, Canada.

Ferguson, G. (in press). Remote acculturation and the birth of an Americanized Caribbean youth identity on the Islands. In J. L. Roopnarine & D. Chadee (Eds.), *Caribbean psychology: Developmental, health, social, and clinical issues* (pp. 97–118). Washington, DC: American Psychological Association.

Ferguson, G.M., & Bornstein, M.H. (2012). Remote acculturation: The "Americanization" of Jamaican Islanders. *International Journal of Behavioral Development, 36*(3), 167–177. doi:10.1177/0165025412437066

Flinn, M. (1992). Paternal care in a Caribbean village. In B. Hewlett (Ed.), *Father-child relations: Cultural and biosocial contexts* (pp. 57–84). New York: Aldine de Gruyter.

Gershoff, E.T. (2002). Corporal punishment by parents and associated child behaviors and experiences: A meta-analytic and theoretical review. *Psychological Bulletin, 128*, 539–579.

Glick Schiller, N., Bach, L., & Blanc-Szanton, C. (1992). Transnationalism: A new analytic framework for understanding migration. *Annals of the New York Academy of Science, 645*, 1–24. doi:10.1111/j.1749-6632.1992.tb33484.x

Glick Schiller, N., Darieva, T., & Gruner-Domic, S. (2011). Defining cosmopolitan sociability in a transnational age: An introduction. *Ethnic and Racial Studies, 34*(3), 399–418. doi: 10.1080/01419870.2011.533781

Greenfield, P. M., Keller, H., Fuligni, A., & Maynard, A. (2003). Cultural pathways through universal development. *Annual Review of Psychology, 54*, 461–490.

Halcon, L., Blum, R.W., Beuhring, T., Pate, E., Campbell-Forrester, S., & Venema, A. (2003). Adolescent health in the Caribbean: Risk and protective factors. *American Journal of Public Health, 93*, 456–460.

Hassan, G., Rousseau, C., Measham, T., & Lashley, M. (2008). Caribbean and Filipino adolescents' and parents' perspectives of parental authority, physical punishment, and cultural values and their relation to migratory status. *Canadian Ethnic Studies, 40(2)*, 171–186.

Holmes, E.K., Galovan, A. M., Yoshida, K., & Hawkins, A. (2010). Meta-analysis of effectiveness of resident fathering programs: Are family life educators interested in fathers? *Family Relations, 59*, 240–252.

Hughes, D., Rodriguez, J., Smith, E.P., Johnson, D.E., Stevenson, H.C., & Spicer, P. (2006). Parents' ethnic-racial socialization practices: A review of research and directions for future study. *Developmental Psychology, 42*, 747–770.

Jensen, L.A., Arnett, J.J., & McKenzie, J. (2011). Globalization and cultural identity developments in adolescence and emerging adulthood. In S.J. Schwartz, K. Luyckx, & V.L. Vignoles (Eds.), *Handbook of identity theory and research* (pp. 285–301). New York: Springer.

Khaleque, A., & Rohner, R.P. (2012a). Pancultural associations between perceived parental acceptance-rejection and psychological adjustment of children and adults: A meta-analytic review of worldwide research. *Journal of Cross-Cultural Psychology, 43*, 784–800.

Khaleque, A., & Rohner, R.P. (2012b). Transnational relations between perceived parental acceptance-rejection and personality dispositions of children and adults: A meta-analytic review of worldwide research. *Personality and Social Psychology Review,16*, 103–115.

Lansford, J.E. (2010). The special problem of cultural differences in effects of corporal punishment. *Law and Contemporary Problems, 73*, 89–106. Retrieved from http://scholarship.law.duke.edu/lcp/vol73/iss2/5

Leo-Rhynie, E. (1997). Class, race, and gender issues in child rearing in the Caribbean. In J.L. Roopnarine & J. Brown (Eds.), *Caribbean families: Diversity among ethnic groups* (pp. 25–55). Norwood, NJ: Ablex.

Leo-Rhynie, E., & Brown, J. (2013). Child rearing practices in the Caribbean in the early childhood years. In C. Logie & J.L. Roopnarine (Eds.), *Issues and perspectives in early childhood education in the Caribbean* (pp. 30–62*)*. La Romaine, Trinidad and Tobago: Caribbean Publishers.

Leo-Rhynie, E., Minott, C., Gift, S., McBean, M., Scott, A-K., & Wilson, K. (2009). *Competencies of children in Guyana, rural Jamaica and St. Vincent and the Grenadines making the transition from pre- to primary school with special emphasis on gender differences.* Dudley Grant Memorial Trust for Caribbean Child Support Initiative of the Bernard van Leer Foundation. Kingston, Jamaica.

Letiecq, B. L. (2007). African American fathering in violent neighborhoods: What role does spirituality play? *Fathering, 5*(2), 111–128.

Lipps, G., Lowe, G. A., Gibson, R. C., Halliday, S., Morris, A., Clarke, N., & Wilson, R. N. (2012). Parenting and depressive symptoms among adolescents in four Caribbean societies. *Child & Adolescent Psychiatry & Mental Health, 6,* 31–42.

Logie, C., & Roopnarine, J. L. (Eds.). (2013). *Issues and perspectives in early childhood development and education in Caribbean countries.* La Romaine, Trinidad: Caribbean Publishers.

Maharaj, R. G., Nunes, P., & Renwick, S. (2009). Health risk behaviours among adolescents in the English-speaking Caribbean: A review. *Child and Adolescent Psychiatry and Mental Health, 3(1),* 3–10.

Marshall, E., & Van Der Wolf, K. (2013). The perceptions of child-rearing among Surinamese teachers and parents. *International Journal of Parents and Education, 7,* 1–7.

Mason, G., & Satchell, N. (2016). Interpersonal violence in the Caribbean: Etiology, prevalence, and impact. In J. L. Roopnarine & D. Chadee (Eds.), *Caribbean psychology: Developmental, health, social, and clinical issues* (pp. 205–233). Washington, DC: American Psychological Association.

Oser, F. K., Scarlett, G., & Bucher, A. (2006). Religious and spiritual development throughout the life span. In W. Damon & R. M. Lerner (Eds.), Handbook of child psychology: Vol. 1. Theoretical models of human development (6th ed., pp. 942–998). Hoboken, NJ: Wiley.

Putnick, D., Bornstein, M. H., Lansford, J. E., Chang, L., Deater-Deckard, K., Di Giunta, L., . . . Bombi, A. S. (2012). Agreement in mother and father acceptance-rejection, warmth, and hostility/rejection/neglect of children across nine cultures. *Cross-Cultural Research, 46,* 191–223.

Ramkissoon, M. W. (2002). *The psychology of fathering in the Caribbean: An investigation of the physical and psychological presence of the Jamaican father.* Unpublished master's thesis, The University of West Indies, Mona, Jamaica.

Ricketts, H., & Anderson, P. (2008). The impact of poverty and stress on the interaction of Jamaican caregivers with young children*. International Journal of Early Years Education, 16* (1), 61–74.

Rohner, R. P., & Khaleque, A. (Eds.). (2005). *Handbook for the study of parental acceptance and rejection.* Storrs, CT: Rohner Research Publications.

Roopnarine, J. L. (2013). Fathers in Caribbean cultural communities. In D. Shwalb, B. Shwalb, & M. E. Lamb (Eds.), *Fathers in cultural context* (pp. 203–227). New York: Rutledge.

Roopnarine, J. L., Brown, J., White, P. S., Riegraf, N. B., Crossely, D., Hossain, Z., & Webb, W. (1995). Father involvement in childcare and household work in common-law low income dual-earner and single-earner Jamaican families. *Journal of Applied Developmental Psychology, 16,* 35–52.

Roopnarine, J.L., & Evans, M., & Pant, P. (2011). Parent-child relationships in African and Indian Caribbean families: A social psychological assessment. In D. Chadee & A. Kostic (Eds.), *Social psychological dynamics* (pp. 147–171). Mona, Jamaica: The University of the West Indies Press.

Roopnarine, J.J., & Jin, B. (2016). Family socialization practices and childhood development in Caribbean cultural communities. In J.L. Roopnarine & D. Chadee (Eds.), *Caribbean psychology: Indigenous contributions to a global discipline* (pp. 71–96). Washington, DC: American Psychological Association.

Roopnarine, J.L., Jin, B., & Krishnakumar, A. (2014a). Do Guyanese mothers' levels of warmth moderate the association between harshness and justness of physical punishment and preschoolers' prosocial behaviours and anger? *International Journal of Psychology, 49*(4), 271–279. doi:10.1002/ijop.12029

Roopnarine, J.L., Krishnakumar, A., Metindogan, A., & Evans, M. (2006). Links among parenting styles, academic socialization, and the early academic and social skills of pre-kindergarten and kindergarten-age children of English-speaking Caribbean immigrants. *Early Childhood Research Quarterly, 21*, 238–252.

Roopnarine, J.L., Krishnakumar, A., Narine, L., Logie, C., & Lape, M.E. (2014b). Relationships between parenting practices and preschoolers' social skills in African, Indo, and mixed-ethnic families in Trinidad and Tobago: The mediating role of ethnic socialization. *Journal of Cross-Cultural Psychology, 45*(3), 362–380. doi:10.1177/0022022113509884

Roopnarine, J. L., & Krishnakumar, A., & Xu, Yi-Li (2009). Beliefs about mothers' and fathers' roles and the division of childcare and household labor in Indo Caribbean immigrants with young children. *Cultural Diversity and Ethnic Minority Psychology, 15*, 173–182.

Roopnarine, J.L., Logie, C., Davidson, K.L., Krishnakumar, A., & Narine, L. (in press). Caregivers' knowledge about children's development in three ethnic groups in Trinidad and Tobago. *Parenting Science and Practice.*

Roopnarine, J.L., Wang, Y., Krishnakumar, A., & Davidson, K. (2013). Parenting practices in Guyana and Trinidad and Tobago: Connections to preschoolers' social and cognitive skills. *Interamerican Journal of Psychology, 47*(2), 313–327.

Samms-Vaughn, M. (2005). *The Jamaican pre-school child: The status of early childhood development in Jamaica.* Kingston, Jamaica: Planning Institute of Jamaica.

Sanghavi, T. (2010). *Factors influencing Asian Indian American children's academic performance.* Unpublished doctoral dissertation, Syracuse University.

Saraswathi, T.S., & Dutta, R. (2010). India. In M. Bornstein (Ed.), *Handbook of cultural developmental science* (pp. 465–483). New York: Psychology Press.

Seetahal, D. (2014, April 24). Corporal punishment and children, *Trinidad Express*, Port of Spain, Trinidad and Tobago.

Sharpe, J., & Schafe, S. (in press). Mental health in the Caribbean. In J. L. Roopnarine & D. Chadee (Eds.), *Developmental, health, social, and clinical psychology: Contributions from Caribbean psychology.* Washington, DC: American Psychological Association.

Simey, T.S. (1946). *Welfare and planning in the West Indies.* London, UK: Oxford University Press.

Smith, R. (1957). *The Negro family in British Guiana.* London, UK: Routledge and Kegan Paul.

Spijk, J.V., Rosenberg, C., Janssens, W. (2008). *RCP impact evaluation in St. Lucia.* Amsterdam, Netherlands: Amsterdam Institute for International Development.

UNDP Caribbean Human Development Report. (2012). *Human development and the shift to better citizen security.* Retrieved from http://hdr-caribbean.regionalcentrelac-undp.org/images/PDF/caribbean_hdr2012.pdf

U.S. Census Bureau. (2014). Measuring America: Decennial Censuses 1990–2000. Retrieved from http://www.census.gov/prod/www/decennial.html

U.S. Census Bureau. (2013). American Community Survey 2009–2013. Retrieved from http://www.census.gov/acs/www/

Wachs, T.D., Chang, S.M., Walker, S.P., & Gardner, J.M.M. (2007). Relation of birth weight, maternal intelligence and mother-child interactions to cognitive and play competence of Jamaican two-year old children. *Intelligence, 35,* 605–622.

Whiting, B.B., & Whiting, J.W. (1975). *Children of six cultures: A psycho-cultural analysis.* Cambridge, MA: Harvard University Press.

Wong, C.A., Eccles, J.S., & Sameroff, A.J. (2003). The influence of ethnic discrimination and ethnic identification on African-Americans adolescents' school and socioemotional adjustment. *Journal of Personality, 71,* 1197–1232.

7

Parents and Childcare in South Korean and Japanese Families

Jung-Hwan Hyun, Jun Nakazawa, David W. Shwalb, and Barbara J. Shwalb

This chapter focuses on contemporary and traditional issues concerning parents, children, and families in the Republic of Korea (South Korea) and Japan. North Korean society is excluded from this chapter because research on parents and childrearing is available only for South Korea (referred to as "Korea" throughout the chapter). We discuss Korea and Japan together here because of their geographical proximity in East Asia (only 124 miles between the cities of Busan, ROK, and Fukuoka, Japan), because of their shared cultural, historical, and religious heritage (Fairbank, 1965), and because they are both economically and technologically advanced and Westernized Asian societies. In addition, the social, economic, and historical contexts of contemporary parenting and child development, and the changing roles of women and men have many similarities (and notable differences) between Koreans and Japanese, as we have noted in previous literature reviews on East Asian fathering (e.g., Shwalb, Nakazawa, Yamamoto, & Hyun, 2010) and Asian childrearing (e.g., Shwalb, Shwalb, Nakazawa, Hyun, Le, & Satiadarma, 2009).

Table 7.1, adapted from the *CIA World Factbook,* illustrates some of the demographic similarities between these two societies. For example, they share a very slight sex ratio imbalance (with more male births), a relatively high mean population age, low fertility rates, highly urbanized populations, high per capita incomes, low infant mortality rates, high life expectancies, and relatively small land masses. It is particularly interesting for us to observe differences in parents and childrearing between the two societies in light of their shared cultural heritage and demographic characteristics.

Table 7.1 Selected Demographic Characteristics of Korea and Japan

	Population	M/F Sex Ratio (births)	Mean Age	Fertility Rate	Percentage of Urban Population	Per Capita GDP	Infant Mortality (/1000)	Life Expectancy	Land Area (Sq km)
South Korea	49,039,986	1.07	40.2	1.25	83.2%	$33,200	3.93	79.8	99,720
Japan	127,103,388	1.06	46.1	1.4	91.3%	$37,100	2.13	84.46	377,915

Source: *The World Factbook* (https://www.cia.gov)

SOUTH KOREA

A 37-year-old father and his wife both work as school teachers, and they have two daughters, one 8-year-old and the other 10-months-old. This father feels uncertain about his ability to raise his children as he does not know if their development is normal and because the current environment is different from the times when he was growing up. He is unsure if he is taking care of the children correctly or understands their needs, but he loves them because they are his children and he has a sense of accomplishment as a father. He feels a little sorry for his children in that his sources of satisfaction come mostly from outside of family life. His approach to childrearing is very different from that of his wife, which sometimes causes conflicts between the two. As a father, he needs his wife to recognize his involvement, and encouragement from his wife indeed enhances his pleasure as a nurturing father. He feels joy from his relationships with the children and wants his wife to make the children aware of this involvement and to praise his efforts.

The father in this case story exemplified many of the widespread feelings, expectations, and problems of South Korean fathers. In sum, he was dedicated to his childrearing responsibilities, yet his difficulty in understanding children's thoughts and feelings made him doubt his ability as a parent. In addition, Korean society at large generally values men's efforts at work more than their childrearing efforts and abilities. This father sensed that his childrearing behavior and understanding of the children differed from that of his wife, but he felt special pleasure when she recognized his value as a parent.

Trends in Korean Family Life

Changing Paternal Role. Korean fathers were by tradition responsible for the lives of their dependents as patriarchs, while mothers were in charge of childcare and housework. However, the structure and function of these family roles changed in response to evolving socioeconomic conditions. Specifically, childrearing in the 21st century became the joint responsibility of both husband and wife, and men are now typically expected to take an active role in childcare. This trend has been observed in the contexts of (a) an increase in dual-income households, (b) a new belief that childrearing and housework should be shared fairly between husband and wife, (c) the prevalence of nuclear families, and (d) an increase in single-father households resulting from a growing divorce rate (Kwon, 2013).

The traditional ideal of an authoritative and strict figure has been replaced by a stronger desire to be a friend-like, intimate father who expresses as much love and concern for his children as mothers do (Nam & Chung, 2013). This change appears to be particularly true of fathers who, as children in the 1970s and 1980s, lived through a period of social, cultural, and economic stress. Many desire to be the liberated and friend-like parent they had wished their own patriarchal fathers had been. A recent survey of 279 mothers and 288 fathers of infant children found that the contemporary image of the ideal Korean father has changed. Specifically, 35.8% of men indicated that fathers should be the child's playmate while a comparable 31.5% believed in counseling the child (respecting the child's ideas; understanding his or her thoughts and feelings), and 18.9% advocated for emotional support (expressing encouragement and love for the child; expressing many emotions and acting like a friend). The roles of financial provider (4.6%) and disciplinarian (4.3%) were relatively less important to these men's image of the ideal father. Mothers' perceptions of the ideal father were quite similar to those of their husbands (35.2% for playmate, 34.5% for counselor, 18.6% to provide emotional support, 1.7% to provide for one's dependents, and 5.2% to discipline the child) (Kim, 2011).

By comparison, children's perceptions of their fathers' roles have provided somewhat different results. First, in a study of 900 elementary school students, the most common image of fathers among children was that of "economic provider," followed in order of frequency by fathers as "exhausted by work" and "like a friend." The latter image of fathers as friends was especially notable among girls' compared with boys' images (Cho, 2010, 2011). Elsewhere, a survey of 400 junior and senior high school students indicated that the predominant images they have of their fathers include that of an economic provider, a mature personality, and a counselor to his children. In another gender comparison, more girls reported images of their fathers as loving and gentle, whereas boys took more notice of their fathers as exhausted by work and inaccessible, especially in their high school years (Choi & Cho, 2005). Finally, a sample of 359 university students (Lee & Oh, 2011) perceived fathers as devoted to their families and sacrificing for children, although the level of their reported father-child intimacy was low.

Changing Maternal Role. Since 1980, higher education of women have become normative, with 82.4% attending college in 2012 as opposed to 63.9% in 1999; women now have a higher college attendance rate than men's 81.6%. In addition, married women's participation rate in the labor force increased from 14% in the 1970s to 41% in 2010 and 43.5% in 2012, resulting in a dramatic shift to two-income households. As a result, the traditional place of mothers at home is now called into question and married couples typically expect to share housework and childcare (Chu, 2010; Kim & Chong, 2003).

Motherhood was by tradition the most central aspect of female identity, but in the current environment young women typically agree that marriage "requires employment" or "is an option." For example, Nam and Chung (2013) described the growing tendency for married women to have no children. Kong and Lee (2012) reported that the percentage of married women between the ages of 20 and 44 years with no children was 7.2% in 2005 but had already increased to 9.0% in 2009. This occurred for various reasons such as having negative experiences growing up (e.g., abuse by parents, marital conflict between one's parents), a sense that it is a burden to be a parent (e.g., in both childbearing and childrearing), personal values (e.g., no longer equating marriage with childbearing), awareness of negative aspects of raising children (e.g., the burden of education and childcare expenses), desire for self-realization and personal growth, and infertility. The 21st-century South Korean household is thus characterized by a growing tendency to have only one or two children, or no children at all. At the same time, the average age of marriage has gradually increased among Korean women. The National Statistical Office (2014) reported that the average age of marriage increased from 24.8 years in 1990 to 26.5 years in 2000 and to 29.8 years in 2014. This means that women's modal age for their first childbirth has been delayed into their 30s (Kwon, 2004).

Waning of Preference for Boys. The 21st century also witnessed a shift in societal values toward favoring sons over daughters. That is, the Confucian ideology that led parents to prefer male children for the sake of passing on the family lineage or obtaining assistance with work has weakened. Indeed, a 2010 report showed that 37% of fathers would rather have a daughter than a son (*Dong-A Ilbo*, 2010). In light of this trend toward a preference for daughters, the past demographic problem of a gender imbalance (i.e., overabundance of boys) is resolving itself. We believe that this trend reflects a loss of boys' instrumental value for working at home, serving parents in old age, and extending the family line. Instead, parents now seek emotional satisfaction from their children regardless of the child's gender.

Contemporary Korean Childrearing Conditions

Childrearing by Fathers. According to a 2012 report of the Korea Institute for Health and Social Affairs, 39.3% of fathers reported that they want to spend more time playing with their children (Park, 2013). Investigations of family life between 1999 and 2009 by the Korean Women's Policy Institute of Gender Equality and Family confirmed a gradual increase in time spent in childcare by fathers, although this time was still less in comparison with mothers' time with children (Ahn, Lee, & Lee, 2013). Another time use study, conducted on 2,693 individuals in 2009, documented that fathers spent an average 44 minutes per day during the week playing with or taking care of their children, and 166 minutes on weekend days (Ahn et al., 2013). The same study showed that for decisions and problem solving concerning childrearing or education, 59.5% of couples discussed issues jointly, while 37.4% of respondents replied that the wife made decisions alone, and only in 3.0% of couples did husbands make decisions alone (Park, 2013).

In another 2013 study, men's preferences for the types of activities they engage in during childcare had shifted from traditional practices: "play with the child (80.5%)" was the most common response, followed by "support the formation of life habits" (70.1%), "soothe the child when s/he cries" (67.6%), "provide milk" (60.65%)," read a picture book" (60.1%), "put to sleep" (58.9%), "give a bath" (54.8%), "change diapers" (54.7%), "provide weaning food" (48.4%), and "cook for the child" (19.25%) (Hyun, 2013). Elsewhere, in a 2009 daily time use survey, husbands spent an average of only 24 minutes a day on housework while wives spent 2 hours and 38 minutes. The main domestic activities of men in this sample included cleaning, shopping, and cleaning up after meals (Lee & Son, 2013).

Fathers' Work/Family Conflict. In recent years, the term "work-life balance" has become popular in Korea. Parents are becoming more aware on how much time they invest between family life and employment (Chae & Lee, 2013; Kim, 2005), and many Korean men are finding it difficult to balance between the two. This discord is largely due to financial reasons as men report excessive stress and long hours at work (Kim, 2011; Song et al., 2010). In a study of 288 fathers of infants, the most frequently mentioned factor that hinders them from performing their roles at home was workplace issues (58.7%), followed by lack of interest, motivation, or skills to be a nurturing father. Many such fathers felt (as in the preceding case story) they lacked the ability and knowledge to be fathers, and some also mentioned personality issues such as irritability (Kim, 2011).

Mothers' Problems with Work-Life Balance. With the increase of women joining the workforce, employed mothers are also facing a conflict between family life and work. The employment rate of women was

39.3% on average in the 1970s, but it surpassed 50% in this century and reached 53.5% in 2012 (Min, 2013). The employment rate among married women was 43.4% in 2011, and we expect that it will continue to increase in the future (Statistics Korea, 2011). Comparing age groups, the employment rate of women apparently drops sharply in their 30s but increases again in their 40s, a trend Koreans call an "M-type curve" (Statistics Korea, 2013). The main reason for this discontinuity is that mothers are primarily responsible for the upbringing of children. In research on the actual reasons for career discontinuity among Korean women, 47% of mothers gave marriage as their reason, followed by childcare (28.7%) and pregnancy or childbirth (20%). Many of these working mothers reported that because of physical fatigue and a lack of time due to their multiple roles and dedication to childcare, they quit their jobs during the period of childrearing. Korea has a parental leave system, but as we shall discuss later, it has not been highly utilized or accepted by employers (Yang & Shin, 2011).

Research on the Roles of Parents in Korean Child Development

Influence of Fathers. A survey of 565 fathers of young children (ages 2–5 years) found that men's role performance was related to their marital satisfaction (Jang & Lee, 2008). In addition, men's participation in childcare was associated with a higher sense of child support efficacy (Kim & Kim, 2011) and knowledge of caregiving (Hwang, Chong, & Woo, 2005). Fathers who earned higher income, obtained higher education levels, and worked in executive rather than manual occupation experienced greater satisfaction and were more involved in childrearing than their counterparts. At the same time, their preschool children also exhibited better social skills, manners, and more respect for social norms and values (Chung & Park, 2013).

Paternal degree of involvement in childrearing can impact the child's development in prosocial behavior (Seol & Moon, 2006), leisure activities, learning, self-esteem, and adaptability at school (Kim & Jang, 2007). In addition, research has demonstrated a close relationship between fathers' functional communication (Yoon & Oh, 2005), affectionate behavior, emotional expression, and preschoolers' social abilities (Woo & Chong, 2003). Others studies have also confirmed that fathers play an important role in the social development of children and adolescents (Hong, 2007; Song & Hyun, 2006). For example, a directive-oriented communication style has been found to be correlated with lower social skills in children. In one study, while both girls and boys encountered problems adapting to school life, those whose fathers were more open and receptive in expression of intentions to their children experienced smoother adaptation in schools than their counterparts (Baek & Kwoon, 2004).

Influence of Mothers. Kim and Lee's study (2014) considered the relationship between infants' temperament (*N* = 70 2-year olds), the attitudes of mothers toward childrearing, and children's behavioral problems. Their results showed a relationship between mothers' attitudes and their perceptions of infants' temperament. Reports of aggressive behavior, oppositional behavior, emotional anxiety, and withdrawn behavior among their infants were more commonly reported by mothers who were control-oriented rather than autonomy-oriented in their attitudes toward childrearing. In another examination of mother-infant relations (*N* = 1,735 infants), Kim, Lee, and Sung (2013) studied childrearing methods and childrearing knowledge and focused on mothers' psychological characteristics (self-esteem, self-efficacy, depression) in relation to childrearing cognitions, childrearing stress, and the childcare system. Mothers in this sample who had high self-esteem and self-efficacy also responded appropriately and affectionately to infants' requests and showed a warm interest in their babies. They also expressed confidence in the childcare system. Here the factor that most strongly influenced mothers' childrearing behavior was their level of childrearing stress, followed by their self-esteem, self-efficacy, and childrearing knowledge.

Another study by Park and Kim (2014) examined the effects of mothers' perfectionistic beliefs and attitudes toward childrearing on their preschool children's social competence (*N* = 277). Their perfectionistic beliefs about children's creativity were associated with children's social competence. Meanwhile, Kim and Sung's study (2013; *N* = 493) of mothers and their four-to-five-year-old preschoolers found a positive correlation between maternal role satisfaction and their children's positive emotional development.

Childcare Issues Facing Korean Society

Unmarried Mothers: Social Isolation and Discrimination. It has been reported that 1.5% of children in Korea are born to unmarried mothers, but it is difficult to ascertain the precise number due to social stigma attached to childbirth outside of marriage (Kim, 2013). In Korean society, the legal status of a birth is important (OECD, 2011), and childbirth and childrearing outside of legal marriages are frowned upon as immoral and destructive to the ideal family life. In the context of strong familism, many elderly or middle-aged people who retain a paternalistic mentality view childbirth and pregnancy of unmarried women as unethical and deviant (Kim, 2013). As a result, unmarried mothers face social discrimination and are ostracized by their families. In a survey of 554 unmarried mothers, 89.0% reported experiences of a severe level of discrimination, particularly in the workplace, school, neighborhood, and wider community (Kim, Sun, Kim, & Jung, 2009).

Because of the social stigma, prejudice, and discrimination that unmarried mothers face, social problems associated with child abandonment, abortion, infanticide, and international adoption have gained greater attention (Kim, 2008). Abortion is illegal in Korea, but it continues to take place in private, and estimates show that between 340,000 and 1.5 million abortions occur on an annual basis. These abortion numbers are striking given that, in 2008, there were only 500,000 live births in Korea (Kim, 2013). It is further estimated that among teenage pregnancies, as many as 70% opt for abortion rather than childbirth (Baek et al., 2012). On the other hand, when a Korean woman gives birth to a child, she has the option of giving the child away for purposes of adoption, raising the child herself, or relying on her parents to raise the child. Over two-thirds of adoptions of Korean children take place abroad, and most are children of unmarried mothers (98.5% in 2005, 92.2% in 2012) (Kim, 2013).

Low Birth Rate. A low birth rate poses a serious social problem in Korea (similar to what we will discuss later for Japan), leading to concerns over the financial burden of an aging population and the weakened economic competitiveness due to a diminishing workforce. The total fertility rate of Korean women was 4.05 children in 1970 but then dropped suddenly to 2.57 children in 1981 and 2.1 in 1985. By the year 2005 it had declined even further to only 1.08 children. Although this rate has risen gradually since then, the 2012 birth rate of 1.30 was still the lowest among the nations of the Organization for Economic Co-Operation and Development (OECD) (Statistics Korea, 2013). While this trend is caused by a complex interplay of various economic, social, and policy factors, the increasing costs of education and childrearing may be the primary reason that Korean parents are hesitant to have more children (Nam & Chung, 2013).

Korean parents' willingness to bear the high cost of education, especially for private schools, is based on the strong belief that education leading to the attendance of a prestigious university is crucial for success in society. A study by the LG Economic Research Institute concluded that many parents follow a formula of "prestigious university = success = happiness" (*Newswire*, 2011). In addition, increased employment of women and change in the perceived instrumental value of children has brought about "marriage evasion" (Im, 2013). Nevertheless, the stress and burdens of the parental role, lack of social infrastructure to support childrearing (Lee, 2006; Nam & Chung, 2013), and conflict between work and family life (Hong, 2010) remain significant problems.

Childrearing in Multicultural Families. Koreans traditionally had a strong identity as a culturally and racially homogeneous people. However, due to an increase of foreign labor and international marriages since the 1990s, Korea began to shift toward a complex and multicultural society where various races and cultures coexist. Interracial marriages grew from 3.5% of total marriages in Korea in 2000 to 13.6% in 2005. This rate decreased to 10.8% in 2009 and 10.5% in 2010 but has stabilized at over 10% since 2004. Moreover, in 2013, there were 25,963 cases of international marriages, which constitutes 8.0% of the 322,807 marriages in Korea (Korean National Statistical Office, 2013). Over 70% of international marriages are between a foreign woman and a Korean man (72.0% in 2006; 75.5% in 2009), and this trend is more notable in rural than urban Korea (Statistics Korea, 2010). Such a phenomenon led to an increasing number of multicultural children who accounted for 10.7% of the inhabitants of the overall foreign population in 2010, and 87.2% of this subpopulation were below the age of 12 (Kim & Jang, 2012).

Grandparents and the 2.5-Generation Nuclear Family. Recently, there have been three predominant styles of grandparenting in Korea. In the first style, grandparents assume the role of "sharer of childrearing" and live with their married daughters, helping them take care of the grandchildren. The second style, called "childcare assistant," is found when grandparents reside only a short distance from their married daughter and provide childcare to the grandchild. In a contrasting third style, the grandparents live too far away from their daughters (often in cases of divorce) to assist with childcare and instead become "surrogate mothers" in place of the daughter. Among these three, the second style of "childcare assistants" is associated with what Koreans call the "new nuclear family" or the "2.5 generation family" (Lee & Lee, 2012). In the 2.5 generation family, the married daughter asks her own parents to take temporary care of the grandchildren. It is also common for such grandparents to provide financial support (Bae, Roh, & Kweon, 2008).

According to a 2010 survey by the Sansei Economic Research Institute, 64.5% of Korean working parents had grandparents' support in raising their children (Jung & Kim, 2012). Another survey, carried out in 2011 in Gyeonggi Province, showed that for children under the age of 3 the percentage of families with grandparents who provided childcare (37.7%) was higher than that among families that sent their children to daycare centers. Here, the younger the child the more pronounced was this tendency to utilize grandparents over institutional childcare (Lee & Lee, 2012).

Grandparent/grandchild families. Societal interest in grandparents began to increase in the 1990s, with the growing number of 2.5 generation families. Looking at the prevalence of this type of family, there were 35,194 grandparent/grandchild families in 1995, and by 2010 there were 69,175 such families, a doubling of numbers within 15 years (Hwang, 2011). It is expected that this trend will continue. However, Korean grandparent/grandchild families suffer from various problems such as limited economic assistance and declining health. Financial support from the government is restricted when the grandchild's parents are still alive, and as such, many grandparent/grandchild families live in poverty even though the parents do not reside with them. In addition, childrearing has been found to induce considerable strain on some grandparents' health (Lee, Park, & Jang, 2010).

Social Policies

Family-Friendly Policies to Support Work/Family Balance. We live in an era where a "family-friendly social environment" is urgently required so that married women can comfortably balance family life and work, and so that fathers can perform their roles at home (Song et al., 2010). Roughly 10 years ago, the Korean government began to prepare institutions to construct such a positive institutional environment. Companies have also begun to play a role in the societal shift toward a family-friendly balanced lifestyle between work and home. The 2007 law further promoted this balance, encouraging residents and institutions to develop family-friendly workplaces and communities and to share in the social responsibility toward families and their dependents. Family-friendly communities in particular would have sufficient space and facilities so that communities could play a role in supporting children in day nurseries and the elderly in nursing homes.

Korean policies that promote paternal participation in childcare emphasize (a) a system to certify family-friendly companies, (b) reduction of work hours, and (c) an expansion of childcare participation opportunities (Park, 2013). The government is attempting to address the issues of a low-fertility and aging society in its first 2006–2010 plan, and now has established a second plan for 2011–2015, which calls for family-friendly corporate management strategies and company childcare facilities (Kim, 2011). However, these policies and priorities have faced stiff opposition and have been far from successful. While a Task Force for Women and Families was established in 2008, its application toward public employers and larger companies has not yet extended into the general and private corporate sector. This is because the policy calls for voluntary compliance, and in the profit-centered corporate world there has not been sufficient incentive for private companies to comply. In addition, South Korean workers continue to work the longest number of hours (2,256 annually) of any OECD member, and the goal of achieving a 40-hour work week remains problematic. Third, the current system of childcare leave does not distinguish between mothers and fathers, and pays only 40% of normal wages up to a maximum amount of about US$1,500 monthly. Given these circumstances, most fathers find it unfeasible to take childcare leave.

Overall the rate of utilization of childcare leave among Korean women is 30.4%, with 90 days allowed for childbirth leave and up to a year of childcare leave permitted by law. The overall childcare leave rate among men is currently only 3.3% (Statistics Korea, 2013). This indicates that the government goal of realizing a suitable work-family life balance is still far from realistic. It is also worth mentioning that Korean government policies to balance work and family life and to make companies more family-friendly may actually be intended to maintain productivity. That is, the actual motivation of the government may not be pro-family or pro-fathering, but may actually reflect a stronger desire to increase the relative size of the workforce and numbers of young people in an aging society for the sake of national economic competitiveness.

Day Nurseries and Childcare Leave. A 2013 investigation of women's reasons for leaving work pointed to marriage (45.9%), followed by childcare issues (29.2%), childbirth and pregnancy (21.2%), and their children's education (3.7%) (Statistics Korea, 2013). These data suggested the importance of the work-family life balance issue. They also illustrate that for women to be able to work and care for their children, companies must be more cognizant of the need for adequate childcare facilities.

Meanwhile, a majority of fathers gave the following reasons not to take childcare leave: "The workplace culture where the atmosphere of being watched makes me anxious (30.8%)," or "low childcare leave payments make it economically impractical" (22.6%), according to the Korean Institute for Health and Social Affairs (2012). In a study of mostly male personnel managers at 402 companies (*Kyunghyang Shinmun*, 2014), 72.1% had negative views about childcare leave. Their reasons included: "hiring for an undetermined period rather than just hiring manpower is problematic" (60%), concerns whether employment will be continued if one married (52.8%), and "we do not recommend childbirth or childcare leave" (47.5%). These data show that the corporate view of childcare leave is still negative and remains the primary obstacle to a better work-family life balance. The next biggest obstacle was the insufficient number of childcare facilities.

One important difference between the situations in Japan and Korea is that in Korea, the problem is not a lack of daycare facilities. Rather, it is the fact that there is a severe lack of *public* Korean daycare facilities, which are considered desirable in consideration of lower tuition, physical size of the center, the center's environment, health, safety, and curriculum issues, and workplace daycare. Over 90% of Korean daycare centers are public and established either by the national state or region government, and only 5.33% of the Korean daycare centers are private facilities, compared with about 50% in Japan. In this context, where children wait longer to get into a public nursery school, about 100,000 children are now on waiting lists for public daycare in Seoul alone. A survey by the Health and Welfare Ministry (2012) indicated that 48.7% of working women reported, "I had to quit my job because I had no place to leave my child." As a result of this situation, the Korean government required that companies with either 500 or more workers or 300 or more full-time working women install workplace nurseries, but only 49.7% of such companies complied with that regulation in 2013 (*Kukmin Ilbo*, 2014). Thus, in Korea, the problem is not a lack of daycare facilities (as in Japan), but rather, a lack of workplace and public daycare facilities that parents trust.

JAPAN

Taro Hinomoto (age 36) and his wife Hanako (35) have a four-year-old son. They work at different companies in the Tokyo metropolitan area. Four years ago, Hanako's pregnancy was welcomed by both her and Taro's parents. Taro went to a fathering class at a community health center to learn how to help his pregnant wife and to care for an infant. Hanako took childcare leave, but Taro did not due to work obligations. When she returned to work, it was difficult for them to find a day nursery for their son, and the grandparents were unable to help with childcare as they lived outside the Tokyo metropolitan area. Therefore, there was no alternative but to utilize a day nursery, but it was difficult to pick their son up at daycare before 5 PM. Taro assists with the cooking and childcare on Saturdays and Sundays. Recently, Hanako became pregnant with their second child, and Taro wants to take childcare leave this time.

In today's younger generation, men like Taro who perform household tasks and childrearing are viewed favorably, and their involvement is seen as quite natural. This case story also illustrates the increased involvement of women in the labor market and the social trend toward gender equality. However, during recent economic downturns, employment has taken precedence over housework and childcare, so that young fathers are torn between work and family responsibilities. It remains very difficult for men to take childcare leave, and the day nursery (Shwalb, Shwalb, Sukemune, & Tatsumoto, 1992) is the primary means of childrearing support for working mothers. As we shall see later, an insufficient number of available day nurseries remains an urgent problem in Japan.

Cultural Context of Japanese Parenting

Families and Childrearing in 21st-Century Japan. Japan's post–World War II economic "bubble" burst in the 1990s. Since then, a long recession in the context of failed economic policies in the 1990s, the Kobe Earthquake of 1995, the international financial crisis of 2008, and the Tohoku earthquake-tsunami-nuclear disaster of 2011 have severely damaged Japan's economic and industrial systems. During an era of world economic globalization, chronic economic woes have led to an increased use of temporary workers that is undermining the Japanese tradition of lifetime employment.

As in Korea, the Japanese now confront a falling birth rate together with an aging population. The total fertility rate continues to decline after reaching its low point of 1.26 in 2005. The number of Japanese children is now rapidly decreasing and the number of newborn children in 2012 (1.04 million) was well below half of that in 1949 (2.70 million—Ministry of Health, Labor and Welfare, 2013). The reasons for limiting pregnancies were similar to those reported in Korean research (National Institute of Population and Social Security Research, 2010) including "the cost of childrearing and children's education" (60.4%), followed by "want to avoid having children as an older mother" (35.1%), "difficulty to endure the psychological and physical burdens of childrearing" (17.4%), "hinders my employment" (16.8%), and "difficult to get husband's help with housework and childrearing" (10.9%). As for aging, the percentage of people over age 65 in the population was only 4.9% in 1950 but increased to 17.4% by 2000 and 25.1% in 2013; the government expects this trend to continue (Ministry of Health, Labor, & Welfare, Statistics and Information Department, Statistics and Information Department, 2014).

Changing Roles of Mothers and Fathers. The spread of higher education among women (the college-university entrance rate of women is 55.5% and that of males is 50.8%; Ministry of Education, Culture, Sports, Science and Technology, 2013) and women's increased participation in the workforce has made them more central to Japanese society. For example, the number of stay-at-home mothers is in decline and the percentage of women who agreed that staying at home is the ideal life course was 34% in 1987 but only 19.7% in 2010. Meanwhile, the lengthy recession and collapse of the Japanese employment system encouraged fathers to view both work and family life as important. With increasing numbers of mothers at work, the roles of fathers expanded from that of exclusive economic provider to include childrearing and housework (Nakazawa & Shwalb, 2013; Shwalb, Nakazawa, Yamamoto, & Hyun, 2010).

Current Conditions of Japanese Childrearing

Maternal Childrearing: Compatibility between Household and Work. Compatibility between household and work, termed "life-work balance" (as stated earlier for Korean parents) is an important issue for Japanese working mothers. Especially after returning from maternity leave, mothers have to coordinate their time and roles between home and workplace, and how they regulate their emotional responses to these dual roles can have significant mental health implications. Hasegawa's study (2010) found that the amount of time mothers spent on childrearing, and household work together with their private time had all reportedly decreased after returning to work from childcare leave. However, childrearing time experienced the least decrease compared to other activities, suggesting that working mothers still prioritized childrearing. The study also indicated an increase in their emotional sense of urgency, but mothers' feelings of depression and fatigue were stable as they adapted after returning to work.

Makino (1982) defined childrearing anxiety (*ikuji fuan*) as a "vague fear and/or accumulated anxiety about the child in the present or future, and concerning methods or results of childrearing" (p. 34). Childrearing anxiety was recognized by scholars and clinicians in the 1980s and remains an important psychological problem for mothers in Japan; in the past, fathers were considered to be secondary parents and, for years, were left out of the discussion regarding childrearing anxiety. Studies have indicated various factors contributing to childrearing anxiety. For instance, raising children alone without support (especially from the children's father) places an enormous psychological burden on some mothers, making it difficult for them to perceive childrearing as a positive experience. Furthermore, a mother might experience conflicting motivations between wanting to take care of her own child and wishing to value her own way of life. In two large-scale studies between 1980 and 2003, Harada (2008) found that successive cohorts of fathers became more cooperative in regards to childrearing across these decades. However, the percentage of mothers who had no childcare experiences before they had their own children increased from 41% to 55%. Mothers' irritation with their children also increased over this same period (from 11% to 32% for mothers of 1.5-year-old children, and from 17% to 44% for mothers of 3-year-olds). In addition, mothers increasingly reported social isolation, for example, the rate of mothers of four-month-olds who reported that they had no neighbors to talk with or ask about childrearing increased from 16% to 32%. Thus, the percentage of mothers who had no prior experiences with childcare, experienced social isolation, or felt irritated with their children increased historically. Meanwhile, a 1990s study comparing fathers and mothers indicated that mothers received information about childrearing from a wider variety of sources, whereas fathers had a more restricted social network with whom to share experiences and knowledge regarding childrearing (Shwalb, Kawai, Shoji, & Tsunetsugu, 1995).

Men's Childrearing Attitudes and Behavior. In a study of 1,300 mothers, fathers, and adults without children, 45% of the sample agreed that "both father and mother should actively share and participate in the childrearing" (Chuochosasha, 2012). This rate has gradually increased over the years (34.7% in 2010; 39.1% in 2011), while agreement with the statement that "fathers should concentrate on work, and mothers should concentrate on childrearing" was only 8.5% in 2012.

Although societal attitudes have shifted dramatically, fathers' use of time in household and childrearing activities has not followed the same trend (similar again to what we observed earlier in this chapter for Koreans).

Japanese fathers remain relatively infrequent participants in childrearing. For example, data from the Cabinet Office, Gender Equality Bureau (2013a) showed that fathers on average spent only 67 minutes daily with children under the age of 6 years in 2011, including 39 minutes in childrearing. This represented a daily increase of 7 minutes when compared to 2006, but it was significantly less time than in the other comparative countries (U.S. household time = 171 minutes, including 65 minutes of childrearing; U.K. household time = 166 minutes, including 60 minutes of childrearing; Sweden household time = 201 minutes, including 67 minutes of childrearing). The Japanese fathers' role in childrearing may actually resemble that of a support or assistant for mothers. As to which factors would improve men's participation in childrearing, the research of Chuouchosasha (2012) discovered that many chose the following options: "Fathers need to recognize themselves more as agents of childrearing" (56.4%), "improvement of the work environment, including shorter work hours" (52.3%), "government support to encourage fathers' participation in childrearing" (40.7%), and "change the mentality that childrearing is women's work" (32.7%). The Japanese have gradually accepted fathers' participation in childrearing and household work, but behavioral changes have lagged behind pro-fathering attitudes. Moreover, support of fathers' participation from the corporate environment and government remains insufficient.

Non-Parental Childrearing: Grandparents and Local Government Support. As the Japanese population has aged, older people who can attend to their grandchildren are living longer and are healthier. As in Korea, grandparents who live with or near the parents can readily assist with childrearing. According to the National Institute of Population and Social Security Research (2010), 51–52% of Japanese parents since 2005 had received a grandmother's daily or frequent support for their first child under the age of 3. Meanwhile, the percentage of parents who lived with their children's grandparents was 37.8% in rural areas but only 17.2% in urban Japan. Because most nuclear families in large cities had no relatives in the neighborhood, they could not depend on grandparents or other extended family members for childrearing. These parents mainly relied on themselves to handle childrearing tasks or depended on day nurseries for institutional support. Nearly all (97%) dual-income couples with children older than one year reported some type of third-party childcare support (grandmothers: 59%, day nurseries: 33%, others: 5%). Seventy-one percent of re-employed or stay-at-home wives received support (from grandmothers: 17%, day nurseries: 19%, others: 35%).

Conceptual and Theoretical Issues

People from collectivistic societies like Japan tend to view themselves as deeply embedded in surrounding social relationships, and their behaviors are strongly influenced by their perception of others' emotions and acts (Markus & Kitayama, 1991). That is, whereas some individualistic Western cultures tend to emphasize individual self-expression and an independent construal of self, Japanese culture values behavioral coordination with the social groups and an interdependent construal of self (Shwalb, Nakazawa, & Shwalb, 2005). These general collectivistic and interdependent characteristics are applicable to Korean society as well, although to some extent, Japanese and Koreans also value individualistic and independent traits, just as some observers consider both South Korea and Japan to be part of "the West" (Shwalb et al., 2010).

How do such cultural factors influence childrearing? Working mothers have to manage various interpersonal problems, such as with day nursery teachers or coworkers when their children are ill. In these situations, an interdependent construal of self may increase mothers' tendency to be more sensitive to others' evaluations and more likely to avoid conflict with others, behaviors that may induce psychological stress. Shi and Katsurada (2010) found that working mothers' interdependent construal of self was associated with more childrearing anxiety, whereas Japanese mothers with a more independent construal of self underwent less childrearing anxiety. Indeed, Japanese cultural norms and values lead mothers to seek mutual accommodation in relationships. As a result, more interdependent construal of self among mothers may lead them to worry excessively about others' evaluations, suppress their own needs, and feel stressed by human relationships.

Azuma's cross-national research (1994) showed that American mothers (with a more independent construal of self) emphasized more on assertive verbal skills with their children, whereas Japanese mothers (with a more interdependent construal of self) stressed more on obedience to adults, manners, and emotion regulation. We wonder if this contrast will continue to exist in the next generation when the children in Azuma's study become adults. More recently, Mori's cross-cultural comparison (2012) indicated that attachment to parents influenced the self-identity formation of American and Japanese university students, suggesting to Mori that identity formation was mediated by an independent versus interdependent construal of self. Specifically, attachment to the mother was associated positively with an interdependent construal of self in both Japan and the United States, but it was also related negatively to independent construal of self in the United States. Mori further concluded that fathers had less influence on students' identity formation than mothers in both Japan and the United States. Thus, Japanese interdependence fostered more coordinated and stable relationships with others, but also led to the suppression of the individual self, affected childrearing anxiety and the mental health of working mothers, and contributed to the ego identity of university students in a negative way.

Research on Parenting Practices and Styles

Effects of Parenting on Intellectual Development. As we described earlier for Koreans, the Japanese tend to be highly oriented toward academic achievement. What kind of parenting promotes children's intellectual development and academic achievement? In a unique study, Sato and Uchiyama (2012) sent two picture books once a month over a three-month period to mothers of nine-month-old children, and asked them to read the books to their children. Analysis of mother-child interactions with 12-month-olds showed that reading picture books facilitated an active approach by mothers. Praise by mothers, children's smiling, and sharing of emotions between mothers and babies occurred more frequently in the shared book reading group than in a control group.

As Japanese culture values an interdependent construal of self, it is important for children to implicitly understand the mother's thoughts and emotions from her ambiguous behavior. Azuma (1994) wrote that Japanese mothers take an "absorbent childrearing" approach in that they do not teach children explicitly, but rather encourage children to understand the situation and behave autonomously. In a newer and related study, Kazama, Hirabayashi, Karasawa, Tardif, and Olson (2013) compared mothers and their four-year-old children in the United States and Japan and found that among American mothers, there was no relation between parenting style and children's "theory of mind" and their understanding of others' emotions. Among Japanese mothers, however, praise of children was positively related to children's "theory of mind" scores. An ambiguous parenting style (e.g., the mother does not address the child's behavior as good or bad) emphasized children's understanding without being told things explicitly, and this style was negatively related to children's "theory of mind" scores and understanding of others' emotions. Children raised by the "understanding without being told" parenting approach may thus find it difficult to understand others.

In Toyama's analysis (2011) of mothers' communication when they were solving problems with their 5–6-year-old children, mothers' child-centered remarks (e.g., adding a complementary or suggestive statement to the child's opinion) were positively related with the children's theory of mind scores. In contrast, the mothers' child-leading utterances (e.g., not waiting for children to express their opinions or guiding the child toward the mother's opinion) were negatively related to the children's scores. Finally, the mother's comments about their children's past experiences and her flexibility in changing her explanations were positively related to children's scores. These results imply that mothers' understandable suggestions, based on children's past experiences and knowledge, facilitated children's theory of mind and understanding of others.

Kikuchi, Matsumoto, and Sugawara (2011) examined parental expectations for the following types of preparation for entrance to elementary school: "learning skills (teach writing to their child)," "learning attitude (teach the attitude of listening to the teacher talk)," "basic life habits (support autonomy)," and "opportunity for activities (provide many new experiences)." Mothers valued "opportunity of activities" more, while fathers emphasized "learning skills" more. These expectations were higher among parents of five-year-olds than parents of four-year-olds, and the expectation for "learning attitude" and "basic life habits" increased in importance for parents of five-year-olds, especially fathers. In general, fathers in this sample had higher expectations for school readiness guidance than did mothers.

Effects of Parenting on Social Development. Motoshima (2013) found that negative emotional expressiveness in the family when children were nine-months-old (e.g., complaining about a family member's behavior) had an effect on maternal depression nine months later, and it also led to children's problem behavior at 30 months of age. On the contrary, positive emotional expressiveness in the family (e.g., giving encouragement when a family member was sad) when the child was 9 months old had an effect on mothers' responsibility at 18 months, but this responsibility was not related to subsequent problem behavior among the children at 30 months of age. Here, the causal relationship between emotional expressiveness in the family and children's problem behavior was mediated by mothers' depression.

In early childhood, regulation of aggressive behavior and self-regulated behavior become important for one's adjustment to peer relations. Nakamichi and Nakazawa (2003) examined the relationship between parenting style and aggressive behavior of kindergarten children. While there were no differences among children based on mothers' parenting styles, the children of authoritarian fathers were evaluated as more aggressive by classroom teachers than the children of the authoritative and permissive fathers. Nakamichi (2013) also examined the connection between parenting style and self-regulation behavior (self-assertion and self-control). As to self-assertion, authoritarian and authoritative fathers' sons were more assertive than permissive fathers' sons. For self-control, authoritative mothers' children (both girls and boys) showed more self-control than children with authoritative and permissive parental styles. In Nakamichi's view, fathers' permissiveness apparently may have weakened the boys' assertiveness while mothers' authoritativeness promoted children's self-control.

Effects of Parenting on Adjustment. A third influence of Japanese parents relates to the children's psychological health and adjustment. A good example of such complex influences can be found in a research project conducted by Ujiie, Ninomiya, Igarashi, Inoue, Yamamoto, and Shima (2010) who found that spousal conflict was a positive predictor of parents' cold behavior toward junior high school children and a negative predictor of warm behavior. Parental warmth led to children's perception of parents' warmth, and cold parental behavior positively predicted children's perception of distance from one's parents. Finally, children's perception of parental warmth negatively predicted children's depression, whereas their perception of parental distance showed the opposite effect. Parental behavior, influenced by spousal conflict, was one determinant of children's depression, as mediated by children's perceptions.

The preceding Japanese data on parental influences may be summarized as follows. First, mothers' child-centered, supportive, and flexible parenting seemed to promote young children's cognitive development, including theory of mind, while ambiguous parenting inhibited such development. Next, authoritative parenting seemed to promote children's social development. In addition, parents' negative emotional expression within the family was related to children's depression and problem behaviors. Additionally, expectations for learning tended to differ between mothers and fathers, although there are no data as yet on the effects of these differences on child development.

As in American and other Western research, authoritative Japanese parenting is associated with adaptive child development, and this trend differs from Chinese data where authoritarian parenting appears to promote child development (Bornstein, 2006). In general, Japanese mothers promote closeness within the mother-child dyad, and they tend to be permissive with the children (Befu, 1986; Kojima, 1986). Living in a culture with a stable child-centered pattern of childrearing, children of authoritative parents may learn to behave and think autonomously, and this environment also promotes their cognitive development. However, Japanese mothers and fathers appear to have different effects on child development. It may be interesting in future research to examine the cause of these differences and the combined effects of mothers and fathers on child development.

Social Policies

The *Ikumen* Project and "New" Japanese Fathers. The Japanese government (as we mentioned earlier for the Korean context) has promoted the use of day nurseries for working mothers and campaigned to increase fathers' participation in housework and childrearing. The Ministry of Health, Labour and Welfare (2010) also initiated the "*Ikumen* Project." *Ikumen* (childrearing men) was coined by combining *iku* (rearing) and men, and *ikumen* refers to men who enjoy childrearing and fulfill themselves through such activity. The motto of this project is "childrearing men change families and society." The current goal of the Ikumen Project focuses on increasing the percentage of fathers who take childcare leave from work, from 1.23% in 2008 to 10% in 2017 and to 13% in 2020. A second goal is to increase the percentage of women who continue to work after having their first baby, from 38% in 2005 to 55% in 2017.

However, there has been very little change thus far in the number of fathers who take paternal leave. According to the Cabinet Office (2013b), the (few) men who want to take childcare leave tended to have parents who likewise endorsed the belief that men should take part in housework and childrearing. Saito (2012) interviewed a small sample of 21 "new" fathers who took childcare leave, and found that they had very flexible attitudes toward gender roles. They also possessed household skills like cooking, washing, and cleaning up prior to marriage. Their wives also had flexible gender role attitudes, and were open to the arrangement where the husband assumes a domestic role and the wife takes a position of the wage earner. Their desire to be independent of parental support, and the husband's willingness to take responsibility for childcare induced the men to take childcare leave. However, they did not feel that paternal leave was accepted or evaluated positively in the workplace. Yet they believed that the current societal attitude, which places more value on wage labor than housework and childcare, will change soon. Finally, these fathers believe that responsibility for childcare should be shared by husband and wife.

If one considers childcare leave and daycare as means of childrearing support within the Japanese social system, the percentage of mothers taking childcare leave rose to 18.2% in 2005–2007 from 6.2% in 1985–1989. Meanwhile, paternal childcare leave increased marginally, from 0.2% to 0.6% between 1995 and 2007, because the work world of men had not advanced sufficiently.

Daycare. Disparities between usages of parental leave versus day nurseries are significant in Japan. Day nursery usage increased to 34.9% by 2005–2007 from 18.9% in 1990–1994. These numbers continue to rise in recent years. In 2011, with 42.2% of 3–5-year-olds and 24.4% of 0–2 year-olds attended day nurseries and 50% attended kindergarten (Cabinet Secretariat, 2013). Expectations of mothers to work have risen so much that there is an insufficient supply of daycare centers, and children now have to wait until availability opens up (these children are called *taiki jido*). This indicates a dire need for new government policies to extend the hours of childcare time in kindergartens and to combine day nurseries and kindergartens (the latter more comparable to American preschools—Shwalb et al., 1992) into new "child centers."

PREDICTIONS FOR THE FUTURE

Korean Childrearing

We forecast that Korean society will continue to see an increase in dual-income families, a weakening of paternalism, an improved recognition of the rights of women, and a general change of consciousness that emphasizes individualism over familism. Such trends should result in an increased role for the father in the home, specifically in relation to housework and childcare. Korean parents generally believe that raising children at home is healthier for the children developmentally than leaving them in daycare facilities until the age of 3 (Hyun, 2013). Therefore, many infants are raised at home rather than in daycare. Accordingly, an increasing number of grandparents will be relied on to raise their grandchildren so that parents of infants will not have to take time off from employment. As two-income households increasingly become the norm and more families turn to grandparents for childrearing, the 2.5-generation household will grow in prevalence in Korea.

Despite many political, social, and economic changes in 21st-century Korea, we still can observe the deep-rooted mentality of the corporate profit motive and the belief that family harmony takes precedence over the growth of the individual. At the same time, we can see the general demise of the principles of filial piety, preference for sons, rigid gender roles, and strict adherence to the family lineage. With regard to filial piety, courtesy to parents and responsibility toward the elderly were once taken for granted, but this duty has now been reduced generally to children's obligation to study hard. For this reason, Korean society has become extremely centered on education and entrance examinations for prestigious schools. As an outgrowth of this mentality, the primary measure of parenting nowadays is the academic achievement of one's children. In the future, we predict that Korean parents will gain confidence in their own childrearing methods and focus on raising children to impart a healthy spirit, recognizing that the current overemphasis on academics may be erroneous.

Japanese Childrearing

Japan is now experiencing negative population growth, and with the decline in the birth rate, parents are adopting more protective attitudes toward their children. We expect that, in the future, mothers will need to increasingly share housework and childcare duties with fathers. Fathers' participation in childrearing is progressing due to government policies and increasing recognition of the need for their participation. In addition, childcare classes will become necessary not only for fathers but also for grandparents and mothers. As in Korea, grandparents will need to learn about contemporary childrearing methods and new attitudes for childcare. In addition, it is likely that the percentage of stay-at-home mothers will decline, and childcare in day nurseries will become the norm. This will require also that the quality of institutional care and early childhood education improve in the years ahead. In sum, we believe that Japanese childcare will change from a focus on maternal care to multiple caregiving by mothers, fathers, grandparents, and daycare centers.

Social Change. As in Korea, the declining number of children and increasing number of elderly Japanese will continue and result in a smaller labor force and lower national productivity. Even though Japan is on track to recovery financially in the short term, it faces many challenges derived from a long economic recession, natural disasters, and a nuclear plant catastrophe. First, Japan has to halt its birthrate decline. To that end, it is important to reduce parents' economic burden for childrearing and education, to provide government support for childrearing, and to improve the work environment for women. Encouraging fathers' involvement in childrearing should be another national priority; it is important not only to change men's attitudes but also to change the psychology of men's workplaces and the broader social system.

We expect that life expectancy will continue to increase in Japan from its current, already very high average of 86.41 years for females and 79.94 years for males (Ministry of Health, Labor and Welfare, 2014). As a result of these trends, middle-aged Japanese will have opportunities to interact at the same time with their children and parents who are healthy and high-functioning. This is a new situation in Japan, which Onodera (2011) examined by dividing a sample of 40–65-year-old women (average: 51.3 years old) into three groups with (a) parents who were still well, (b) parents who received medical care, and (c) parents who were deceased. Among these three groups, Onodera found that women whose parents were well and whose parent were receiving medical care had negative feelings and were more annoyed with their parents, while women whose parent were deceased did not have such negative feelings. Their relationships with their mothers after marriage often became negative due to discord between their husbands and mothers, and to differing values between the women and their mothers. It is important to note that the participants in Onodera's study were born after World War II and grew up in a society that valued individual fulfillment, whereas their mothers were raised in a generation when women were responsible for housework and childrearing. This change in values has the potential to bring about greater generational conflicts. As an aging society, the Japanese have many social and psychological issues associated with the elderly, such as childrearing by grandparents, a discrepancy between childrearing values of parents and grandparents, and role reversal of dependency between parents and their adult children.

Similarities between Korean and Japanese Parents and Their Changing Childrearing Practices

In both Korea and Japan we have observed numerous similar tendencies: (a) a reduction in the authority of fathers, (b) an increase in both attitudes and behavior among the younger generation favoring participation of fathers in childcare, (c) increases in maternal employment, age of marriage for women, and maternal age at birth of the first child, (d) a decrease in the birth rate, (e) a growing preference for daughters rather than sons, (f) problems of balance between work and family life, and (g) changes in the involvement of grandparents. In the contexts of economic and corporate modernization, Westernization, democratization, the assimilation of Confucian values into modern life, and advances in female employment and education, there has been a growing awareness in both countries of domestic equality between women and men, and consequently, men are more than ever encouraged to participate in childcare and housework. At the same time, for reasons we have enumerated, with fewer children in most Korean and Japanese families, these children compete fiercely in the realm of education for the sake of their families. This ongoing trend should continue to be associated with marrying and childbearing at a later age along with an increased reliance on grandparents.

CONCLUSIONS

Trends of childrearing in Korea and Japan reveal that economic globalization and retreat from traditionalism have produced similar changes in both countries. These tendencies may or may not generate the same effects in other societies. However, the intensification of academic competition has given rise to an increase in investment in education and a declining birthrate in China and some other Asian nations; it will be interesting to observe how these developments extend throughout Asia and elsewhere. Finally, no matter how much governments publicly seek to change the environment of childrearing, it may be economic influences, stemming chiefly from the corporate environment, that constrain changes in parenting. We conclude that the psychological transformation of today's younger generation in both Korea and Japan is undeniable and profound. In this context, it will be interesting to see how current changes in parenting affect how today's children will think and behave when they someday become parents.

ACKNOWLEDGMENT

We acknowledge the support of the Psychology Department of Southern Utah University (Britt Mace, Chair). This chapter is dedicated to Mar-Sun Yi, Sayuri Nakazawa, and Lucy Bo Gorder.

REFLECTIVE QUESTIONS

1. What are some of the similarities and differences between parents and childrearing in Korea and Japan? How do the authors explain these comparisons?

2. In what ways are the environments in which children grow up in Korea and Japan similar and different?
3. How does childrearing compare between that described in this chapter and that in your society or other societies?
4. How would you generally describe the roles of mothers and fathers in child development, in Korea and Japan? Do these roles differ between the two societies?
5. How does research on parents and childrearing in countries like Korea and Japan help us to understand these issues better worldwide?
6. Does anything you read about parents or childrearing in Korea or Japan seem culturally "unique" to you, or do most of the descriptions sound like parents or childrearing in any country?
7. Why is it difficult to make comparisons between parents and childrearing in different countries?

SUGGESTED READINGS

South Korea

Books and Articles

Bumpass, L. L. (2004). *Marriage, work, and family life in comparative perspective: Japan, South Korea, and the United States.* Honolulu, HI: University of Hawaii Press.

Lee, P. H., de Bary, W. T., & Choe, Y. (Eds.). (2000). *Sources of Korean tradition, Vol. 2: From the sixteenth to the twentieth centuries.* New York: Columbia University Press.

Shwalb, D. W., Nakazawa, J., Yamamoto, T., & Hyun, J.-H. (2010). Fathering in Japan, China, and Korea: Changing context, images, and roles. In M. E. Lamb (Ed.), *The role of the father in child development* (5th ed., pp. 341–387). Hoboken, NJ: Wiley.

Websites

The Korean Association of Child Studies: http://www.childkorea.or.kr/en/
Korean Institute of Child Care and Education: http://www.kicce.re.kr/eng/
Korea Institute for Health and Social Affairs: https://www.kihasa.re.kr/html/jsp/english/main.jsp

Japan

Books

Shwalb, D. W., Nakazawa, J., & Shwalb, B. J. (Eds.). (2005). *Applied developmental psychology: Theory, practice, and research from Japan.* Charlotte, NC: Information Age Publishing.

Shwalb, D. W., & Shwalb, B. J. (Eds.). (1996). *Japanese childrearing: Two generations of scholarship.* New York: Guilford Press.

Shwalb, D. W., Shwalb, B. J., & Lamb, M. E. (Eds.). (2013). *Fathers in cultural context.* New York: Routledge.

Stevenson, H. W., Azuma, H., & Hakuta, K. (Eds.). (1986). *Child development and education in Japan.* New York: Freeman.

Websites

"Fathering Japan": http://www.fathering.jp/

"Gender Equality Bureau, Cabinet Office": www.gender.go.jp/english_contents/index.html

"Ikujiren: Let's take time for childrearing, both males and females!" http://www.eqg.org/index-e.html

REFERENCES

South Korea

Ahn, S.M., Lee, K.Y., & Lee, S.M. (2013). Fathers' parenting participation and time. *Korean Family Resource Management Association, 17*(2), 93–119.

Bae, J.H., Roh, S.K., & Kweon, K.S. (2008). Current practices of grandparents raising grand children and their needs for support. *Journal of Future early Childhood Education, 15*(1), 379–410.

Baek, H.J., Kim, J.Y., Kim, H.Y., Bang, E.R., Kim, H.J., & Lee, J.Y. (2012). Research on comprehensive countermeasures for youth single-parent families I: A general report. *Korean Youth Policy Institute, 12,* 1–168.

Baek, K.S., & Kwon, Y.S. (2004). The effect of parent-adolescent communication types on the adaptation of adolescent school life. *Korean Journal of Adolescent Welfare, 6*(2), 87–99.

Chae, H.Y., & Lee, K.Y. (2013). A qualitative study on men's experiences of work-life balance: Focusing on men in dual-income families with children under the age of six. *Family Environment Research, 51*(5), 497–511.

Cho, S.H. (2010). Children's images about their father. *Korean Journal of Play Therapy, 13*(2), 81–95.

Cho, S.H. (2011). The relationship between children's father image and communication. *Korean Journal of Play Therapy, 14*(1), 75–91.

Choi, M.S., & Cho, S.H. (2005). Adolescents' image about their father. *The Korea Journal of Youth Counseling, 13*(1), 55–69.

Chu, B.W. (2010). A study on the methods of forming a family-friendly values orientation in the low childbirth & aged society. *Korean Elementary Moral Education Society, 34,* 226–252.

Chung, K.J., & Park, M.R. (2013). The relation between fathers' participation in nurturing and children's social morality. *Korean Journal of Child Care and Education, 80,* 43–64.

Dong-A. Ilbo. (2010). January 13.

Fairbank, J.K. (1965). *East Asia: The modern transformation.* Boston, MA: Houghton Mifflin.

Hankook-Ilbo Newspaper. (2013, April 16). Seoul, Korea: Author. Retrieved from http://www.hankookilbo.com

Health and Welfare Ministry. (2012). *Female employees and welfare conditions.* Retrieved from http://www.mw.go.kr/

Hong, K.H. (2007). A study of fathers' linguistic patterns and pre-school children's development of sociability. *Bulletin of Dongnam Health College, 25*(1), 49–64.

Hong, S.A. (2010). Dual income families and support for life-work balance. *Welfare Trends, 137,* 18–21.

Hwang, M.J. (2011). A study on the effect of grandparents' parenting stress and grandchildren's environmental adaptation on the satisfaction with family relations. *Journal of the Korean Society and Child Welfare, 35,* 7–35.

Hwang, S.Y., Chong, Y.S., & Woo, S.K. (2005). Fathers' involvement in parenting, role satisfaction, and young children's social competence as a function of socio-demographic variables. *Korean Journal of Human Ecology, 14*(4), 521–529.

Hyun, J. H. (2013). A study on childrearing and the value of the child in mothers' perceptions. *Journal of Child Research Institute in Seoul Theological University, 12,* 41–55.

Hyun, J.H. (2013, August). *Childrearing by Korean fathers.* Paper presented at the annual convention of the Japanese Association for Educational Psychology, Tokyo, Japan.

Im, S.Y. (2013). Factors that influence the intentions of married couples to have additional children. *Korean Journal of Kukje Theology,* 485–511.

Jang, S.K., & Lee, J.H. (2008). Young children's self-perceived competence according to fathers' parenting efficacy and participation in child rearing. *The Journal of Korea Open Association for Early Childhood Education, 13*(2), 73–89.

Jung, K.M., & Kim, M.K. (2012). The recognition of grandmother and mother in the role expectations of child rearing. *Korean Education Inquiry, 30*(3), 63–79.

Kim, G.R. (2011). The philosophy and value of work-life balance. *The Journal of Chungnam National University, 15,* 1–18.

Kim, H., & Lee, S.E. (2014). The effects of infants' temperament and mothers' child-rearing attitudes on infants' problem behaviors in child care centers. *Korean Council for Children's Rights Journal of Korean Council for Children & Rights, 18*(1), 123–146.

Kim, H.H. (2005). The effect of paternal involvement on the self-esteem in early adolescence. *Korean Journal of Child Studies, 26*(5), 311–330.

Kim, H. Y. (2008). How shall policies deal with unmarried mothers: Documentation of the current situation. Korean Women's Development Institute, 47th Proceedings of the Women's Policy Forum. Retrieved from http://eng.kwdi.re.kr/index.do.

Kim, H.Y. (2013). Social exclusion and discrimination against unwed mothers. *Gender and Culture, 6*(1), 7–41.

Kim, H.Y., Sun, B.Y., Kim, E.Y., & Jung, J.H. (2009). *The unwed mother's life world and a policy agenda.* Seoul, Korea: Korean Women's Development Institute.

Kim, J.H., Lee, J.Y., & Sung, J.H. (2013). The influences of mother's psychological characteristics and parenting related factors on two-year-old infants' development: The mediating role of parenting styles. *Korean Journal of Child Studies, 34*(6), 77–96.

Kim, J.H., & Sung, J.H. (2013). The effects of marital conflict and mother's parent satisfaction and parenting behavior on preschoolers' emotional intelligence. *The Korean Journal of Developmental Psychology, 26*(2), 87–105.

Kim, J.J., & Kim, Y.M. (2011). Effects of socio-psychological characteristics and childhood experiences on fathering practices. *The Journal of Child Education, 20*(1), 113–129.

Kim, J. O., & Chong, Y. S. (2003). Father's role satisfaction and child-rearing behavior. *Journal of Human Ecology, 7*(1), 141–161.

Kim, M. I., & Jang, Y. A. (2007). The effect of father's child-rearing behavior and child-rearing involvement perceived by children on the children's self-esteem and school adjustment. *Korean Journal Community Living Science, 18*(3), 379–390.

Kim, N. H. (2011). Early childhood parents' perceptions of good father's roles and social roles for good fathering. *Journal Future Early Childhood Education, 18*(2), 79–98.

Kim, N. H., & Jang, S. J. (2012). A study on child-rearing attitudes, involvement levels, and self-efficacy of young children's fathers in multicultural families. *Korean Journal of Early Childhood Education, 16*(4), 121–138.

Kim, S. K. (2002). *The social and economic impact of low birth rate and long- and short-term government policies.* Seoul, Korea: Korean Ministry of Health and Welfare.

Kong, M. H., & Lee, S. Y. (2012). Childless women's experience of making the decision not to have children. *Korean Journal of Family and Culture, 24*(2), 39–63.

Korean Institute for Health and Social Affairs. (2012). *National survey research on the falling birth rate and aging of society.* Seoul, Korea: Author.

Korean National Statistical Office (2013). Current state of international marriages. Retrieved from http://kostat.go.kr/portal/english/index.action.

Kukmin Ilbo. (2014, April 30). Social affairs. Retrieved from http://www.kukmindaily.co.kr/.

Kwon, I. S. (2013). Trends and perspectives of studies on paternal parenting in pediatric nursing. *Child Health Nursing Research, 19*(2), 69–75.

Kwon, J. D. (2004). The historical background of Korean family centralism. *The Study of Confucianism, 20,* 15–44.

Kyunghyang Shinmun (2014, May 22). Men's motivation to take paternal childcare leave. Retrieved from http://english.khan.co.kr/.

Lee, C. S., Park, M. J., & Jang, E. S. (2010). The effects of coping with stress, social support, and self-esteem on depression of adolescents of grandparent-grandchild families. *Korean Journal of Family Relations, 15*(1), 1–21.

Lee, H. J., & Oh, Y. J. (2011). Impacts of father-children relationship perceived by the college student children on their social problem resolving ability and happiness. *Korean Journal of Family Welfare, 16*(1), 157–173.

Lee, J. R., & Son, S. H. (2013). Mothers' work-family conflict in dual-earner families with young children: The role of resources and perceptions related to work and child care. *Korea Associational Journal of Family Relations, 18*(1), 93–114.

Lee, S. S. (2006). Causes of low fertility and future policy options in Korea. *Health and Welfare Policy Forum, 111,* 5–17.

Lee, Y. M., & Lee, J. E. (2012). A comparative study on the perception of traditional child-rearing practices between the parents' generation and grandparents' generation. *Asia Studies Review, 29,* 267–299.

Min, J. W. (2013). The employment conditions of working mothers in relation to the use of childrearing support services. *Korea Institute of Child Care and Education,* 1–18.

Nam, J. E., & Chung, C. H. (2013). A study on low fertility through child-rearing based on articles from the mid of 1980s to the 2000s. *Korean Journal of Early Childhood Education, 33*(2), 53–78.

National Statistical Office. (2014). Statistics Korea—2013. *Current conditions of births and child care leave.* Seoul, Korea: Author. Retrieved from [A marriage rate] http://kostat.go.kr/portal/english/index.action.

Newswire: Korea Press Release Network. (2011, August 16). *Korean lifestyle and values of people in their 20s: 2011.* Retrieved from https://www.newswire.co.kr/

OECD. (2011). OECD family database. Paris: OECD. Retrieved from www.oecd.org/social/family/database

Park, J.S. (2013). Gauging gender equality in terms of household labor division and gender-role perception. *Health and Welfare Policy Forum, 199,* 28–38.

Park, Y.Y., & Kim, L.J. (2014). The influence of mother's perfectionism and parenting beliefs on preschooler's social competence. *Journal of Korean Child Care and Education, 10*(1), 183–199.

Seol, G.O., & Moon, H.J. (2006). Relationships between father's involvement in child-rearing, psychological life position, and child's prosocial behavior. *Journal of the Korean Home Economics Association, 44*(7), 1–9.

Song, H.R., Ko, S.K., Park, J.Y., Kwon, H.J., Kim, Y.K., & Jin, M.J. (2010). Men's father-role in the context of a family friendly environment. *The Journal of Korean Family Resource Management Association, 14*(4), 341–361.

Song, Y.H., & Hyun, O.K. (2006). Children's sociality and perceptions of fathering practice in middle childhood and early adolescence. *Korean Journal of Child Studies, 27*(5), 19–34.

Statistics Korea. (2011). *Dual income families and women's career breaks: Aggregate statistical results.* Retrieved from http://kostat.go.kr/portal/korea/kor_nw/2/3/3/index.board?bmode=read&aSeq=252676

Statistics Korea. (2013). *Women's economic activities and participation in the work population.* Retrieved from www.index.go.kr/egams/stts/jsp/potal/stts/PO_STTS_IdxMain.jsp?idx_cd=1572

Woo, S.K., & Chong, Y.S. (2003). The relationships between parents' emotional expressiveness and children's social competence. *Research Institute of Human Ecology, Chungbuk National University, 7*(1), 99–119.

Yang, S. N., & Shin, C.S. (2011). Work-family conflicts: Challenges of working mothers with young children. *The Journal of Korea Institute for Health and Social Affairs, 31*(3), 70–103.

Yoon, M.A., & Oh, Y.J. (2005). Study on parent-adolescent child communication types and self-efficacy. *The Journal of Child Education, 14*(1), 115–129.

Japan

Azuma, H. (1994). Nihonjinn no shitsuke to kyouiku [Japanese socialization and education]. Tokyo, Japan: University of Tokyo Press.

Befu, H. (1986). The social and cultural background of child development in Japan and the United States. In H.W. Stevenson, H. Azuma, & K. Hakuta (Eds.), *Child development and education in Japan* (pp.13–27). New York: Freeman.

Bornstein, M.H. (2006). Parenting science and practice. In W. Damon & R.M. Lerner (Editors in Chief), and K.A. Renninger & I.E. Sigel (Eds.), *Handbook of child psychology, Vol. 4: Child psychology in practice* (pp. 893–949). Hoboken, NJ: Wiley.

Cabinet Office. (2013a). *Gender equality 2013 white book.* Retrieved from www.gender.go.jp/about_danjo/whitepaper/h25/gaiyou/index.html

Cabinet Office. (2013b). *Prompt report of research on work and life balance.* Retrieved from http://wwwa.cao.go.jp/wlb/research/wlb_h2511/follow-up.pdf#search

Cabinet Secretariat. (2013). *Joint meeting of Cabinet and ruling party about free early childhood education.* Retrieved from www.cas.go.jp/jp/seisaku/youji/dai2/sankou1.pdf

Chuouchosasha. (2012). *Opinion research about father's participation in childrearing: Report no. 659.* Retrieved from www.crs.or.jp/backno/No659/6592.htm

Harada, M. (2008). The past, present and future of childrearing. *Sodachinokagaku, 10,* 33–37.

Hasegawa, Y. (2010). Adjustment of time allocation and daily emotional experience during the transition to the role of working mother. *Japanese Journal of Psychology, 81,* 123–131.

Kazama, M., Hirabayashi, H., Karasawa, M., Tardif, T., & Olson, S. (2013). Ambiguous parenting and four-year-olds' understanding of others: A comparison between mothers in Japan and the U.S. *Japanese Journal of Developmental Psychology, 24,* 126–138.

Kikuchi, T., Matsumoto, S., & Sugawara, M. (2011). Parental expectations towards preschool: A longitudinal study from age four to five. *Japanese Journal of Developmental Psychology,* 22, 55–62.

Kojima, H. (1986). Child rearing concepts as a belief-value system of the society and the individual. In H.W. Stevenson, H. Azuma, & K. Hakuta (Eds.), *Child development and education in Japan* (pp. 39–54). New York: Freeman.

Makino, K. (1982). "Childcare anxiety" of mothers of infants and young children. *The Journal of Family Education Research Center, 3,* 35–56.

Markus, H.R., & Kitayama, S. (1991). Culture and self: Implications for cognition, motivation and self. *Psychological Review,* 98, 224–253.

Ministry of Education, Culture, Sports, Science and Technology. (2013). *Basic research on Japanese schools in 2013.* Tokyo, Japan.

Ministry of Health, Labor & Welfare (2010). *Outline of Ikumen Project.* Retrieved from http://www.mhlw.go.jp/bunya/koyoukintou/ikumen_shiryou/dl/ikumen_gaiyou.pdf

Ministry of Health, Labor & Welfare. (2013). *Research on demographics.*

Ministry of Health, Labor & Welfare, Statistics and Information Department. (2014). Vital statistics in Japan: Trends up to 2012.

Mori, I. (2012). Comparison of ego-identity between young Japanese and American people. *Japanese Journal of Adolescent Psychology, 24,* 31–43.

Motoshima, Y. (2013). Family expressiveness and young children's behavior problems: Role of maternal depressive symptoms and sensitivity. *Japanese Journal of Psychology, 84,* 199–208.

National Institute of Population and Social Security Research (2010). *The 14th national basic birth research.* Retrieved from www.ipss.go.jp/ps-doukou/j/doukou14/doukou14.asp

Nakamichi, K. (2013). Effects of childrearing styles on young children's self-regulation. *Bulletin of the Education Faculty, Shizuoka University, 63,* 109–121.

Nakamichi, K., & Nakazawa, J. (2003). Maternal/paternal childrearing style and young children's aggressive behavior. *Bulletin of the Faculty of Education of Chiba University, 51,* 173–179.

Nakazawa, J., & Shwalb, D.W. (2013). Fathering in Japan: Entering an era of involvement with children. In D.W. Shwalb, B.J. Shwalb, & M.E. Lamb (Eds.), *Fathers in cultural context* (pp. 42–67). New York: Routledge.

Onodera, A. (2011). The relationship between middle-aged daughters' feelings toward their fathers/mothers and subjective well-being. *Mejiro Journal of Psychology, 7,* 1–14.

Saito, S. (2012). Empirical research on the awareness of fathers who took the paternal leave. *Journal of Ohara Institute for Social Research, 647/648,* 77–88.

Sato, A., & Uchiyama, I. (2012). The effects of shared book reading on mothers' behavior with infants: A longitudinal intervention to increase reading frequency. *Japanese Journal of Developmental Psychology, 23,* 170–179.

Shi, X., & Katsurada, E. (2010). Distress of mothers with young children, in relation to their interdependent/independent self-construal and social support. *Journal of Developmental Psychology, 21,* 138–146.

Shwalb, D. W., Kawai, H., Shoji, J., & Tsunetsugu, K. (1995). The place of advice: Japanese parents' sources of information about child health and development. *Journal of Applied Developmental Psychology, 16,* 645–660.

Shwalb, D. W., Nakazawa, J., & Shwalb, B. J. (Eds.). (2005). *Applied developmental psychology: Theory, practice, and research from Japan.* Charlotte, NC: Information Age Publishing.

Shwalb, D. W., Nakazawa, J., Yamamoto, T., & Hyun, J.-H. (2010). Fathering in Japan, China, and Korea: Changing context, images, and roles. In M. E. Lamb (Ed.), *The role of the father in child development* (5th ed., pp. 341–387). Hoboken, NJ: Wiley.

Shwalb, D. W., Shwalb, B. J., Nakazawa, J., Hyun, J.-H., Le, H.V., & Satiadarma, M. P. (2009). Child development in East and Southeast Asia: Japan, Korea, Vietnam, and Indonesia. In M. H. Bornstein (Ed.), *Handbook of cultural developmental science* (pp. 445–464). New York: Psychology Press.

Shwalb, D. W., Shwalb, B. J., Sukemune, S., & Tatsumoto, S. (1992). Japanese non-maternal childcare: Past, present and future. In M. Lamb, K. Sternberg, C.-P. Hwang, & A. Broberg (Eds.), *Childcare in context* (pp. 331–353). Hillsdale, NJ: Erlbaum.

Toyama, K. (2011). Relation between 5- to 6-year-old children's theory of mind and their mothers' use of mind-related words. *Japanese Journal Educational Psychology, 59,* 427–440.

Ujiie, T., Ninomiya, K., Igarashi, A., Inoue, H., Yamamoto, C., & Shima, Y. (2010). Parental behavior and children's perceptions as mediators of the effects of marital conflict on children's depressive symptoms. *Japanese Journal of Developmental Psychology, 21,* 58–70.

Part III

THREE THEMES IN CHILDREN'S LIVES: GENDER ROLES, SIBLINGS, AND BECOMING AN ADOLESCENT

8

Gender Roles in Childhood and Adolescence

Deborah L. Best and Caitlin D. Bush

It is a Friday evening and Mr. and Mrs. Finney are in search of a babysitter for their two young children, Allison and Hunter. Their usual sitter just called in sick and the Finneys already have plans for the evening. In a frantic rush they visit a trusted child care website. They find that a local sitter named Cameron is available for the evening and after reviewing excellent references they hire Cameron. Thirty minutes later the doorbell rings at the Finney household. Mr. Finney goes to the front door and opens it to find a teenage boy standing on the doorstep. The boy introduces himself as Cameron, the sitter they have requested for the evening. Mr. Finney attempts to contain his shock as he invites Cameron into the house, but it is evident that he is surprised that the sitter is a male. Apparently he and his wife did not read the reviews carefully, he thinks to himself, because they certainly would not have hired a MALE babysitter to care for Allison and Hunter.

It is apparent that gender is a dominant consideration in many Western middle-class families' babysitter selection process and that a male performing such a job violates typical gender role expectations (Chaker, 2014). Although ideas about gender and the way gender is discussed are shifting, hesitance to hire a male babysitter or "manny" is a trend that permeates American society and has become a recent topic of interest across journals and discussion boards in other countries as well. In a role-play experiment examining whether sex and sexual orientation matter in decisions on child care, participants were most likely to choose a heterosexual female as a babysitter. Participants also indicated that both homosexual men and women were knowledgeable about child care, but they were least likely to choose a heterosexual male as a babysitter as such a role is a supposed violation of traditional sex-role expectations (Regan & Ramirez, 2000).

The ways in which gender is perceived and discussed may be evolving, but one thing certainly has not changed: as psychologists interested in development and culture, gender inevitably remains of critical consideration. Gender is one of the most salient physical features distinguishing human beings. As proof of its salience, what is the first question that is asked following the announcement of the birth of a healthy child? "Is it a boy or a girl?" This gender label affects almost every aspect of that child's subsequent life.

As infants, girls and boys are so similar that they are often difficult to distinguish from one another. However, throughout early childhood and into adolescence, boys and girls develop distinct differences in appearance, mannerisms, ways of talking, styles of dress, interests and games, and preferred playmates. Children learn the gender role for their sex—the behaviors and social roles that are expected of males and females in their particular society.

Munroe and Munroe (1975/1994) noted that in all known human societies there are modal sex differences in physical characteristics (e.g., primary and secondary sex characteristics), behavior, and at the adult level a division of labor. For children, sex differences are reported in child behavior (e.g., in 45 countries, nurturance, responsibility, obedience, self-reliance, achievement, independence; Barry, Bacon, & Child, 1967), and in child training (34 of 35 countries with full ratings). Sexual dimorphism appears very early in life (e.g., higher basal metabolism, more muscle development, higher pain threshold of male neonates, differential responses to early life stress; Davis & Pfaff, 2014; Rosenberg & Sutton-Smith, 1972) and continues, resulting in the well-known adult physical differences (e.g., for males, greater height, more massive skeleton, higher muscle-to-fat ratio, higher blood oxygen capacity, more body hair, primary and secondary sex characteristics; D'Andrade, 1966). Both physical and behavioral differences have been well documented across cultural groups (Munroe & Munroe, 1975/1994), suggesting that sex and gender have a pervasive influence on almost every aspect of individual and communal life.

Gender researchers (Ruble & Martin, 1998; Verhofstadt & Weytens, 2013) often differentiate between the words "sex," referring to the biological aspects of masculinity/femininity, and "gender" referring to the psycho-socio-cultural aspects that are constructed by culture. Unfortunately, this creates an unnecessary dichotomy between biological and environmental influences (Fausto-Sterling, 2000; Hoyenga & Hoyenga, 1993).

BIOLOGICAL ASPECTS OF GENDER

Even though gender and sex are often treated categorically, many biological differences between males and females are on a continuum rather than falling into a clean dichotomy (Kessler & McKenna, 1978). For example, people differ in levels of testosterone, some are at the higher end of the continuum with most males, others at the lower end with most females, and still others range across the middle at levels that are below the typical male but above the typical female. In most biological definitions of gender, chromosomes, hormones, gonads, and external anatomy are the determinative factors.

Biological Determinism

When similarities between genders are found across cultures, they are often used as support for the role of genes and hormones, which implies genetic or biological determinism. Biological determinism assumes that a biological influence leads to an irreversible sex difference, making biology the necessary and sufficient cause of sex differences. Biology is neither. The long-standing nature-nurture controversy within developmental psychology has shown that biology does not cause behavior and that such a notion is quite naive.

Sex chromosomes or sex hormones are neither necessary nor sufficient to cause behaviors; they simply change the probability of occurrence of certain behaviors in various environments (Hoyenga & Hoyenga, 1993). The gene-behavior pathway is bidirectional (Gottlieb, 1983), and somewhat like people inherit genes, they may "inherit" environments by living close to parents and family.

Probabilistic Epigenesis

Genes and environment may act similarly on growth and development, and at all times, the developmental process reflects their interaction (Gottlieb, 1976, 2007). Life history strategies (evolutionary patterns of adaptation that differ by developmental stage) can be altered by both genes and developmental environments (Hoyenga & Hoyenga, 1993), affecting brain anatomy, the child's intellectual abilities and traits, and leading to stability and change. In the sexually dimorphic process, gender is the added factor that affects the form of the interaction between genes and environmental context.

PSYCHO-SOCIO-CULTURAL ASPECTS OF GENDER

Psychological aspects of gender refer to behavioral differences between males and females, how they interact with people and things in their environments. The gender of rearing usually determines gender identity, gender roles, gender stereotypes, gender-role ideology, and other cultural-environmental aspects of gender, and these are the focus of the present chapter.

Multidimensional View of Sex-Typing

Sex-typing, the development of gender-related differences in children, changes continuously with age and is a multidimensional process including constructs and content areas (Huston, 1983). Ruble and Martin (1998) identified six areas (biological gender, activities and interests, personal-social attributes, gender-based social relationships, stylistic and symbolic content, and gender-related values) and four content aspects (beliefs, self-perception, preferences or attitudes, behavioral tendencies). Although gender-related differences are found in all areas, few studies have addressed the interrelationships among the areas, and even fewer of these relationships have been examined cross-culturally (e.g., two exceptions, examination of gender stereotypes and self- and ideal-self descriptions of adolescents by Cheung Mui-ching [1986] and Williams and Best [1990).

Cultural Influences on Gender Development

Even though biological factors may impose predispositions and restrictions on development, sociocultural factors are important determinants of gender development (Best & Williams, 1993; Munroe & Munroe, 1975/1994). Culture has profound effects on behavior, prescribing how babies are delivered, how girls and boys are socialized, how they are dressed, what is considered intelligent behavior, what tasks girls and boys are taught, and what roles adult women and men will adopt. Children's behaviors, even behaviors that are considered biologically determined, such as walking and other motor milestones, are governed by culture (Super, 1976). Cultural universals in gender differences are often explained by similarities in socialization practices, while cultural differences are attributed to differences in socialization.

Children grow up within other people's scripts, which guide their actions long before the children themselves can understand or carry out the culturally appropriate actions. For developmental researchers, one of the crucial tasks is to identify the mechanism responsible for the changes seen across time. This means that researchers must unpackage broadly defined cultural variables to identify what aspects or processes are responsible for the development of particular behavioral outcomes. Gender should be examined not only in relation to culture (e.g., social systems, practices, myths, beliefs, rituals), but also in the context of the history and economics of the society

(Mukhopadhyay & Higgins, 1998). Identification of the mechanisms within a culture that are responsible for age-related developmental change must also account for variation between individuals within the cultural group as well as variation between cultures.

Not only is the subject of study, the child or parent, changing across time, but that change takes place in a cultural system that is itself changing. Thus, developmental change is the emerging synthesis of several major factors interacting over time, what Cole (1999) refers to as a bio-social-behavioral shift–changes in the relations between a child's biological makeup, the social world in which he or she lives, and the resulting behaviors that occur. Several illustrative examples of this interplay are: (a) a mother's influence on her child's prenatal development through the foods and other substances that she ingests (biological) or (b) the songs she sings during the final weeks of pregnancy (social, cultural), which can be heard in utero and become preferred (DeCasper & Fifer, 1980); (c) the cultural practices that surround the birth of a child in various societies that are relevant to the discussion of gender, (d) a parent's interpretation (e.g., Is it a boy or is it a girl?) of the child's biological sex characteristics following birth.

Even when particular behaviors are assumed to be heavily biologically determined, cultural practices can play an important role in shaping them. For example, lengths of sleeping bouts are modified by culturally determined demands on mothers' time, and the course of sitting and walking are influenced by childcare practices (Super & Harkness, 1982). Cultural practices shape children to fit differing life circumstances.

SOCIALIZATION OF BOYS AND GIRLS

Parents

"Baby X" studies (e.g., sex of the infant is not known to study participants) in the United States have shown that parents and young adults treat infants differently depending on whether they think they are interacting with a girl or a boy (Rubin, Provezano, & Luria, 1974; Sidorowicz & Lunney, 1980). Boys are described as big and strong, and are bounced and handled more physically than girls who are described as pretty and sweet, and are handled more gently. Even before birth after finding out their child's sex via ultrasound, parents described girls as "finer" and "quieter" than boys who were described as "more coordinated" than girls (Sweeney & Bradbard, 1989). Parental presumptions such as these reflect the impact of culture on parents' memory of their own past and their assumptions about their child's future. However, culture is dynamic and changes across time. In the United States, parents of the 1950s would never have assumed their daughters would grow up to be soccer players in college, but many 21st-century parents would certainly have this expectation.

Such parental expectations are not peculiar to the United States. Greenfield and her colleagues (Greenfield, Brazelton, & Childs, 1989) report that shortly after birth, Zinacanteco babies in Mexico are given objects that are gender appropriate. A father reported giving his son three green chilies to hold so he would know to buy chili when he grew up. Parents assume that things in the future will be as they have been in the past, an assumption of continuity.

Behavioral differences between girls and boys are often attributed to differences in socialization. Barry, Bacon, and Child (1957) examined socialization practices in over 100 societies and found that generally boys are reared to achieve and to be self-reliant and independent while girls are reared to be nurturant, responsible, and obedient. However, when Hendrix and Johnson (1985) reanalyzed these data, they found no evidence of a general sex differentiation in socialization, with similar emphases in the training of girls and boys to be self-reliant and independent.

In a meta-analysis, Lytton and Romney (1991) examined 158 North American studies of socialization and found the only significant effect was for the encouragement of sex-typed behaviors. In 17 additional studies from other Western countries, there was a significant sex difference for physical punishment with boys receiving a greater portion than girls. Differential treatment of boys and girls decreased with age, particularly for disciplinary strictness and encouragement of sex-typed activities.

Overall, socialization studies suggest that there may be subtle differences in how parents treat boys and girls. These differences are only occasionally significant, perhaps due to the ways the behaviors are measured or which parent is being observed. Fathers play an especially important role in signaling the types of behaviors they consider appropriate, particularly for their sons who have fewer accessible male role models and for whom deviations are considered more undesirable (Langlois & Downs, 1980). Even if parents do not differentiate between daughters and sons, the same parental treatment may affect girls and boys differently. Research in the United States suggests that gender lessons are finely focused on specific behaviors and that learning often occurs during transitional periods, such as toddlerhood or adolescence, when new abilities first emerge (Beal, 1994).

Parents' behaviors communicate the importance of gender via their reactions to their children's behavior and by the organization of activities within the family. Parent behaviors, as well as that of peers, teachers, and other socialization agents, help shape sex-appropriate behaviors, toy choices, playmates, and other activities. Peers, task assignment, care-giving, and the educational environment are among the cultural influences that help to socialize children's gender role behaviors.

Peers

Throughout childhood and adolescence, peers play an important role in socialization. In some cultures, boys and girls are separated by the end of infancy (Fouts, Hallam, Purandare, 2013; Whiting & Edwards, 1988), and in others, children play freely within mixed age and gender groups (Rogoff, 1990). Peer influence increases as children grow older, helping to structure the transition between childhood and adulthood (Edwards, 1992). Maccoby (1998) suggests that peers may play as important a role as parents, if not more so, in the socialization of gender roles.

Maccoby (1998) has identified three major gender-linked phenomena in children's social development: gender segregation, differentiation of interaction styles, and group asymmetry. In many cultures (Whiting & Edwards, 1988), sometimes as early as age 3, and somewhat later in other cultures (Harkness & Super, 1985), there is a powerful tendency for children to seek out playmates of their own sex and to avoid children of the other sex, and this tendency strengthens throughout grade school. These segregated playgroups differ in their interaction styles and activities. Boys strive for dominance, play rough, take risks, "grandstand," and are reluctant to reveal weaknesses to each other. In contrast, girls self-disclose more, try to maintain positive social relationships, and avoid open conflict. Same-sex playgroups provide children with useful socialization experiences and the venue for construction of social norms, but there is an asymmetry in these groups. Compared with girls' groups, boys' groups are more cohesive, more exclusionary, and more separate from adult culture.

In preschool children, sex similarity appears to influence playmate selection even beyond the role of activity similarity (Martin et al., 2013). Maccoby (1998) found that behavioral compatibility, avoidance of aggression or rough-and-tumble play, and matching activity levels also cannot by themselves account for gender segregation of playgroups. She proposes an interplay between biology (differences in metabolic rate, activity level, arousability, maturation rates of language and inhibitory mechanisms, prenatal hormones), socialization (role of fathers, more emotion-oriented talk with girls, role of peer-group, cultural practices), and cognition (self-identity, cultural stereotypes, scripts). Segregation of play groups leads to different activities and toy choices, which in turn may lead to differences in intellectual and emotional development (Block, 1983).

Examination of peer interactions of 2- to 10-year-olds from the Six Culture Study and from six additional samples (Edwards, 1992; Edwards & Whiting, 1993) showed a robust, cross-culturally universal same-gender preference that emerges after age 2. By middle childhood gender segregation is found frequently, perhaps in part motivated by a desire for self-discovery

(Edwards, 1992). Agemates who resemble the child in abilities and activity preferences also provide the greatest opportunity for competition and conflict. Although interest in opposite-sex peers increases in adolescence, a preference for same-sex peers is evident throughout adolescence and into adulthood (Mehta & Strough, 2010).

Gender segregation also results from culturally prescribed adolescent initiation rites, which are found in many cultures. Initiation rites are designed to separate initiates from their families, to socialize them to culturally appropriate sexuality, dominance, and aggression, to create peer group loyalty, and to solidify political ties. Collective rituals, more common for boys than girls, are found more frequently in warrior societies that emphasize gender differences in adult activities (Edwards, 1992). Western education has begun to change initiation rites, but vestiges remain in many cultures, such as circumcision celebrations for young Turkish boys.

Task Assignment

Examining children's learning environments in various cultures shows how cultural differences in socialization processes affect the development of gender roles. Learning environments were investigated in the Six Culture Study (Edwards & Whiting, 1974; Minturn & Lambert, 1964; Whiting & Edwards, 1973), which examined aggression, nurturance, responsibility, and help and attention-seeking behaviors of children aged 3 to 11 in Okinawa (Japan), the Mixtecans in Mexico, the Philippines, India, the Gusii in Kenya, and the United States. Fewer gender differences were found in the three groups (United States, the Philippines, Kenya) where both boys and girls cared for younger siblings and performed household chores. In contrast, more differences were found where boys and girls were treated dissimilarly (India, Mexico, Okinawa) with girls assuming more responsibility for siblings and household tasks. Indeed, the fewest gender differences were found between American girls and boys who were assigned few childcare or household tasks. More recently, similar patterns have been found in the United States where gender differences in household responsibilities vary between ethnic and socioeconomic groups (Giles, Cantin, Best, Tyrrell, & Gigler, 2014).

Bradley (1993) examined children's labor in 91 Standard Cross-Cultural Sample cultures (Murdock & White, 1969) and found that children younger than age 6 perform little work whereas children older than 10 perform work similar to that of same gender adults. Both boys and girls do women's work (e.g., fetching water) more frequently than men's (e.g., hunting), and children tend to do chores that adults consider demeaning or unskilled. Women monitor children's work while simultaneously socializing with their daughters. These joint tasks provide help for the mother, which she also needs. Parents report that along with providing care in parents' old age, children's labor is an important benefit of having children (Kağitçibaşi, 1982b).

Caregiving

Analyzing data from 186 societies, Weisner and Gallimore (1977) found that in most cases mothers, female adult relatives, and female children are the primary caregivers for infants. However, when infants reach early childhood, older girls and boys share caretaking responsibilities. Sibling caregivers play an important socialization role in societies where 2–4-year-olds spend more than 70% of their time every day with their child nurses (see Maynard's chapter 9 in this volume). Because mothers in such societies spend much of their time in productive activities, they are not devoted exclusively to mothering (Minturn & Lambert, 1964) even though children in all cultures see mothers as responsible for children.

Indeed, Katz and Konnor (1981) found that in 20% of 80 cultures they surveyed, fathers were rarely or never near their infants. Father-infant relationships were close in only% of the cultures, but even when close, fathers spent only 14% of their time with their infants and only gave 6% of the actual caregiving. Paternal interactions with children are more likely to be characterized by physical play than by socialization, caregiving, and didactic play (Schoppe-Sullivan, Kotila, Jia, Lang, & Bower, 2013).

Father absence has been associated with their sons showing impaired social behaviors (Balcom, 1998; Katz & Konner, 1981; Whiting, 1965). Sons who experience lengthy father absence due to war (Stolz, 1954) or sea voyages (Gronseth, 1957) show effeminate overt behaviors, high levels of dependence, excessive fantasy aggression, as well as some overly masculine behaviors. Compared with father-present children, father-absent children are more aggressive (Amato & Keith, 1991) but only father-absent boys showed less stereotyped sex-role behaviors (Stevenson & Black, 1988).

Fathers pay less attention to female offspring than to males and promote sex-typed activities more than mothers (Lytton & Romney, 1991). Fathers begin engaging in such gender-typed activities with their children as early as age 2, before children have established a distinct understanding of gender roles (Leavell, Tamis-LeMonda, Ruble, Zosuls, & Cabrera, 2012). While mothers are equally involved in the caregiving for sons and daughters, fathers tend to be more involved as caregivers of sons (Rohner & Rohner, 1982). Mackey (Mackey, 1981) observed parents and children in public places in 10 different cultures and found that girls were seldom with adult males while boys were frequently in all-male groups, and these differences increased with age.

Education

Educational settings also greatly influence the development of children's gender roles. Observations in classrooms of Japanese and American fifth graders revealed that teachers paid more attention to boys, particularly negative attention, and the greater attention was not due to off-task or bad behavior (Hamilton, Blumenfeld, Akoh, & Miura, 1991).

Parents' beliefs about academic performance can also have a profound impact on children's achievements. Serpell (1993) found that education was considered to be more important for Zambian boys than girls, and fathers made schooling arrangements even though mothers were primarily responsible for childcare. In China, Japan, and the United States, mothers expect boys to be better at mathematics and girls to be better at reading (Lummis & Stevenson, 1990) even though they perform equally well in some aspects of both disciplines.

CULTURAL PRACTICES THAT INFLUENCE BEHAVIORS OF MALES AND FEMALES

The previous section examined specific aspects of socialization, but there are broader distal cultural influences on gender that provide an important context for gender-role learning. Among these practices are the status of women, gender division of labor, religious beliefs and values, economic factors, and political participation.

Status of Women

Ethnographic evidence suggests that women's "status" is multidimensional and includes economic indicators, power, autonomy, prestige, and ideological dimensions (Mukhopadhyay & Higgins, 1988; Quinn, 1977). Asymmetry in status between men and women may be due to women's reproductive roles and physical differences as well as the complexity of the society (Ember, 1981).

What is considered masculine and feminine may differ across cultures, but the literature suggests two possible cultural universals: At least to some degree, every society assigns traits and tasks according to gender (Munroe & Munroe, 1975); and, in no society is the status of women superior to that of men, while the reverse is common (Hoyenga & Hoyenga, 1993; Population Crisis Committee, 1988).

Gender Division of Labor

Analysis of ethnographic records of jobs and tasks in 244 different societies found that men were involved with hunting, metal work, weapon making, and travel further from home while women were responsible for cooking and food preparation, carrying water, caring for clothing, and making things used in the home (D'Andrade; 1966). Women's participation in subsistence activities was consistent with childrearing activities (Segal, 1983), and men had major childrearing responsibilities in only 10% of the 80 cultures examined (Katz & Konner, 1981).

Recent decreases in infant mortality and advances in technology have made it possible for women to participate more extensively in the labor force outside the home (Huber, 1986). However, compared with men, women remain economically disadvantaged and are paid 70 to 90% less than their male counterparts, with even lower ratios in some Asian and Latin American countries (International Labor Organization, 2009). Even in societies where women are active in the labor force, there has not been a commensurate reduction in their household duties (The World Bank Group, 2013). Across 29 countries, including the United States, Switzerland, Sweden, Mexico, Italy, Japan, Poland, and China, the overwhelming majority of household work is performed by women, regardless of the extent of their occupational demands (Organisation for Economic Co-operation and Development, 2014).

The difficulty in eliminating gender divisions in labor is illustrated by the Israeli kibbutz, established in the 1920s where there was a deliberate attempt to develop egalitarian societies (Rosner, 1967; Spiro, 1995). Initially there was no sexual division of labor. Both women and men worked in the fields, drove tractors, worked in the kitchen and in the laundry. However with time and increases in the birthrate, women found they could not undertake many of the physical tasks that men were capable of doing. Women soon found themselves in the roles they had tried to escape—cooking, cleaning, laundering, teaching, caring for children. Somewhat surprisingly, the kibbutz attempts at equitable division of labor had little effect on the children. Kibbutz-raised children and Swedish children showed no differences in how they conceptualized typical female and male sex-role behaviors or in their sex-typed self-attributions (Carlsson & Barnes, 1986).

Religious Beliefs and Values

Religious and cultural views of gender roles and family honor influence perceptions of women and their working outside the home (Rapoport, Lomski-Feder, & Masalia, 1989), as well as the role models children see. For instance, ideals of personal and family honor in Latin America and the Middle East link the manliness of men (*machismo*, *muruwwa*) with the sexual purity of women (*vergüenza,'ird*), and these influence the division of labor within the family and work outside the home (Youssef, 1974). Some religious communities prescribe proper roles and behavior for males and females, and children are brought up in ways consistent with these views.

Economic Factors

Economic factors appear to influence gender-related cultural practices. Bride price, a compensation for the loss of a daughter's economic contributions to her family (Heath, 1958), is found more frequently where her contributions are substantial. Dowry accompanies the bride when her economic contributions to her family are relatively small. Cronk (1993) theorized that relative to females, the reproductive success of males is affected more by socioeconomic factors, particularly in societies where men may have more than one wife and where they must pay a bridewealth for their wives. Consequently, when parents have high socioeconomic status so that sons can pay for wives, males are favored, but when parents have low status, females are favored because they can be married off to wealthier, higher-status neighbors.

Sex-biased parental investment in children may be affected by socioeconomic conditions (Cronk, 1993). Among the Mukogodo of central Kenya who are at the bottom of the regional hierarchy of regional wealth and prestige, the male-female birth ratio is about equal, but the 1986 census recorded 98 girls and 66 boys under age 4. Although there is no evidence of male infanticide, it is likely that boys' much higher death rate is due to favoritism toward girls. Compared with sons, daughters are breast-fed longer, are generally well fed, and visit the doctor more often. Because men in the Mukogodo area can have as many wives as they can afford, women are in short supply and as a result they all find husbands.

In sharp contrast, in many other traditional parts of the world (e.g., India, China, Turkey, Korea) cultural practices favor boys who are highly valued by their families and whose birth leads to great rejoicing (Kağitçibaşi, 1982a). Bride-burning (Ghadially & Kumar, 1988), wife beating (Flavia, 1988), and female infanticide (Krishnaswamy, 1988) are cultural practices that demonstrate the lack of concern for women in some traditional Indian cultures. In the United States (Pooler, 1991; Puri, Adams, Ivey, & Nachtigall, 2011) and in non-Western countries (Bandyopadhyay, 2003), preference for boys continues to be strong even though many of the religious traditions and economic circumstances that created the preference for sons no longer apply in contemporary society.

Female Political Participation

Across cultures, men are more involved in political activities and possess greater power than women (Coffe & Bolzendahl, 2010; Ember, 1981; Ross, 1985). The long-standing stereotyped dichotomy of public/male versus private/female suggests that men are in the public eye, active in business, politics, and culture, while women stay at home, caring for home and family

(Peterson & Runyan, 1993). However, this dichotomy is not supported by cross-cultural studies showing women actively working and in public life outside the home and men being more involved with their families (del Mar Alonso-Almeida, 2014; Meil, 2013).

Moreover, young girls now conceptualize the female gender role to encompass both homemaking and employment outside the home, especially when there is a more egalitarian distribution of household labor (Croft, Schmader, Block, & Baron, 2014). Children's images of women reflect the change in conditions and attitudes toward women around the world.

THEORIES OF SEX ROLE DEVELOPMENT

Even though there is theoretical disagreement about the sources of influence and the course of gender role development, most theories recognize the role of gender information readily available in the child's culture. While maturational theories have gone out of vogue, many of the assumptions about the role of biological influences remain important and have been incorporated into other, more current theories of gender role development, such as evolutionary theory and social role theory.

Evolutionary Theories

Growing out of early 19th-century Darwinian (1872) reasoning, evolutionary theory posits that the forces of natural selection shape the morphological features of the organism, which in turn shape behavioral and psychological tendencies (Dixon & Lerner, 1999; Kenrick & Luce, 2000). Humans and animals inherit brains, bodies, and specific behavioral mechanisms that are equipped to adapt to their environments and to solve the recurrent problems confronted during their ancestral past. Evolutionary success is measured not by survival but ultimately by reproductive success. Sexual selection (e.g., attracting a mate; Geary, 1998) and differential parental investment (e.g., nutritional cost of carrying fetus, provision of food, protection from predators; Trivers, 1985) may account for many of the sex differences found throughout the animal kingdom.

Sex differences in physical development and reproductive life history are linked to sex differences in social behaviors, such as mate preferences (Buss, 1989), aggression (Daly & Wilson, 1988), sexuality (Daly & Wilson, 1988), and child care (Geary, 1998). Some evolutionary theorists assume that cultural variation in behavior results from a flexible genetic program unfolding in variable environments (Kenrick & Luce, 2000; Öhman, 1986).

In an effort to strengthen their arguments, evolutionary theorists dealing with gender have borrowed experimental psychology's concept of preparedness, which grew out of research with animal taste aversion and with the development of human phobias (Rozin & Kalat, 1971; Seligman, 1971). They propose that males and females enter the world biologically prepared to experience their environments differently and these experiences shape sex-appropriate behaviors (Kenrick & Luce, 2000). While this is an interesting application, there presently are no data to support the extension of the preparedness mechanism from the learning of food avoidance (poison) and fear responses (e.g., from the predatory defense system—fear of snakes, spiders; from dominance/submissiveness system—social fears) to gender-related social behavior.

Many current researchers find the broad outline of evolutionary theory to be correct but point to the difficulty in testing the propositions and assumptions. Perhaps the most serious weakness of evolutionary approaches is that they do not account for the precise developmental mechanisms by which gender-differentiated values and norms are transmitted to individuals within a cultural group.

Social Role Theory

According to social role theory, the differences between male and female behaviors are a result of the different social roles that they play, which in turn are based on the sexual division of labor. The division of labor and the gender hierarchy of power and status are a function of the differences in reproductive activities and the physical size and strength of women and men (Wood & Eagly, 1999), with differences typically favoring men (Eagly, Wood, & Diekman, 2000). The contrasting social positions of men and women result in differing gender roles (Ross, 1977), which include both beliefs (descriptive norms) and expectations (injunctive norms; Cialdini & Trost, 1998) about what men and women do. Because women are more frequently associated with the domestic role, the characteristics thought to exemplify homemakers are ascribed to women in general. Likewise, characteristics thought to typify providers are ascribed to men in general (Eagly et al., 2000). Cultural expectations promote conformity to gender roles and influence how people think about themselves and their perceptions of masculinity and femininity. Indeed, gender stereotypes often become the rationalizations that justify differential sex role distributions (Williams & Best, 1982/1990).

Critics of social role theory point out that physical sex differences are not the entire story. Social role theory fails to explain why the two social structures, sexual division of labor and gender hierarchy, are common in most cultural groups. Furthermore, the mechanisms are not identified by which social structures influence individuals and groups within various cultural settings.

One support for social role theory comes from Van Leeuwen's (1978) ecological model of sex differences in behavior. She proposes that in sedentary, high-food-accumulating societies training for males and females differs greatly and females are trained to be nurturant and compliant. Inversely, in low-food-accumulating societies (e.g., hunting societies), there is little division of labor by sex with both men and women contributing to subsistence. Thus, there is no need to train either females or males to be nurturant and compliant. Cross-cultural variations in gender-related variables are most likely a product of socialization practices that vary in their degrees of compliance training.

Social Learning Theory

In the 1960s, Sears and his colleagues (Sears, Maccoby, & Levin, 1957; Sears, Rau, & Alpert, 1965) revised Freud's notions of sex role development to be consistent with learning theory's principles of reinforcement and modeling. Accordingly, sex-typed behaviors resulted from differential parenting behaviors, warmth and emotional support from mothers, and control and discipline from fathers. Bandura (Bandura, 1969; Bussey & Bandura, 1984) and Mischel (1970) expanded the cognitive aspects of social learning theory by emphasizing the role of modeling and expectations in the differential treatment of boys and girls.

Because observational learning is a powerful process, modeling is important in the development of sex-typing. Gender stereotypes can be passed from parent to child, from one generation to the next, and from one child to another (Endendijik et al., 2013; Hoyenga & Hoyenga, 1993). Girls are systematically exposed to fewer same-sex models with power and prestige than are boys, a process that certainly affects the development of stereotypes.

While there is substantial cross-cultural evidence that social learning is an important part of gender role learning, by itself, social learning is not a sufficient explanation. Cross-culturally, there is wide variation in the differential treatment of boys and girls, which is not consistently tied to differential behaviors (Bronstein, 1984; Lamb, Frodi, Hwand, Frodi, & Steinberg, 1982; Russell & Russell, 1987). Task assignment and role models in children's cultural context provide differential learning opportunities for boys and girls and encourage distinct behaviors. Indeed, childhood culture and peer group socialization may be a more important carrier of social change than are parents.

Cognitive Stage Theories

Even though Piaget used biological concepts, he did not believe that the invariant stages of cognitive development were wired into the genetic code. Children interacted with their environments demonstrating increasingly more sophisticated ways of thinking. Development was an active construction process in which children developed schemes, or action structures, to deal with their environments (Ginsberg & Opper, 1969). The environment influenced development through children's physical experience (manipulations of objects) and social interactions (Ginsberg & Opper, 1969).

Building on Piaget's ideas, Kohlberg (1966) developed a cognitively oriented theory of gender development. Children seek out information and experiences that are appropriate for their own sex, and their understanding of gender develops through a series of stages from gender identity or labeling (achieved by 2½ years), through gender stability (by 3½ years), and finally gender consistency or constancy (by 4½ to 5). The impact of external forces and experiences on children's developing gender-role orientation is governed by the child's emerging cognitive structure.

The Munroes (Munroe, Shimmin, & Munroe, 1984) tested cognitive-developmental theory in a cross-cultural study with children in American Samoa, Belize, Kenya, and Nepal. They expected that gender classification would be more salient for children in cultures that emphasized sex-differentiated socialization practices (e.g., Kenya, Nepal). Because the latter stages of gender understanding depend on cognitive structural factors, they were expected to be less influenced by culture and should appear at approximately the same time for all groups. They found that contrary to expectations, the culture-specific predictions were not confirmed, but findings did support cognitive development theory in cross-cultural context.

While gender development researchers recognize the importance of cognitive factors, it has been difficult to demonstrate an antecedent relationship between the stages of gender identity and sex-typed behaviors (Bussey, 1983). Children appear to learn sex-appropriate behaviors before they can translate these behaviors into words. Golombok and colleagues (Golombok, Rust, Zervoulis, Golding, & Hines, 2012) actually found continuity in sex-typed behavior from age 3 to 13 for both boys and girls. Furthermore, there appears to be a two-process model for boys (acceptance of masculine behavior, rejection of feminine behavior) and a one-process model for girls (acceptance of same-sex behavior only). It would be interesting to see whether these same gender identity acquisition processes are found across different cultural groups.

Gender Schema Theories

Schema theorists assume that individuals develop notions about gender, and these ideas organize and bias their behavior, thinking, and attention to information in their environments (Martin & Halverson, 1981). Environmental information about what it means to be male or female stimulates the creation of gender schemas or theories, which in turn facilitate gender-related processing of newly incoming information (Martin, 2000). As a result, children come to see themselves and others in terms of gender distinctions—boys-girls, females-males, masculinity-femininity, women-men. Gender stereotypes are used to evaluate the appropriateness of behaviors.

The cognitive-developmental approach to gender proposes a multidimensional model (Huston, 1983; Ruble & Martin, 1998) of gender-related constructs from gender identity, gender stereotypes, gender scripts, self-perceptions of masculinity and femininity, and expectations about others' gender appropriate behaviors. Interrelationships among these constructs have been hypothesized, but only a few have been tested developmentally or cross-culturally, and even fewer have been related to gendered behaviors (e.g., interaction styles, segregation of play groups, Maccoby, 1998; gendered appearance rigidity, gender identity, Halim et al., 2014).

Differences in Male and Female Gender-Related Behaviors

Research across cultures has shown consistent patterns of differences in the behaviors of males and females in four areas: nurturance, aggression, proximity to adults, and self-esteem. These will be reviewed briefly.

Nurturance

In the classic Six Culture Study, Edwards and Whiting (1980) found that between ages 5 and 12, gender differences in nurturance were most consistent in behavior directed toward infants and toddlers rather than in behavior directed toward mothers and older children. Because infants elicit more nurturant behavior than do older children, girls who spent more time with infants displayed more nurturance than boys who did not interact as much with infants.

These findings are consistent with Barry et al.'s (1957) findings across 110 cultures that found that compared with boys, girls were socialized to be more nurturant (82% of cultures), obedient (35% of cultures), and responsible (61% of cultures). Boys, on the other hand, were socialized to be more achieving (87% of cultures) and self-reliant (85% of cultures) than girls. In 108 cultures, Welch, Page, and Martin (1981) found more pressure for boys to conform to their roles than girls who also had greater role variability.

Aggression

Cross-culturally, prepubertal boys have consistently shown higher levels of aggression, competitiveness, dominance-seeking, and rough-and-tumble play than girls (Ember, 1981; Hay et al., 2011; Munroe et al., 2000). When examining data from the Six Culture Study and additional African samples, Whiting and Edwards (1988) found sex differences in aggression and dominance, but contrary to their earlier findings, aggression showed no decrease with age and was more physical among the oldest boys. In playground observations in Ethiopia, Switzerland, and the USA (Omark, Omark, & Edelman, 1975), boys were more aggressive than girls, and similar patterns were found in four !Kung Bushmen villages of Africa's Kalahari Desert and in London (Blurton Jones & Konner, 1973). A meta-analysis of studies in 12 countries revealed that boys exhibit more frequent direct aggression than girls, although there were no significant gender differences in displays of indirect aggression (Card, Stucky, Sawalani, & Little, 2008).

Mothers in the Six Culture Study generally react similarly to boys' and girls' aggression, but there was some differential aggression training in Okinawa and the United States suggesting the father's role in socializing boys' aggression (Minturn & Lambert, 1964). In Western European countries, there are gender differences in the forms of aggression. Initially, males are more restrained but when they act, they are more violent (Ramirez, 1993) than females who are more emotional and use shouting and verbal attacks (Burbank, 1987).

Proximity to Adults and Activity

Observing 5–7-year-olds at play in eight cultures (Australian Aboriginal, Balinese, Ceylonese, Japanese, Kikuyu, Navajo, Punjabi, Taiwanese), Freedman (1976) determined that boys ran in larger groups, covered more physical space, and engaged in more physical and unpredictable activities than girls who were involved in more conversations and games with repeated activities. Usually, girls are found closer to home (Draper, 1975; Munroe & Munroe, 1971; Whiting & Edwards, 1973). Boys interact more with other boys and girls interact more with adults (Blurton Jones & Konner, 1973; Omark et al., 1975; Whiting & Edwards, 1973). Both task assignment (Whiting & Edwards, 1973) and behavioral preferences may contribute to these gender differences (Draper, 1975).

Self-Esteem

Even though gender role attributions are similar, girls seem less satisfied with being girls than boys are with being boys (Burns & Homel, 1986), and boys perceive themselves to be more competent than girls (van Dongen-Melman, Koot, & Verhulst, 1993). Girls may report slightly lower self-esteem than boys, but the difference is often not significant (Farrugia, Chen, Greenberger, Dmitrieva, Macek, 2004; Kling, Hyde, Showers, Carolin, & Buswell, 1999). Adolescent girls in Nepal, the Philippines, and

Australia had lower opinions of their physical and mathematical abilities than boys, but girls in Australia and Nigeria felt more competent in reading (Watkins & Akande, 1992). Nigerian boys believed they were more intelligent than did girls (Olowu, 1985).

Childhood Disorders

Along with differences in usual social behaviors, childhood disorders also show distinct gender differences in prevalence rates. For example, Attention Deficit Hyperactivity Disorder (ADHD) is more prevalent in boys, with boys manifesting symptoms of hyperactivity, inattention, impulsivity, and externalizing problems more often than girls (Gershon, 2002). Autism is also predominantly diagnosed in boys, although the specific biological bases underlying this male sex bias are still unclear (Becker, 2012). Conduct disorder is yet another childhood disorder with higher prevalence in the male population (Maughan et al., 2004). Although more boys are diagnosed with childhood disorders than girls, girls are more likely to experience depression in adolescence (Nolen-Hoeksema, 2001). Similarly, eating disorders are also more commonly found in adolescent girls than boys (Micali, Ploubidis, De Stavola, Simonoff, & Treasure, 2013). Differences in these disorders could be considered more extreme manifestations of the gender differences seen in children's social behaviors.

In summary, differences between girls and boys in nurturance, aggression, and mobility are robust and consistently found across cultures (Ember, 1981), but self-esteem differences are less consistent. These gender differences in social behaviors are also reflected in the unhealthy behaviors they display. Culture shapes children's social behaviors by determining the company they keep and the activities that engage their time. Such experiences can minimize, maximize, or even eliminate gender differences in social behaviors.

GENDER ROLES AND STEREOTYPES

Gender roles and behaviors develop within the context of cultural stereotypes about male-female differences. In the United States, children as young as 19 months of age begin using gender labels to stereotype objects as masculine or feminine (Zosuls et al., 2009), and by age 3 to 4, children use stereotypic labels accurately with toys, activities, and occupations (Guttentag & Longfellow, 1977).

Italian children associated toys representing domestic activities with a female silhouette while they connected toys representing technology, warfare, locomotion, and construction to a male silhouette (De Caroli & Sagone, 2007). In Africa, similar gender stereotyping of toys is found where girls play with dolls and boys construct vehicles and weapons (Bloch & Adler, 1994). By age 4 to 5, Sri Lankan village children exhibit gender differences in play, similar to those found with British children (Prossner, Hutt, Hutt, Mahindadasa, & Goonetilleke, 1986). Boys display more negative behaviors and more fantasy object play, while girls show more fantasy person play. Although cultural factors may determine the content of children's play, only a few behaviors show culturally specific forms.

Development of Sex-Trait Stereotypes

Children in the United States acquire knowledge of sex-trait stereotypes somewhat later than stereotypic knowledge of toys and occupations (Best et al., 1977; Williams & Best, 1982/1990). Using the Sex Stereotype Measure II (SSM II) to assess children's knowledge of adult-defined stereotypes, research with European American children revealed a consistent pattern of increasing knowledge from kindergarten through high school, similar to a typical learning curve. Stereotype knowledge increases dramatically in the early elementary school years and scores plateau in the junior high years. African American children's scores also increase with age but are lower than those of the European American children, reflecting subcultural variation in stereotype knowledge.

Stereotypes are more differentiated in the early years and become more flexible from age 5 to 11 (Banse, Gawronski, Rebetez, Gutt, & Morton, 2010; Biernat, 1991). Children show a growing recognition of the similarities between the sexes that may lead to the incorporation of gender-incongruent information into their gender stereotypes and self-construals (Hanover, 2000).

Cross-Cultural Findings

Williams and Best and their colleagues (1982/1990) administered the SSM II to 5-, 8-, and 11-year-olds in 25 countries. Across all countries, the percentage of stereotyped responses rose from around 60% at age 5 to around 70% at age 8. Strong, aggressive, cruel, coarse, and adventurous were consistently associated with men at both age levels, and weak, appreciative, softhearted, gentle, and meek were consistently associated with women.

Male and female stereotype scores were unusually high in Pakistan and relatively high in New Zealand and England. Scores were atypically low in Brazil, Taiwan, Germany, and France. Although between countries there was variation in the rate of learning, there was a general developmental pattern in which stereotype acquisition begins prior to age 5, accelerates during the early school years, and reaches adult levels during the adolescent years.

Girls and boys learned the stereotypes at the same rate, but there was a tendency for male-stereotype traits to be learned somewhat earlier than female traits. In 17 of the 24 countries studied, male stereotype items were better known than female items. Germany was the only country where there was a clear tendency for the female stereotype to be better known than the male. In contrast, female stereotype items were learned earlier than male items in Latin/Catholic cultures (Brazil, Chile, Portugal, Venezuela) where the adult-defined female stereotype is more positive than the male (Neto, Williams, & Widner, 1991; Tarrier & Gomes, 1981).

In predominantly Muslim countries, five-year-olds associate traits with the two sexes in a more highly differentiated manner and they learn the stereotypes, particularly the male items, at an earlier age than in non-Muslim countries. Initially, children in predominantly Christian countries are slower in learning the stereotypes, perhaps reflecting the less-differentiated nature of the adult stereotypes, particularly in Catholic countries.

Using a combined measure of traits and roles, Albert and Porter (1986) examined the gender stereotypes of 4–6-year-olds in the United States and South Africa and found stereotyping increased with age. South African children stereotyped the male role more than did American children, but there were no country differences for the female role. South African children from liberal Christian and Jewish backgrounds stereotyped less than children from more conservative religious groups. In the United States religious background was not a factor.

Looking at older children, 11 to 18 years of age, Intons-Peterson (1988) found that compared with American children, Swedish children attributed more instrumental qualities to women. Stereotypes of women and men were more similar in Sweden than in the United States, perhaps reflecting the egalitarian Swedish culture. Surprisingly, in Sweden ideal occupational choices differed by gender with young Swedish women reporting interests in service occupations, such as flight attendant, hospital worker, nanny, and young Swedish men reporting interests in business occupations. In contrast, ideal occupations for the sexes overlapped in the United States with both groups listing doctor/dentist/attorney, and business executive as their top choices. Given the similarities found across diverse countries with the differing measures used, sex stereotypes appeared to be universal with culture modifying rate of learning and minor aspects of content.

Conclusions and Future Challenges

Gender differences have fascinated social scientists for decades, and with the growing interest in culture, questions regarding the joint effects of these variables should continue to intrigue researchers for years to come. It is remarkable to see that pancultural similarities in sex and gender greatly outweigh the cultural differences that are found. Indeed, the ways in which male-female relationships are organized are remarkably similar across social groups. With the many technological advances that have shrunk the world, longitudinal studies within societies undergoing rapid socioeconomic development should address concomitant changes in gender roles and behaviors.

In spite of the fact that females and males are biologically more similar than different, persons in traditional or modern, industrialized societies can expect to live qualitatively different lives based upon their sex. The relatively minor biological differences between the sexes can be expanded or reduced by cultural practices and socialization, resulting in gender differences in roles and behaviors that are generally modest but in some cases culturally important. Furthermore, few researchers have studied the relationship between cultural practices, such as initiation rites—a typical anthropological topic—and the development of the individual—a topic usually confined to the psychological domain.

The range of variation and diversity in familial and peer relationships seen across cultural groups provides an exceptional opportunity for examining gender-related social development. Future studies across cultural groups should investigate how social relationships and behaviors change with age and identify the mechanisms that contribute to the development of gendered behaviors. Cross-cultural researchers have only begun to explore these social and behavioral issues with children in other societies.

REFLECTIVE QUESTIONS

1. Although gender has traditionally been studied as a dichotomous variable, an increasing number of individuals in some Western countries are identifying as transgender, agender, pangender, and so on. How will this shift impact the way gender is studied cross-culturally, considering different cultures may accept and utilize such identities at different times?
2. What are the best ways to support children and adolescents engaged in gender roles that may be considered nontraditional in their respective cultures (i.e., boy babysitters in Western middle-class culture)?
3. There have already been significant changes in the gender division of labor as the global economy has evolved. In what ways will future global economic changes impact the gender division of labor and thus gender roles?
4. While the five theories of sex role development discussed in this chapter offer strong theoretical perspectives, what other variables of sex role development remain to be addressed?

SUGGESTED READINGS

Books and Articles

Blakemore, J. E. O., Berenbaum. S. A., & Liben, L. S. (2009). *Gender development.* New York: Taylor & Francis.

Endendijk, J. J., Groeneveld, M. G., van Berkel, S. R., Hallers-Hallboom, E. T., Mesman, J., & Bakermans-Kranenburg, M. J. (2013). Gender stereotypes in the family context: Mothers, fathers, and siblings. *Sex Roles, 68*(9–10), 577–590.

Golombok, S., Rust, J., Zervoulis, K., Golding, J., & Hines, M. (2012). Continuity in sex-typed behavior from preschool to adolescence: A longitudinal population study of boys and girls aged 3–13 years. *Archives of Sexual Behavior, 41*(3), 591–597.

Sherif-Trask, B. (2014). *Women, work, and globalization: Challenges and opportunities.* New York: Routledge/Taylor & Francis.

Websites

Gender Corncerns International: http://www.genderconcerns.org/

International Labor Organization: http://www.ilo.org/employment/areas/gender-and-employment/lang—en/index.htm

Inter-Parliamentary Union, Democracy through Partnership between Women and Men: http://www.ipu.org/iss-e/women.htm

UNICEF: Basic Education and Gender Equality: http://www.unicef.org/education/

United Nations Human Development Programme–Gender Development Index (GDI): http://hdr.undp.org/en/content/gender-development-index-gdi

World Economic Forum–Global Gender Gap Report 2013: http://www.weforum.org/issues/global-gender-gap

REFERENCES

Albert, A. A., & Porter, J. R. (1986). Children's gender role stereotypes: A comparison of the United States and South Africa. *Journal of Cross-Cultural Psychology, 17,* 45–65.

Amato, P. R., & Keith, B. (1991). Parental divorce and the well-being of children: A meta-analysis. *Psychological Bulletin, 110,* 26–46.

Balcom, D. A. (1998). Absent fathers: Effects on abandoned sons. *The Journal of Men's Studies, 6*(3), 283–296.

Bandura, A. (1969). Social learning theory of identificatory processes. In D. A. Goslin (Ed.), *Handbook of socialization theory and research* (pp. 213–262). Chicago, IL: Rand McNally.

Bandyopadhyay, M. (2003). Missing girls and son preference in rural India. *Health Care for Women International, 24*(10), 910–26.

Banse, R., Gawronski, B., Rebetez, C., Gutt, H., & Morton, J. (2010). The development of spontaneous gender stereotyping in childhood: Relations to stereotype knowledge and stereotype flexibility. *Developmental Science, 13*(2), 298–306.

Barry, H., III, Bacon, M. K., & Child, I. L. (1957). A cross-cultural survey of some sex differences in socialization. *Journal of Abnormal and Social Psychology, 55,* 327–332.

Barry, H., III., Bacon, M.K., & Child, I.L. (1967). Definitions, ratings and bibliographic sources of child-training practices of 110 cultures. In C.S. Ford (Ed.), *Cross-cultural approaches* (pp. 293–331). New Haven, CT: HRAF Press.

Beal, C.R. (1994). *Boys and girls: The development of gender roles.* New York: McGraw-Hill.

Becker, K.G. (2012). Male gender bias in autism and pediatric autoimmunity. *Autism Research, 5*(2), 77–83.

Best, D.L., & Williams, J.E. (1993). Cross-cultural viewpoint. In A.E. Beall & R.J. Sternberg (Eds.), *Perspectives on the psychology of gender* (pp. 215–248). New York: Guilford.

Best, D.L., Williams, J.E., Cloud, J.M., Davis, S.W., Robertson, L.S., Edwards, J.R., Giles, H., & Fowles, J. (1977). Development of sex-trait stereotypes among young children in the United States, England, and Ireland. *Child Development, 48*, 1375–1384.

Biernat, M. (1991). Gender stereotypes and the relationship between masculinity and femininity: A developmental analysis. *Journal of Personality and Social Psychology, 61*, 351–365.

Bloch, M.N., & Adler, S.M. (1994). African children's play and the emergence of the sexual division of labor. In J.L. Roopnarine, J.E. Johnson, & F.H. Hooper (Eds.), *Children's play in diverse cultures* (pp. 148–178). Albany, NY: State University of New York Press.

Block, J.H. (1983). Differential premises arising from differential socialization of the sexes: Some conjectures. *Child Development, 54*, 1335–1354.

Blurton Jones, N.B., & Konner, M. (1973). Sex differences in behavior of London and Bushman children. In R.P. Michael & J.H. Crook (Eds.), *Comparative ecology and behavior of primates* (pp. 690–749). London, UK: Academic.

Bradley, C. (1993). Women's power, children's labor. *Cross-Cultural Research, 27*, 70–96.

Bronstein, P. (1984). Differences in mothers' and fathers' behaviors toward children: A cross-cultural comparison. *Developmental Psychology, 20*, 995–1003.

Burbank, V.K. (1987). Female aggression in cross-cultural perspective. *Behavior Science Research, 21*(1–4), 70–100.

Burns, A., & Homel, R. (1986). Sex role satisfaction among Australian children: Some sex, age, and cultural group comparisons. *Psychology of Women Quarterly, 10*, 285–296.

Buss, D. M. (1989). Sex differences in human mate preferences: Evolutionary hypotheses tested in 37 cultures. *Behavioral and Brain Sciences, 12*, 1–49.

Bussey, K. (1983). A social-cognitive appraisal of sex-role development. *Australian Journal of Psychology, 35*, 135–143.

Bussey, K., & Bandura, A. (1984). Influence of gender constancy and social power on sex-linked modeling. *Journal of Personality and Social Psychology, 47*, 1292–1302.

Card, N.A., Stucky, B.D., Sawalani, G.M., & Little, T.D. (2008). Direct and indirect aggression during childhood and adolescence: A meta-analytic review of gender differences, intercorrelations, and relations to maladjustment. *Child Development, 79*(5), 1185–1229.

Carlsson, M., & Barnes, M. (1986). Conception and self-attribution of sex-role behavior: A cross-cultural comparison between Swedish and kibbutz-raised Israeli children. *Scandinavian Journal of Psychology, 27*, 258–265.

Chaker, A. M. (2014). More teenage boys get jobs as babysitters, find parents are fans. *Wall Street Journal,* May 7, 2014. Retrieved from wsj.com/news/articlesSB10001424052702304831304579544422380463420

Cheung Mui-ching, F. (1986). Development of gender stereotypes. *Educational Research Journal, 1,* 68–73.

Cialdini, R.B., & Trost, M.R. (1998). Social influence: Social norms, conformity, and compliance. In D.T. Gilbert, S.T. Fiske, & G. Lindzey (Eds.), *The handbook of social psychology* (4th ed., Vol. 2, pp. 152–192). Boston, MA: McGraw-Hill.

Coffe, H., & Bolzendahl, C. (2010). Same game, different rules? Gender differences in political participation. *Sex Roles, 62* (5–6), 318–333.

Cole, M. (1999). Culture in development. In M. H. Bornstein & M. E. Lamb (Eds.), *Developmental psychology: An advanced textbook* (4th ed., pp. 73–123). Mahwah, NJ: Erlbaum.

Croft, A., Schmader, T., Block, K., & Baron, A. (2014). The second shift reflected in the second generation: Do parents' gender roles at home predict children's aspirations? *Psychological Science, 25*(7), 1418–1428.

Cronk, L. (1993). Parental favoritism toward daughters. *American Scientist, 81,* 272–279.

Daly, M., & Wilson, E.O. (1988). *Sex, evolution, and behavior* (2nd ed.). Belmont, CA: Wadsworth.

D'Andrade, R. (1966). Cultural meaning systems. In R.A. Shweder & R.A. LeVine (Eds.), *Culture theory: Essays on mind, self and emotion* (pp. 88–122). New York: Cambridge University Press.

Darwin, C. (1872). *The expression of emotions in man and animals.* London, UK: Murray.

Davis, E.P., & Pfaff, D. (2014). Sexually dimorphic responses to early adversity: Implications for affective problems and autism spectrum disorder. *Psychoneuroendocrinology, 49,* 11–25.

De Caroli, M., & Sagone, E. (2007). Toys, sociocognitive traits, and occupations: Italian children's endorsement of gender stereotypes. *Psychological Reports, 100* (3, Pt 2), 1298–1311.

DeCasper, A.J., & Fifer, W.P. (1980). Of human bonding: Newborns prefer their mothers' voices. *Science, 208,* 1174–1176.

del Mar Alonso-Almeida, M. (2014). Women (and mothers) in the workforce: Worldwide factors. *Women's Studies International Forum, 44,* 164–171.

Dixon, R.A., & Lerner, R.M. (1999). History and systems in developmental psychology. In M.H. Bornstein & M.E. Lamb (Eds.), *Developmental psychology: An advanced textbook* (pp. 3–45). Mahwah, NJ: Erlbaum.

Draper, P. (1975). Cultural pressure on sex differences. *American Ethnologist, 2*(4), 602–616.

Eagly, A.H., Wood, W., & Diekman, A.B. (2000). Social role theory of sex differences and similarities: A current appraisal. In T. Eckes & H.M. Trautner (Eds.), *The developmental social psychology of gender* (pp. 123–174). Mahwah, NJ: Erlbaum.

Edwards, C. P. (1992). Cross-cultural perspectives on family-peer relations. In R.D. Parke & G.W. Ladd (Eds.), *Family-peer relationships: Modes of linkages* (pp. 285–315). Mahwah, NJ: Erlbaum.

Edwards, C.P., & Whiting, B.B. (1974). Women and dependency. *Politics and Society, 4,* 343–355.

Edwards, C.P., & Whiting, B.B. (1980). Differential socialization of girls and boys in light of cross-cultural research. *New Directions for Child Development, 8,* 45–57.

Edwards, C. P., & Whiting, B. B. (1993). "Mother, older sibling, and me": The overlapping roles of caretakers and companions in the social world of 2–3 year olds in Ngeca, Kenya. In K. MacDonald (Ed.), *Parent-child play: Descriptions and implications* (pp. 305–329). Albany, NY: State University of New York Press.

Ember, C. R. (1981). A cross-cultural perspective on sex differences. In R. H. Munroe, R. L. Munroe, & B. B. Whiting (Eds.), *Handbook of cross-cultural human development* (pp. 531–580). New York: Garland.

Endendijk, J. J., Groeneveld, M. G., van Berkel, S. R., Hallers-Hallboom, E. T., Mesman, J., & Bakermans-Kranenburg, M. J. (2013). Gender stereotypes in the family context: Mothers, fathers, and siblings. *Sex Roles, 68*(9–10), 577–590.

Farruggia, S. P., Chen, C., Greenberger, E., Dmitrieva, J., & Macek, P. (2004). Adolescent self-esteem in cross-cultural perspective: Testing measurement equivalence and a mediation model. *Journal of Cross-Cultural Psychology, 35*(6), 719–733.

Fausto-Sterling, A. (2000). *Sexing the body: Gender politics and the construction of sexuality.* New York: Basic Books.

Flavia. (1988). Violence in the family: Wife beating. In R. Ghadially (Ed.), *Women in society: A reader* (pp. 151–166). New Delhi, India: Sage.

Fouts, H. N., Hallam, R. A., & Purandare, S. (2013). Gender segregation in early-childhood social play among the Bofi foragers and Bofi farmers in Central Africa. *American Journal of Play, 5*(3), 333–356.

Freedman, D. G. (1976). Infancy, biology, and culture. In L. P. Lipsitt (Ed.), *Developmental psychology* (pp. 35–54). New York: Halsted, Wiley.

Geary, D. C. (1998). *Male, female: The evolution of human sex differences.* Washington, DC: American Psychological Association.

Gershon, J. (2002). A meta-analytic review of gender differences in ADHD. *Journal of Attention Disorders, 5*(3), 143–154.

Ghadially, R., & Kumar, P. (1988). Stress, strain, and coping styles of female professionals. *Indian Journal of Applied Psychology, 26*(1), 1–8.

Giles, A. C., Cantin, K. D., Best, D. L., Tyrrell, H. P., & Gigler, M. E. (2014, February). *Filial responsibilities of Anglo and Hispanic children in the United States.* Paper presented at the Society for Cross-Cultural Research conference, Charleston, SC.

Ginsberg, H., & Opper, S. (1969). *Piaget's theory of intellectual development: An introduction.* Englewood Cliffs, NJ: Prentice-Hall.

Golombok, S., Rust, J., Zervoulis, K., Golding, J., & Hines, M. (2012). Continuity in sex-typed behavior from preschool to adolescence: A longitudinal population study of boys and girls aged 3–13 years. *Archives of Sexual Behavior, 41*(3), 591–597.

Gottlieb, G. (1976). Conceptions of prenatal development: Behavioral embryology. *Psychological Review, 83,* 215–234.

Gottlieb, G. (1983). The psychobiological approach to development. In P.H. Mussen (Ed.), *Handbook of child psychology,* Vol. 2 (M.M. Haith & J.J. Campos, Vol. Eds.), *Infancy and developmental psychobiology* (pp. 1–26). New York: Wiley.

Gottlieb, G. (2007). Probabilistic epigenesis. *Developmental Science, 10,* 1–11.

Greenfield, P.M., Brazelton, T. B., & Childs, C. P. (1989). From birth to maturity in Zinacantan: Ontogenesis in cultural context. In V. Bricker & G. Gosen (Eds.), *Ethnographic encounters in southern Mesoamerica: Celebratory essays in honor of Evon Z. Vogt* (pp. 177–216). Albany, NY: Institute of Mesoamerican Studies, State University of New York.

Gronseth, E. (1957). The impact of father absence in sailor families upon the personality structure and social adjustment of adult sailor sons. Part I. In N. Anderson (Ed.), *Studies of the family* (Vol. 2, pp. 97–114). Göttingen, Germany: Vandenhoeck and Ruprecht.

Guttentag, M., & Longfellow, C. (1977). Children's social attributions: Development and change. In C. B. Keasey (Ed.), *Nebraska Symposium on Motivation* (pp. 305–341). Lincoln, NB: University of Nebraska Press.

Halim, M. L., Ruble, D. N., Tamis-LeMonda, C. S., Zosuls, K. M., Lurye, L. E., & Greulich, F. K. (2014). Pink frilly dresses and the avoidance of all things "girly": Children's appearance rigidity and cognitive theories of gender development. *Developmental Psychology, 50,* 1091–1101.

Hamilton, V. L., Blumenfeld, P. C., Akoh, H., & Miura, K. (1991). Group and gender in Japanese and American elementary classrooms. *Journal of Cross-Cultural Psychology, 22,* 317–346.

Heath, D. B. (1958). Sexual division of labor and cross-cultural research. *Social Forces, 37,* 77–79.

Hanover, B. (2000). Development of the self in gendered contexts. In T. Eckes & H. M. Trautner (Eds.), *The developmental social psychology of gender* (pp. 177–206). Mahwah, NJ: Erlbaum.

Harkness, S., & Super, C. M. (1985). The cultural context of gender segregation in children's peer groups. *Child Development, 56,* 219–224.

Hay, D. F., Nash, A., Caplan, M., Swartzentruber, J., Ishikawa, F., & Vespo, J. D. (2011). The emergence of gender differences in physical aggression in the context of conflict between young peers. *British Journal of Developmental Psychology, 29,* 158–175.

Hendrix, L., & Johnson, G. D. (1985). Instrumental and expressive socialization: A false dichotomy. *Sex Roles, 13,* 581–595.

Hoyenga, K. B., & Hoyenga, K. T. (1993). *Gender-related differences: Origins and outcomes.* Boston, MA: Allyn & Bacon.

Huber, J. (1986). Trends in gender stratification, 1970–1985. *Sociological Forum, 1,* 476–495.

Huston, A. C. (1983). Sex-typing. In P. H. Mussen (Ed.), *Handbook of child psychology* (4th ed., Vol. 4, pp. 387–467). New York: Wiley.

International Labour Organization. (2009). Global Employment Trends for Women, p. 19. Retrieved from http://www.unwomen.org/en/what-we-do/economic-empowerment/facts-and-figures#notes

Intons-Peterson, M. J. (1988). *Gender concepts of Swedish and American youth.* Hillsdale, NJ: Erlbaum.

Kağitçibaşi, Ç. (1982a). Old-age security value of children: Cross-national socioeconomic evidence. *Journal of Cross-Cultural Psychology, 13,* 29–42.

Kağitçibaşi, Ç. (1982b). The changing value of children in Turkey. Honolulu, HI: East-West Center.

Katz, M. M., & Konner, M. J. (1981). The role of the father: An anthropological perspective. In M. E. Lamb (Ed.), *The role of the father in child development* (2nd ed; pp. 155–185). New York: Wiley.

Katz, M. M., & Konner, M. J. (1981). The role of the father: An anthropological perspective. In M. E. Lamb (Ed.), *The role of the father in child development* (2nd ed; pp. 155–185). New York: Wiley.

Kenrick, D. T., & Luce, C. L. (2000). An evolutionary life-history model of gender differences and similarities. In T. Eckes & H.M. Trautner (Eds.), *The developmental social psychology of gender* (pp. 35–63). Mahwah, NJ: Erlbaum.

Kessler, S. J., & McKenna, W. (1978). *Gender: An ethnomethodological approach.* New York: Wiley.

Kling, K. C., Hyde, J. S., Showers, C. J., & Buswell, B. N. (1999). Gender differences in self-esteem: A meta-analysis. *Psychological Bulletin, 125,* 470–500.

Kohlberg, L. (1966). A cognitive-developmental analysis of children's sex-role concepts and attitudes. In E. E. Maccoby (Ed.), *The development of sex differences* (pp. 82–173). Palo Alto, CA: Stanford University Press.

Krishnaswamy, S. (1988). Female infanticide in contemporary India: A case study of Kallars of Tamil Nadu. In R. Ghadially (Ed.), *Women in Indian society: A reader* (pp. 186–195). New Delhi, India: Sage.

Lamb, M. E., Frodi, A. M., Hwand, C. P., Frodi, M., & Steinberg, J. (1982). Mother- and father-infant interaction involving play and holding in traditional and nontraditional Swedish families. *Developmental Psychology, 18,* 215–221.

Langlois, J. H., & Downs, C. (1980). Mothers, fathers and peers as socialization agents of sex-typed play behavior in young children. *Child Development, 51,* 1217–1247.

Leavell, A., Tamis-LeMonda, C. S., Ruble, D. N., Zosuls, K. M., & Cabrera, N. J. (2012). African American, White, and Latino fathers' activities with their sons and daughters in early childhood. *Sex Roles, 66*(1–2), 53–65.

Lummis, M., & Stevenson, H. W. (1990). Gender differences in beliefs and achievement: A cross-cultural study. *Developmental Psychology, 26,* 254–263.

Lytton, H., & Romney, D. M. (1991). Parents' differential socialization of boys and girls: A meta-analysis. *Psychological Bulletin, 109,* 267–296.

Maccoby, E. E. (1998). *The two sexes: Growing up apart, coming together.* Cambridge, MA: Belnap Press.

Mackey, W. C. (1981). A cross-cultural analysis of adult-child proxemics in relation to the Plowman-Protector Complex: A preliminary study. *Behavior Science Research, 3/4,* 187–223.

Martin, C., Kornienko, O., Schaefer, D. R., Hanish, L. D., Fabes, R. A., & Goble, P. (2013). The role of sex of peers and gender-typed activities in young children's peer affiliative networks: A longitudinal analysis of selection and influence. *Child Development, 84*(3), 921–937.

Martin, C. L. (2000). Cognitive theories of gender development. In T. Eckes & H. M. Trautner (Eds.), *The developmental social psychology of gender* (pp. 91–121). Mahwah, NJ: Erlbaum.

Martin, C. L., & Halverson, C. F. (1981). The effects of sex-typing schemas on young children's memory. *Child Development, 54,* 563–574.

Maughan, B., Rowe, R., Messer, J., Goodman, R. & Meltzer, H. (2004). Conduct disorder and oppositional defiant disorder in a national sample: Developmental epidemiology. *Journal of Child Psychology and Psychiatry, 45,* 609–621.

Mehta, C. M., & Strough, J. (2010). Gender segregation and gender-typing in adolescence. *Sex Roles, 63*(3–4), 251–263.

Meil, G. (2013). European men's use of parental leave and their involvement in child care and housework. *Journal of Comparative Family Studies, 44*(5), 557–570.

Micali, N., Ploubidis, G., De Stavola, B., Simonoff, E., & Treasure, J. (2013). Frequency and patterns of eating disorder symptoms in early adolescence. *Journal of Adolescent Health, 54*(5), 574–581.

Minturn, L., & Lambert, W.W. (1964). *Mothers of six cultures: Antecedents of child rearing*. New York: Wiley.
Mischel, W. (1970). Sex-typing and socialization. In P.H. Mussen (Ed.), *Carmichael's manual of child psychology* (Vol. 2, pp. 3–72). New York: Wiley.
Mukhopadhyay, C.C., & Higgins, P.J. (1998). Anthropological studies of women's status revisited: 1977–1987. *Annual Review of Anthropology, 17,* 461–495.
Munroe, R.L., Hulefeld, R., Rodgers, J.M., Tomeo, D.L., & Yamazaki, S.K. (2000). Aggression among children in four cultures. *Cross-Cultural Research, 34,* 3–25.
Munroe, R.L., & Munroe, R.H. (1971). Effect of environmental experiences on spatial ability in an East African society. *Journal of Social Psychology, 83,* 3–10.
Munroe, R.L., & Munroe, R.H. (1975/1994). *Cross-cultural human development.* Prospect Heights, IL: Waveland Press.
Munroe, R.H., Shimmin, H.S., & Munroe, R.L. (1984). Gender understanding and sex role preference in four cultures. *Developmental Psychology, 20,* 673–682.
Murdock, G.P., & White, D.R. (1969). Standard cross-cultural sample. *Ethnology, 8,* 329–369.
Neto, F., Williams, J.E., & Widner, S.C. (1991). Portuguese children's knowledge of sex stereotypes: Effects of age, gender, and socioeconomic status. *Journal of Cross-Cultural Psychology, 22,* 376–388.
Nolen-Hoeksema, S. (2001). Gender differences in depression. *Current Directions in Psychological Science, 10*(5), 173–176
Öhman, A. (1986). Face the beast and fear the face: Animal and social fears as prototypes for evolutionary analysis of emotion. *Psychophysiology, 23,* 123–145.
Olowu, A.A. (1985). Gender as a determinant of some Nigerian adolescents' self-concepts. *Journal of Adolescence, 8,* 347–355.
Omark, D.R., Omark, M., & Edelman, M. (1975). Formation of dominance hierarchies in young children: Action and perspective. In T. Williams (Ed.), *Psychological anthropology* (pp. 289–315). The Hague, Netherlands: Mouton.
Organisation for Economic Co-operation and Development. (2014). Balancing paid work, unpaid work and leisure.http://www.oecd.org/gender/data/balancingpaidworkunpaidworkandleisure.htm
Peterson, V.S., & Runyan, A.S. (1993). *Global gender issues.* Boulder, CO: Westview Press.
Pooler, W.S. (1991). Sex of child preferences among college students. *Sex Roles, 25,* 569–576.
Population Crisis Committee. (1988, June). *Country rankings of the status of women: Poor, powerless, and pregnant* (Issue Brief No. 20). Washington, DC: Author.
Prossner, G.V., Hutt, C., Hutt, S.J., Mahindadasa, K.J., & Goonetilleke, M.D.J. (1986). Children's play in Sri Lanka: A cross-cultural study. *British Journal of Developmental Psychology, 4,* 179–186.
Puri, S., Adams, V., Ivey, S., & Nachtigall, R.D. (2011). "There is such a thing as too many daughters, but not too many sons": A qualitative study of son preference and fetal sex selection among Indian immigrants in the United States. *Social Science & Medicine, 72,* 1169–1176.
Quinn, N. (1977). Anthropology studies of women's status. *Annual Review of Anthropology, 6,* 181–225.
Ramirez, J.M. (1993). Acceptability of aggression in four Spanish regions and a comparison with other European countries. *Aggressive Behavior, 19,* 185–197.
Rapoport, T., Lomski-Feder, E., & Masalha, M. (1989). Female subordination in the Arab-Israeli community: The adolescent perspective of "social veil." *Sex Roles, 20,* 255–269.

Regan, P.C., & Ramirez, C. (2000). Decisions on child care: Do sex and sexual orientation matter? *Psychological Reports, 86*(3, Pt 1), 922–924.

Rogoff, B. (1990). *Apprenticeship in thinking: Cognitive development in social context.* New York: Oxford University Press.

Rohner, R.P., & Rohner, E.C. (1982). Enculturative continuity and the importance of caretakers: Cross-cultural codes. *Behavior Science Research, 17,* 91–114.

Rosenberg, B.G., & Sutton-Smith, B. (1972). *Sex and identity.* New York: Holt, Rinehart, and Winston.

Rosner, M. (1967). Women in the kibbutz: Changing status and concepts. *Asian and African Studies, 3,* 35–68.

Ross, L. (1977). The intuitive psychologist and his shortcomings: Distortions in the attribution process. In L. Berkowitz (Ed.), *Advances in experimental social psychology* (Vol. 10, pp. 173–220). New York: Academic Press.

Ross, M.H. (1985). Female political participation: A cross-cultural explanation. *American Anthropologist, 88,* 843–858.

Rozin, P., & Kalat, J.W. (1971). Specific hungers and poison avoidance as adaptive specializations of learning. *Psychological Review, 78,* 459–486.

Rubin, J. Z., Provezano, F. J., & Luria, Z. (1974). The eye of the beholder: Parents' views on sex of newborns. *American Journal of Orthopsychiatry, 44,* 512–519.

Ruble, D.N., & Martin, C. L. (1998). Gender development. In W. Damon (Series Ed.) & N. Eisenberg (Vol. Ed.), *Handbook of child psychology:* Vol. 3, *Social, emotional, and personality development* (5th ed., pp. 933–1016). New York: Wiley.

Russell, G., & Russell, A. (1987). Mother-child and father-child relationships in middle childhood. *Child Development, 58,* 1573–1585.

Schoppe-Sullivan, S. J., Kotila, L. E., Jia, R., Lang, S. N., & Bower, D. J. (2013). Comparisons of levels and predictors of mothers' and fathers' engagement with their preschool-aged children. *Early Child Development and Care, 183* (3–4), 498–514.

Sears, R.R., Maccoby, E.E., & Levin, H. (1957). *Patterns of child rearing.* Palo Alto, CA: Stanford University Press.

Sears, R.R., Rau, L., & Alpert, R. (1965). *Identification and child rearing.* Palo Alto, CA: Stanford University Press.

Segal, E.S. (1983). The structure of division of labor: A tentative formulation. *Behavior Science Research, 18,* 3–25.

Seligman, M.E.P. (1971). Phobias and preparedness. *Behavior Therapy, 2,* 307–320.

Serpell, R. (1993). *The significance of schooling: Life-journeys in an African society.* New York: Cambridge University Press.

Sidorowicz, L. S., & Lunney, G. S. (1980). Baby X revisited. *Sex Roles, 6,* 67–73.

Spiro, M.E. (1995). *Gender and culture: Kibbutz women revisited.* New Brunswick, NJ: Transaction Publishers.

Stevenson, M.R., & Black, K.N. (1988). Paternal absence and sex role development: A meta-analysis. *Child Development, 59,* 793–814.

Stolz, L.M. (1954). *Father relations of war-born children.* Palo Alto, CA: Stanford University Press.

Super, C.M., (1976). Environmental effects on motor development: The case of African infant precocity. *Developmental Medicine and Child Neurology, 18,* 561–567.

Super, C.M., & Harkness, S. (1982). The infants' niche in rural Kenya and metropolitan America. In L.L. Adler (Ed.), *Cross-cultural research at issue* (pp. 47–55). New York: Academic Press.

Sweeney, J., & Bradbard, M.R. (1989). Mothers' and fathers' changing perceptions of their male and female infants over the course of pregnancy. *Journal of Genetic Psychology, 149,* 393–404.

Tarrier, N., & Gomes, L.F. (1981). Knowledge of sex-trait stereotypes: Effects of age, sex, and social class on Brazilian children. *Journal of Cross-Cultural Psychology, 12,* 81–93.

Trivers, R.L. (1985). *Social evolution.* Menlo Park, CA: Benjamin/Cummings.

van Dongen-Melman, J. E. W. M., Koot, H. M., & Verhulst, F. C. (1993). Cross-cultural validation of Harter's self-perception profile for children in a Dutch sample. *Educational and Psychological Measurement, 53,* 739–753.

Van Leeuwen, M. S. (1978). A cross-cultural examination of psychological differentiation in males and females. *International Journal of Psychology, 13,* 87–122.

Verhofstadt, L. L., & Weytens, F. (2013). Biological sex and gender role identity as predictors of spousal support provision: A scenario-based study. *Journal of Gender Studies, 22(2),* 166–177.

Watkins, D., & Akande, A. (1992). The internal structure of the self description questionnaire: A Nigerian investigation. *British Journal of Educational Psychology, 62,* 120–125.

Weisner, T. S., & Gallimore, R. (1977). My brother's keeper: Child and sibling caretaking. *Current Anthropology, 18,* 169–190.

Welch, M.R., Page, B.M., & Martin, L.L. (1981). Sex differences in the ease of socialization: An analysis of the efficiency of child training processes in preindustrial societies. *Journal of Social Psychology, 113,* 3–12.

Whiting, B.B. (1965). Sex identity conflict and physical violence: A comparative study. *American Anthropologist, 67* (Special publication), 123–140.

Whiting, B.B., & Edwards, C.P. (1973). A cross-cultural analysis of sex differences in the behavior of children aged 3 to 11. *Journal of Social Psychology, 91,* 171–188.

Whiting, B.B., & Edwards, C.P. (1988). *Children of different worlds: The formation of social behavior.* Cambridge, MA: Harvard University Press.

Williams, J.E., & Best, D.L. (1982/1990). *Measuring sex stereotypes: A multination study* (rev. ed., 1990). Newbury Park, CA: Sage.

Williams, J.E., & Best, D.L. (1990). *Sex and psyche: Gender and self viewed cross-culturally.* Newbury Park, CA: Sage.

Wood, W., & Eagly, A.H. (1999). *The origins of the division of labor and gender hierarchy: Implications for sex differences in social behavior.* Unpublished manuscript.

The World Bank Group (2013). Gender at work: A companion to the world development report on jobs. http://www.worldbank.org/content/dam/Worldbank/Event/Gender/GenderAtWork_web2.pdf

Youssef, N.H. (1974). *Women and work in developing societies.* Berkeley, CA: Institute of International Studies.

Zosuls, K.M., Ruble, D.N., Tamis-LeMonda, C.S., Shrout, P.E., Bornstein, M.H., & Greulich, F.K. (2009). The acquisition of gender labels in infancy: Implications for genre-typed play. *Developmental Psychology, 45*(3), 688–701.

9

Sibling Interactions

Ashley E. Maynard

Imagine a group of indigenous Maya siblings playing in the backyard while their mother is at work in the house:

> *Six-year-old Xunka' says, "Come here Pati! Let's play here!" Patricia, age 2, walks over to Xunka', and their four-year-old brother Esteban enters to sit with them. He says, "Let's play!" Xunka' is tearing leaves off a branch to serve as pretend-tortillas as Patricia and Esteban both watch her. Patricia and Esteban both pick up some leaves and imitate Xunka'. Esteban then quits the tortillas making and exits. Xunka' says, "Wait then. I'm going . . . I'm going to make it this way—better," and then goes to pound the leaves and make them better. Xunka' sees that Patricia is doing nothing and demands from a distance that she pat tortillas. "You pat . . . pat tortillas! Pat tortillas!" Xunka' herself pounds leaves with a rock on top of a wooden surface, away from Patricia. Xunka' says, "The tortillas came out thick," and then she comes closer to Patricia and notices that Patricia has taken the wrong leaves off the wrong branch. "Not this," she says, "Just the little ones! Just the little ones! There aren't any . . . (mumbles)" Xunka' continues, "Where did the stone go?" and looks for the stone. She looks at what Patricia is doing and says, "It's finished already Pati. Not yet." Xunka' stops Patricia from making any more tortillas as she prepares little tortillas out of leaves for Patricia. Xunka' ends the cooking and they play with some glue and paper.*

This episode demonstrates the ways that siblings organize each other's interactions in ways that reflect their developmental capabilities and relative status. A scene like this might happen in many places in the world, but there is one important difference: Maya siblings are socialized by their parents to take care of their younger charges. Children learn from a young age how to manage sibling interactions—an important lifelong bond. The ways they manage these interactions are culturally influenced and shaped by socialization practices around them.

There is a notion in the developmental literature that the child's internal model of relationships uses the parent-child dyad (usually the mother-child dyad) as a prototype (Azuma, 1994; Dunn, 1992; Lebra, 1994). But parents, of course, are not the only source of guidance in children's development. Siblings also socialize each other (Rogoff, 1991; Stewart, 1983; Tobin, Wu, & Davidson, 1989; Zukow, 1989a). Interactions with siblings serve important functions in development because they allow children to practice roles and to observe more skilled partners (Rogoff, 1990).

The role of siblings in early childhood socialization has received much attention in psychology and anthropology (e.g., Abramovitch, Corter, & Lando, 1979; Kendrick & Dunn, 1980; Nuckolls, 1993a; Weisner, 1987; Zukow, 1989a; Zukow-Goldring, 1995, 2002). Research in Western cultures has focused on the effects of a new sibling on the mother's relationship with the firstborn (e.g., Kendrick & Dunn, 1980), on the role of siblings in children's cognitive development (e.g., Teti, Bond, & Gibbs, 1988; Zukow, 1989b), and on the role of siblings in children's social and emotional development (e.g., Dunn, 1989; Dunn & Munn, 1986; Howe & Ross, 1990; Teti & Ablard, 1989; Whiting & Edwards, 1988). The study of sibling relationships in non-Western cultures has added to our understanding of the role that siblings may play in development (Marshall, 1983; Nuckolls, 1993b; Whiting & Edwards, 1988; Whiting & Whiting, 1975). Extensive studies of sibling caretaking in many agrarian and foraging societies highlight the role of siblings as guides for one another in cultural practices (Broch, 1990; DeLeon, 2008; Maynard, 2002; Minks, 2008; Rabain-Jamin, Maynard, & Greenfield, 2003; Rindstedt, 2001; Weisner & Gallimore, 1977; Zukow-Goldring, 1995, 2002).

In many of the world's cultures the sibling relationship is an ideal relationship, forming the prototype for other social relationships outside the family (Marshall, 1983; Maynard, 1999b; Nuckolls, 1993b; Weisner, 1993a). In such cultures, siblings maintain lifelong bonds and obligations to one another. For example, in the Zinacantec Maya culture of Chiapas, Mexico, the older brother-younger brother relationship serves as a prototype for relationships outside the family. People know how to behave in terms of status, a concept that stems from the older brother-younger brother paradigm (Vogt, 1969). In this chapter, I explore the significant roles that siblings play in each other's lives around the world, emphasizing cultural influences on sibling interactions. In the first section, I consider the cultural context that surrounds sibling relationships with a focus on sibling caretaking practices as a form of social support used in many cultures. I then examine the impact that siblings have on each other's development in several domains: social and emotional development, cognitive development, and play.

THE ROLE OF CULTURE IN SIBLING INTERACTIONS

Wherever children develop in the world, sibling relationships are important, though the degree of importance varies across cultures and throughout the lifespan. Because they are biologically related and close in age, siblings may be especially effective at helping each other understand the cultural practices they are exposed to in development. Different cultures define how siblings should interact with each other and with other relatives and neighbors; what resources, including both material and personnel, they should have individually; what should be shared among them; and how they should work and sleep (Weisner, 1989b; Whiting & Edwards, 1988). All of these aspects of interaction are influenced by people's cultural values. Ecocultural theory provides a framework for understanding the important impact that siblings have on one another.

Ecocultural Theory

In ecocultural theory, development is an ecological-cultural project (Weisner, 1984) influenced by the interaction between the surrounding ecology and cultural practices for the care and raising of children (LCHC, 1986; Super & Harkness, 1986; Weisner, 1989a; Whiting & Edwards, 1988). The major premise is that the entire package of culture influences the developing child. This includes, for example, each family member's role in the family subsistence activities, how much time the siblings spend together, and whether or not older siblings are responsible for the care of the younger ones, all of which affect sibling relationships and a child's ultimate development. There are various ecocultural influences on sibling interactions including availability of personnel to care for children, cultural beliefs about sex roles and goals for child development, and whether or not a sibling group shares lifelong obligations to each other, such as economic reciprocity and arrangement of marriages (Weisner, 1987).

The role of siblings is an important part of the ecocultural project, and, conversely, the cultural place is primary in the study of sibling relationships (Weisner, 1993). Taken-for-granted cultural values may affect sibling interactions and the role that siblings have in each other's lives. In those cultures where independence is a primary goal for child development, such as the United States (Greenfield, 1994), siblings will find themselves more independent of one another. By comparison, in cultures where interdependence is a primary goal for development, siblings may be more dependent on one another for their social, cognitive, and biological needs (Kim & Choi, 1994; Zukow, 1995, 2002). Raising the issue of the cultural place brings forth many more questions about sibling relationships. First, who is a sibling? What is the form that the sibling relationship should take? How should siblings relate to one another during childhood and adulthood? Once culture is seen as a set of practices adapted to local conditions, it becomes clear that the sibling relationship is part of a complex system of cultural practices that are adapted to a cultural place.

The Sibling Relationship: Who Is a Sibling?

Biological and evolutionary theories tell us that siblings are those individuals who share parents and therefore approximately 50% of their genes. Linguistics and ecocultural theory have a different answer to the question of who is a sibling: It depends on the cultural place. In the United States, Europe, and other Western cultures, siblings are defined as those people who share parents, and therefore, on average, 50% of their genetic material. The English language goes so far as to denote a special term for a stepsibling, who is the child of a spouse of one's step parent, conceived from another union. In this case no genes are shared. In the American system of genealogy, cousins—sharing even less genetic material than siblings—are often even less involved in each other's lives.

This is not the case in many cultures of the world, where aunts, uncles, cousins, and siblings-by-baptism may be considered as important as genetic siblings. These siblings are sometimes called "classificatory siblings" by Western researchers to indicate a kinship category (Nuckolls, 1993b; Watson-Gegeo & Gegeo, 1989). In some cultures, such as in the Solomon Islands and some parts of India, people who are not genetic siblings, and therefore share a smaller percentage (or none) of their genes, may be referred to as siblings and have the same obligations as genetic siblings (Watson-Gegeo & Gegeo, 1989; Zukow-Goldring, 2002). In Pukapuka Atoll in Oceania, there is a sibling term (*taina*) that is applied in modern times not only to those with blood relations, but also to other members of the village, members of the same church, and "created kin" (Hecht, 1981, p. 61). In Pukapuka, taina are expected to share resources. In the Marquesas Islands, cousins may be considered to be a part of the sibling group or they may be considered part of separate groups (Kirkpatrick, 1981). Marquesan siblings are expected to share resources and workload, and to engage each other in an informal way. Thus who is classified as a sibling, and what the relationship should therefore entail, is relative to the cultural place.

It is likely that parents socialize children according to their developmental goals for the siblings' future relationships, whether they are related by blood or not. This finding might fit within an evolutionary framework if it were interpreted as a way to increase possible resources in one's ecocultural niche. Nongenetically related siblings who have obligations to one another may ensure each other's success and survival. It is important for researchers interested in doing sibling research to find out who among a group are considered siblings, what their relationship entails, and what their future obligations might be to one another.

Influences on Sibling Interactions

In American culture, the parent-child relationship is more primary than the sibling relationship (Weisner, 1993). Parents often look for ways to reduce sibling rivalry and foster positive sibling relationships (Mendelson, 1990; Stoneman & Brody, 1993). Parents manage the sibling relationship, rather than siblings managing their own relationship. Stoneman and Brody (1993) propose a family systems model of sibling relations within the family context. In their study of American families, they find several variables important in fostering positive sibling relationships: direct parental behavior, which children imitate; parental discipline; intrafamily differences in parenting as experienced by the siblings; and consistency of parenting strategies with all siblings. The focus here is on the parents trying to influence siblings to get along, in an environment of fairness. Individual needs and goals are considered primary in the children's development.

In Western cultures, sibling interactions are affected by parents' presence, and having a sibling changes the way an earlier born child interacts with the parents. In American homes, mothers' presence has been found to reduce the quantity of sibling interactions (Pepler, Abramovitch, & Corter, 1981). Kendrick and Dunn (1980) found that the arrival of a second child affects the first child's interactions with the mother in children growing up in England. When the mother was interacting with the new baby, there was an increase in confrontation and nurturance with the first child. When mothers were busy with the new baby, there was a decrease in attention to the first child compared to before the birth of the new baby. Howe and Ross (1990) found that American sibling interactions were more negative when the mother paid attention to one child at the expense of the other. Attachment style may influence the effects of a new sibling on an earlier-born child's distress. Securely attached infants were found to be less distressed by their mothers' attentiveness to a younger sibling than less securely attached infants (Teti & Ablard, 1989).

In non-Western cultures the sibling relationship is often more primary than the parent-child relationship, and parents worry less about fostering positive sibling relationships, usually because the siblings work out their own relations rather well, without intervention from adults (Martini, 1994;

Whiting & Edwards, 1988; Zukow-Goldring, 1995, 2002). Abaluyia children of Kenya, for example, automatically seek siblings or other peers for support as much or more than the mother (Bryant, 1992; Weisner, 1987). This may be because mothers are working and children are accustomed to relying on each other for social support more than their American counterparts. Abaluyia children are sibling caretakers meaning that older children help take care of their younger siblings. Older children are assigned roles to ensure the safety and well-being of younger children. Sibling caretaking is a widely used practice in which children rely on each other for social support. The practice of sibling caretaking has important influences on the ways that siblings relate to one another.

Sibling Caretaking

Sibling caretaking is a primary form of childcare in many agrarian societies (Weisner & Gallimore, 1977; Whiting & Edwards, 1988; Zukow-Goldring, 1995, 2002). In the practice of sibling caretaking, older siblings are responsible for the care of their younger siblings. This care may range from keeping the child happy and entertained while an adult is within earshot to feeding, bathing, and taking full responsibility for the child's complete safety and well-being while the adult is away. Care by older siblings frees adult caretakers to perform subsistence tasks such as cooking or working in a field. Sibling caretakers do more than just provide basic biological needs of their charges; they also socialize each other into cultural practices and settings (Maynard, 2002; Rogoff, 1991; Stewart, 1983; Zukow-Goldring, 1995, 2002).

Siblings may provide special care because they are related to the child genetically and they are in the same relative age cohort compared to the parents. Children seem to benefit, both cognitively and socially, from interacting with caregivers other than their parents (Hill, 1991). In cultures with sibling caretaking, both the caregiver and the sibling being cared for benefit from such care. Sibling caregiving promotes interdependence and prosocial behavior in children (Weisner & Gallimore, 1977; Whiting & Edwards, 1988).

Adults' Roles in Guiding Sibling Caretaking

Adults in societies in which there is child-caretaking do not consider that they are shirking their duties as caregivers (Whiting & Edwards, 1988; Whittemore & Beverly, 1989). Parents closely supervise sibling caretaking and typically give children increasingly complex tasks, initiating them into the role of child caretaker (Whiting & Edwards, 1988; Weisner, 1989b; Zukow-Goldring, 1995). For instance in the Maya community of Nabenchauk in Chiapas, Mexico, a child of three years might get a clean cloth for the mother to diaper the infant or fetch a bar of soap as the mother bathes the younger infant sibling. An older child might actually bathe the infant herself.

The responsibilities that parents give to children reflect the children's developing abilities and their interest in new babies. Children start to take more interest in younger children around the age of 4 (Weisner, 1993a), and most sibling caretakers range in age from 5 to 10 years (Zukow-Goldring, 1995, 2002). This appears to be an affordance of evolution, given that natural birth spacing in non-industrialized hunter-gatherer societies is 3–4 years. As the older sibling is maturing, she (and sometimes he) will become quite interested in the infant, wanting to be more involved in its care. As the child matures cognitively and emotionally, he or she becomes ready to take care of younger siblings (Weisner, 1993a; Whiting, 1977). Sibling caretakers exhibit many of the same behaviors as parents, showing that they have internalized cultural models for caretaking behaviors (Zukow, 1989b). While it appears that children who take the role of caretaker for a younger sibling are being prepared for adult roles (Essman, 1977; Weisner, 1987), adults do not always describe the delegation of caretaking and instruction in caretaking as training the child caretaker for a future parenting role (Whittemore & Beverly, 1989).

In many cultures parents hold good caretaking skills in high regard. Among the Kwara'ae of Melanesia, for example, children are rewarded for being good sibling caretakers (Watson-Gegeo & Gegeo, 1989). Children who are good at caretaking gain higher status. In Kwara'ae society, child caretakers play a bigger role than parents in introducing their younger siblings to cousins and other children with whom they will have relationships throughout their lives. As a whole, the Kwara'ae village is a much richer environment for children and families because there are distributed resources that are not found in each individual household. This probably promotes a sense of reliance on shared resources and a long-term connection among age-mates who will grow together as a community throughout their lives.

Sibling caretaking plays an important role in foraging societies as well. Among the Murik of Papua New Guinea, children learn to care for each other as parents socialize them to pay attention to their relative status (the older-younger distinction) and to share food (Barlow, 2013). Foraging societies in Africa also emphasize sibling caretaking and the sharing of resources (Ottenberg, 1968).

The Study of Sibling Care in Europe and the United States

Sibling caretaking relationships have also been studied in Europe and the United States, with a predominantly different set of methods. As opposed to the ethnographic approaches employed in more agrarian cultures, most studies in Europe and the United States have relied on questionnaire and behavioral inventory studies to ask questions about sibling caretaking. In a questionnaire and inventory study of both parent and sibling caretaking behaviors, Bryant (1989) related sibling care to children's social and emotional development and places sibling caretaking practices in the web of family caretaking practices. She asked how the sibling interactions relate to the parents' caretaking interactions. She found seven factors in caretaking practices: paternal support, sibling nurturance, sibling challenge, paternal and sibling punishment, maternal and sibling concern, paternal protectiveness, and paternal indulgence. Her quantitative results suggest a stronger effect of sibling interactions compared to parent-child interactions in social and emotional development.

There have been few ethnographic studies of sibling caretaking in the United States and Europe. Notable examples are the study of siblings in Orchard Town, a pseudonym for a community studied by Beatrice and John Whiting in their Six Cultures Study (Whiting & Whiting, 1975), a study of African American working-class children (Ward, 1971), and a study of children in South Carolina (Heath, 1983). Further study of sibling interactions in activities in the United States and Europe, through a more ethnographic approach, would help to elucidate this important relationship.

Summary

Sibling caretaking practices are adapted to an ecocultural place. An evolutionary view helps explain the use of the help of older children to take care of the younger ones: attentional and physical resources (for labor) are used where they are more likely to ensure the survival of offspring. In agrarian societies, adults, capable of hard work, use their energy and strength for the work of supporting the family as they socialize siblings to care for their younger charges. The socioeconomic situation interacts with the cultural goals for children's development.

THE IMPACT OF SIBLING INTERACTIONS ON SOCIAL AND COGNITIVE DEVELOPMENT

Siblings have been found to affect each other's social development as well as their cognitive development. There is an ongoing question in the literature about the relationship between family size and cognitive success. In this section the effects of siblings on social and cognitive development will be considered, along with issues raised by evolutionary theory such as the effect of number of siblings and sibling conflict.

Social Development

Sibling interactions are a major arena for children to learn about social support and the social world more generally. Children need to figure out how other family members, and still others in the world outside of the home, will behave and respond in various situations. They also need to understand others' feelings in order to behave appropriately. The sibling relationship is one in which young children exhibit relatively mature skills of cooperation, sharing and comforting, conciliation and teasing (Dunn, 1992; Martini, 1994; Maynard, 2002; Watson-Gegeo & Gegeo, 1989; Weisner & Gallimore, 1977; Zukow-Goldring, 1995, 2002). Sibling interactions are associated with aspects of prosocial behavior in both the family and school contexts in the preschool period (Dunn, 1992). These capabilities may be importantly fostered in sibling interactions (Dunn & Munn, 1986).

There are social benefits for both older and younger siblings. Older siblings may learn the skills of caretaking, including providing nurturance and guidance. Younger siblings receive this care and benefit from it. The older sibling plays a role as a model for the younger sibling. Younger siblings pay a lot of attention to older siblings as they look for appropriate ways to behave and as they look for ways to participate in activities (Dunn & Kendrick, 1982; Martini & Kirkpatrick, 1992; Zukow, 1989b). Younger siblings imitate older siblings more than they are imitated (Pepler, Abramovitch, & Corter, 1981), and they receive guidance from older brothers or sisters (Maynard, 2002; Zukow, 1989b), rather than the other way around. When urban American children had positive images of their older siblings, the sibling relationship served as a buffer for adjustment in such areas as delinquency, academic success, and mental health (Widmer & Weiss, 2000).

Parents in various cultures around the world believe it is important for children to be competent in giving and receiving social support, and they may train children in various social practices (Lebra, 1994; Watson-Gegeo & Gegeo, 1989; Weisner, 1989b; Zukow, 1989a; Zukow-Goldring, 1995, 2002). Two areas in which children receive such training are sharing and cooperation. In American society, sharing is often considered a source of conflict among siblings (Mendelson, 1990). In many agrarian societies, children learn to share from a very early age, and sharing is not a source of conflict in the sibling group. For example, Solomon Islanders train infants to share as early as six months of age (Watson-Gegeo & Gegeo, 1989). Watson-Gegeo and Gegeo (1989) describe the development of children's sharing in the Solomon Islands; children share on request by 18 months of age, share without any prompting by 3 years, and, by the age of 6, give food willingly to a younger sibling if there is not enough food for everyone. Martini and Kirkpatrick (1992) also describe early sharing among children in the Marquesas Islands; indeed by the age of 3 Marquesan siblings share with each other freely.

In addition to sharing, cooperation between siblings has been found to promote prosocial behaviors. Cooperation may take different forms in different cultures. In societies valuing independence and personal choice, such as in the United States, cooperation may be based on an ethic of compromise or on taking turns at getting one's wishes: "I get what I want this time and you'll get what you want next time." In agrarian societies, cooperation may be based more on a social hierarchy. Older siblings have higher status and get more respect from younger siblings. For this respect they provide care and nurturance to the younger siblings. Younger siblings, on the other hand, become accustomed to listening to and following the will of an older child (Ochs, 1988; Zukow-Goldring, 1995, 2002). Overall, it appears that cooperation with siblings leads to cooperation in other types of interactions. For example, Dunn and Munn (1986) found that British children who grew up with a sibling who cooperated with them in a high proportion of their interactions became more cooperative than children whose siblings did not cooperate as much with them.

Cognitive Development

Interacting with siblings also has influences on a child's cognitive development. As with social development, most cognitive benefits of interacting with siblings are not unidirectional. Interacting with siblings increases cognitive functioning for both parties involved (Botvin & Murray, 1975; Cicirelli, 1975). Children may display cognitive capacities earlier with their siblings than with other peers or adults or when they are alone (Azmitia & Hesser, 1993; Weisner, 1989b). For example, Weisner (1989b) found that children sometimes display cognitive and social capacities earlier in interaction with their siblings than with an experimenter in a laboratory situation. This could be because children relate more to siblings than to experimenters. Or this could be because sibling caretakers break down activities into their component parts and provide models of appropriate conduct to children (Zukow, 1989b). Both siblings and adult caretakers in Zukow's Mexican and American samples used scaffolding in their interactions with young children, but sibling caretakers accommodated to children more than they did to adults. These findings suggest an important role of siblings in cognitive development.

There are two major domains where siblings have been found to play a role in each other's cognitive development; these include perspective taking and providing guidance or teaching.

Perspective Taking

Perspective taking involves understanding the point of view of another person. Children may be asked to indicate what someone else can see (Piaget, 1951) or how someone else would feel in a given situation (Eisenberg & Mussen, 1989). Sibling nurturance has been found to predict American children's later social perspective taking (Bryant, 1987) and to affect children's school behaviors and adjustment (Gallimore, Tharp, & Speidel, 1978; Weisner, Gallimore, & Jordan, 1988).

Positive sibling relations are related to perspective taking skills of the older child (Howe & Ross, 1990). If the older child can appropriately assess the younger child's point of view or desires, sibling relations may be more positive. However, perspective taking may not be necessary for children to respond appropriately to a child's needs. Although on the surface it seems necessary to take the perspective of a sibling in distress in order to respond appropriately, Howe and Ross (1990) found that sibling response to distress was related to the intensity of the younger sibling's upset, and not to perspective-taking abilities. It may be that early attention to distress leads to the development of perspective-taking abilities at a cognitive level as children try to meet the needs of their younger siblings more efficiently and sensitively.

Interacting with siblings enhances children's perspective taking (Lewis, Freeman, Kyriakidou, Maridaki-Kassotaki, & Berridge, 1996; Perner, Ruffman, & Leekam, 1994; Ruffman, Perner, Naito, Parkin, & Clements, 1998). Lewis and colleagues (Lewis et al., 1996) found that children who interacted with an extended kin network, including multiple siblings, were precocious in their acquisition of false belief compared with children who interacted with a more limited kin group. In their studies in Japan and England, Perner and his colleagues found that the more siblings a child has, the more likely he or she is to understand the classic false belief task. That is, children with more siblings have a better understanding that others may hold beliefs that are actually false relative to the true state of the world, and that beliefs may change according to changes in the world. Having a *younger* sibling does not appear to influence children's performance on the false belief task (Perner et al., 1994).

Sibling Teaching

Siblings can be especially effective teachers of their younger siblings because they are related, they are emotionally close, and they are also close in age. Older siblings often serve as guides or models for their younger siblings (Maynard, 2002; Zukow-Goldring, 1995, 2002). Older siblings may accrue advantages in cognitive functioning from teaching their younger siblings (Meisner & Fisher, 1980) and younger siblings receive the benefits of guidance. In the peer tutoring literature, it has been shown that peer tutoring can benefit both the tutor and the tutee (Goldenberg & Gallimore, 1991; Weisner et al., 1988). Sibling teaching probably has similar effects.

The scope of past research on sibling teaching is limited. Dunn and Kendrick (1979) mention that they have noticed older siblings teaching and caring for their younger siblings, but they do not describe these interactions. Most studies have focused at one age, usually a sibling teacher aged 6 and a target child aged 18 months to 4 years. One study of young children's semantic development compared six-year-old siblings approach to teaching with that of mothers in a picture categorization task (Perez-Granados & Callanan, 1997). Mothers labeled categories and objects more than siblings. The target children, age 4, labeled more objects and categories themselves when they were working with their mothers than they did when they were working with their siblings.

Most studies of sibling teaching have been conducted in laboratory settings (e.g., Cicirelli, 1972, 1973; Stewart, 1983) with protocols designed for experimental control but perhaps lacking in ecological validity. Some researchers have studied sibling interaction in children's home environments (e.g., Lamb, 1978; Pepler et al., 1981), but they have not considered what develops in the process of teaching younger siblings.

Ethnographic studies of sibling interactions indicate that siblings do teach each other to do everyday things. Sibling caretakers introduce younger siblings to new languages, language routines, and appropriate ways to behave (Ochs, 1988; Watson-Gegeo & Gegeo, 1989; Zukow-Goldring, 1995, 2002). In this way, they teach their younger siblings to become competent members of their cultures. In a study in Central Mexico, Zukow (1989a) described examples of older siblings engaging their younger charges in more advanced play than what the younger ones had been previously engaged in on their own. In the Marquesas, Martini (1994) found that sibling caretakers socialize each other to become competent at managing stratified social roles, respecting the complex social hierarchy of Marquesan culture. Maynard (2002) used ethnographic video data to examine the development of sibling teaching in the context of caretaking interactions. Older siblings aged 3–11–years were observed as they engaged their younger, two-year-old siblings in everyday activities. They provided verbal and nonverbal guidance to incorporate the two-year-olds into the sibling group activity. The oldest sibling caretakers, ages 8–11, were able to structure tasks, provide necessary materials, simplify tasks into doable parts, guide the bodies of learners, and provide both verbal and nonverbal feedback to help their youngest siblings do a task. The six- and seven-year-olds could also set up materials, but their teaching involved many directives without much task simplification, explanations, or feedback. The three- to five-year-old children mainly served as observational models, engaging in side-by-side activities with learners. Maynard (2004) found that sibling-teaching at home is affected by older siblings' school attendance: Maya children who have gone to school change the way they teach their younger siblings. The growing body of ethnographic work elucidates the ways that siblings engage each other in everyday teaching activities.

Questions Raised by Evolutionary Theory Concerning Cognitive and Social Development in the Sibling Group

An evolutionary theory of siblings suggests that a person is more likely to help a sibling who shares half of his genes, than an unrelated person. Evolutionary theory raises the question of how siblings will behave as they compete with each other for resources while protecting them as carriers of half of each other's genes. From a classic evolutionary perspective, the number of siblings one has should increase conflict because of diminishing resources. Taken another way, however, the number of siblings may also have an impact on children's social and cognitive development—a greater number of siblings could be either an impediment for resources or a resource itself.

Number of Siblings

In the United States, a debate has gone on for many years regarding the issue of family size and children's educational performance. Several researchers concluded that having more siblings led parents to over-divide their material and attentional resources among siblings, resulting in a pattern of first-borns outperforming later-borns on SATs, and other measures of cognitive ability (Downey, 1995; Zajonc, 1986). Zajonc (1986) concluded that, in terms of cognitive development, it was better for a child to come from a smaller family rather than a larger one. However, recent research in both agrarian cultures and the United States has shown that there are positive effects, in both social and cognitive development, of having more than one sibling.

Much research shows that children's social and cognitive development can be enhanced by having more than one sibling. For example, Tambashe and Shapiro (1996) found that women in Zaire who grew up with more siblings had easier social transitions into marriage in adulthood. Children with more siblings were found to achieve success on false belief tasks earlier than children with fewer siblings (Lewis et al., 1996). Children who had multiple siblings who were both older than and younger than they were showed advanced theory of mind abilities (Peterson, 2001). Maynard (2002) found that children with a greater number of older siblings were the beneficiaries of more opportunities for complex, scaffolded instruction than those children who had a smaller number of older siblings. In her Zinacantec Maya sample, Maynard found that siblings in multi-age playgroups each served as teachers for young 2-year-olds in ways that exhibited their developmental capabilities: 3–5-year-olds served as observational models; 6–7-year-olds served to bring necessary items and provide some verbal instruction; and 8–11-year-olds provided appropriate verbal and nonverbal help, including sensitive scaffolding of tasks. Thus, the two-year-old siblings with more than one older sibling were able to take advantage of more of these available teaching characteristics than children with only one older sibling. The scaffolding of the two-year-old's learning is distributed among all the older siblings of a particular group.

Having more than one sibling available for care of the younger ones is also beneficial for parents who go away from home to work, as in many cultures in Africa (e.g., the Abaluyia of Kenya). Children in these cases are left in the complete care of siblings while parents work (Weisner & Gallimore, 1977). The sibling relationship becomes central to children's daily routines, and maintaining positive sibling relationships, therefore, becomes critical. Siblings must learn to manage conflict when it arises.

Sibling Conflict

Sibling relationships are not always smooth and easy. The more siblings there are available, the more potential for conflict exists among them. Siblings may find themselves dominated by others or in conflict with others over material goods. The ways that sibling conflict is characterized varies across cultures. In agrarian societies, sibling groups are usually stratified in a hierarchy where older siblings have authority over the younger ones (Zukow, 2002). Older children assume responsibility for the happiness and well-being of the younger siblings. That responsibility often entails the wielding of power. Older siblings can tell younger siblings what to do to avoid harm, to stay out of the way of adult work, and to behave well (Weisner & Gallimore, 1977; Whiting & Edwards, 1988). Younger children learn to accept that authority and follow the lead of the older siblings. The sibling group maintains homeostasis through this accepted authority system, rarely requiring intervention from adults.

In Great Britain and the United States, sibling conflict is characterized as a struggle based on sibling rivalry (Mendelson, 1990). Conflict is thought of as something that helps an individual to develop particular socioemotional skills and to internalize rules for social conduct (Zukow, 2002). The sibling relationship is typically managed by the parents who intervene to help resolve sibling conflicts. Thus homeostasis is maintained by the parents as the children gradually internalize social rules.

Summary

Across the world, siblings must learn to get along with each other and with others they meet in contexts outside the home. Siblings learn social and cognitive skills as they interact together. Just as having more than one sibling may be beneficial in guiding the youngest sibling's learning, having more than one sibling may give children more opportunities to deal with greater conflict, to observe a wider range of emotional profiles, and to therefore develop greater agility with social skills. Having more than one sibling may be a resource or an impediment, depending on the particular ecocultural context. The relationship between number of siblings, birth spacing, and the distribution of resources needs to be investigated in both within- and between-culture studies to separate cultural values from economic issues.

SIBLINGS AT PLAY

Play serves important social and cognitive functions in children's development (Corsaro & Schwarz, 1991; Lancy, 1996; Scales, Almy, Nicolpoulou, & Ervin-Tripp, 1991). Play permits children to explore their environment, to learn about objects, and to solve problems (Garvey, 1990). In play, children learn to understand others and to practice roles they will assume as they mature (Corsaro, 1985; Haight & Miller, 1993; Vygotsky, 1978).

Play, as with other domains of development, is also affected by ecocultural models and values; for example, whether or not play is supported by parents and how much parents participate affect the role of play in siblings' lives. In agrarian societies, play occurs predominantly outside the realm of adult activities (Farver, 1999; Gaskins, 1999; Martini, 1994; Maynard, 2002; Watson-Gegeo & Gegeo, 1989; Zukow, 1989b). Children may play while adults work. As long as children do not interfere with adult work, play is usually tolerated and sometimes encouraged. A notable exception are the Yucatec Maya, described by Gaskins (1996, 1999). Gaskins finds that Yucatec Maya families do not support play. For example, Yucatec parents do not provide toys or engage in behaviors that otherwise encourage play.

Play can be a very powerful engine for sibling interactions. In a Vygotskian view, play is a way for the child to deal with real-life situations. Interacting with siblings and peers in play helps children take on roles and participate in cultural practices (Vygotsky, 1978; Zukow-Goldring, 1995, 2002). Indeed, even though much of children's play is imaginary, we observe that much of children's play is based on real-life events. Play often reproduces the adult world within the context of peer culture. It is with play that children "come to grasp, refine and extend features of the adult world in the creation of their own peer world" (Corsaro, 1985, p. 62). Children express their understandings of their worlds in their play activities. They also develop new ways of being in the culture.

Children develop cultural knowledge through role-play (Vygotsky, 1978). Role-play indicates their conception and use of social information like status, roles, and norms (Corsaro, 1985; Martini, 1994; Maynard, 1999a, 1999b; Vygotsky, 1978; Zukow-Goldring, 1995, 2002). Play provides an arena for children to practice what they know, to teach, to learn, and to try out future roles. In the case of the Yucatec Maya where play is not a predominant form of role practice, future roles are practiced by the early assumption of chores and participation in household work (Gaskins, 1996, 1999).

Older siblings often structure younger children's play (Gaskins, 1999; Martini, 1994; Maynard, 2002; Watson-Gegeo & Gegeo, 1989; Zukow-Goldring, 1995, 2002). Zukow (1984, 1986) used ethnographic data to demonstrate that play with siblings was significantly more advanced than play with adult caregivers. Older siblings were adept at engaging toddler siblings in elaborate role-playing scenes from everyday life. In the Zinacantec Maya community studied by Maynard (1999a, 1999b, 2002), siblings structure play activities for their younger charges to keep them out of the way of adults and to keep them entertained and happy. The long-term cognitive and social effects of sibling play are being studied longitudinally.

CONCLUSION

No matter where they are developing in the world, siblings have an impact on each other's lives. Sibling caretaking provides a special glimpse into the potential for children to guide and teach each other as they become competent members of their cultures. Sibling interactions influence many areas of children's development including their social, cognitive, linguistic, and play development. It is important to consider sibling relationships in the study of human development. We must understand how the sibling relationship relates with other relationships in the larger family and societal contexts.

The study of sibling interactions can add greatly to our understanding of human development. For example, an innovative study by Whaley and her colleagues (Whaley, Sigman, Beckwith, Cohen, & Espinosa, 2002) contradicts the prevailing view that African children in Kenya participate in less *en face* interaction with their caregivers than their American counterparts. By taking into account siblings and caregivers other than the mother, Whaley and her colleagues showed that Kenyan and American children actually receive roughly the same amount of *en face* communication. Previous studies of infant-caregiver interactions had apparently focused solely on mother-infant interaction, without taking into account the role of sibling caretakers in Kenyan society. Because they understood the role of siblings and other caregivers in their Kenyan subjects' lives, Whaley and her colleagues were able to show that Kenyan siblings provide some types of care that their mothers do not provide. The focus for research thus shifts from a Kenyan "interaction deficit" to a deeper question about the pervasive role of interactions with infants, the ways that such interactions support development, and the ways that care is distributed among people in a society. Future studies of sibling interactions in their cultural contexts will help us understand human development as a set of adaptations to particular ecocultural niches.

REFLECTIVE QUESTIONS

1. Think about your own upbringing. If you had siblings, what role did your siblings play in your development? If you did not have siblings, how did you learn to negotiate with peers?
2. Why do you think sibling rivalry is so prevalent in the United States?
3. If you were to have more than one child, how would you want them to interact with and care for each other? In childhood? In adulthood?

SUGGESTED READINGS

Books and Articles

Cicirelli, V. G. (1995). Sibling relationships in cross-cultural perspective. In V. G. Cicirelli (Ed.), *Sibling relationships across the life span* (pp. 69–85). New York: Springer. Retrieved from http://link.springer.com/chapter/10.1007/978–1–4757–6509–0_6

Maynard, A. E., & Tovote, K. E. (2009). Learning from other children. In D. Lancy, S. Gaskins, & J. Bock (Eds.), *The anthropology of learning in childhood* (pp. 181–205). Lanham, MD: AltaMira Press.

Websites

International Association for Cross-Cultural Psychology: www.iaccp.org
Society for Psychological Anthropology: www.aaanet.org/sections/spa
Jean Piaget Society: www.piaget.org

REFERENCES

Abramovitch, R., Corter, C., & Lando, B. (1979). Sibling interaction in the home. *Child Development, 51,* 1268–1271.

Azmitia, M., & Hesser, J. (1993). Why siblings are important agents of cognitive development: A comparison of siblings and peers. *Child Development, 64,* 430–444.

Azuma, H. (1994). Two modes of cognitive socialization in Japan and the United States. In P. Greenfield & R. Cocking (Eds.), *Cross-cultural roots of minority child development* (pp. 275–84). Hillsdale, NJ: Erlbaum.

Barlow, K. (2013). Attachment and culture in Murik society: Learning autonomy and interdependence through kinship, food, and gender. In N. Quinn & J. M. Mageo (Eds.), *Attachment reconsidered: Cultural perspectives on a Western theory* (pp. 165–188). New York: Palgrave Macmillan.

Botvin, G. J., & Murray, F. B. (1975). The efficacy of peer modeling and social conflict in the acquisition of conservation. *Child Development, 46,* 796–799.

Broch, H. B. (1990). *Growing up agreeably: Bonerate childhood observed.* Honolulu, HI: University of Hawaii Press.

Bryant, B. (1987). Mental health, temperament, family, and friends: Perspectives on children's empathy and social perspective taking. In N. Eisenberg & J. Strayer (Eds.), *Empathy and its development* (pp. 245–270). New York: Cambridge University Press.

Bryant, B. (1989). The child's perspective of sibling caretaking and its relevance to understanding social-emotional functioning and development. In P. G. Zukow (Ed.), *Sibling interaction across cultures: Theoretical and methodological issues* (pp. 143–164). New York: Springer-Verlag.

Bryant, B. K. (1992). Sibling caretaking: Providing emotional support during middle childhood. In F. Boer & J. Dunn (Eds.), *Children's sibling relationships: Developmental and clinical issues* (pp. 55–69). Hillsdale, NJ: Erlbaum.

Cicirelli, V. G. (1972). The effect of sibling relationship of concept learning of young children taught by child-teachers. *Child Development, 43,* 282–287.

Cicirelli, V. G. (1973). Effects of sibling structure and interaction on children's categorization style. *Developmental Psychology, 9,* 132–139.

Cicirelli, V. G. (1975). Effects of mother and older sibling on the problem-solving behavior of the younger child. *Developmental Psychology, 11*(6), 749–756

Corsaro, W. A. (1985). *Friendship and peer culture in the early years.* Norwood, NJ: Ablex.

Corsaro, W. A. & Schwarz, K. (1991). Peer play and socialization in two cultures: Implications for research and practice. In B. Scales, M. Almy, A. Nicolopoulou, & S. Ervin-Tripp (Eds.), *Play and the social context of development in early care and education* (pp. 234–54). New York: Teachers College Press.

DeLeon, L. (November, 2008). Authority, attention, and affect in directive/response sequences in Zinacantec Mayan siblings. Paper presented in Jennifer Reynolds and Lourdes DeLeon, Siblings socializing siblings: The social organization of sibling activities, styles, and affect in cross-cultural perspective. Symposium presented at the 107th annual meeting of the American Anthropological Association, San Francisco, CA.

Downey, D. B. (1995). When bigger is not better: Family size, parental resources, and children's educational performance. *American Sociological Review, 60*(5), 746–761.

Dunn, J. (1989). Siblings and the development of social understanding in early childhood. In P. G. Zukow (Ed.), *Sibling interaction across cultures. Theoretical and methodological issues* (pp. 106–116). New York: Springer-Verlag.

Dunn, J. (1992). Sisters and brothers: Current issues in developmental research. In F. Boer & J. Dunn (Eds.), *Children's sibling relationships: Developmental and clinical issues* (pp. 1–17). Hillsdale, NJ: Erlbaum.

Dunn, J., & Kendrick, C. (1979). Interaction between young siblings in the context of family relationships. In M. Lewis & L. A. Rosenblum, *The child and its family* (pp. 143–168). New York: Plenum Press.

Dunn, J., & Kendrick, C. (1982). *Siblings: Love, envy, and understanding.* Cambridge, MA: Harvard.

Dunn, J., & Munn, P. (1986). Siblings and the development of prosocial behaviour. *International Journal of Behavioral Development, 9*, 265–284.

Eisenberg, N., & Mussen, P. (1989). *The roots of prosocial behavior in children*. New York: Cambridge University Press.

Essman, C. S. (1977). Sibling relations as socialization for parenthood. *Family Coordinator, 26*(3), 259–262.

Farver, J. A. M. (1999). Activity setting analysis: A model for examining the role of culture in development. In A. Göncü (Ed.), *Children's engagement in the world: Sociocultural perspectives* (pp. 99–127). New York: Cambridge University Press.

Gallimore, R., Tharp, R. G., & Speidel, G. E. (1978). The relationship of sibling caretaking and attentiveness to a peer tutor. *American Educational Research Journal, 15*(2), 267–273.

Garvey, C. (1990). *Play* (Vol. 27). Cambridge, MA: Harvard University Press.

Gaskins, S. (1996). How Mayan parental theories come into play. In S. Harkness & C. Super (Eds.), *Parents' cultural belief systems: Their origins, expressions, and consequences* (pp. 345–363). New York: Guilford Press.

Gaskins, S. (1999). Children's daily lives in a Mayan village: A case study of culturally constructed roles and activities. In A. Göncü (Ed.), *Children's engagement in the world: Sociocultural perspectives* (pp. 25–61). New York: Cambridge University Press.

Goldenberg, C., & Gallimore, R. (1991). Changing teaching takes more than a one-shot workshop. *Educational Leadership, 49*, 69–72.

Greenfield, P.M. (1994). Independence and interdependence as developmental scripts: Implications for theory, research, and practice. In P.M. Greenfield & R. R. Cocking (Eds.), *Cross-cultural roots of minority child development* (pp. 1–39). Hillsdale, NJ: Erlbaum.

Haight, W., & Miller, P. (1993). *The ecology and development of pretend play*. Albany, NY: SUNY Press.

Heath, S. B. (1983). *Ways with words: Language, life and work in communities and classrooms*. Cambridge, England: Cambridge University Press.

Hecht, J. A. (1981). The cultural contexts of siblingship in Pukapuka. In M. Marshall (Ed.), *Siblingship in Oceania: Studies in the meaning of kin relations* (pp. 53–77). Ann Arbor, MI: The University of Michigan Press.

Hill, M. (1991). The role of social networks in the care of young children. In M. Woodhead, P. Light, & R. Carr (Eds.), *Growing up in a changing society* (pp. 97–114). London: Routledge, in association with The Open University.

Howe, N., & Ross, H. S. (1990). Socialization, perspective-taking, and the sibling relationship. *Developmental Psychology, 26*(1), 160–165.

Kendrick, C., & Dunn, J. (1980). Caring for second baby: Effects on interaction between mother and firstborn. *Developmental Psychology, 16*(4), 303–311.

Kim, U., & Choi, S. (1994). Individualism, collectivism, and child development: A Korean perspective. In P. Greenfield & R. Cocking (Eds.), *Cross-cultural roots of minority child development* (pp. 227–257). Hillsdale, NJ: Erlbaum.

Kirkpatrick, J. (1981). Meanings of siblingship in Marquesan society. In M. Marshall (Ed.), *Siblingship in Oceania: Studies in the meaning of kin relations* (pp. 17–51). Ann Arbor, MI: The University of Michigan Press.

Lamb, M. E. (1978). Interactions between eighteen-month-olds and their preschool-aged siblings. *Child Development, 49*(1), 51–59.

Lancy, D. (1996). *Playing on the mother ground: Cultural routines for children's development*. New York: Guilford Press.

LCHC (Laboratory of Comparative Human Cognition). (1986). Contribution of cross-cultural research to educational practices. *American Psychologist, 41*, 1049–1058.

Lebra, T. S. (1994). Mother and child in Japanese socialization: A Japan–US comparison. In P. M. Greenfield & R. R. Cocking (Eds.), *Cross-cultural roots of minority child development* (pp. 259–274). Hillsdale, NJ: Lawrence Erlbaum Associates, Inc.

Lewis, C., Freeman, N.H., Kyriakidou, C., Maridaki-Kassotaki, K., & Berridge, D.M. (1996). Social influences on false belief access: Specific sibling influences or general apprenticeship? *Child Development, 67*, 2930–2947.

Martini, M. (1994). Peer interactions in Polynesia: A view from the Marquesas. In J. L. Roopnarine, J. E. Johnson, & F. H. Hooper (Eds.), *Children's play in diverse cultures* (pp. 73–103). Albany, NY: SUNY Press.

Martini, M., & Kirkpatrick, J. (1992). Parenting in Polynesia: A view from the Marquesas. In J. L. Roopnarine & D. B. Carter (Eds.), *Parent-child socialization in diverse cultures* (Vol. 5) (pp. 199–222). Norwood, NJ: Ablex.

Maynard, A.E. (1999a). *Cultural teaching: The social organization and development of teaching in Zinacantec Maya sibling interactions*. Unpublished doctoral dissertation, University of California Los Angeles.

Maynard, A.E. (1999b). The social organization and development of teaching in Zinacantec Maya sibling play. In S. Gaskins (Chair), Symposium presented at the meeting of the American Anthropological Association. Chicago, IL.

Maynard, A.E. (2002). Cultural teaching: The development of teaching skills in Zinacantec Maya sibling interactions. *Child Development, 73*(3), 969–982.

Maynard, A.E. (2004). Cultures of teaching in childhood: Formal schooling and Maya sibling teaching at home. *Cognitive Development, 19*(4), 517–536.

Meisner, J.S., & Fisher, V.L. (1980). Cognitive shifts of young children as a function of peer interaction and sibling status. *The Journal of Genetic Psychology, 136*, 247–253.

Mendelson, M.J. (1990). *Becoming a brother: A child learns about life, family, and self.* Cambridge, MA: MIT Press.

Minks, A. (2008). Socializing rights and responsibilities: Domestic play among Miskitu siblings on the Atlantic Coast of Nicaragua. Paper presented at the 107th annual meeting of the American Anthropological Association, San Francisco, CA.

Nuckolls, C.W. (1993a). *Siblings in South Asia: Brothers and sisters in cultural context.* New York: Guilford.

Nuckolls, C.W. (1993b). An introduction to the cross-cultural study of sibling relations. In C.W. Nuckolls (Ed.), *Siblings in South Asia: Brothers and sisters in cultural context* (pp. 19–41). New York: Guilford.

Ochs, E. (1988). *Culture and language development: Language acquisition and socialization in a Samoan village.* Cambridge, MA: Cambridge.

Ottenberg, S. (1968). *Double descent in an African society: The Afikpo Village-group.* Seattle, WA: University of Washington Press.

Pepler, D.J., Abramovitch, R., & Corter, C. (1981). Sibling interactions in the home: A longitudinal study. *Child Development, 52*(4), 1344–1347.

Perez-Granados, D.R., & Callanan, M.A. (1997). Conversations with mothers and siblings: Young children's semantic and conceptual development. *Developmental Psychology, 33*(1), 120–134.

Perner, J., Ruffman, T., & Leekam, S.R. (1994). Theory of mind is contagious: You catch it from your sibs. *Child Development, 65*, 1225–1238.

Peterson, C. C. (2001). Influence of siblings' perspectives on theory of mind. *Cognitive Development, 15*(4), 435–455.

Piaget, J. (1951). *The origins of intelligence in children.* New York: International Universities Press.

Rabain-Jamin, J., Maynard, A. E., & Greenfield, P. (2003). Implications of sibling caregiving for sibling relations and teaching interactions in two cultures. *Ethos, 31*(2), 204–231.

Rindstedt, C. (2001). *Quicha children and language shift in an Andean community.* Unitryck, Sweden: Linköping.

Rogoff, B. (1990). *Apprenticeship in thinking.* New York: Oxford University Press.

Rogoff, B. (1991). The joint socialization of development by young children and adults. In M. Lewis & S. Feinman (Eds.), *Social influences and socialization in infancy* (pp. 253–280). New York: Plenum Press.

Ruffman, T., Perner, J., Naito, M., Parkin, L., & Clements, W. A. (1998). Older (but not younger) siblings facilitate false belief understanding. *Developmental Psychology, 34*(1), 161–174.

Scales, B., Almy, M., Nicolopoulou, A., & Ervin-Tripp, S. (1991). *Play and the social context of development in early care and education.* New York: Teachers College Press.

Stewart, R. B. (1983). Sibling interaction: The role of the older child as teacher for the younger. *Merrill Palmer Quarterly, 29*(1), 47–68.

Stoneman, Z., & Brody, G. H. (1993). Sibling relations in the family context. In Z. Stoneman & P. Waldman Berman (Eds.), *The effects of mental retardation, disability, and illness on sibling relationships: Research issues and challenges* (pp. 3–30). Baltimore, MD: Paul H. Brookes.

Super, C. M., & Harkness, S. (1986). The developmental niche: A conceptualization at the interface of child and culture. *International Journal of Behavioral Development, 9*, 1–25.

Tambashe, B. O., & Shapiro, D. (1996). Family background and early life course transitions in Kinshasa. *Journal of Marriage and the Family, 58*(4), 1029–1037.

Teti, D. M., & Ablard, K. E. (1989). Security of attachment and infant-sibling relationships: A laboratory study. *Child Development, 60*(6), 1519–1528.

Teti, D. M., Bond, L. A., & Gibbs, E. D. (1988). Mothers, fathers, and siblings: A comparison of play styles and their influence upon infant cognitive level. *International Journal of Behavioral Development, 11*(4), 415–432.

Tobin, J. J., Wu, D. Y. H., & Davidson, D. H. (1989). *Preschool in three cultures: Japan, China, and the United States.* New Haven, CT: Yale University Press.

Vogt, E. Z. (1969). *Zinacantán: A Maya community in the highlands of Chiapas.* Cambridge, MA: Harvard University Press.

Vygotsky, L. S. (1978). *Mind in society.* New York: Cambridge University Press.

Ward, M. (1971). *Them children: A study in language learning.* New York: Holt, Rinehart & Winston.

Watson-Gegeo, K. A., & Gegeo, D. W. (1989). The role of sibling interaction in child socialization. In P. G. Zukow (Ed.), *Sibling interaction across cultures. Theoretical and methodological issues* (pp. 54–76). New York: Springer-Verlag.

Weisner, T. S. (1984). Ecocultural niches of middle childhood: A cross-cultural perspective. In W. A. Collins (Ed.), *Development during middle childhood: The years from six to twelve* (pp. 334–369). Washington, DC: National Academy Press.

Weisner, T. S. (1987). Socialization for parenthood in sibling caretaking societies. In J. B. Lancaster, J. Altmann, A. S. Rossi, & L. R. Sherrod (Eds.), *Parenting across the life span: Biosocial dimensions* (pp. 237–270). Hawthorne, NY: Aldine.

Weisner, T. S. (1989a). Cultural and universal aspects of social support for children: Evidence from the Abaluyia of Kenya. In D. Belle (Ed.), *Children's social networks and social supports* (pp. 70–90). New York: John Wiley & Sons.
Weisner, T. S. (1989b). Comparing sibling relationships across cultures. In P. G. Zukow (Ed.), *Sibling interaction across cultures. Theoretical and methodological issues* (pp. 11–25). New York: Springer-Verlag.
Weisner, T. S. (1993). Ethnograpic and ecocultural perspectives on sibling relationships. In Z. Stoneman & P. W. Berman (Eds.), *The effects of mental retardation disability, and illness on sibling relationships: Research issues and challenges.* (pp. 51–83). Baltimore, MD: Paul H. Brookes.
Weisner, T. S., & Gallimore, R. (1977). My brother's keeper: Child and sibling caretaking. *Current Anthropology, 18*(2), 169–190.
Weisner, T. S., Gallimore, R., & Jordan, C. (1988). Unpackaging cultural effects on classroom learning: Native Hawaiian peer assistance and child-generated activity. *Anthropology and Education Quarterly, 19*(4), 327–353.
Whaley, S. E., Sigman, M., Beckwith, L., Cohen, S. E., & Espinosa, M. P. (2002). Infant-caregiver interaction in Kenya and the United States: The Importance of multiple caregivers and adequate comparison samples. *Journal of Cross-Cultural Psychology, 33*(3), 236–247. doi:10.1177/0022022102033003002
Whiting, B. B., & Edwards, C. P. (1988). *Children of different worlds: The formation of social behavior.* Cambridge, MA: Harvard University Press.
Whiting, B. B., & Whiting, J. M. (1975). *Children of six cultures: A psycho-cultural analysis.* Cambridge, MA: Harvard University Press.
Whiting, J. W. (1977). A model for psychocultural research. In H. Liederman, S. Tulkin and A. Rosenfeld (Eds.), *Culture and infancy: Variations in the human experience* (pp. 29–48). New York: Academic Press.
Whittemore, R. D., & Beverly, E. (1989). Trust in the Mandinka way: The cultural context of sibling care. In P. G. Zukow (Ed.), *Sibling interactions across cultures: Theoretical and methodological issues* (pp. 26–53). New York: Springer-Verlag.
Widmer, E. D., & Weiss, C. C. (2000). Do older siblings make a difference? The effects of older sibling support and older sibling adjustment on the adjustment of socially disadvantaged adolescents. *Journal of Research on Adolescence, 10*(1), 1–27.
Zajonc, R. B. (1986). The decline and rise of scholastic aptitude scores: A prediction derived from the confluence model. *American Psychologist, 41*(8), 862–867.
Zukow, P. G. (1986). The relationship between interaction with the caregiver and the emergence of play activities during the one-word period. *British Journal of Developmental Psychology, 4*, 223–234.
Zukow, P. G. (1989a). *Sibling interaction across cultures. Theoretical and methodological issues.* New York: Springer-Verlag.
Zukow, P. G. (1989b). Siblings as effective socializing agents: Evidence from Central Mexico. In P. G. Zukow (Ed.), *Sibling interaction across cultures. Theoretical and methodological issues* (pp. 79–105). New York: Springer-Verlag.
Zukow-Goldring, P. (1995). Sibling caregiving. In M. H. Bornstein (Ed.), *Handbook of parenting, Vol. 3: Status and social conditions of parenting* (pp. 177–208). Hillsdale, NJ: Erlbaum.
Zukow-Goldring, P. G. (2002). Sibling caregiving. In M. H. Bornstein (Ed.), *Handbook of parenting. Vol. 3, Status and social conditions of parenting* (2nd ed., pp. 253–286). Mahwah, NJ: Erlbaum.

10

Adolescents in the Majority World

Katelyn E. Poelker and Judith L. Gibbons

Alex (a pseudonym) is a 17-year-old girl who lives with her family on the Guatemalan south coast. She attends a bilingual (Spanish-English) school. In a typical day she finds it hard to get up at 5 am. But she rouses herself, spends the day in school, and arrives back home where she does homework and talks to her boyfriend on WhatsApp. *On an ideal day, she would* drive *to school, then go to the nearest town where with friends she would talk or watch movies, then go home to sleep. She says that technology is important where she lives because smart phones are the major way to keep in touch with friends; she uses a computer primarily for homework, and only rarely for accessing social media. In the future, Alex's main goal is to be happy. She wants to study industrial design, make creative things, or do something that helps others. If she could send a message to other teenagers around the world, it would be, "Stop worrying about what others think."*

Paolo is a 17-year-old boy who lives with his family in Guatemala City, where he attends a private school. In his typical day he prepares for school, hangs around with his friends, studies, goes back home, and spends his free time doing sports, reading, and watching television. On an ideal day he would eat good food, rest, and have a quiet peaceful day either alone or with people he likes. Paolo sees technology as a tool for living life, for staying in touch. He says it can be pretty addictive, for example, not being able put down your phone at dinner. Paolo would like the quality of life (for all) to increase in the future, and he would like to live in a free world. He feels as though he belongs to a global community of teenagers, and he quoted Walt Whitman, that he feels he "belong(s) to something greater." Paolo does not know what he wants to do for a career, but it is something he wants to decide. If Paolo could send a message to teenagers around the world, it would be, "If they feel like they are alone, there are other people who are like them. They are not truly alone; they just feel like they are."

Both Alex and Paolo feel close to their parents, and somewhat different from their peers. Alex feels different because she likes to be alone and her peers are always in groups. Paolo sees himself as more critical and analytical than his peers. Both are uncertain about their future careers, but place high value on education and plan to go to university. Both see success as being happy and satisfied with oneself. And both are cognizant of the challenges that adolescents face in Guatemala today, primarily economic, but also lack of access to education and opportunities, and increased competition for lucrative jobs.

There are 1.2 billion adolescents (ages 10 through 19) in today's world (UNICEF, 2012). They make up approximately 17% of the world's population. Of the global teenagers, 90% live in majority world countries (also known as developing countries, low- and middle-income countries, or the global south, UNICEF, 2012). Yet, adolescents from the majority world are vastly underrepresented in the psychological literature. An analysis of papers published in the *Journal of Research on Adolescence* from 1992 through 2010 revealed that during most of those years only about 5% of the articles addressed adolescents in the majority world. In the peak years of 2009 and 2010, the percentage reached only 27% (Raffaelli, Lazarevic, Koller, Nsamenang, & Sharma, 2013). The purpose of this chapter is to update a chapter published in 2004 (Gibbons, 2004) that reviewed the conditions of adolescents in the developing, now referred to as majority, world. Here we focus on the changes in adolescents' lives, including the new challenges young people face in the areas of health, education, family, work, technology, and globalization.

Recently adolescents, especially those in the majority world, have come to the attention of scientists and practitioners. In 2011, UNICEF devoted its annual issue on the *State of the World's Children* to the life stage of adolescence. The next year UNICEF published a follow-up report, "Progress for children: A report card on adolescents" (UNICEF, 2012). The *Journal of Research on Adolescence* published a special issue on adolescents of the majority world in 2013. In addition, the medical journal *Lancet* sponsored the *Lancet Series on Adolescent Health* in 2012 (Resnick, Catalano, Sawyer, Viner, & Patton, 2012). Most recently, the World Health Organization published a report titled "Health for the World's Adolescents: A second chance in the second decade" (WHO, 2014a). Taken together, those reports provide a broad outline of the conditions of adolescents in different regions of the world.

Most marked is the diversity of the adolescent experience. Within low- and middle-income countries, adolescents differ by economic condition, which ranges from extreme poverty to relative wealth. In addition, adolescent differences according to age and gender are important, with girls at elevated risk for health problems due to early pregnancy and older boys at elevated risk for being victims of violence (Blanc & Bruce, 2013). Also, the specific contexts of adolescents' lives, including urban or rural residence, vary widely. For example, in Ghana, most urban adolescents have access to the Internet through Internet cafes (Borzekowski, Fobil, & Asante, 2006), and they use the Internet to access health information. On the other hand rural adolescent boys who herd cattle in East Africa use cellphones to communicate about water sources and good grazing lands (Santos, 2010). Some adolescents live in particularly difficult circumstances. Many live in poverty and some have experienced trauma, such as domestic and war-related violence, or have been orphaned by AIDS, leaving them vulnerable to psychological disorders such as PTSD (Familiar et al., 2013; see also Aptekar & Oliver, chapter 15, this volume). Despite living in difficult circumstances many adolescents in the majority world show resilience, based in part on cultural and relational support, flexibility, and personal agency (Cameron et al., 2013).

In this chapter we will address adolescents' social relationships, education, work, lifestyle and leisure, gender differences, physical and psychological health and well-being, use of technology and exposure to globalization, and the difficult circumstances in which some teens live. Because of space consideration the chapter omits discussions of sports-related and political activities and interests. We conclude with a call for the application of psychological knowledge to the everyday problems many adolescents face.

HOW ADOLESCENTS SPEND THEIR TIME

The settings in which adolescents spend their time provide the social, physical, and cultural contexts for development. Adolescents spend most of their time engaged in three domains: school, paid and unpaid work, and leisure or recreational time (Lloyd, Grant, & Ritchie, 2008; Ritchie, Lloyd, & Grant, 2004). The proportion of time allotted to each of those categories depends on factors such as gender, school enrollment, economic condition, and culture.

Education and work status appear to set the tone for how adolescents spend their time. School occupies much of the time of many adolescents around the world; however, the time spent on academic activities varies greatly. Ritchie et al. (2004) reported that South African adolescents spent 5 hours a day, and Kenyan adolescents 10 hours a day on academic activities. Education and work may compete for adolescents' time. Adolescents who work as well as attend school spend less time on education-related activities than those who do not work (Teixeira, Fischer, Nagai, & Turte,

2004). Adolescents who do not attend school spend most of their time working (Lloyd et al., 2008; Ritchie et al., 2004).

With respect to work, adolescent boys are more likely to work for pay than are girls (Zapata, Contreras, & Kruger, 2011). By way of contrast girls typically spend more time engaged in domestic work than do boys (Amin & Chandrasekhar, 2009; Lloyd et al., 2008; Ritchie et al., 2004; Zapata et al., 2011). This pattern was evidenced regardless of school enrollment status. For girls not enrolled in school, household chores occupied from 5 to 7 hours per day, whereas for their male counterparts chores consumed only 30 minutes to 3 hours (Ritchie et al., 2004), leaving more time for recreational activities.

Other demographic variables are related to adolescents' time use. Adolescents living in rural communities in Bangladesh participated in more domestic chores than did their urban counterparts (Amin & Chandrasekhar, 2009). As might be expected, children and adolescents from economically disadvantaged families spent more time working than did those from families with more resources (Amin & Chandrasekhar, 2009).

With respect to leisure time, there are significant gender differences in both the quantity of leisure time and its use. Boys of the majority world have more time for leisure and recreational activities than do girls (e.g., Lloyd et al., 2008; Mete, 2010; Ritchie et al., 2004). In addition, boys more often play sports and engage in group activities. Girls reported leisure activities such as reading and collecting; girls who played sports were involved in individual sports such as swimming (Gibbons, Lynn, & Stiles, 1997). Work and school responsibilities may limit free time; working students in Brazil reported significantly less time for recreational activities than did nonworking students (Teixeira et al., 2004); they also slept approximately two hours less each night than nonworking students.

In sum, ecological niches that include cultural, economic, and educational opportunities and constraints, in connection with the demands of the transitional period from childhood to adulthood, dictate how adolescents spend their time.

EDUCATION

Schools for children and adolescents of all ages provide a unique environment to foster learning, friendship, and under optimal conditions, safety and security; however, there are immense challenges to attendance for children and adolescents living in the majority world. Abu, a 13-year-old from Tanzania, commented on one challenge, "We share one textbook between many students so you never have the chance to read for yourself. The teachers are so overwhelmed they only teach a few lessons, the rest you have to read and learn on your own" (UNICEF, 2011a, p. 25). Learning on one's own can be challenging when textbooks are in poor condition and must be shared among multiple students.

According to a recent report by UNICEF (2012), there are 531 million secondary students worldwide (up from 196 million in 1976). Although this may seem like a large number, it signals that only 60% of adolescents who are secondary school age are actually enrolled in secondary education. The percentage of eligible adolescents enrolled in secondary schools are even lower in the most economically challenged parts of the world like sub-Saharan Africa, such as Tanzania, where only one-third of adolescents attend school. Secondary school completion rates in Tanzania are also quite low, greatly limiting the pool of qualified individuals for skilled jobs. In 2002 only 8% of adolescents were enrolled in secondary school; this number had grown to over 30% in 2010 (UNICEF, 2011a). The UNICEF report (2011a) also reminds us that while great strides are being made with respect to primary school enrollment, matriculation rates into secondary school are still problematic.

Many adolescents leave school because they cannot afford the cost of attending, whether that includes transportation expenses or uniforms. Research from Paraguay (Organización Internacional del Trabajo & Dirección General de Estadística, Encuestas & Censos del Paraguay, 2013), Tanzania (UNICEF, 2011a), and Fiji supports this claim (ILO, 2010). For example, Latifah, a 13-year-old Tanzanian, was unable to continue attending school because she did not have the approximately $2 to repair her school uniform (UNICEF, 2011a). A 16-year-old girl from Fiji said she had dropped out of school two years earlier because the cost of her daily transportation to and from school had been $10 (ILO, 2010).

Gender disparity in school attendance has been an important focus of international education initiatives for years. In general, there are more boys enrolled in secondary schools than girls in the majority world with the exceptions of North Africa, East Asia, and the Pacific where gender parity (or equal enrollment between sexes) has been reached (UNICEF, 2012). In Latin America and the Caribbean, however, UNICEF (2012) reports that the pattern is reversed, as more girls are attending secondary school than are boys.

An initiative in Bangladesh is a reminder of an important struggle specific to secondary school girls; that is, how does a girl manage to maintain her school attendance when she is menstruating (UNICEF, 2013b)? At a school in rural Bangladesh, administrators noticed an alarming decline of female enrollment of 48% over seven years. Due to a combination of lack of knowledge about menstruation and few sanitary facilities at the school, many girls could not handle the stress that accompanied this event each month, so they dropped out altogether. McMahon et al. (2011) found similar challenges for girls in Kenya. Focus-group discussions were dominated by the negative feelings that accompany menstruation including those of fear and shame. Girls felt that teachers and other girls began to view them differently with the onset of menstruation. With respect to absenteeism, teachers noted a similar pattern as the one found among Bangladeshi girls for even their most promising students.

With some assistance, the Bangladeshi school was able to install several new bathrooms and also provide resources (e.g., counselors and necessary supplies) to encourage girls to return to school. This effort was a resounding success, as girls now comprise 66% of students (UNICEF, 2013b). Sharmin, a 13-year-old school girl and a wonderful success story for the program, remembered her first period saying, "I planned to stop coming to school, but learning about how normal the phenomenon is was helpful to me" (UNICEF, 2013b, Support for Young Girls, through Women, paragraph 1). Although this is only one example of a circumstance that contributes to the lack of gender parity in secondary school enrollment, it suggests oftentimes the solutions are not terribly complicated to implement and still result in desired outcomes.

Another initiative in India (Beaman, Duflo, Pande, & Topolova, 2012) provided reassuring support for community-based efforts to empower women, resulting in increased school enrollment for girls ages 11 to 15. The authors selected villages where positions on the village council were reserved specifically for women, a *pradhan* (these villages were randomly selected by the Indian government) and villages where no such specification was enforced. Although in both types of villages parents had higher aspirations for their sons compared to daughters, the discrepancy was smaller in villages with a female leader on the council. There was an increase in girls' educational aspirations if they lived in a village with a *pradhan*. It is important to note that having female village council leaders did not decrease aspirations for boys, but raised them for girls. In fact, by the time of the second election period, gender parity in villages with a female council member was achieved.

Despite the number of advances and efforts to increase school enrollment in the majority world, many difficulties remain. Implementing sound educational practices is especially challenging for indigenous groups like the Maasai of Kenya and Tanzania (Poirier, 2012). Many influences from outside their culture (starting with colonization by the British and more recently demands by the Tanzanian and Kenyan governments) have forced the Maasai to adapt a more modern lifestyle, including compulsory education. This newly imposed compulsory education takes away from the traditional education (e.g., how to be good wives and mothers for girls and successful warriors and shepherds for boys) that is highly valued by the Maasai community. Many fear the emphasis on a Western school education threatens the very structure of the Maasai society. There is often a disconnect, according to Serpell (2011), between how parents think their children should be educated to be successful members of their communities and what schools provide. These conflicts between what parents view as best for their children's futures and the role of Western classroom–based education are not easily reconciled and may contribute to the low rates of secondary school enrollment that are found internationally.

Given the limited resources of many families in the majority world, parents rely heavily on their older children to care for their younger siblings (Zukow-Goldring, 2002; see Maynard's chapter on siblings in this volume [chapter 9]). A study by Yi et al. (2012) investigated the impact of sibling caretaking on the adolescent caretakers with respect to their school performance and reports of depression in Cambodia. Although Yi and colleagues (2012) argue that some research suggests positive outcomes associated with caretaking for siblings (e.g., development of cooking and caretaking abilities, more developed social skills), they note that the benefits of these experiences will not likely surface until later in life. Not all consequences of being in the caretaker role, moreover, are positive. Adolescents responsible for taking care of younger siblings reported lower school performance and for boys only, a greater perceived likelihood of dropping out of school. Along with the Bangladeshi effort (UNICEF, 2013b) mentioned earlier, Beaman et al.'s (2012) work, along with Yi et al.'s (2012) study, serves as a reminder that contextual factors can play a large role in educational issues, especially for girls.

As the preceding research shows, there is great diversity in the conditions and challenges students face in schools with respect to their location, gender, and socioeconomic class. These factors create different experiences for the students in these situations and oftentimes, the less than optimal circumstances result in high dropout rates and low matriculation from primary to secondary school (UNICEF, 2012). When looking forward, it seems that investing in education will be one of the most important goals for majority world nations in order to provide meaningful opportunities for adolescents, helping them to invest in their futures (see the chapter on literacy development by Wagner, Zahra, & Lee, chapter 4, in this volume).

WORK

There are 168 million children under 18 in the world who work in market activities (International Labour Organization, ILO, 2013). Of those children, the majority are adolescents, and half of them work under hazardous conditions. The work of children and adolescents is considered child labor only when it has "a negative impact on [their] physical and psychological development" (ILO, 2014, p. 8). Around the world children and adolescents often contribute to their families by engaging in household work or unpaid agricultural work. When conditions are optimal (i.e., with age-appropriate hours and safe working conditions), engagement in tasks can contribute positively to development; unfortunately adolescents' work is often arduous, hazardous, and prolonged.

Adolescents in the majority world often work to either support their families or pay for their own schooling, including uniforms and transportation. A study in Lao revealed that most adolescents reported that the reason they engaged in market work was to supplement the family income (ILO & Lao Statistics Bureau, 2012). In Paraguay, the primary reason reported by adolescents was to cover the expenses and debts of the household (Organización Internacional del Trabajo & Dirección General de Estadística, Encuestas & Censos del Paraguay, 2013). That motivation is revealed in this description of the life of 15-year-old Pethias from Zambia,

> To add to the family income, Pethias draws water for families that live a kilometer from the borehole. He also goes to work in the nearby fields to cultivate or weed. He gets only the equivalent of three US cents per day for working in a field for two to three hours. His money goes to buy food for the day and occasionally other groceries. (Save the Children, 2012, p. 41)

Adolescents may also work specifically to support their own schooling. Three children from one family in Fiji worked weekends in a farmer's vegetable and fruit farm, earning $5 each daily, in order to pay their bus fare to school (ILO, 2010).

Depending on the conditions and the hours worked, adolescents often forgo education for work, limiting their future options. The competition between school and work has been demonstrated for youth in Bolivia (Zapata, Contreras, & Kruger, 2011), Ethiopia (Admassie, 2003), Nicaragua (Buonomo Zabaleta, 2011), Paraguay (Organización Internacional del Trabajo & Dirección General de Estadística, Encuestas & Censos del Paraguay, 2013), and Egypt (Assaad, Levison, & Zibani, 2010). An adolescent boy from Ethiopia said, "I work for my living; I am not able to manage my time for studies" (Save the Children, 2012, p. 38). Among Egyptian girls, their participation in household work negatively predicted schooling (Assaad et al., 2010). The work-school tradeoff is illustrated in this quote from an 11-year-old boy in Fiji, "I left school last month. . . . Now I help my uncle in the farm. . . . I like farming [but] I [would] also like to go to school" (ILO, 2010, p. 88). Flory, 15, from Guatemala said, "I would have liked very much to have continued school, because I know education is very important for me; if I'd only known, if I'd continued in school, I wouldn't be working. Education costs a lot" (UNICEF, 2009, p. 3).

When work is defined as market activities, boys work more frequently and longer hours than do girls (Zapata et al., 2011). When both market and domestic tasks are included, girls work more than boys (Zapata et al., 2011). In Vietnam, children and adolescents' household chores included tidying the house, doing laundry or cooking, and babysitting or shopping. Girls did more of all of those tasks than did boys (ILO, 2014).

The largest employment sector for adolescents in the majority world is agriculture, including farming, fishing, forestry, and livestock production (ILO, n.d.). Most adolescents who work in agriculture are boys working as unpaid family members. Agricultural work can contribute to adolescents' well-being by contributing to the family's food supply, increasing self-esteem, and promoting skill development. In Zambia even teachers saw advantages to children leaving school during the rainy season to tend fields; they claimed that children gained knowledge about agriculture, learned self-reliance, responsibility, and hard work, and also contributed to food for the family (Serpell, 1993). Under adverse conditions, however, work can limit children's access to education and damage health (ILO, n.d.). In addition, like domestic work described later, work in agriculture is often unprotected by law.

A major form of work for adolescent girls is domestic work. The numbers of adolescent domestic workers are unknown, because the employment is invisible and unregulated. However, in India, it is estimated that one in five children under 14 works as a domestic outside the family (UNICEF, 2004). Worldwide, more girls under 16 are engaged in domestic service than any other kind of employment (UNICEF, 2004). In Ethiopia, as in many other countries, "many children are brought to the city from rural areas by their relatives with promises of an education, but made to work as full-time domestic servants once they arrive (Save the Children, 2012, p. 25). Girls working as domestics away from the protection of their families are vulnerable to exploitation and physical and sexual abuse; they work long hours and may have their pay or food withheld (Erulkar & Medbib, 2007). Hezzel, 15, from Nicaragua said,

> Being a domestic worker is a risk. The men of the house always want to abuse you; they touch us and if we don't let them they threaten to kick us out. Also, the employer, if it is her son or husband, believes them and you're humiliated and fired. (UNICEF, 2009, p. 3)

A 14-year-old domestic worker in Addis Ababa said, "Most of the time, the child of the employer beats me without reason. When I ask him why he does that, he beats me again" (Erulkar & Madbib, 2007, p. 251). A qualitative study of young domestic workers in Malawi revealed that the major theme was surviving; young women said that poverty had driven them to domestic work and their goal was simply to endure it (Mkandawire-Valhmu, Rodriguez, Ammar, & Nemoto, 2009).

Although worldwide adolescents are at risk for engaging in work that is hazardous or exploitative, paradoxically older adolescents and young adolescents who need to work may have difficulty finding satisfying work. Youth (ages 15 to 24) in Guatemala are engaged primarily in the informal sector (Programa de las Naciones Unidas para el Desarrollo, PNUD, 2012), in work that is unregulated and precarious. The story of a Guatemalan adolescent who left school and migrated to the city to work in the informal sector, in a street stall selling CDs and DVDs, illustrates his search for more productive and lucrative work. He says he has dreams to set up his own barbershop in his home village (PNUD, 2012). Migration, most often from rural areas to urban areas and sometimes internationally, is common for youth seeking employment (Juárez, LeGrand, Lloyd, Singh, & Hertrich, 2013). Migrant adolescents and young adults face unique challenges because of their age-related vulnerabilities and the fact that they often migrate alone.

In sum, although exploitative child labor has been decreasing around the world, many adolescents still labor in deplorable conditions (ILO, 2013). Moreover, the work they do competes for more valuable activities, such as school attendance. Much of the work done by adolescents is hidden and without legal or parental protection. Striving to move out of poverty, many adolescents in the majority world anticipate a difficult future. On an Internet youth forum, an adolescent from Nepal blogged, "[I] have no energy to change the world because I'm going to be busy in fulfilling basic needs of me and my family" (Koirala DP, 2013, paragraph 10).

SOCIAL RELATIONSHIPS

Parents and peers form the social fabric of the lives of adolescents. They are the individuals adolescents learn from and learn with, who provide support and security, and with whom they have fun. For Vietnamese adolescents, feeling important to one's family was the strongest predictor of adolescents' own confidence in a rewarding future career (Nguyen, Cohen, & Hines, 2011). Positive peer relationships were associated with adolescents' beliefs that they will grow up to achieve their goals and have a happy family with financial stability. Both peers and parents are central to adolescents' social development, but likely take on different meanings and have different implications across the various cultural contexts in which adolescents live.

Parents

Some important characteristics of families internationally revealed by the World Family Map (2013) help to shape our understanding of the role of parents and families across cultures. For example, although rates of single-parenting are increasing, most children and adolescents around the world live in two-parent households, especially in Asia and the Middle East, while in the Americas, Europe, and sub-Saharan Africa single parent households are more common. These living arrangements have implications for adolescents' well-being. Arends-Kuenning and Duryea (2006) found that among adolescents from Brazil, Ecuador, Nicaragua, and Panama those living in single parent households headed by mothers (20% of the sample) were significantly less likely to attend school than were adolescents in families headed by both parents, by fathers, or even those not living with any family members. This finding is attenuated when controlling for income and parental education, suggesting that adequate financial resources can help compensate for the challenges faced by mothers raising children alone. Maternal education was a superior predictor of adolescent educational achievement compared to paternal education, particularly in Nicaragua, the poorest of the four countries included in the study.

Despite the changing landscape of an adolescent's social world with more time spent with peers (both same and opposite sex), the relationships between parents and children remain critical for adolescents' sense of stability (Laursen & Collins, 2009). A study on adolescent self-disclosure in Costa Rica, Thailand, and South Africa revealed eight main reasons why they share information about personal lives with their parents, including: "I tell him or her so she won't worry about me" and "I tell her or him so that she or he will be able to protect me from danger or trouble" (Hunter, Barber, Olsen, McNeely, & Bose, 2011, pp. 457–458). Adolescents whose parents exhibited more positive parenting characteristics (e.g., acceptance) and more parental control were more likely to disclose information than adolescents whose parents were lower in these domains.

Research in Thailand also supports the importance of parental involvement for adolescent well-being. For example, adolescents whose parents are more aware of their daily activities and set more rules engage in less risky behavior (e.g., smoking; Miller et al., 2011). In addition, fewer reports of mental health problems among Thai adolescents were associated with higher levels of parental involvement (Tammariello, Gallahue, Ellard, Woldesemait, & Jacobsen, 2012). Examples of involvement included checking homework and taking the time to understand the adolescent's struggles, suggesting simple interactions are associated with meaningful benefits.

The World Family Map (2013) also identified family mealtime as a specific protective factor for children and adolescents, calling it a "direct measure of positive family progress" (p. 37); eating meals together as a family is consistently associated with adolescent well-being (Fulkerson et al., 2006). The report indicates that family mealtime occurs most frequently (i.e., an adolescent eats the main meal with their parents several times per week) in Europe, but also quite often in Central and South American households.

The lack of data from other low-income countries in Africa and Asia, however, prohibits us from drawing global conclusions.

On a related note with respect to parental influence on career aspirations, a study with Indonesian adolescents suggests parents' own hopes for their children are related to how adolescents perceive their own future careers (Sawitri, Creed, & Zimmer-Gembeck, 2014). More specifically, parents' goals for their adolescents' futures predicted adolescents' aspirations six months later. In addition, at the second time point adolescents with high aspirations reported spending more time on career planning. Finally, the authors note that the alignment between parents' and adolescents' aspirations was important for adolescent career exploration. That is, adolescents were more likely to explore career options if they had high goals for themselves and felt they were consistent with those their parents had for them. Studies like this one are excellent examples, in collectivistic cultures in particular, of the role parents can play in shaping their adolescent children's futures.

Research with Filipino and Guatemalan adolescents whose parents were migrant workers underscores the impact of parental absence on adolescent health (Lykes & Sibley, 2013; Smeekens, Stroebe, & Abakoumkin, 2012). Adolescents who had a parent working out of the country had poorer physical and emotional health (e.g., higher stress and feelings of loneliness) than those whose parents worked domestically, particularly when the mother was the parent abroad (Smeekens et al., 2012). When Guatemalan adolescents were asked to create stories about why parents must move abroad to work, one group wrote, "The daughter was sad because her mother left her with just her aunts. And every week she called her on the phone, but she said that it's not the same when she is with her mom as when she is with her aunts" (Lykes & Sibley, 2013, p. 574). Despite efforts by parents to give their children a better life by providing for them financially, Smeekens et al. (2012) suggest that the negative health outcomes that are associated with parental separation may offset the potential financial benefits.

Although adolescents may not have so much difficulty getting along with their parents as many might think, adolescence is a pivotal point in development that may result in occasional stressful conflicts with parents. A study by Seiffge-Krenke et al. (2013) investigated adolescent coping ability with parental and peer stress in four majority world (Costa Rica, Korea, Pakistan, and Turkey) and two minority world (Czech Republic and Germany) countries. As expected, parental stress was more common than peer stress. For Costa Rican, Turkish, and Korean adolescents, parental stress was higher than peer-related stress. Adolescents from the Czech Republic, Germany, and Pakistan reported the opposite pattern. Moreover, adolescents from all countries reported many healthy coping strategies (e.g., seeking support). The authors concluded that stress because of parental conflicts may be interpreted differently across cultures; majority world adolescents may perceive parental involvement and input as a source of support (rather than stress), a pattern that is opposite to the more prevalent reaction in the minority world (Seiffge-Krenke et al., 2013).

Parents play a central role in the lives of their adolescent children all over the world. The aforementioned research converges in many ways with the parenting literature conducted in the minority world (e.g., benefits of family mealtime). Other issues, though, are more specific to adolescents living in the majority world. Few, if any, adolescents from the minority world have to navigate the unique challenges that come with having parents as migrant workers, for example. In conclusion, although certain issues surrounding the parent-adolescent relationship may be different across cultures, research suggests a fundamental need for parental presence in the lives of their adolescent children, as well as the negative implications of their absence.

Peers

Peers, like parents, are among the most important fixtures in the social world of the adolescent in many cultures. In part, greater time spent with peers is due to the increased opportunities for independence that are presented to adolescents in many parts of the world (Dijkstra & Veenstra, 2011). Schools are popular venues for children and adolescents to build peer relationships and allow them the chance to flourish and develop into meaningful connections (Chen, French, & Schneider, 2006). And as Chen et al. (2006) note, various facets of the culture contribute to the nature of peer relationships (e.g., a society's individualistic versus collectivistic orientation, size and intimacy of peer groups, and the extent of adolescents' other responsibilities that may decrease their time for leisure). Because much of the research on peer relationships in a cultural context was presented in the earlier version of this chapter (see Gibbons, 2004), the empirical evidence presented here reflects only the most pertinent developments in this line of research since that time (see also chapter 9 on siblings by Maynard in this volume).

Some peer relationships are romantic in nature and underscore the increasingly important role that romantic partners play in adolescents' lives (Collins, 2003). Dhariwal and Connolly (2013) investigated romantic relationships in India and among Indian immigrants to Canada. In India, late adolescents' own views on their romantic relationships are often secondary to their parents'; however, given the spread of technological communication via modernization, this is beginning to change. Technological advances have facilitated the spread of Western media and ideals, which in contrast to Indian portrayals showcase the benefits of being involved in a romantic relationship. Results indicated similar levels of romantic desire for all cultural groups (i.e., immigrants, the traditional group attending a single-sex college, and a transitional group attending a co-educational college). However, autonomy in romantic relationships increased as the environment became more Western (with traditional college students as the least Westernized group). A similar pattern was found for media use. Overall, girls reported less use of Western media than boys. Those living in Canada and attending a co-educational college had more friends of the opposite sex than those attending the traditional college. This study has implications for how globalization is affecting the lives of adolescents as well as different views of romantic relationships based on cultural context.

Bullying. Bullying has received increasing attention among international researchers studying adolescents. Bullying typically occurs via two types of aggression, physical and verbal (Craig et al., 2011). While direct physical aggression is more common in younger children, indirect or verbal aggression becomes more frequent by adolescence. In a 40-country study on bullying, Craig et al. (2011) found that 10.7% of participants reported being bullies themselves, an additional 12.6% reported bullying others, and 3.6% were both bullies and bullying victims. Although the sample in this study was drawn from minority world countries, the widespread endorsement of involvement in these issues suggests it is a truly international youth crisis. Work by Elamé and colleagues (2013) suggests the bullying based on ethnicity for adolescent immigrants is particularly problematic for adolescents from African and Middle Eastern countries.

A study on bullying in Brazilian schools revealed that bullying occurs for a variety of reasons (Grossi & Dos Santos, 2012). Some of the examples from the adolescent focus groups included "There was a guy who used to call me fat. I do not like that" and "Usually the fights are because of boyfriends" (Gross & Dos Santos, 2012, p. 132). The authors did note some success with interventions in the schools (called restorative circles) that allowed adolescents a safe place to attempt to resolve conflicts with peers. Unlike research with Western participants, a study on direct and indirect aggression with Indian adolescents provided evidence for a negative relationship between indirect or relational aggression and popularity (Bowker, Ostrov, & Raja, 2011). The authors suggest this may be the case given India's strong collectivistic orientation as relational aggression undermines the relationships that are central to a collectivist culture. Direct or physical aggression had a positive relation with popularity. Bowker et al. (2011) suggest that this traditionally unaccepted form of aggression in individualistic Western society might be a more acceptable way to negotiate conflict with peers in collectivistic India.

HEALTH

Adolescent health research has burgeoned since the earlier version of this chapter was written (Gibbons, 2004). The health problems that afflict adolescents differ from those of younger children, and include substance abuse, mental health, and sexual health problems (Fatsui & Hindin, 2010; Resnick, Catalano, Sawyer, Viner, & Patton, 2012). According to the World Health Organization (WHO, 2014a), over 1.3 million adolescents died in 2012, mostly from preventable causes. Road injury, HIV/AIDS, and self-harm (i.e., suicide) were the three most common causes of adolescent death. Boys and older adolescents suffer higher mortality rates; boys are more likely than girls to be victims of violence. As Patton et al. (2010) note in their review of adolescent health, mortality rates do not tell the complete story. Instead, disability-adjusted live years lost (DALYs) are more telling indicators of health (WHO, 2014a). For adolescents, unipolar depressive disorders, road injuries, and anemia are the top three health issues that lead to DALYs (WHO, 2014a). Psychological disorders, specifically depressive disorders, are responsible for adolescents missing more school and work than are physical health concerns. There are also important geographic differences; not surprisingly mortality rates are high for adolescents in sub-Saharan Africa, and deaths due to violence are particularly common in Latin America (Patton et al., 2012). Suicide occurs more often in regions undergoing political unrest and economic downturn (Kim & Singh, 2004). These regional differences oftentimes speak to the broader cultural climate. Due to the large number of studies published on a variety of health-related topics, the information presented here is only a brief introduction to a topic that could easily fill many more pages.

Physical Health

An important component of physical health is nutrition and healthy eating. As the 2012 UNICEF report on adolescents notes, nutrition is a complex problem with significant numbers of adolescents both under- and overweight. Being an underweight girl is quite common in South Asia, where in India, for example, 40% of adolescent girls are underweight. In addition, there are 21 countries (e.g., Cambodia, Ghana, and Senegal) around the world where more than 33% of adolescent girls (ages 15–19) are anemic, a condition caused by a lack of iron in their diet (UNICEF, 2012). Doku, Koivusilta, Raisamo, and Rimpelä (2011) conducted a study of Ugandan adolescents' eating patterns and found associations with socioeconomic status (SES). Adolescents of parents with more education were more likely to eat breakfast. Unfortunately, many adolescents reported skipping breakfast because there was insufficient food in the household.

The authors noted the striking contrast to the reasons Western adolescents report for skipping this meal (e.g., they are too busy, dieting).

Although obesity has traditionally been labeled as a vice of high-income countries, research suggests it is affecting increasing numbers of majority world adolescents (United Nations, 2011). According to the World Health Organization (WHO, 2014b), children and adolescents living in LMICs face a "double burden" of health problems given that obesity due to the low cost of many high-fat and high-sugar foods occurs alongside infectious diseases and undernutrition. A 2012 UNICEF report revealed that in a sample of 11 majority world countries, more than 20% of the girls were overweight.

In addition to a poor diet, lack of physical exercise is one of the contributing factors to being overweight or obese. Several studies have brought attention to this issue. In a study of adolescents living in 34 countries, Githold, Cowan, Autenrieth, Kann, and Riley (2010) reported that only 23.8% of boys and 15.4% of girls met the requirement for adequate physical activity. Moreover, 33% of adolescents engaged in sedentary activities for at least three hours each day.

Ugandan adolescents who attended public school (presumably of lower SES) spent less time each week engaged in physical activity than those who attended private school (presumably of higher SES; Doku et al., 2011). The decline in physical activity among adolescents in Vietnam is illustrated in a study by Trang, Hong, and Dibley (2012). Over the course of five years, adolescents actively commuted (e.g., walked, rode their bike) to school less frequently. Girls were less likely to actively commute to school than boys, possibly due to parents' wish to protect their daughters (Trang et al., 2012). The decline in physical activity parallels the decrease found in high-income countries. Research by Bastos, Araújo, and Hallal (2008) and de Vargas Nunez Coll, Knuth, Bastos, Hallal, and Bertoldi (2014) documented a similar decline in physical activity for Brazilian adolescents with 70% not engaging in sufficient activity. Like Vietnamese adolescents (Trang et al., 2012), Brazilian participants were less likely to walk or bike to go to school (de Vargas Nunez Coll et al., 2014).

Mental Health

As noted earlier, mental health is critical during adolescence (e.g., Resnick et al., 2012). WHO (2014a) reports that the onset of approximately 50% of mental health problems occurs before 14 years of age. Moreover, if mental health problems are not addressed when they first emerge, they can carry over into adulthood (UNICEF, 2012). Unfortunately, in many parts of the majority world, adequate mental health services are not readily available, increasing the likelihood these early adolescent onset problems will continue into the future. Moreover, treatment and intervention for psychological disorders in adolescents around the world can be challenging because there is lack of agreement on diagnostic criteria, in part due to poor measures (Patton et al., 2012), and emic or indigenous expression of disorders.

For adolescents, depression is responsible for more productive days lost than any physical illness (WHO, 2014a). In a descriptive study of depression in Zambian adolescents, Neese, Pittman, and Hunemorder (2013) reported some culturally specific or emic components of the disorder. Perceived stress was correlated with both somatic and depressive symptoms, which were themselves correlated. Active coping such as talking with others about problems, contrary to expectations based largely on research with Western samples, was correlated (positively) only with depressive symptoms. The authors conclude that in collectivistic cultures openly discussing one's problems is rare, not socially acceptable, not helpful, and sometimes harmful. Neese et al. (2013) argue that discussing problems may lead to greater suffering because direct expression of negative experiences may cause increased feelings of distress.

The role of protective factors in Ugandan adolescents suffering from anxiety and/or depression was investigated by Haroz, Murray, Bolton, Bentancourt, and Bass (2013). Results indicated that participants' engagement in prosocial acts was associated with fewer symptoms of anxiety and depression. Social support, however, was not related to a reduction in either depressive or anxious symptoms. The authors note that this might be due to the conflict-ridden environment and the inconsistent or poor quality social support adolescents may receive as a result of the tumultuous circumstances.

Eating disorders, although they have severe physical consequences, are considered a psychological disorder; moreover, they are likely influenced by culture (e.g., the role of food in the culture, the ideal body size; Hood, Vander Wal, & Gibbons, 2009). Once considered a problem only in the minority world, given the spread of Western media and the sometimes dangerously "thin ideal" it portrays, eating disorders are becoming more widespread across cultures (Hood et al., 2009). In a 2004 study on eating disorders in Belize, Anderson-Fye (2004) reported a low incidence of eating disorders in adolescent Belizean girls. However, those girls who did report disordered eating were those who came in frequent contact with U.S. tourists.

Latin American adolescents endorsed the thin ideal with nearly 40% of adolescents in the middleweight category expressing a desire to be thinner, even though the majority of boys and girls in this group were already thin (McArthur, Holbert, & Peña, 2005). In a qualitative study black South African adolescent females noted the difference between "sick skinny" (associated with diseases like AIDS) and "nice skinny" (which was seen as attractive; Morris & Szabo, 2013, p. 340). One participant remarked, "All the popular girls are thin" (Morris & Szabo, 2013, p. 340). The girls noted that Western celebrities were seen as endorsing the thin ideal. Moreover, their white peers contributed to the pressure to be thin, saying,

> White girls are obsessed about their weight and we spend a lot of time with them, so we start comparing ourselves to them and that is where the pressure is coming from. We think if SHE is fat, then what am I?" (Morris & Szabo, 2013, p. 340)

Substance Abuse

Adolescence is a popular time for experimenting with drugs and alcohol (UNICEF, 2012). Data show that Latin American and Caribbean adolescents have the highest rates of tobacco use worldwide, with approximately a quarter of boys and girls ages 13–15 in these regions indicating they had used tobacco in the past month. Similar rates of alcohol use were reported in same-age adolescents in other majority world countries surveyed (UNICEF, 2012). Data from the United Nations Office on Drugs and Crime (UNODC) in 2009 reported by UNICEF (2012) revealed that somewhere between 149 and 272 million adolescents had used illegal drugs that year, and that the drug use had greatly contributed to the HIV/AIDS epidemic. Aside from tobacco use in Latin America and the Caribbean, drugs and alcohol are typically used more by boys than by girls (UNICEF, 2012). Those patterns were upheld in a study with Guatemalan adolescents ages 12–18 (Foulger, Page, Hall, Crookston, & West, 2013). Both tobacco and alcohol use were reported more frequently by boys, with 36.% of urban boys and 30.7% of urban girls reporting consumption of at least one alcoholic beverage in the past 30 days. Moreover, urban adolescents, regardless of gender, reported engaging in these risky behaviors more often than their rural counterparts. Fougler et al. (2013) argue the urban/rural trend is likely due to increased media exposure that popularizes and promotes these risky behaviors in urban settings. Research by Carney, Myers, Louw, Lombard, and Fisher (2013) with adolescents in South Africa suggests that substance abuse does not occur in isolation and, under certain circumstances, can be related to delinquency. Lai et al. (2013) established that peer acceptability significantly predicted drug use and delinquency in South African youth, suggesting that these behaviors occur as a part of adolescent culture and depend (at least partially) on peer endorsement. Finally, Thai adolescents who are high in sensation seeking are likely to drink as a way to cope with their problems (Siviroj, Peltzer, Pengpid, Yungyen, & Chaichana, 2012).

Reproductive and Sexual Health

Along with experimentation with drugs and alcohol during this developmental period, becoming sexually active and engaging in risky sexual behavior is a reality for many of the world's adolescents (UNICEF, 2012). Adolescent girls give birth to 11% of the babies born each year; moreover, 95% of adolescent pregnancies occur in the majority world (United Nations Population Fund, UNFPA, 2013). Even though adolescent births are declining, the health complications that can arise for adolescent girls who give birth are troubling (Population Reference Bureau, 2013; UNICEF, 2012). Health complications can include fistulas and increased risk of sexually transmitted diseases (STDs); many health risks are especially elevated for mothers under the age of 15 (UNFPA, 2013).

The effects of giving birth during adolescence are long lasting and stay with adolescent mothers much longer than the length of the pregnancy itself as Tarisai, a Zimbabwean mother at 16, remarks, "All of a sudden the world became a lonely place. I felt excluded from my family and the community; I no longer fitted in as young person, nor did I fit in as a woman" (UNFPA, 2013, p. 10). In addition, adolescent mothers are at elevated risk for dropping out of school, resulting in decreased earning potential in the long term for her and her child (UNFPA, 2013).

Results of qualitative studies by Steele (2011), Saluksy (2013), and Swartz and Bana (2009) remind us that adolescent pregnancy and parenting (as mothers and as fathers) is a complex issue, whose consequences are not well represented with statistics alone. In Steele's (2011) study with mothers, some participants revealed they are viewed more positively by others after becoming mothers, while others face religious consequences and stigmatization after having children outside of marriage. Young mothers from the Dominican Republic echoed the same complexity, sharing feelings of both pride and shame. Anabele, who became a mother at 13, explained, "I felt really really bad. . . . Bad because I was very young to have a child right then and leave my studies. I felt . . . good because I was going to have a girl and this is a gift that God gives someone, their children" (Salusky, 2013, p. 602). Although adolescent girls sometimes view motherhood as a gift, the consequences are likely to play a large role in adolescents' daily lives, limiting their future education and employment. WHO has created six guidelines to help manage the consequences of adolescent pregnancy in an effort to improve options and positive outcomes for young women (Chandra-Mouli, Camacho, & Michaud, 2013).

Although research on adolescent pregnancy focuses almost exclusively on young mothers and their children, the experience affects many young fathers as well. Swartz and Bana (2009) offer a rare look into their perspective. Although some young fathers explained that they wanted to have children at a young age, others mentioned that feelings of invincibility were responsible. Onathi provides insight into his thought process, "I was drinking. I didn't use condoms—I told myself, 'Nah man, it won't happen. Why happen to me? Like, it's not my first time not using a condom, so it won't happen to me'" (Swartz & Bana, 2009, p. 34). And still others expressed that a lack of knowledge was responsible. Lwandile states clearly, "It comes to a lack of knowledge—it's whereby you don't know what will be the consequences of what you have done" (Swartz & Bana, 2009, p. 33). Some of the struggles for young fathers are similar to those for mothers. Siya noted, "I am prepared to drop out of school for a year" (Swartz & Bana, 2009, p. 25).

HIV/AIDS affects adolescent boys and girls on an even larger scale than adolescent pregnancy with an estimated 2.2 million of the world's adolescents ages 10–19 infected with HIV (UNICEF, 2012). Nearly two million of HIV-positive adolescents live in sub-Saharan Africa alone. Lack of condom use is problematic for both HIV and pregnancy, with low usage rates worldwide for both married and unmarried adolescents (UNICEF, 2012). Using condoms is sometimes seen as a sign of untrustworthiness between adolescent sexual partners, which likely further discourages their use (Martson & King, 2006).

Data suggest that less than half of adolescents have appropriate knowledge of HIV/AIDS in some of the most severely affected areas like Kenya, Mali, and Haiti, contributing greatly to its high prevalence (Population Reference Bureau, 2013). Boys are likely to have a more sophisticated understanding of HIV, and girls are more likely to become infected (Population Reference Bureau, 2013). A study in Zambia provides evidence for this lack of HIV/AIDS knowledge, as well as a limited understanding of basic sexual and reproductive health issues, with some girls asking "How do girls become pregnant?" (Warenius et al., 2007, p. 537). Boys asked equally troubling questions like "Can girls produce sperm?" (Warenius et al., 2007, p. 537). Not surprisingly, adolescents expressed feeling alone and without the necessary resources to discuss their concerns. Ugandan adolescents relayed similar concerns regarding lack of support in their quest for knowledge of these issues, as well as difficulty in critically evaluating misleading messages about sexual health from media and other sources (Rijsdijk, Lie, Bos, Leerlooijer, & Kok, 2012).

ADOLESCENTS IN DIFFICULT CIRCUMSTANCES

Although many adolescents around the world live in less-than-ideal conditions, some live in particularly dire circumstances. They may suffer from poverty, disease, and/or the loss of parental protection. Some adolescents are trafficked, forced to engage in sex work, or fight wars. Other adolescents experience natural or man-made disasters, live on the street, work long hours for no or little pay, or migrate under dangerous conditions.

The root cause of most difficulties for teenagers in the majority world is poverty (see Gielen's chapter 3 in this volume). We document this claim for adolescents living in three types of difficult conditions—sex workers, AIDS orphans, and street children. A study in Fiji documented many kinds of exploitative child labor, all of which stemmed from poverty (ILO, 2010). The primary reason that children gave for engaging in sex work was that they need the money. A 16-year-old girl said,

> I live with my aunty and uncle in Suva, sometimes my parents are late in sending money for my schooling. I learnt from my friends that I can easily make a lot of money if I sell myself. I am now able to pay my busfare and buy other school things. (ILO, 2010, p. 52)

When children engaged in sex trade were asked about their hopes for the future, most simply wanted a better, safer life, free from sex work (ILO, 2010). In India, sex work as part of the Devadasis system (a tradition in which parents dedicate a girl to the service of a deity) may be considered normative behavior that is respected by the girls' families (Orchard, 2007). However, even in that unusual situation girls feel pressure to financially support their families who depend on them (Orchard, 2007). In other words, even under the most favorable, socially sanctioned conditions, sex work is stressful.

A group that has received a great deal of attention is children who are orphaned by AIDS. The great majority of children "orphaned" by AIDS are single orphans, in that they have lost one parent; only about 10% are double orphans (Monasch & Boerma, 2004). Of the double orphans, the great majority is absorbed into the extended family; many live with grandparents (Maundeni, 2009). About 2% of orphaned children live in child-only households (Richter & Desmond, 2008). The model child-only household is headed by a 15-year-old boy, and about 20% of those households reported that a child had been hungry because of a lack of food during the past six months (Richter & Desmond, 2008). Dire as the circumstances were for child-only households, they were on the whole better off than households of young single adults (Richter & Desmond, 2008). In sum, although AIDS orphans have received a great deal of international attention, the numbers of adolescents who head child-only households is relatively small; the difficulties they report stem in large part from poverty.

Although street children often report having left home because of family conflicts and abuse, the challenges they face are primarily economic—how to find food, shelter, and clothing (Aptekar & Stoecklin, 2014; see also Aptekar & Oliver's chapter 15 on war-traumatized and street children in this volume). According to Aptekar and Stoecklin, street children of the majority world are mostly boys and many are resilient and innovative in surviving on the street. As they reach mid- to late adolescence, however, they face additional challenges because they are no longer considered children, but instead, thugs or gang members. The most effective transition they can make to adulthood involves using the skills engendered in street life to become small-scale entrepreneurs.

In sum, many adolescents in the majority world live in particularly difficult situations, with those situations provoked or worsened by severe poverty. The problems they endure may leave them with emotional scars and with fewer chances of escaping poverty in adulthood.

GLOBALIZATION AND TECHNOLOGY

"*Estoy conectado; luego existo.*" [I am connected; therefore I exist]. This quote by Jeremy Rifkin (2010, p. 573) commenced a report on the state of youth in Guatemala (PNUD, 2012, p. 100). It embodies the central role that technology has come to play in the lives of the world's adolescents, cultivating their connections in an increasingly global world. Since the first version of this chapter was published in 2004 (Gibbons, 2004), few advances rival the infiltration of technology and the sense of connectedness, both locally and globally, it affords. Data from the World Bank (2014) suggest that in LMICs there were 82 mobile or cellular phone subscriptions for every 100 people in 2012.

Data from the United Nation's International Telecommunications Union (ITU, 2014b) revealed that, for example, in 2012 (the most recent year for which data are available), 18.1% of Hondurans used the Internet, up over 7% from two years earlier. In 2012, in Vietnam nearly 40% of the population used the Internet, an increase of nearly 10% since 2010 and an over 39% increase since 2000. Data from the ITU in 2012 suggested that 27.6% of majority world households have computers at home, a number that has nearly doubled since 2005 (ITU, 2014a).

As the psychological literature suggests, though, the story and implications of globalization are far more complex than usage and access statistics reveal. For adolescents, these changes in communication are reflected in the nature of their relationships and in the way they relate to others who live down the street or 2,000 miles away. Jensen (2003) discussed some of those implications for adolescents and stressed the emergence of a multicultural identity and cultural identity formation for adolescents. Globalization, she argued, has afforded adolescents exposure, through both direct experiences and media, access to other cultures, and that globalization stands to affect this age group in particular given their passion for technology and media-related activities. Adolescence, as noted by Jensen and discussed earlier, is also a time for identity formation in which exploring options, cultivating autonomy, and forming personal opinions on issues ranging from religion to politics may result in a tolerance for new perspectives and beliefs. This openness, she argued, contributes greatly to the multicultural identity assumed by many adolescents.

Due in large part to globalization, adolescents are often exposed to Western media, which promotes a more modern perspective on traditional cultures, oftentimes forcing adolescents to adopt multiple identities to accommodate both past and current customs. Indian adolescents noted the influence of Western values on many aspects of their lives including food, clothing, religion, and social roles (Rao et al., 2013). One adolescent summed the changes up well saying, "We are changing for the good. Earlier Indian culture was too strict and people had to follow values and traditions, which didn't make much sense" (Rao et al., 2013, p. 15). Armenian adolescents shared similar ideas with respect to views on marriage (Huntsinger, 2013). Nearly a quarter of urban Armenian adolescents said they would not marry at all and even more referenced delaying their plans to wed until they had completed other milestones (e.g., graduating from university). Those modern views were endorsed despite the traditional and still common practice of arranged marriages in Armenia.

Another byproduct of globalization has been the spread of U.S. and Western culture with respect to popularity of name brand goods including Nike and Coca Cola (Larson, 2002). Brazilian adolescents with diverse SES backgrounds were interested in luxury brand items because owning them brought a level of status and happiness (de Araujo Gil, 2009). An Indian adolescent in another study explained, "Nowadays we only believe in purchasing expensive bikes and buying branded stuff" (Rao et al., 2013, p. 15). The global recognition of brands like Nike contributes to the status that adolescents associate with wearing them (de Araujo Gil, 2012).

Data from a study with Brazilian adolescents (Pedrozo, 2011) supports these conclusions, while explicitly bringing awareness to the social exclusion that can occur when adolescents do not own possessions deemed as cool or desirable by their peers. The condescension that underlies this participant's comment is a clear example, "I bought a mobile [phone] . . . with a camera . . . imagine if I'm going to have a mobile without a camera" (Pedrozo, 2011, p. 117). Unfortunately, the reality is that many adolescents (or their families) cannot afford such luxuries. Social exclusion resulting from a lack of material status symbols is particularly problematic in a country like Brazil where socioeconomic differences between social classes are so clear. Research with U.S. adolescents would support the importance of material goods as status symbols and common, but unsuccessful buffers for low self-esteem, especially during early and mid-adolescence (Chaplin & John, 2007, 2010). As globalization continues to affect the world's youth, materialistic values and consumption of material goods represent an important area for future research with adolescents in the majority world.

The previously reviewed literature reveals the overarching consequences of globalization for adolescents. The spread of materialism is a compelling example of the global affecting the local (Larson, 2002). Although the implications of our increasingly global world are diverse for the youth of the majority world, the technology is the driving force behind these changes. As the quote at the start of this section reveals, technology, for some adolescents, has become so enmeshed in their daily lives that they see it as necessary for their existence.

Research suggests that adolescents in different parts of the majority world may use cell phones and other technology for different purposes. For example, research in Africa on technology with adolescents has focused on cell phones as a means for conveying health information (e.g., Mitchell, Bull, Kiwanuku, & Ybarra, 2011; Nwagwu, 2007; van Heerden, Norris, & Richter, 2010). For example, 51% of Ugandan adolescents indicated they were somewhat or extremely likely to access information about an AIDS prevention program via text (Mitchell et al., 2011). Among girls in Nigeria who were not in school, Nwagwu (2007) found that the Internet was used by 55% as their most frequently used source of health information, despite fewer nonstudents having home Internet access than students. Only friends were reported more frequently as an information resource for out-of-school adolescent girls. Van Heerden et al.'s (2010) study with South African youth revealed that 66% of participants owned cell phones. Overall nearly three-fourths of adolescents indicated they would prefer to answer questions about personal health information in a face-to-face interview versus with their cell phone. However, participants who had personal experience with electronic communication through texting or video calling were more likely to prefer a cell phone–based survey. This study is important because it suggests there are limits to adolescents' preference for technology over more traditional methods, yet certain experiences (e.g., using Skype) may help individuals to become more comfortable with some uses of technology.

A UNICEF (2013a) report on social media usage in Kenya, including the popular social networking site Facebook, highlighted reminders about safety issues that can arise from making digital connections on social media. The report noted that girls from poorer, more rural areas were particularly vulnerable. For example, 18% of both 12–14-year-olds and 15–17-year-olds reported sharing personal contact information with someone online that they had never met in real life. Data reveal varying levels of discretion with these issues; one girl remarked, "All my friends on FB, [Facebook] I have met first, as in they ask if I'm on FB and ask what name I use on FB then they send a request from there" (UNICEF, 2013a, p. 32), while another appeared to use more questionable methods when deciding whom to connect with: "The feeling is 50–50. I might confirm or not depending on how good the person looks" (UNICEF, 2013a, p. 33). In a potentially more threatening situation, over a quarter of 15–17-year-old participants reported meeting someone in person after knowing them solely online initially. Data from this initiative in Kenya suggested that adolescents who are more experienced on the Internet are more likely than less experienced users to engage in risky Internet behavior.

The research presented earlier highlights the diverse ways in which globalization and technology have altered aspects of majority world adolescents' lives. Globalization has helped expose adolescents to other perspective and values, thereby creating a multicultural identity, pushing them to incorporate diverse worldviews and evaluate their own (Jensen, 2003). Majority world adolescents are now bombarded with images and advertisements for Western products, which is another way they are challenged with incorporating minority world culture into their everyday lives. Technology may be an excellent way to communicate health information especially on important matters of sexual and reproductive health (Mitchell et al., 2011; Nwagwu, 2007; van Heerden et al., 2010). Globalization and technology are domains that will continue to have a remarkable impact on adolescents worldwide for years to come. Future research should continue to focus on the impacts these phenomena have on adolescents.

CONCLUSION

Research reviewed here reveals the diverse and unique circumstances experienced by majority world adolescents in their everyday lives. Their time is often divided mostly between work and school, leaving limited time for leisure. Oftentimes, work takes place in less-than-ideal conditions and prohibits adolescents from continuing and completing their education, as the need to provide economic support for their families is paramount. Gender parity in educational opportunity is becoming more common worldwide, as schools are becoming increasingly sensitive to issues that specifically affect their female students. Parents play an important role in their adolescent children's lives despite their increasing autonomy. Peers are also central to the continuing social development of adolescents, although research suggests bullying is a major international concern. Unfortunately, some of the world's adolescents must live under particularly difficult circumstances as AIDS orphans, sex workers, and street children. Finally, in the 12 years since the first edition of this chapter, issues of adolescent health, both physical and mental, as well as the impact of globalization and technology have risen to the fore as we look to the future for majority world adolescents. Understanding the challenges adolescents face as global citizens in a highly connected world will be essential for researchers of majority world adolescents in the years to come.

Many of these same ideas were highlighted by the adolescents whose comments were featured at the start of this chapter. Both majority world adolescents were focused on the future, acknowledging the lives they desired were achievable only through hard work and staying in school. They also expressed a desire to hold careers with meaning and promise that will better their communities and those around them. In addition, they both noted their parents were among their favorite people to spend time around. The desire for more freedom, expressed in different ways by both Alex and Paolo, is also a hallmark of adolescence. In addition, the pair noted their connection to technology, specifically its importance for schoolwork as well as for entertainment and connecting with friends. It is likely, too, that technology is at least partially responsible for facilitating their identity as members of a global community. When asked what they would wish if given three wishes today, their responses were a combination of personal desires and wishes for all humanity, again supporting this idea of global connectedness. Finally, both Alex and Paolo noted that adolescents should not be afraid to be themselves and to remain true to who they are regardless of who others think they should be or how others think they should act.

Future research should focus on the issues most likely to affect adolescent well-being and their futures. Research aimed at improving adolescent health, including reducing the rates of both communicable and non-communicable diseases, violence, and adolescent maternal health are of particular importance. In addition, the influence of technology on globalization and adolescents' cultural and global identity is paramount, as it is becoming increasingly clear that many of the world's youth are bearers of multiple cultures. As important as the discovery of new knowledge about majority adolescents is the application of knowledge to improving their well-being. Interventions, however, must be developmentally and culturally informed (Wuermli, Tubbs, Petersen, & Aber, 2015). Because majority world adolescents comprise a significant portion of the population, the topics central to their healthy development deserve the attention of researchers, policy makers, and service providers in the years to come.

REFLECTIVE QUESTIONS

1. Although primary school rates are increasing, secondary school enrollment remains a challenge for adolescents worldwide. What are some ways to address the choice many adolescents face between continuing their education and dropping out of school to work, helping to support their families financially?
2. What strengths and resiliencies shown by adolescents in the majority world can inform adolescents of the minority world?

3. In what ways can the use of technology foster and support adolescent development and well-being? In what ways does technology present a risk? How can researchers and those who work directly with adolescents best promote healthy use of technology and address the concerns?
4. What are the best ways to support majority world adolescents as they reconcile popular, modern cultures in connection with still revered traditional values and practices?

SUGGESTED READINGS

Books and Articles

International Labor Organization. (ILO; 2013). Making progress against child labor: Global estimates and trends 2000–2012. Retrieved from http://www.ilo.org/wcmsp5/groups/public/@ed_norm/@ipec/documents/publication/wcms_221513.pdf

Jensen, L. A. (2003). Coming of age in a multicultural world: Globalization and adolescent cultural identity formation. *Applied Developmental Science, 7*(3), 189–196.

Lloyd, C. B., Grant, M., & Ritchie, A. (2008). Gender differences in time use among adolescents in developing countries: Implications of rising school enrollment rates. *Journal of Research on Adolescence, 18*(1), 99–120.

UNICEF. (2012). Progress for children: A report card on adolescents. Retrieved from http://www.unicef.org/media/files/PFC2012_A_report_card_on_adolescents.pdf

World Health Organization. (WHO; 2014a). Health for the world's adolescents: A second chance in the second decade. Retrieved from http://apps.who.int/adolescent/second-decade/files/1612_MNCAH_HWA_Executive_Summary.pdf

Websites

Population Reference Bureau: http://www.prb.org/

UNICEF on adolescents: http://www.unicef.org/adolescence/

World Health Organization (WHO) on adolescents: http://www.who.int/maternal_child_adolescent/topics/adolescence/en/

REFERENCES

Admassie, A. (2003). Child labour and schooling in the context of a subsistence rural economy: Can they be compatible? *International Journal of Educational Development, 23*(2), 167–185.

Amin, S., & Chandrasekhar, S. (2009). Looking beyond universal primary education: Gender differences in time use among children in rural Bangladesh. *Poverty, Gender, and Youth, 17*, 1–21.

Anderson-Fye, E. P. (2004). A "Coca Cola" shape: Cultural change, body image, and eating disorders in San Andrés, Brazil. *Culture, Medicine and Psychiatry, 28*, 561–595.

Aptekar, L. & Stoecklin, D. (2014). *Street children and homeless youth.* New York: Springer.

Arends-Kuenning, M., & Duryen, S. (2006). The effect of parental presence, parents' education, and household hardship on adolescents' schooling and work in Latin America. *Journal of Family and Economic Issues, 27*(2), 263–286.

Assaad, R., Levison, D., & Zibani, N. (2010). The effect of domestic work on girls' schooling: Evidence from Egypt. *Feminist Economics, 16*(1), 79–128.

Bastos, J.P., Araújo, C.L.P., & Hallal, P.C. (2008). Prevalence of insufficient physical activity and associated factors in Brazilian adolescents. *Journal of Physical Activity and Health, 5,* 777–794.

Beaman, L., Duflo, E., Pande, R., & Topalova, P. (2012). Female leadership raises aspirations and educational attainment for girls: A policy experiment in India. *Science, 335,* 582–586.

Blanc, A.K., & Bruce, J. (2013). Commentary: Explicit attention to age and gender disparities is key to understanding adolescent experiences and outcomes. *Journal of Research on Adolescence, 23*(1), 191–192.

Borzekowski, D.L.G., Fobil, J.N., & Asante, K.O. (2006). Online access by adolescents in Accra: Ghanaian teens' use of the internet for health information. *Developmental Psychology, 42*(3), 450–458.

Bowker, J.C., Ostrov, J.M., & Raja, R. (2011). Relational and overt aggression in urban India: Associations with peer relations and best friends' aggression. *International Journal of Behavioral Development, 36*(2), 107–116.

Buonomo Zabaleta, M. (2011). The impact of child labor on schooling outcomes in Nicaragua. *Economics of Education Review, 30,* 1527–1539.

Cameron, C.A., Theron, L., Tapanya, S., Li, C., Lau, C., Liebenberg, L., Unger, M. (2013). Visual perceptions on majority-world adolescent thriving. *Journal of Research on Adolescence, 23*(1), 149–161.

Carney, T., Myers, B.J., Louw, J., Lombard, C., & Flisher, A.J. (2013). The relationship between substance abuse and delinquency among high-school students in Cape Town, South Africa. *Journal of Adolescence, 36,* 447–455.

Chandra-Mouli, V., Camacho, A.V., & Michaud, P.A. (2013). WHO guidelines on preventing early pregnancy and poor reproductive outcomes among adolescents in developing countries. *Journal of Adolescent Health, 52,* 517–522.

Chaplin, L.N., & John, D.R. (2007). Growing up in a material world: Age differences in materialism in children and adolescents. *Journal of Consumer Research, 34,* 480–493.

Chaplin, L.N., & John, D.R. (2010). Interpersonal influences on adolescent materialism: A new look at the role of parents and peers. *Journal of Consumer Psychology, 20,* 176–184.

Chen, X., French, D.C., & Schneider, B.H. (2006). Culture and peer relationships. In X. Chen, D.C. French, & B.H. Schneider (Eds.), *Peer relationships in cultural context* (pp. 3–20). New York: Cambridge University Press.

Child Trends. (2013). World family map: Mapping family change and child well-being outcomes. Retrieved from http://worldfamilymap.org/2013/wp-content/uploads/2013/01/WFM-2013-Final-lores-11513.pdf

Collins, W.A. (2003). More than myth: The developmental significance of romantic relationships during adolescence. *Journal of Research on Adolescence, 13*(1), 1–24.

Craig, W., Harel-Fisch, Y., Fogel-Grinval, H., Dostaler, S., Hetland, J., Simons-Morton, B., . . . HBSC Bullying Writing Group. (2009). A cross-national profile of bullying and victimization among adolescents in 40 countries. *International Journal of Public Health, 54*, 216–224.

de Araujo Gil, L. (2009). *Impact of self on attitudes toward luxury items among teens in Brazil.* Unpublished doctoral dissertation, East Lansing, MI: Michigan State University.

de Vargas Nunez Coll, C., Knunth, A.G., Bastsos, J.P., Hallal, P.C., & Bertoldi, A.D. (2014). Time trends of physical activity among Brazilian adolescents over a 7-year period. *Journal of Adolescent Health, 54*, 209–213.

Dhariwal, A., & Connolly, J. (2013). Romantic experiences of homeland and diaspora South Asian youth: Westernizing processes of media and friends. *Journal of Research on Adolescence, 23*(1), 43–56.

Doku, D., Koivusilta, L., Raisamo, S., & Rimpelä, A. (2011). Socio-economic differences in adolescents' breakfast eating, fruit and vegetable consumption and physical activity in Ghana. *Public Health Nutrition, 16*(5), 864–872.

Eksi, A., Peykerli, G., Saydam, R., Toparla, D., & Braun, K.L. (2008). Vivid intrusive memories in PTSD: Responses of child earthquake survivors in Turkey. *Journal of Loss and Trauma, 13*, 123–155.

Elamé, E. (2013). *Discriminatory bullying: A new intercultural challenge.* New York: Springer.

Erulkar, A., & Mekbib, T.A. (2007). Invisible and vulnerable: Adolescent domestic workers in Addis Ababa, Ethiopia. *Vulnerable Children and Youth Studies: An International Interdisciplinary Journal for Research, Policy, and Care, 2*(3), 246–256.

Familiar, I., Murray, L., Gross, A., Skavenski, S., Jere, E., & Bass, J. (2013). Posttraumatic stress symptoms and structure among orphan and vulnerable children and adolescents in Zambia. *Child and Adolescent Mental Health,* 1–8.

Fatsui, A.O., & Hindin, M., J. (2010). Adolescents and youth in developing countries: Health and development issues in context. *Journal of Adolescence, 33*, 499–508.

Forsthe, R., Heaton, T.B., & Haas, D.W. (2004). Adolescents' expectations for higher education in Bogotá, Colombia, and La Paz, Bolivia. *Youth & Society, 36*(1), 56–76.

Foulger, L., Page, R.M., Hall, P.C., Crookston, B.T., & West, J.H. (2013). Health risk behaviors in urban and rural Guatemalan adolescents. *International Journal of Adolescent Mental Health, 25*(1), 97–105.

Fulkerson, J.A., Story, M., Mellin, A., Leffert, N., Neumark-Sztainer, D., & French, S.A. (2006). Family dinner meal frequency and adolescent development: Relationships with developmental assets and high-risk behaviors. *Journal of Adolescent Health, 39*, 337–345.

Gibbons, J.L. (2004). Adolescents in the developing world. In U.P. Gielen & J. Roopnarine (Eds.), *Advances in applied developmental psychology: Childhood and adolescence in cross-cultural perspective* (pp. 255–276). Westport, CT: Greenwood/Ablex.

Gibbons, J.L., Lynn, M., & Stiles, D.A. (1997). Cross-national gender differences in adolescents' preferences for free-time activities. *Cross-Cultural Research, 31*(1), 55–69.

Grossi, P.K., & Dos Santos, A. M. (2012). Bullying in Brazilian schools and restorative practices. *Canadian Journal of Education, 35*(1), 20–136.

Guthold, R., Cowan, M.J., Autenrieth, C.S., Kann, L., & Riley, L.M. (2010). Physical activity and sedentary behavior among schoolchildren: A 34-country comparison. *The Journal of Pediatrics, 157*(1), 45–49.

Haroz, E.E., Murray, L.K., Bolton, P., Betancourt, T., Bass, J.K. (2013). Adolescent resilience in northern Uganda: The role of social support and prosocial behavior in reducing mental health disorders. *Journal of Research on Adolescence, 23*(1), 138–148.

Hunter, S. B., Barber, B. K., Olsen, J. A., McNeely, C. A., & Bose, K. (2011). Adolescents' self-disclosure to parents across cultures: Who discloses and why. *Journal of Adolescent Research, 26*(4), 447–478.

Huntsinger, C. (2013). Armenian adolescents and globalization. *Society for Research on Adolescence.* Retrieved from http://www.s-r-a.org/announcements/online-newsletter/2013–10–25-armenian-adolescents-and-globalization-0

International Labor Organization (ILO; n.d.). Child labor in agriculture. Retrieved from http://www.ilo.org/ipec/areas/Agriculture/lang—en/index.htm

International Labor Organization. (ILO; 2010). Child labor in Fiji: A survey of working children in commercial sexual exploitation, on the streets, in rural agricultural communities, in informal and squatter settlements and in schools. Retrieved from http://www.ilo.org/wcmsp5/groups/public/@asia/@ro-bangkok/@ilo-suva/documents/publication/wcms_155659.pdf

International Labor Organization. (ILO; 2012). Viet Nam national child labor survey 2012 main findings. Retrieved from http://www.ilo.org/wcmsp5/groups/public/—asia/—-ro-bangkok/—-ilo-hanoi/documents/publication/wcms_237833.pdf

International Labor Organization. (ILO; 2013). Making progress against child labor: Global estimates and trends 2000–2012. Retrieved from http://www.ilo.org/wcmsp5/groups/public/@ed_norm/@ipec/documents/publication/wcms_221513.pdf

International Labor Organization & Lao Statistics Bureau. (2012). Report on the National Child Labour Survey 2010 of Lao DPR. Retrieved from http://www.ilo.org/ipecinfo/product/download.do?type=document&id=21256

International Telecommunications Union. (ITU; 2014a). ITU key 2005–2014 ICT data. Retrieved from http://www.itu.int/en/ITU-D/Statistics/Pages/stat/default.aspx?utm_source=twitterfeed&utm_medium=twitter

International Telecommunications Union. (ITU; 2014b). Percentage of individuals using the internet. Retrieved from http://www.itu.int/en/ITU-D/Statistics/Pages/stat/default.aspx?utm_source=twitterfeed&utm_medium=twitter

Jensen, L. A. (2003). Coming of age in a multicultural world: Globalization and adolescent cultural identity formation. *Applied Developmental Science, 7*(3), 189–196.

Juárez, F., LeGrand, T., Lloyd, C. B., Singh, S., & Hertrich, V. (2013). Youth migration and transitions to adulthood in developing countries. *The ANNALS of the American Academy of Political and Social Science, 648*(6), 6–15.

Kim, W. J., & Singh, T. (2004). Trends and dynamics of youth suicide in developing countries. *The Lancet, 363*, 1090.

Koirala, D. P. (2013, August). Yeah! I'm also a youth but have no energy to change the world [Web log post]. Retrieved from http://www.voicesofyouth.org/es/posts/yeah—i-m-also-a-youth-but-have-no-energy-to-change-the-world

Lai, M. H., Graham, J. W., Caldwell, L. L., Smith, E. A., Bradley, S. A., Vergnani, T., & Larson, R. W. (2002). Globalization, societal change, and new technologies: What they mean for the future of adolescence. *Journal of Research on Adolescence, 12*(1), 1–30.

Laursen, B., & Collins, W. A. (2009). Parent-child relationships during adolescence. In R. M. Lerner & L. Steinberg (Eds.), *Handbook of adolescent psychology* (Vol. 2, pp. 3–42). Hoboken, NJ: John Wiley & Sons.

Lloyd, C. B., Grant, M., & Ritchie, A. (2008). Gender differences in time use among adolescents in developing countries: Implications of rising school enrollment rates. *Journal of Research on Adolescence, 18*(1), 99–120.

Lykes, M.B., & Sibley, E. (2013). Exploring meaning-making with adolescents "left behind" by migration. *Educational Action Research, 21*(4), 566–581.

Markey Hood, M., Vander Wal, J., & Gibbons, J.L. (2009). Culture and eating disorders. In S. Esshun & R. Gurung (Eds.), *Culture and mental health: Sociocultural influences, theory, and practice* (pp. 273–295). Malden, MA: Blackwell.

Martson, C., & King, E. (2006). Factors that shape young people's sexual behavior: A systematic review. *The Lancet, 368*, 1581–1586.

Matthews, C., & Wagner, L. (2013). Linking life skills and norms with adolescent substance use and delinquency in South Africa. *Journal of Research on Adolescence, 23*(1), 128–137.

Maundeni, T. (2009). Care for children in Botswana: The social work role. *Society Work & Society, 7*, Retrieved from http://www.socwork.net/sws/article/view/41/344

McArthur, L.H., Holbert, D., & Peña, M. (2005). An exploration of the attitudinal and perceptual dimensions of body image among male and female adolescents from six Latin American cities. *Adolescence, 40*(160), 801–816.

McMahon, S.A., Winch, P.J., Caruso, B.A., Obure, A.F., Ogutu, E.A., Ochari, I.F., & Rheingans, R.A. (2013). "The girl with her period is the one to hang her head": Reflections on menstrual management among schoolgirls in rural Kenya. *BMC International Health and Human Rights, 11*(7), 1–10.

Mete, C. (2010). Children's work study and leisure time in five countries: Implications for human capital accumulations. Retrieved from http://www2.econ.iastate.edu/faculty/orazem/TPS_papers/Mete_Children_Work_Study_Leisure.pdf

Miller, B.A., Byrnes, H.F., Cupp, P.K., Chamratrithirong, A., Rhucharoenpornpanich, O., Fongkaew, W., . . . Zimmerman, R.S. (2011). Thai parenting practices, family rituals and risky adolescent behaviors: Alcohol use, cigarette use and delinquency. *International Journal of Adolescent Health, 4*(4), 367–378.

Mkandawire-Valhmu, L., Rodriguez, R., Ammar, N., & Nemoto, K. (2009). Surviving life as a woman: A critical ethnography of violence in the lives of female domestic workers in Malawi. *Health Care for Women International, 30*, 783–801.

Monasch, R., & Boerma, J.T. (2004). Orphan and childcare patterns in sub-Saharan Africa: An analysis of national surveys from 40 countries. *AIDS, 18* (Suppl. 2), S55–S65.

Morris, P.F., & Szabo, C.P. (2013). Meanings of thinness and dysfunctional eating in black South African females: A qualitative study. *African Journal of Psychiatry, 16*, 338–342.

Neese, A.L., Pittman, L.D., & Hunemorder, R., (2013). Depressive symptoms and somatic complaints among Zambian adolescents: Associations with stress and coping. *Journal of Research on Adolescence, 23*(1), 118–127.

Nguyen, H., Cohen, E., & Hines, A. (2012). Brief report: Do peer relationships matter to Vietnamese adolescents' and young adults' development of identity. Toward a working theory of identity development in a changing culture. *Journal of Adolescence, 35*, 1501–1504.

Nwagwu, W.E. (2007). The internet as a source of reproductive health information among adolescent girls in an urban city in Nigeria. *BMC Public Health, 7*(354). doi:10.1186/1471–2458–7–354

Okello, J., Nakimuli-Mpungu, E., Muisi, S., Broekarte, E., & Derluyn, I. (2013). War-related trauma exposure and multiple risk behaviors among school-going adolescents in Northern Uganda: The mediating role of depression symptoms. *Journal of Affective Disorders, 151*, 715–721.

Orchard, T. R. (2007). Girl, woman, lover, mother: Towards a new understanding of child prostitution among young Devadasis in rural Karnataka, India. *Social Science & Medicine, 64*, 2379–2390.

Organización Internacional del Trabajo & Dirección General de Estadística, Encuestas & Censos del Paraguay. (2013). Magnitud y characterísticas del trabajo infantil y adolescente en el

Paraguay [Magnitude and characteristics of child and adolescent labor in the Paraguay.]. Retrieved from http://www.dgeec.gov.py/Mag.%20y%20ctca%20del%20trabajo%20infantil%20y%20adolescent%20en%20el%20py.pdf

Patton, G. C., Coffey, C., Cappa, C., Currie, D., Riley, L., Gore, F, Degenhardt, L., . . . Ferguson, J. (2012). Health of the world's adolescents: A synthesis of internationally comparable data. *The Lancet, 379*, 1665–1675.

Patton, G. C., Viner, R. M., Linh, L. C., Ameratunga, S., Fatsui, A. O., Ferguson, J., & Patel, V. (2010). Mapping a global agenda for adolescent health. *Journal of Adolescent Health, 47*, 427–432.

Pedrozo, S. (2011). To be "cool" and not to be "cool": Young people's insights on consumption and social issues in Rio de Janeiro. *Journal of Youth Studies, 14*(1), 109–123.

Poirier, L. (2012). Molding the non-Maasai: Pastoralist encounters with modern education. Retrieved from http://www.lpoirier.myrpi.org/wp-content/uploads/2013/07/PoirierSeniorProject2012.pdf

Population Reference Bureau. (2013). The world's youth 2013 data sheet. Retrieved from http://www.prb.org/pdf13/youth-data-sheet-2013.pdf

Programa de las Naciones Unidas para el Desarrollo (PNUD; 2012). Guatemala: ¿Un país de opportunidades para la juventud? Informe nacional de desarrollo humano 2011/2012 [A country of opportunities for the youth? National Human Development Report 2011/2012]. Retrieved from http://desarrollohumano.org.gt/sites/default/files/INDH%202011_2012.pdf

Raffaelli, M., Lazarevic, V., Koller, S. H., Nsamenang, A. B., & Sharma, D. (2013). Introduction: Special issue on adolescents in the majority world. *Journal of Research on Adolescence, 23*(1), 1–8.

Rao, M. A., Berry, R., Gonsalves, A., Hostak, Y., Shah, M., & Roeser, R. W. (2013). Globalization and the *identity remix* among adolescents. *Journal of Research on Adolescence, 23*(1), 9–24.

Resnick, M. D., Catalano, R. F., Sawyer, S. M., Viner, R., & Patton, G. C. (2012). Seizing the opportunities of adolescent health. *The Lancet, 379*, 1564–1566.

Richter, L. M., & Desmond, C. (2008). Targeting AIDS orphans and child-headed households? A perspective from national surveys in South Africa, 1995–2005. *AIDS Care, 20*(9), 1019–1028.

Rifkin, J. (2010). *The empathic civilization: The race to global consciousness in a world in crisis.* New York: Penguin.

Rijsdijk, L. E., Lie, R., Bos, A. E. R., Leerloijer, J. N., & Kok, G. (2012). Sexual and reproductive health and rights: Implications for comprehensive sex education among young people in Uganda. *Sex Education: Sexuality, Society, and Learning, 13*(4), 409–422.

Ritchie, A., Lloyd, C. B., & Grant, M. (2004). Gender differences in time use among adolescents in developing countries: Implications of rising school enrollment rates. *Policy Research Working Papers, 193*, 1–34.

Salusky, I. (2013). The meaning of motherhood: Adolescent childbearing and its significance for poor Dominican females of Haitian descent. *Journal of Adolescent Research, 28*(5), 591–614.

Santos, R. (2010). The Maasai tribe goes mobile. *2010 Global Marketing.* Retrieved from http://2010globalmarketing.wordpress.com/2010/07/24/695/

Save the Children. (2012). Voices from urban Africa: The impact of urban growth on children. Retrieved from http://www.savethechildren.org/atf/cf/%7B9def2ebe-10ae-432c-9bd0-df91d2eba74a%7D/SAVETHECHILDREN-VOICESFROMURBANAFRICA-REPORT2012.PDF

Sawitri, D. R., Creed, P. A., & Zimmer-Gembeck, M. J. (2014). Longitudinal relations of parental influences and adolescent career aspirations and actions in a collectivistic society. *Journal of Research on Adolescence.* Advance online publication. doi: 10.1111/jora.12145

Seiffge-Krenke, I., Persike, M., Karaman, N. G., Cok, F., Herrera, D., Rohail, I, . . . Hyeyoun, H. (2013). Stress with parents and peers: How adolescents from six nations cope with relationship stress. *Journal of Research on Adolescence, 23*(1), 103–117.

Serpell, R. (1993). *The significance of schooling: Life-journeys in an African society.* Cambridge, UK: Cambridge University Press.

Serpell, R. (2011). Social responsibility as a dimension of intelligence and as an educational goal: Insights from programmatic research in an African society. *Child Development Perspectives, 5*(2), 126–133.

Siviroj, P., Peltzer, K., Pengpid, S., Yungyen, Y., & Chaichana, A. (2012). Drinking motives, sensation seeking, and alcohol use among Thai high school students. *Social Behavior and Personality, 40*(8), 1255–1262.

Smeekens, C., Stroebe, M. S., & Abakoumkin, G. (2012). The impact of migratory separation from parents on the health of adolescents in the Philippines. *Social Science & Medicine, 75,* 2250–2257.

Steinberg, L., Lamborn, S. D., Darling, N., Mounts, N. S., & Dornbusch, S. M. (1994). Over-time changes in adjustment and competence among adolescents from authoritative, authoritarian, indulgent, and neglectful families. *Child Development, 65,* 754–770.

Swartz, S., & Bhana, A. (2009). *Teenage tata: Voices of young fathers in South Africa.* Cape Town, South Africa: Human Sciences Research Council (HSRC).

Tammariello, A., E., Gallahue, N. K., Ellard, K. A., Woldesemait, N., & Jacobsen, K. H. (2012). Parental involvement and mental health among Thai adolescents. *Advances in School Mental Health Promotions, 5*(4), 236–245.

Teixeira, L. R., Fischer, F. M., Nagai, R., & Turte, S. L. (2004). Teen at work: The burden of double shift on daily activities. *Chronobiology International, 21*(6), 845–858.

Trang, N. H. H. D., Hong, T. K., & Dibley, M. J. (2012). Active commuting to school among adolescents in Ho Chi Minh City, Vietnam: Changes and predictors in a longitudinal study, 2004 to 2009. *American Journal of Preventative Medicine, 42*(2), 120–128.

UNICEF. (2004). Efforts against child labour often overlook domestic workers. Retrieved from http://www.unicef.org/media/media_21576.html

UNICEF. (2009). The invisible face of child labour in Latin America and the Caribbean. Retrieved from http://www.unicef.org/lac/Boletin-desafios8-CEPAL-UNICEFeng(2).pdf

UNICEF. (2011a). Adolescence in Tanzania. Retrieved from http://www.unicef.org/adolescence/files/TANZANIA_ADOLESCENT_REPORT_Final.pdf

UNICEF. (2011b). *The state of the world's children 2011. Adolescence: An age of opportunity.* Retrieved from http://www.unicef.org/sowc2011/pdfs/SOWC-2011-Main-Report_EN_02092011.pdf

UNICEF. (2012). *Progress for children: A report card on adolescents.* Retrieved from http://www.unicef.org/media/files/PFC2012_A_report_card_on_adolescents.pdf

UNICEF. (2013a). *A private public space: Examining the use and impact of digital and social media among adolescents in Kenya.* Retrieved from http://www.intermedia.org/wp-content/uploads/2013/09/A-Private-Public_Voices-of-Youth-Kenya-study.pdf

UNICEF. (2013b). *Simple solutions to keep girls in school in Bangladesh.* Retrieved from http://www.unicef.org/infobycountry/bangladesh_70622.html

United Nations. (2011). *Non-communicable diseases deemed developmental challenge of "epic proportion."* Retrieved from http://www.un.org/News/Press/docs/2011/ga11138.doc.htm

United Nations Population Fund. (UNFPA, 2013). *Motherhood in childhood: Facing the challenge of adolescent pregnancy.* Retrieved from http://www.unfpa.org/webdav/site/global/shared/swp2013/EN-SWOP2013-final.pdf

van Heerden, A.C., Norris, S.A., & Richter, L.M. (2010). Using mobile phones for research in low and middle income countries: Preliminary findings from the birth to twenty cohort, South Africa. *Journal of Adolescent Health, 46*, 302–304.

Warenius, L., Petterson, K.O., Nissen, E., Höjer, B., Chisimiba, P., & Faxelid, E. (2007). Vulnerability and sexual and reproductive health among Zambian secondary school students. *Culture, Health, and Sexuality, 9*(5), 533–544.

World Bank. (2014). *World development indicators: Power and communications.* Retrieved from http://wdi.worldbank.org/table/5.11#

World Health Organization. (WHO; 2014a). Health for the world's adolescents: A second chance in the second decade. Retrieved from http://apps.who.int/adolescent/second- decade/files/1612_MNCAH_HWA_Executive_Summary.pdf

World Health Organization. (WHO; 2014b). Obesity and overweight. Retrieved from http://www.who.int/mediacentre/factsheets/fs311/en/.

Wuermli, A.J., Tubbs, C.C., Petersen, A.C., & Aber, C.L. (2015). Children and youth in low- and middle-income countries: Toward an integrated developmental and intervention science. *Child Development Perspectives, 9*, 61–66.

Yi, S., Poudel, K.C., Yasuoka, J., Palmer, P.H., Yi, S., Yanagisawa, S., & Jimba, M. (2012). Sibling care, school performance, and depression among adolescent caretakers in Cambodia. *Asian Journal of Psychiatry, 5*, 132–136.

Zapata, D., Contreras, D., & Kruger, D. (2011). Child labor and schooling in Bolivia: Who's falling behind? The roles of domestic work, gender, ethnicity. *World Development, 39*(4), 588–599.

Zuckow-Goldring, P. (2012). Sibling caregiving. In M.H. Bornstein (Ed.), *Handbook of parenting* (2nd ed., vol. 3, pp. 253–286). Mahwah, NJ: Lawrence Erlbaum Associates.

Part IV

TRANSNATIONAL AND IMMIGRANT CHILDREN

11

Growing Up Internationally, and How It Shapes a Child

Gene H. Bell-Villada

In memoriam Audrey Dobek-Bell, 1945–2013, my loving spouse, who passed away during the planning stages of this chapter.

The phrase in my title "Growing up Internationally" can cover a wide and diverse range of developmental dynamics. For this purpose, I would like to begin my overview with a brief look at a couple of individual cases, each of them an identifiable if extreme instance of two somewhat different growth patterns and outcomes.

The first of these subjects is myself, Gene H. Bell-Villada. The second one, a college senior whom I shall call "Vanesa," sat for a 45-minute interview with me in my office on November 22, 2013, specifically in connection with this projected chapter.

Here is my own story, in brief. I was born in Haiti of an Anglo-Saxon father—a businessman-adventurer from Kansas and Missouri—and a Chinese-Filipina mother from Honolulu. A year following my birth, my parents moved with me to nearby Puerto Rico. There my younger brother Kanani and I would eventually attend a Catholic school that was run and staffed in part by American priests and nuns, and was aimed at and designed for local pupils. The curriculum was largely U.S.-based. "Dick and Jane" books were among our initial reading fare. (The institution, I now realize, was essentially a "mission school.") Then, during my eighth grade, my father abandoned my loving yet hapless mother for a sexy, blonde Cuban; next, he more or less abducted Kanani and me, and finally went on to place us in a military boarding school in distant Havana, where much of the course content, naturally, was Cuban-inflected, and the language of instruction was exclusively Spanish.

During much of those early years, my parents would inculcate in us the idea that we were both American kids. After all, we had U.S. passports and progenitors (albeit from colonial Hawaii in the case of my mom), and our home language was English. We attended an American school (of sorts), nine whole years for me; we saw countless Hollywood movies (never Mexican ones) with subtitles and understood all the dialogue; we watched the budding medium of 1950s American television (sent with two weeks' delay via kinescope); and we mostly ate canned peaches and pears rather than tropical guavas or passion fruits. Our entire, subjective frame of reference was United States, and we identified ourselves as such. Yet at the same time the overwhelming majority of our everyday social life was in Spanish as we interacted with local children—Puerto Ricans, later Cubans—and occasionally with their parents, although, strictly speaking, we didn't "belong" to either of those island nations' societies. We were living, fragmented fashion, in two, three separate worlds without realizing it.

In my junior year, Kanani and I transferred to American schools in Caracas, Venezuela, where our father had previously resettled. It was my maiden entry into anything resembling a "regular American" scholastic setting, with classes all in English, a U.S. curricular focus, no uniform dress, and, most important of all, a dominant presence of a "typically American" student body (and I mean the classically WASP look and style of that time: fair hair, crew-cuts, and plaid shirts for the generally lanky, all-white boys; plaid skirts, pumps or loafers on shapely young legs, and short blond hair in a spray or a bouncy perm for the all-WASP girls; and a casual, informal, slightly bumptious manner for members of both sexes). At the same time, approximately a third of the school population consisted of Latin Americans (Venezuelans mostly), along with a smattering of Europeans.

And from the start, in my everyday social interactions, I found myself gravitating toward the Latin students. Our "gringo" classmates I saw largely as alien (even though in their dealings with me they were perfectly cordial and polite). For the first time in my life I was attending school with "my fellow Americans," yet I hardly felt myself one of them. And I vaguely remember chatting about these matters with my midwestern father on the balcony of our fifth-floor apartment early that academic year, probably on a weekend afternoon. Almost offhandedly, I reflected to him, "I guess I'm a Latino at heart," words he echoed quizzically but didn't follow up on. It was my earliest insight into an identity dilemma that has stayed with me to this day.

My other individual subject, Vanesa, was born in a city in the Antioquia region of Colombia, where she spent her first 10 years and went to Catholic school. When arriving legally with her parents in Queens, New York (her father worked for a restaurant chain), she was initially shocked at the rough, tough nature of the public-education environment, a change that often had her crying to herself at nights. Though the student body at her school was diverse, she was one of just three Latina pupils. People of all sorts, in school and elsewhere, tended to think she was from Mexico, and they'd perceive her and address her as such. Later, Vanesa's family moved to Florida, where, in a predominantly white setting, she at times felt the lingering presence of Southern racism and, on more than one occasion, heard the derogatory term "Spiks."

Vanesa, a bright student, eventually came to Williams College on a generous scholarship, and fellow students now thought of her as a recent arrival from Colombia. For her first couple of years in that rarefied campus atmosphere, she had few "regular" white American friends. As a way of coping with these issues, she took several courses that focused on identity questions and also read a lot on the topic. She did not consider studying abroad for her junior year because, being at the time in something of a dejected state, she was concerned that she might choose not to come back.

To my expected question as to whether she felt Colombian or American, Vanesa had a complicated reply. She does indeed feel Colombian, has wanted to be Colombian, and loves her country. On her mother's side she has 15 relatives living there, and sees them almost yearly. Still, when she is back visiting the land of her origins, while her numerous kin treat her with love, they also at first refer to her as "la gringa" (North American or English-speaking woman). And oftentimes Vanesa speaks more slowly than and dresses differently from them, and can thus feel somewhat "in limbo" (her word).

At the same time Vanesa reflects, "It pains me to say so, but I'm American." After a process of 10 years' waiting for a green card, such a feeling was inevitable. Her social circles, moreover, now comprise a number of friends who don't know Spanish. As for the future, Vanesa at first considered becoming an immigration lawyer, though she now senses that her ideals of justice might clash with the reality of law studies and the tasks of lawyering. Currently she contemplates being a teacher of English as a Second Language (perhaps a way of bridging her two worlds).

So, shifting gears, over the next few pages I'll be addressing the broader topic of growing up internationally. My experience and Vanesa's, it goes without saying, are significantly different, a matter that will also merit special attention. Of course, most educators and most educated people, belonging as they do to a generally cosmopolitan environment, are international in some way. The audience of this volume, I'm sure, has its share of immigrants, or children of immigrants, and that fact will shape one's diverse cultural loyalties and identities. The same goes for those readers who are either political exiles or the children of refugees. Even those with standard U.S. backgrounds, however, are likely to have had international experiences, whether they be pursuing studies abroad anytime between high school and postgraduate investigations for a thesis, or serving a stint in the Peace Corps or at an international school, or speaking a foreign language at home, or maybe even having a romantic partner as well as in-laws who hail from elsewhere. Finally, much of research in the physical sciences and social sciences qualifies as an enterprise that cuts across national borders and is, ipso facto, international.

My own case history, though, represents a particular form of international experience that is still scarcely recognized in the public arena. It's a two-step process. I'm referring to those individuals who spend significant portions of their childhoods overseas, and who then move on to their passport countries either for academic reasons or because their parents return home. In the American case, these kids tend to be the offspring of religious missionaries, corporate employees, career diplomats, military personnel, international educators, expatriate artists, or adventurers of some sort. For the returnee children, the entirety of the experience, both Act One, overseas, and Act Two, Stateside, can result in some confusion, some uncertainty as to what one is, where one belongs. Given their backgrounds they certainly qualify as international students, yet with their U.S. passports they are not foreign students, even though some of their peers may perceive them as such. They are also, in some measure, cosmopolites, but may be enrolled or employed in a milieu in which cosmopolitanism is not normally recognized or valued.

I'd like to cite a telling statistic: In any given year since 1950, there have been at least a quarter of a million American children attending overseas schools (Bell-Villada, 2005, pp. xvii–xviii). Some of them may actually have been born abroad, of American parents, and then pursued their entire elementary and secondary education outside the United States. And what does one call these individuals? As children they are not, strictly speaking, expatriates, since it was not their choice to live *ex patria*, but that of their parents. By the same token, once settled on U.S. soil, they're not exactly immigrants either, inasmuch as they speak unaccented American English, have gone through some version of the U.S. school curriculum, and, most important of all, have American citizenship and passports, with all the rights appertaining to.

There are a number of technical terms that serve to designate these subjects. The most prominent among them is Third Culture Kids, or TCKs for short. The phrase was minted in the 1950s by Ruth Hill Useem, a sociologist at Michigan State University. Useem at the time had been stationed in newly independent India with her family, doing social research on Indians who had pursued higher education in Western countries. Eventually she became aware of another set of developmental patterns in her three children within their Indian environment. The term she coined thus indicates a phenomenon that is "third" in that it combines aspects of both the host culture and the passport culture, without necessarily belonging to either of them (Useem & Downie, 2005). The phrase, I should emphasize, has nothing to do with the Third World and its political connotations.

Third Culture Kids, the idea as well as the term, is now common currency among international educators. It is also subject to modification. Hence, when referring to TCKs who are no longer kids, the phrase *Adult* Third Culture Kids is employed. There's now a best-selling book by David Pollock and Ruth Van Reken called *Third Culture Kids: The Experience of Growing Up among Worlds* (1999/2001), and about equal parts psychology, sociology, and self-help. In addition, the twosome refer to those kids who repatriate to their passport countries as "hidden immigrants," since they literally immigrate to a land they may have scarcely lived in, yet are not necessarily perceived as migrants by their fellow citizens. Further breathing life into this terminology, there exists a close study of such adults, a volume bearing the title *Hidden Immigrants* by Linda Bell (1997) [no relation].

Two other terms: first, "Global Nomads," coined by Norma McCaig, who grew up the daughter of a pharmaceutical executive in the Philippines and South Asia. Though a TCK herself, she felt less than comfortable with the noun "kid" when designating adult men and women (McCaig, 2005). Finally, I will mention my own little term, which I used as the title for my memoir, *Overseas American: Growing Up Gringo in the Tropics* (2005). I dreamt up the phrase by analogy with "overseas Chinese," the formula by which the Chinese regularly refer to their ethnic brethren who are not residing either in the mainland republic or in Taiwan.

Each of these appellations has strengths and distinct emphases of their own. "Third Culture Kids," however, has the added advantage of comprising the host as well as the passport countries, the overseas as well as the returnee component, suggesting how both form a new, separate, ongoing entity within a child who has been thus shaped. It captures a process, a dialectic, as it were.

Vanesa's case brings yet another dimension to the experience. The question arises: In what measure do immigrant children qualify as Third Culture Kids? Concerning school-age Latin Americans in the United States—who, for reasons of physical proximity and relatively accessible air travel, may well be going back and forth with some frequency—the term would certainly seem partly applicable. In this regard, TCK writer Ruth Van Reken (coauthor of the eponymous book) has, in a more recent study, proposed the term "Cross-Cultural Kid" (or "CCK") to designate "a person who is living in—or meaningfully interacting with—two or more cultural environments for a significant period of time in the developmental years of childhood (up to age 18)" (Van Reken, 2011, p. 33).

Among the numerous instances Van Reken cites are an African American girl who was bused to a white Catholic school where she learned to speak "white English," then needed to return to black dialect at home for fear of appearing "uppity"; or the son of Chinese immigrants who felt enough integrated at his Indianapolis school yet also entered "an all-Chinese world" whenever he spoke with his monolingual mother and grandmother (p. 31). Van Reken furnishes a lengthy list of possible categories of such subjects, among them: children who attend an international school in their native land; "children who cross national borders on a regular basis";[1] children who are international adoptees; and even "domestic TCKs," that is, "children whose parents have moved in or among various subcultures within that child's home country" (p. 35). Many Hispanics in the United States such as Vanesa are thus arguably examples either of Third Culture Kids or of Van Reken's "Cross-Cultural Kids," and I shall deal with them here.

I should make the obvious point that these terms are not American specific, even though the U.S. case is unique in its range and extent. There are, for instance, Japanese Third Culture Kids. The Japanese language even has special labels for them, first *Kaigaishijo* (meaning "while abroad") and *Kikokushijo* (meaning "on return"), as Ann Baker Cottrell, a specialist on the topic, points out (p. 57). Within Japan, the topic reportedly is seen and dealt with as a problematical issue in its own right, with separate university exams and even dedicated schools set up to provide training for returnee children.

Moreover, between 1970 and 1990, "the number of overseas Japanese schools was increased three fold and supplemental Japanese schools six fold" (Cottrell, 2005, p. 68). Still, by the year 2000, only 31% of Japanese kids abroad were attending such institutions. The simple reason was that a majority of parents placed a higher priority on their children acquiring English and assimilating Western culture, especially if the families were posted in Europe or North America (less so if assigned elsewhere). On the other hand, these youthful returnees having absorbed such Westernized ways as "questioning, self-assertion, direct eye contact and informal speech offend sensibilities in a society that cares deeply about conformity" (p. 71). Paradoxically, their more fluent English makes them a special breed, a desirable commodity, even as their knowledge of the subtleties of their native language may be relatively deficient and expose them to prejudice, discrimination, or worse while back home. One important difference with American TCKs is that Japanese ones are almost exclusively corporate children, or, more rarely, the offspring of diplomats. For obvious reasons, since 1945, there have been no overseas Japanese "military brats." Nor are the Japanese given to religious proselytizing, hence the absence of "missionary kids" from Japan.

European TCKs, by contrast with Americans and Japanese, have scarcely been singled out or studied. In one of few such instances, Anu Warinowski takes a detailed look at expatriate families from Finland, whose children, with minimal previous linguistic training, may find themselves thrust into an English-language school. Moreover, the institutional components of the entire new system—"curriculum, admissions, testing, counseling, and . . . social situations" (p. 298)—inevitably will differ from those of the child's native Finland. Within the family fold, Warinowski remarks, Finnish children overseas often end up hardly using their original language, if at all. As expected, there is but a smattering of Finnish schools abroad, and though distance learning does exist, fewer than 10% of the kids in Warinowski's study actually availed themselves of the service (p. 307). Curiously, those Finnish children who attended the local schools seemed to fare better psychologically, given that they were faced with only one rather than two alien cultures—the host country's and the international school's—to negotiate.

In this regard, Warinowski pointedly and eloquently notes the case of a Finnish boy named Ilpo (originally cited by Pollock and Van Reken in their book) who had attended an international school in Taiwan, and whose less-than-proficient skills in Finnish led him to enroll in an American university rather than in a Finnish one. He later encountered difficulties finding work back home for "lack of Finnish occupational vocabulary" (p. 298).

From the foregoing, an obvious inference to be drawn is that the more powerful a nation is on the world stage, the more TCKs it will generate. Indeed, in an earlier era, what we now see as the TCK phenomenon was associated with European colonialism. The British and French governments encouraged their nationals to settle overseas, with a view to "civilizing" their colonies. In the process these settlers had offspring who may have been TCKs without realizing it. Think of those Brits brought up in India or Africa, or French raised in Indochina and Algeria, who, when they went back to the supposed and longed-for "mother country," oftentimes found that they didn't fully belong there. As a concrete example, I have in mind the English novelist Penelope Lively, who in the mid-1990s published a beautiful memoir with the highly suggestive title *Oleander, Jacaranda: A Childhood Perceived* (1994). In it she recalls a happy youth in British-occupied Egypt, where she loves the country and its people, but where she is told that actually England is her country. Well, when she does at last "go back" to England for boarding school, she hates the place, hates the climate, the manners, and the everyday life.

The United States, of course, was not a full-fledged world power until 1945. Its sphere of influence was rather Latin America, where in fact U.S. schools had been in place from early on in the 20th century. In addition there were the religious missionary efforts that constituted a culture unto itself. Pearl Buck, the Nobel Prize–winning novelist, and Henry Luce, the media tycoon who founded Time-Life, were both of them the children of missionaries in China. In the years since, as we know, American economic, military, and cultural power around the world has attained unprecedented scale and heights. American business abroad, and the 700 to 1,000 U.S. military bases across the globe, add up to a total entity larger than most nation-states. The entire complex thus serves as a natural breeding ground for TCKs. And that will be my focus for the next few pages.

The title of my chapter, again, is "Growing Up Internationally, and How It Shapes a Child." I should state from the outset that there's no single way in which any given kid is shaped by an international childhood, nor more than there is a one-size-fits-all way in which a small-town child is formed by his or her locally rooted upbringing. The parents' circumstances and occupations, the family life, the country or countries where they are stationed, and the children's own temperament and talents all play a role in the formative process. I'll get to some of those differences shortly, but certain common, almost predictable results bear mention.

First, if you're in a country where the language is accessible, chances are you'll gain some familiarity, proficiency, even fluency in that language. Bilingualism in such a setting is a natural, even desirable possibility, more a norm than an exception, more a thing valued than an oddity. Not a few language teachers I know, including myself, grew up with this advantage and have made a career and a lifestyle out of such a background. Obviously this is a more likely outcome if you are reared in a Hispanic, Francophone, or German-speaking country, less so if you grow up as a privileged foreigner in an Arabic-speaking or Slavic or Japanese environment. I know some bright, young TCKs who've been raised in Cairo and Warsaw, and they admit to little more than a rudimentary knowledge of Egyptian Arabic or of Polish. With a multilingual upbringing, of course, you eventually will have to make long-range language choices—the humorous subject of "Le français," a poem by Maya Goldstein Evans that serves as end paper to the TCK collection *Writing Out of Limbo*, coedited by Nina Sichel and me (p. 476).

Another, less tangible advantage of an international childhood is that you acquire a kind of reflex, unconscious cosmopolitanism. Not being grounded in any particular location, you become an everyday anthropologist who sees cultures from a distance and constantly compares them, if at times unfairly, to the detriment of one and the benefit of another. In time, you begin to be aware that any given nation's customs and practices are by no means natural or universal but local, traditional, perhaps arbitrary. The culture of your passport is thus simply one of many, even if you may prefer it to that of others. A certain adaptability is the result, and much of your future will consist of negotiating these perceptions of difference and maybe ultimately making a living from them. Studies have in fact shown a high proportion of Adult TCKs working in some international field or other.

At the same time there can arise a kind of compensation effect whereby the TCK becomes a professional, even chauvinistic defender of the passport country. This is the case with Henry Luce, who in his magazine empire coined the jingoistic phrase, "the American century." Or that of Newt Gingrich, who spent some years with his military father in France and Germany and wrote his doctoral thesis on the Belgian Congo, but, after being denied tenure as a history professor, threw in his lot with a more aggressively nationalistic political project, attacking candidates John Kerry and Mitt Romney for speaking French, for instance. Or Bob Barr, who, after growing up in Malaysia, Pakistan, Panama, Peru, Iraq, and Iran, spent a decade using his language skills as an analyst for the CIA, and eventually became a conservative congressman and the 2008 presidential candidate for the Libertarian Party.

Getting back to more mundane TCK matters, every human institution can have its downside, and the TCK experience is no exception. Many an individual raised overseas is known to lament the many moves that have led to a lack of stable, continuous, early friendships, and even an incapacity to forge lasting bonds. Difficulties crop up in the hidden immigrant phase. You might have thought of yourself as fully American, and find out that that is not so. Your peers make casual references to pop culture or to current events, and you've no idea what they're talking about. By the same token, you can't allude in much detail to your own childhood and adolescence, inasmuch as in this milieu they are alien, or meaningless. Or people might perceive such reminiscences as bragging, showing off. And you're in turn surprised at the American gaps in knowledge about the world outside U.S. borders.

Meanwhile, the less savory aspects that you discover about your passport country end up contradicting the somewhat idealized image you may have entertained about it while living overseas. When my brother and I first arrived in the United States in 1959, we rode Greyhound buses from Key West all the way to Santa Fe, New Mexico, during a time when racial segregation in the Southern states was absolute. And at the stations, as we read the signs stating starkly, "WHITE BATHROOM" and "COLORED BATHROOM," we wondered which one of them was appropriate for our yellow-brown skin and Asian features. Cautiously, over the next few days we'd venture into the white-designated areas, though our initial concerns were not unfounded. Indeed, during a lunch stop in Little Rock, Arkansas, my brother was stealthily followed into the bathroom by a trio of white roughnecks. They stood about in silence as he did his number-one business. As he departed the urinal, they surrounded him threateningly. Thinking fast, he addressed them in rapid-fire Spanish, sashayed toward the door without having washed his hands, and left the courageous warriors somewhat nonplussed.

Like many a TCK, I was "returning" to the country of my citizenship for my undergraduate studies. For years I'd imagined campus life as an endless round of earnest rap sessions dealing with great books and big ideas. There certainly was some of that, but there were also such things as fraternities and their overt racism, philistine anti-intellectualism, and sexism, their loud parties and occasional street violence, as well as the overall culture of casual sex—topics known to many of us, and invoked by my coeditor Nina Sichel in her chapter "Outsider," in *Writing Out of Limbo*. I also remember my first roommate, a tall, lanky sort with a blond brush cut and a couple of pimples in his sunken cheeks. His D plus grade average had earned him suspension from his fraternity, yet he still thought of non-frat people as "rinky-dink." He'd routinely employ the "n" word when alluding to blacks, refer to Venezuela and other countries I'd lived in as "those Mexican countries," and from his lips I first heard about "camel jocks," the pejorative term for Arabs. He found laughable my love of classical music, and when I'd have friends visiting the room, he'd introduce himself saying, "Hi, Seymour Butts here!" or "I'm Dick Bender!" (I got to be known humorously as "the man with the crude roommate.") Such, then, were among my initial encounters with campus life in this land.

Returnee TCKs can also be subject to the occasional culture clash. The two contributing editors to our *Limbo* book have stories in that regard. Elaine Orr, a writer who grew up of Baptist missionary parents in Nigeria, recalls her coming back to Arkansas to finish high school; at one point a beautiful white cheerleader asks her where she's from; Elaine replies, "West Africa." The cheerleader makes a face, whispers "queer," and walks away (Orr, 2005, p. 396). In another instance, our fourth editor and also a writer, Faith Eidse, was raised by Christian missionaries in Congo; she remembers being, in her own words to me, "an inexpensive date" in college, always ordering just soup when eating out, "because everything else on the menu seemed like enough food and money to feed a small village"; and of course there was her bewilderment at seeing 50 varieties of chocolate bars or cheese at grocery stores. Yet another missionary girl had shared with Congolese playmates the preferred pastime of going barefoot for walks in the jungle; when she came to the States for university, she'd ask her dates to join her in a barefoot stroll in the woods. It goes without saying that they thought of her as daffy.

In my case, after so many moves, during my first couple of years as a student at the University of Arizona, I took to answering the standard "Where are you from?" question with—if only for simplicity's sake—"Venezuela." As a result my peers would deal with me via stereotypes: I was dubbed "the Caracas Kid" or I was asked if I'd been involved with all those revolutions down there; or was told, "Gee, you don't *look* like a Latin lover!"

Linguistic misunderstandings can occur. As some readers probably know, in Spanish it's not considered bad manners to address someone by their physical traits. Well, I'll never forget the time I greeted a female classmate in the hall, saying, "Hello, cute one." A male friend looked at me and said, "You're crazy!" As knowledgeable readers might guess, all I'd been doing was to translate directly the casual phrases, "¡Hola, guapa!" and "¡Hola, mona!", clueless about the fact that they did not, in fact, translate. Another time I greeted a fellow musician, "Hi there, redhead." (In my mind, "¡Hola, pelirrojo!") He replied, "Hi, blackhead," and added, "Aha! Got you on that one!"

I cite such incidents as just a few small examples of the disorientation that can result when TCKs start dealing with early adult life in what is their official homeland. There are more extreme instances, such as one woman, a foreign service kid who had moved every one or two years by the time she was a senior in high school, and who ended up finding refuge as a Buddhist nun (Anora Egan, 2004). In the worst-case scenarios, a TCK's confused and fractured self can lead to a fall through the cracks, a spiral into alcoholism, and other sorts of personal loss. (I have known or know about a couple of them myself.) We don't hear that much about these individuals because, quite simply, they don't write about it, and they haven't been the subjects of major studies thus far. In this regard I must confess that I was a rather unbalanced, ungrounded, and more than slightly crazy young TCK during my first 10 to 15 years in the United States. The gradual healing process began only with an intellectual space that I envisioned and claimed for myself in the late 1960s, as well as with my marriage to Audrey in 1975. In addition, my memoir *Overseas American* was an instrument of nine years' deep reflection and personal discovery that helped me tease out the conflicting strands from my past and give it a shape. The book was, shall we say, my writing cure.

There are many varieties of TCK experience, and I'd like to spend these next few pages considering a number of well-defined TCK groups. By far the most complex are the missionary kids, or MKs. As children, MKs live as part of the societies to which their religious parents have been assigned, in Third World locations, generally. They grow up playing with native kids with whom they oftentimes will attend class, perhaps at the mission school. They usually learn at least one of the local languages, becoming fully bi- or multilingual. Then, every four or five years, their entire family is sent on a paid, 12-month furlough back in the States, where the children enroll at a public school for the duration. At year's end, they return to the field, though not necessarily to the previous country. (See Emily Hervey's chapter "Returning to My Parents' Foreign 'Home'" in *Writing Out of Limbo* for a lucid summing-up of the process.) A study by Laila Plamondon, also included in our anthology, suggests that those furloughs may actually increase the kids' confusion, that it may be wiser to have them spend their full 17 years abroad consecutively than live in this constant back-and-forth. Once the MKs do finally settle for good in the United States, the confusion becomes permanent, as yet another chapter, by Nancy Henderson-James, suggests, and they may spend the rest of their lives figuring out their relationship to the mission country or countries, as well (Henderson-James, 2005). About half of them lose their religious faith, though they tend to retain their parents' humanitarian values of service.

Another group is that of the armed service kids, or "military brats." They tend to grow up moving from one humungous base to another, both within the United States and overseas, but all within a single, larger Defense Department bubble. There is an entire novel, *The Great Santini*, by Pat Conroy, that captures the unreality of such a world, though without the foreign component. It was subsequently made into a Hollywood movie under the same title, with Robert Duvall as the protagonist. And one of our anthology contributors, Donna Musil, who had moved 12 times on three continents following her Army dad, put together the first documentary film ever about the experience, entitled *Brats: Our Journey Home*, and narrated by singer-songwriter Kris Kristofferson, whose own father, in turn, was an Air Force general. As the singer himself notes, in the military you grow up not in a country but a state of mind. Similarly, when Donna, the director, asks some of her interviewees where they are from, they reply, for instance, "From?" or "From everywhere!" or "I'm . . . not." Until they go off to college, armed forces children may have known no other life, and the entire shift to civilian ways takes some adaptation. For high school military brats whose parents have been discharged or retired, even mundane things like prom dates and student-body elections suddenly seem like alien phenomena, and moreover all hitherto-taken-for-granted base privileges come to an end.

Yet one more TCK grouping consists of what are called corporate kids, or, more informally, "biz kids." When I was living in Caracas, Venezuela, the biz kids were almost a breed apart. They attended a special, high-quality grammar school, staffed with excellent teachers, and funded and subsidized by the oil firms. In addition, the entire families had their bi-annual travel expenses to visit relatives back home defrayed by the companies. Later on, for high school, the young charges were sent to prestigious private academies up in the States, the tuition for which, by then, the family breadwinners could afford. Many of these biz kids, I should note, scarcely learned much Spanish, and local events hardly impinged on them. Generally speaking, corporate children do not experience the dilemmas and confusions that MKs or military brats often do. They live lives that are privileged and frequently happy, with relatively few social or cultural dissonances to speak of. Significantly, there are no book-length memoirs or reflections written by corporate kids, inasmuch as major conflict or dissonance is missing from their circumstances. Living in a luxurious paradise, after all, does not provide much in the way of narrative suspense. Of course there are exceptions, some of which I'm personally acquainted with, but this is how I remember that neo-colonial world.

Three other, less-privileged groups can receive only a more passing, anecdotal, sketchy glance here, inasmuch as I am not aware of any systematic researches about them.

First, there are the offspring of small businesspeople, parents who've relocated to a foreign land where they perceive money-making opportunities for an ambitious entrepreneur. Venezuela with its oil wealth attracted such free-wheeling elements in my time. (China today seems to be playing that role, as fortune-seekers from the world over show up, sometimes with their digital gadgets and designer briefcases.) During my two years as a student at the Colegio Americano de Caracas, among my schoolmates there were sons and daughters of the owners of, for instance, a local hardware store, a set of laundries, a Dale Carnegie franchise, an import-export outfit (my father), and a potato-chip or spaghetti factory. The male children might occasionally lend a hand with the business operations. Some learned Spanish; others did not.

As a group these kids were not cohesive, were not bound together by the corporate ties, prep-school status, and country-club memberships that gave the more affluent "biz kids" their highly visible collective identity. Whenever the latter would descend on Caracas for their Christmas break and summer vacations, the socioeconomic gap between the two sectors became manifest, and the small-enterprise children would slightly resent the returnees' wealth, refer to them as "snobs."

International educators have kids, too, and these form another, somewhat less conspicuous group. (Significantly, unlike the "MKs" or the "military brats," there is no set term, let alone a nickname, for designating them.) In another era, their mothers might have gone into teaching in order to supplement the family income—or simply to be active in the public arena. (At my Colegio Americano, in keeping with the times, most all of the teachers were female.) A yet smaller cluster consists of the career educators, upper-level administrators who may move from one school to another. A former classmate of mine happened to be the daughter of our school principal. Not surprisingly, she reports always having felt apart from the rest of the students. After all, from family discussions at home, she possessed "inside information" about our teachers, privileged knowledge that discretion could not allow her to bring up with her peers, and that inhibited her socially. Even today, when attending alumni reunions or receiving reports about them, she will read or overhear things that render her uncomfortable. (In a familiar enough trajectory, she herself became a high school Spanish teacher in upper New York State.)

In another case, my senior-year English teacher, Charmian Mock, was herself TCK. Raised in the U.S. Philippines, where she met her future husband Charles, she spent time at the Los Baños internment camp as a result of the Japanese invasion and occupation of 1941–1945; she actually married her spouse at the camp. When the Mocks eventually moved to Caracas, she joined the Colegio Americano faculty. Following the passing away of her husband in 1964, Charmian and her children moved to Spain, where she accepted positions as director of a couple of American schools. Not surprisingly, two of her sons also became international educators, teaching at and then running a series of institutions in Spain (again), Pakistan, Honduras, the Philippines, Indonesia, Taiwan, and South Africa. And *they* in turn have kids who've taught in the Philippines (again), Peru, Spain (again), Japan, Dubai, Ethiopia, and Saudi Arabia. Naturally, the children of the children were themselves all raised overseas. The pattern thus seems open-ended.

Charmian's son Joe, currently stationed in the Philippines, has strong attachments still to Venezuela and Pakistan. Yet it is Spain where, he informed me in an e-mail message, "I think I feel more at home than anywhere else." Nevertheless, he has come to realize that "I am somewhere deep down culturally American." Though not nationalistic, he accepts his responsibilities as a U.S. citizen and votes in national elections ("I care very much about who is in the White House, because I know how important it is to the rest of the world"). At the same time he maintains close ties to the Cape Cod area, where his father's peoples were from, and where the many relatives meet for family reunions.

The lack of a wide-ranging, representative survey notwithstanding, one might venture to speculate that international educators are potentially true "citizens of the world." After all, they have as their vocation, indeed their mission, to disseminate and preserve knowledge, and thus deal directly with cultural issues rather than with money, guns, or power.

Finally, there are the children of political exiles, kids who, to some extent or other, might retain attachments to their parents' home country, yet inevitably build ties with the language and culture of their land of expatriation. While formal studies of childhood development in this group are virtually nonexistent, personal memoirs are a matter of record. In the American case we are speaking of U.S. leftists and their offspring who, during what is known (somewhat inaccurately) as "the McCarthy era," fled elsewhere, some to Marxist states, some not. (Novelist Richard Wright, for instance, moved to France and raised his two daughters there. Others settled in, for instance, Canada, Mexico, or Puerto Rico.) One such reminiscence, by Ann Kimmage, bears the provocative title *An Un-American Childhood.* The author spent 11 of her youthful years with her left-wing parents in postwar Czechoslovakia (where she was a member of the Young Communist

Pioneers), and then two years in Mao's China, just before the incipient stages of the Cultural Revolution. The family returned to the United States in the early 1960s, when things had started loosening up. Kimmage, though disillusioned by the errors and excesses of what she had witnessed in both countries, ended up thinking of herself more as Czech than American (causing some tensions with her parents, who did not learn the language and were homesick for New York City and America); she never ceased feeling loyal to the Czech world and its cultural traditions.

From what we saw earlier in the chapter, then, it can be seen that the term TCK covers a fairly broad gamut of experiential patterns. A MK will have been raised quite differently from a corporate kid or a child of political exile, yet they all qualify as TCKs. Meanwhile, in the last couple of decades or so, we've entered a whole new setting for what I call the Third Culture Kid condition, namely the rise and spread, since 1989, of what has been dubbed "globalization": the increased interconnectedness of the world through international finance and trade, through entertainment media and information technology, through employment outsourcing and voluntary legal migration, and with English as the dominant lingua franca. The trend was vividly summed up in the catchy title of *New York Times* columnist Thomas Friedman's 2005 best seller, *The World Is Flat.*

As a side result of this inexorable wave, educational institutions across the globe have been seeing an increasing international and cultural diversity within their student ranks. From my recent experiences at Williams College, for instance, I can cite a South Korean student, son of an executive at a Korean multinational firm, and a product of the American school in Warsaw, Poland; or a son of Afghan immigrants who also lived a while in Chile; or a daughter of Chinese parents who, during her infancy, had emigrated with the entire family to Argentina and later relocated to the United States; or another Chinese girl, born in Texas, but whose father, in her 11th year, decided to move back to China and work in business, and where she too attended international schools. Many of these budding minds presumably have not yet worked out in full their personal identities within this new, still-fluid and developing situation; they may well spend years sorting out the various strands in their cultural makeup.

The matter of Vanesa, whose case I cite at the start of this chapter, brings me to yet another sort of cross-cultural developmental trajectory (to build on Ruth Van Reken's phrase). Vanesa's experience in certain ways can be regarded as typical. At this time the United States has, demographically speaking, the third-largest Hispanic population in the world (after Mexico and Spain). Their collective histories range from that of the rooted, settled, Spanish-speaking ethnics of rural New Mexico—with an ancestry going back centuries, long before the Anglo expansion that followed the Mexican War—to yesterday's immigrants arriving by foot, by rail, by truck, by raft, or by air, mostly from Mexico but also from Central America and any of the other republics, as well as individuals from Puerto Rico who move to the mainland US. In addition there are the Cubans who, being designated as "fleeing from Communism," are routinely, automatically given refugee status under the McCarran-Walter Act upon their arrival on U.S. soil. Any casual visitor to the enclaves of "Little Havana" in Miami, or of the many "Little Mexicos" in Texas or California, would feel scarcely aware of being within the political borders of the United States.

The steady flow of immigration by Hispanics, whether or not documented, and of course the higher Latino birth rate combine to result in the constant growth of that population segment, to the point that it has surpassed African Americans as the largest "minority" group in the United States. Its young people tend necessarily to live in two worlds, speaking English at school but oftentimes Spanish at home and especially with relatives in the Old Country. Many of them come and go, then come and go, under varying circumstances, between north and south. Some blending, blurring, and confusion are thus inevitable. At the anecdotal level, I have conversed with many an individual like Vanesa, who will recall with some ambivalence their trips to the lands of their birth; relatives or childhood friends there see them at least initially as "gringas"; here in the States they're perceived as alien Hispanics of some sort, and some American interlocutors may be unable to distinguish the country of their origin from Mexico or Puerto Rico. In the worst of cases they might be labeled "Spiks," the derogatory term for Latinos.

Over the past several decades there has emerged a rich body of narrative literature that hones in on this dilemma. There is the novel *Hot Land, Cold Season* (1961; English translation, 1973) by the Puerto Rican writer Pedro Juan Soto (1928–2002), which deals with a "Nuyorican" adolescent who goes to the island with high hopes of becoming rooted in the "homeland," only to find out, to his deep disappointment, that his time in New York no longer helps him nor brings him much standing "back home," as it were. Finally he decides to fly back to El Norte. The author himself, I should note, experienced this double bind, though he did finally end up staying in Puerto Rico.

In a more dramatic instance, the Afro-Puerto Rican writer and activist Piri Thomas (1928–2011), who narrates his own classic memoir *Down These Mean Streets* (1967), has never yet set foot in the Caribbean. "Borinquen" (Puerto Rico's original, indigenous place name and an alternate signifier in the daily discourse of its residents) is but a nostalgic memory for his parents, who have made their lives in East Harlem and later on Long Island. Young Piri is torn apart by his mixed Puerto Rican inheritance and his dark skin color as he travels throughout a racist America from Babylon (New York State) all the way to Texas, with a stint in the Merchant Marine in-between.

In the case of the well-known memoir by Esmeralda Santiago, *When I Was Puerto Rican* (1993), the title verb in past tense, "was," already conveys in brief a transformation from island immigrant into something else—a U.S.-based artist in this case. The same can be seen in *Family Installments* (1982), an autobiographical novel both touching and funny, by the late Edward Rivera (1939–2001), in which a youth from the rural town of Orocovis (Puerto Rico) moves with his family to New York City, where he will slowly, tentatively find his way as an apprentice U.S. man of the pen. Such examples of the *Bildungsroman* demonstrate a repeated trajectory of Puerto Rican island identity struggles in El Norte, followed by a possible cultural integration into El Norte.

The same can be seen in the literature of Chicanos—a noun applied at times to Mexican Americans (the term having welled up as a kind of ethnic battle cry in the 1970s). *Pocho* (1959) by José Antonio Villarreal (1924–2010), the first novel published in English by a Chicano author, tells of the gradual Americanization, in north-central California, of a sensitive but also somewhat prickly protagonist, Richard Rubio, who is in turn the eldest born of an undocumented Mexican immigrant couple in the 1920s. Along similar lines there is the Cuban segment of this literary trend. The very beautiful novel by Cristina García, *Dreaming in Cuban* (1992), focuses on embattled Cuban American adolescent Pilar Puente and her struggles to reconcile her family roots back on the island with her history as a child immigrant and her life as a budding art student in Manhattan.

On the other hand, Richard Rodriguez in *Hunger of Memory* (1982) chooses to slough off completely his Mexican and Hispanic heritage—and reject bilingual education and Affirmative Action policies into the bargain. The position brought him plaudits from the conservative establishment in the United States—praise that would not repeat itself when, in *Days of Obligation* (1992), Rodriguez was to re-explore his Mexican roots and become frank about his homoerotic orientation. Finally, there is Junot Diaz: A masterful Dominican American novelist and short-story writer, he has succeeded in fashioning an entire bi-national and bicultural geography of Dominicans settled in New Jersey, immigrants (or children thereof) who nonetheless feel some deep need to maintain contact, either sporadic or continuous, with the island of their forebears. The rich, vibrant, energetic "Spanglish" prose crafted by Diaz for his virtuoso story-telling serves as a potent symbol of the double identity in which his troubled characters live and love, grow and die. His novel, *The Brief Wondrous Life of Oscar Wao*, it bears reminding, won the 2008 Pulitzer Prize for fiction.

This new, imaginative literature springing from U.S. Latino authors serves as a notable manifestation of a large-scale cultural and human presence that is taking shape within the United States, and that children and parents, educators and counselors, psychologists and sociologists can expect to be coping with in decades to come. The process is ongoing, and there is no sign of its subsiding very soon. Concerning identity, in many a high-school or college classroom there are countless students wondering to themselves, "Am I gringo, or Latino? Both, or neither?" Such questions are inevitable from these Cross-Cultural Kids (to cite Ruth Van Reken once again), with their international childhoods across the Americas, a situation that qualifies as a special variant of the TCK phenomenon.

Meanwhile, as TCK trends continue, we are going to see more and more TCKs in visible positions. The 2008 presidential election is a case in point. President Barack Obama has a personal history that relates directly to this chapter. As far as I know, Obama is the first U.S. chief of state who fits the profile of a TCK. His late father was Kenyan; his mother was a white woman from Kansas. And he was born in Hawaii, spending his first five, formative years there. Sometime after his parents divorced, in his second year, Obama's mother married an Indonesian man. The boy next went on to live four years in Indonesia, where he attended local schools and learned the language fluently. The adult Obama's best-selling first book, *Dreams from My Father* (1995), besides its glow as a humane and beautifully crafted piece of literature, is in fact a TCK memoir that crops up as required reading for undergraduate courses on the subject. In its climax, the twenty-ish author discovers who he is as he sits in deep reflection under a tree in Kenya. Obama's electoral rival, in turn, Senator John McCain, was born at an air naval base in the Panama Canal Zone, and is hence a product of overseas U.S. empire, though he's obviously not a full-fledged TCK. And I've already made mention of the third party, Libertarian candidate, Bob Barr and his complex life path. Another instance I'll add to the list is that of Timothy Geithner, the Secretary of the Treasury 2009–2013, who grew up in Zimbabwe, Zambia, India, and Thailand, graduating from the International School in Bangkok. Press pundits have liked to note some personal affinity between Obama and Geithner on the basis of their overseas backgrounds.

Well, in conclusion, we've every reason to assume that the twofold phenomenon of growing up internationally and its long-term developmental effects will remain part of our larger existence, not just in the United States, but in the rest of the world as well. Granted, international childhoods as a social fact might not be featured in the mass media. "Third Culture Kids" and other such terms might not yet be household words. However, those of us involved in foreign language and international studies, such as myself, know that it's there, that it's not going away or dropping from sight, and that its presence will most likely increase, with more instances of amazingly mixed backgrounds, more varieties of cultural confusion, and, just incidentally, more need for counseling, understanding, and research. Whatever we choose to call it, TCK, if I may rhymingly daresay, is here to stay, and we should be ready for it in the years to come.

REFLECTIVE QUESTIONS

1. The United States and Canada are commonly—and accurately—described as "nations of immigrants." In your view, to what degree do the children of immigrants qualify as Third Culture Kids or as Cross-Cultural Kids? Conversely, how are TCKs both similar to and different from "regular" immigrants?
2. Might TCKs qualify as another, unrecognized "minority group?"
3. Are Hispanic immigrant children Third Culture Kids? Or are they CCKs? Or neither? Why or why not? When and when not?
4. Under what circumstances would African American or Asian American children be considered TCKs or CCKs?
5. Can you suggest other sorts of TCKs or CCKs besides the ones mentioned in this chapter?
6. Have you ever spent a year or more studying or working in a foreign country? How did the experience shape your view of yourself and of your passport country?
7. Are you personally acquainted with any Third Culture Kids or Cross-Cultural Kids? If so, arrange a brief interview with one or two of them and ask about their life history, their cultural identity, their loyalties, and where they feel they belong (if anywhere . . .). Sum up your findings in a page or two, using the biographical and autobiographical portions of this chapter as models.
8. Do you think you might be a TCK or a CCK? If so, write a page or two in which you tell about and reflect on the issue!

NOTE

1. In this connection, it is worth noting that the specialty "Borderlands Studies" has become an entire subdiscipline in its own right. Hence, an Association for Borderlands Studies and a journal by that name have both existed since 1976; they were launched, logically enough, in San Diego, near the U.S.-Mexico border.

SUGGESTED READINGS

There is now a fairly extensive scholarly literature available on Third Culture Kids, most of it from small presses or from academic publishers such as Praeger.

The seminal book on the topic is David Pollock and Ruth Van Reken's (1999/2001) *Third Culture Kids: The Experience of Growing up among Worlds*. The volume features definitions, individual profiles, and in-depth analyses, along with extensive advice for parents and children.

Several anthologies have brought together under one cover some foundational essays (those by e.g. Ruth Hill Useem, Norma McCaig) that are now standard references on the subject, as well as specially commissioned pieces, some academic, some personal. The subtitle of Faith Eidse and Nina Seichel's edited volume, *Unrooted Childhoods: Memoirs of Growing up Global* (2004) spells out the subjective approach of the work's contents. The book contains essays by recognized authors such as Pat Conroy,

Ariel Dorfman, Marie Arana, Isabel Allende, and Pico Iyer, but also reminiscences by fifteen other, less-known writers. A more recent collection, *Writing out of Limbo: International Childhoods, Global Nomads, and Third Culture Kids*, Eds. Gene H. Bell-Villada and Nina Sichel (2011), gathers 30 essays and a poem—combining classic texts and personal remembrances, rigorous scholarly investigations and cultural reflections, all of them exploring some chosen aspect of TCK life and development.

Carolyn D. Smith has carried out some pioneering empirical research in *The Absentee American: Repatriates' Perspectives on America* (1991). She followed it up with *Strangers at Home: Essays on the Effects of Living Overseas and Coming "Home" to a Strange Land* (1996), a compilation of 13 major articles on the TCK experience. Linda Bell's *Hidden Immigrants: Legacies of Growing up Abroad* (1997) deals with the issue via a series of extended interviews with TCKS.

For military children, see Mary Edwards Wertsch's classic, *Military Brats: Legacies of Childhood Inside the Fortress* (1991), and also Morten Ender, ed., *Military Brats and Other Global Nomads: Growing up in Organization Families* (2002).

The field is rich in TCK memoirs. Among them are *American Chica: Two Worlds, One Childhood* by Marie Arana (2001); *Overseas American: Growing up Gringo in the Tropics* by Gene H. Bell-Villada (2005); *Heading South, Looking North: A Bilingual Journey* by Ariel Dorfman (1998), *Gods of Noonday: A White Girl's African Life* by Elaine Neil Orr (2003); *Don't Let's Go to the Dogs Tonight: An African Childhood* by Alexandra Fuller (2001); *Oleander, Jacaranda: A Childhood Perceived* by Penelope Lively (1994); and *Under My Skin* by Nobel laureate Doris Lessing (1994).

There exists a growing body of TCK fiction. *Wide Sargasso Sea* (1966) by Jean Rhys (who grew up in the tiny British Caribbean colony of Dominica) is such an example *avant la lettre*. Barbara Kingsolver, herself a TCK, captures the strangeness of the condition in her celebrated novel *The Poisonwood Bible* (1998) and also more recently in *The Lacuna* (2009). Bell-Villada discusses both these authors in his essay, "On Jean Rhys, Barbara Kingsolver, and Myself: Reflections on a Problem That Has No Set Name," in *Writing Out of Limbo.*

Finally, for the first book-length study ever of TCK fiction, see Antje M. Rauwerda (2012), *The Writer and the Overseas Childhood: The Third Culture Literature of Kingsolver, McEwan and Others.*

REFERENCES I

The following references are chapters included in: Bell-Villada, G.H., & Sichel, N. (2011), with Eidse, F., & Orr, E.N. (Eds.). *Writing out of limbo: International childhoods, global nomads, and third culture kids*. Newcastle upon Tyne, UK: Cambridge Scholars.

Cottrell, A.B. (2005). Explaining differences: TCKs and Other CCKs, American and Japanese TCKs (pp. 57–77).

Evans, M.G. *Le français* (poem) (p. 476).

Henderson-James, N. (2005). The religious lives of adult missionary kids (pp. 232–245).

Hervey, E. (2005). Returning to my parents' foreign "home" (pp. 165–179).

McCaig, N. (2005). Raised in the margin of the mosaic: Global nomads balance worlds within (pp. 46–56).

Musil, D. (2005). On making BRATS (pp. 455–474).

Orr, E.N. (2005). The stranger self: A pattern in narrative (pp. 391–410).

Plamondon, L. (2005). Four third culture kids: One portrait (pp. 263–277).

Sichel, N. (2005). Outsider (pp. 196–208).
Useem, R. H., & Downie, R. (2005). Third culture kids (pp. 18–24).
Van Reken, R. (2005). Cross-cultural kids: The new prototype (pp. 25–44).
Warinowski, A. (2005). Finnish expatriate families and their children: A complementary viewpoint (pp. 291–312).

REFERENCES II

Bell, L. (1997). *Hidden immigrants: Legacies of growing up abroad.* Notre Dame, IN: Cross-Cultural Publications.
Bell-Villada, G. H. (2005). *Overseas American: Growing up gringo in the tropics.* Jackson, MS: University Press of Mississippi.
Bell-Villada, G. H., & Sichel, N., with Eidse, F. & Orr, E. N. (Eds.). (2011). *Writing out of limbo: International childhoods, global nomads, and third culture kids.* Newcastle-on-Tyne, UK: Cambridge Scholars.
Conroy, P. (1976). *The great Santini.* New York: Random House.
Diaz, J. (2007). *The brief wondrous life of Oscar Wao.* New York: Riverhead Books.
Egan, A. (2004). Breath roots. In F. Eidse & N. Sichel (Eds.), *Unrooted childhoods: Memoirs of growing up global* (pp. 209–224). Yarmouth, ME: Intercultural Press.
Friedman, T. (2005). *The world is flat: A brief history of the twenty-first century.* New York: Farrar, Straus, Giroux.
García, C. (1992). *Dreaming in Cuban.* New York: Ballantine.
Kimmage, A. (1996). *An un-American childhood.* Athens, GA: University of Georgia Press.
Lively, P. (1994). *Oleander, jacaranda: A childhood perceived.* New York: HarperCollins.
Orr, E. N. (2003). *Gods of noonday: A white girl's African life.* Charlottesville, VA: University of Virginia Press.
Pollock, D., & Reken, R. V. (1999/2001). *Third culture kids: The experience of growing up among worlds.* London, UK: Nicholas Brealey.
Rivera, E. (1982). *Family installments: Memories of growing up Hispanic.* New York: Morrow.
Rodriguez, R. (1982). *Hunger of memory: The education of Richard Rodriguez.* Boston, MA: D. R. Godine.
Rodriguez, R. (1992). *Days of obligation: An argument with my Mexican father.* New York: Viking.
Santiago, E. (1993). *When I was Puerto Rican.* New York: Addison-Wesley.
Smith, C. D. (1991). *The absentee American: Repatriates' perspectives on America.* Westport, CT: Praeger.
Smith, C. D. (1996*). Strangers at home: Essays on the effects of living overseas and coming "home" to a strange land.* Putnam Valley, NY: Aletheia.
Soto, P. J. S. (1973). *Hot land, cold season* (Trans. Helen Lane). New York: Dell.
Thomas, P. (1967). *Down these mean streets.* New York: Knopf.
Villarreal, J. A. (1959). *Pocho.* New York: Doubleday.

12

Adaptation of Immigrant Children, Adolescents, and Their Families

John W. Berry and Paul Vedder

Brian, a 16-year-old, had moved to the Netherlands when he was 12. He was born on the sunny island of Curacao in the Caribbean, a few miles off the Venezuelan coast. His parents decided to emigrate, because the economic prospects for themselves and for their children were bad. Brian had been a good student in Curacao and put in a lot of effort to excel in the Dutch language, the national language of the Netherlands. He had been very excited about emigrating and felt that he was well prepared to follow his dream to go to good schools and eventually become a famous surgeon.

In the Netherlands the family moved in with an aunt and her five children in Hoogvliet, near Rotterdam. Not only was the place cramped, none of his cousins seemed to approach living in the Netherlands as a challenge worth spending special efforts on. They all spoke their native Creole, Papiamento and hung out with other Caribbean youth. Worse still, they mostly were enrolled in lower educational tracks and never spoke enthusiastically about school and the opportunities it would open to realize a dream of a desirable job career. Brian nevertheless enjoyed the first half year of his new school. Teachers supported his enthusiasm, but with time he started failing examinations and increasingly experienced that the things he had learned in school in Curacao were not considered worth much in the Netherlands. His grades were never really good and eventually the school advised him and his parents that he should continue his school career at a junior vocational high school. From then on Brian's development and aspirations took a sharp turn completely opposite to his original dreams. In his new school he was instantly labeled as another Caribbean rowdy macho youth. He could not connect to non-Caribbean kids and could hardly do anything other than live up to the new label of a rowdy macho Caribbean. Sixteen years old now, he was sent to a youth prison for stabbing and gravely injuring another Caribbean boy.

Shamila, Brian's younger sister, hated it when she, then 10 years old, heard that the family would emigrate to the Netherlands. She was furious about losing her friends and grandmother. Once in the Netherlands, she refused at first to make new friends. Instead, she developed a very strong relationship with both her mother and her aunt. They told and showed her how to live a safe and happy life in the Netherlands. Her love for dance and music made it easy for her to connect with all fellow students, from all kinds of cultural backgrounds. Of course, she saw what happened to Brian and she tried to help, but it also made her decide that she would not want to hang out with Caribbean girls only, let alone Caribbean boys. Supported by mother and aunt in her efforts to be autonomous and open to connect with all girls who enjoyed music and dance, she enjoyed her leisure as much as her school. She was anxious to go to university and study law as this would certainly create opportunities to help Brian.

In these two young people, we see two very different trajectories of how immigrant youth may orient themselves to their new life. The contrast and tension between the Caribbean and the Netherlands cultures confront and are confronted by Brian and Shamila in very different ways. Brian cannot resolve them, whereas Shamila, supported by friends, mother and aunt, can. In this chapter we will outline some of these ways to live with and between two cultures, and show how these different ways have personal, social, and educational consequences.

INTRODUCTION

The examination of the migration and adaptation of families and their children is a core area of cross-cultural and intercultural psychology. The central issues are how, and how well, they are able to reestablish their lives in a new society. The psychological examination of these issues uses the concepts of acculturation, acculturation strategies (of both migrants and of the receiving society), and the psychological and sociocultural adaptation of the children and their families. These phenomena are closely linked to changes in the children's educational settings, especially to the goals that caregivers strive to attain for the children from these environments. Other factors that impact these acculturation and adaptation phenomena include the developmental changes in youth, changes in family relationships (especially between the parents and the child) in terms of stress and support, and the discrimination and clash of different value orientations experienced in the society of settlement. All these factors are embedded in the broader political, social, and cultural characteristics that migrants bring with them, as well as in the political, economic, and educational institutions in the society of settlement. In this chapter, we first examine the larger social contexts for the settlement, acculturation, and adaptation of migrant families and their children. We then review selected psychological studies of these phenomena, highlighting the cultural transmission processes, both intra- and intergenerational, that shape children's and adolescents' lives. Finally, we seek to discern general principles from the research findings that might serve as a basis for developing and implementing settlement and educational policies in the societies of settlement.

In many Western countries, the situation of immigrant youth and their families in their societies of settlement has become a topic of major importance in public discourse and research over the past few years (Bornstein & Cote, 2006; Chuang & Moreno, 2011; Lansford, Deater-Deckford, & Bornstein, 2007). Many researchers and policy makers have raised concerns regarding the sense of belonging and the degree of participation that immigrant youth develop with respect to their heritage cultures and to their new societies. In particular, second-generation youth are faced with the challenge of how to live with, and between, their parents' cultural heritage and community and that of their peers in the new society.

The study of immigrant acculturation and adaptation has a long history in the social and behavioral sciences (Berry, 1997; Sam & Berry, 2006/2015). Recent international research (e.g., Berry, Phinney, Sam, & Vedder, 2006; Berry & Sabatier, 2010; Sabatier & Berry, 2008) has shown that immigrant youth manage their orientations to these two cultural communities in highly variable ways. They also achieve different levels of adaptation in the psychological and social domains of their lives. Of particular importance is whether there is a relationship between these two issues. In other words, if there is a certain acculturation pattern that is consistently associated with better adaptations, then there may be a basis for designing policies and programs that can promote more positive outcomes for immigrant youth and their families.

International comparative studies of acculturation and adaptation involve analyzing a number of societies of settlement and immigrant groups. This comparative approach has many advantages including the ability to examine the generalizability of findings by comparing and contrasting settlement contexts and immigrant groups. In this way, we seek to discover general principles that can be extracted from a variety of acculturation arenas. Additionally, as noted earlier, it may be possible to generate "best practice" policies and programs for immigrant youth in general. However, if research findings indicate more context-specific outcomes, then efforts can be devoted to sorting out the reasons behind such variations.

Following this Introduction section, the structure of the remainder of this chapter is as follows. The next section presents a conceptual introduction to studies of acculturation and adaptation. The third section reviews studies of acculturation and adaptation in contexts that are relevant to parents, children, and adolescents. This includes studies of families, of institutions relating to the care and education of immigrant children, and of the wider community where immigrants reside in. In the final section, we extract from the research findings presented earlier to bring together a general set of principles and rules that can serve as a basis for developing and implementing settlement and educational policies in the societies of settlement.

ACCULTURATION AND ADAPTATION

Acculturation is the process of cultural and psychological changes that takes place as a result of contact between cultural groups and their individual members (Redfield, Linton, & Herskovits, 1936). Such contact and change usually occur during colonization, military invasion, migration, and sojourning (i.e., tourism, international study, and overseas posting). This is the process that continues after the initial contact in societies where ethnocultural communities maintain features of their heritage cultures. Over time, groups and individuals from both sides make various adaptations in order to live in the culture-contact settings. This process can occasionally be stressful, but it often results in some form of mutual accommodation that both parties have created in order to live together in relative harmony. Following an initial period of working with colonized peoples, recent acculturation research has focused on how immigrants (both voluntary and involuntary) changed following their entry and settlement into receiving societies. Most recently, research has examined how ethnocultural groups and individuals relate to each other and change as a result of their attempts to live together in culturally plural societies (see Sam & Berry, 2006 for an overview of this literature). Nowadays, as globalization results in the growth of trade and the need for political relations, all peoples in contact play important roles in facilitating this development: Indigenous national populations are experiencing a form of neo-colonization as new waves of immigrants, sojourners (especially guest workers), and refugees gather to establish large ethnocultural populations in these countries.

Graves (1967) introduced the concept of psychological acculturation, which refers to a participant in a culture-contact situation who undergoes changes induced by both the external (usually dominant) culture and the changing culture (usually nondominant) of which the individual is a member. There are two reasons for keeping the cultural and psychological levels distinct. The first is that from a cross-cultural psychology perspective, individual human behavior interacts with the cultural context within which it occurs; hence separate conceptions and measurements are required at the two levels (Berry, Poortinga, Breugelmans, Chasiotis, & Sam, 2011). The second reason is that not every individual enters into, participates in, or changes in the same way during their acculturation; there are vast individual differences in psychological acculturation, even among individuals who have the same cultural origin and live in the same acculturative arena (Sam & Berry, 2006).

The concept of *adaptation* is used to refer to *how well* immigrants engage in their new lives. Not all immigrants adapt equally well in their new societies. A distinction has been made between *psychological* and *sociocultural* adaptation (Ward, 1996). Psychological adaptation refers to personal qualities of well-being including self-esteem, life satisfaction, and the absence of psychological symptoms (i.e., depression and anxiety). Sociocultural adaptation refers to qualities of relationships between the acculturating individuals and their social contexts; these include knowledge of life skills, achievements in the school or work environments, and the lack of behavioral problem in the community (i.e., truancy, addictions, and antisocial behaviors). In this chapter, we examine both the psychological and sociocultural adaptation of immigrant adolescents.

Acculturation Framework

This framework provides a map that outlines and links cultural and psychological acculturation as well as identifies the two (or more) groups in contact (Berry, 2003). These are some of the factors that need to be conceptualized and measured in acculturation research (see Figure 12.1). At the cultural level (on the left), we need to understand the key features of the two original cultural groups prior to their major contact and the pre-contact variations among the groups that are now attempting to live together following migration. Migrants bring cultural and psychological qualities with them to a new society that already has its own preexisting standards. The compatibility (or incompatibility) in religion, values, attitudes, personality, and other characteristics between the two cultural communities in contact needs to be examined as a basis for understanding the acculturation process that is set in motion. It is also important to understand the nature of their contact relationships; it may be the domination of one group over the other or an attitude of mutual respect or hostility.

At the cultural level, we need to understand the resulting cultural changes in both groups that emerge during the process of acculturation. Acculturation is a two-way interaction, resulting in actions and reactions to the contact situation that affect all cultural parties involved (Horenczyk, Jasinskaja-Lahti, Sam, & Vedder, 2013). In many cases, most change takes

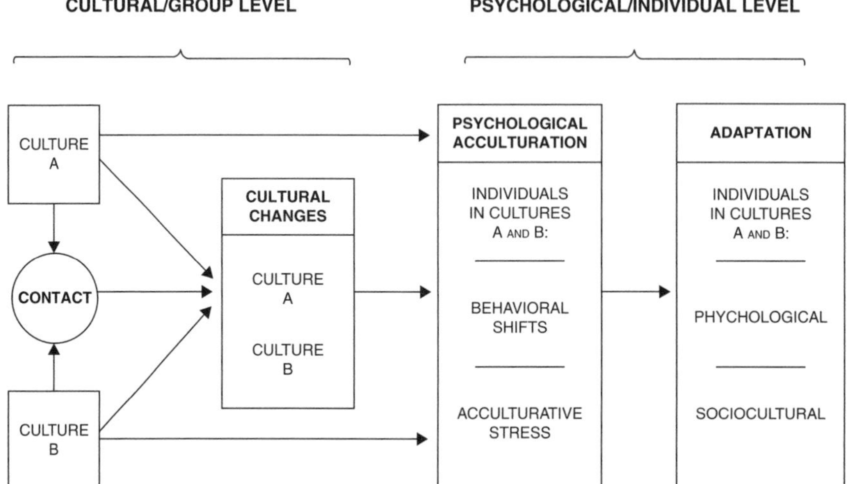

Figure 12.1 General Acculturation Framework

place in nondominant communities; however, all societies of settlement (particularly their metropolitan cities) experience massive transformations following years of receiving migrants. These changes can be minor or substantial, ranging from being easily accomplished to being a source of major cultural disruption. Gathering this information would require extensive ethnographic, community-level work.

At the individual level, we need to consider the psychological changes that individuals in all groups undergo and their eventual adaptation to their new situations. Identifying these changes requires sampling a population and studying individuals who are variably involved in the process of acculturation. The changes can be a set of rather easily accomplished behavioral shifts (e.g., in ways of speaking, dressing, and eating) or they can be more problematic, producing acculturative stress (Berry, 1976; Berry, Kim, Minde, & Mok, 1987) as manifested by uncertainty, anxiety, and depression. This approach has been reviewed by Berry (2006) and remains one of the main methods of understanding the challenges and coping responses in immigrant populations.

In the past few years, the concept of acculturation has been extended, refined, and scrutinized. In particular, the limitation of the concept to only *two* groups has been criticized as too simplistic: In most plural societies, ethnocultural groups engage in multiple intercultural interactions and are not limited to just those with the larger society. Berry and Sabatier (2010, 2011), for instance, showed that immigrant youth in Montreal were able to engage with two cultural groups in the larger society (e.g., the French- and

English-speaking Canadians). The issue of interest was not which group they engaged more (French or English) but the extent to which they wished to engage members of either cultural community that differed from their own.

Social constructivists have also criticized the field as being overly positivistic with too little regard for understanding the lived experiences of acculturating people (Chirkov, 2009). On the extreme end, they attribute the phenomena of acculturation as being largely constructed by the researcher. In a response to this critique, Berry (2009) advocated for a dual approach, one that accepts both the natural sciences' and the cultural sciences' ways of advancing our knowledge of human behavior in context as valid methodologies. He argued that dismissing the positivist traditions of the natural sciences and replacing them with social constructionist concepts and methods constitutes a regressive step in the search to improve our understanding of acculturation.

Acculturation Strategies

When we refer to *how* immigrant youth acculturate, we are addressing the fact that not all immigrants acculturate in the same way. Using the concept of *acculturation strategies,* we explore variations in preferences and behaviors among acculturating individuals by using the concepts of *assimilation, integration, marginalization,* and *separation* for immigrant youth. To explicate these terms, Figure 12.2 displays them within two parallel

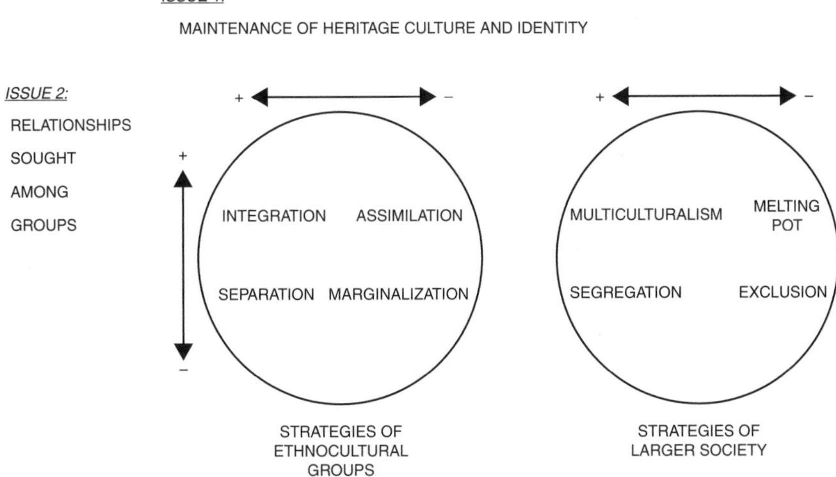

Figure 12.2 Four Acculturation Strategies in Ethnocultural Groups and Four Acculturation Expectations in the Larger Society

acculturation spaces; on the left are the acculturation strategies of nondominant groups (e.g., immigrants and ethnocultural groups), and on the right are the acculturation expectations held by the larger national society.

Early research assumed that acculturating individuals would orient themselves either to one group or to the other, in a sense of choosing between them. This perspective aligned acculturating individuals on a single dimension with preferring one's heritage culture on one end to desiring the society of settlement on the other (e.g., Gordon, 1964). However, Berry (1974, 1980) proposed an alternative, two-dimensional model that has been validated in a number of later studies (e.g., Ryder, Alden, & Paulhus, 2000). In this view, Berry proposed that everyone experiencing acculturation holds attitudes toward two distinct and fundamental aspects of acculturation: *cultural maintenance* and *intercultural contact.* For each issue, a dimension is shown, with a positive orientation at one end and a negative one at the other. In addition to these two basic dimensions, Berry (1980) included a third dimension: the power of groups to decide which way they preferred to acculturate. Hence, the strategies shown in the two circles interact with each other because the preferences of the larger society may constrain or promote possible choices in ethnocultural groups.

Among immigrants (on the left of the figure), *acculturation strategies* are based on the intersection of these two issues: to what extent do immigrants or other nondominant groups wish to maintain (or give up) their cultural attributes, and to what extent do they wish to have contact with (or avoid) others outside their group. When examined among the population at large (e.g., the dominant or national group on the right), views about how immigrants and other nondominant ethnocultural groups should acculturate have been termed *acculturation expectations* (Berry, 2003). Thus, for members of the nondominant immigrant ethnocultural group, the main question is, "How shall *we* deal with these two issues?" while for the larger national society the question is, "How should *they* (e.g., immigrants and ethnocultural groups) deal with them?"

These two issues define an acculturation space (the circles) within which individuals occupy a preferred attitudinal position. Each sector of the circles in Figure 12.2 carries a name that has a long-standing usage in acculturation studies. From the ethnocultural groups' point of view (on the left), the *assimilation* attitude describes individuals who do not wish to maintain their cultural heritage and seek daily participation with other cultures in the larger society. In contrast, the *separation* alternative is used to define ethnocultural group members who value holding on to their original culture and, at the same time, wish to avoid interaction with others. When there is an interest in both maintaining one's original culture and interacting with other groups, this is referred to as *integration*. Here, individuals maintain a degree of cultural integrity while at the same time seeking to participate as an integral part of the larger society. Finally, marginalization refers to persons who perceive little possibility or indicate no interest in cultural maintenance (often for reasons of enforced cultural loss) and little interest in having relations with other groups (often for reasons of discrimination).

The right side of Figure 12.2 uses the concept of *acculturation expectations* held by the larger society (Berry, 2003). Assimilation, when sought by the dominant group, is termed the *melting pot.* When separation is enforced by the dominant group, it is called *segregation.* Marginalization, when imposed by the dominant group, is *exclusion.* Finally, for integration, when diversity is a widely accepted feature of the society as a whole, including all the various ethnocultural groups, it is called *multiculturalism.*

Social Contexts for the Settlement, Acculturation, and Adaptation of Migrant Families and Their Children

This section is divided into three subsections dealing with institutions (e.g., health care centers and schools), families, and the wider community for children's well-being and development. In regards to the institutions, we mainly focus on issues of access and the quality of the service that they deliver. The family is considered from the perspective of family structure and family functioning. The wider society is analyzed through discrimination and exclusion imposed on children through adults and peers.

Educational and Health Care Institutions

Some Preliminary Remarks. International comparative studies on academic achievements yield the general impression that immigrant children perform worse than their national contemporaries (Alba, Sloan, & Sperling, 2011; OECD, 2006) although there are some exceptions to this generalization (see the chapter on Chinese-American immigrants by Ho & Gielen, chapter 13, in this volume). With respect to academic achievement, we know that the human capital (e.g., skills, knowledge, social networks) is available in a family before immigration does play an important and continuing role in the new country of settlement (Dustmann, Frattini, & Lanzara, 2012). When it comes to other aspects of adaptation such as physical health and problematic behavior, children who recently immigrated to industrialized Western countries start off with less respiratory problems and with less antisocial behavior, although they may be bothered by more worries and anxiety (Jackson, Kiernan, & McLanahan, 2012). Such findings are interesting but are not our primary concern here; we are more interested in whether immigration and the initiating acculturation makes a difference in adaptation outcomes and their development. The observations that respiratory problems are less prevalent in immigrant children may have a genetic basis or be related to breathing in cleaner air in their region of origin. Notwithstanding the possibility that not all adaptation characteristics of immigrants can be explained in reference to immigration and acculturation related phenomena, we focus here on issues of access to institutions in the societies of settlement that are meant to promote health, well-being, and the development of cognitive resources.

Since emigration is an ongoing process, educational and health care institutions will always be challenged by the fact that immigrant children and families may not be knowledgeable or simply have no access to these institutions due to their status and limited rights in the country of residence. Moreover, Crosnoe and Fuligni (2012) commented that in the Western world, transnationalism of immigrants allows country hopping between the country of settlement and the region of origin. As a result, aside from the influx of new immigrants, earlier immigrants may renew their immigration, thus continuing to form a group of newcomers that challenges the institutions.

Access and Accessibility. There seems to be one group for which the situation is quite straightforward: undocumented immigrants. Most wealthy countries perceive undocumented immigrants as bringers of sickness and other misery (Gordon, 1983). Yet, they may or may not be fully eligible to access the institutions that can prevent or cure such sickness and misery (De Genova, 2013; Mendoza, 2009). Instead these undocumented immigrants are excluded, a consequence that causes further damage to their health and well-being (Bean, Leach, Brown, Bachmeier, & Hipp, 2011; Tankimovich, 2013). As for the exclusion of uninvolved citizens who feel threatened, fear of threat is bad for the fearing as well (Kunst, Sam, & Ulleberg, 2013).

The picture for the documented immigrants is less clear. Specifically addressing the educational and occupational achievement of immigrant children in the United States, Portes and Fernández-Kelly (2008) summarize it with the help of a telling title: "No margin for error." This title expresses that not all is bad and worrisome, but there is need and opportunity for efforts toward the improvement of the situation. They mention immigrants' human capital, the reception of immigrants in the United States, and the composition of the families as major factors that affect how children fare in the new society. Here we will consider the human capital as well as the immigrants' reception. The family composition or structure will be elaborated in the next subsection.

Human Capital and Reception. The concept of human capital refers to the skills, knowledge, and social networks possessed by persons and their primary socializers. Frequently, parental education is used as a proxy (e.g., Baum & Flores, 2011). As stated before, differences in human capital that already existed before the families' immigration, to a large extent, are carried forward in immigrant adolescents' performance in school and in the labor market. These differences explain why immigrant students who came with their parents from certain Asian and African countries perform academically well, whereas their peers from Latin America and the Caribbean perform less well (Pong & Landale, 2012). A comparable situation with the same explanation can be found in European studies (e.g., Dustmann et al., 2012). According to Baum and Flores (2011), the human capital in the country remains stable because immigrant families are insufficiently capable to accumulate more human capital on their own, and the new society does not provide them with the support that they would need to do so. Parents do not know how to effectively navigate in the new society. In this context and based on data from OECD-countries, Willms (2003) concluded that children growing up with foreign-born parents run an elevated risk for dropping out from schools and developing problematic behaviors. Parents are not always aware of what they need to do to help their children prepare and behave well in school. Furthermore, most may not have the time to help their children or the financial means to enroll their children in high-quality centers for early childhood education and schools. Their voices are not heard by teachers, for instance, to influence curricular choices that would better suit their children's learning needs to prepare them for further and higher studies and well-paying jobs (Crosnoe, 2013; Karoly & Gonzalez, 2011; Kim, 2009). Alba et al. (2011) even argued that not only are schools not responsive to the voices of what they call low-status immigrants, but schools are influenced by national well-to-do parents who make sure that schools do not accommodate the needs of low-status immigrant children (also see Kim, 2009).

A study conducted in Israel by Leopold and Shavitt (2013) found that even though immigrant and national students scored similarly on a test of reading comprehension, their teachers graded them differently on class reading assignments. They concluded that teachers and schools favor students of whom they assume that their parents' human capital does connect well with the cognitive, linguistic, and social competences required in school. In short, schools and teachers may be biased against immigrant children based on their prejudices about immigrant children's human capital.

We stated previously that some aspects of the development and health of immigrant children are better than those of their national contemporaries, even for those who came from backgrounds with little human capital that can be exploited in the new country of settlement by parents and their children. This phenomenon is referred to as the "immigrant paradox" (Alegria et al., 2008; Crosnoe, 2013; Sam, Vedder, Liebkind, Neto, & Virta, 2008). The relative health and adaptation advantage that they have, however, is short lived: The immigrant children and their parents cannot hold on to this advantage. How this is possible is explained in the theory of segmented assimilation (Portes & Zhou, 1993). Stated simply, the children are highly adaptive to the contexts to which they have access: On average they live in relatively worse neighborhoods with cheaper housing and higher levels of danger, interacting with other neighborhood children who do not fare well in schools. Moreover, they tend to adopt unhealthy eating lifestyles and engage in risk behaviors (Buscemi, Beech, & Relyea, 2011; Portes & Fernández-Kelly, 2008). Referring to the situation of immigrant children in Canada, Beiser, Hou, Hyman, and Tousignant (2002) wrapped it up as follows: Immigrants left their region of origin and arrived in their country of settlement in poverty, but with an aspiration to fare better; however, their reception and the new situations to which they have access, and to which they have to adapt are such that they cannot escape poverty and the many health risks that accompany it.

Portes and Fernández-Kelly (2008) clarified that segmented assimilation does not always refer to problematic situations and outcomes, but rather it depends on the quality of the situation of reception. If immigrants succeed in finding a secure, safe, and healthy place to live and are surrounded by families with ample human capital, they may integrate into the social and economic mainstream. Apart from the impact of the context of reception, immigrant children may experience resources that shelter them from risks and stimulate them toward positive adaptation outcomes. The same scholars found that maintenance of parental authority and strong family discipline may prevent children from mimicking the behavior of others who practice unhealthy living habits. Having significant figures such as teachers, friends, or older siblings may have the same preventative effects. They can model a better perspective in life and offer advice on how to accomplish their goals. Additionally, the availability of and engagement in sponsored and well-organized programs can also serve as another resource. These programs help children acquire various skills and knowledge, encouraging them to spend time out of school in a challenging but safe environment. However, these life-changing resources are not readily available to many. For instance, in a sample of 5,262 early adolescents, Portes and Fernández-Kelly (2008) found that only 50 had access to them; in other words, less than 1% enjoyed and benefitted from such resources.

Family Relationships and Family Functioning

Studies on family relationships may focus on either family structure or family functioning, or both. We will first address changes in family structure and their consequences in an acculturation context and then attend to family functioning.

Bean, Eurelings-Bontekoe, and Spinhoven (2007) discovered that changes in structure play a vital role in the functioning of immigrant children. From a sample of nearly six hundred 11- to 17-year-old refugee youths from Africa and Asia who came to the Netherlands without their parents, half of them had prolonged and serious psychological problems, a finding that was established with the Child Behavior Checklist (CBCL) and the Teacher Report Form (TRF). They also found that the intensity of problems co-varied with the number of their reported traumatic experiences such as war and the loss of friends and kin. Comparable findings were reported by Seglem, Oppedal, and Raeder (2011) who analyzed the mental health of unaccompanied asylum seeker minors in Norway. Pinto-Wiese and Burhorst (2007) compared two groups of children who were referred to a mental health clinic. The first group had 70 African and Asian youth and their parents who had fled their region of origin and had requested asylum in the Netherlands; the other group contained 59 adolescents who had fled the same regions, but without their parents. Almost 80% of the youths in this latter group had lost their parents; some had even witnessed the murder and mutilation of their family members. These samples had been referred to the clinic, and hence it was not surprising that the prevalence of post-traumatic stress disorder and anxiety disorders was high in both groups. The two groups differed in that youth without parents reported more frequent and more prolonged depressive moods and psychoses. These differences can likely be explained by the youth's limited coping opportunities and the absence of parental support in the second group. The differences and the explanation also clarify that changes in family structure may refer to changes in family responsibilities and roles, in that these can no longer be fulfilled.

Reflecting on these studies of asylum-seeking adolescents, it may seem as if trauma is the primary cause of the mental health problems in refugee adolescents and that acculturation, in a sense, is the consequence, not the cause of traumatic experiences. However, it is important to realize that for refugees, trauma and acculturation are closely linked. In many cases, acculturation did not begin when emigration started but rather, it started in the war-struck region where they lived. Often the violence experienced is embedded in the conflicts between different ethnic or religious groups that live in the region. Refugees from these regions were involved in violent acculturation conflicts that made them flee, and such flight caused them to experience grave culture loss. The consequences are seriously and continuously manifested in the new country of settlement.

Suárez-Orozco, Bang, and Kim (2011) present evidence that the processes and adaptation consequences described for refugee youth are also found in immigrant youth who lived separately from one or both parents as a result of their parents having decided to emigrate first, functioning as trailblazers. Children and parents may then reunite after one or several years. Their study showed that the level of depressive symptoms reported by children increased with longer separation.

Euser, Van IJzendoorn, Prinzie, and Bakermans-Kranenburg (2011)'s study on immigrant family functioning found that parents' aggression toward children is more prevalent in low SES families that fled from regions in which they suffered from economic hardship or violence. The stress related to emigration, economic hardship, physical and mental suffering, and possibly the loss of kin or good friends may express itself by way of thwarting the parental competence to provide a loving and caring home situation for the children. If others do not provide the necessary support, the parents may live in uncertainty about a stable and healthy future for themselves and their children for a long time.

Family functioning and family structure are not only under pressure in families in which parents and children are separated temporarily or forever. Mesman, Van IJzendoorn, and Bakermans-Kranenburg (2012) reviewed research on the importance of parental sensitivity to children's educational and developmental needs as well as their ability to provide warmth and security for their children's well-being and healthy development. They concluded that parental sensitivity is important in all families regardless of ethnicity. However, there is a dependency on acculturation. Both the process of migration and the eventual minority position in terms of resources or problems encountered in the new country of settlement explained parental stress which, in turn, was related to parents' sensitivity. As a result of their minority position, these families frequently work long days to make sure there is sufficient family income (Bacallao & Smokowski, 2007; Dyson, Qi, & Wang, 2013). As such, they have little opportunity to look after their children and interact in a sensitive way with them.

A final strand of research to be reviewed in this subsection relates to the quality of family relationships and family functioning. It is about the so-called acculturation gap-distress model and intergenerational value discrepancies. Archambault, Janosz, Fallu, and Pagani (2009) showed that conflicts between parents and children or stress in children due to relational problems at home contribute to students' disengagement and problematic behavior in school. The acculturation gap-distress model, however, is not about any conflict between adolescents and their parents. It specifically refers to the differences and tensions between parents and their children with respect to the orientation toward or appreciation of their own ethnic group and culture as well as the orientation to the dominant group and its culture in the country of residence. Most studies on the acculturation gap show that parents are usually more oriented toward the ethnic culture than their children are and that children tend to accommodate more toward the new society of settlement (Telzer, 2010; Vedder, Berry, Sabatier, & Sam,

2009). The acculturation gap is typically studied in immigrant families and not in national families.

Intergenerational value discrepancies are typical of growing up in all families, which help the children to develop autonomy and create a life of their own. Studies that focus on value discrepancies in acculturating families (Kwak, 2003; Phinney, Kim-Jo, Osorio, & Vilhjalmsdottir, 2005; Vedder & Oortwijn, 2009) predominantly focus on the responsibilities or obligations that children have with respect to other family members, particularly the parents. These issues involve the children's rights to unsupervised time spent in building relationships or particularly starting those with intimate characteristics.

Studies on the acculturation gap-distress model are inconclusive as to whether it has negative, positive, or no consequences for children's well-being, although researchers do agree that such gaps may lead to some conflicts between parents and their offspring (Glick, 2010; Phinney & Vedder, 2006; Telzer, 2010). It may be that such conflicts actually are "acceptable disagreements" that, as suggested by Steinberg (1990), may be considered part of normal developmental processes. Reviewing research on the acculturation gap-distress model that, in a sense, repeats and underlines Steinberg's conclusion, Telzer (2010) clarified that most studies focus on intergenerational differences with respect to the host culture and that immigrant youth commonly have stronger preferences and better knowledge of the host culture than their parents. She labeled these differences as "benign," expected, and hence normative. In her review, she concluded that studies in which parents and children do not agree about the value of their ethnic culture and the retention of corresponding practices and customs reveal more family dysfunctions and problematic behaviors in children. Because the situation in which parents hold stronger preferences for the host culture than their children is also unexpected, this type of difference might also lead to family conflicts and behavioral problems of the children. In Telzer's view, the crucial issue is whether or not the differences are expected by the parents, adolescents, and children involved. When differences are not expected, they will probably be accompanied by conflicts. Costigan and Dokis (2006) suggest an alternative though related explanation; they comment that scholars should distinguish acculturation issues that are related to school, work, or everyday contacts from those that are more emotional and personally significant like intimate relationships. In their study they hardly found any differences between parents and children regarding common matters, whereas the differences concerning the so-called private issues were large. Studies investigating such discrepancies confirmed a link with adolescents' problem behaviors such as substance use, violence, and depression (Lorenzo-Blanco, Unger, Baezconde-Garbanati, Ritt-Olson, & Soto, 2012; Unger, Ritt-Olson,

Wagner, Soto, & Baezconde-Garbanati, 2009; Vedder & Oortwijn, 2009). In short, when immigrant parents and children do not agree on the relevance and importance of values, customs, rules, and practices that really matter to them in the acculturation context, there will likely be conflicts, family dysfunction, and negative adaptation outcomes in the children.

Discrimination

Discrimination is an intricate and intrusive experience for immigrants. For them, it primarily refers to the quality of the context of reception. Earlier we mentioned discrimination in terms of limited access to institutional and personal resources that would be conducive to immigrants' health, well-being, and social participation and in terms of biased teacher evaluations that would make immigrant students' school life unnecessarily difficult. In the international study of immigrant youth done by Berry et al. (2006), discrimination was seen as the single most important factor that explained the psychological and sociocultural adaptation of immigrant youth. Reviews on discrimination and health and adaptation outcomes all have a simple message: Discrimination is an experience that is bad for health, mental well-being, and social adjustment (Paradies, 2006; Priest et al., 2013; Vedder & Van Geel, 2012). Here we deal with two questions: (a) Is it personal or is it contextual? And (b) Does discrimination refer to evaluations based on seemingly irrelevant characteristics; what are these characteristics and are they really irrelevant?

Personal or Contextual. Most studies on discrimination do not allow for conclusions about the direction of influence or whether there is any influence at all. They state that persons who report discrimination also report more health problems, lower levels of well-being, and more worrying qualities of social adjustment (Priest et al., 2013). It could well be that immigrants who experience suboptimal health, low well-being, and alienation from desirable forms of social participation blame this on the society and label this "discrimination." Most studies offer this as a plausible option because they use measures of perceived, self-reported discrimination. This, however, does not make discrimination a less important issue. Discrimination as a contextual process and as a personal illusion is both bad for persons experiencing it. To clarify the negative impact of discrimination as a personal illusion, we refer to the work of Portes and Zhou (1993) and Ogbu and Simons (1998), who analyzed the position of members of subversive youth cultures. Groups sharing such a youth culture often are mono-ethnic. Experiences of discrimination and ruminating about them with peers may strengthen bonds with one's own group (Branscombe, Schmitt, & Harvey, 1999). These youths may or may not have experienced a bad reception, but whatever their actual experience has been, they agree that they did not receive a fair chance of success in their new society of settlement regardless of how much effort and other resources they used and still use to earn that chance. They attribute this to exclusion and discrimination by the national majority and label, for instance, attending and being involved in school a "white thing." The consequences of such an attitude are problematic in school and career settings. They can lead to higher chances of dropping out or engaging in criminal activities.

An important qualification is needed here: Many immigrant youth with a strong ethnic identity have many national friends and positive attitudes toward the society of settlement and its institutions (Marks et al., 2007).

In any case, the confusion about the source of discrimination (contextual or personal) does not make everything obsolete that hitherto was said about the negative consequences of a bad reception and treatment of immigrants. Studies that allow conclusions to be drawn about the direction and influence of discrimination may be scant, but they do support the conclusion that discrimination precedes and leads to poor health and adaptation outcomes (Priest et al., 2013).

Discrimination and Justified or Unjustified Distinctions between Persons. Stevens (2007) and Stevens, Clycq, Timmerman, and Van Houtte (2011) analyzed educational inequality, respectively, in Great Britain and the Netherlands, concluding that the less successful school careers of many immigrant children can be explained by the lower national language proficiency of these children. Dustmann and colleagues (2012) contend that in OECD (Organization for Economic Co-operation and Development) countries, the problematic educational position of immigrant children is best explained by the fact that many immigrant children at home speak their native ethnic language that is different from the national language used in school. Dustmann et al. suggest that the frequent use of the ethnic language is indicative of a limited availability of or access to important cognitive and linguistic resources in the family. Nevertheless, language proficiency is frequently mentioned as the reason for immigrant children's relatively weak school performance. Stevens and colleagues explicitly state that language proficiency is a quality of immigrant students that is relevant for a broad range of, if not all, school subjects. The students simply do not satisfy the requirements formulated by curriculum planners and teachers. These criteria are used for all students irrespective of their ethnic background, and hence using language proficiency to distinguish groups of students or individual students is not considered an act of discrimination. It is remarkable that Stevens and colleagues do not define the lack of fit between student proficiency and curricular requirements as an educational challenge or even as an educational responsibility. To shed further doubt on the justification of their conclusion, we turn now to studies on peer acceptance and victimization. Before doing so, however, it is important to qualify the role of ethnic language use. Frequently using the ethnic language in the immigration context may be indicative of lacking adaptive competences of many immigrant families, but even so, other families may find ways to compensate for these limitations. They may, like many Asian families in the United States now, use other resources like demanding educational strategies, creating a climate of unquestionable and relentless effort and stamina in their offspring (Zhou, 2009; see also chapter 13).

Studies have repeatedly demonstrated that in schools, both immigrant students (Kao & Vaquera, 2006; Titzmann, Silbereisen, & Schmitt-Rodermund, 2007) and national students (Kao & Joyner, 2004; Baerveldt, Zijlstra, De Wolf, Van Rossem, & Van Duijn, 2007) show a preference for intraethnic friendships. Referring to kindergartners in Switzerland, Von Grünigen, Perren, Nägele, and Alsaker (2010) found that such a preference raises the risk of victimization due to an absent or dwindling circle of friendly peers who can have a protective or sheltering function. The negative consequences of the lack of sheltering friends can be severe, sometimes even lethal (Van Geel, Tanilon, & Vedder, 2014). Von Grünigen and colleagues (2010) studied the criteria used by children for excluding or rejecting other children and found that acceptance of other children co-varied with children's proficiency in the dominant local language: lower proficiency meant lower acceptance. This statement held true for immigrant children as well as national children. Immigrant children, however, were at additional risk because they or their parents were not born in Switzerland. One may ask here whether the researchers who explained that immigrant students' educational position is largely determined by language proficiency would also suggest that kindergartners are not actually discriminating as long as they base their rejection of immigrant peers on a "relevant" characteristic like proficiency in the local language.

In educational settings, the educational task and responsibility in democratic countries is to optimize children's developmental chances, so that their human capital increases and societies have strong resources to warrant health, well-being, and prosperity for all its members. Arguing about whether or not certain characteristics can be justified as discrimination seems improper from an educational perspective if the consequences conflict with the aforementioned goal.

GENERAL PRINCIPLES AND EDUCATIONAL POLICIES

We have presented a variety of rules or principles that we will summarize here and consider possible policy implications. The first principle may appear to conflict with the notion that general principles can feed into policies for settlement and education. There are vast individual differences in acculturation strategies and in the psychological and sociocultural adaptation of immigrant youth, even when they belong to the same ethnocultural groups and grow up in a comparable situation of reception. However, the general finding from a meta-analysis (Nguyen & Benet-Martínez, 2013) concludes that those who pursue the integration acculturation strategy ("bi-cultural," in their terms) achieve more positive adaptations. Personal characteristics, personal histories, personal emotions, and meaning-making activities as well as access to support and other resources from kin and the own community have an impact on the acculturation and adaptation processes and outcomes. Despite this general finding, individual experiences in particular acculturation contexts may require very specific attention to each individual case. This has an important implication, which, supposedly paraphrasing Abraham Lincoln, is: "A particular policy might work for all immigrants some of the time, and it might work for some immigrants all of the time, but no policy will work for all immigrants all of the time." This statement suggests that general policies may be important, but their value is determined by implementation efforts that take the needs for context and person-specific adaptations into consideration.

Research has repeatedly shown that acculturation requires adaptation and learning efforts by immigrants who need the support from their own ethnocultural community as well as the larger society. This kind of support is likely to come without complaints from those who offer it, provided that the climate of reception stays positive and optimistic and that giving help is respected by others and appreciated by the immigrants. Conducive to such a constructive, optimistic attitude is to draw repeated attention to the notion that while acculturation and support of acculturating persons may occasionally be stressful, it nevertheless tends to result in some form of mutual accommodation and comes with positive adaptation outcomes for the immigrants.

In this process, undocumented immigrants run a high risk of experiencing undesirable and disappointing outcomes. More than other immigrants, they experience isolation and exclusion that are detrimental to their health and well-being. These exclusionary practices have a basis in incorrect views on what immigrants come to do in their new country of settlement, together with a fear of unknown customs, of high financial costs for the receiving community, or a combination of the two. We have pointed out that such erroneous views and fears are not only harmful to the immigrants but also to those who hold such views and fears. Politicians and proponents of the maintenance of the national culture would be well advised to make sure that they avoid representing immigrants and their acculturation in writing, speech, and pictures in ways that induce incorrect views and fear in the national community. Those who seek to thrive by using wrong representations and by inducing fear should be informed time and again of the living conditions, wealth, and health of immigrants as well as being aware of their own fears.

Exclusion and the propagation of a divide between cultural groups in society create an environment that tolerates discrimination, and such discrimination has grave consequences for immigrants' mental and physical health (Berry & Sam, 2013). It is important to stop discrimination.

For professionals in institutions that cater to the educational needs and well-being of immigrants and their offspring, it is important to realize that as long as the current countries of reception remain wealthier and safer than countries of origin, immigration will continue. In this situation, educational and health care institutions will always be challenged by children and families who are not knowledgeable about these institutions. Thinking about solutions and ensuring that immigrants have access and are supported and successful in their efforts to find the help they need is not just a temporary challenge, but a long-term one. Such efforts are not wasted because they take shape in new expertise, attitudes, and tools that may need some adaptation under new circumstances, but continue to be useful for generations to come.

Time and again studies have clarified that it is important for immigrants to feel that they may hold on to their ethnic culture, provided they also constructively take part in the tasks that have to be accomplished and that are needed for sustaining the health and welfare of the new country in which they live. This integrative strategy is particularly important in the family context. For instance, learning the national language takes time. It is not realistic to expect parents to use the national language for family interactions. It is important during all stages of children's development that parents can fully engage in their lives and that they can clearly and fluently express their thoughts as well as their feelings. Additionally, it is important that parents and children alike learn to use the new national language. This is important for their opportunities for social participation but also for their personal development and health. Growing up multilingual is an educational program that comes nearly free and is an important resource for international contacts and mental health (Ramírez-Esparza & García-Sierra, 2014). Moreover, in addition to language, the maintenance of other cultural ethnic components and a wish to interact with members and institutions of the society of settlement are the ingredients of the acculturation strategy labeled integration. Many studies have shown that in Western democratic societies, this strategy is predictive of positive adaptation outcomes. Also akin to the notion of culture maintenance is what we pointed out in the subsection on human capital and reception about parental authority and strong family discipline. These make it less likely that children come under the influence of other children and adults who model behavior likely to interfere with their social adjustment and health. Instead they preferably meet friends and adults who function as models of healthy behavior and show them challenging perspectives in life and how to best realize them.

ACKNOWLEDGMENT

Work on this chapter by John Berry was prepared within the framework of the Basic Research Program at the National Research University Higher School of Economics (HSE), and supported within the framework of a subsidy granted to the HSE by the Government of the Russian Federation for the implementation of the Global Competitiveness Program.

REFLECTIVE QUESTIONS

This chapter has highlighted the situation in which immigrant children are required to make sense of the two (or sometimes more) cultural worlds in which they live. We have proposed that it is now possible to establish some generalizations that are rooted in adequate conceptual clarity and enough research-based evidence to implement some general practices that will assist immigrant children in meeting this challenge, and in improving their psychological, social and educational outcomes.

1. In your view, what is the validity of these assertions, with respect to:
   a) Their conceptual adequacy,
   b) Their empirical basis, and
   c) The practical proposals?
2. Would you suggest alternatives for, or qualifications of, the generalizations presented? Clarify and give some examples.

SUGGESTED READINGS

Books and Articles

Alba, R., & Waters, M. (Eds.). (2011). *The next generation; Immigrant youth in a comparative perspective.* New York: New York University Press

Berry, J. W., Phinney, J. S, Sam, D. L. &Vedder, P. (Eds.). (2006). *Immigrant youth in cultural transition: Acculturation, identity and adaptation across national contexts.* Mahwah, NJ: Erlbaum.

Bornstein, M. H., & Cote, L. R. (Eds.). (2006). *Acculturation and parent-child relationships: Measurement and development.* Mahwah, NJ: Erlbaum.

Sam, D. L., & Berry, J. W. (Eds.). (2006/2015). *Cambridge handbook of acculturation psychology*. Cambridge, UK: Cambridge University Press.

Websites

Future of Children translates social science research about children and youth into information that is useful to policy makers, practitioners, the media, and students. It is not just about immigrant children, but its site regularly also publishes about the education and development of immigrant children. You can find its site at: http://www.princeton.edu/futureofchildren/index.xml

The Organisation of Economic Cooperation and Development's website hosts an abundance of information on immigration, immigrants, and their well-being. Visit, for instance, http://www.oecd.org/general/searchresults/?q=immigrants&cx=012432601748511391518:xzeadub0b0a&cof=FORID:11&ie=UTF-8

Urban Institute researchers study and report on gender inequalities, racial segregation, and the disparities these cause in education, housing, employment, income, and health care. Their site can be found at: http://www.urban.org/race/index.cfm

REFERENCES

Alba, R., Sloan, J., & Sperling, J. (2011). The integration imperative: The children of low-status immigrants in the schools of wealthy societies. *Annual Review of Sociology, 37*, 395–415.

Alegria, M., Canino, G., Shrout, P. E., Woo, M., Duan, N., Vila, D., Torres, M., Chen, C., & Meng, X-L. (2008). Prevalence of mental illness in immigrant and non-immigrant U.S. Latino groups. *American Journal of Psychiatry, 165*, 359–369.

Archambault, I., Janosz, M., Fallu, J-S., & Pagani, L. S. (2009). Student engagement and its relationship with early high school dropout. *Journal of Adolescence, 32*, 651–670.

Bacallao, M. L., & Smokowski, P. R. (2007). The costs of getting ahead: Mexican family systems after immigration. *Family Relations, 56*, 52–66.

Baerveldt, C., Zijlstra, B., De Wolf, M., Van Rossem, R., & Van Duijn, M. A. (2007). Ethnic boundaries in high school students' networks in Flanders and the Netherlands. *International Sociology, 22*, 701–720.

Baum, S., & Flores, S. M. (2011). Higher education and children in immigrant families. *The Future of Children, 21*, 171–193.

Bean, F., Leach, M. A., Brown, S. K., Bachmeier, J. D., & Hipp, R. (2011). The educational legacy of unauthorized migration: Comparisons across U.S.-immigrant groups in how parents' status affects their offspring. *International Migration Review, 45*, 348–385.

Bean, T., Eurelings-Bontekoe, L., & Spinhoven, P. (2007). Course and predictors of mental health of unaccompanied refugee minors in the Netherlands: One year follow-up. *Social Science & Medicine, 64*, 1204–1215.

Beiser, M., Hou, F., Hyman, I., & Tousignant, M. (2002). Poverty, family process, and the mental health of immigrant children in Canada. *American Journal of Public Health, 92*, 220–227.

Berry, J. W. (1974). Psychological aspects of cultural pluralism: Unity and identity reconsidered. *Topics in Culture Learning, 2*, 17–22.

Berry, J. W. (1976). *Human ecology and cognitive style: Comparative studies in cultural and psychological adaptation*. New York: Sage/Halsted.

Berry, J. W. (1980). Acculturation as varieties of adaptation. In A. Padilla (Ed.), *Acculturation: Theory, models and findings* (pp. 9–25). Boulder, CO: Westview.

Berry, J. W. (1997). Immigration, acculturation and adaptation. *Applied Psychology: An International Review, 46*, 5–68.

Berry, J. W. (2003). Conceptual approaches to acculturation. In K. Chun, P. Balls-Organista, & G. Marin (Eds.), *Acculturation* (pp. 3–37). Washington, DC: APA Press.

Berry, J. W. (2006). Stress perspectives on acculturation. In D. L. Sam & J. W. Berry (Eds.), *The Cambridge handbook of acculturation psychology* (pp. 43–57). Cambridge, UK: Cambridge University Press.

Berry, J. W. (2009). A critique of critical acculturation. *International Journal of Intercultural Relations, 33*, 361–371.

Berry, J. W., Kim, U., Minde, T., & Mok, D. (1987). Comparative studies of acculturative stress. *International Migration Review, 21*, 491–511.

Berry, J. W., Phinney, J. S., Sam, D. L., & Vedder, P. (Eds.). (2006). *Immigrant youth in cultural transition: Acculturation, identity and adaptation across nations*. Mahwah, NJ: Erlbaum.

Berry, J. W., Poortinga, Y. H., Brugelmans, S., Chasiotis, A., & Sam, D. L. (2011). *Cross-cultural psychology: Research and applications.* Cambridge, UK: Cambridge University Press.

Berry, J. W., & Sabatier, C. (2010). Acculturation, discrimination, and adaptation among second generation immigrant youth in Montreal and Paris. *International Journal of Intercultural Relations, 34*, 191–207.

Berry, J. W., & Sabatier, C. (2011). Variations in the assessment of acculturation attitudes: Their relationships with psychological wellbeing. *International Journal of Intercultural Relations, 35*, 658–669.

Berry, J. W., & Sam, D. L. (2013). Accommodating cultural diversity and achieving equity: An introduction to psychological dimensions of multiculturalism. *European Psychologist, 18*, 151–157.

Bornstein, M. H., & Cote, L. R. (Eds.). (2006). *Acculturation and parent-child relationships: Measurement and development.* Mahwah, NJ: Erlbaum.

Branscombe, N. R., Schmitt, M. T., & Harvey, R. D. (1999). Perceiving pervasive discrimination among African Americans: Implications for group identification and well-being. *Journal of Personality and Social Psychology, 77*, 135–149.

Buscemi, J., Beech, B. M., & Relyea, G. (2011). Predictors of obesity in Latino children: Acculturation as a moderator of the relationship between food insecurity and body mass index percentile. *Journal of Immigrant Minority Health, 13*, 149–154.

Chirkov, V. (2009). Introduction to the special issue on critical acculturation psychology. *International Journal of Intercultural Relations, 3*, 87–93.

Chuang, S., & Moreno, R. (Eds.). (2011). *Immigrant children: Change, adaptation, and cultural transformation*. Lanham, MD: Lexington.

Costigan, C., & Dokis, D. (2006). Similarities and differences in acculturation among mothers, fathers, and children in immigrant Chinese families. *Journal of Cross-Cultural Psychology, 37*, 723–741.

Crosnoe, R. (2013). *Preparing the children of immigrants for early academic success.* Washington, DC: Migration Policy Institute.

Crosnoe, R., & Fuligni, A. (2012). Children from immigrant families. *Child Development, 83*, 1471–1476.

De Genova, N. (2013). Spectacles of migrant "illegality": The scene of exclusion, the obscene of inclusion. *Ethnic and Racial Studies, 36*, 7, 1180–1198.

Dustmann, C., Frattini, T., & Lanzara, G. (2012). Educational achievement of second-generation immigrants; an international comparison. *Economic Policy, 27*(69), 143–185.

Dyson, L., Qi, J., & Wang, M. (2013). At the interface of ethnicity and recent immigration: Family functioning of Chinese with school-age children in Canada. *Journal of Child and Family Studies, 22*, 1061–1073.

Euser, E. M., Van IJzendoorn, M. H., Prinzie, P., & Bakermans-Kranenburg, M. J. (2011). Elevated child maltreatment rates in immigrant families and the role of socioeconomic differences. *Child Maltreatment, 16*, 63–73.

Glick, J. E. (2010). Connecting complex processes: A decade of research on immigrant families acculturation: Parenting and intergenerational relations. *Journal of Marriage and Family, 72*, 498–515.

Gordon, M. M. (1964). *Assimilation in American life. The role of race, religion and national origins.* New York: Oxford University Press.

Gordon, P. (1983). Medicine, racism and immigration control. *Critical Social Policy, 3*, 6–20.

Graves, T. (1967). Psychological acculturation in a tri-ethnic community. *South-Western Journal of Anthropology, 23*, 337–350.

Horenczyk, G., Jasinskaja-Lahti, I., Sam, D. L., & Vedder, P. (2013). Mutuality in acculturation: Towards an integration. *Journal of Psychology/Zeitschrift für Psychologie, 221*, 205–213.

Jackson, M. I., Kiernan, K., & McLanahan, S. (2012). Immigrant–native differences in child health: Does maternal education narrow or widen the gap? *Child Development, 83*, 1501–1509.

Kao, G., & Joyner, K. (2004). Do race and ethnicity matter among friends? Activities among interracial, interethnic, and intra-ethnic adolescent friends. *Sociological Quarterly, 45*, 557–573.

Kao, G., & Vaquera, E. (2006). The salience of racial and ethnic identification in friendship choices among Hispanic adolescents. *Hispanic Journal of Behavioral Sciences, 28*, 23–47.

Karoly, L. A., & Gonzalez, G. C. (2011). Early care and education for children in immigrant families. *The Future of Children, 21*, 71–101.

Kim, Y. (2009). Minority parental involvement and school barriers: Moving the focus away from deficiencies of parents. *Educational Research Review, 4*, 80–102

Kunst, J. R., Sam, D. L., & Ulleberg, P. (2013). Perceived islamophobia: Scale development and validation. *International Journal of Intercultural Relations, 37*, 225–237.

Kwak, K. (2003). Adolescents and their parents: A review of intergenerational family relations for immigrant and non-immigrant families. *Human Development, 46*, 115–136.

Lansford, J., Deater-Deckard, K., & Bornstein, M. H. (Eds.). (2007). *Immigrant families in contemporary society*. New York: Guilford.

Leopold, L., & Shavitt, Y. (2013). Cultural capital does not travel well: Immigrants, natives and achievement in Israeli schools. *European Sociological Review, 29*, 450–463, doi:10.1093/esr/jcr086

Lorenzo-Blanco, E. I., Unger, J. B., Baezconde-Garbanati, L., Ritt-Olson, A., & Soto, D. (2012). Acculturation, enculturation, and symptoms of depression in Hispanic youth: The roles of gender, Hispanic cultural values, and family functioning. *Journal of Youth and Adolescence, 41*, 1350–1365.

Marks, A. K., Szalacha, L. A., Lamarre, M., Boyd, M. J., & García Coll, C. (2007). Emerging ethnic identity and interethnic group social preferences in middle childhood: Findings from the Children of Immigrants Development in Context (CIDC) study. *International Journal of Behavioral Development, 31*, 501–513.

Mendoza, F. S. (2009). Health disparities and children in immigrant families: A research agenda. *Pediatrics, 124*, 187–195.

Mesman, J., Van IJzendoorn, M. H., & Bakermans-Kranenburg, M. J. (2012). Unequal in opportunity, equal in process: Parental sensitivity promotes positive child development in ethnic minority families. *Child Development Perspectives, 6*, 239–250.

Nguyen, A., & Benet-Martínez, V. (2013). Biculturalism and adjustment: A meta-analysis. *Journal of Cross-Cultural Psychology, 44*, 122–159.

OECD (2006). *Where immigrant students succeed: A comparative review of performance and engagement in PISA 2003*. Paris: OECD.

Ogbu, J. U., & Simons, H. D. (1998). Voluntary and involuntary minorities: A cultural ecological theory of school performance with some implications for education. *Anthropology and Education Quarterly, 29*, 155–188.

Paradies, Y. (2006). A systematic review of empirical research on self-reported racism and health. *International Journal of Epidemiology, 35*, 888–901.

Phinney, J., Kim-Jo, T., Osorio, S., & Vilhjalmsdottir, P. (2005). Autonomy and relatedness in adolescent-parent disagreements: Ethnic and developmental factors. *Journal of Adolescent Research, 20*, 8–39.

Phinney, J., & Vedder, P. (2006). Family relationship values of adolescents and parents: Intergenerational discrepancies and adaptation. In J. Berry, J. Phinney, D. Sam., & P. Vedder (Eds.), *Immigrant youth in cultural transition: Acculturation, identity and adaptation across national contexts* (pp. 167–184). Mahwah, NJ: Erlbaum.

Pinto Wiese, E. B., & Burhorst, I. (2007). The mental health of asylum-seeking and refugee children and adolescents attending a clinic in the Netherlands. *Transcultural Psychiatry, 44*, 596–613.

Pong, S.-L., & Landale, N. L. (2012). Academic achievement of legal immigrants' children: The roles of parents' pre- and postmigration characteristics in origin-group differences. *Child Development, 83*, 1543–1559.

Portes, A., & Fernández-Kelly, P. (2008). No margin for error: Educational and occupational achievement among disadvantaged children of immigrants. *Annals of the American Academy of Political and Social Science, 620*, 12–36.

Portes, A., & Zhou, M. (1993). The new second generation: Segmented assimilation and its variants. *Annals of the American Academy of Political and Social Science, 530*, 74–96.

Priest, N. A., Paradies, Y., Trenerry, B., Truong, M., Karlsen, S., & Kelly, Y. (2013). A systematic review of studies examining the relationship between reported racism and health and wellbeing for children and young people. *Social Science & Medicine, 95*, 115–127.

Ramírez-Esparza, N., & García-Sierra, A. (2014). The bilingual brain: Language, culture and identity. In V. Benet-Martínez & Y. Hong (Eds.), *The Oxford handbook of multicultural identity* (pp. 35–56). Oxford, UK: Oxford University Press.

Redfield, R., Linton, R., & Herskovits, M. (1936). Memorandum on the study of acculturation. *American Anthropologist, 38*, 149–152.

Ryder, A. G., Alden, L. E., & Paulhus, D. L. (2000). Is acculturation unidimensional or bidimensional? A head-to-head comparison in the prediction of personality, self-identity, and adjustment. *Journal of Personality and Social Psychology, 79*, 49–65.

Sabatier, C., & Berry, J. W. (2008). The role of family acculturation, parental style and perceived discrimination in the adaptation of second generation immigrant youth in France and Canada. *European Journal of Developmental Psychology, 5*, 159–185.

Sam, D. L., & Berry, J. W. (Eds.). (2006/2015). *Cambridge handbook of acculturation psychology*. Cambridge, UK: Cambridge University Press.

Sam, D., Vedder, P., Liebkind, K., Neto, F., & Virta, E. (2008). Immigration, acculturation and the paradox of adaptation in Europe. *European Journal of Developmental Psychology, 5*, 138–158

Seglem, K.B., Oppedal, B., & Raeder, S. (2011). Predictors of depressive symptoms among resettled unaccompanied refugee minors. *Scandinavian Journal of Psychology, 52*(5), 457–464.

Steinberg, L. (1990). Autonomy, conflict, and harmony in the family relationship. In S.S. Feldman & G. Elliot (Eds.), *At the threshold: The developing adolescent* (pp. 255–276). Cambridge, MA: Harvard University Press.

Stevens, P. (2007). Researching race/ethnicity and educational inequality in English secondary schools: A critical review of the research literature between 1980 and 2005. *Review of Educational Research, 77*, 147–185.

Stevens, P., Clycq, N., Timmerman, Ch., & Van Houtte, M. (2011). Researching race/ethnicity and educational inequality in the Netherlands: A critical review of the research literature between 1980 and 2008. *British Educational Research Journal, 37*, 5–43.

Suárez-Orozco, C., Bang, H.J., & Kim, H.Y. (2011). I felt like my heart was staying behind: Psychological implications of family separations & reunifications for immigrant youth. *Journal of Adolescent Research. 26*, 222–257.

Tankimovich, M. (2013). Barriers to and interventions for improved tuberculosis detection and treatment among homeless and immigrant populations: A literature review. *Journal of Community Health Nursing, 30*, 83–95.

Telzer, E. (2010). Expanding the acculturation gap-distress model: An integrative review of research. *Human Development, 53*, 313–340.

Titzmann, P.F., Silbereisen, R.K., & Schmitt-Rodermund, E. (2007). Friendship homophily among diaspora migrant adolescents in Germany and Israel. *European Psychologist, 12*, 181–195.

Unger, J.B., Ritt-Olson, A., Wagner, K.D., Soto, D.W., & Baezconde-Garbanati, L. (2009). Parent–child acculturation patterns and substance use among Hispanic adolescents: A longitudinal analysis. *The Journal of Primary Prevention, 30*, 293–313.

Van Geel, M., Vedder, P., & Tanilon, J. (2014). Relationship between peer victimization, cyberbullying and suicide in children and adolescents: A meta-analysis. *Pediatrics, 168*(5), 435–442.

Vedder, P., Berry, J., Sabatier, C., & Sam, D. (2009). The intergenerational transmission of values in national and immigrant families: The role of zeitgeist. *Journal of Youth and Adolescence, 38*, 642–653.

Vedder, P., & Oortwijn, M. (2009). Adolescents' obligations towards their family: Intergenerational discrepancies and adaptation in three cultural groups in the Netherlands. *Journal of Comparative Family Studies, 40*, 699–717.

Vedder, P., & Van Geel, M. (2012). Immigrant children and discrimination. *Contributions to Human Development, 24*, 99–121

Von Grünigen, R., Perren, S., Nägele, C., & Alsaker, F.D. (2010). Immigrant children's peer acceptance and victimization in kindergarten: The role of local language competence. *British Journal of Developmental Psychology, 28*, 679–697.

Ward, C. (1996). Acculturation. In D. Landis & R. Bhagat (Eds.), *Handbook of intercultural training* (2nd ed., pp. 124–147). Newbury Park, CA: Sage.

Willms, J.D. (2003). *Student engagement at school, a sense of belonging and participation: Results from PISA 2000.* Paris: OECD.

Zhou, M. (2009). *Contemporary Chinese America; Immigration, ethnicity, and community transformation.* Philadelphia, PA: Temple University Press.

13

Chinese American Adolescents and Emerging Adults in New York City: Striving for a Place in the Sun

Jennifer Ho and Uwe P. Gielen

Born and raised in New York City, 16-year-old Sophia Ling (a pseudonym like all names in this chapter) had two unevenly shaped eyes—the double-lidded eye proclaimed her "American side" while the other proclaimed her "Asian side"—representing the duality of living in two cultural worlds. Growing up as a minority, Sophia disliked being grouped in with Chinese stereotypes and was unsure what it meant to be a Chinese American. Her parents had immigrated illegally to the United States to pursue better economic opportunities, a sacrifice that Sophia understood only too well. "Grow up, earn money, and send us back to China" was her parents' mantra, and she felt it to be her duty to fulfill their wish despite her own lack of attachment to her ethnic country of origin. Her parents heavily emphasized education but were not involved in her academic endeavors. Furthermore, they expected her to fulfill her household duties as a woman: expectations that were not imposed on her brother. Sophia placed extreme pressure on herself to excel and pursue a life of independence. Through the years, her perspective had slowly shifted, and just as she was beginning to accept her physical appearance, she had found ways to gain more confidence in herself and reconcile her dual identity.

In this chapter, we discuss how Chinese American adolescents and young adults such as Sophia Ling attempt to come to terms with their multicultural identities which are jointly shaped by growing up in a minority Chinese immigrant family and by their attempts to create a future for themselves in the larger American mainstream society. We examine their family lives, evaluate the considerable demands their parents tend to place upon them, and then ask: What emotional price might some of these young people have to pay for their elevated educational aspirations and achievements?

Substantial numbers of Chinese came to the United States in the 1850s in the wake of the California Gold Rush. Working as indentured laborers in the mining industry and subsequently on the transcontinental railroads, they soon found themselves the steady target of racial exclusion and anti-Chinese riots. To escape some of the persecution, a few thousand Chinese moved to New York where during the last three decades of the 19th century they founded New York's oldest Chinatown, in Manhattan. By the 1890s, about 12,000–13,000 racially isolated Chinese eked out a meager living in the New York area.

As late as 1950, only about 18,000 Chinese lived in Manhattan's Chinatown, an impoverished, inward-looking and hierarchically organized society that included many bachelors. But all of this would change dramatically after 1965, the year when the U.S. Congress passed the Immigration and Nationality Act, also known as the Hart-Cellar Immigration Act. This revolutionary act of legislation changed the very nature of immigration into the United States. Whereas laws prior to 1965 almost exclusively favored European immigrants, the post–Hart-Cellar period saw a rapidly expanding influx of immigrants from Latin America and Asia. Large numbers of ethnic Chinese or *Han* immigrants began to arrive from Taiwan, Hong Kong, Vietnam, Mainland China, Malaysia, and elsewhere. By 1990 the U.S. Census Bureau counted 238,919 Chinese in New York City and in 2013, their number had reached 558,000 (U.S. Census Bureau, 2014). Even so, these already-very large numbers are generally believed to seriously underestimate the Chinese population since many undocumented Chinese immigrants attempt to avoid any contact with census workers. Having been smuggled into the United States by so-called snakeheads or else overstaying their visitor's visas, they try to live beneath the radar screen of the authorities (Keefe, 2010). Altogether, the number of persons of Han descent in the larger New York Metropolitan Area probably now surpasses 800,000, making it the largest "Chinese Metropolitan Area" outside Asia.

A traditional entrance door for immigrants, over three million of New York City's 8.4 million residents are foreign-born. Around 49% of all New Yorkers speak a language other than English at home (U.S. Census Bureau, 2012). As one of the most ethnically, culturally, and linguistically diverse metropolises in the world, the city hosts numerous ethnic neighborhoods ranging from Hispanic and Chinese to Russian and Arabic (Kiersz, 2014). In fact, Asian Americans comprise the third-largest ethnic minority in New York City after African Americans and Hispanics. And so, with the Chinese population expanding dramatically, the city's Chinatowns have continued to grow rapidly both in number and in size. Today, New York can boast of three major Chinatowns in Flushing-Queens, Sunset Park-Brooklyn, and Lower Manhattan as well as five smaller ones that are scattered throughout the boroughs.

Many Chinese American children in New York City grow up in working-class and lower middle-class environments, with hopes of rising above the low socioeconomic status that tends to be the fate of so many of their parents. In the public view, these students shine brightly in the academic realm, but little research has offered a qualitative inquiry into their thoughts, feelings, and psychological health. This chapter provides a glimpse into the family dynamics of these Chinese Americans and the psychosocial adaptations they undergo as they attempt to reconcile their ethnic cultures with the American mainstream.

Our observations and analyses derive not only from current literature but also from our own studies that include 86 in-depth interviews with Chinese American adolescents and emerging adults as well as 82 autobiographical essays by high school and college students. While many other studies of Chinese Americans have investigated middle-to-high–income families, our research projects include many young people who grew up in low-income households. The purpose of our studies is to provide vivid portraits and authentic documentation based upon firsthand accounts of Chinese American New Yorkers. In our interviews, we explored a variety of topics such as moving from East Asia to New York; growing up in often modest circumstances; assuming various roles in one's family; being reared as a "satellite baby"; the nature of parent-child relationships; gender roles and gender-related body images; questions of identity; the interviewees' emotional attachments and emotional health; and their educational involvements and successes.

Our research focuses on 1st, 1.5, and 2nd-generation immigrants who have either spent a major portion or all of their youth in New York City. In this context, we define 1st-generation immigrants as those who were born overseas but subsequently migrated to New York, 1.5 generation immigrants were born overseas but arrived in the new country before adolescence, and 2nd-generation immigrants are those born in New York to immigrant parents. This special focus means that we will not explore the lives of foreign college and graduate students who spent their youth in China nor do we examine here the lives of the many Fujianese working-class immigrants who have been arriving in the city in their 20s or 30s and tend to speak little if any English. Finally, this chapter does not aim to encapsulate the diversity of experiences within the Chinese American community across the United States and Canada that includes many upper-middle class residents in the suburbs and so-called Asian "ethnoburbs."

We are interested here in the lives and subjective experiences of immigrant Chinese Americans adolescents and emerging adults who are coming of age in the Big Apple. We believe that the meeting in their hearts and minds between the Chinese and American cultures is not only a manifestation of the accelerating process of globalization but also represents an intimate and sustained encounter between the world's two most influential sociocultural visions. Although the family lives we analyze in this chapter are varied, tied to New York, and often modest in nature, they can nevertheless tell us something important about the global encounter between East and West: As so often in recent cultural psychology, the story we tell is "glocal" (i.e., simultaneously global and local) in nature.

FROM ASIA TO NEW YORK CITY

Whereas recent Chinese immigrants have come to New York from a considerable variety of provinces in China as well as from other Asian countries, most families prior to the 1970s originated in the Taishan (Toishan) area and some other towns and villages located in the southern Guangdong Province. Speaking Taishanese or the related Cantonese dialect, these families and their descendants continue to make up the nucleus of the "Old Chinatown" in Manhattan, with Mott Street as its center. In the 1980s and 1990s, they were joined by often well-educated immigrants from Taiwan, Hong Kong, Vietnam, Malaysia, and elsewhere. Feeling no close kinship to the working-class Taishanese, many of these immigrants began to settle in Little Asia, a multiethnic area centered on the Flushing area in Queens. This wave of immigrants was followed by still another group of families and individuals originating in the Min River Delta in Fujian Province. Speaking entirely different dialects such as the Fuzhou dialect, these newcomers began to grow roots around the East Broadway area, thereby creating Manhattan's "New Chinatown." Other Fujianese (also called Fukienese) moved to Brooklyn where, together with Taishanese and Cantonese speakers, they helped to create a new but rapidly expanding Chinatown in the Sunset Park area.

Altogether, the Chinese immigrant community in New York is highly diverse in terms of geographical origins, languages and dialects spoken, date of arrival, immigration status, the degree of exposure to American mainstream culture, social class, cultural and political orientations, and various other characteristics. Nevertheless and regardless of their immigration status, most adolescents we interviewed called themselves "Chinese" or "Asian American" in order to distinguish themselves from those they labeled "Americans"—such as non-Hispanic Whites. This linguistic usage suggests that they perceive themselves as members of a distinct minority group that has not quite arrived yet in the new society. At the same time they perceive themselves as being quite distinct from African Americans and Hispanics not only in their physical appearance but at times also in their behavioral tendencies. This statement holds true especially for the less-assimilated parents who may convey skeptical opinions about these groups to their teenagers and hope that they will not marry one of "them."

McGlinn's report (2002) on Chinese Americans in the United States distinguished Chinese immigrants from Taiwan and Hong Kong from those from Mainland China. He discovered that the median household income of Taiwanese or Hong-Kong families was nearly 50% higher than that of families from China. Furthermore, 43% of immigrants from China arrived with less than a high school education compared to 12% of Taiwan/Hong Kong immigrants. Whereas better-off immigrants from Hong Kong and Taiwan typically settle down in middle-class areas of Queens, Manhattan's Upper West Side, and suburban New Jersey, Long Island, and California, Chinese from the more rural regions of the Guangdong and Fujian Provinces are often compelled to work in New York's Chinese ethnic enclaves because they offer varied job opportunities as well as communal support. While these ethnic enclaves continue to serve as the favored destination spots for many incoming Chinese immigrants, a large proportion of them has dispersed across the metropolitan area over the years. This holds true especially for the economically successful "uptown Chinese," whereas the largely working-class and lower middle-class families residing in Manhattan Chinatown are sometimes referred to as "downtown Chinese" (Kwong, 1996), although some of them do not like this designation.

Chinese immigrants have been coming to New York for a variety reasons including economic prosperity, social mobility, better educational opportunities for their children, and sometimes also for political and religious reasons. Seventeen-year-old Julia Ho aptly summed up the American dream embraced by those crossing the country's borders:

> My family came because they wanted better job opportunities and a better life for their children. Coming to the United States was this goal that everyone wanted to achieve because there was just this ideal [of making a lot of money] that was associated with the United States.

Indeed, the pursuit of this goal has led thousands to leave the comforts of their homes behind in the search for Golden Mountain, a hopeful Chinese term for the United States that was first coined during the Californian gold rush. Today, however, while New York has experienced considerable economic recovery since the 2009 recession, the 2013 poverty rate of Chinese in New York City has remained at a high 21.2%, well above the country's average of 15.8% and the national Chinese population's average of 15.9%. While there exist an increasing number of economically well-off Chinese especially in Queens, the median income of a Chinese household in New York City continues to remain below the city and national average, and its working-class Chinese population remains the largest in the nation. They are, however, less likely than other ethnic groups to utilize government subsidies such as welfare payments nor do they tend to be politically very active. For these and other reasons, their poverty and acculturation struggles remain largely concealed from the general public.

ADAPTING FAMILY ROLES

Leaving the comforts of their communities behind, first-generation immigrants also lose their social roles that provided them with a sense of belonging in society. Feelings of loss and incompetence are common as they navigate a whole new world, fighting against discrimination and marginalization in the workforce (Suárez-Orozco & Suárez-Orozco, 2001). While parents struggle to establish economic stability, their children face a different sort of challenges at school and in the social realm. Like their parents, they are no strangers to racism and prejudice. 1.5 and 2nd-generation children in particular grow up in a unique environment of divergent cultures. Most adolescents we met described living two different identities that they alternate between home and school: At home, they speak one of the Chinese dialects and attempt to live up to the values their parents endorse; at school, they don the character of the American teenager—at least up to a point. As they navigate through the confusing maze of seemingly divergent cultural rules, psychological distress can arise when they are unable to resolve these separate identities into a coherent whole.

On the whole, first-generation immigrants remain closer to the Chinese culture, whereas second-generation immigrants become more Americanized. Those immigrants who came to the United States in their teens often struggle with the English language, remain fluent in spoken and written Chinese, like to watch Chinese TV programs and listen to Chinese or Korean pop music, form friendships with other Chinese and Asian teenagers, and find it easy to understand and sympathize with their Chinese parents (Jia, 2004). In contrast, many American-born Chinese teenagers and young adults move away from some important aspects of their parents' culture, speak their parents' Chinese dialect only imperfectly, and cannot read Chinese characters. Their world is much more Americanized: They tend to have both Asian and non-Asian friends with whom they converse in English, may think of their parents as old-fashioned and out of touch with their own teenage world, and at times perceive themselves as more American than Chinese. Indeed, a few of them commented ironically in their interviews that they were a "twinkie" or "banana": externally yellow, but internally white. Still others have learned to live comfortably in the two cultural worlds by forging an "integrated identity," and they tend be optimistic and well adjusted (cf. Berry & Vedder, chapter 12, this volume). As several studies have shown, language proficiency in both Chinese and English and pride in one's ethnic culture are positively correlated with self-esteem. Moreover, Tsai, Ying, and Lee (2001) found that for Chinese American women, self-esteem was largely associated with pride in their ethnic culture whereas language proficiency was more salient for men.

Nevertheless, immigration places enormous stress on the relationship between parents and children and can significantly alter the family dynamic. The pressure of having to survive in a new land inevitably places the immigrant family in a precarious position of having to redefine and alter the responsibility of each member. Boundaries between the roles of children and those of adults may thus become blurred, with the child sometimes taking on parental responsibilities well beyond their age.

Mo Li Kao came to the United States at the age of 14 from Taiwan, living with her relatives before her mother joined her four years later. They lived in Flushing, a neighborhood known as "Little Asia" that includes a considerable Taiwanese population which meant that her mother could communicate with others. Mo Li, now a social worker, spoke about the poverty surrounding immigration and the familial obligations:

> The reality is I took care of everything. [My mother] was a cleaning lady in Taiwan, and it was very difficult for her to make a living. Over here [in the U.S.] as a housekeeper, while they didn't pay a lot—I mean, $800 a month—it was a lot more than what she was making in Taiwan. It was tough for her, and I think coming here actually was easier, even though compared to a lot of other people, it still seemed hard. Like when we first moved to Flushing, we lived in a room the size of an office. It was the cheapest accommodation we could get, so we shared the kitchen and bathroom with 10 other people. But in Taiwan, we had our own apartment. . . . My stepfather was still in Taiwan. We were sending money back for him, but he was still kind of not making it or fell into a great depression of some sort and had like a temporary psychotic break. He stabbed himself a few times and nearly died. . . . I said to my mom, "I think you should go home and take care of him. You married this guy." [But] she was too scared. She was too scared to give up her 800-dollars-a-month job. And so, I dropped out of school and went back to take care of him until he was well enough, and then I brought him over. . . . [We are] not close, but we're not distant. I mean, once you sign the papers, you're family, you know.

Many of our Chinese American interviewees possessed a similar sense of familial obligation, learning to become independent early on and taking on responsibilities beyond their age. While the parents work long hours to establish themselves in the new country, the children have to maneuver through the school system on their own, learning social norms and doing homework with little parental guidance. Once the child achieves a fair grasp of the language and the norms of the community, the parents may come to rely on the child to help them navigate the new world. Language brokering—a practice expected of some children in immigrant families whereby they serve as linguistic (and cultural) mediators between their parents and the outside world—becomes a major aspect in the parent-child relationship. Their duties typically involve translating and fulfilling various administrative duties such as checking mail and buying groceries. Older siblings usually hold the additional responsibilities of looking after their younger siblings and helping them with homework.

Julia: The Chinese friends I have are more Americanized, more second generation. They were born here and some of their parents came here at an early age, so they can speak English fluently or at least they can kind of understand bits and pieces. I feel like it's easier for them in a way because their parents already had this experience of the United States that they can pass on to them, but it's different for me because I sort of support my parents socially.

Interviewer: Socially? How is that?

Julia: Well, after being here for 18 years, they still can't speak any English, so ever since I was about 7 years old and in 2nd grade, I have been attending parent-teacher conferences, going to court, taking care of utility bills, even the most basic things.

Interviewer: So you had to grow up really quick. Do you wish like you had more of a childhood?

Julia: I guess so, but I feel like my past was kind of a blur. I don't remember being depressed or anything, but . . .

Interviewer: It's just the way life was?

Julia: Yes.

REARING "SATELLITE BABIES"

The makeup of a traditional Chinese family frequently involves grandparents living with their children's families. Despite the growth of urban cities constraining living spaces, the practice of involving multiple caregivers is still endorsed today as it also serves to relieve the burden of childcare from working parents. This type of three-generation childcare arrangement functions well when the family members live in close geographic proximity within a given cultural and linguistic context, but it becomes much more problematic when it is implemented across the Pacific Ocean. Indeed, for Chinese parents who cannot afford to raise their children, the practice of sending their children back to China to live with relatives remains an unpleasant alternative (Bohr & Tse, 2009). Termed "satellite babies," these children are shuttled between vastly different cultures and are being physically separated from caregivers multiple times until the parents are financially stable to care for them.

Such practices can be psychologically traumatic in the child's developmental trajectory that can later manifest in behavioral and emotional problems in life although systematic longitudinal research on Chinese satellite children is missing. For instance, although Chinese immigrants have lower rates of violence than most other groups, 17-year-old Julia recounted her troubling brother who constantly got into grapples at school. He ended up being expelled after smashing a classmate's head into the wall. Julia spoke sadly about her brother's violent behavior and attributed his aggressive temperament to having been sent away as a child:

Julia: My brother went to school in China for two years, and when he came back my parents already had another baby. I think even to this day those four or five years apart have made my parents care for him just a little less. Even though he is still their kid, just the fact that he was away for that time makes them not love him as much. I think he feels that he is being victimized in a way.

Interviewer: Does he remember being sent back?

Julia: Yes, and this actually happens to a lot of Fujianese kids. All of my cousin's kids are with their grandparents in China, and they get brought back something like seven or eight years later. When they come back, they are just kids, but I don't know how they could be close as a family after that.

Interviewer: There is no real connection?

Julia: No, they definitely don't treat them the same way.

Interviewer: Do the kids ever ask why their parents got rid of them?

Julia: I don't think the kids ever say that, but they certainly wonder about it.

Interviewer: Do you think they feel abandoned?

Julia: Yes.

Interviewer: Has your brother ever said anything?

Julia: No, I don't think he knows how to express it in those words. I think the only way he knows how to express himself is through retaliation.

Unlike children raised by parents, satellite babies undergo a traumatic exchange of caretakers at an early age. Some may experience abandonment more than once in their lives as their parents initially hand them to grandparents to only take them back later. Some of these children may see the parents "as strangers who had stolen him away to a strange land," and they may require intensive psychological aid to help them adjust to the shifting, oftentimes confusing changes in their environments (Bernstein, 2009, p. 1). The psychological consequences that result from such practice can be serious, including behavioral problems such as head banging, tantrums, and acting out. Appropriate attention needs to be focused on this population with the goal of reestablishing the parent-child attachment bond and addressing the children's psychological needs.

PARENTING AND FAMILIAL RELATIONSHIPS

Emotional Expression

Parental emotional restraint and a perceived lack of affection in the family are some of the most common complaints that some of our participants raised. The family stress model delineated by Benner and Kim (2010) demonstrated how the stress of immigration and acculturation can place an increased strain on the parents' emotional state, thus affecting their parenting performance and causing them to grow less in tune with their children's emotional needs. Even so, the relationship between the older and younger generations involves a two-way dynamic: Many Chinese parents, while maintaining a miserly attitude toward most commodities, would not hesitate to shell out money for their children's school books and afterschool fees. In exchange, most participants acknowledged their parents' efforts and expressed a profound sense of obligation to return this generosity.

Having spent the first four years in another person's care, 18-year-old Nancy Xian recalled the desire to impress her parents and gain their approval, but her parents failed to acknowledge her efforts. "Tough love," she justified. Like many Fujianese, her parents emphasized hard work and held traditional beliefs that children should take care of them later in life. Being raised in this environment has affected Nancy's perspective on social relationships. She felt she had no best friends, only mere acquaintances. Despite the lack of affection in the family, Nancy claimed she nevertheless felt obligated to help the family relieve their financial burden and therefore became financially independent after high school.

Gender Roles and Body Image

During the course of development, identity formation is contingent on the gender roles imposed by the residing culture. However, children of immigrants often grow up negotiating their gender between conflicting cultural expectations. Chinese parenting practices are often heavily influenced by patriarchal Confucian and post-Confucian values (Qin, 2009). Girls were traditionally expected to play more subordinate roles such as cleaning and childrearing, whereas boys were (and often still are) expected to carry on the family name. Although such strict gender delineation has blurred over the years, as social reforms have gradually permeated and changed time-honored practices in China, gender-specific expectations and discrimination are still evident in a good many Chinese families. This holds especially true for working-class families whose origins can be traced back to rural and small-town China but tends to be less evident in more educated middle-class families from big and more globalized cities such as Shanghai, Taipei, or Hong Kong.

Chinese parents typically keep a close eye on their daughters, encouraging them to stay at home while discouraging interactions with boys. Dating early is not only seen as a distraction from schoolwork but also as a shameful reflection of the family's failure to properly rear their daughter. For Chinese American adolescents, upholding their parents' expectations becomes difficult in New York's high schools where sexuality is ubiquitous. Furthermore, social acceptance often involves materialistic acquisitions, a concept that contradicts the traditional Chinese value of frugality. Qin's study (2009) discovered that, when faced with these conflicting messages, girls tend to internalize their parents' expectations and socialization. As difficult as it may be, they are able to structure their identity in contrast to the image of their more fashionable and popular peers. Most of our female participants echoed these findings, sacrificing transient popularity for academic excellence. However, some added that their parents have lower expectations of their abilities to succeed when compared to their brothers. Performing household chores is also one of the expected duties imposed on some of the female interviewees.

Traditional Chinese Confucian values for boys emphasize "education, self-cultivation, and gentleness" (Qin, 2009, p. 42). Contrary to predominant American attitudes, masculinity in Chinese culture stresses high educational attainment rather than physical prowess. As Qin pointed out, the Chinese boy is taught to use "his wits, not his fists" (2009, p. 42). This can pose a serious conflict for Chinese American boys who have to navigate the American social realm. Like the girls, boys feel the pressure to excel academically; however, unlike the girls, they seem to have a harder time internalizing their parents' values. In addition to warding off social pressure to not appear a "nerd," boys in school are expected to participate in physically demanding sports (Qin, 2009). Unfortunately, their naturally smaller statures place them at a physical disadvantage compared to their non-Asian peers, and a considerable number of them have reported incidences of being bullied and demeaned (Rosenbloom & Way, 2004). Even so, some of our male participants agreed that, if they were girls, they would not be accorded certain privileges at home. The price for such privileges comes with the enormous pressure of having to carry on the family name. For those who are homosexuals, there lies the additional difficulty of coming out to their parents for fear of bringing them shame.

Benjamin was a proud gay Chinese American who spoke extensively about the (in his view) unwarranted expectations in the Chinese American community to become "normal." He talked at length about his passion to inspire Chinese Americans to fight against stereotypes and be open to others and themselves. Living in a loving middle-class family, Benjamin also admitted the pressure of being the only son in the family, and he felt he would never be able to live up to his parents' expectations due to his homosexuality. Like many male Chinese in particular, he was not very communicative about personal issues. Instead, he found a safe haven in being involved in political movements where he could interact with like-minded, passionate people. He hoped to become a positive influence in the Asian American community by becoming a professor.

Beyond readily voiced prohibitions against dating for the girls, sexuality is rarely discussed among Chinese families. Rather, Asian parents tend to convey their opinion about sex indirectly, but children are able to pick up these subtle cues, acknowledging their parents' discouraging attitude regarding dating without recalling explicit conversations with them. Indeed, Asian American teenagers are less likely to recall having discussions about sex with their parents than their non-Asian peers (Kim & Ward, 2007). While language barriers may be one factor supporting the lack of communication, sexuality remains an awkward or taboo topic in many Asian families. Whereas boys rarely receive sexual information, girls often report receiving too much information from their mothers about the negative consequences of sex and pregnancies (Kim & Ward, 2007). The messages that boys and girls receive are also inherently different: While boys may be educated about safer sex, girls are often blatantly warned against being victimized by men and are taught to avoid them altogether. For instance, parents' stress on academic achievement renders dating to be a form of distraction from the single-minded search for success. Faced with the disparaging outlook of dating at home, Chinese American adolescents struggle to redefine their perspective on sexuality in the American environment where sexuality is omnipresent in both the media and schools. Despite the cross-generation conflict, Asian American teenagers seem to have adopted some of their parents' values, initiating sexual activity at later ages and having fewer sexual partners in their lifespan compared to other ethnic groups (e.g., Kao & Martyn, 2014).

American media propagate a form of unattainable beauty that many female adolescents strive hopelessly to achieve (Kasinitz, Mollenkopf, Waters, & Holdaway, 2008). The hopelessness of this effort is even more pronounced among Chinese American adolescents who do not physically align with the American conceptualization of beauty:

Vivian: It's just sometimes when I'd watch TV, I'd be like, oh, I wanna be that person, just like a fantasy world, really.

Interviewer: Anything but Chinese, is that it?

Vivian: Yeah.

Interviewer: How do you feel about that today?

Vivian: I'm actually pretty okay with it now. In my school there's an Asian cultural society, and they talk about issues like this and once you get it in and you have a group of people that feel the same way, I think it's easier to accept it.

Interviewer: So is this common among young Chinese girls that they want to be anything but Chinese?

Vivian: Yeah, I think that's why they dye their hair or they wear colored contact lenses to change themselves pretty much. I don't think they explicitly think or say that, but when they use those products or when they dress that way, I think yeah they're trying to assimilate into white culture pretty much.

Interviewer: Do you believe that's the perception that other people have of Chinese people? Or is this your perception of Chinese people?

Vivian: I think it's . . . mine. . . . But now that you ask, I hope other people don't have this outlook on us. I'm not actually sure.

Benjamin Wong shared a similar story of trying to fit into mainstream America as a Chinese American:

Benjamin: I think that body image is something that's not talked about a lot of the times because it is [connected to an] individual sense of insecurities. I think these things are necessary to talk about because no one talks about them, especially inside the Chinese community. When my aunt says I look like everyone else, I know that outside the Chinese community, even more people think that all Asians or all Chinese people look alike. Whenever I see different Chinese people who are younger, males or females, with no fashion sense, glasses, moppish hair, or fattish, I know what it is like to feel like a nerd and to be susceptible to the brunt of many different stereotypes and jokes, and being teased.

Interviewer: What did people use to say to you?

Benjamin: That's the thing. No one really ever said too much about it, although I heard that one person said I was the third ugliest male in the class in my Catholic elementary school. . . . The thing about race and being Chinese is it's very hard to pinpoint when it affects certain things. It's that feeling where sometimes you go, "Does my race have something to do with things like that?" I think it definitely did. Yeah.

Interviewer: Reading your essay, it seemed like you were on the outside looking in.

Benjamin: I always feel that way; it's hard to always feel completely inside something. When I was younger, there was a certain community within my family, but as we got older, I became more politicized about issues of race, gender, sexuality, class, and all these different types of things. My different family members didn't. There are all these different facets of me that I feel are never completely encapsulated within a certain group of friends or peers or loved ones. I always kind of feel semi-outside.

Chinese American girls and boys face many pressures and gender trends comparable to those of other ethnic groups. Perhaps as a result of being more closely supervised and the more consistent internalization of their parents' values, girls tend to perform better academically than boys and are also less likely to drop out of school or to "get into trouble" (Kasinitz et al., 2008). Boys face the pressure of conforming to the American mainstream norm of being physically stronger and aggressive, traits determined to a significant extent by genetics that are out of their control. This may contribute to feelings of resentment or a sense of helplessness that can lead to greater difficulty in internalizing parental expectations and more behavioral problems both at school and at home.

Compliance

Chinese Americans encounter stereotypes as being too passive or overly compliant. Many participants voiced their concerns about Asians being too shy and lacking self-confidence, traits that conflict with the American emphasis on boisterous assertiveness. Although compliance may initially bring forth connotations related to weakness, studies have found that the development of compliance is essential in the process of socializing and imparting moral values to children. How children then internalize the process provides a script for how to adjust and adapt to changing environment stimuli.

In Huang and Lamb's comparative study (2014) of Taiwanese, Chinese immigrant, and British children, the authors observed two forms of compliance: committed compliance and situational compliance. Committed compliance is based on the stable internalization of parental motivation and values, whereas situational compliance occurs when children comply with parental wishes without internalizing the desired motivation. Examining how parental practices across cultures impact compliance style, the authors found that Western rearing customs generally encourage parents to adopt a "child-centered" perspective that promotes increasing sensitivity to the child's needs while decreasing control (p. 511). In comparison, self-control and compliance with authority are both explicitly and implicitly a part of the Chinese culture. As the authors noted, children are consistently praised for being well behaved (*guai*) or obedient (*ting hua*), values Chinese parents endorse in a more consistent and absolute manner than Anglo-Saxon parents. Indeed, this study replicated findings that, when compared to their English counterparts, the Chinese and Taiwanese mothers exhibited more controlling behaviors that are consistent with the Confucian value that children be obedient to their parents. The results showed that only situational compliance, and not committed compliance, differed significantly among the three groups. Taiwanese children exhibited the most situational compliance in which, when under pressure to obey, they demonstrated higher obedience, self-control, and compliance.

The finding that Chinese immigrant children demonstrated less situational compliance than their Taiwanese counterparts suggests that they had internalized not only Chinese beliefs but also assimilated to the norms of the mainstream Western society where they reside. Similarly, parents undergo various degrees of acculturation. Far from their original hometown, immigrants lose the stable community supports that provide childrearing advice. We have found that, while some parents continue to rigidly apply childrearing practices modeled from their own childhood experiences, others may modify their rearing behaviors to be more in line with the Western emphasis on individualism. Although many interviewees complained about their parents' attempt to dictate their social lives (e.g., forbidding dating, playing with friends, or staying out late), they also conceded that their parents had little actual, physical control over them. Still, the Chinese parenting style of consistent control facilitates the internalization of the value of education in their children, and the results are reflected in Chinese American adolescents investing more time in studying than their non-Asian peers even in the absence of parental supervision.

Asakawa (2001) delineated that the process of internalization involves three basic psychological needs for autonomy, competence, and relatedness to parents. The study generally supported other findings that, compared to their white Americans, Asian Americans exhibited higher levels of competence in areas concerning academic and work activities, allowing them to internalize their cultural values of hard work and education. Asakawa also added that Asian parents from intact families are more likely to assert greater control and involvement over their children's academic pursuits. However, unlike their white American peers whose own educational aspirations are correlated with performance, Asian American children's academic performance was more associated with parents' expectations than their own. In other words, regardless of whether the parents are involved in school, children tend to perform better in schools if education is a value that the parents heavily emphasized. This latter explanation fits most of our Chinese American participants who, though lacking parental help in the academic realm, have nevertheless internalized their parents' educational expectations.

Control

The American emphasis on freedom may lead mainstream parents to adversely react to the word "control" by associating it with coercion and loss of autonomy. However, this is simply not the case: Motivation comes from a variety of sources, and high control does not necessarily entail the loss of autonomy. There is some evidence that, unlike Western children who derive their motivation from making personal decisions, Asian American children are more motivated by others' choices (Bao & Lam, 2008). What this suggests is that motivation is not influenced in a straightforward manner by the existence of freedom of choice; rather, interpersonal relatedness between the parent and child tends to facilitate the internalization of motivation and values. However, the need for freedom of choice does appear to be more salient among children who have a limited socioemotional connection with their parents in order to establish a sense of personal autonomy.

Some studies have shown that whereas Asian parents heavily emphasize academic achievement, they can do so while still maintaining warmth and open communication with their children (Juang, Qin, & Park, 2013). Baumrind's (1971) well-known classification of parenting styles as either "authoritarian" or "authoritative" greatly undervalues the diversity of parenting practices across cultures. Compared to Western values emphasizing individualism, independence building, and parental warmth, Chinese childrearing practices follow modernized Confucian principles such as collectivism, parental obedience and control, and emotional restraint that do not align well with the American emphasis on individualism (Chao, 1994; Cheah, Zhou, Leung, & Vu, in prep.; Chen & Luster, 2002; Ho, 1986). Even so, Chinese parents can offer their children a sense of safety and satisfaction without endorsing overt American gestures of hugs and words. Chao (2001) has suggested that authoritative parenting styles may work better for whites and second-generation Asian immigrants but not for first-generation Chinese Americans who are used to what Westerners deem an "authoritarian" style. Indeed, most of our participants, while not receiving the overt American warmth they see their peers enjoy, nevertheless retained some level of obligation toward their parents to help them financially in the future, a belief that American mainstream adolescents are less likely to endorse.

Motivation

Motivational beliefs differ across cultures. In a sample of ninth graders, Eaton and Dembo (1997) found that although Asian Americans (mostly Chinese) held lower situational self-efficacy beliefs than their Caucasian counterparts, they consistently outperformed Caucasians and demonstrated higher motivation across a variety of tasks. Academic success is touted among most Asian immigrant families, and failure to achieve can result in family shame and parental punishment. American parenting styles have generally encouraged positive feedback and reinforcement to enhance children's self-esteem. However, Eaton and Dembo's research implies that self-esteem is not necessarily a crucial component for success. The Caucasian students in their study may have overestimated their abilities, a form of self-illusion that can disrupt positive performance. In contrast, the lower sense of self-efficacy among the Asian American sample may have derived not merely from low self-esteem, but even more from having more stringent internal standards, higher goals, and a culturally valued emphasis on humility: traits that spur Asian Americans to work harder and perform better than their non-Asian peers in academic and probably also in certain non-academic situations.

Taken together, a clear majority of our research participants displayed an inherent understanding of the sacrifice and hardships that their parents endured while and after immigrating to the United States. This knowledge further augments many students' tendency to strive for success in the hopes of rising above their socioeconomic status and supporting their parents financially in the future. This sense of obligation, called *filial piety* (*hsiao* or *xiao*), is one of the most valued qualities in Confucianism; it encourages appreciation for the tangible and intangible gifts that parents have bestowed upon their children, and the sense of duty to pay back signifies respect, humility, and gratefulness.

Sixteen-year-old Dung is aware of her parents' sacrifices and the hardships they endured when migrating to America. She recounted how her parents, with only a middle-school education, had managed to complete the necessary immigration paperwork to escape the destructive refugee camps in Vietnam during the late 1970s:

> They make a lot of sacrifices for me in general. In fact the whole idea of them coming here was the biggest sacrifice. They sacrificed nearly their lives [because] they could have died easily by trying to come here. And day in, day out now like today, they sacrifice their hours. My dad gets out of the house at five in the morning and doesn't come home 'til like eight at night. My mom gets out at nine, and doesn't come home 'til like 10. So they both sacrifice long

> hours of work trying to get the most money [so that] I don't have to work. They don't want me to work. They want me to go to school, and they want me to be successful in the educational system here.

Even 12-year-old Yang Wang—our youngest interviewee—understood that Chinese parents often do not enjoy the immediate reward of their immigration. As much as Chinese culture emphasizes filial piety, it seems to equally place a strong obligation on parents to offer the best opportunities for the next generation:

Interviewer: Why did your family come to the United States?

Yang: I guess to have a better life for my brother and me.

Interviewer: Do you feel they made a sacrifice when they came to America?

Yang: Yeah. My dad was an engineer which was like high-paying, and he went to like the highest rated college in China, but now, when he came to America, he had to work in a restaurant. So it's like a really big difference.

Interviewer: So did your parents ever mention making a sacrifice to you?

Yang: Well, they could already have been pretty rich, like have a lot of money in China, even here in America if it wasn't for like tuition bills and all.

Interviewer: Now, do you feel a little bit stressed or anxious that you have to do well in school because your parents spent so much on tuition bills?

Yang: Yeah.

EMOTIONAL ATTACHMENT

Qin (2006) observed that a difference in cultural expectations can result not only in parent-child alienation but also in psychological maladaptation. Unlike children who grew up among peers experiencing similar upbringings, Chinese American children may derive mixed messages from what their parents teach and what their non-Asian school peers endorse. Qin coined the term "parallel dual frame of reference" to illustrate how both parents and children endorse different anticipation about each other: Parents yearn that their children act in accordance with Chinese teachings, whereas children also hold expectations on how their parents should behave.

Immigrant parents face the difficult task of modifying their childrearing practices in a new country. The manner in which Chinese immigrant mothers tend to raise their children is neither identical to their Chinese counterparts in China nor does it simply follow the mainstream practices of white parents. One study has shown that Chinese immigrant parents, estranged from the community where they had grown up, tend to exert less emotional, more traditional, and more familiar forms of parenting when compared to parents in China where more liberal practices have slowly permeated mainstream society (Wang, 2013). This pattern also emerged in another study focusing on Taiwanese immigrant families in which the immigrant mothers exerted more authoritarian control over their children than their native counterparts (Huang & Lamb, 2014).

Similar to their children, immigrant parents stand at the crossroads of two divergent cultures, and in the realm of parenting, several studies have demonstrated that immigrant parents who are aware of and better at negotiating with the new culture tend to have better relationships with their children (Chiu, 1987; Lin & Fu, 1990; Qin, 2008). Middle-class, highly educated immigrant parents have the financial resources to learn the new language and social norms. On the other hand, struggling working-class parents may experience more difficulty. Not only do they have less time to spend with children, they frequently also lack the linguistic and cultural means to fully integrate into mainstream society. For them the nation's Chinatowns provide ethnic enclaves where they do not need to acquire proficient English to go about their daily lives.

Moreover, the Chinese American working-class parents originally came to the United States with the intention of "making it," but that ambition frequently creates a dilemma for them. On the one hand, they are forced to work numerous hours at poorly paid jobs to enable their children to go to school and hopefully on to college. This holds even truer for those parents who were smuggled into the country by snakeheads and who therefore tend to owe large amounts of money to family members and friends who had originally helped them pay off the smugglers. Their difficult monetary situation, in turn, forces them to work even longer hours. At the same time it means that they have hardly any time left for their children. In response, some will decide to send their young children overseas as satellite babies—and yet that decision can easily undermine family cohesion, the children's sense of contentment and happiness, and their mastery of the English language. In addition, some adolescents grow up as "latchkey children," that is children who return to an empty home after school because their parents are at work. In either case, attachment between the parents and the children may be undermined and cause some children to develop feelings of depression, loneliness, and even abandonment.

On a more positive note, in Chinatown's blended, yet divergent, cultural environment, many second-generation Chinese Americans develop useful skills to navigate successfully both within the mainstream community and within their Chinese families. Placed in this demanding situation, they learn to embody different motivational values and forms of adaptation that allow them to endorse and negotiate between the two cultures, thereby adopting an integrated bicultural identity (Berry & Vedder, chapter 12, this volume). More generally, Chinese American children must learn to endure the stresses deriving from processes of acculturation and cultural reconciliation. While most of them understand the parental sacrifices and are willing to fulfill their filial obligation, a good many of our participants did report a certain lack of emotional attachment to their parents.

For instance, Cameron's father grew up in an impoverished area in Guangzhou (Canton), Guangdong Province of China. He dreamt of America as the "freedom" path toward a better life, but when he arrived reality did not meet his expectations. Formerly a teacher in China who commanded respect, his father began to work as a delivery man earning a meager salary in New York. Cameron is fully aware of the sacrifice his parents had made immigrating, but while he is sympathetic, he does not feel emotionally close with them:

Cameron: I'm pretty private about my school work.

Interviewer: So is every aspect of your life kept hidden from your father?

Cameron: Not like every aspect. I mean it's not like hidden. It's not purposely hidden. It's just that I don't feel the need to expose it.

Interviewer: And your mother?

Cameron: She doesn't need to know either.

Interviewer: So do you feel that you've never really had an emotional connection with your parents?

Cameron: No, no. I mean I care for them and everything, but you know I just don't talk to them about school or anything.

Another issue that Chinese American families encounter is the language and cultural barriers between the parents and the child. Twenty-year-old Pearl Wu described her struggles:

> It's just we're really not that open with each other. Moreover, my Chinese isn't one hundred percent and there is some vocabulary I can't pick up on. I can't just go up to them and ask them questions. It's weird if I do that. We are not like an Americanized family that you would see on TV where the daughter goes and asks her mother about anything she wants to. It's more like a "Oh-hello" kind of a relationship. But it's not like we don't get along. . . . I think that if the parents were the ones who just came to America from China, and those kids are the first ones here, that relationship with those parents wouldn't really "mix" because the kids have something else going on than what their parents would have wanted them to have in China. I don't really know how to explain that. . . . It's just Asian parents aren't really that open. It's stricter. You should do well in school and that's that.

Raised by her grandparents, 20-year-old Sandy Hsu experienced a similar emotional distance: "I love my parents. They work so hard. I understand what they're going through . . . trying to keep a roof over my head. [But] I won't say [we have] a close relationship." As a child, Sandy felt neglected and lonely, experiencing bouts of depression that she kept to herself. Although she was grateful and understood her parents' sacrifice, she could not help but feel detached from them. Her parents' unhappy marriage has affected her outlook on social relationships, acknowledging that she had trust issues. She felt she could not meet her parents' expectation both physically (to be a "pretty, skinny, smart" Asian girl) and academically, and the pressure made her self-conscious and insecure. Although they do not project any obligations, she still felt obligated to take care of them. Over the years, she had been trying to be more independent and gain more confidence in herself.

Not every Chinese parent endorses such a style, although the same emphasis on education can be generally seen through most interviews, as is the following observations by 19-year-old Carrie Wei:

Carrie: I think that [my parents] would be better off if they had stayed in Taiwan. My dad lived in a big house in Taiwan, and now we live in a small apartment in Manhattan. I think the quality of life would have been better in Taiwan, but the opportunities for growth are much better in the United States.

Interviewer: Do you feel that your parents made a sacrifice when they came here?

Carrie: Yeah. They could have found jobs easily in Taiwan since they speak Chinese fluently, whereas going to the United States, their English isn't very good. I feel they definitely made a sacrifice in terms of their job.

Interviewer: I'm guessing your parents mentioned their sacrifice to you?

Carrie: They have mentioned it, but it's not like they remind us about it a lot. My parents are really great because they just want us to do well. They're not going to complain about what they sacrificed. I have a lot of Asian friends whose parents force them to study a lot. They force them to go to prep schools. My parents weren't that harsh on me and my sisters in terms of grades, but we all just want to do well on our own. We were lucky in that our parents weren't forcing good grades down our throats. We just wanted to do well anyway.

Some other interviewees, however, perceived their parents to be overly strict and unbending while holding unrealistic expectations. They also complained that their parents do not recognize their achievements and that they suffered the humiliation of being compared with more successful relatives and peers. Chinese parents are also less prone to express affection to their children overtly, something that many interviewees picked up as a clearly recognizable difference between them and their American peers. "We don't go around saying I love you. We don't hug. We don't kiss on the cheek or anything," Pearl observed. However, it is an aspect of behavior that many said they would change when raising their future children. Their intentions are supported by research findings indicating that parental acceptance and warmth in Chinese (and other) families are correlated with positive child mental health and adaptation when compared to child-perceived parental neglect and rejection (Li, 2015a, 2015b; see also chapter 5 by Ahmed et al. in this volume).

Yet even with the cultural and familial tension among Chinese American families, many of our participants did not resent their parents. Rather, it seems that like Pearl, they have accepted many of their parents' values as well as their hopes, inspiring a strong sense of confidence in their abilities to achieve social mobility and rise out of poverty.

> Well, they do so much for me. They've struggled a lot. They expect your children to take care of you. I don't have a problem with it because, financially, we're struggling right now, which is why I can't wait to get my career going and get that paycheck to help them out, to relieve them of some stress. So I'm not obligated, I just want to.

EMOTIONAL HEALTH

Parent-child acculturation discrepancy is related to negative child adjustment and poorer mental health outcomes in immigrant children (Ho, 2014). As children gain more proficiency in the English language, more so than their knowledge of their ethnic Chinese dialect, they may find it more difficult to communicate with their parents. This can cause a critical emotional deficiency in their developmental growth as parents are not able to offer their children the support they need. Parents' inability to provide emotional support is further compounded by the long hours parents spend away from home because of work. It is not exaggerated to say that a good many parents—and especially so the working-class fathers—become "working machines" to pay back debts while trying to save money for their children's education and, hopefully, establish their own modest restaurant or business.

"For a long time, I was kind of detached from my emotions," Mo Li said, "like I was kind of described like that I see the world through kind of like a . . . like the world looked like a fish tank to me." This form of emotional detachment is not uncommon in our Chinese American participants. In addition, the adolescent years are racked by developmental challenges, and so we have heard frequent instances of depression and anxiety. These mental health issues are troubling, even more so since they remain frequently unknown even to their Chinese peers and the parents. "I don't want to bother my parents with my problems since they already have to struggle so hard," interviewees told us in this context. Others indicated that we were the first ones to hear about of their emotional problems because of their fear that if they told their best friend(s) about them, they might become the object of gossip and thereby bring shame upon their family.

Teachers are frequently unknowing participants in the circular process of racial discrimination and bullying that many Asian Americans face especially in New York's poorer neighborhood schools where Asians often form a minority (Rosenbloom & Way, 2004). Zhou Peverly, Xin, Huang, and Wang (2003), for instance, reported that in their New York–based study, a sample of first-generation Chinese American adolescents displayed more negative attitudes toward their teachers than comparable samples of European American adolescents and students in China. They also reported higher levels of depression and stress than the other two groups; in part because they were the recipients of racial harassment by their non-Asian peers. They typically suffered these harassments in silence, neither telling their teachers nor their parents because they believe that they will not be understood by them. Their silence is not a sign of psychological strength but a resigned belief that they have no one to depend on.

ACADEMIA

Because many Chinese American children and young adults have deeply internalized their parents' relentless emphasis on the practical as well as symbolic value of education, it comes as no surprise that they are frequently successful in the academic realm. Chinese students typically spend more than twice as many hours studying than their non-Chinese peers on a weekly basis (University of California—San Diego, 2011). Many Chinese families believe that their children's admission into a top-tier college is the key to financial mobility. Moreover, in the past two decades, the three most important public elite high schools in New York City have seen a dramatic increase in the admission rate of Asian Americans. Admission to these often extremely selective high schools is strictly based on the score a student receives on a citywide entrance examination. As of 2013–2014, Asian Americans dominate the academic scene in a number of top schools, comprising 73% of the student body at the famous Stuyvesant High School, 62% at the influential Bronx High School of Science, and 61% at Brooklyn Technical High School. These percentages are staggering given that Asian Americans comprise a mere 15.6% of the New York City public student population (between the ages of 5 and 17) (NYC Department of Education, 2014).

Kasinitz et al. (2008) compared 24–32-year-old New Yorkers from eight ethnic groups, including a group of second-generation Chinese. Of all the groups, the Chinese were the most likely to score in the upper performance quintile of the public high school they attended. Moreover, they were also the most likely to have received at least a BA (64%) and the least likely to have dropped out of high school—a finding that held true above all for the Chinese girls. In these achievements, they substantially outpaced native-born whites although the average level of their parents' education and income was substantially below that of the white parents.

Hsin and Xie's study (2014) threw into serious doubt the idea that Asian Americans are genetically predisposed to excel in schools. Rather, the major factors that exert the strongest impact on academic achievement involve a special kind and intensity of cultural orientation as well as immigration status, not their socio-demographic characteristics or superior cognitive abilities. "Cultural orientation, immigrant selectivity, and adaptive strategies that emphasize education for upward mobility all play a part in shaping AA youth's outlook toward the value of effort in attaining achievement" (p. 8420), the authors state. New York City's Chinatowns also offer a plethora of tutoring classes and college preparatory resources, both reinforcing the importance of academic success and providing the means to do so. Additionally, the "model minority" status that Asian Americans hold in the eyes of many can also have the indirect effect of bolstering confidence and the ability to succeed just as negative stereotypes can hinder other minority youths from reaching their full potential.

Indeed and across the country, among the major ethnic groups, Asian Americans are most likely to have graduated with at least a bachelor's degree. On a national level, 70.3% of Chinese in 2007 had a bachelor's degree, a percentage much higher than that of whites (32.6%), blacks (17%), and Hispanics (11.2%). However, this does not hold true in New York City where Chinese (39%) fell far behind whites (63%) but still outranked blacks (31%) and Hispanics (23%). These statistics represent the many rural and working-class immigrants who arrived in the United States with limited education throughout the 1970s to 1990s, and who in many cases would become the parents of the adolescents and emerging adults in our study. The wave of immigration was not evenly distributed throughout the United States. Whereas most educated and wealthier Chinese are scattered throughout the country, with a concentration on the West Coast and some suburban areas on the East Coast, New York City exerted a natural pull for those who came from a less educated background. Indeed, most of our participants had working-class or lower middle-class parents from small towns and rural areas in China who were working toward the American dream by providing their children with the opportunities they themselves would never enjoy.

In Chinese societies, parents entrust teachers with the complete authority to supervise the students in their respective classrooms, while they structure the learning environment at home by making sure that the often extensive homework is completed. However, in the United States, American parents tend to play more active roles within the school grounds in a variety of ways, for example, by joining the Parent-Teacher Association or addressing complaints directly to the teacher. Compared to other ethnic groups, Chinese parents may seem to adopt a passive approach when it comes to advocating for their children in schools. They may also downplay the importance of extracurricular activities such as sports that, in American society, serve as the ladder to peer group acceptance and fame.

However, as heavily as Chinese immigrant parents emphasize academic success, their ability to assist their children in this process is severely limited in this new land. Their frequent lack of English proficiency, unfamiliarity with the American educational system, and having to work long hours place them decidedly in a disadvantaged position when attempting to play a more active role in their child's school life; moreover they may feel hesitant about confronting school administrators whose language and cultural background they tend not to share. Above all, these Chinese-speaking parents push their children to achieve what was impossible for themselves, and they therefore cannot serve as distinct role models or supervisors of their children's educational efforts. Yet for all of that they are often surprisingly effective in inculcating their high expectations in their children.

Despite their inability to assist with schoolwork, the values and motivations that Chinese parents instill in their children have far-reaching consequences. Compared to other ethnic groups, young Chinese adults are more willing to stay home, defer sexual gratifications, and marry at a later age, thus saving money, reducing debt, and having the time and resources to obtain higher education and build a solid financial foundation (Chen & Kim, 2009; Kasinitz et al., 2008). Their willingness to delay marriage, and thus childbirth, stems from their focus on achieving financial stability before starting a family. The low birth rates among the Chinese American population serve individual families well in that they can pool their resources together to achieve social mobility, but the larger, inadvertent consequence is that fewer children in the next generation are able to launch off of their predecessors' success.

CONCLUSIONS

In the foregoing we have attempted to depict the inner emotional world of immigrant Chinese American adolescents and emerging adults in the context of their (more or less) bicultural environment. Given the complex circumstances that have surrounded them since their early years, their often-mixed emotions and subtle assessments of themselves and their relationships to loved ones may not come as a complete surprise. Many of them deeply respect the many sacrifices their parents have made for them, yet they may also feel a certain affective distance to them. A few others, such as Sophia, whose self-observations we noted in the beginning of this chapter, experience a deep ambivalence about their parents' culture of origin that reaches into the very depths of their body image. Most of them have internalized the rigid educational expectations of their parents and, indeed, their educational successes as a group are outstanding. But we also found that many of them are paying an emotional price for their successes. A significant portion of them did report that attempting to meet such sky-high internal and external expectations caused them to suffer from self-doubts, bouts of depression, and social anxieties. Indeed, although Chinese children tend to work hard in school, the boys in particular often dislike their schools. In a comparative study of 411 immigrant students' adaptation in school, Qin-Hilliard (2003) found that among various cultural and gender groups, Chinese boys were the *least* likely to experience positive attitudes toward school. At the same time, they spent considerably more time on homework than, for instance, their Dominican peers who were much more likely to be distracted by outside jobs.

Similar tensions between reported family conflicts, self-reported adjustment, and academic achievement were observed by Qin, Rak, Rana, and Donnellan (2012) in their comparison of high-achieving Chinese and European American ninth graders at an extremely selective magnet school located in New York. The Chinese American students, many of whom came from poor families, reported lower levels of family cohesion and psychological adjustment, but higher levels of family conflict than their economically better-off European American peers. Furthermore, the ethnic differences in psychological adjustment vanished once the researchers controlled for the variables of perceived family cohesion and conflict. This points to difficult family conditions as a key reason for the Chinese students' lower levels of psychological adjustment. To this it may be added that because the Asian students dominated the school's student body, it is unlikely that the obtained results were influenced by perceived racial handicaps at the school.

To grow up as a Chinese American child and adolescent in New York City, then, can be an emotionally difficult experience. But despite the stresses of economic hardship, acculturation, linguistic handicaps, cross-generational negotiation, racial-ethnic minority status, prejudice and discrimination, and pubescent development, many of our Chinese American adolescents demonstrated powerful resilience in the face of these adversities. Most of them are on their way to success, which suggests that they will not have to endure their parents' harsh working conditions and hard scrabble lives. They are bound to make a major contribution to the life of the city and, more generally, to the country's overall welfare. New York City has always been a place where immigrants step ashore (or get off the plane), buckle down, and attempt to realize the American dream either for themselves or, if that is not possible, for their children. Most Chinese American "children" we interviewed were prepared to endorse this demanding tradition, do everything they could to fulfill their parents' dreams, and secure a place in the sun for themselves and their loved ones. But, for too many of them, their journey on this promising path has been, and will be, accompanied by considerable inner and outer struggles.

ACKNOWLEDGMENT

The authors are deeply indebted to Jonathan Palumbo, who did many of the interviews cited, and to Ting Lei, co-principal investigator of our interview study.

REFLECTIVE QUESTIONS

1. How and why did the Chinese originally end up in New York City, and why do so many Chinese immigrants continue to settle down in the Big Apple?
2. What are some of the main pressures that Chinese American teenagers and young adults face in New York City?
3. What are some of the family dynamics that predominate in Chinese American immigrant families from a working-class background?
4. What impact do gender roles have on the adjustment and educational success of Chinese American immigrant adolescents?
5. What are some of the differences in the cultural and emotional adjustment of first- and second-generation immigrants?
6. Chinese American students often do well in school. What are some of the reasons for their success and what is the emotional price they may have to pay for it?

SUGGESTED READINGS

Books and Articles

Kasinitz, P., Mollenkopf, J. H., Waters, M. C., & Holdaway, J. (2008). *Inheriting the city: The children of immigrants come of age.* New York: Russell Sage Foundation. This is the leading comparative study of second-generation, immigrant young adults in New York City.

Qin, D. B. (2009). Being "good" or being "popular": Gender and ethnic identity negotiations of Chinese immigrant adolescents. *Journal of Adolescent Research, 24*(1), 37–66. Qin is the author of several research-based articles on Chinese immigrant children and adolescents that are relevant to this chapter.

Rosenbloom, S. R., & Way, N. (2004). Experiences of discrimination among African American, Asian American, and Latino adolescents in an urban high school. *Youth & Society, 35*(4), 420–451. The authors investigated a lower-tier public neighborhood high school in New York City, finding that Asian American students reported extensive physical and verbal harassment by their non-Asian peers.

Sung, B.L. (1987). *The adjustment experience of Chinese immigrant children in New York City.* New York: Center for Immigration Studies. Although now outdated in a few respects (e.g., the earlier prevalence of violent Chinatown gangs in the 1980s), this remains the most detailed study of Chinese immigrant children in the Big Apple.

Zhou, M. (2009). Conflict, coping, and reconciliation: Intergenerational relations in Chinese immigrant families. In N. Foner (Ed.), *Across generations: Immigrant families in America* (pp. 21–46). New York: New York University Press. This chapter presents a well-balanced sociological analysis of intergenerational relationships among Chinese Americans.

Website

Qin, D.B. (2013). *Other side of the model minority story: Psychological & social adjustment of Chinese Americans.* Retrieved from https://www.youtube.com/watch?v=Zc7382cgiko.

REFERENCES

Asakawa, K. (2001). Family socialization practices and their effects on the internalization of educational values for Asian and White American adolescents. *Applied Developmental Science, 5*(3), 184–194.

Bao, X.-h., & Lam, S.-f. (2008). Who makes the choice? Rethinking the role of autonomy and relatedness in Chinese children's motivation. *Child Development, 79*(2), 269–283.

Baumrind, D. (1971). Current patterns of parental authority. *Developmental Psychology Monographs, 4*(1, Pt. 2).

Benner, A. D., & Kim, S. Y. (2010). Understanding Asian American adolescents' developmental outcomes: Insights from the family stress model. *Journal of Research on Adolescence, 20,* 1–12.

Bernstein, N. (2009). Chinese-American children sent to live with kin abroad face a tough return. *The New York Times.* Retrieved from http://www.nytimes.com/2009/07/24/nyregion/24chinese.html?pagewanted=all&_r=0.

Bohr, Y., & Tse, C. (2009). Satellite babies in transitional families: A study of parents' decision to separate from their infants. *Infant Mental Health Journal, 30*(3), 265–286.

Chao, R.K. (1994). Beyond parental control and authoritarian parenting: Understanding Chinese parenting through the cultural notion of training. *Child Development, 65,* 1111–1119.

Chao, R.K. (2001). Extending research on the consequences of parenting style for Chinese Americans and European Americans. *Child Development, 72,* 1832–1843.

Cheah, C.S.L., Zhou, N., Leung, C.Y.Y., & Vu, K.T.T. (in prep.). Why and how U.S. immigrant mothers engage in parenting control and the role of their acculturation. In S.S. Chuang, C. Costigan, & U.P. Gielen (Eds.), *Parenting and parent-child relationships among immigrant families around the world.* New York: Springer.

Chen, F.-M., & Luster, T. (2002). Factors related to parenting practices in Taiwan. *Early Child Development and Care, 172,* 413–430.

Chen, G.A., & Kim, S.C. (2009). Sexuality. In N. Tewari & A.N. Alvarez (Eds.), *Asian American psychology: Current perspectives* (pp. 247–271). New York: Taylor & Francis Group.

Chiu, L.H. (1987). Child-rearing attitudes of Chinese, Chinese-American, and Anglo-American mothers. *International Journal of Psychology, 22,* 409–4119.

Eaton, M.J., & Dembo, M.H. (1997). Differences in the motivation beliefs of Asian American and non-Asian students. *Journal of Educational Psychology, 89,* 443–440.

Ho, D.Y.F. (1986). Chinese patterns of socialization: A critical review. In M.H. Bond (ed.), *The psychology of the Chinese people* (pp. 1–37). New York: Oxford University Press.

Ho, G.W.K. (2014). Acculturation and its implications on parenting for Chinese immigrants: A systematic review. *Journal of Transcultural Nursing, 25*(2), 145–158.

Hsin, A., & Xie, Y. (2014). Explaining Asian Americans' academic advantage over whites. *Proceedings of the National Academy of Sciences of the United States of America. 111*(23), 8416–8421. Retrieved on April 14, 2015, from http://www.pnas.org/content/111/23/8416.full.pdf.

Huang, C.-Y., & Lamb, M.E. (2014). Are Chinese children more compliant? Examination of the cultural difference in observed maternal control and child compliance. *Journal of Cross-Cultural Psychology, 45*(4), 507–533.

Jia, G. (2004). The acquisition of English and maintenance of first language by immigrant children and adolescents in North America. In U.P. Gielen & J. Roopnarine (Eds.), *Children and adolescence: Cross-cultural perspectives and application* (pp. 350–373). Westport, CT: Praeger.

Juang, L.P., Qin, D.B., & Park, I.J.K. (2013). Deconstructing the myth of the "tiger mother": An introduction to the Special Issue on Tiger parenting, Asian-heritage families, and child/adolescent well-being. *Asian American Journal of Psychology, 4*(1), 1–6.

Kao, T.-S.A., & Martyn, K.K. (2014). Comparing White and Asian American adolescents' perceived parental expectations and their sexual behaviors. *Sage Open,* April–June 2014, *4*(2), 2158244014535411.

Kasinitz, P., Mollenkopf, J.H., Waters, M.C., & Holdaway, J. (2008). *Inheriting the city: The children of immigrants come of age.* New York: Russell Sage Foundation.

Keefe, P.R. (2010). *The snakehead: An epic of the Chinatown underworld and the American dream.* New York: Anchor.

Kiersz, A. (2014). Here's the most commonly spoken language in every New York neighborhood that isn't English or Spanish. *Business Insider.* Retrieved from http://www.businessinsider.com/nyc-non-english-language-maps-2014–8

Kim, J.L., & Ward, L.M. (2007). Silence speaks volumes: Parental sexual communication among Asian American emerging adults. *Journal of Adolescent Research, 22*(1), 3–31.

Kwong, P. (1996). *The new Chinatown* (rev. ed.). New York: Hill and Wang.

Li, X. (2015a). Interpersonal acceptance-rejection research in Chinese populations (Part One). *Interpersonal Acceptance, 9*(1), 2–5.

Li, X. (2015b). Interpersonal acceptance-rejection research in Chinese populations (Part Two), *Interpersonal Acceptance, 9*(2), 2–7.

Lin, C.C., & Fu, V.R. (1990). A comparison of child-rearing practices among Chinese, immigrant Chinese, and Caucasian-American parents. *Child Development, 56,* 429–433.

McGlinn, L. (2002). Beyond Chinatown: Dual immigration and the Chinese population of metropolitan New York City, 2000. *Middle States Geographer, 35,* 110–119. Retrieved from http://geographyplanning.buffalostate.edu/MSG%202002/13_McGlinn.pdf

NYC Department of Education. (2014). *School quality guide 2013–2014.* Retrieved on April, 14, 2015, from http://schools.nyc.gov/OA/SchoolReports/2013-14/School_Quality_Guide_2014_HS_K430.pdf

Qin, D.B. (2006). Our child doesn't talk to us anymore: Alienation in immigrant Chinese families. *Anthropology and Education Quarterly, 37,* 162–179.

Qin, D.B. (2008). Doing well vs. feeling well: Understanding family dynamics and the psychological adjustment of Chinese immigrant adolescents. *Journal of Youth and Adolescence, 37,* 22–35.

Qin, D.B. (2009). Being "good" or being "popular": Gender and ethnic identity negotiations of Chinese immigrant adolescents. *Journal of Adolescent Research, 24*(1), 37–66.

Qin, D.B., Rak, E., Rana, M., & Donnellan, B. (2012). Parent-child relations and psychological adjustment among high-achieving Chinese and European American adolescents. *Journal of Adolescence, 35,* 863–873.

Qin-Hillard, D.B. (2003). Gendered expectations and gendered experiences: Immigrant students' adaptation in school. *New Directions for Youth Development, 100,* 91–109.

Rosenbloom, S.R., & Way, N. (2004). Experiences of discrimination among African American, Asian American, and Latino adolescents in an urban high school. *Youth & Society, 35*(4), 420–451.

Suárez-Orozco, C., & Suárez-Orozco, M.M. (2001). *Children of immigration.* Cambridge, MA: Harvard University Press.

Tsai, J.L., Ying, Y., & Lee, P.A. (2001). Cultural predictors of self-esteem: A study of Chinese American female and male young adults. *Cultural Diversity and Ethnic Minority Psychology, 7*(3), 284–297.

United States Census Bureau. (2012). Languages spoken at home: 2012 American Community Survey 5-Year Estimates. Retrieved from http://factfinder2.census.gov/faces/tableservices/jsf/pages/productview.xhtml?pid=ACS_12_5YR_S1601&prodType=table

United States Census Bureau. (2014). State and county quick facts: New York (city), New York. Retrieved from http://quickfacts.census.gov/qfd/states/36/3651000.html

University of California—San Diego (2011). Is there a "tiger mother" effect? Asian students study twice as many hours, analysis finds. *ScienceDaily.* Retrieved from www.sciencedaily.com/releases/2011/05/110505103345.htm.

Wang, Q. (2013). Chinese socialization and emotion talk between mothers and children in native and immigrant Chinese families. *Asian American Journal of Psychology, 4*(3), 185–192.

Zhou, Z., Peverly, S.T., Xin, T., Huang, A.S., & Wang, W. (2003). School adjustment of first generation Chinese-American adolescents. *Psychology in the Schools, 40*(1), 71–84.

Part V

DIFFICULT CIRCUMSTANCES AND ADJUSTMENTS

14

Violence against Girls

Janet A. Sigal, Carrol S. Perrino, Florence L. Denmark,
Emily A. A. Dow, Renata Strashnaya,
Talia Zarbiv, and Felicia Wright

Between 1997 and 2013, there were approximately 1,400 cases of child abuse in Rotherham, England, including sexual assault and sex trafficking within England. The following case study describes one of the sex trafficking victims named Lucy (Bennhold, 2014):

> *The abuse began when Lucy was 12 years old. Male teenagers would flirt with Lucy and other girls in a shopping mall after school. "Over time, older men were introduced to the girls while the boys faded away. Soon they were getting rides in real cars and were offered vodka and marijuana. One man in particular, a Pakistani twice her age and the leader of the group, flattered her and bought her drinks and even a mobile phone. Lucy liked him. The rapes started gradually, once a week, then every day in many different locations and "once, in an apartment where she was locked naked in a room and had to service half a dozen men lined up outside."*
>
> *Escape was difficult because they said "If you don't come back we will rape your mother and make you watch." Even so, just before her 14th birthday, Lucy informed her mother who informed the police. "Two police officers came to collect the (bags of) clothes as evidence. . . ." "A few days later, they called to say that the bags had been lost." Once, she said, when they thought she might go to the police, a man . . . "dragged her into his car . . ., and put a gun to her head. . . . Keep your mouth shut, he said. . . . Next time there will be a bullet inside." The police and Council members who were contacted treated the girls with contempt and in some cases even claimed that the sex had been "consensual" although the girls were very young. Very few cases were prosecuted. Lucy and her family moved away for over a year to protect her. After many years of psychological distress, she now consults with the police and other organizations.*

Cases such as Lucy's are unfortunately not uncommon. A recent report from the United Nations Children's Fund (UNICEF, 2014) found especially high rates in Africa, and noted that

> At least one in eight adolescent girls in all West and Central African countries except two (Nigeria and Sao Tome and Principe) with available data reported experiences of forced sexual intercourse or other sexual acts at some point during their lives. Prevalence rates of sexual violence are above 10 per cent in all countries of Eastern and Southern Africa with available data, except for Comoros and Mozambique. When it comes to recent exposure to sexual violence, up to 12 per cent of adolescent girls aged 15 to 19 in all countries with available data reported victimization in the last year. The highest rates of past-year victimization are found in the Democratic Republic of the Congo (10 per cent), Uganda (9 per cent) and Equatorial Guinea and Zambia (8 per cent each). (p.66)

Sexual violence is only one form of several acts of violence against girls found in the world today. More broadly, violence against girls is a human rights violation that prevents girls from being educated, achieving fulfillment, and sometimes leading them to fear for their lives. This chapter cannot cover the numerous forms of violence against girls; therefore we will focus on those forms of violence that are of special global relevance including physical punishment and abuse, child marriages (which are conceptualized as coerced or forced since children are incapable of making marriage choices at such young ages), sex trafficking leading to lasting physical and psychological damage, and honor crimes or honor killings representing the most extreme form of violence against girls.

Our chapter begins with an overview of selected theories followed by a discussion of those four types of violence against girls noted earlier, including definitions, methodological issues, causes, and consequences of this violence. We conclude with a description of different approaches to prevention or interventions designed to reduce or eliminate violence against girls.

THEORIES

According to social learning theory children learn by observing and internalizing their parents' or caregivers' behaviors and learn which behaviors achieve desirable results. If inappropriate behaviors are modeled for children in the home or through the media, violent strategies can be learned and subsequently replicated. Therefore, this explanation suggests that boys who witness violence in childhood are more likely to grow up and become abusers, whereas girls who view the abuse of their mothers may become victims themselves (Johnson, 1995).

Another major approach to explain violence against girls is the concept of patriarchy. Frequently this theory is associated with a feminist perspective and describes a system of male domination and female subordination. Patriarchal systems exist both at the macro level in institutions (e.g., government, law, and religion) and at the micro level in families or communities. In some patriarchal cultures there is support for male violence against girls (Olson, 1997).

Other theories focus on the psychopathology of the male abuser, with implications that interventions should address abusive men (Saunders, 1996). Dutton, Saunders, and Starzomski (1994) identified the borderline or antisocial personality structure as an important personality characteristic associated with abuse. Borderline individuals have a distrustful sense of the self that stems from childhood experiences of loss or abandonment. These men often fail to develop a sense of responsibility and tend to see people as either all good or all bad. For instance, if they perceive a girl as "bad" that may serve as an impetus for violence against the girl. Moreover, the antisocial abuser tends to experience a sense of inner calmness while battering.

Systems theory offers another explanation of the role of interpersonal factors that characterize violent men who abuse girls and women. The family is seen as a dynamic organization of interdependent parts that continually interact with one another. If violence is rewarded within this system, then it is likely to reoccur at home or elsewhere. If it is punished, on the other hand, it may be eliminated (Cahn & Lloyd, 1996).

PHYSICAL CHILD ABUSE

Abusing children physically constitutes a violation of their human rights. The experience of physical abuse can be confusing to children and have lasting negative effects. Additionally, children often do not have the physical capacity to fight back when the abuse is clearly unwarranted. Despite this violation of human rights, defining physical child abuse (PCA) is challenging, especially on an international level where cultural differences are widespread. International prevalence rates of PCA vary from country to country, and definitions of child abuse often reflect the prevalent cultural norms and attitudes about families and parenting. The process for identifying PCA also varies, and so do cultural and ethnic risks and outcomes for PCA. Despite the United Nations efforts to address the human rights of children through the Convention on the Rights of the Child (CRC), the legal ramifications for engaging in PCA are vastly different across the globe.

Definitions

Children are constantly developing, and their experiences and environments help guide these changes. In the bio-ecological model presented by Urie Bronfenbrenner, the child is embedded in relationships and transactions that are influenced and shaped by the cultural context (Bronfenbrenner & Morris, 2006; Cicchetti & Valentino, 2006). According to this model, hypotheses about attachment relationships with parents or primary caregivers can be influenced by the community in which that relationship is formed. Similarly, child development is influenced by specific morals and ethics found within a community.

In order to fully capture the experiences of PCA and its consequences, it is essential to understand the cultural and environmental demands a child may experience. Therefore, the definition of abuse must be culturally defined.

Researchers have called for better definitions of abuse (Cyr, Michel, & Dumais, 2013, p. 144), as there is often a struggle to differentiate corporal punishment from physical abuse. Using a definition originally developed by Strauss (1994), Gershoff (2002) defined corporal punishment as "the use of physical force with the intention of causing a child to experience pain *but not injury* for the purpose of correction or control of the child's behavior" (p. 540). Alternatively, Whipple and Richey (1997) suggested that "physical discipline" lies on a continuum of parenting practices where physical abuse is the extreme form (p. 439).

For example, spanking is a rather debatable parenting practice, and it can be reasoned that it is a cultural parenting tool used to help address a child's inappropriate or rule-breaking behavior. To highlight the continuum between discipline and abuse, Whipple and Richey (1997) suggest that some parents argue that it is an adequate form of discipline while others would say that it is a form of physical abuse. To help operationalize this distinction, Hawkins and colleagues (2010), in their research on ethnic difference, differentiated between "injurious spanking" and PCA (p. 244). Injurious spanking was defined as hitting that caused bruises, cuts, and/or welts. The definition of physical abuse included more severe acts of violence, liking punching, throwing/pushing, or choking.

In addition to definitional concerns in the empirical literature, there are problems in how to measure PCA in and of itself, as well as outcomes of experiencing PCA. It is unclear from the research how corporal punishment—non-abusive parenting practices as defined by Gershoff—can impact child development (Gershoff, 2002). Morally and ethically, as psychological researchers we cannot use the gold standard of experimental design in an effort to better understand PCA, (i.e., have a treatment and control group, randomize group membership, and measure specific outcomes of PCA).

Despite these definitional and measurement problems, what constitutes the observable or operationalized variables of PCA is value-dependent. Researchers in the past decade have begun to incorporate such values into their research on PCA (e.g., Chou, Su, Wu, & Chen, 2011). For example, Bril and Sabatier (1986) studied the cultural influences of parenting practices on motor development in Mali. Children from West African cultures are exposed to rather aggressive massage and manipulation in early infancy. Mothers can be seen dangling a young infant by the arm, or pushing an infant's leg to their forehead. Outside of this context, observing this kind of behavior between a mother and an infant may be noted as a form of child abuse and parents may be reported for endangering the life of the child. However, there are positive effects of this early motor experiences: Children exposed to this kind of parenting develop locomotion skills and gross motor skills earlier compared to other same-aged cohorts (see Adolph, Karasik, & Tamis-LeMonda, 2009, for a review). They walk at a younger age, their arm, hand movements develop earlier, and their overall motor development is formed at an earlier age. In another example, children in urban China are restricted in their motor development (Mei, 1994). Infants are often restricted by using a variety of swaddling methods. This procedure, too, could be seen as a form of child abuse. It is clear from these examples that researchers must consider cultural influences when defining child abuse, and operationalizing it.

Similarly, perceptions—not just behaviors—about child abuse must be examined. For example, in Taiwan, a cultural distinction may be drawn between strict discipline with violent acts, where the violent acts may have no consequential injuries; however, if there are lasting effects of the violent acts, for example, where a child may need medical attention, then the discipline is perceived as abuse (Chou et al., 2011, p. 59).

The United Nations Convention on the Rights of the Child (CRC) is an international document that details the human rights, including the civil, political, economic, social, health, and cultural rights, of children. Governments of countries that have signed the CRC are required to demonstrate how they are creating legislation and policy consistent with the CRC. Currently, 194 countries have signed the CRC including every member of the United Nations except South Sudan and the United States; Somalia recently signed the CRC. Article 19 in the CRC states that any country that ratifies the CRC "shall take all appropriate legislative, administrative, social and educational measures to protect the child from all forms of physical or mental violence, injury or abuse, neglect or negligent treatment, maltreatment or exploitation, including sexual abuse, while in the care of parent(s), legal guardian(s) or any other person who has the care of the child" (Convention on the Rights of the Child, 1990). However, there is no explicit definition of what abuse is in the document. The World Health Organization (2014), in contrast, does define child abuse on its website, and it includes "all forms of physical and emotional ill-treatment, sexual abuse, neglect, and exploitation that results in actual or potential harm to the child's health, development or dignity" (p. 1). The lack of international definitions and clarity makes it challenging for researchers to study the effects of child abuse.

Prevalence

In light of the recognition that cultural differences in PCA are abundant, a 2013 meta-analysis sought to understand the large variation of PCA internationally and provide a worldwide estimate of child abuse (Stoltenborgh et al., 2013b). A review of 111 publications found several moderating variables that explain the variation in prevalence rates of PCA internationally. Based on the meta-analysis, an overall prevalence rate for PCA of 17.7% was found with a 95% confidence interval ranging from 13.0% to 23.6%. First, when the definition of PCA was broad, there was an increase in prevalence rates. Second, there was a decrease in prevalence rates when abuse was measured within a limited time period, for example, up to one year, as opposed to a greater time period, for example, between 0 and 18 years of age. Third, the number of questions about the PCA influenced the prevalence rate: studies that asked more questions about the abuse reported higher prevalence rates. Fourth, more recent publications reported lower prevalence rates of PCA; it is thought that this finding is in light of recent efforts to better define PCA. Lastly, there were no geographic differences with respect to prevalence rates.

The lack of geographic, or regional, differences among the 111 studies could be explained on the basis of a variety of methodological reasons, including sampling differences. However, the authors suggest that the "large variability of prevalence rates within the continents may have overshadowed differences between continents" (p. 88). Similarly, they note that future studies of prevalence rates should not substitute the concepts of culture, ethnicity, and economic status for one another (p. 89; also see Cry et al., 2013, p. 145). Culture, ethnicity, and economic status are unique concepts that capture different aspects of the community.

Risk Factors

In a 2002 meta-analysis on corporal punishment in the United States, Gershoff reviewed 88 studies to better understand the effects of corporal punishment on child behaviors. Gershoff identified several behavioral outcomes, as well as higher-order context variables that influenced this relationship. These variables mimicked the ecological approach, with variables representing the interactional context (e.g., characteristics of the misbehavior, parental goals), the relational context (e.g., characteristics of the child, parent, family), and the social-cultural context (e.g., stress, SES, ethnicity). These variables introduce important considerations when understanding PCA on the international level. Following is a review of international evidence about these various risk and protective factors in the context of PCA. Risk factors for PCA can be categorized into four different types using the ecological approach: demographic, familial, parental, and child (Belsky & Vondra, 1989). It is important to demonstrate how mediating variables related to child abuse are either risk or protective variables (Cry et al., 2013, pp. 145–146).

Demographic. Demographics are perhaps the most studied variable in child abuse. Internationally, though, demographic characteristics are often relative, and cross-cultural comparisons can sometimes be challenging. Ethnic differences have been established in a population-based study in the United States (Hawkins et al., 2010). Youths who had identified as African American or Hispanic had higher self-report rates of PCA in comparison to youths who identified as Caucasian, even when considering other demographic information such as age or family income. Much of the research that focuses on ethnic differences uses agency data (e.g., Child Protective Services); agency data have a tendency to over-represent minorities, and under-represent population statistics. Hawkins, et al., used self-report data in an effort to capture more accurate figures.

Poverty/Low SES. It is often thought that parents who are struggling economically have higher rates of stress (e.g., Deater-Deckard, Bates, Dodge, & Pettit, 1996). Stoltenborgh and colleagues (2013b) suggest that a higher level of parental stress increases the use of physical discipline, which in turn increases the likelihood for PCA (p. 82). In a large Canadian population-based study, growing up in poverty predicted (along with other factors of interest) increased rates of PCA (MacMillan, Tanaka, Duku, Vaillancourt, & Boyle, 2013).

Familial. Familial characteristics include features of interactions and relationships the child may have with the entire family. Exposure to interpersonal violence (e.g., between parents) increases the likelihood a child will experience PCA (e.g., Annerback, Svedin, & Gustafson, 2010; Finkelhor, Turner, Ormrod, & Hamby, 2010). Additionally, a large family also may increase the likelihood to experience PCA (Stith et al., 2009). On the contrary, growing up in a single-parent home also can be detrimental (Brown, Cohen, Johnson, & Salzinger, 1998; MacMillan et al., 2013; Stith et al., 2009). Additionally, families that live in relative isolation may use physical abuse more frequently (Cicchetti & Valentino, 2006). Cultural norms must also be considered: If physical abuse within the family is normative in the culture, it is more likely to be used (Chou et al., 2011; Gracia & Herrero, 2008; Lansford, Dodge, Pettit, & Bates, 2010).

Immigrant Status. Families that are immigrating may use physical abuse more frequently compared to acculturated families. Chinese immigrants to Taiwan have higher incidence rates of abuse compared to the national prevalence rate for Taiwan (Chou et al., 2011). Another example from the Netherlands found that traditional and nontraditional immigrants to the Netherlands were both at high risk for PCA (Alink, Euser, van IJzendoorn, & Bakermans-Kranenburg, 2013). Euser and colleagues (2011) found similar results with differences between the types of immigrant family to the Netherlands: Traditional immigrants who had lower education status and nontraditional immigrant family structures were more likely to use PCA. Nontraditional immigrant families were those emigrating from countries like Central Asia or South America; traditional immigrant families are those emigrating from countries that have a history of immigrating to the Netherlands, such as Turkey or Morocco. For nontraditional immigrants, parenting stress was a primary variable that influenced the rate of PCA. It was hypothesized that many of these nontraditional immigrant families were refugees, and the stress they were experiencing may be a reflection of PTSD related to their refugee status.

Child Factors. Multiple psychosomatic symptoms in children may be an indicator for PCA. A Swedish, population-based study found that nearly two-thirds of children who experienced PCA also reported at least one psychosomatic symptom (e.g., headache, dizziness, loss of appetite), and one-third reported at least three psychosomatic symptoms, even when specific variables were controlled (e.g., chronic condition, school performance, involvement with bullying) (Jernbro, Svensson, Tindberg, & Janson, 2012). Using the same nationally representative data set, Svensson, Bornehag, and Janson (2011) found that Swedish children with a chronic condition were more likely to experience physical abuse; however, there was variability based on economic status, specifically low income.

Gender Differences. While this chapter is focused on violence against girls, as the title suggests, it is useful to briefly discuss gender differences in the context of physical punishment. The recent UNICEF (2014) document reports rates as high as one in four boys experiencing some form of physical violence in their teenage years (p. 52). However, UNICEF also notes that there are more limited global data on boys and physical punishment than there are for girls. Researchers have sought to understand gender differences in experiencing physical violence. For example, in a study using self-report data in St. Croix, where corporal punishment is an acceptable cultural parenting practice, results showed that boys were often hit or "beaten" more strongly compared to girls (Mathurin, Gielen, & Lancaster, 2006, p. 320). However, both boys and girls viewed their punishment as equally harsh. Additional gender differences were found in personality traits, and such traits were both antecedent and consequence of the experience of physical punishment. This is simply one example of many in discussing gender differences in physical punishment, and it highlights the interacting effects of parenting practices, cultural acceptability, and gender related variables as both outcomes and potential precipitants. Unfortunately, a further review of gender differences is beyond the scope of this chapter.

Protective Factors

Families that have strong social networks are less likely to use non-normative physical punishment and therefore are less likely to be abusive (Korbin, 1991). Positive perceptions of abuse can also be considered a protective factor for the child (Chou et al., 2011). Chou and colleagues note that the cultural perceptions of abuse in Taiwanese-Chinese immigrants became a "rationalized attribution": Children understood that the abuse was in a specific context and was used for a specific reason. This lessened the likelihood of PTSD in the sample; the positive cultural bias toward harsh abuse was a protective factor against negative outcomes of experiencing physical violence, such as PTSD (p. 65).

Conclusions

PCA is affected by many factors but culture is a determining feature associated with global definitions and risk factors. The distinction between physical punishment and physical abuse is not always clear, and cultural norms determine what is acceptable globally. However, it is important to identify what would be considered abusive parenting internationally in order to develop prevention programs that may help to mitigate any potential negative outcomes.

CHILD MARRIAGES, ABDUCTIONS, AND KIDNAPPINGS

Definition

The International Women's Health Coalition (IWHC) cited the United Nations Convention on the Rights of the Child (CRC) as defining a child as anyone under 18 years old (IWHC, 2008, p. 1). There was some mention in the CRC that a child could be labeled an adult prior to age 18 in some countries, but generally that is the accepted classification of a child. Therefore child marriages involve a girl younger than 18.

Although there is general acceptance of the definition of a child marriage as involving girls younger than 18, there still is confusion about the distinction between child marriages and forced marriages. The IWHC views all child marriages as "forced marriages" since children have not reached the developmental stage to fully grasp the concept of marriage, and do not have the power to refuse to marry at an early age. However, Chantler (2012) reported that in the United Kingdom, for example, children who are 16 or older can freely enter into "arranged marriages" in which the consent of the partners to the marriage is required. According to Chantler, arranged marriages are different from coerced marriages. Forced marriages involve a lack of consent and imply marriage under "duress" which can include threats of physical harm, psychological abuse, or even abductions.

In this chapter, we will adapt the general guideline of defining child marriage as occurring when at least one of the couple (usually the girl) is under 18 years old, and view that type of marriage as "forced or coerced." According to the IWHC (2008), child forced marriages are a violation not only of the girls' human rights but also their "sexual and reproductive health" (p. 1).

There was a recent horrific and relevant international incident related to child abductions, and possibly to forced marriages in Nigeria on April 14, 2014. Over 270 girls were kidnapped from their school in Chibok, Borno State in violation of international law (e-mail Communication: Joint Statement on the Abduction of School Girls in Nigeria, UNWomen.org, April 30, 2014). The kidnappings were carried out by Boko Haram, an armed rebel group in Nigeria as a protest against education of girls (Kristof, 2014). Following the abductions, there were rumors that many of the abducted girls had been "sold" to members of the militant group as "wives." A protest by parents of the abducted girls sparked a worldwide support movement "Bring Back Our Girls," which has been spreading through social media. The Nigerian government, after considerable local and international pressure, has reached out to other countries for assistance in rescuing the girls.

Incidence of Child Marriages

As is the case in most types of violence against girls, methodological issues limit the conclusions that can be drawn from data on global incidence of child marriages. The major issue is extensive underreporting. Since child marriages are illegal in many countries (e.g., in India, Speizer & Pearson, 2011), respondents are hesitant to report having been married before the legal age of 18. Representative samples are often difficult to obtain, and anonymity may not be understood by participants who fear that honest responses could be reported to the authorities.

However, there is some evidence that early marriage is widespread particularly in some areas of the world. This practice was reported to be particularly prevalent in South Asia and sub-Saharan Africa. Chantler (2012) cited a UNICEF estimate based on 100 countries that proposed that millions of women worldwide had been married as a child or an adolescent. Ghosh (2011) focused on Malda, a part of West Bengal, India, and found that over 55% of the girls in that area were married by age 15, mostly to much older men. Ertem, Saka, Ceylan, Deger, and Çiftçi (2008) identified a comparable percentage of child marriages in Mardin, Turkey.

The UNICEF (2014) report notes that "South Asia has the highest proportion of married adolescent girls (29 percent), followed by West and Central Africa (25 percent), Eastern and Southern Africa (21 percent) and Latin America and the Caribbean (19 percent) (p. 131). Data from more than 60 low- and middle-income countries indicate that an estimated 20 percent of married or cohabiting girls aged 15 to 19 are with a man who is at least 10 years older. The age gap between spouses is particularly high in Mauritania and Nigeria, where 60 percent and 52 percent, respectively, of married or cohabiting adolescent girls are with a man who is at least 10 years older than they are" (p. 131).

Causes or Explanations of Child Marriages

There are at least two major explanations of child or early marriages which have been proposed by a number of researchers. The first presumed cause was identified as stemming from gender discrimination in a report by UNICEF (2014). Ghosh (2011) examined an extension of this interpretation of the cause of early marriages in a study in Malda, India. Through a variety of methods, including interviews and group discussions with 380 respondents, Ghosh found that "90% of the fathers, mothers and elders . . . consider marriage as essential for girls" (p. 207). Ghosh also reported that many girls in the sample did not support the view of marriage being a necessity for girls. A major explanation of the advocacy for early marriages for girls among parents and elders was the patriarchal nature of the community, an extreme form of discrimination against girls. Men were dominant in the culture and held all the power in the community. Girls were less valued than boys in the family, and this form of discrimination fostered a positive attitude toward child marriages for daughters. If marriage was the only opportunity available for girls, education or schooling would be seen as inappropriate since it might produce attitudes and behaviors that would conflict with the girls' "subordinate position" in the home and the community. Associated with the patriarchal culture was a concern for the "sexual purity" of girls. The honor of the family is tied to the "chastity" of its female members. If girls are married as children, there would be few opportunities for young girls to "stray."

Similarly, Ertem et al. (2008), in a study using surveys and interviews of over 870 married women 15–49, in Mardin, Turkey, confirmed the importance of the patriarchal culture for reinforcing male dominance as well as the concern about the sexual behavior of girls. Location in Turkey (particularly rural areas) and ethnicity (e.g., in Kurdish areas) were other important factors associated with positive attitudes toward child or adolescent marriages. Over 60% of families pushed girls into these marriages at young ages without the girls' consent or approval.

The second major cause or interpretation of the prevalence of early or child marriage was economic. Poverty is a primary reason why girls are married off at young ages especially if there are several girls in a family. Girls are considered a "burden" particularly in large families. If there is an early marriage, girls cease to be a drain on the family's finances.

Consequences of Child Marriages

A major health consequence of child marriages is a detrimental impact on sexual and reproductive health (Ertem et al., 2008; IWHC, 2008). Girls who marry at early ages are at an increased risk for pregnancy complications that may adversely affect maternal and child health and may contribute to maternal and infant mortality. Child wives often become sexually active quickly, and their bodies are not fully developed or equipped for this activity. In addition, if husbands are much older, they may have had many sexual experiences, and therefore, the risk of the wife contracting a sexually transmitted disease increases (Gangoli, McCarry, & Razak, 2009). Another adverse consequence of child marriages was discovered by Speizer and Pearson (2011) in their study in Rajasthan, a part of India. Using interviews and a modified version of the Conflict Tactics scale to measure intimate partner violence (IPV), the authors found that women married as adolescents were more likely to have been victims of intimate partner violence than women married at or above 18 years old.

Other negative effects of child marriage include the prevention of young wives from attending school so they become very dependent on their husbands and their husbands' families (IWHC).

Overall, even though there are laws preventing child marriages in many countries, there is considerable variation in the minimum age required for marriage particularly in developing countries (IWHC). For example, Ghosh (2011) found that in India, despite the passage of the "Prohibition of Child Marriage Act, 2006," it is not routinely enforced or else there are extensive exceptions to the law (pp. 201–202).

HONOR CRIMES AND HONOR KILLINGS

Honor crimes and honor killings of young and adolescent girls occur in many parts of the world but are more frequent in the Middle East, North Africa (MENA), and selected countries in Asia (Kulczycki & Windle, 2011). Elakkary et al. (2014) suggested, however, that the range of countries has expanded even to developed nations such as the United States and the United Kingdom.

There are still examples of honor killings in recent years. For example, Burgess (2013) reported that a father in Yemen "burned his daughter to death" after discovering that she had been communicating with her fiancé before they were married. In another example, a "Romeo and Juliet" saga has been happening in Afghanistan (Norland, 2014). Two young people in a farm area wanted to marry but the daughter's father threatened to kill her if she married against his wishes. The young couple eloped and still are "on the run" away from both her father and the police.

Definition

An "honor crime" or "honor killing" generally is "defined as the killing of a female, typically by a male perpetrator, because of perceived or actual misconduct of the victim who has dishonored or shamed her family and clan by actually or allegedly committing an indiscretion" (Devers & Bacon, 2010, p. 360). In the case of girls the "indiscretion" could consist of being a victim of rape or kidnapping, or refusing to marry a much older man. The honor killing is considered necessary and "legitimate" in order to restore the honor of the family (Elakkary et al., 2014).

Incidence and Methodological Issues

Elakkary et al. cited a report by the UN Population Fund that approximately 5,000 women a year globally are victims of honor killings. This figure is clearly an underestimation, since there are numerous methodological issues that bring the figure into question. Many honor crimes occur without being reported to the authorities. Even if the crime is reported, the age of the victim often is obscured so the incidence of this form of violence against girls is even more difficult to establish. In a major review of 40 relevant studies, Kulczycki and Windle (2011) found that most of the studies were based on secondary data, not direct interviews or surveys. Since these crimes are usually not reported, figures from police reports and other public data sources are bound to be inaccurate. Honor crime victims also are often reported as having "disappeared" or "having committed suicide" rather than being honor crime victims. Research involving direct questions of respondents (e.g., Araji & Carlson, 2001) generally found that individuals had heard about honor killings but respondents did not acknowledge that anyone in their family had committed an honor killing (Kulczycki & Windle, 2011). Thus, inconsistencies and underestimates of the incidence of honor killings persist.

Attitudes toward Honor Killings

Eisner and Ghuneim (2013) examined attitudes toward honor killings by administering anonymous surveys including scenarios describing transgressions of girls and women, to over 850 high school boys and girls in Amman, Jordan. The authors found that a relatively high percentage of adolescents in their sample showed support for killing girls or women who had "dishonored" their families. In particular, boys who supported traditional values, including "obedience to authority, patriarchism and Islamic conservatism" (pp. 9–10), were more likely to condone the killings for transgressions described in the survey. Another factor was that "moral neutralization of violence" was associated with strong "justification of honor crimes" (p. 10). In other words, honor killings were not identified as crimes by some respondents but as a means of restoring the honor of the family. Although the authors cited limitations of the study, including the representativeness of the sample, the results demonstrated the importance of cultural factors in supporting honor killings.

Causes and Consequences

As described in the preceding section, Eisner and Ghuneim (2013) identified the patriarchal culture as particularly associated with support for honor killings. In this culture, as Kulczycki and Windle (2011) suggested, male dominance and female subordination reinforce traditional gender norms. Eisner and Ghuneim further discussed the power of the father over girls in patriarchal societies. Girls must be chaste and their sexual purity must be protected. Girls must not interact with boys at all until they enter into a marriage arranged by their father. If they "stray" (e.g., are raped or have a boyfriend), they must be violently punished by the family to restore their honor. Generally the girl, not the boy involved in the transgression, is the person who is punished.

Patel and Gadit (2008) reported that there are numerous physical and psychological consequences of living in this type of honor culture or community. Girls may live in fear because they do not know when they will become victims of honor crimes, and may suffer from depression and anxiety.

Although laws against honor crimes exist in many countries, Devers and Bacon (2010) suggested that often the police and other authorities respond more positively to the perpetrator than to the victim. Elakkary et al. (2014) surveyed laws in several countries, including Egypt, Lebanon, Libya, Syria, Turkey and Yeman, and found that men who had committed honor killings were mostly given lenient sentences because of "provocative behavior" by the girl who is murdered. In effect, girls in these cultures are blamed for being murder victims.

CHILD SEX TRAFFICKING

Definition

Konstantopoulos et al. (2013) cited the generally accepted UN definition of sex trafficking (UN Protocol to Prevent, Suppress and Punish Trafficking in Persons, Especially Women and Children, 2000) as "the recruitment, transportation, transfer, harboring or receipt of persons by means of the threat or use of force, or other forms of coercion, of abduction, of fraud, of deception, of the abuse of power or of a position of vulnerability . . . for commercial sex or other forms of sexual exploitation" (p. 1195). The Protocol states that "children transported for exploitative work are considered trafficking victims whether or not they have been deceived" (Ray, 2007, p. 73).

The UN Office on Drugs and Crime (UNODC) concluded that almost every nation is connected with trafficking either as the place where trafficking victims are "recruited" through coercion or fraud countries which are "transit" locations through which trafficking victims are transported, or nations which are "destinations" for trafficking victims (UNODC, 2014, p. 1). The Future Group (2007) described the "typical" trafficking scenario: A young girl from a poor family in Southeast Asia, for example, is convinced to accompany a trafficker (a friend, relative, or acquaintance) to a "better life." At the destination country she is forced to hand over her passport, is physically and sexually abused, and is sold into prostitution to pay off her "debt" to the trafficker. Since she is totally dependent on the trafficker for basic needs, the debt is never repaid.

Incidence of Sex Trafficking of Girls

Accurate estimates of the number of girl children who are victims of sex trafficking are impossible to obtain since the process is secretive, particularly since sex trafficking has become a highly profitable criminal enterprise (The Future Group, 2007). Methodological issues contribute to the extensive underestimation of this type of violence against girls. Trafficking victims fear reporting their plight to the authorities for several reasons. Traffickers typically use physical force, coercion, and manipulative control over their victims, which would lead to fear of retaliation if the girls attempt to escape. If they have been transported to another country, the victims will be afraid to report to the police because they might be deported. The trafficking victims also are totally dependent on the traffickers and sometimes do not even realize that they are victims.

Magesa, Shimba, Magombola, Bakari, and Ramadhan (2014) described girls as the primary targets of trafficking. Davy (2013) cited the 2009 UNICEF report, which indicated that "globally 10 million children, mainly girls are subjected to various forms of sexual exploitation" (p. 42). Davy also distinguished between internal trafficking, for example, from rural areas to urban centers in a country as opposed to transnational trafficking across country borders. Gozdziak (2008) identified Asia, West Africa, Eastern Europe, and Latin America as global regions that play a major role in the sex trafficking of girls. However, no global area is immune from playing some part in the process.

Causes of Sex Trafficking of Girls

The Future Group (2007) estimated that "trafficking is the third largest criminal industry in the world" (p. 1). Therefore, Davy (2013) suggested, it is important to examine both the "supply side" of victims' motivations and familial conditions, as well as the "demand side" of trafficking of girls. Three studies related to this issue identified poverty as the major cause of the "supply side" of the problem. Davy (2013), using interviews and other methods, requested information from professionals in different organizations, as well as UN employees in Thailand and Cambodia. Extreme poverty, lack of economic opportunities, and lack of education were highlighted as major causes of girls becoming vulnerable to commercial sex exploitation.

In a study by Konstanopoulos et al. (2013) the researchers identified eight global cities that were places of sex trafficking either as an origin, transit, or destination location, and interviewed over 270 professional in "anti-trafficking work" (p. 1196). Although financial hardship and low education were relevant issues, the authors also cited dysfunctional family relationships, abusive childhood experiences, and "sexual objectification" as contributing factors to victims' vulnerability to trafficking.

In another study, Magesa et al. (2013) interviewed girl trafficking survivors, anti-trafficking professionals, and community individuals from the Arusha Municipality in Tanzania. The researchers also found that poverty was a major cause of being trafficked as well as poor and dysfunctional parenting. The practice of child forced marriages also contributed to girls' vulnerability since some of the girls had run away from the child marriages and had been captured by the sex traffickers.

In terms of the "demand" side of sex trafficking, increased global and within-nation demand for "fresh faces" in the sex trade, the ease of travel to "sex tourist destination countries," and the impact of organized crime has made sex trafficking more profitable (Davy, 2013).

Consequences of Sex Trafficking of Girls

Rafferty (2008) identified numerous consequences of sex trafficking of girls mainly due to the coercive and abusive physical and psychological tactics used by traffickers. Trauma and injuries stemming from physical abuse, cognitive deficits from lack of schooling, unwanted pregnancies and negative physical outcomes from early pregnancies, as well as possibilities of contracting sexually transmitted diseases are among the consequences described by Rafferty. Psychological effects include depression, anxiety, lowered "self-esteem," and "self-blame" (p. 14). Gozdziak, Bump, Duncan, MacDonell, and Loiselle (2006) also identified depression as a major consequence for victims of sex trafficking.

Despite international laws and efforts by international organizations including the UN, sex trafficking of girls continues to be a widespread crime transcending national and international boundaries. Anti-trafficking organizations and international crime fighting organizations should focus both on rescuing trafficked children and on capturing and punishing sex traffickers. Anti-trafficking laws should address not only traffickers but also individuals who are "sex tourists."

CONCLUSIONS

In this chapter we have reviewed various forms of violence against girls. Although these types of violent acts vary in terms of somewhat less violence to extreme violence, there are commonalities. All these forms of violence are violations of the human rights of girls and sometimes boys preventing them from leading fulfilling lives. Another common factor is that parents or families are implicated in many of these types of violence. Physical punishment of girls which can turn into abuse generally is committed by parents. Child marriages are arranged by parents, and honor crimes are committed by families to control the behavior of girls in the family. Sometimes girls are married at young ages to prevent them from engaging in inappropriate sexual behavior. Honor crimes or killings occur as a response by families to actual or suspected transgression on the part of daughters to "restore the honor" of the family. Parents sometimes are even involved in sex trafficking of girls when the family accepts money to "sell" their girl child to a sex trafficker.

Strongly patriarchal cultures are implicated in many of these forms of violence against girls, including child marriages and honor killings. Poverty and lack of education are other common factors in many of the described forms of violence. Finally, in many cases, punishment of the perpetrators of violence against girls either does not occur or is very lenient, even in the case of honor killings.

In the final section of our chapter, we will review recommendations for reducing or eliminating violence against girls.

PROGRAMS TO MITIGATE THE VIOLENCE AGAINST GIRLS

In the previous sections of this chapter, violence against girls has been dramatically illustrated. The portrait painted is tragic. Attacks by Boko Haram, and specifically the abduction of the girls from the boarding school in Chibok, Borno state, Nigeria, have horrified the world. Let's look at programs and policies that offer the potential to change the landscape and promote achievement of the protection of girls' rights, what the UN mandated in the Convention on the Rights of the Child (UNGA, 1989).

Lee-Rife and her associates (2012) analyzed the effectiveness of interventions from 1973 to 2009 across the globe that focused on preventing child marriage. These programs were organized into levels of methodological rigor, high, medium or low, with outcomes (knowledge, attitudes, behavior and policy) designated as positive, mixed, or no change. Using this as a guide, we have selected two programs in which methodological issues were carefully addressed justifying both evidence-based conclusions and implications. These might well serve as models for future interventions for various forms of violence against girls, with sustainability also addressed as a critical issue.

Ethiopia

The Amhara region of northern Ethiopia has been identified as having one of the highest rates of child marriage; 50% of girls are married by 15, a suitable site for the Berhane Hewan ("Light for Eve") project (Erulkar & Muthengi, 2009). A pilot study was conducted in 2002–2004 in Mosebo village with Enamirt village serving as the control. Not only were the risk factors for child marriage noted, but girls rejecting their arranged marriages were also found to flee to urban areas where they became easy victims of the sex traffickers. The primary purpose of the project was to keep unmarried girls, aged 10–19 years, in formal schooling, delay arranged marriages, as well as provide both married and unmarried girls in the same age group support systems to reduce social isolation and allow interaction with same-sex friends and designated female adult mentors. The girls who were in school were provided with necessary school materials. Those who were not in school were given the opportunity to go to school. Those who chose not to were given access to the basic literacy and numeracy Ethiopian Ministry of Education's curriculum, as well as livelihood skills including agricultural techniques, husbandry knowledge, and training in construction of household items. Girls who were sexually active were given information about the use of existing reproductive health services.

In discussions to develop the program, community members suggested a payment to help families delay making marriage arrangements for economic reasons, and thus a goat or sheep was given to both the girl and her family if she stayed in school and delayed marriage over the course of the two-year project period. The trained mentors first introduced the community to the project and then approached all 10–19-year-old girls in

Mosebo village. The mentors were 20–28-year-old females with at least a 10th-grade education who received appropriate training.

Community dialogue in the form of community conversations is common in this region. This is an accepted social custom in which the community gathers to confront problems and find solutions. Attendees participated regardless of demographic characteristics. As part of the project, trained facilitators led discussions to confront the tradition of early marriage, HIV/AIDS, family planning, and safe motherhood.

Initial outcomes were recorded separating the girls by age, 10–14 years and 15–19 years. Whereas the younger girls mostly (65%) participated in the formal schooling component, only 37% of the older girls pursued formal schooling. About 23% of the project participants regardless of age participated in the informal education group. Almost 75% of both age groups attended at least one of the community conversations.

Social network contacts expanded for the project participants as did literacy and school attendance. The odds ratio for the younger girls to be in school as compared to the control changed from 0.6 before the project to 3.0 after participating, thereby indicating a 300% greater chance of remaining in a formal education setting for the Mosebo girls. There was no difference for the 15–19 year old girls. The results of participating in the project for ever-marrying differed by age. The younger girls were much less likely to ever marry as compared to the controls, odds ratio of 0.1, while the older girls were more likely to marry, odds ratio of 2.41. Contraceptive usage for sexually active girls showed that project participants were 288% more likely to use contraceptives as compared to the controls. The primary impact of this multifaceted project on crucial social, educational, and health behaviors is clear.

The program was then made available to three additional districts, including about 11,000 girls, but perhaps the impact of Berhane Hewan is best illustrated in the feature story of Zufan Fentahun (UNFPA, 2013), married to an older man as a toddler. After participating in the program following the initial pilot, she indicated that

> The programme was a lifeline to me. It has transformed my life as well as that of my family. If Berhane Hewan were not here, I would have borne children at a very young age and would have been poor.— Zufan Fentahun (Ethiopia's girl empowerment, 2012, paragraph 3)

Instead her life has taken a very different trajectory. She pushed her parents to annul her marriage based on violation of her rights, obtained the annulment, and is now earning money. In this she has been using funds generated through breeding the animals obtained for remaining unmarried in the program, buying a cow and raising vegetables. She is able to pay the costs of her education.

India

The International Center for Research on Women conducted a survey in Bihar and Jharkhand, India, and found that girls who were married before age 18 were twice as likely to be beaten, slapped, or threatened by their husbands in comparison to girls who married at an older age (ICRW, 2005). It was also found that the girls married at an early age were less likely to talk to their husbands about contraception and childbearing. Studies from other countries like Peru and Bangladesh reported similar findings such that child brides are more likely to be a victim of domestic violence (Flake, 2005; UNICEF, 2005) and show signs of child sexual abuse and posttraumatic stress disorder (PTSD; Khan & Lynch, 1997).

Raj, Saggurti, Balaiah, and Silverman (2009) conducted a study to examine the prevalence of child marriages in India and to assess if there have been any significant changes in the past decade. Their results indicated that almost half (44%) of women ages 20–24 in India were married before age 18. Roughly 23% of the sample were married before age 16 and 3% were married before age 13.

It has been reported that the best predictor of determining when a girl will be married is education (Jain & Kurz, 2006). In India, a decline in early marriage has been associated with increased school enrollment (Hussain & Bittles, 1999). Due to the strong association of education levels with fewer early marriages, programs have been developed to increase education and overall life skills of adolescent girls. One such program was carried out by the Institute for Health Management Pachod (IHMP), which is located in Maharashtra, India. In this particular region is the Aurangabad district, which has a median age of marriage of 14.5 years. The IHMP started the first series of this program in 1998–1999 in hopes of increasing the age of marriage. The organization predicted that a girl's year-long participation in a life skills program could help increase the age of marriage by one year.

The life skills course took place every weekday for approximately one hour and covered topics such as social issues, government, life skills, child health, and nutrition and health. Participants also taught basic literacy to girls who were illiterate and not participating in the program. One unique aspect of the program was that parents and community members were part of the intervention development process. The program was designed using a pre-post case control design. Two health centers were randomly assigned to be the program and control areas. Villages near the health centers were divided geographically into units. The program area had a total of 35 units and the control had 36 units. Each unit had a population between 1,000 and 1,500 persons. Teachers from the program kept track of the participants once they completed the year-long life skills course and monitored who got married in the following year.

Results from the implementation of the life skills course indicated that the average age for marriage for girls in the program area rose from 16 to 17. Moreover, the percentage of married girls under the age of 18 significantly decreased from 80.7% to 61.8%. The most noteworthy finding is that it included the whole program area and not solely the girls who participated in the program. In other words, the influence of the program was not only on the participants but also on the community. Participants in the program gained life skills and also self-confidence.

> Even if my parents arrange my marriage, I will not agree until I am 18 years old. I will convince my parents about this and I am confident that they will listen to me.—Sheetal Gajwate, 14 years old (IHMP, n.d, slide 29)

Programs that educate girls may help reduce the detrimental effects of early child marriage. Education of young girls may not only improve their life skills and self-esteem but it will also hopefully impart additional changes that will impact a generation.

REFLECTIVE QUESTIONS

1. What are some common characteristics among the different types of violence against girls?
2. What is the role of culture in global violence against girls?
3. How does gender inequality perpetuate the different types of violence against girls discussed in this chapter?
4. Who are most likely to perpetrate violence against girls?
5. What are some solutions to eliminate violence against girls?

SUGGESTED READINGS

Books and Articles

Stoltenborgh, M., Bakermans-Kranenburg, M. J., & van IJzendoorn, M. H. (2013). The neglect of child neglect: A meta-analytic review of the prevalence of neglect. *Social Psychiatry and Psychiatric Epidemiology, 48*, 345–355.

United Nations Children's Fund (UNICEF), Division of Data, Research and Policy (2014). *Hidden in plain sight: A statistical analysis of violence against children.* New York: UNICEF.

United Nations General Assembly. (1989). *Convention on the Rights of the Child.* Retrieved from http://www.unicef.org/crc/index_30160.html.retrieved 5/14/2014

Websites

Child physical abuse:

1. Child Safe Network: http://www.childsafe-international.org/
2. International Society for the Prevention of Child Abuse and Neglect: http://www.ispcan.org/

Sex trafficking of children:
1. Children's Organization of Southeast Asia: http://www.cosasia.org/
2. Coalition Against Trafficking in Women http://www.catwinternational.org/
3. ECPAT International: http://www.ecpat.net/
4. Emancipation: http://www.emancipaction.org/index.htm
5. The Future Group: http://www.thefuturegroup.org
6. Global Alliance against Traffic in Women: http://www.gaatw.org/

Honor killings:
1. Honor Based Violence Awareness Network: http://hbv-awareness.com/

Child marriages, forced marriages and abductions:
1. Forced Marriage Unit: https://www.gov.uk/forced-marriage
2. Tahiri Justice Center: http://www.tahirih.org/

Honor-based violence and forced marriage:
1. AHA (Ayaan Hirsi Ali) Foundation: http://theahafoundation.org/
2. The Iranian and Kurdish Women's Rights Organisation (IKWRO): http://ikwro.org.uk/
3. Karma Nirvana: http://www.karmanirvana.org.uk/

REFERENCES

Adolph, K. E., Karasik, L. B., & Tamis-LeMonda, C. S. (2009). Moving between cultures: Cross-cultural research on motor development. In M. H. Bornstein (Ed.), *Handbook of cross-cultural developmental science* (pp. 61–88). New York: Taylor & Francis Group.

Alink, L. R., Euser, S., van IJzendoorn, M. H., & Bakermans-Kranenburg, M. J. (2013). Is elevated risk of child maltreatment in immigrant families associated with socioeconomic status? Evidence from three sources. *International Journal of Psychology, 48,* 117–127.

Annerbäck, E. M., Svedin, C. G., & Gustafsson, P. A. (2010). Characteristic features of severe child physical abuse—a multi-informant approach. *Journal of Family Violence, 25,* 165–172.

Araji, S. K., & Carlson, J. (2001). Family violence including crimes of honor in Jordan: Correlates and perceptions of seriousness. *Violence against Women, 7,* 586–621. doi:10.1177/10778010122182613

Belsky, J., & Vondra, J. (1989). Lessons from child abuse: The determinants of parenting. In D. Cicchetti & V. Carlson (Eds.), *Child maltreatment: Theory and research on the causes and consequences of child abuse and neglect* (pp. 153–202). New York: Cambridge University Press.

Bennhold, K. (2014, September 1). Years of rape and "utter contempt." *The New York Times.* Retrieved from http://www.nytimes.com/2014/09/02/world/europe/reckoning-starts-in-britain-on-abuse-of-girls.html?_r=0

Bril, B., & Sabatier, C. (1986). The cultural context of motor development: Postural manipulations in the daily life of Bambara babies (Mali). *International Journal of Behavioral Development, 9,* 439–453.

Bronfenbrenner, U., & Morris P. (2006). The bioecological model of human development. In R. M. Lerner & W. Damon (Eds.), *Theoretical models of human development.* Vol. 1, *Handbook of child psychology* (pp. 793–828). New York: Wiley.

Brown, J., Cohen, P., Johnson, J.G., & Salzinger, S. (1998). A longitudinal analysis of risk factors for child maltreatment: Findings of a 17-year prospective study of officially recorded and self-reported child abuse and neglect. *Child Abuse and Neglect, 22,* 1065–1078.

Burgess, T. (2013, October 24). Honor killing: Father burns 15-year-old daughter to death for talking to fiancé. *Examiner.* Retrieved from http://www.examiner.com/article/honor-killing-father-burns-15-year-old-daughter-to-death-for-talking-to-fiance

Cahn, D.D., & Lloyd, S.A. (Eds.). (1996). *Family violence from a communication perspective.* Thousand Oaks, CA: Sage.

Chantler, K. (2012). Recognition of and intervention in forced marriage as a form of violence and abuse. *Trauma Violence Abuse, 13,* 176–183. doi:10.1177/1524838012448121

Chou, C.Y., Su, Y.J., Wu, H.M., & Chen, S.H. (2011). Child physical abuse and the related PTSD in Taiwan: The role of Chinese cultural background and victims' subjective reactions. *Child Abuse and Neglect, 35*(1), 58–68.

Cicchetti, D., & Valentino, K. (2007). Toward the application of a multiple-levels-of-analysis perspective to research in development and psychopathology. *Minnesota Symposia on Child Psychology, 34,* 243–284.

Convention on the Rights of the Child. (1990). Retrieved from http://www.ohchr.org/Documents/ProfessionalInterest/crc.pdf.

Cyr, C., Michel, G., & Dumais, M. (2013). Child maltreatment as a global phenomenon: From trauma to prevention. *International Journal of Psychology, 48,* 141–148.

Davy, D. (2013). Understanding the motivations and activities of transnational advocacy networks against child sex trafficking in the Greater Mekong Subregion: The value of cosmopolitan globalization theory. *Cosmopolitan Civil Societies Journal, 5,* 41–68.

Deater-Deckard, K., Dodge, K.A., Bates, J.E., & Pettit, G.S. (1996). Physical discipline among African American and European American mothers: Links to children's externalizing behaviors. *Developmental Psychology, 32,* 1065–1072.

Devers, L.N., & Bacon, S. (2010). Interpreting honor crimes: The institutional disregard towards female victims of family violence in the Middle East. *International Journal of Criminology and Sociological Theory, 3,* 359–371.

Dutton, D.G., Saunders, K., Starzomski, A., & Bartholomew, K. (1994). Intimacy-anger and insecure attachment as precursors of abuse in intimate relationships. *Journal of Applied Social Psychology, 24,* 1367–1386. doi:10.1111/j.1559–1816.1994.tb01554.x

Eisner, M., & Ghuneim, L. (2013). Honor killing attitudes amongst adolescents in Amman, Jordan. *Aggressive Behavior, 39,* 405–417. doi:10.1002/ab.21485

Elakkary, S., Franke, B., Shokri, D., Hartwig, S., Tsokos., M. & Puschel, K. (2014). Honor crimes: Review and proposed definition. *Forensic Science, Medicine, and Pathology, 10,* 76–82. doi:10.1007/s12024–013–9455–1

Ertem, M., Saka, G., Ceylan, A., Deger, V., & Çiftçi, S. (2008). The factors associated with adolescent marriages and outcomes of adolescent pregnancies in Mardin, Turkey. *Journal of Comparative Family Studies, 39,* 229–239.

Erulkar, A., & Muthengi, E. (2009). Evaluation of Berhane Hewan: A program to delay child marriage in rural Ethiopia. *International Perspectives on Sexual and Reproductive Health, 35,* 6–14.

Ethiopia's girl empowerment programme worth emulating. (2012). Retrieved from http://esaro.unfpa.org/public/public/cache/offonce/news/pid/12901;jsessionid=B6B4F382029B6D557608D39C8895A3F5.jahia01#sthash.UHqITVyr

Euser, S., Alink, L. R., Pannebakker, F., Vogels, T., Bakermans-Kranenburg, M. J., & Van IJzendoorn, M. H. (2013). The prevalence of child maltreatment in the Netherlands across a 5-year period. *Child Abuse & Neglect, 37,* 841–851.

Finkelhor, D., Turner, H., Ormrod, R., & Hamby, S. L. (2010). Trends in childhood violence and abuse exposure: Evidence from 2 national surveys. *Archives of Pediatrics & Adolescent Medicine, 164,* 238–242.

Flake, D. F. (2005). Individual, family, and community risk markers for domestic violence in Peru. *Violence against Women, 11,* 353–373.

The Future Group. (2007). *Human trafficking: A human security crisis of global proportions.* Retrieved from http://www.thefuturegroup.org/id20.html

Gangoli, G., McCarry, M., & Razak, A. (2009). Child marriage or forced marriage? South Asian communities in North East England. *Children & Society, 23,* 418–429. doi:10.1111/j.1099–860.2008.00188.x

Gershoff, E. T. (2002). Corporal punishment by parents and associated child behaviors and experiences: A meta-analytic and theoretical review. *Psychological Bulletin, 128,* 539–579.

Ghosh, B. (2011). Child marriage, society and the law: A study in a rural context in West Bengal, India. *International Journal of Law, Policy and the Family, 25,* 199–219. doi:10.1093/lawfam/ebr002

Gozdiak, E. M. (2008). On challenges, dilemmas, and opportunities in studying trafficked children. *Anthropological Quarterly, 81,* 903–923. doi:10.1353/anq.0.0033

Gozdiak, E. M., Bump, M., Duncan, J., MacDonnell, M., & Loiselle, M. B. (2006). The trafficked child: Trauma and resilience. *Forced Migration Review, 25,* 14–15.

Gracia, E., & Herrero, J. (2008). Is it considered violence? The acceptability of physical punishment of children in Europe. *Journal of Marriage and Family, 70,* 210–217.

Hawkins, A. O., Danielson, C. K., de Arellano, M. A., Hanson, R. F., Ruggiero, K. J., Smith, D. W., . . . Kilpatrick, D. G. (2010). Ethnic/racial differences in the prevalence of injurious spanking and other child physical abuse in a national survey of adolescents. *Child Maltreatment, 15,* 242–249.

Hussain, R., & Bittles, A. H. (1999). Consanguineous marriage and differentials in age at marriage, contraceptive use, and fertility in Pakistan. *Journal of Biosocial Science, 31*(1), 121–138.

ICRW. (2005). Development Initiative on Supporting Healthy Adolescents (DISHA) project: *Analysis of quantitative baseline survey data conducted in 2004.* Washington, DC: ICRW.

Institute of Health Management, Pachod Life Skills Presentation. (n.d). Retrieved from http://www.ihmp.org/lifeskills_presentation.html

International Women's Health Coalition. (2008). *Child marriage: Girls 14 and younger at risk.* New York: IWHC.

Jain, S., & Kurz, K. (2006). *ICRW research on prevalence and predictors of child marriage in developing countries* (in progress).

Jernbro, C., Svensson, B., Tindberg, Y., & Janson, S. (2012). Multiple psychosomatic symptoms can indicate child physical abuse–results from a study of Swedish school children. *Acta Paediatrica, 101,* 324–329.

Johnson, M. P. (1995). Patriarchal terrorism and common couple violence: Two forms of violence against women. *Journal of Marriage and the Family, 57,* 283–294.

Khan, N., & Lynch, M. (1997). Recognizing child maltreatment in Bangladesh. *Child Abuse and Neglect, 21,* 815–818.

Konstantopoulos, W. M., Ahn, R., Alpert, E. J., Cafferty, E., McGahan, A., Williams, T., & Korbin, J. E. (1991). Cross-cultural perspectives and research directions for the 21st century. *Child Abuse & Neglect, 15,* 67–77.

Konstantopoulos, W. M., Ahn, R., Alpert, E. J., Cafferty, E., McGahan, A., Williams, T. P., Castors, J. P., Wolferstan, N., Purcell, G., & Burke, T. F. (2013). An international comparative public health analysis of sex trafficking of women and girls in eight cities: Achieving a more effective health sector response. *Journal of Urban Health, 90,* 1194–1204.

Kristof, N. D. (2014, May 4). Bring back our girls. *The New York Times,* p. 11.

Kulczycki, A., & Windle, S. (2011). Honor killings in the Middle East and North Africa: A systematic review of the literature. *Violence against Women, 17*(11), 1442–1464. doi: 10.1177/1077801211434127

Lansford, J. E., Dodge, K. A., Pettit, G. S., & Bates, J. E. (2010). Does physical abuse in early childhood predict substance use in adolescence and early adulthood? *Child Maltreatment, 15,* 190–194.

Lee-Rife, S., Malhotra, A., Warner, A., & Glinski, A. (2012). What works to prevent child marriage: A review of the evidence. *Studies in Family Planning, 43,* 287–303.

MacMillan, H. L., Tanaka, M., Duku, E., Vaillancourt, T., & Boyle, M. H. (2013). Child physical and sexual abuse in a community sample of young adults: Results from the Ontario Child Health Study. *Child Abuse & Neglect, 37,* 14–21.

Magesa, R., Shimba, C., Magombola, D., Bakari, V., & Ramadhan, A. (2014). Girl trafficking: Causes, experiences and challenges encountered: A case of Arusha Municipality. *Journal of Developing Country Studies, 4,* 80–89.

Mathurin, M. N., Gielen, U. P., & Lancaster, J. (2006). Corporal punishment and personality traits in the children of St. Croix, United States Virgin Islands. *Cross-Cultural Research, 40*(3), 306–324.

Mei, J. (1994). The Northern Chinese custom of rearing babies in sandbags: Implications for motor and intellectual development. In J. H. A. van Rossum & J. I. Laszlo (Eds.), *Motor development: Aspects of normal and delayed development.* Amsterdam, Netherlands: VU Uitgeverij.

Nordland, R. (2014, April 22). Afghan newlyweds, facing threats, find brief respite in mountains. *The New York Times,* pp. A4, A10.

Olson, L. C. (1997). On the margins of rhetoric: Audre Lorde transforming silence into language and action. *Quarterly Journal of Speech, 83,* 49–70. doi:10.1080/00335639709384171

Patel, S., & Gadit, A.M. (2008). Karo-Kari: A form of honour killing in Pakistan. *Transcultural Psychiatry, 45,* 683–694. doi:10.1177/1363461508100790

Rafferty, Y. (2008). The impact of trafficking on children: Psychological and social policy perspectives. *Child Development Perspectives, 2,* 13–18. doi: 10.1111/j.1750-8606.2008.00035.x

Raj, A., Saggurti, N., Balaiah, D., & Silverman, J. G. (2009). Prevalence of child marriage and its effect on fertility and fertility-control outcomes of young women in India: A cross-sectional, observational study. *The Lancet, 373,* 1883–1889.

Ray, N. (2007). Wither childhood? Child trafficking in India. *Social Development Issues, 29*, 73–83.

Saunders, D.G. (1996). Feminist-cognitive-behavioral and process-psychodynamic treatments for men who batter: Interaction of abuser traits and treatment models. *Violence and Victims, 11*, 393–414.

Speizer, I.S., & Pearson, E. (2011). Association between early marriage and intimate partner violence in India: A focus on youth from Bihar and Rajasthan. *Journal of Interpersonal Violence, 26*, 1963–1981. doi: 10.1177/0886260510372947

Stith, S.M., Liu, T., Davies, L.C., Boykin, E.L., Alder, M.C., Harris, J.M., . . . Dees, J. (2009). Risk factors in child maltreatment: A meta-analytic review of the literature. *Aggression and Violent Behavior, 14*, 13–29.

Stoltenborgh, M., Bakermans-Kranenburg, M.J., & van IJzendoorn, M.H. (2013a). The neglect of child neglect: A meta-analytic review of the prevalence of neglect. *Social Psychiatry and Psychiatric Epidemiology, 48*, 345–355.

Stoltenborgh, M., Bakermans-Kranenburg, M.J., van IJzendoorn, M.H., & Alink, L.R. (2013b). Cultural–geographical differences in the occurrence of child physical abuse? A meta-analysis of global prevalence. *International Journal of Psychology, 48*, 81–94.

Straus, M.A. (1994). *Beating the devil out of them*. Livingston, NJ: Transaction.

Svensson, B., Bornehag, C.G., & Janson, S. (2011). Chronic conditions in children increase the risk for physical abuse–but vary with socio-economic circumstances. *Acta Paediatrica, 100*, 407–412.

UNFPA. (2013). Award-winning programme gives Ethiopian girls a safer transition to adulthood. Retrieved on May 14, 2014, http://www.unfpa.org/public/cache/offfonce/home/news/pid/12659

UNICEF. (2005). *Early marriage: A harmful traditional practice*. New York: UNICEF.

UNICEF. (2012, April). *Progress for children: A report card on adolescents*. Retrieved from http://www.unicef.org/media/files/PFC2012_A_report_card_on_adolescents.pdf

United Nations Children's Fund (UNICEF), Division of Data, Research and Policy. (2014). *Hidden in plain sight: A statistical analysis of violence against children*. New York: UNICEF.

United Nations General Assembly. (1989). *Convention on the Rights of the Child*. Retrieved from http://www.unicef.org/crc/index_30160.html.retrieved 5/14/2014.

United Nations Office of Drugs and Crime. (2000). Protocol to prevent, suppress and punish trafficking in persons, especially women and children. Retrieved from http://www.osce.org/odihr/19223?download=true on September 20, 2015.

United Nations Office on Drugs and Crime. (2014). *Human trafficking*. Retrieved from http://www.unodc.org/unodc/en/human-trafficking/what-is-human-trafficking.html

Whipple, E.E., & Richey, C.A. (1997). Crossing the line from physical discipline to child abuse: How much is too much? *Child Abuse & Neglect, 21*, 431–444.

World Health Organization. (2014). *Health topics: Child maltreatment*. Retrieved from http://www.who.int/topics/child_abuse/en/

15

Cultural Nuances and Other Particulars That Impact Street Children and War-Traumatized Adolescents

Lewis Aptekar and Lisa Oliver

Michael's mother poses in front of her tent at Kaliti, a camp for displaced people outside of Addis Ababa, Ethiopia. She has made a home for the past six years for her son Michael and his friends. Looking at her photo, it is easy to see that absolute poverty—the kind of poverty where there is not enough protein, and often not enough calories—has made her look twice her age. But, look closely into her eyes and they stare back with absolute resolve.

On my first encounter, Michael is still a teenager barely holding enough weight; his eyes bulging as if they had been injected with air. Through our interactions, it became evident that Michael and his mother's alliance were less melded by necessity, than driven by love, and that she was Michael's immunization to life.

For the past 15 years Michael sporadically writes letters. The first letter comes on his return from the front of the civil war and includes a picture of him arm-in-arm with his friend, Solomon. For several years, there is no letter. Then, a letter arrives with an announcement. He has been accepted into a job training program to study electricity. Fast forward a few years, and an e-mail with a photo of his baby. And, another new life and cycle has begun.

Michael's life and his letters are, and should be, a reminder of the vagaries of life: each an object of contemplation. Michael was not one of the statistics. He was not killed as was Simon, a Kenyan street boy you will meet later, under the belief he had no mother who loved him. And, Michael did not die like his best friend, Solomon, of AIDS. Nor, thankfully, was Michael a fallen youthful warrior. I like to think that Michael survived and prospered because of his mother's love, or because he had friends, or because of his wisdom to help others that are worse off than himself in spite of his potentially dim circumstances. But, these might only be the happy musings of an aged humanitarian helper. I look forward to seeing him on Facebook.

DEVELOPMENTAL DISPARITIES AMONG STREET CHILDREN

The children that the United Nations International Children's Emergency Fund (UNICEF) refers to as "in particularly difficult circumstances" are those whose suffering entails the highest risk to mental health (1986). They include children traumatized by war, or natural and technological disasters, and those living and working without parents (otherwise known as street children). Other children also face especially difficult circumstances, either from extreme poverty, severe malnutrition, forced prostitution, labor exploitation, or excessive family violence. Each of these additional groups faces their own trials and tribulations, so much so that they are beyond the scope of this chapter. The two areas that are the focus of this chapter, street children and war-traumatized adolescents, have their own particular set of developmental difficulties and challenges.

In 1989, UNICEF estimated 100 million children growing up on urban streets around the world; then, in 2002 UNICEF reported the latest estimate of street children to be as high as 100 million (UNICEF, 2002). A few years later, UNICEF reported that it was impossible to quantify the exact number of street children in the world (UNICEF, 2005). It is unclear whether the amount of street children is growing globally or whether there is increased awareness of street children and therefore a more accurate count (Thomas de Benítez, 2011). Street children have been defined according to two dimensions, the time spent in the street and the absence of contact with responsible adults (UNICEF, 1987). This definition characterizes street children as prematurely living and working without parents, a bit like premature adults. They are, in essence, living in two worlds, one characterized by childhood dependence and the other by adult independence. There are several problems with this definition; partially simple facts, while other areas ignored how the children perceived their experiences and the cultural context of childhood (Aptekar, 1994). By understanding street children within a cultural context (and taking into consideration gender distinctions), the Western viewpoint that presents street children as victims of abuse/neglect, or as delinquents ready for reeducation, should be reexamined. As a result, how they have learned strategies for coping in economically (and sometimes emotionally) challenging circumstances comes to the forefront.

The perspective that abusive parents are the root of the problem for street children can be labeled as ethnocentric. Oftentimes, in the West, parents are seen as the source of abuse, whereas in non-Western cultures parental abuse is not as prominent as abuse from society. Take, for example, how the numerous instances of political contexts invoking the "superior interests of the state" have led to the most painful forms of child abuse. During the "Dirty War" in Argentina, children were tortured and killed from 1976 through1983 under military dictatorship (Bradley, 2008). And, over 400 children were kidnapped or born in captivity then raised by the original captors (Bradley, 2008). Children in Syria are being used as sniper targets and human shields (AFP United Nations, 2013). A United Nations report has found that in addition to the thousands of children who have been injured, killed, or displaced as part of the war, the Syrian government and allied militia are responsible for countless killings, maiming, and torture (*United Nations*, 2014, February 22). Children as young as 11 years old have been put into prisons where they are tortured by abhorrent methods (United Nations, 2014, February 5). In these cases, abuse comes under government or state authority.

The importance of the state as an agent of child abuse is also evident in the case of China's one-child policy. Children born to families that already have a child are "out of plan" and amount to nearly 40% of the annual births (Aptekar & Stoecklin, 1997). Yet, by virtue of the state's policy, they do not officially exist. Hidden by parents who fear sanctions for having an excess birth, an unknown number of children remain unregistered, and therefore deprived of social services. Also, as a result of the one-child policy, the gender distribution is skewed toward males since urban couples perform sex selection because they are allowed only one child (Hesketh, Liu, & Xing, 2005). Thus, while Chinese parents positively desire a child's birth, the birth is dictated by the state in stigmatizing terms. These examples illustrate that worldwide child abuse is not solely, or even mainly, a consequence of the wrongdoing due to a few psychopathological parents; it can also be a product of state policy.

The original definition of "street children" claimed that these children came from poor families, almost always headed by women living in urban areas of the developing world (Aptekar & Ciano, 1999). Parents either neglected the children, which led to the children leaving home and going to the streets, or the children were actively thrown out of the house. Not only did this beg the question of why only a small percentage of poor and neglected/abused children turned to the streets, while the vast majority did not, but it also ignored the fact that as many as 90% of street children in developing cultures maintain contact with their families, and most of them contribute a portion of what they earn to their families (Aptekar & Stoecklin, 2014). Over the years, research showed that rather than being abandoned, street children almost always left home in a measured manner, initially staying away for a night or two; then, the children would gradually add to the nights spent away from their homes (Aptekar, 1988, 1989, 1994). Steadily, the amount of time they spent with other street children increased until they were fully matriculated into the street culture.

The general view and assumed characteristics of street children were that they were either pitiful and in need of help or delinquent and in need of incarceration. However, it has been reported that as a group, many street children were better off than their counterparts living at home (Aptekar & Stoecklin, 2014). A study in Guatemala and Colombia that compared the degree of malnutrition between street children and their poor counterparts who lived at home found that street children had living conditions on the street that were often better than those at home (Connolly, 1990). Another study in Honduras found similar results (Wright, Kaminsky, & Wittig, 1993). In South Africa, street children ate more nutritiously, while simultaneously escaping the daily abuse they might have faced at home (Donald & Swartz-Kruger, 1994). In Brazil, it was reported that street children were both more intelligent and less likely to abuse drugs than their poor, stay-at-home counterparts (Baizerman, 1988). So, it is possible, at least when considering the context of developing countries, instead of succumbing to abuse or neglect, becoming a street child might also be considered a positive coping strategy even if filled with difficulty. In a developmental context, street children can be seen as a case in which adolescence begins earlier and ends sooner than what would be considered ideal in the West (Aptekar, 1992; Aptekar & Stocklin, 1997).

STREET CHILDREN: STREET BOYS VERSUS STREET GIRLS

When the term "street children" is used, who is it referring to? Essentially, street children are young people—too young from their society's perspective—who are living without parental or adult supervision in the cities of the developing world. One of the most fundamental mistakes of the original view of street children is that the category referred to all street children instead of specifying street boys and street girls. Thus, the differences between the genders were minimized. However, when one considers the statistics, it is clear that there is a predominance of street boys in the developing world, 90% in many African countries, over 80% in Jamaica and other Caribbean countries, and more than 75% worldwide (Aptekar, 1994; Aptekar & Ciano, 1999). A recent report on urban street children in the Republic of Georgia also reported that of the 1,600 street children most were primarily boys ranging from 5 to 14 years of age (Wargan & Dershem, 2009). This striking gender difference is important for another reason. Since in many cultures girls are more likely to be abandoned and abused than boys (Aptekar & Ciano, 1999), if being a street child is mainly the result of neglect or abuse, then one may expect a much higher proportion of street girls. However, the gender bias was not the only overgeneralized statement about street children. Another bias describes the families of alleged street children. Three hypotheses point to family dysfunction as the major reason for the origins of street children: (a) that urban poverty leads to a breakdown of family and moral values; (b) that aberrant families abandon, abuse, or neglect their children; and (c) that street children are an inevitable adverse side effect of modernization (Aptekar, 1988).

In a study conducted in Nairobi, Kenya (Aptekar, Cathey, Ciano, & Giardino, 1995; Aptekar & Ciano, 1999), a mother of four boys and two girls lived with four of her six children in one room no bigger than a small bedroom in an American middle-class home. Two blankets, hung up by clothespins, divided the room. Behind one blanket was the mother's loft, behind the other, three levels of shelves, each of which was used for a bed. In one corner was a small one-burner propane stove that was surrounded by two pots and a stool. The only source of light in the house was from the front door. Open sewage ran from the front door, through the walkway, and down to the front of the house, where it met the drainage from other homes.

The mother was nearly able to support herself and her children by selling illegal beer. She never attended school, had no job skills, and was illiterate. Her two oldest boys, half-brothers well into their teens, both lived and made a living on the streets. They came home periodically, usually with a gift, and were very welcome. Their mother had taught them they could stay at home without making a contribution until shortly before puberty. Her two oldest boys accepted this concept since they preferred the streets to their home, particularly since they knew they could come home when they needed to.

One cultural interpretation of this mother's situation would describe her as irresponsible and immoral. However, she can also be seen as coping adequately and teaching her children coping strategies. She taught her two oldest boys to make their own way, she found a means to feed the other four children at home, and she fulfilled her hopes of educating as many of her children as possible by using the sale of illegal brew to pay for the children's school fees. In short, the children's period of dependence ended early and their adolescent independence was accelerated. The cultural notion that single poor mothers were, by virtue of being single and poor, irresponsible and incapable of raising moral and productive children, represents a culturally ethnocentric point of view (Aptekar & Ciano, 1999).

To pejoratively label these families, in large part because mothers have developed their own cultural criteria for the supervision and protection of their children, forces a compounding rather than a resolution to the problem. Not only does the pejorative attitude condemn the resilient efforts of mothers, but it also dismisses the fact that unmarried mothers can raise children without a husband. Indeed, it even discounts the biased perspective that street children only leave unhealthy homes, such as girls who have been physically or sexually abused.

It is by looking more closely at street boys and street girls, rather than street children, those erroneous notions of family deviance become easier to understand. Research has found that most (but not all) street boys are taught by their mothers to cope with the necessity of having to live in a very limited economic environment by becoming independent at a far earlier age than the dominant society deems appropriate (Aptekar, 1992, 1994). Thus, when compared to other poor boys and to the other boys in the family, street boys are more resilient, since boys with fewer resiliencies are unable to leave home.

The opposite situation exists for street girls. Mothers teach their daughters how to cope with the vagaries of poverty by staying at home, and out of the streets. Thus, street girls (for the most part) are often more psychopathological than their sisters who stay at home. These girls begin street life much later than boys, usually not before they are 10 years of age, and the opportunities to make a living on the street are limited (Rurevo & Bourdillon, 2003). Even though they may appear to be alone, they are most often being supervised by an older sibling (Aptekar, 1988). As poverty overtakes a family, income from children becomes more essential, protection of girls diminishes, and they then find their way onto the streets in greater numbers (Rurevo & Bourdillon, 2003). Regardless of age, and especially when they became pubescent, girls are perceived (and evaluated) in sexual terms. It is common for girls to emulate their mothers and supplement income with the trade of sex (Rurevo & Bourdillon, 2003). By the time they are young women, street girls follow in their mother's footsteps by having children, usually many and by different men who as a rule do not view them as legitimate wives, and thus do not value them worthy of continued financial support (Aptekar, 1988).

Since boys are expected to bring income into the house by living on the streets, while girls are expected to stay at home and help with the household chores, the street boys and street girls relate to their families of origin differently. They also probably come from different types of families. It is quite common for street boys to remain connected to their mothers; indeed, they often contribute part of their incomes to their mothers. On the other hand, because girls are taught that they are supposed to remain at home, street girls often have distant and more difficult relationships with their families of origin (Aptekar & Ciano, 1999; Aptekar et al., 1995).

Taken together, all of this information suggests that street boys commonly are on the streets because they have been brought up to be independent, while street girls are on the streets because they are fleeing a very difficult situation. Their mental health is therefore considerably worse than that of the boys. Considering that all over the developing world the majority of street children are male, it can be speculated that contrary to popular opinion, the vast majority of street children are not as likely to be psychopathological, or otherwise delinquent and drug-abusing. Many have been taught and have developed adequate coping strategies which allow them to function at least as well as their poor counterparts who spend less time in public view. These coping strategies include finding a niche in the economic market thereby giving them sufficient income to eat and clothe themselves. They are also able to find and take advantage of programs that serve them, and are sufficiently informed about their physical health to stay reasonably healthy. They form close friendships with their peers and find themselves in many cases belonging to strong communities. At the same time, they consistently maintain some form of connection to their family of origin.

There are important gender differences that must be considered. The reasons this population is on the streets cannot be explained by poverty alone. The results of the philosophy of the state and of wars fought by ethnic or political groups also contribute to the prevalence of street children. In the past 10 years, perhaps the most important reason for children going to the streets in the developing world is because they have been orphaned due to war or HIV/AIDS (Nyawasha & Chipunza, 2012).

VARIATIONS BETWEEN THE DEVELOPING AND THE DEVELOPED WORLDS

The second major problem with the original statements about street children is that the differences between street children in the developed and the developing worlds are ignored. In the developed world, one quickly notes that there appear to be as many, if not more, female street children as male street children. And, when one looks into the background of these children, one discovers that many do not come from poor, one-parent families. Instead, their origins are often middle class and their family structure is what might be considered the ideal nuclear family, including two parents and a couple of siblings (Aptekar & Stoecklin, 2014).

In the developed world, street children are pushed out of their families often because of abuse that comes from one or more of their psychopathological parents or guardians; frequently, both poverty and abuse are cited as the major reasons children take to the streets in the United States (Smollar, 1999). An additional factor, and one that seems to account for a good deal of the male street children in the developed world, is homosexuality. Adolescent males are simply either afraid to "come out" to their parents and flee, or if they do "come out" they are forced out of their homes; and, they have the highest risk of self-destructive acts, including suicide (Kruks, 1991; Kurtz, Kurtz, & Jarvis, 1991).

There are also far fewer street children in the developed world. This has less to do with mental health or poverty of families (in fact, the mental health of the families of origin of the street children might be better in the developing world than in the developed world), than it has to do with the power of the civil community (Aptekar & Stoecklin, 2014). In the developed world, the state is wealthy enough to police the streets and support enough facilities so children who do not conform to the rules and regulation of what is considered appropriate child or adolescent development are confined. In the developed world, street boys are not raised for early independence as they are in many developing countries, and they do not have the skills or experiences to help them cope when on the streets. Their mental health is considerably more precarious than that of their developing world male counterparts. There are no significant mental health differences between developed world girls on the streets and street girls in developing worlds (Aptekar & Stoecklin, 2014). Sadly, both suffer.

There are also a couple of other important parallels between developed and developing world street children. Adolescents all over the world are living more and more under an international culture that is influenced by the West, mostly due to exposure via movies, music, and multinational corporations. No matter where one goes (even the most remote places on Earth), no matter how poor the people are, one always seems to find some evidence of Western influence. Even in a small rural Indian village a day north of Bombay (present-day Mumbai) where there is extreme poverty, the village has a communal satellite dish that gives street children the opportunity to connect with the world and idealize what they see (Aptekar, 1998). It is clear that one of the easiest ways to make a conversation with a street child in either the developed or developing world is to talk about Nike shoes, or the latest rock group. No matter how poor the children may be, they find a way to obtain the goods they see on television, or make adjustments to what they have so items look like what they have seen and remember.

Another parallel between street children in the developed world and street children in the developing world is that, as difficult as life is for all street children, the worst problem they face is public animosity (Aptekar, 1994; Aptekar & Abebe, 1997). In the case of girls, this often takes the form of sexual abuse. For boys, they are treated rudely or worse actually physically assaulted. In many places in the world, street children have been assassinated for no more than petty crimes and haughty behavior (Aptekar & Ciano, 1999). Similar to the majority of the public in many parts of the world, police reservists have construed a scenario about street children that does not include loving parents, a good character, or continuous contributions and connections with family.

The dominant culture often assumes that street children lack character and adequate parenting. Street children, in nearly all cultures in the world, have become symbols of moral judgment because they violate the norms that most cultures give to children. Street children do not usually live under the same roof as their parents; they work instead of going to school, and make decisions for themselves. What makes the climate so volatile is that the phenomenon of children taking on the roles of adults are peaking at a time when many societies are moving away from traditional codes of conduct. These codes originated by birthright and long-accepted roles of authority. Now, conduct is based on rational values, democratic choices, and a worldwide adolescent culture based on Western entertainment media. Murderers of street children often justify their actions in self-righteous moral terms, seeing themselves as heroes in cultures rapidly approaching moral decay.

Street children have become cultural scapegoats, portrayed as carriers of all the large-scale social problems, including inequality of income, changing family values with concomitant alterations in the roles of men and women, and the reduction in personal security in the context of an overly romanticized past. The press in many countries must share the blame for contributing to public outrage. The press dramatizes the "bad boy" image of street children and intimidate the public. The image emphasizes worst-case scenarios, such as the youngest of children on the streets, the severely intoxicated, and the most delinquent of youngsters. While this approach sells newspapers and raises money, it does not contribute to an accurate assessment of the situation. Ultimately, the period of adolescence is determined more by dominant society's definition of appropriate behavior for people under the age of majority. Adolescence is less a period of status related to the well-being or the capabilities of teenagers, than to extraneous cultural factors that come from other societal factors. Street children do not usually conform to dominant society's expectations or definitions.

DEVELOPMENTAL CONTRASTS OF WAR-TRAUMATIZED ADOLESCENTS

In the past 15 years, the frequency of wars has increased, and there have been more and more civilians casualties (UNICEF, 2014). Nearly 90% of the war-related deaths have been noncombatants, approximately half being children (UNICEF, 1986). In the past dozen years, more than two million children have been killed in wars, and nearly five million more have been disabled (UNICEF, 2014). In addition, approximately 12 million children were made homeless and another 1 million children were orphaned or now living without their parents (UNICEF, 1997). Furthermore, the horrors of wars—where rape and decapitation of children and women were documented as a purposeful policy—have increased (UNICEF, 2014). War has become more purposeful, at whatever human costs, the goal is to win.

Targeting health workers to prevent heath care, destroying schools to prevent education, and ruining places of religion to prevent spirituality are just a few tactics employed.

The emotional result of these events has been surprisingly difficult to ascertain. The classical symptoms of posttraumatic stress disorder (PTSD) are recurrent distressing mental imagery expressed through sleep disturbance, intrusive daytime thoughts, and/or phobic responses. In addition, there can be an exaggerated startle response, problems with concentration, sleep disturbance, reckless or self-destructive behavior, and angry outbursts (DSM-5, 2013). There are problems with trying to find these classic symptoms within children traumatized by war. Some highly traumatized adolescents do not show any classic PTSD symptoms. This might be because symptoms manifest themselves differently depending on the culture and therefore can go unnoticed, which has been the case with some war-traumatized adolescents coming from a developing world to the West as refugees. Also, young children have a limited ability to verbally describe their symptoms accurately so a PTSD assessment is particularly challenging (Loeb, Stettler, Gavila, Stein, & Chinitz, 2011).

Several studies of highly traumatized Cambodian children and adolescents living as refugees in the United States did not reveal classic PTSD symptoms (Kinzie, Sack, Angell, Manson, & Rath, 1986). The participants of these studies were severely traumatized due to experiencing the death of family members. They witnessed the killings of relatives, they were beaten, and they were starved. It was speculated that the relative absence of Western PTSD symptoms was related to the participants' past cultural reactions to education and teachers (Kinzie et al., 1986). The American schoolteachers helped these youngsters find part-time jobs. They promoted Cambodian culture in their schools, and provided ample opportunities to help them learn about American culture. Under their cultural framework, it would have been impolite not to adjust to school since their teachers were doing so much to help them. In fact, this resilient approach was contrasted with what has been found in developed countries, where adolescents are more likely to respond to trauma by acting out in delinquency and drug abuse (Kinzie et al., 1986). Wisely, it was noted that although the responses of the Cambodian children and adolescent refugees were not in line with the traditional Western definition of PTSD, these children were still under a great deal of posttraumatic stress (Kinzie et al., 1986). In addition, it was found that depressive symptoms and drug and alcohol abuse were commonly experienced.

Another reason for the lack of a PTSD diagnosis might be that Westerners working in the developing world do not notice different symptoms that may be culturally motivated or are subtle and rarely found in the West, yet still debilitating. Possible culturally influenced symptoms may include elective mutism, hysterical blindness, dizziness and wind-like substance attacks (Hinton, Hinton, Eng, & Choung, 2012), and other dissociative disorders like shaking or falling down. Sometimes, the psychosocial manifestations of trauma may also include a pathological difficulty in facing new challenges, and various problems associated with engaging unnecessarily in self-destructive relationships with people (Aptekar & Giel, 2002; Aptekar, Paardekooper, & Kuebli, 2000). In any case, the more extensive the period of time that an individual is forced to suffer trauma symptoms, the greater the risk for loss of self (Quinn & Quinn, 2011). It has been found that childhood trauma may also increase the potential for victimization and PTSD in adults (Grinage, 2003). While these symptoms may not meet the diagnostic criteria for PTSD, they certainly contribute to the process of coming to terms with the larger issues of grief and recovery faced by war traumatized adolescents.

It can also be difficult to know whether adolescents in some cultures actually have psychological disorders as they are defined and understood in the West. Or, whether they are possessed by spirits which is how the incident is described in their own cultures. It can be difficult to determine if there are differences between the two. This is why "culturally sensitive assessment and treatment should ideally include the assessment of culturally salient somatic symptoms and cultural syndromes" (Hinton, Kredlow, Bui, Pollack, & Hoffmann, 2012, p. 147). Another question concerns the effects of living where the horrendous is commonplace. In the 1980s, for example, a large percentage of the population was killed in Cambodia, and in Rwanda 14% of the population was slaughtered in three months (Veale, Taylor, & Linehan, 2000). In Mozambique, 48% of the healthcare facilities and 45% of the schools were destroyed (Veale et al., 2000). Do the adolescents in these places become accustomed to suffering? Or, do they suffer just as much as would be expected as someone from the West where these tragedies have not been experienced recently? Can resilience or coping strategies mask psychological disorders?

Rutter (1990) points out that resilience (and by inference, psychological disorders such as PTSD) are not merely a fixed reaction to particular traumatic events—that is, the compounded amount and severity of trauma cannot be used to predict behavior. Instead, reactions to trauma are mitigated or exaggerated by the person's perception of events. For example, among adolescents exposed to war from Ireland, (Conroy, 1987; Hosin & Cairns, 1984), Palestine (Baker, 1990; Punamaki, 1988, 1989), and South Africa (Straker, 1991), there were considerable psychological differences in response to war trauma. Those who believed that the cause was just and that fighting for it was appropriate exhibited much less psychopathology than the adolescents in the same traumatic circumstances who did not have political convictions.

A group of war-traumatized, displaced Ethiopian adolescents in a refugee camp called Kaliti surprisingly exhibited much less psychopathology than expected (Aptekar et al., 2000). In this study, 7 of 10 suffered from lack of water, and 6 of 10 from lack of food, a third of them had witnessed the death of a family member, nearly a third felt that they were near death themselves, while a quarter viewed their experience as torture. Given their terrible ordeal, a case could have been made to expect a good deal of psychopathology. Instead, a relative lack of psychopathology was found and attributed to several factors. One was the importance and value the community received from their spiritual beliefs; they were actively religious. Even after the war-traumatized adolescents came to terms with the loss of their loved ones and the demise of their material lives, with faith and philosophy they were able to cope.

Another mitigating factor was the adolescents' ability to take some solace in comparing their adolescence to that of their parents'. By comparison, they felt they had much to be thankful for. They recalled that their parents were routinely prevented from playing with the opposite sex and even from playing with those of their own gender. Their fathers were made to work under the direct guidance of their grandfathers. If they were allowed to play with other boys, they were considered to be straying from their chores. Their mothers were confined to their homes. In contrast, these adolescents had the benefits of living in close contact with other adolescents. Their parents granted them more personal choices of lifestyle and, most importantly, the parents of these adolescents allowed them to interact with one another across gender lines. This was similar with what was found among Eritrean orphans traumatized by war and famine (Wolff, Tesfai, Egasso, & Aradom, 1995). What accounted for the well-being of the Ethiopian adolescents was not individual counseling, but the child-centered group care they received. This care was characterized by changing traditional roles that allowed for an earlier end to adolescence (Aptekar et al., 2000) and a shift in cultural perspective due to the circumstances.

The parents of these adolescents gave them authority to respond to their circumstances. Traditionally, taking care of those who were in need was a role assigned to elders, but in Kaliti this role was taken over by adolescents (Aptekar et al., 2000). One reason for this was that many of the elders were no longer alive. By helping others, these adolescents were not only taking over adult roles far earlier than tradition dictated, but they were also able to help themselves. This is also consistent with the literature. For instance, Folkman (1997) reported that the act of providing care to terminally ill patients was not just a depressing and difficult psychological process, but also infused with positive mental health. Adolescent caregivers, in caring for and coming to terms with the grim reality of their loved ones, actually found they were also maturing and finding their own meaning in life

(Aptekar et al., 2000) at a younger age. These adolescent caregivers were engaged in fulfilling the culturally meaningful goal of helping their loved ones die in dignity. As Frankl (1963) pointed out among Holocaust survivors, adequate mental health (even in relative terms) came to those who were able to create some redeeming value from the losses that were so omnipresent. Miller (1996) found a lack of PTSD among Guatemalan adolescent refugees in Chiapas, Mexico, and suggested that the reason for this was the personal meanings they found in their circumstances. The importance of the community in aiding the psychological well-being of war-traumatized adolescents has been found among Rwandan genocide survivors (Geltman & Stover, 1997). Ultimately, Rwandan genocide survivors were able to come to terms with their experience due to the community's ability to change its social values rather than depending on traditional mental health services, which focused on helping individuals cope with what they had experienced (Geltman & Stover, 1997). It appears that cultural community beliefs can support well-being and mental health.

Data Collection Issues When Working with Street Children and War-Traumatized Adolescents

When conducting research with both street children and war-traumatized adolescents, it is particularly important to collect both quantitative and qualitative data, and use what has been referred to as a triangulation of methods. This means selecting three or more methods, each of which is chosen to offset some of the inherent problems of the others (Segall, 1983). A mixed methods approach can draw from the strengths of quantitative and qualitative approaches while minimizing their respective limitations (Johnson, Onwuegbuzie, & Turner, 2007). It has even been asserted that a mixed methods approach can produce data that are unattainable via a solely quantitative or qualitative perspective (O'Cathain & Thomas, 2006).

While it is common to follow the appropriate cross-cultural methodology in many areas, sometimes the practical realities that can lead to invalid data are ignored. An example would be a research protocol that includes translating testing materials developed in the West, establishing local norms, and training local individuals to gather data. This entails utilizing translated Western-influenced tests to gather data in an area with a different cultural perspective while making use of data collectors who also bring their own cultural biases. Developing tests in one culture and administering the tests to a population with a completely different cultural perspective can be problematic.

When the data collectors finally went to gather data, they proceeded in groups of four, carrying with them the papers they needed to administer the protocol. The children knew when they were coming and that they would pay the children to take the tests. The data collectors were chosen from the brightest and most competent university students in the local culture. As a result, they came from privileged backgrounds, and were not familiar with the living conditions of the adolescents in the refugee camp (note, the sample population could have easily been street children). Due to this and other social class differences, the researchers tended to stay by themselves. They all sat together in one tent to collect the data, ate lunch together, and left together at the end of the day. In fact, the very training they undertook to prepare themselves for this work solidified them as a social group, which increased their lack of intermingling with the traumatized adolescents. One of the many problems that this setup caused was a decrease in the various types of information that could have been gathered; after all, who wants to talk about personal things when one's peers are in earshot?

Since the research participants were paid to finish the protocol, which took several hours, and because they were so poor, they vied for the option to participate. And, because the test takers did not know the children, they were not aware that some of them bought the names of others. In addition, the sample was drawn from a list made by organizations whose continued funding depended on the size of the population, which led to numbers being inflated. Thus, there were many names of children who were never found. This helped children take the test more than once, which meant getting paid more than once. Unfortunately, it also meant that the data had been invalidated and were being compared to other people with significantly different demographics.

While the children were completing the testing, there was no check for accuracy of responses. Many research participants rushed through their tests since a completed test would equal payment for participating. The children were much more interested in the monetary aspect rather than telling some stranger the accurate details of their awful experiences. In some cases, children lied, making up complete stories about themselves, including past traumas, because they thought that their fictitious circumstances would bring them more aid. Unfortunately, the data collectors were also being paid per completed survey. So, they too had their reasons to get the protocols completed as quickly as possible even at the expense of accuracy.

Many of these research issues could have been avoided had the data collectors and the people in charge of the study worked more closely together, but the preceding example is a paradigm that is too common in this field. Someone in a far-off location plans the research with children in particularly difficult circumstances, and these planners have their own agendas in collecting data. Rarely is the information validated. Needless to say, it is also important to be clear about whether or not the child is being paid to give answers, or is being forced to give answers in return for placement in a program, or to obtain services.

Another source of research bias comes from where the data are collected. Since whether the data are collected on the streets, or in a refugee camp, or in the child's home, or with/without parents present can influence the results, these details must be taken into account. Time also distorts information. The flow of PTSD symptoms, for example, routinely fluctuates, and often does not even manifest itself until a considerable time has passed after the person has been traumatized. By asking the same questions more than once, in more than one place, and at more than one time, it is possible to check for variations in answers, thus increasing reliability.

Increasing the amount of data that are performance related, or of a projective nature, can assist with dispensing many of the problems resulting from a child's distortion of information. Photos can be taken from magazines and used with projective techniques. One can use the photos to elicit the respondents' thoughts about the relationships between the adolescents that the respondents are seeing in the photos, or the wishes that the adolescents in the photos might have for their future. Adolescents, even if they are not literate (which is common in this field), can build their own life story by cutting out photos from magazines and arranging items selectively. While this procedure does not provide standardized data, it may help the researcher gain a sense of how reliable the standardized, but not culturally normed, data are. It should also be pointed out that in addition to a low level of literacy, there is the problem of ascertaining the child's true age, and of course, all standardized tests are normed on age.

Performance-related tests, including projective techniques like sociograms of social networks, as well as drawings of their family or of the important people in their lives, or of their daily life routines, are valuable in judging how accurately the respondents are reporting information. Some homemade projective techniques such as incomplete sentences and the Three Wishes Test are also helpful in this way. In addition, researchers may make use of the Q-sort procedure by asking the children to arrange cards in such a way that they reflect their preferences or their fears in ordinal amounts.

It is also valuable to obtain quantitative data, such as how many children participate in a certain program, or how many pass a certain place in a given period of time. Using random time samplings in collecting ethnographic data—that is, collecting data both during the day and during the night, during the week as well as during the weekends, and in all kinds of weather—helps to reduce the bias of time-skewed data. Random medical examinations of the children can also be used to determine their nutritional level as well as their abuse of drugs. All of this information can be quantified.

Another much overlooked and extremely important method of getting accurate psychological data from these adolescents is the Mental Status Exam (MSE). Essentially, the MSE is the psychological equivalent of a physician's physical exam. The MSE includes an assessment of the child's appearance, memory, thought processes, language abilities, motor behavior, intelligence, and judgment. It also provides information about the child's attitudes toward strangers. While it is true that understanding and interpreting an MSE does take some training, it is certainly not beyond a researcher's grasp to undertake. As soon as the researcher makes contact with a street child, the MSE should begin. The researcher can observe the child's appearance. Is the child clean or dirty? Are there any wounds, and if so, are they cared for or untreated? Does the child have any tremors? Are there any unusual facial distortions or movements, or any stereotypical or repetitive movements or mannerisms? Does the child's pace exhibit other signs of agitation? Or, are the child's movements too slow and labored? Is the amount of eye contact appropriate? What is the child's attitude toward strangers and toward people whom he or she knows? What is the child's speech like? Is the tone appropriate? Is the flow of speech slow or pressured? Is the tone quality unusual? Is the volume appropriate? What is the level of vocabulary? Does the child have a problem finding words and the names of well-known objects? Is he or she misusing words?

There are other areas to observe, such as the children's mood, and over time their range of moods. One can ask about their goals and evaluate how realistically they perceive themselves as well as their insight into their problems, and what kinds of judgments they are making about their lives. Certain games can be played with them that will help ascertain their level of simple arithmetic, or their memory. It is impossible to arrive at an accurate understanding of these adolescents without obtaining various sources of data. In the aggregate, it is particularly important to understand society's attitude toward the adolescents and to understand the historical context of the children being studied. Information can also be gleaned from archival data such as press reports and written documents from governments and nongovernmental organizations, and from civil and criminal laws. It is valuable to see how the children are presented by the media.

Focus groups composed of parents, of persons who worked with the children, and of those who do not know them at all can yield important information. This method was utilized to help define street children from several perspectives, and the results showed that different people's knowledge and attitudes about street children contributed to their estimates of their numbers, which ranged from 1,000 to 100,000 in Nairobi, and from 5,000 to 1.5 million in Kenya (Aptekar & Ciano, 1999). The themes for the focus groups can be chosen by the participants or by the issues brought up by the children, or by research questions. The adolescents can be present or absent.

Two additional problems are particularly important and unfortunately too widespread in this field. Authors routinely overgeneralize their findings by moving from a small and often nonrandom sample to a statement that suggests a much larger population. For example, a nonrandom sample of 40 street boys may lead to a (false) statement like "*Nearly* all street children are HIV positive or addicted to drugs." Second, there are problems with verifying numbers. No matter how much the author discounts the validity of his or her numbers by saying that they were obtained from invalid standardized tests, the reader still tends to believe in them, if for no other reason than to use them in his or her own literature reviews. Then, the next person down the line uses them more easily, and so forth.

Research Dilemmas Associated with Street Children and War-Traumatized Adolescents

A particular problem related to conducting research with street children is obtaining a sample. Obtaining a sample depends upon knowing the dimensions of the population, which of course is related to a clear definition of who is being studied. For instance, there has been confusion between the terms "street children" and "working children" (e.g., children who at a young age are on the streets working during the day, but return to their families at night). This confusion is exacerbated because it is probably not accurate to distinguish between street children and working children because the definitions include components on a continuum that often changes with such circumstances as family dynamics, economic circumstances, and other influencing factors (Aptekar, 1994).

Another problem is the bias toward inflating the numbers of street children (which can also be true of war-traumatized adolescents). There are several reasons why numbers are inflated. The higher the number, the larger the problem, and the larger the problem, the more likely donors are to contribute funds. Once funds are flowing there will be more programs, and each of these employs several people, who are apt to inflate the numbers. Finally, the press is biased toward increasing the numbers, which it often does by reporting worst-case scenarios (e.g., the youngest child on the street, the most drug-dependent, the severest delinquent acts). These are examples of what sells newspapers. There is a field of research in this area, one that falls under the rubric of the sociology of information or the sociology of knowledge (Aptekar & Stoecklin, 2014).

A process that helped to establish a valid procedure for choosing a sample of street children was utilized in Kenya (Aptekar & Ciano, 1999). It began with a map of Nairobi. Then, by using former street children and others who were working with street children, areas in the city that had high concentrations of street children were identified. This was laid over the map of the city and numbered grids were drawn onto this new map. Local people who were known by the street children were asked to walk these areas each night for two weeks. Sleeping places (which in Kenya are called *choums*) were used to define households. Households are usually the central concept in a census and were lacking in former estimates of street children in a particular space. The *choums* were then placed on the map of the city. This gave areas of the city with high and low concentrations of street children. The map was then divided into equal grids, which were then labeled with high or low concentrations of households. A stratified random sample of the high and low areas of households for collecting census data was then selected.

The census takers collected data on the numbers of street children in each *choum* in the randomly selected areas for three successive nights, and then at weekly intervals for three weeks. Each data collection team had the same structured interview format. All of this helped to ascertain a rough estimate of the numbers of street children, the degree to which they moved from household to household, and gender ratio. Each census team was composed of two people. Since street children are not known to be good reporters of demographic information, such as age and family circumstances, while one member of the team asked the child's age, the other team member made an independent estimate of the child's age. Similar procedures were also employed for comparing the children's stated tribal affiliation with physical characteristics and language skills. The degree of discrepancy gave some idea about the validity of information the child was supplying, and by using this procedure three times, there was some notion of reliability. The census data were then ready to be used for an estimation of the population, which in turn was used to determine how large the samples had to be in order to arrive at useful statistical comparisons.

Having an estimate of the number of street children in the population can help to ascertain several important pieces of information. For example, an estimate of the number of street children using the programs that were being offered could be made. The program records could now be used to match up the children with the specific *choums* they were living in, which programs they were visiting, and the consistency of their visits. In this case, a surprising realization emerged: There were more than enough programs available for the current number of street children. This miscalculation of existing programs was based upon inflated estimates of the number of street children. The real issue was the lack of organized services. Another result of the inflated estimation of street children was the presence of more feeding programs than was necessary. Consequently, the children networked with each other so they knew which feeding program to go to on a particular day.

As part of the study, a stratified random sample of street children with differing degrees of street experience was selected, ranging from children who had just arrived to the streets to those who had been on the streets for a while (Aptekar & Ciano, 1999). When the degree of street experience was coupled with various measures of mental health, whether mental health was impacted by the length of time on the streets became more understandable. In trying to determine why some poor children become street children and why within a single family only some of the children become street children, a sample of siblings who stayed at home was utilized as a type of control group. Though it was quite easy to choose an adequate-sized sample of street boys, it was nearly impossible to get a large enough random sample of street girls. So, street girls were not randomly chosen.

In the case of street children, it was found that they were not reliable informants in ethnographic conversations nor on paper-and-pencil tests (Aptekar & Ciano, 1999). Like other nomadic entertainers (Berland, 1982), street children make their living by manipulating their audiences; they either beg or devise schemes to get work. The data collector is rarely exempt from their skills. Unfortunately, much too much emphasis is placed on administering questionnaires, and questionnaires are particularly insensitive to this issue. Hutz and Koller (1999) discuss similar findings and additional methodological issues when conducting research with street children.

It is a common strategy to stress the importance of creating trust and building a relationship or rapport with street children (and for that matter with war-traumatized children) before conducting research with them. Yet, it is very rare for anyone who interacts with street children to have such a unique relationship where the distortion of facts is not evident. In some cases, a relationship based on trust or friendship is just as likely to lead to increased distortion as it is to reduce it because the more the children are familiar with you, the more adept they are at manipulating information to get what they want from you. There are some data collectors who overromanticize the children which may create a biased belief that resilience is the main protecting agent, while other researchers overdramatize situations and portray the children as being much worse off than they actually are.

To help with this distortion, more than one person should be utilized to collect data. Researchers should routinely match the children's answers given to different data collectors to look for overlap. Within the study in Kenya, data collectors from different academic disciplines, ethnic groups, genders, social status, and ages were engaged; the results showed how street children responded differently to different people when asked the same question. In fact, some correlations were stronger between data collectors than the information gleaned from different children (Aptekar & Ciano, 1999).

The following are "Ten Commandments" (not to be taken with religious zeal) for prospective researchers in the field of street children: (a) Think about how your ethnocentrism defines the nature of childhood; (b) Do not judge how the children of poor families cope in the context of their culture; (c) Avoid pitying the children or overestimating their resilience; (d) Be clear about how the sample was drawn and who the children are; (e) Do not forget gender differences; (f) Use both narrative and numbers, but understand the shortcomings of each; (g) Do not accept or assume that everything the children say to you is factual; (h) Use projective methods, performance based tests, and observe their mental status; (i) Collect data regarding how the children are perceived in their society; and (j) Do not over generalize your results.

Personal Hurdles When Supplying Mental Health Services: Scenarios to Ponder

There was an elderly priest who had been working with street children for nearly four decades (Aptekar et al., 1995). Each Monday night, he conducted work on the streets of a large Africa city with several young men and women who were interested in learning how to work with street children. It was always a pleasure to accompany him while he would visit various groups of children. A typical rainy evening included stopping to talk with a group of about a dozen boys who were living at the back of a dead-end alley, encouraging them to get help, buying them each a bag of chips, and then moving on to the next group of children who received essentially the same treatment. As was the custom at the end of each evening, the visits would be discussed over chicken and chips. On one particular evening on the way home, a group of seven girls about 13 to 15 years old came into the street, stopped the car, and pointed to one girl who had stayed behind in the shadows. This girl clearly had a high fever and was delusional. She may have been suffering from malaria, or an overdose of drugs, or possibly even syphilis. Whatever the reason for the girl's illness, the group of girls implored the priest to take their sick companion to the hospital. He refused and told them he would check on her in the morning. As he continued to drive, the question was asked as to why he left the girl in such a crisis. He said that it was past 10.00 p.m., and if he took her to the hospital, he would not get home until past 1.00 a.m. He continued to say that he had mass to give at 6.00 a.m. and a full day of street work already planned for the next day. He said, "I have to draw the line somewhere."

When the priest left this sick young girl alone in the rainy night, the initial reaction was an immediate deep sense of betrayal because he was not living up to the moral standards of his calling. It was surprisingly easy to evaluate 40 years of good work by a single late-night decision. Only later did the following painful fact become clear: When working with this population of adolescents there are always more troubled children than there are resources to help them. At some point everyone has to turn his or her back, if for no other reason than to move forward to the next day. The priest's refusal to administer to the sick child, a decision learned from decades of experience, was based on the greater good. With a quick judgmental perspective that was heavily Western biased, a cultural viewpoint about the righteous life and what was appropriate and inappropriate to helping street children was made. In spite of the fact that each time a program for street children was visited, no matter what continent or hemisphere, people spoke disparagingly about another program across town. They also spoke badly about people helping in a different style than their own. Religious assail the secular, tough disciplinarians complain about the easygoing, those in favor of offering shelter but not family fight against those who favor fostering, and on and on.

Quick judgments are inappropriate for several reasons. There is little correlation between a program's official policy and the way the child experiences the program. Street children are also very different from each other, and their needs change over time. There is, in short, plenty of room for nearly all philosophies and nearly every style of help. And, regardless of the philosophy or style of help, all aid is beneficial. What keeps diversity, experimentation, and variety from flourishing in the work with street children can often be traced to ethnocentric values emphasizing that only programs based on Western approaches should be utilized and are valuable.

In fact, the question is larger. Whether or not to give help, what kind of help, and how to deliver it is a major problem for the humanitarian aid worker (Aptekar, 2013). In fact, it is far more difficult to help than one might expect (Aptekar & Giel, 2001). After seeing a videotape made of the refugee camp on the outskirts of Addis Ababa in Ethiopia and wanting to help, an American friend donated $200. It was easy to distribute a portion of the funds to particular groups in need, one of which was a collection of about 120 adolescent orphans. However, before a meeting with the adolescent orphan group started, there was jockeying for favor. One young man claimed to be an orphan but was not on the list of eligible orphans. He kept demanding that he be given something. There were two members of the camp's sports team who had fractured their legs while playing in a game. They stayed in the tent and kept asking for money. They claimed that because they were on the camp's sports team, they deserved compensation. One young woman, who was partially paralyzed, probably due to a stroke, waited outside in the rain to ask for transport money to go to the doctor.

After the meeting with the orphans, there was still a portion of the donation to distribute so the help of four additional individuals was solicited to assist with the decision making. First to present his case was Asnake, a 21-one-year-old war-orphaned boy who was working as a waiter earning 100 birr per month (at the time, the exchange rate was about 7 birr per U.S. dollar). A week earlier, he had missed a meeting with the orphans due to work, so was not on the list, and therefore had missed the opportunity to receive 50 birr that had been given to the other orphans. As a result, he was offered only 20 birr.

The next to come was a young man in his early 20s wearing a red Indiana University sweatshirt. He came in with a prescription for an antibiotic. He looked healthy so he was not given any money. An indigent young mother was given 5 birr to get something to eat. Then, a woman breast-feeding a baby presented her case and she was also given 5 birr for food. Around the middle of the process, a young man with mental health problems showed up. He stood in the doorway, blocking the way for others to enter and refusing to leave unless he was given money. He claimed that he needed money for school and transportation; he displayed his clavicle which was protruding, and said it was dislocated. He demanded money to go to the doctor. He was reminded that the day before he had been given money to visit the psychiatric hospital, but did not go. He refused to leave. Finally, one helper gave him a birr, but this was not enough. He still refused to budge. The standoff lasted several minutes before he was offered another birr. Finally he left, but only for a short time. He returned twice disrupting the process and taking time away from the other individuals.

Abush, a young man who lost a leg when he stepped on a mine, came in next looking for money for transport to a job prospect. He was refused. Then, a woman who wanted money for transport to visit her children who were being fostered in Addis was turned down. This process of seeing people and making judgments about their claims continued for a couple of hours. As can be expected, as word got out that money was being disseminated, the crowd grew larger. Each person had a case, but eventually the money was gone with many people still queuing. Unfortunately, many people said that they had been promised an audience, and in fact this was true for some of them. They all believed they deserved help and certainly felt that they needed it. Sadly, the criteria used to determine who actually received some money were grim. Furthermore, it was likely that the neediest were not even able to get out of bed to ask.

It was logistically impossible (and this still begs the question of one's professional and moral responsibilities) to give each of them what they wanted. As a result, there were questions that needed answering. Is it better to give to only some people and face the challenge of favoritism? Or, should the money have been given to the camp committee with the expectation that "administrative fees" would be deducted and therefore lost to those who really needed it? In either case, and not unimportantly, how do you stop giving once you start? When you see children who can benefit so much from something that is so very little to you, how can you not give? No matter the country or culture, every time when a child who is skinny, dirty, and ragged asks for food, it is difficult not to look into your pockets or want to buy something for him or her to eat. Once you start to distribute food or change, every time, within seconds, children begin to run from out of nowhere and soon there is a mob surrounding you. What started out as an exchange with one, or a few children, has now turned into a horde of children demanding more food and insisting that you have more money to give them. An innocent act of kindness can quickly turn into a scary, frenzied situation.

The bottom line is that people have to accept that no matter how well meaning, it is impossible to meet all demands; they must comprehend that the only way to help any of them is to understand that not everyone is going to be helped. What one needs in this line of work is a heavy, impenetrable coat of armor. Another scenario to ponder involves Sister Mary, from the Italian Comboni Order, the order that specialized in working with "outcastes." Sister Mary provided a feeding program for the indigent in the same neighborhood. During an initial conversation, Sister Mary shared that it was difficult to work in this field (whether with street children or with war refugees) because, at a fundamental level, one could never finish the job. Usually, when people say that it is difficult to work in this field, they either mean that it is difficult to work with the government or that it is difficult because the people never stop asking for help. No matter what they are given, they are never satisfied. At first, it appeared this was Sister Mary's meaning but later it became clear that she was actually saying that God's work was never done.

While leaving Sister Mary's compound one day, there was a young woman with a 10-month-old baby waiting to see her. The baby had been completely burned all over her face. A soiled white piece of cotton cloth was wrapped around her head as if she had a toothache, but it was still possible to see a gag-inducing red pimple protruding from the cornea of one eye. As the woman reached out to say hello to Sister Mary, she displayed the fingers of her hands that were burned to the stubs. Sister Mary welcomed the young woman in her arms and complained to her that the baby had a runny nose. Sister Mary developed a way of helping, probably as subconsciously as consciously, to keep her going. She persisted by finding a way to ignore the incurably obvious and embracing the barest of possibilities. The most important goal, and in many cases the most difficult, is to find a way to stay in the field. Since this work can be so overwhelming and disturbing, without the ability to do more, only the least-sensitive remain.

Making Difficult Cultural Choices

Apart from the logistical issues that take place when trying to help, other problems occur and exist due to cultural differences. Perhaps the first place to focus upon is the United Nations Convention on the Rights of the Child (commonly abbreviated as CRC), which offers a promising opportunity for helping street and war-traumatized children since it "articulates the rights more completely and provides a set of guiding principles that fundamentally shapes the way in which we view children" (UNICEF, 2013, April 4, p. 1). However, the CRC may also pose similar problems that laws crossing cultural barriers encounter. By taking into account the cultural variations and diversity in children's lives, the CRC can contribute to defining what is universal about children's rights. It can clarify when certain behaviors are abusive regardless of the cultural beliefs that promote them. On the other hand, because the CRC is a global promise, it also incorporates some exceptions to Western practices which may be considered appropriate child development in order to avoid an ethnocentric perspective.

Many people in the West have a concept of child development based on a stereotyped bias that all children are innocent and in need of constant attention. Although this type of child might commonly be found in many cultures, to assume this is the case for children across all cultures poses problems. So, the definition of childhood and adolescence may be one area to focus upon in order to determine how to help today's street children. For example, in the developing world, there are many instances that may seem like unusually harsh forms of training for early dependence to a person with a Western perspective. In many developing worlds, 10-year-old children are expected to earn a living, take care of their own basic needs, and contribute to the general welfare of their family. Although these 10-year-old individuals may be capable, they are not (and perhaps should not be) given the privileges and responsibilities of adults. Is this perspective and practice out of compliance with the CRC, and should they therefore now be considered abused?

When individuals who are accustomed to material comforts work with street children, they often bring with them many preconceived notions about children which are often ethnocentric and moralistic, and therefore can be challenged. For example, it is far too easy for a person from the West to employ Western morality and make the assumption that street children are deprived. The following is a narrative of a fairly typical workday for two Colombian street children (Aptekar, 1988). Every morning, Roberto and Antonio, two 11-year-old Colombian street children, go to the El Paradiso restaurant to wash the front sidewalk with a hose in exchange for leftover food (*sobres*). On one particular day, Antonio slings a plastic bag of *sobres* over his shoulder, then the two of them go to a quiet side street and sit down in the shade. They empty the *sobres*, which are lumped together in a mass about the size of a small pillow, eat a bit then take the rest to a blind man to trade for a few pesos and a couple of cigarettes. The boys then board a bus en route to the cemetery. They ask the driver to let them ride for free since they have no money, are starving, and need to beg for food. On the bus, Roberto puts a pitiful expression on his face and begins to soulfully sing about the difficulties of having and supporting a sick mother. The song concludes, "Can you give my mother a few pesos so she can go to the doctor?" Roberto receives a few pesos, enough to pay for their ride to the cemetery. Meanwhile, Antonio lodges himself in the exit well, stands in the way of exiting passengers, and offers his hand to them so they might climb down more easily. Most of the passengers ignore him, some are indignant and make comments to the bus driver, while a few find his performance amusing (or possibly heartfelt) and give him a coin. Once at the cemetery, the two boys meet a few older friends and exchange some of the bus money with them for a ladder. The boys carry the ladder over to an area where relatives are visiting graves of loved ones. Roberto and Antonio rent out the use of the ladder since it is nearly impossible to place wreaths on the higher gravesites without a ladder.

In the evening, the boys go to the *sexta* (or Sixth Avenue, an avenue of fashionable shops and restaurants in the fashionable side of town), where, because of their disordered and disheveled appearance, the boys are perceived as a menace. After receiving some malignant looks and rude comments from people, they stop on a side street, where a young and rather affluent couple is dining. When the boys ask them for food, the couple try to ignore them. The two boys, sensing that they are intruding on a special occasion, become more insistent, since they believe they may be paid to leave the diners alone. Finally, the man who is dining tells them in a loud voice to leave. This only emphasizes to the boys that they are winning the battle of nerves. The diner calls the waiter for help, who halfheartedly tells the boys to go. However, they are back in a few moments. Roberto approaches the table from one side, asking once more for something to eat, while Antonio comes from the other side and grabs a piece of meat off the woman's plate. Running and laughing, they recede into the darkened street (Aptekar, 1988).

These two boys exhibit a peripatetic way of life; they stalk different places to find items that can be sold for more value in another place. They rotate between routines and places known for their lucrative possibilities. They live in a group in which they have emotional ties only among themselves, and they travel among the sedentary. In comparison, the daily routine of a typical 11-year-old American child is in stark contrast. So, which example is the norm internationally and cross-culturally? How can a value be placed on either example?

The very term "street children," a name given by the sedentary middle class, hides its own paradox. Streets are a public environment, whose degree of safety depends upon the control of the civic politic, but children belong to the family, a private environment considered off-bounds to public scrutiny. The term "street children" is thus an oxymoronic moniker that reveals the origins of this form of exaggerated hostility toward them. What endangers street children, more than their poverty or the lack of adult supervision, is the degree to which they are treated with hostility, and this can be understood only in the context of the unique environment in which they need to make a living.

The CRC can serve poor children by defining behaviors toward children that are universally reprehensible and drawing the line between cultural relativism and child neglect/abuse. However, the various articles and rights defined by the CRC can also lean toward cultural hegemony. For example, although the CRC states that all children should have the benefit of their childhood and not be forced into premature adult responsibilities, the question remains, at what point should a child be considered an adult? Is it influenced by age? Or, possibly experience? The escapades of Roberto and Antonio suggest that many street children, rather than being passive recipients of abuse/neglect, are more like young adults; they use their knowledge of human behavior to survive. Instead of perceiving the children as the pathological result of abuse or neglect, they can rather be perceived as well adapted due to their ability to turn impoverished conditions into economic opportunities. By assuming the right to live as they choose (either attending or not attending school, entering public restaurants for something to drink or eat, by becoming intoxicated when and where they desire, and by working to support themselves), poor children have taken on many of the behaviors associated with adulthood. However, street children have made these decisions in full public view and have often received sanctions which in many cases are of immense proportion.

An article of the CRC incorporates what has been described as the child's right to childhood (i.e., certain inalienable rights). In the case of poor children this perspective is difficult to apply unless the public is educated about young children assuming adulthood earlier than certain cultural expectations allow. If this can be accomplished, then a peace in the troubled space where street children assume adult roles and where the public views and responds to them with such fear and anger may be negotiated. Many poor working children put to test the question of cultural relativism in childrearing. While some studies have shown how miserable their childrearing is, others point to the children's resilience in the face of adversity (Aptekar & Stoecklin, 2014). Perhaps the truth lies somewhere in-between, and brings up the following questions: Are the lives of poor working and street children abusive? Or, do they live in an appropriate but culturally different set of circumstances? Coming to terms with the apparent dichotomy between cultural relativism and universalism is at the heart of helping street children. Redirecting public concern should be one of the necessary tasks for working with street children. Unfortunately, changing the behavior of poor children is the focus for all but a handful of the tens of thousands of people devoted to helping street children. This leaves the important work of changing society's attitudes toward poor children almost completely neglected. Whether this is because direct care is easier to administer and evaluate than community development is not clear, but whatever the reason for ignoring public health, the difficulty of changing the public's perception is not easy.

Sometimes cultural hegemony is easy to accept, but it is rarely unanimously accepted. In other cases, particularly in the field of mental health, cultural hegemony is subtler, but so prevalent that to bridge cultural differences is professionally taxing and morally ambiguous. Every couple of months in Ethiopia in the mid-1990s, the Christian Relief and Development Association (CRDA; a self-styled mega–nongovernmental organization composed of all the groups working with refugees in Ethiopia) held a meeting to coordinate programs. The idea of this association was to avoid duplication of services while functioning as a focal organization for donors and the government. CRDA had written a report that called for giving priority assistance to women and children. While their rationale was based on Western gender relations that would be helpful in getting funding from Western donors, the approach made less sense in the local cultural context.

In local terms, a case in the opposite direction could easily be made that the men should receive the priority. The women were already working in a food-for-work project (a public project funded by donor countries), and were involved with their traditional roles in childrearing and heading the household. The women were already too busy, though better off than the men who sat and played cards, chewed *chat,* and were unable to find work, though desperate for it. Although it was possible to view the behavior of these young men as culturally appropriate to their cultural gender roles, it was also possible to see them as emasculated from their culture's gender specific roles and possibly suffering from clinical depression. As young men, they had moved from their rural homes into the cities and competed successfully to gain access to the miniscule salaried economy, some in the military and many in what might be referred to as the military-industrial economy. They had worked on tasks that were far greater even in imagination than they had ever dreamed of. They had learned to be mechanics for tanks and transport vehicles, and some worked on airplanes and naval ships. In the civilian sector, they had refined oil, learning and assuming command of the technology that it required. Some had earned enough to buy homes, electrify them, and have refrigerators. Their children were fed and clothed, and attended school. Their family had medical care. They were a part of the small Ethiopian middle class.

Now, these same men had lost the power to support their families. They were no longer warriors or providers, nor part of a team of men working together to reach a challenging goal. These men were war victims, not physically wounded, but certainly injured (their behavior was similar to patients in a hospital daycare recovery room) and deserving of attention. Giving priority to children and women would make the men even more withdrawn and less involved. This would place yet more stress and responsibility on the women in their families. Even the families who were able to make it intact through this ordeal would most likely find themselves in greater stress and disharmony.

When the assumption of female and child priorities was challenged, many in the CRDA meeting countered by saying that if money was given to the men, then the men would use it for drink. However, the women would use the money appropriately. Ethiopian men (and also by implication, men of the Third World) are treated pejoratively. If this accusation is true, then this is even more reason why men should be targeted for help. In other cases, cultural factors may impede understanding and treatment of mental health problems.

It was estimated that 2.6 million Ethiopian adults and about 3 million children suffered from psychiatric disorders (Araya & Aboud, 1993). There are long-standing descriptors for mental illness in Ethiopia, which included people who wandered naked on the streets and talked to themselves *(ibd, kewes). Wofefe* referred to people whose mood fluctuated suddenly. *Bisichit* described people who were greatly irritable, intensely gloomy, or severely anxious. *Abshiu* referred to people who were aggressive because of being intoxicated (see Araya & Aboud, 1993; Kortman, 1987, for additional terms). Therefore, the cultural reason given for behaviors made treatment a problem, but not the difference in the symptoms of mental disorder. In the West, mental disorders are assumed to come from childhood experiences, ongoing mental stressors, and physiological dispositions, while in Ethiopia mental illness is believed to be caused by evil spirits (the main ones being the *buda* and the *zar* [Vecchiato, 1993a, 1993b]). As a result, very few Ethiopians with mental disorders are served in secular offices. Almost all the mental health services are offered in churches, or in areas designated for spiritual value. Ethiopian healers, the cultural equivalent of Western clinicians, go through training by passing through rites of passage within a religious context. This is very different than attending graduate school. While the healer's training calls for accepting the unknown, the Westerner is trained to find rational truth. In short, the Ethiopian healer is more likely to receive insight into the clinical process from prayer than from academic conferences.

As a result of these cultural differences, clients have different expectations. In the West, a client forms an alliance with a "professional" healer, and expects this help to be based on secular natural science theories and principles. When an Ethiopian client has (what in the West would be called) a mental health problem, he or she goes to a healer. The client is likely to supplicate himself or herself to God (or to other forms of the supernatural).

Ethiopian clients will acknowledge their own weaknesses and give themselves to the all-powerful healer, while in the West clients look forward to reasoned dialogue between counselor and client. The Western client expects therapy to include occasional emotional arousal, but mostly he or she expects to have controlled verbal recollections of past and current events. In contrast, Ethiopian clients expect to be taken over by spiritual possession. In the West, clients expect to learn to react to social situations differently, control their behavior, and make cognitive changes. Ethiopian clients expect to be told what to do, which is often done in an elaborate ceremony that is considered irrational in the West. In short, the philosophy behind mental health services in the West is secular humanism and the therapy democratic, while in Ethiopia the philosophy is religious and the practice authoritarian (Kleinman, 1988). To work in this context often means denying what one knows to be right, while accepting what one knows to be incorrect.

If you are one of the many mental health workers who research or work with street children or adolescents traumatized by war, you may wish to consider adopting the following perspectives: (a) Examine your culturally bound beliefs about child development; (b) Embrace alternative family structures as legitimate; (c) Do not confuse poverty with psychopathology; (d) Accept that there are many young people in adult roles; (e) Work with street children and war-traumatized adolescents without forcing them to accept your moral point of view; (f) Refrain from quick judgment against others who work with street children and war-traumatized adolescents but operate from different cultural points of view; (g) Give psychotherapy only to those who need it, give the rest of the children practical help; (h) Focus on the child, not the drug; (i) Do your best to increase income generation and self-efficacy; and (j) Educate the public (one of the most difficult and potentially most rewarding of tasks you can undertake).

CONCLUSION

This chapter has stressed the importance of understanding trauma in reference to street children and war-traumatized adolescents' phenomenological interpretation of it. Phenomenological factors can mitigate antecedent traumas and severity of current situational difficulties to produce less than the expected amount of psychopathology. This seemed to be particularly true for the adolescents in the refugee camp and for street children. And, it may help to explain why many antecedent traumatic factors have been mentioned as ameliorating and exaggerating psychopathology in adolescent development (Aptekar & Stoecklin, 1997; Losel & Bliesener, 1990).

There are, however, two variables that have been found to be mitigating factors in several different cultures. One of these is a stable psychological relationship with at least one parent, or at least having a parent or an adult caretaker present and calm in the midst of trauma (Ajdukovic & Ajdukovic, 1993; Garbarino, Kostelny, & Dubrow, 1991a, 1992; McCallin & Fozzard, 1990; McFarlane, 1990; Zeidner, Klingman, & Itzkovitz, 1993). In other words, resiliency can still be fostered and developed even within extreme stress and trauma. This seems to hold particularly true for children and preadolescents, the clear effects waning with age (see Terr, 1990, 1991). What this chapter has shown is that community and peers are vitally important.

The second mitigating factor found in the literature is that positive interpersonal relations with people, when combined with an active approach to problem solving, are particularly helpful in reducing psychopathology (Garbarino et al., 1991a, 1991b; Hobfoll et al., 1991; Ressler, Boothby, & Steinbeck, 1988; Saylor, 1993; Wertleib et al., 1990). It appears that for both war-traumatized and street children, this is particularly important. Certainly, street children find solace with other young adults, living what in the West might be called a premature adulthood. The same can be said of the adolescents in the refugee camp. By being able to freely associate with each other (in sharp contrast to the past), they were able to greatly improve their capacity to cope.

After exploring some of the developmental distinctions of street children and war-traumatized adolescents, this chapter examined research and intervention problems and then offered some suggestions for clinical work. The reader ultimately should not lose sight of the fact that working in this field addresses some essential research questions for the social scientist. The question of applicability hits in its fullest form to the researcher. What value, if any, is there in conducting research with street children and war-traumatized adolescents? What might constrain or facilitate the transfer of research into policy and practice? For the practitioner, the assumption and responsibility of privilege may be put to the test. How do counselors balance professionalism and social responsibility? Fortunately, the field also offers many opportunities to better understand not only the miscellany of adolescent behavior, but also the cross-cultural diversity of attitudes toward children and adolescents.

REFLECTIVE QUESTIONS

1. What are possible cultural nuances that may impact street children and war-traumatized adolescents?
2. How does gender influence street children?
3. Are there cultural overlaps between street children and war-traumatized adolescents from various countries?
4. How is adolescence changed by being a street child?

SUGGESTED READINGS

Books and Articles

Aptekar, L. (2013). *In the lion's mouth: Hope and heartbreak in humanitarian assistance* (2nd ed.). Bloomington, IN: Xlibris.

Aptekar, L. (2013). Street children, AIDS orphans, and unprotected minors: What you read is not what you see. In M. Hashemi. & M. Sanchez-Jankowski (Eds.), *In children in crisis: Ethnographic studies in international contexts* (pp. 9–24). New York: Routledge.

Aptekar, L. (2013). To give or not to give, confessions of a humanitarian aid worker. In D. Vakoch (Ed.), *Altruism in cross-cultural perspective* (pp. 151–159). New York: Springer.

Aptekar, L., & Stoecklin, D. (2014). *Street children and homeless youth: A cross-cultural perspective.* New York: Springer.

REFERENCES

AFP United Nations. (2013, June 13). Children used as human shields in Syria war, says United Nations. Retrieved from http://english.alarabiya.net/en/News/middle-east/2013/06/13/Children-used-as-human-shields-in-Syria-war-says-U-N-.html

Ajdukovic, M., & Ajdukovic, D. (1993). Psychological well-being of refugee children. *Child Abuse & Neglect, 17,* 843–854.

American Psychiatric Association. (2013). *The diagnostic and statistical manual of mental disorders* (5th ed.). Arlington, VA: American Psychiatric Association.

Aptekar, L. (1988). *Street children of Cali.* Durham, NC: Duke University Press.

Aptekar, L. (1989). Characteristics of the street children of Colombia. *Child Abuse and Neglect: The International Journal, 13*(3), 427–439.

Aptekar, L. (1992). Are Colombian street children neglected? The contributions of ethnographic and ethnohistorical approaches to the study of children. *Anthropology and Education Quarterly, 22*(4), 326–349.

Aptekar, L. (1994). Street children in the developing world: A review of their condition. *Cross-Cultural Research, 28*(3), 195–224.

Aptekar, L. (2013). To give or not to give, confessions of a humanitarian aid worker. In D. Vakoch (Ed.), *Altruism in cross-cultural perspective* (pp. 151–159). New York: Springer Press.

Aptekar, L., & Abebe, B. (1997). Conflict in the neighborhood: Street children and the public space. *Childhood, 4*(4), 477–490.

Aptekar, L., Cathey, P. J., Ciano, L., & Giardino, G. (1995). Street children in Nairobi, Kenya. *African Urban Quarterly, 10,* 1–26.

Aptekar, L., & Ciano, L. (1999). Street children in Nairobi, Kenya: Gender differences and mental health. In M. Rafaelli & R. Larson (Eds.), *Developmental issues among homeless and working street youth: New directions in childhood development* (pp. 35–46). San Francisco, CA: Jossey-Bass.

Aptekar, L., & Giel, R. (2002). Walks in Kaliti life in a destitute shelter for the displaced. In J. De Jong (Ed.), *War and violence: Public mental health in the sociocultural context* (pp. 337–366). New York: Plenum-Kluwer.

Aptekar, L., Paardekooper, B., & Kuebli, J. (2000). Adolescence and youth among displaced Ethiopians: A case study in Kaliti camp. *International Journal of Group Tensions, 29*(1–2), 101–134.

Aptekar, L., & Stocklin, D. (1997). Growing up in particularly difficult circumstances: A cross-cultural perspective. In J. Berry, P.R. Dasen, & T.S. Saraswathi (Eds.), *Handbook of cross-cultural psychology. Volume 2, Basic processes and development psychology* (2nd ed., pp. 377–412). Boston, MA: Allyn & Bacon.

Aptekar, L., & Stoecklin, D. (2014). *Street children and homeless youth: A cross-cultural perspective.* New York: Springer Press.

Araya, M., & Aboud, F. (1993). Mental illness. In H. Kloos & A. Zein (Eds.), *The ecology of health and disease in Ethiopia* (pp. 493–506). Boulder, CO: Westview.

Baizerman, M. (1988). Street kids: Notes for designing a program for youth of and on the streets. *Child Care Worker, 6*(11), 13–15.

Baker, A. M. (1990). The psychological impact of the Intifadah on Palestinian children in the occupied West Bank and Gaza. *American Journal of Orthopsychiatry, 60*(4), 496–505.

Berland, J. (1982). *No five fingers are alike.* Cambridge, MA: Harvard University Press.

Bradley, C. (2008). Babies of the disappeared. *New Statesman, 137,* 19–20.

Connolly, M. (1990). Adrift in the city: A comparative study of street children in Bogota, Colombia, and Guatemala City. In N. Boxhill (Ed.), *Homeless children: The watchers and the waiters* (pp. 129–149). New York: Haworth Press.

Conroy, J. (1987). *Belfast diary.* Boston, MA: Beacon Press.

Donald, D., & Swartz-Kruger, J. (1994). The South African street child: Developmental implications. *South African Journal of Psychology, 24*(4), 169–174.

Folkman, S. (1997). Positive psychological states and coping with severe stress. *Social Science Medicine, 45,* 1207–1221.

Frankl, V. (1963). *Man's search for meaning.* New York: Washington Square Press.

Gabarino, J., Kostelny, K., & Dubrow, N. (1992). *Children in dangerous environments: Coping with the consequences of community violence.* San Francisco: Jossey-Bass.

Gabarino, J., Kostelny, K., & Dubrow, N. (1991a). *No place to be a child: Growing up in a war zone.* Lexington, MA: Lexington Books.

Gabarino, J., Kostelny, K., & Dubrow, N. (1991b). What children can tell us about living in danger. *American Psychologist, 46,* 376–383.

Geltman, P., & Stover, E. (1997). Genocide and the plight of children in Rwanda. *Journal of the American Medical Association, 277*(4), 289–294.

Grinage, B. (2003). Diagnosis and management of post-traumatic stress disorder. *American Family Physician, 68*(12), 2401.

Hesketh, T., Lu, L., & Xing, Z. W. (2005). The effect of China's one-child family policy after 25 years. *New England Journal of Medicine, 353,* 1171–1176. doi: 10.1056/NEJMhpr051833

Hinton, D.E., Hinton, A.L., Eng, K.T., & Choung, S. (2012). PTSD and key somatic complaints and cultural syndromes among rural Cambodians: The results of a needs assessment survey. *Medical Anthropology Quarterly, 26*(3), 383–407.

Hinton, D.E., Kredlow, M.A., Bui, E., Pollack, M.H., & Hoffmann, S.G. (2012). Treatment change of somatic symptoms and cultural syndromes among Cambodian refugees with PTSD. *Depression & Anxiety, 29*(2), 148–155.

Hobfoll, S., Spielberger, C., Breznitz, S., Figley, C., Folkman, S., Leper-Green, B., . . . van der Kolk, B. (1991). War related stress: Addressing the stress of war and other traumatic events. *American Psychologist, 46,* 848–855.

Hosin, A., & Cairns, E. (1984). The impact of conflict on children's ideas about their country. *Journal of Psychology, 118,* 161–168.

Hutz, C., & Koller, S. (1999). Methodological and ethical issues in research with street children. In M. Raffaelli & R. Larson (Eds.), *Homeless and working youth around the world: Exploring developmental issues* (pp. 59–70). San Francisco, CA: Jossey-Bass.

Johnson, R. B., Onwuegbuzie, A. J., & Turner, L. A. (2007). Toward a definition of mixed methods research. *Journal of Mixed Methods Research, 1*(2), 112–133.

Kinzie, J., Sack, W., Angell, R., Manson, S., & Rath, B. (1986). The psychiatric effects of massive trauma on Cambodian children, Part 1: The children. *Journal of American Academy of Child Psychiatry, 25,* 370–376.

Kleinman, A. (1988). *Rethinking psychiatry.* New York: Free Press.

Kortman, F. (1987). Popular, traditional, and professional mental health care in Ethiopia. *Transcultural Psychiatric Research Review, 24,* 255–274.

Kruks, G. (1991). Gay and lesbian homeless/street youth: Special issues and concerns. *Journal of Adolescent Health, 12,* 515–518.

Kurtz, P., Kurtz, G., & Jarvis, S. (1991). Problems of maltreated runaway youth. *Adolescence, 26,* 543–552.

Loeb, J., Stettler, E. M., Gavila, T., Stein, A., & Chinitz, S. (2011). The child behavior checklist PTSD scale: Screening for PTSD in young children with high exposure to trauma. *Journal of Traumatic Stress, 24*(4), 430–434.

Losel, F., & Bliesener, T. (1990). Resilience in adolescence: A study of the generalizability of protective factors. In K. Hurrelemann & F. Losel (Eds.), *Health hazards in adolescence* (pp. 299–320). New York: Walter de Gruyter.

McCallin, M., & Fozzard, S. (1990). *The impact of traumatic events on the psychological well-being of Mozambican women and children.* Geneva, Switzerland: International Catholic Child Bureau.

McFarlane, A. C. (1990). An Australian disaster: The 1983 bush fires. *International Journal of Mental Health, 19,* 36–47.

Miller, K. (1996). The effects of state terrorism and exile on indigenous Guatemalan refugee children: A mental health assessment and an analysis of children's narratives. *Child Development, 67*(1), 89–106.

Nyawasha, T. S., & Chipunza, C. (2012). An assessment of psychosocial and empowerment support intervention for orphans and vulnerable children in Zimbabwe. *Journal of Human Ecology, 40*(1), 9–16.

O'Cathain, A., & Thomas, K. (2006). Combining qualitative and quantitative methods. In C. Pope & N. Mays (Eds.), *Qualitative research in health care* (3rd ed., pp. 102–111). Oxford, UK: Blackwell.

Punamaki, R. (1988). Historical-political and individualistic determinants of coping modes and fears among Palestinian children. *International Journal of Psychology, 23,* 721–739.

Punamaki, R. (1989). Factors affecting the mental health of Palestinian children exposed to political violence. *International Journal of Mental Health, 18,* 63–79.

Quinn, T., & Quinn, E. (2011). Trauma and the developmental course of PTSD postdeployment. In D. Kelly, S. Barksdale, & D. Gitelson (Eds.), *Treating young veterans: Promoting resilience through practice and advocacy* (pp. 23–32). New York: Springer.

Ressler, E., Boothby, N., & Steinbock, D. (1988). *Unaccompanied children: Care and protection in wars, natural disasters, and refugee movements.* New York: Oxford University Press.

Rurevo, R., & Bourdillon, M. (2003). Girls: The less visible street children of Zimbabwe. *Children, Youth and Environments, 13,* http://www.colorado.edu/journals/cye/13_1/Vol13_1Articles/CYE_CurrentIssue_Article_Girls_Rurevo_Bourdillon.htm

Rutter, M. (1990). Pychosocial resilience and protective mechanisms. In J. Rolf, A. Masten, D. Cicchetti, K. Neuchterlein, & S. Weintraum (Eds.), *Risk and protective factors in the development of psychopathology* (pp. 181–214). Cambridge, UK: Cambridge University Press.

Saylor, C. (Ed.). (1993). *Children and disaster.* New York: Plenum Press.

Segall, M. (1983). On the search for the independent variable in cross-cultural psychology. In S.H. Irvine & J. Berry (Eds.), *Human assessment and cultural factors* (pp. 122–137). New York: Plenum.

Smollar, J. (1999). Homeless youth in the United States: Description and development issues. In M. Raffaelli & R. Larson (Eds.), *Homeless and working youth around the world: Exploring developmental issues* (pp. 47–58). San Francisco, CA: Jossey-Bass.

Straker, G. (1991). *Faces in the revolution: The psychological effects of violence on township youth in South Africa.* Cape Town, South Africa: David Phillip.

Terr, L. (1990). *Too scared to cry.* New York: Harper and Row.

Terr, L. (1991). Childhood traumas: An outline and overview. *American Journal of Psychiatry, 148,* 10–20.

Thomas de Benítez, S., (2011). *State of the world's street children: Research.* London, UK: Consortium for Street Children.

UNICEF. (1986). *Children in situations of armed conflict.* E/ICEF.CRP.2. New York: UNICEF.

UNICEF. (1987). *The state of the world's children: 1987.* Oxford, UK: Oxford University Press.

UNICEF. (1997). *The state of the world's children: 1997.* Oxford, UK: Oxford University Press.

UNICEF. (2013, April 4). *Understanding the convention on the rights of the child.* Retrieved from http://www.unicef.org/crc/index_understanding.html

UNICEF. (2002). *The state of the world's children 2003: Child participation.* New York: United Nations Children's Fund (UNICEF).

UNICEF. (2005). *The state of the world's children 2005: Childhood under threat.* New York: United Nations Children's Fund (UNICEF).

UNICEF. (2014). *The state of the world's children 2014 in numbers: Ever child counts.* New York: United Nations Children's Fund (UNICEF).

United Nations. (2014, February 5). Office of the Special Representative of the Secretary-General for Children and Armed Conflict. http://childrenandarmedconflict.un.org/first-un-report-on-children-in-syrias-civil-war-paints-picture-of-unspeakable-horrors/

United Nations. (2014, February 22). Security Council unanimously adopts resolution 2139. Retrieved from www.un.org/press/en/2014/sc11292.doc.htm.

Veale, A., Taylor, M., & Linehan, C. (2000). Psychological perspectives of 'abandoned' and 'abandoning' street children. In C. Panter-Brick & M.T. Smith (Eds.), *Abandoned children* (pp. 131–145). Cambridge, UK: Cambridge University Press.

Vecchiato, N. (1993a). Illness, therapy, and change in Ethiopian possession cults. *Journal of International African Institute, 63*(2), 176–195.

Vecchiato, N. (1993b). Traditional medicine. In H. Kloos & Z. Zien (Eds), *The ecology of health and disease in Ethiopia* (pp. 157–178). Boulder, CO: Westview.

Wargan, K., & Dershem, L. (2009). Don't call me a street child: Estimation and characteristics of urban street children in Georgia. *UNICEF* Report March 2009. http://www.unicef.org/georgia/Street_children_survey.eng%281%29.pdf

Wertleib, D., Weigel, C., Springer, T., & Feldstein, M. (1990). Temperament as a moderator of children's stressful experiences. *American Journal of Orthopsychiatry, 57,* 234–245.

Wolff, P., Tesfai, B., Egasso, H., & Aradom, T. (1995). The orphans of Eritrea: A comparison study. *Journal of Child Psychology and Child Psychiatry and Allied Disciplines, 36*(4), 633–644.

Wright, J. D., Kaminsky, D., & Wittig, M. (1993). Health and social conditions of street children in Honduras. *American Journal of Diseases of Children, 147,* 279–283.

Zeidner, M., Klingman, A., & Itzkovitz, R. (1993). Anxiety, control, social support, and coping under threat of missile attack: A semi-projectile assessment. *Journal of Personality Assessment, 60,* 435–457.

16

Developmental Psychopathology: Multicultural Challenges, Findings, and Applications

Thomas M. Achenbach

"Psychopathology" is often thought of in terms of particular diagnostic categories, such as Attention Deficit Hyperactivity Disorder (ADHD) as defined by the American Psychiatric Association's (2013) *Diagnostic and Statistical Manual-5th Edition* (DSM-5) or the World Health Organization's (1992) *International Classification of Diseases-10th Edition* (ICD-10). The DSM-5 and ICD-10 define many kinds of maladaptive functioning in terms of diagnostic categories. For most categories, the criteria are the same for people of all ages, both genders, and different cultural backgrounds. The criteria are also the same whether assessment data are obtained from self-reports, reports by others, clinical observations, or other sources.

Among people who work with troubled children, it is widely recognized that psychopathology must be understood in relation to particular developmental periods. (I use the term "children" to include ages from infancy to adulthood.) This is because certain behaviors that are adaptive at one developmental period may be maladaptive if they occur at earlier or later developmental periods. Equally important, certain behaviors may be more typical of one gender than the other and more typical of children of one cultural group than another group. Furthermore, children's behavior may vary from one context and interaction partner to another. For example, a teacher may report that a child fails to pay attention in class, whereas the child's parent reports intense concentration on video games. Reflecting contextual variations in children's behavior and the effects of informant characteristics, meta-analyses and other kinds of studies have found important discrepancies between parent, teacher, and self-reports of children's problems (Achenbach, McConaughy, & Howell, 1987; De Los Reyes, 2011; Rescorla et al., 2013, 2014).

Rather than defining psychopathology in terms of the same categorical criteria from infancy to adulthood, developmental approaches assess behavioral, emotional, and social characteristics in relation to adaptive and maladaptive functioning within particular developmental periods. Developmental approaches may thus assess different characteristics during early childhood, middle childhood, adolescence, and adulthood. Developmental approaches also take account of possible differences related to gender, context, and cultural background by assessing representative samples of each gender, as reported by different informants, in different societies. The findings are then used to construct models for psychopathology.

This chapter presents ways in which a particular developmental approach to psychopathology differs from the approach embodied in the DSM-5 and ICD-10, plus points of contact between the different approaches. The chapter focuses mainly on multicultural findings and applications of the findings to helping children and their parents, including birth, adoptive, step, and foster parents. Parents are typically the most important adults in children's lives. Because parents affect children's adaptive and maladaptive functioning, efforts to help children should include assessment of parents' functioning.

To set the stage, a vignette illustrates some key multicultural issues highlighted by the research presented in this chapter. After presenting the research, I will describe applications of the findings to helping the family portrayed in the vignette. All names and other personal identifying data are fictitious. Societies are designated as A and B to avoid stereotyping particular societies and cultural groups.

CASE VIGNETTE

The Cross family emigrated from their home Society A to host Society B, which was very different from Society A. Their son, Robert, was six years old when they emigrated. Robert became more completely acculturated to Society B than his parents, who continued to speak their native language at home. When Robert was 11, his teacher became so concerned about sharp declines from his previously good school work, his failure to pay attention, and his sad demeanor that she consulted the school psychologist. The school psychologist met with Robert's parents to discuss the school's concerns. Mr. and Ms. Cross had also become concerned about Robert's declining school work, but they felt he needed stricter discipline to keep him from being distracted by social activities with peers. However, because they were highly motivated to improve Robert's school performance, they accepted the school psychologist's recommendation for an evaluation by a mental health clinic that emphasized a family-based approach.

At the clinic, Mr. and Ms. Cross were asked to fill out assessment forms to describe Robert and themselves. Because they were not sufficiently proficient in the language of host Society B, they elected to fill out translations in their native language. Robert filled out the Society B version of the Youth Self-Report (YSR). With the consent of Mr. and Ms. Cross, Robert's teacher filled out the Teacher's Report Form (TRF). As detailed later, computer software was used to display scales scored from all the forms in relation to multicultural norms for Robert's age and gender, based on ratings obtained from population samples of Society A parents and Society B teachers and youths. Before returning to Robert's case, I will present research challenges and findings that have culminated in practical applications of multicultural assessment to children and parents in many societies.

DIAGNOSTICALLY BASED RESEARCH IN DIFFERENT SOCIETIES

This section highlights research that has reported the percentage of children who qualified for particular diagnoses in particular population samples from different societies. The diagnoses were based on standardized diagnostic interviews (SDIs) that have been developed to operationalize criteria for DSM and/or ICD diagnoses. Various SDIs are designed for administration to parents and children. Some SDIs, such as the Diagnostic Interview Schedule for Children (DISC; Shaffer, Fisher, Lucas, Dulcan, & Schwab-Stone, 2000), comprise thousands of questions that are structured to elicit yes-versus-no answers about whether a child meets specific criteria for particular diagnoses. Because respondents' answers to the questions directly determine whether diagnostic criteria are met, interviews such as the DISC are called "respondent based." Such interviews can be administered to parents and adolescents by people without clinical training because no clinical probes or judgments are required.

Other SDIs—such as the Kiddie Schedule for Affective Disorders and Schizophrenia (K-SADS; Ambrosini, 2000)—are called "interviewer based," because they must be administered by clinically trained interviewers. The interviewers can rephrase questions to probe interviewees' answers and can apply their clinical judgment when deciding whether a child meets criteria. Still other interviews combine aspects of respondent-based and interviewer-based SDIs. For example, the Development and Well-Being Assessment (DAWBA; Goodman, Ford, Richards, Gatward, & Meltzer, 2000) uses structured questions administered by lay interviewers to obtain responses that are then computer-aggregated to produce tentative diagnoses. Clinicians review the computer output to make the final diagnostic decisions.

Prevalence Estimates of Diagnoses in Different Societies

A review of SDI findings summarized diagnoses obtained for samples of children from 15 societies (Achenbach, Rescorla, & Ivanova, 2012). ("Societies" are geopolitically demarcated populations such as countries but also include societies that are not countries, such as Puerto Rico, Hong Kong, and Flanders, the Flemish-speaking region of Belgium.) The percentage of children who met criteria for at least one psychiatric diagnosis ranged from 1.8% in Goa, India (Pillai et al., 2008) to 50.6% in a study that included three Mainland U.S. areas, plus San Juan, Puerto Rico (Shaffer et al., 1996). The 28-fold difference between the 1.8% prevalence in Goa versus the 50.6% prevalence in the U.S.-Puerto Rican sample suggests that children in India have far less psychopathology than children in the United States and Puerto Rico. However, a study in Bangalore, India (Srinath et al., 2005) yielded a prevalence of 12.0%, while a national U.S. study (Merikangas et al., 2010) yielded a prevalence of 13.1%. These findings suggest a much smaller difference between the prevalence of psychopathology among Indian and U.S. children. Findings from other studies have also revealed large variations in prevalence estimates between and within societies.

Methodological Differences. Examination of the SDI studies revealed many methodological differences, such as the following:

1. Differences in the age ranges of the children who were assessed.
2. Differences in sampling frames, such as households versus schools in local versus regional versus national samples.
3. Differences in sampling designs such as one-stage versus two-stage. (One-stage designs aim to assess all eligible children who are selected from a sampling frame. In two-stage designs, a brief screening instrument is used in Stage 1 to identify children who have relatively high problem scores and children who have lower problem scores. In Stage 2, SDIs are used to assess as many of the high-scoring children as possible, plus a subsample of the low-scoring children.)
4. Differences in completion rates for assessment of the selected children, ranging from 42% in a Swiss study (Steinhausen, Metzke, Meier, & Kannenberg, 1998) to 90% in a Puerto Rican study (Canino et al., 2004).
5. Differences between diagnostic systems, including DSM-III, DSM-III-R, DSM-IV (American Psychiatric Association, 1980, 1987, 1994), and ICD-10 (World Health Organization, 1992).
6. Differences between the numbers of diagnoses that were assessed, ranging from three in an Australian study (Sawyer et al., 2001) to "every DSM-III diagnosis" in a Puerto Rican study (Bird et al., 1988).
7. Differences in whether data were obtained from only the child, only the parent, or some combination of child, parent, and teacher.

8. If data were obtained from more than one informant, differences between the methods for combining the data to decide whether diagnostic criteria were met.
9. Differences between the SDIs that were used.

Considering the many variations among the studies, it is not surprising that prevalence estimates varied greatly. Because neither the DSM nor the ICD specifies assessment procedures or sources of data for determining whether diagnostic criteria are met, the researchers who did the studies had to decide how to obtain data and from whom. In studies that obtained data from more than one informant (parent, child, teacher), the researchers also had to decide how to combine often-contradictory information from different informants into yes-or-no decisions about whether each child met criteria for each diagnosis that was assessed. There are thus many ways in which the methodological differences among the studies—as well as differences between the diagnosticians who made diagnoses from the data obtained in each study—could lead to different prevalence estimates.

Top-Down Approach

The diagnostic constructs on which the prevalence studies focused originated with the committees of experts who formulated the DSM and ICD. After agreeing on the diagnostic categories, the experts formulated criteria for each category. This can be described as a "top-down" approach, because it starts "at the top" with the experts' concepts of disorders and then works down to criteria for each disorder. Because neither the DSM nor the ICD specifies how to operationalize their criteria in terms of specific assessment procedures, the various SDIs operationalize the diagnostic criteria in different ways. The differences in how the diagnostic criteria are operationalized, as well as differences in sources of diagnostic information (parent, child, teacher) and different ways of combining information to make yes-or-no diagnostic decisions could lead to different findings in many kinds of research and clinical applications.

DEVELOPMENTALLY BASED RESEARCH IN DIFFERENT SOCIETIES

Bottom-Up Approach

In contrast to the top-down approach, developmentally based research on children's problems has taken a "bottom-up" approach. The bottom-up approach starts by identifying specific kinds of problems that may warrant professional help for people in particular developmental periods, such as early childhood, middle childhood, adolescence, adulthood, and older adulthood. Items for assessing the problems are selected by testing the power of each candidate item to discriminate between samples of individuals who have been referred for mental health services versus demographically similar individuals who have not been referred for services. Items that are found to perform well are then factor analyzed to identify syndromes of covarying problems, as rated by different kinds of informants. The syndromes can be viewed as manifest indicators of constructs, that is, of latent variables. Rather than being formulated by a top-down expert-judgment approach, the syndromes are thus derived from bottom-up analyses of data obtained by assessing large samples of individuals.

An individual's standing on each syndrome is operationally defined as the sum of informants' ratings of the items comprising the syndrome. Unlike the yes-or-no decisions required for making categorical diagnoses, the summing of problem item ratings yields a continuum of syndrome scores indicating whether an individual has a relatively low, medium, or high level of the problems comprising the syndrome. To provide a metric for evaluating the magnitude of syndrome scores, norms are constructed from the distributions of scores found in large samples of people who are representative of particular populations. The norms tell users whether an individual's score is in the same range as scores for most peers of the individual's gender and age group, as rated by a particular kind of informant, or whether the individual's score is deviant enough to indicate a possible need for professional help.

PROFILES OF SYNDROME SCORES

To help users evaluate individuals' problems for research and clinical purposes, scores on all the syndromes relevant to the individual's developmental level are displayed on profiles in relation to norms for the individual's age, gender, and the type of informant who rated the individual (e.g., parent, teacher, self). Figure 16.1 illustrates a profile of syndromes scored for 11-year-old Robert, who was introduced earlier in the case vignette. The syndromes were scored from Robert's mother's ratings on the Child Behavior Checklist for Ages 6–18 (CBCL/6–18). The eight syndromes in the profile were derived from factor analyses of ratings of thousands of clinically referred and nonreferred children (Achenbach & Rescorla, 2001). Factor analyses of teacher and self-ratings of thousands of children also yielded counterparts of the eight syndromes.

By looking at Figure 16.1, you can see the names of the eight syndromes (in boldface). In the graphic display above the names of the syndromes, you can see how Robert's score on each syndrome compares with *T* scores listed on the left for 6–11-year-old boys rated by their parents. Scores below the bottom broken line in the graphic display are in the normal range

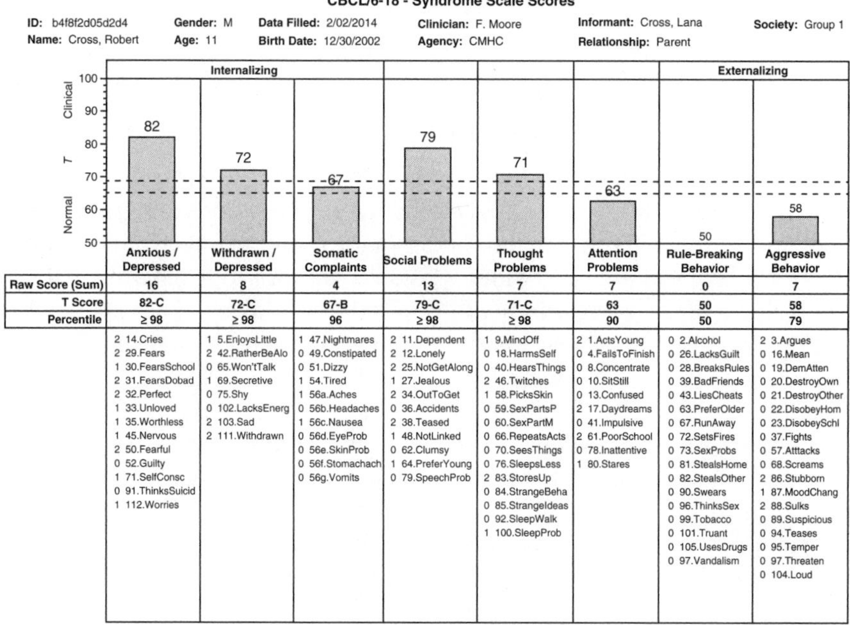

	Anxious / Depressed	Withdrawn / Depressed	Somatic Complaints	Social Problems	Thought Problems	Attention Problems	Rule-Breaking Behavior	Aggressive Behavior
Raw Score (Sum)	16	8	4	13	7	7	0	7
T Score	82-C	72-C	67-B	79-C	71-C	63	50	58
Percentile	≥ 98	≥ 98	96	≥ 98	≥ 98	90	50	79

Figure 16.1 Profile of Syndromes for 11-Year-Old Robert, Based on the Child Behavior Checklist Completed by His Mother

Note: Table copyright 2015 T. M. Achenbach. Reproduced by permission.

(*T* scores <65; <93rd percentile for the normative sample). Scores between the two broken lines are in the borderline clinical range (*T* scores 65–69; 93rd–97th percentiles). And scores above the top broken line are in the clinical range (*T* scores >69; >97th percentile). You can see that Robert obtained scores in the clinical range on the Anxious/Depressed, Withdrawn/Depressed, Social Problems, and Thought Problems syndromes. According to his mother's ratings, Robert thus had considerably more problems in these areas than most boys of his age, as rated by their parents.

Beneath the boldface name of the leftmost syndrome (Anxious/ Depressed), you can see the Raw Score, which is the sum of Robert's mother's ratings of the problem items comprising the syndrome. Beneath the Raw Score is the *T* score, which is 82. The "C" indicates that the *T* score is in the clinical range (*T* >69), which is >97th percentile, as printed beneath the *T* score. Beneath the percentile is a list of abbreviations for the items that comprise the Anxious/ Depressed syndrome. The 0s, 1s, and 2s to the left of the items are Robert's mother's ratings of the items, as follows: *0 = not true (as far as you know), 1 = somewhat or sometimes true,* and *2 = very true or often true,* over the preceding six months. The number before the abbreviated text of each item is the number the item bears on the rating form.

TESTS OF SYNDROMES IN MANY SOCIETIES

The syndromes for ages 6–18 displayed in Figure 16.1, plus syndromes for ages 1½–5 and 18–59, were derived by factor analyzing ratings of thousands of individuals in Anglophone societies, mostly the United States. To test whether these syndromes would be supported by data from other societies, indigenous researchers in 56 non-U.S. societies have used the same family of assessment instruments (in translation where necessary) to obtain ratings of problems for over 100,000 individuals. Confirmatory factor analyses (CFAs) have supported the syndrome models in all the societies, although the fit to data in a few societies was improved by small modifications to some of the syndrome models (Ivanova et al., 2007a, 2007b, 2007c, 2010, 2011, 2015a, 2015b; Rescorla et al., 2012b). The CFA results indicate that the syndromes provide valid models for aggregating ratings of behavioral, emotional, social, and thought problems for individuals in very diverse societies.

COMPARISONS OF SCALE SCORES FROM MANY SOCIETIES

The sums of 0–1–2 ratings for all of an instrument's problem items (Total Problems scale) and for each syndrome on each instrument have been statistically compared across multiple societies (Rescorla et al., 2007a, 2007b, 2007c, 2011, 2012a, 2012b, 2015a, 2015b). For different informants' ratings of individuals at ages 1½–5, 6–18, and 18–59, the findings have revealed the following patterns:

1. There were significant cross-society differences between mean scale scores obtained on each instrument.
2. Although there were statistically significant differences between societal mean scores, there was a great deal of overlap between the problem scale scores obtained by most individuals in each society and in each other society, as illustrated in Figure 16.2.
3. Variance among problem scale scores was considerably greater within each society than between different societies.

The bars in Figure 16.2 depict the CBCL/6–18 5th to 95th percentile Total Problems scores obtained from parents' ratings of children in population samples from the societies listed along the bottom of the graph. The star on each bar represents the mean Total Problems score for a society. By looking at the bars in Figure 16.2, you can see that most scores in every

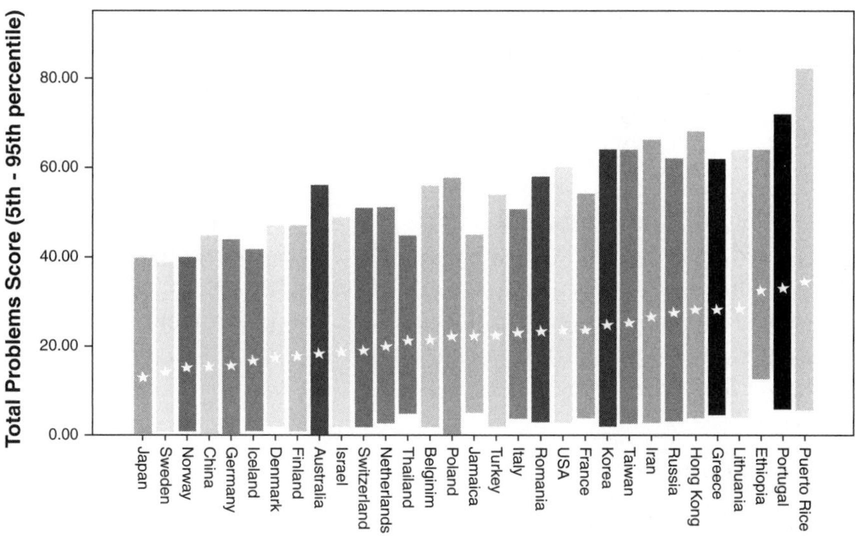

Figure 16.2 Distributions of CBCL/6–18 Total Problems Scores: 5th to 95th Percentiles. Stars Indicate the Mean Total Problems Score for Each Society.

Source: Achenbach (2009). Used by permission.

society overlapped with most scores in every other society. There was considerable overlap even between the scores of the societies with the lowest (Japan) and highest (Puerto Rico) mean Total Problems scores. In other words, no society differed categorically from any other society with respect to the range of scores for the Total Problems scale (nor for any problem scales scored from any of the instruments for ages 1½–5, 6–18, or 18–59).

The evidence for the greater variance within than between societies was that *SD*s for scale scores within societies were much greater than the *SD* of the societal mean scores on every instrument. Individual differences within societies thus accounted for more variance in scale scores than did differences between societies.

A similar conclusion was supported by findings from self-ratings of Neuroticism by students in 45 societies (Stankov, 2011). Stankov found that 95.3% of the variance in Neuroticism scores was accounted for by individual differences, 2.0% of the variance was accounted for by differences between societies, and 2.7% of the variance was accounted for by differences between "culture clusters" of societies, such as those with Confucian cultures.

All the participants in the Stankov study were college students who completed an English language measure of Neuroticism. However, Althoff et al. (2015) performed similar analyses of CBCL/6–18 ratings by population samples of parents of 69,353 6–18-year-olds in 41 societies. The samples from each society were more representative of their societies than Stankov's college student samples, and the parents completed the CBCL/6–18 in the dominant language of their society. The more representative samples assessed in many languages besides English may have contributed to larger effects of societal and cultural differences than what Stankov found. Nevertheless, Althoff et al. found that only 6.3% of the variance in CBCL/6–18 Total Problems scores was accounted for by societal differences, 6.0% was accounted for by cultural differences, and 87.7% was accounted for by individual differences within societies and culture clusters. In other words, far more of the variance in children's CBCL/6–18 problem scores was accounted for by individual differences within societies than by societal or cultural differences.

Emic Questions

The studies by Ivanova et al., Rescorla et al., Stankov, and Althoff et al. were *etic* in that they used the same standardized instruments to assess individuals in different societies. CFA findings supported the syndrome models employed by Ivanova et al. and Rescorla et al. in the participating societies. Moreover, the small percentage of variance in scale scores attributable to societal differences in the Rescorla, Stankov, and Althoff studies suggests that the assessment instruments performed similarly in the participating societies. Nevertheless, the findings do not necessarily answer *emic* questions about societal differences.

One emic question is whether individuals in different societies interpreted items similarly. Although it is not feasible to test whether all participants in all societies identically interpreted every item, Rescorla's studies tested the degree to which the same items tended to receive low, medium, or high ratings in different societies. Rescorla et al. did this by first computing the mean of the 0–1–2 ratings received by each item in each society. For example, Rescorla et al. (2012b) computed the mean of the 0–1–2 ratings received by 112 CBCL/6–18 items in each of 42 societies. They then computed the bi-society correlations between the 112 mean item ratings in Society A versus Society B, Society A versus Society C, and so on, for every pair of societies. (The correlations were *Q* correlations, because they correlated scores on multiple variables from two sources, i.e., mean ratings on 112 items from two societies rather than *R* correlations, which correlate scores on two variables from multiple sources.) Thereafter, Rescorla et al. computed the mean of all the bi-society correlations, which was found to be 0.74.

Mean correlations were likewise computed for ratings of the items on each of the other assessment instruments for ages 6–18, as well as the instruments for ages 1½–5 and 18–59. The results were very similar for all instruments, with mean bi-society correlations ranging from 0.70 for the YSR to 0.78 for the Child Behavior Checklist for Ages 1½–5 (CBCL/1½–5) and the Adult Self-report for Ages 18–59 (ASR). As all the mean correlations were large according to Cohen's (1988) criteria, they provide good evidence that the items functioned similarly in different societies.

Another kind of emic question is whether any society's patterns of scale scores differed from other societies' patterns in ways that suggest a need for emic research. One finding of this sort was that teachers rated boys higher than girls on the Attention Problems syndrome in all societies except Iran, where girls obtained a slightly higher mean Attention Problems score than boys did (Rescorla et al., 2007b).

Because Iran was the only society in which the participating schools were completely segregated by gender (90 boys schools and 90 girls schools participated), it might be speculated that Iranian teachers' ratings of girls were not affected by implicit gender comparisons of the sort that might affect ratings by teachers who see boys and girls in the same classrooms. However, the finding that—unlike parents in other societies—Iranian parents also rated girls higher than boys on Attention Problems suggests a more general difference between ratings in Iran versus other societies.

An additional finding that—like youths in other societies—Iranian boys and girls rated themselves similarly on the Attention Problems syndrome suggests that the findings for Iranian teacher and parent ratings do not necessarily reflect intrinsic Iranian characteristics that differ from those of other societies. In any event, the difference between gender effects in teacher and parent ratings of Attention Problems in Iran versus other societies invites emic research to uncover reasons for the differences. Because etic research can yield findings of this sort that then invite emic research, the two approaches are complementary.

TOOLS FOR APPLYING MULTICULTURAL FINDINGS

The foregoing sections outlined multicultural findings that are now being applied in many societies. Software for scoring the syndromes that have been supported in 56 non-U.S. societies can display scale scores for ages 1½–59 in relation to user-selected multicultural norms specific to the age and gender of the person being assessed, as rated by a particular kind of informant. In addition to the syndrome scales, the software can display individuals' scores on DSM-oriented scales, scales for clinical constructs such as obsessive-compulsive problems and sluggish cognitive tempo, personal strengths, and broad-band scales designated as Internalizing, Externalizing, and Total Problems (Achenbach & Rescorla, 2007a, 2010, 2015).

Constructing Multicultural Norms

The population data analyzed for many societies in the Rescorla et al. (2007a, 2007b, 2007c, 2011, 2012a, 2012b, 2015a, 2015b) studies have been used to construct the multicultural norms implemented by the software. The multicultural norms for problem scales on each instrument were constructed by first computing the mean of the Total Problems scores obtained by all the individuals who were assessed with that instrument in a particular society. Next, all the means of the Total Problems scores were averaged to obtain the *omnicultural mean* (Ellis & Kimmel, 1992; i.e., the mean of the means from all societies that provided data). For all instruments for which multicultural norms have been constructed, the distributions of mean Total Problems scores around the omnicultural mean have been found to be normal, with the mean Total Problems scores for most societies falling within +1 *SD* of the omnicultural mean. The mean Total Problems scores for a few societies fell >1 *SD* below the omnicultural mean, while a few fell >1 *SD* above the omnicultural mean.

For each instrument, sets of multicultural norms were constructed for the societies that had relatively low Total Problems scores (>1 *SD* below the omnicultural mean, designated as “Group 1”), intermediate scores (+1 *SD* from the omnicultural mean, designated as “Group 2”), and high scores (>1 *SD* above the omnicultural mean, designated as “Group 3”). For each problem scale scored from an instrument, Group 1 norms were constructed for each gender in a particular age range by averaging the cumulative frequency distributions from all the Group 1 societies and then assigning normalized *T* scores to raw scale scores on the basis of the percentiles for scores in the averaged distributions.

Applying Multicultural Norms

The Group 1, 2, and 3 norms are programmed into the computer software for displaying scale scores on profiles like the one shown for Robert in Figure 16.1. For societies that have normative data, the appropriate Group 1, 2, or 3 norms are used to generate *T* scores and to display the individual’s scores on the profile in relation to those norms. If normative data are not available for a relevant society, the software displays the Group 2 (default) norms, or the user can elect to have norms displayed that are appropriate for a society like the relevant society. Users can also elect to have an individual’s scale scores displayed in relation to two sets of norms or even three sets of norms in order to see whether the individual’s scores would be clinically deviant according to any of the chosen norm groups. Figure 16.3 summarizes the construction and application of the multicultural norms. Table 16.1 lists the societies for which data on population samples have been used to determine the appropriate multicultural norm group.

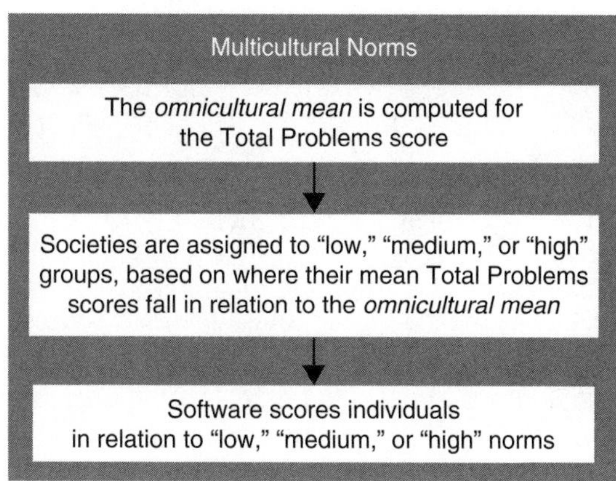

Figure 16.3 Procedure for Constructing and Applying Multicultural Norms
Source: Achenbach & Rescorla (2015). Used by permission.

Table 16.1 Societies for Which Multicultural Norms Are Available

Ages 1½–5		**Ages 6–18**		**Ages 18–59**	
Australia	Kosovo	Algeria	Kosovo	Albania	Korea (South)
Austria	Lithuania	Australia	Lebanon	Argentina	Latvia
Belgium (Flanders)	Netherlands	Bangladesh	Lithuania	Belgium (Flanders)	Lithuania
Chile	Peru	Belgium (Flanders)	Netherlands	Brazil	Poland
China	Portugal	Brazil	Norway	Czech Republic	Portugal
Denmark	Serbia	China	Pakistan	Hong Kong	Serbia
Finland	Singapore	Colombia	Peru	Iceland	Taiwan
France	Spain	Croatia	Poland	Italy	United States
Germany	Taiwan	Denmark	Portugal	Japan	
Iceland	Turkey	Ethiopia	Puerto Rico		
Iran	United Arab Emirates	Finland	Romania		
Italy	United States	France	Russia		
Korea (South)		Germany	Serbia		
		Greece	Singapore		
		Hong Kong	Spain		
		Iceland	Sweden		
		India (Telugu)	Switzerland (German)		

(*Continued*)

Table 16.1 Continued

Ages 1½–5	Ages 6–18		Ages 18–59
	Iran	Taiwan	
	Israel	Thailand	
	Italy	Tunisia	
	Jamaica	Turkey	
	Japan	United States	
	Korea (South)	Uruguay	

Note. Table copyright 2015 T.M. Achenbach. Used by permission.

Cross-Informant Comparisons

Numerous studies cited earlier have revealed important discrepancies between ratings of children's problems by different informants, such as parents, teachers, and the children themselves (Achenbach et al., 1987; De Los Reyes, 2011; Rescorla et al., 2013, 2014). Consequently, no one informant's reports can substitute for reports by other informants. Comprehensive assessment of children's problems therefore requires data from multiple informants. In the case vignette presented earlier in the chapter, Robert's mother and father each completed the CBCL/6–18, while Robert's teacher completed the TRF and Robert completed the YSR. Robert's parents each completed the ASR to describe themselves and the ABCL to describe their spouse.

To provide comparisons of scores obtained from the CBCL/6–18, TRF, YSR, ASR, and ABCL, the Multicultural Family Assessment Module (MFAM; Achenbach et al., 2015) was used to print bar graphs that display *T* scores for the scales that have counterparts on the child and adult forms. The *T* scores are normed for the age and gender of the person being assessed, the type of informant who rated the person being assessed, and the relevant multicultural norm group.

The MFAM comparisons of syndrome scale scores for Robert and his parents are shown in Figure 16.4. Scores for the following seven syndromes are shown on bars for ratings by all eight informants, because these syndromes have counterparts for both the child and adult instruments: *Anxious/Depressed, Withdrawn/Depressed* (designated as *Withdrawn* for the adult forms), *Somatic Complaints, Thought Problems, Attention Problems, Aggressive Behavior,* and *Rule-Breaking Behavior.* Because the *Social Problems* syndrome is scored only from the child forms, bars are shown only for the Social Problems syndrome scored from the CBCL/6–18, TRF, and YSR. Conversely, because the *Intrusive* syndrome is scored only from the adult forms, bars are shown only for the Intrusive syndrome scored from the ASR and ABCL.

Multi-Informant Comparison - Syndrome Scale T Scores

Form	Eval ID	Assessed Person	Age	Informant	Relation	Society	Date
ABC1	01	Cross, Lana	40	Cross, Martin	Spouse	Group 1	02/01/2014
ASR2	02	Cross, Lana	40		Self	Group 1	02/01/2014
ABC3	01	Cross, Martin	40	Cross, Lana	Spouse	Group 1	02/02/2014
ASR4	02	Cross, Martin	40		Self	Group 1	01/31/2014
CBC5	01	Cross, Robert	11	Cross, Martin	Parent	Group 1	01/03/2014
CBC6	02	Cross, Robert	11	Cross, Lana	Parent	Group 1	02/02/2014
TRF7	03	Cross, Robert	11	Hotchkiss, Mary	Teacher	Group 1	02/02/2014
YSR8	04	Cross, Robert	11		Self	Group 1	02/02/2014

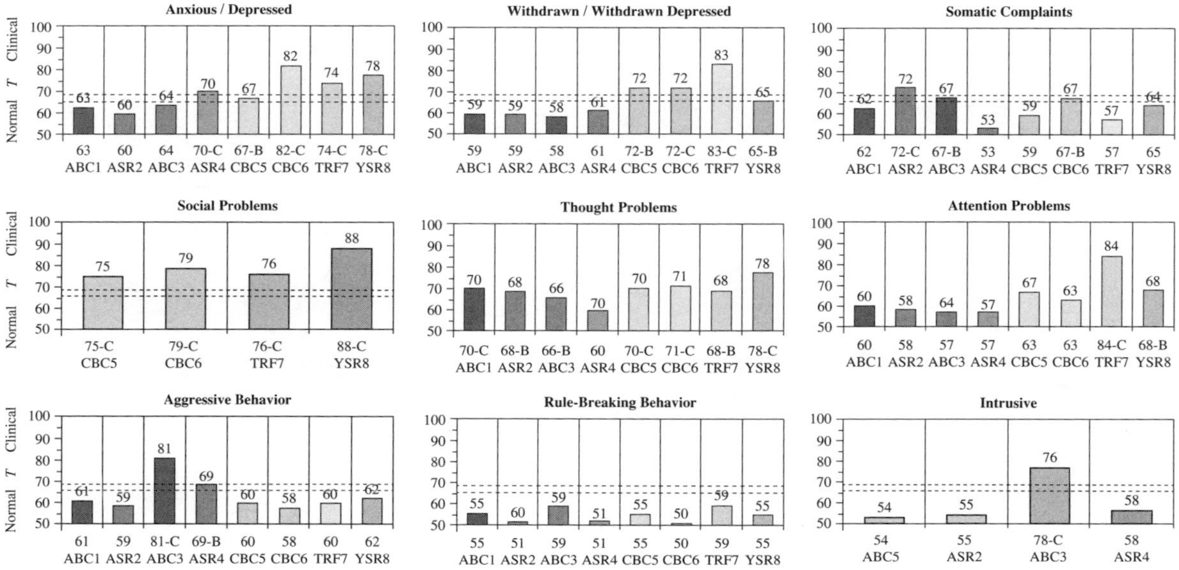

Anxious / Depressed

63	60	64	70-C	67-B	82-C	74-C	78-C
ABC1	ASR2	ABC3	ASR4	CBC5	CBC6	TRF7	YSR8

Withdrawn / Withdrawn Depressed

59	59	58	61	72-B	72-C	83-C	65-B
ABC1	ASR2	ABC3	ASR4	CBC5	CBC6	TRF7	YSR8

Somatic Complaints

62	72-C	67-B	53	59	67-B	57	65
ABC1	ASR2	ABC3	ASR4	CBC5	CBC6	TRF7	YSR8

Social Problems

75-C	79-C	76-C	88-C
CBC5	CBC6	TRF7	YSR8

Thought Problems

70-C	68-B	66-B	60	70-C	71-C	68-B	78-C
ABC1	ASR2	ABC3	ASR4	CBC5	CBC6	TRF7	YSR8

Attention Problems

60	58	57	57	63	63	84-C	68-B
ABC1	ASR2	ABC3	ASR4	CBC5	CBC6	TRF7	YSR8

Aggressive Behavior

61	59	81-C	69-B	60	58	60	62
ABC1	ASR2	ABC3	ASR4	CBC5	CBC6	TRF7	YSR8

Rule-Breaking Behavior

55	51	59	51	55	50	59	55
ABC1	ASR2	ABC3	ASR4	CBC5	CBC6	TRF7	YSR8

Intrusive

54	55	78-C	58
ABC5	ASR2	ABC3	ASR4

B = Borderline clinical range; C = Clinical range; Borken Lines = Borderline clinical range

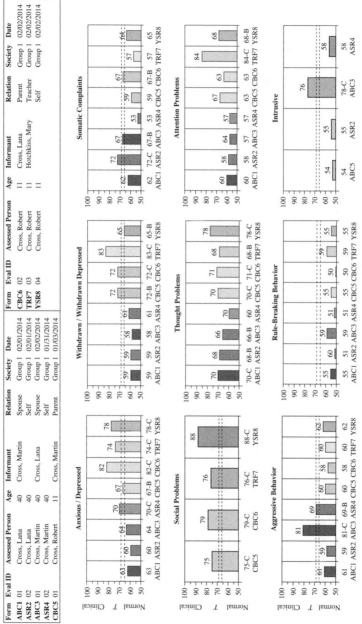

Figure 16.4 Bar Graphs of Syndrome Scores for 11-Year-Old Robert and His Parents

Source: Achenbach and Rescorla (2015). Reproduced by permission.

By looking at the top left-most box in Figure 16.4, you can see that the CBCL/6–18 completed by Robert's mother Lana, the TRF completed by Robert's teacher, and the YSR completed by Robert all yielded scores in the clinical range (above the top broken line, >97th percentile, *T* >69) on the Anxious/Depressed syndrome. By looking again at the top left-most box, you can see that Robert's father Martin also rated himself high enough on the Anxious/ Depressed syndrome to reach the clinical range and rated Robert high enough to reach the borderline clinical range (between the two broken lines, 93rd–97th percentiles, *T* 65–69).

By looking at the top middle box, you can see that Robert scored in the clinical range on the Withdrawn/Depressed syndrome according to ratings by both parents and his teacher, and in the borderline range according to his self-ratings. And by looking at the left-most box in the middle row, you can see that Robert also scored in the clinical range on the Social Problems syndrome according to ratings by both parents, his teacher, and himself. Robert's scores on some other syndromes differed more among the informants. For example, on the Attention Problems syndrome, Robert scored in the normal range according to both parents' ratings but in the clinical range according to his teacher's ratings and in the borderline range according to his self-ratings.

By looking at the left-most box in the bottom row, you can see that Lana rated her husband Martin in the clinical range on the Aggressive Behavior syndrome, while Martin rated himself in the borderline clinical range. In the right-most box of the bottom row, you can see that Lana also rated Martin in the clinical range on the Intrusive syndrome, but Martin rated himself in the normal range. The differences between Lana and Martin's ratings suggest that she saw him as more aggressive and especially as more intrusive than he saw himself.

By showing Lana and Martin the MFAM bar graphs, the mental health practitioner concretely communicated differences in how they saw each other and also in how Robert was seen by different informants. Recognition of such differences is an important ingredient in establishing therapeutic alliances to help Robert.

ASSESSMENT OF PROGRESS AND OUTCOMES

When interventions are implemented for children and families, it is important to reassess a broad spectrum of problems during the course of the interventions in order to determine whether sufficient improvements are made and whether any new problems become evident. If improvements are insufficient and/or if new problems are found, the interventions may need to be changed. Reassessments should also be done after the interventions end to determine whether problems have been ameliorated.

To provide a credible basis for comparing problems reported before, during, and after interventions, the same assessment instruments should be administered prior to the intervention, during the intervention, and after the intervention. Quantitative scales such as those scored from the CBCL/6–18, TRF, and YSR make it possible to measure changes and to test the significance of changes via the standard error of measurement for individual cases and via group statistics for comparing the effects of different interventions. For family-oriented assessment, the MFAM can be used to compare scale scores for children and their parents at each assessment. Translations of the forms, plus multicultural norms for evaluating scale scores, make the MFAM usable with people from many backgrounds in many societies.

SUMMARY AND CONCLUSIONS

This chapter presented a developmental approach to understanding and assessing psychopathology. It compared the top-down, categorical, diagnostically based approaches embodied in the DSM and ICD with the bottom-up, quantitative, empirically based aspects of developmental approaches to psychopathology. It also documented pervasive variations among informants' reports, which argue for systematically obtaining and combining data from multiple informants.

A case vignette was used to illustrate practical issues in multicultural assessment of children's problems, plus practical tools for assessing children and their parents from multiple perspectives.

Diagnostically based research on the prevalence of diagnoses in different societies was reviewed. Estimated prevalence rates varied widely among societies, owing at least partly to great variations in sampling methods, diagnostic criteria and procedures, sources of data, methods for combining data, and the diagnostic interviews that were used.

Developmentally based assessment was presented as it pertained to the construction of standardized assessment instruments, statistical derivation of syndromes from data on thousands of individuals, tests of syndromes in dozens of societies, tests of age, gender, informant, and societal differences in scores, and construction of multicultural norms for ages 1½–59. Practical tools for applying the multicultural findings to clinical cases were illustrated with the MFAM for combining evidence-based assessment of children and their parents. The same tools can be used to assess progress and outcomes in response to interventions.

REFLECTIVE QUESTIONS

1. Compare and contrast the "top-down" and "bottom-up" approaches to psychopathology.
2. What are the differences between developmental and diagnostic approaches to psychopathology?
3. What have multicultural studies found with respect to within-society versus between-society variations in psychopathology?

4. How are multicultural norms for psychopathology constructed?
5. Why does assessment of psychopathology require data from multiple informants?

SUGGESTED READINGS

Books and Articles

Achenbach, T.M., & Rescorla, L.A. (2007). *Multicultural understanding of child and adolescent psychopathology: Implications for mental health assessment.* New York: Guilford Press.

Achenbach, T.M., Rescorla, L.A., & Ivanova, M.Y. (2012). International epidemiology of child and adolescent psychopathology: 1. Diagnoses, dimensions, and conceptual issues. *Journal of the American Academy of Child and Adolescent Psychiatry, 51,* 1261–1272.

Rescorla, L.A., Ivanova, M.Y., Achenbach, T.M., Begovac, I., Chahed, M., Drugli, M.B., . . . Woo, B. (2012). International epidemiology of child and adolescent psychopathology: 2. Integration and applications of dimensional findings from 44 societies. *Journal of the American Academy of Child and Adolescent Psychiatry, 51,* 1273–1283.

Stankov, L. (2011). Individual, country and societal cluster differences on measures of personality, attitudes, values, and social norms. *Learning and Individual Differences, 21,* 55–66.

Websites

ASEBA: Achenbach System of Empirically Based Assessment: www.aseba.org

IACAPAP: International Association for Child and Adolescent Psychiatry and Allied Professions: http://iacapap.org/iacapap-textbook-of-child-and-adolescent-mental-health

REFERENCES

Achenbach, T.M. (2009). *The Achenbach System of Empirically Based Assessment (ASEBA): Development, findings, theory, and applications.* Burlington, VT: University of Vermont Research Center for Children, Youth, and Families.

Achenbach, T.M., McConaughy, S.H., & Howell, C.T. (1987). Child/adolescent behavioral and emotional problems: Implications of cross-informant correlations for situational specificity. *Psychological Bulletin, 101,* 213–232. doi:10.1037/0033–2909.101.2.213

Achenbach, T.M., & Rescorla, L.A. (2001). *Manual for the ASEBA school-age forms & profiles.* Burlington, VT: University of Vermont Research Center for Children, Youth, and Families.

Achenbach, T.M., & Rescorla, L.A. (2007a). *Multicultural supplement to the Manual for the ASEBA school-age forms & profiles.* Burlington, VT: University of Vermont Research Center for Children, Youth, and Families.

Achenbach, T.M., & Rescorla, L.A. (2007b). *Multicultural understanding of child and adolescent psychopathology: Implications for mental health assessment.* New York: Guilford Press.

Achenbach, T.M., & Rescorla, L.A. (2010). *Multicultural supplement to the Manual for the ASEBA preschool forms & profiles.* Burlington, VT: University of Vermont Research Center for Children, Youth, and Families.

Achenbach, T.M., & Rescorla, L.A. (2015). *Multicultural supplement to the Manual for the ASEBA adult forms & profiles.* Burlington, VT: University of Vermont Research Center for Children, Youth, and Families.

Achenbach, T.M., Rescorla, L.A., & Ivanova, M.Y. (2012). International epidemiology of child and adolescent psychopathology: 1. Diagnoses, dimensions, and conceptual issues. *Journal of the American Academy of Child and Adolescent Psychiatry, 51,* 1261–1272.

Achenbach, T.M., Rescorla, L.A., & Ivanova, M.Y. (2015). *Guide to family assessment using the ASEBA*. Burlington, VT: University of Vermont Research Center for Children, Youth, and Families.

Althoff, R.R., Achenbach, T.M., Rescorla, L.A., Ivanova, M.Y., & The International ASEBA Consortium. (2015). Effects of society, culture, and individual differences on assessment of children's mental health problems: Parents' ratings in 41 societies. Submitted for publication.

Ambrosini, P.J. (2000). Historical development and present status of the Schedule for Affective Disorders and Schizophrenia for School-Age Children (K-SADS). *Journal of the American Academy of Child and Adolescent Psychiatry, 39,* 49–58.

American Psychiatric Association. (1980; 1987; 1994; 2013). *Diagnostic and statistical manual of mental disorders* (3rd ed., 3rd ed. rev., 4th ed., 5th ed.). Washington, DC: Author.

Bird, H.R., Canino, G., Rubio-Stipec, M., Gould, M.S., Ribera, J., Sesman, M., . . . Moscoso, M. (1988). Estimates of the prevalence of childhood maladjustment in a community survey in Puerto Rico: The use of combined measures. *Archives of General Psychiatry, 45,* 1120–1126.

Canino, G.J., Shrout, P.E., Rubio-Stipec, M., Bird, H.R., Bravo, M., Ramirez, R., . . . Martinez-Taboas, A. (2004). The DSM-IV rates of child and adolescent disorders in Puerto Rico. *Archives of General Psychiatry, 61,* 85–93.

Cohen, J. (1988). *Statistical power analysis for the behavioral sciences* (2nd ed.). New York: Academic Press.

De Los Reyes, A. (2011). Introduction to the special section: More than measurement error: Discovering meaning behind informant discrepancies in clinical assessments of children and adolescents. *Journal of Clinical Child and Adolescent Psychology, 40,* 1–9. doi:10.1080/15374416.2011.533405

Ellis, B.B., & Kimmel, H.D. (1992). Identification of unique cultural response patterns by means of item response theory. *Journal of Applied Psychology, 77,* 177–184. doi:10. 1037/0021–9010.77.2.177

Goodman, R., Ford, T., Richards, H., Gatward, R., & Meltzer, H. (2000). The development and well-being assessment: Description and initial validation of an integrated assessment of child and adolescent psychopathology. *Journal of Child Psychology and Psychiatry, 41,* 645–655. doi:10.1111/j.1469–7610.2000.tb02345.x

Ivanova, M.Y., Achenbach, T.M., Dumenci, L., Rescorla, L.A., Almqvist, F., Weintraub, S., . . . Verhulst, F.C. (2007a). Testing the 8-syndrome structure of the CBCL in

30 societies. *Journal of Clinical Child and Adolescent Psychology, 36,* 405–417. doi:10.1080/15374410701 444363

Ivanova, M. Y., Achenbach, T. M., Rescorla, L. A., Dumenci, L. Almqvist, F., Bathiche, M., . . . Verhulst, F. C. (2007b). Testing the Teacher's Report Form syndromes in 20 societies. *School Psychology Review, 36,* 468–483.

Ivanova, M. Y., Achenbach, T. M., Rescorla, L. A., Dumenci, L., Almqvist, F., Bilenberg, N., . . . Verhulst, F.C. (2007c). The generalizability of the Youth Self-Report syndrome structure in 23 societies. *Journal of Consulting and Clinical Psychology, 75,* 729–738. doi:10.1037/ 0022–006X.75.5.729

Ivanova, M. Y., Achenbach, T. M., Rescorla, L. A., Harder, V. S., Ang, R. P., Bilenberg, N., . . . Verhulst, F. C. (2010). Preschool psychopathology reported by parents in 23 societies. Testing the seven-syndrome model of the child behavior checklist for ages 1.5–5. *Journal of the American Academy of Child and Adolescent Psychiatry 49,* 1215–1224. doi:10.1016/ j.jaac. 2010.08.019

Ivanova, M. Y., Achenbach, T. M., Rescorla, L. A., Bilenberg, N., Bjarnadottir, G., Denner, S., . . . Verhulst, F. C. (2011). Syndromes of preschool psychopathology reported by teachers and caregivers in 14 societies using the Caregiver Teacher Report Form (C-TRF). *Journal of Early Childhood and Infant Psychology, 7,* 87–103.

Ivanova, M. Y., Achenbach, T. M., Rescorla, L. A., Turner, L. V., Ahmeti-Pronaj, A., Au, A., . . . Zasępa, E. (2015a). Syndromes of self-reported psychopathology for ages 18–59 in 29 societies. *Journal of Psychopathology and Behavioral Assessment, 37,* 171–183.

Ivanova, M. Y., Achenbach, T. M., Rescorla, L. A., Turner, L.V., Árnadóttir, H. A., Au, A., . . . Zasępa, E. (2015b). Syndromes of collateral-reported psychopathology for ages 18–59 in 18 societies. *International Journal of Clinical and Health Psychology, 15,* 18–28.

Merikangas, K. R., He, J. P., Brody, D., Fisher, P. W., Bourdon, K., & Koretz, D. S. (2010). Prevalence and treatment of mental disorders among US children in the 2001–2004 NHANES. *Pediatrics, 125,* 75–81.

Pillai, A., Patel, V., Cardozo, P., Goodman, R., Weiss, H. A., & Andrew, G. (2008). Non-traditional lifestyles and prevalence of mental disorders in adolescents in Goa, India. *British Journal of Psychiatry, 192,* 45–51.

Rescorla, L. A., Achenbach, T. M., Ivanova, M. Y., Dumenci, L., Almqvist, F., Bilenberg, N., . . . Verhulst, F. C. (2007a). Behavioral and emotional problems reported by parents of children ages 6 to 16 in 31 societies. *Journal of Emotional and Behavioral Disorders, 15,* 130–142. doi:10.1177/10634266070150030101

Rescorla, L. A., Achenbach, T. M., Ginzburg, S., Ivanova, M. Y., Dumenci, L., Almqvist, F., . . . Verhulst, F. C. (2007b). Consistency of teacher-reported problems for students in 21 countries. *School Psychology Review, 36,* 91–110.

Rescorla, L. A., Achenbach, T. M., Ivanova, M. Y., Dumenci, L., Almqvist, F., Bilenberg, N., . . . Verhulst, F. C. (2007c). Epidemiological comparisons of problems and positive qualities reported by adolescents in 24 countries. *Journal of Consulting and Clinical Psychology, 75,* 351–358. doi:10.1037/0022–006X.75.2.351

Rescorla, L. A., Achenbach, T. M., Ivanova, M. Y., Harder, V.S., Otten, L., Bilenberg, N., . . . Verhulst, F. C. (2011). International comparisons of behavioral and emotional problems in preschool children: Parents' reports from 24 societies. *Journal of Clinical Child and Adolescent Psychology, 40,* 456–467. doi:10.1080/15374416.2011.563472

Rescorla, L. A., Achenbach, T. M., Ivanova, M. Y., Bilenberg, N., Bjarnadottir, G., Denner, S., . . . Verhulst, F. C. (2012a). Behavioral/emotional problems of preschoolers:

Caregiver/ teacher reports from 15 societies. *Journal of Emotional and Behavioral Disorders, 20,* 68–81. doi:10.1177/1063426611434158

Rescorla, L. A., Ivanova, M. Y., Achenbach, T. M., Begovac, I., Chahed, M., Drugli, M. B., . . . Woo, B. (2012b). International epidemiology of child and adolescent psycho-pathology: 2. Integration and applications of dimensional findings from 44 societies. *Journal of the American Academy of Child and Adolescent Psychiatry, 51,* 1273–1283.

Rescorla, L. A., Ginzburg, S., Achenbach, T. M., Ivanova, M. Y., Almqvist, F., Bilenberg, N., . . . Verhulst, F. C. (2013). Cross-informant agreement between parent-reported and adolescent self-reported problems in 25 societies. *Journal of Clinical Child and Adolescent Psychology, 42,* 262–273.

Rescorla, L. A., Achenbach, T. M., Ivanova, M. Y., Turner, L. V. Au, A., Bellina, M., . . . Zasępa, E. (2015a). Problems and adaptive functioning reported by adults in 17 societies. Submitted for publication.

Rescorla, L. A., Achenbach, T. M., Ivanova, M. Y., Turner, L. V., Árnadóttir, H. A., Au, A., . . . Zasępa, E. (2015b). Collateral reports of problems and cross-informant agreement about adult psychopathology in 14 societies. Submitted for publication.

Rescorla, L. A., Bochicchio, L., Achenbach, T. M., Ivanova, M. Y., Almqvist, F., Begovac, I., . . . Verhulst, F. C. (2014). Parent-teacher agreement on children's problems in 21 societies. *Journal of Clinical Child and Adolescent Psychology, 43,* 627–642.

Sawyer, M. G., Arney, F. M., Baghurst, P. A., Clark, J. J., Graetz, R. J., Kosky, R. J., . . . Zubrick, S. R. (2001). The mental health of young people in Australia: Key findings from the Child and Adolescent Component of the National Survey of Mental Health and Well-being. *Australian and New Zealand Journal of Psychiatry, 35,* 806–814.

Shaffer, D., Fisher, P., Dulcan, M. K., Davies, M., Piacentini, J., Schwab-Stone, M. E., . . . Regier, D. A. (1996). The NIMH Diagnostic Interview Schedule for Children version 2.3. (DISC-2.3): Description, acceptability, prevalence rates, and performance in the MECA study. *Journal of the American Academy of Child and Adolescent Psychiatry, 35,* 865–877.

Shaffer, D., Fisher, P., Lucas, C. P., Dulcan, M. K., & Schwab-Stone, M. E. (2000). NIMH Diagnostic Interview Schedule for Children version IV (NIMH DISC-IV): Description, differences from previous versions, and reliability of some common diagnoses. *Journal of the American Academy of Child and Adolescent Psychiatry, 39,* 28–38. doi:10.1097/00004583–200001000–00014

Srinath, S., Girimaji, S. C., Gururaj, G., Seshadri, S., Subbakrishna, D. K., Bhola, P., & Kumar, N. (2005). Epidemiological study of child & adolescent psychiatric disorders in urban & rural areas of Bangalore, India. *Indian Journal of Medical Research, 122,* 67–79.

Stankov, L. (2011). Individual, country and societal cluster differences on measures of personality, attitudes, values, and social norms. *Learning and Individual Differences, 21,* 55–66.

Steinhausen, H. C., Metzke, C. W., Meier, M., & Kannenberg, R. (1998). Prevalence of child and adolescent psychiatric disorders: The Zurich Epidemiological Study. *Acta Psychiatrica Scandinavica, 98,* 262–271.

World Health Organization. (1992). *Mental disorders: Glossary and guide to their classification in accordance with the Tenth Revision of the International Classification of Diseases* (10th ed.). Geneva: World Health Organization.

Epilogue

Cross-Cultural Human Development: Following the Yellow Brick Road in Search of New Approaches for the 21st Century

Harry W. Gardiner

If I were to describe the current standing of cross-cultural human development and the direction it might take in the early years of the new millennium in only one word—that word would be one that has appeared often in this book: *contextualization.* It refers to the view that behavior cannot be meaningfully studied or fully understood independent of its *ecocultural* context.

This is not an entirely new approach but is firmly rooted in George Herbert Mead's *symbolic interactionism* (1934) as well as Urie Bronfenbrenner's original *ecological systems approach* (1975, 1979, 1989) and his evolving *bioecological model* (1999), to mention just a few of its ancestors. What *is* noteworthy is the frequency with which research linking contextualization and development is appearing in contemporary literature. In the pages that follow, I shall briefly comment on the origins of research on cross-cultural development, consider its relationship to other social sciences, evaluate where it is today, and speculate about its future.

I find myself in agreement with my longtime colleague, John Berry, who, in his autobiography in Michael Bond's book *Working at the Interface of Cultures,* said: "My view is that the ecological perspective is a continuing and evolving theme in thinking about the origins and functions of human diversity, and that a periodic attempt to synthesize and organize such thoughts into frameworks is a useful exercise." This I shall attempt to accomplish in this chapter and for our purpose, I will define *cross-cultural human development* as "cultural similarities and differences in developmental processes and their outcomes as expressed by behavior in individuals and groups" (Gardiner & Kosmitzki, 2011, p. 4).

CULTURE AND DEVELOPMENT

In the early days of this discipline, it was accurately (and frequently) pointed out that developmental psychology was *neither* cross-cultural *nor* interdisciplinary in its approach, while cross-cultural psychology *failed* to be developmental in its approach. For example, in 1981, Theodore Schwartz (1981) wrote that "anthropologists had ignored children in culture while developmental psychologists had ignored culture in children" (p. 4). However, in the past two decades, and particularly since 2010, progress—as described in the current volume—has been dramatic and we may be approaching what I like to call *the age of cross-cultural human development.*

RELATIONSHIP TO OTHER SOCIAL SCIENCES

In an article published two years before the turn of this century, titled "Cross-Cultural Psychology as a Scholarly Discipline," Segall, Lonner, and Berry (1998) posed a question: "Can it still be necessary, as we approach the millennium (as measured on the Western, Christian calendar), to advocate that all social scientists, psychologists especially, take culture seriously into account when attempting to understand human behavior?" (p. 1101). The answer, unfortunately, was yes! However, circumstances have vastly improved and continue to get even better as the authors and editors of this book, and others, clearly demonstrate. (See also Abela & Walker, 2014; Arnett, 2012.)

While cross-cultural psychology and cross-cultural human development both have long historical ties with general psychology, there are also connections to other social sciences, most notably sociology and anthropology. Although they often focus on kindred topics and frequently make use of similar concepts, approaches, and methodologies, the interface between the two disciplines has not always been a smooth one.

While examining the relationship between anthropology and psychology, Gustav Jahoda, an exceptional scholar with close ties to both disciplines and a sincere appreciation and understanding of each, has made the point that "[a]nthropologists have always been concerned with psychology, even if unwittingly. However, this interest has not been reciprocated by psychologists and psychology has, in many respects, remained narrowly culture-bound, largely ignoring the wider perspectives provided by anthropology" (1982, back cover). In more recent years, proponents of these two disciplines have begun to show greater appreciation for each other's points of view, although some are not yet ready to work closely with each other.

I believe an important goal in the future should be to search for threads of common interest between psychology and its sister disciplines and nurture them where they exist. Cooperative research efforts, like many of those cited in this collection, can only help to refine and sharpen our understanding of human behavior and the vital role culture plays in determining similarities and differences. Not to do so is like trying to clap with one hand!

THEORETICAL VIEWS AND PARADIGMS

One of the current debates highlighting efforts aimed at linking psychology and culture, including development, focuses on theorists and researchers employing two divergent approaches: those of *cross-cultural psychology* and those of *cultural psychology.* It is impossible, within the scope of this chapter, to unravel even a few of the threads that weave their way through this debate. There is no question that it will continue to be an important issue and one would do well to know as much as possible about it. In this regard, interested readers are directed to writings by Heine (2011), Keith (2013), and a proposed synthesis offered by Triandis (2000). Hopefully, these divergent views may one day merge or, at the very least, find a way to coexist.

EVOLVING TRENDS

While there is a remarkably expanding literature on cross-cultural human development, it remains a relatively new area and is not yet fully organized. An effort aimed at integrating existing research is found in Gardiner and Kosmitzki's book *Lives Across Cultures: Cross-Cultural Human Development* (2011). Let us briefly focus on two of the evolving trends mentioned there.

Contextual Influences

In a commentary on parenting in diverse cultures, Stevenson-Hinde (1998) proposes a model that allows more accurate measurement and greater understanding of parenting *practices* and *styles* within cultural contexts. Researchers planning studies of cultural similarities and differences in parenting can benefit from consideration of this model. In addition, one would do well to consider the recent work of Coleman (2014), Sorkhabi (2012), and Walker (2014).

Applications to Social Policy Issues

As part of his 1969 presidential address to members of the American Psychological Association, George Miller (1969) encouraged his listeners to "give psychology away." Now, following more than 100 years of developmental research and several decades of gathering information on cultural similarities and differences, I believe the time has come to "give cross-cultural (and cultural) psychology (as well as cultural anthropology) away" by devoting increased attention to successfully applying our theoretical findings to practical social policy issues, many of which have been successfully discussed in earlier chapters of this book.

More than 30 years ago, while teaching and doing research in Thailand, I wrote an article in which I suggested a two-year moratorium on conducting any more psychological research so we could sit back, read what had been done, try to make sense of it, and begin to make practical use of it. I did not think anyone would actually do this and, of course, unfortunately, no one did. Four decades later, I still remain convinced that it is a good idea.

A good beginning, aimed at more closely linking theory and practice (as well as "giving" research away), is the work of Çiğdem Kağitçibaşi and her "Turkish Early Enrichment Project" for mothers and children (2013). Focusing on early childhood care and education, she has transformed her country in ways that will be felt long into the new century. Her work has clearly demonstrated that cross-cultural developmental findings can be used to establish intervention strategies and policy positions relevant to children and families within a variety of cultural contexts.

Another example is the work of Mishra, Sinha, and Berry (1996) examining the psychological adaptation of tribal groups in India. Three groups (the Oraon, Birhar, and Asur), differing in settlement and occupation patterns, were compared in terms of cultural lifestyles, patterns of child socialization, cognitive behavior, and acculturation attitudes and experiences. Similar to Kağitçibaşi's research, the focus was on the application of findings, this time to problems of acculturative stress. The authors successfully introduced strategies for reducing such stress and providing better psychological adaptation. A similar approach could be applied to issues of immigration and problems of refugee resettlement seen almost daily throughout the world. Good starts in this direction are the chapters in this volume found in Part IV: Transnational and Immigrant Children. Readers are also directed to Berry, Poortinga, Breugelmans, Chasiotis, and Sam (2011), Bushong (2013), Chun, Organista, and Marin (2013), and Nguyen (2013).

One part of the world where the application of psychological principles to societal problems *has* been made a priority is Africa (see also Aptekar & Oliver, chapter 15, this volume). Mike Durojaiye (1987, 1993), a pioneer in African cross-cultural psychology (and once an officemate of mine during our doctoral studies at Manchester University in England), has stated, "There is a serious effort to make psychology an indigenous discipline useful to national development" (1987, p. 25). Other important work is Mundy-Castle's early analysis (1993) of rapid modernization and its psychological effects on peoples living in African communities and Nsamenang's studies and proposals (1992) for improving African family life and childrearing practices through the practical use of indigenous findings.

WHERE DO WE GO FROM HERE?

As we look to the future, several important and challenging questions present themselves. What kinds of cross-cultural human development studies need to be carried out in the future? How similar or different should this research be to that currently being conducted? In what ways will these new studies contribute to our understanding of human development and the ever-changing and increasingly complex world in which people live? What implications will future findings have for the design and construction of new developmental theories and how will these new theories affect even newer studies?

While the questions are easy to ask, finding appropriate answers is not. In this context, let me suggest a few possibilities. For example, researchers conducting future developmental studies should seriously consider making greater use of the triangulation design in which multiple concepts and methods are used to study a single phenomenon. A good illustration is a cross-cultural investigation by Dreher and Hayes (1993) consisting of an ethnographic study of marijuana use among rural Jamaican women along with standardized clinical evaluations of the development and health status of their children. In the words of the authors, "The methodological combination of ethnography and standardized instruments is not just a matter of coming at the same question from qualitative and quantitative perspectives. Rather, it is an essential feature of cross-cultural research. Ethnography tells us what questions to ask and how to ask them. The open-ended inquiries commonly associated with ethnography, however, may sacrifice comparability when answers fall into different domains. Standardized instruments, administered in as consistent a manner as possible, enhance comparability but are useful only when preliminary determination of the appropriate range and categories of responses are accompanied by ethnographic observations and interviews" (p. 227).

If you finish reading this chapter and go away with only one piece of information, this is what I would like you to take with you: I look forward to future cross-cultural research efforts focusing on developmental comparisons within cultural contexts that attempt to combine, in part, the ethnographic approaches of the anthropologist, the psychological theories and methodologies of the psychologist, and the social policy concerns of the sociologist.

In addition to highly creative and pioneering studies aimed at breaking new ground, I would like to see more attention given to clarifying, modifying, and extending existing knowledge and theories through careful (and well designed) replication of previous findings. As mentioned earlier, this is a frequently ignored (and often unappreciated) undertaking in which many findings may or may not be confirmed when viewed within *sociocultural settings* other than the ones in which they were originally conducted or at different time periods.

Super and Harkness published an extremely important chapter titled "The Environment as Culture in Developmental Research" (in a 1999 volume edited by Friedman & Wachs, *Measuring Environment Across the Life Span: Emerging Methods and Concepts*), which lays the foundation for answering many of the questions raised in this chapter. Specifically, they outline several methods of data collection that permit measurement of the three subsystems in their developmental niche framework.

LESSONS LEARNED AND WINDOWS OPENED TO THE FUTURE

At the beginning of this chapter, I stated if I were to choose one word to describe the direction that the study of cross-cultural human development would take in the years ahead, it would be *contextualization.* It is clear, from a reading of preceding chapters, that many authors in this volume share this view. In fact, the importance of studying the developmental context in order to better understand behavior is stressed so often that it can be viewed as a common theme connecting many of the contributions.

Another point made earlier in this chapter was the importance of bringing psychology and its sister disciplines closer together by developing interdisciplinary cooperative research efforts involving participants from a variety of cultural backgrounds along with a greater sensitivity to each other's theories, methodologies, unique research difficulties, and central social issues. It is encouraging to note that a number of authors in this volume have done, and are continuing to do, exactly this in their cross-cultural research on children and adolescents. Again, this becomes a general theme and, as such, bodes well for the future of the field: it provides models, as well as rich examples, for others to follow. Existing research that helps in these efforts includes the pioneering work by Georgas, Berry, van de Vijver, Kağitçibaşi, and Poortinga (2006).

Each chapter in this book, written by a variety of researchers—psychologists and anthropologists as well as seasoned leaders and younger scholars—represents the best in historical overviews and literature reviews of topics on the cutting edge of the field. The number and variety of cultural settings presented in these investigations is truly astounding, thereby providing a global perspective on a range of critically important issues not found anywhere else. Although the chapters were written independently and focus on a diversity of topics, approaches, and findings, several additional themes emerge and weave their way throughout the pages of this book. For example, a significant number of authors comment on the lack of well-designed studies from developing countries, the need to look more closely at the daily lives and activities of children, such as greater attention to sibling relationships and parental belief systems, and the importance of viewing behavior in other than Western perspectives.

Again, several authors (Achenbach, Wagner, Zahra, & Lee, Aptekar & Oliver, Gielen, and Roopnarine & Yildirim) join with me in stressing the need to place greater emphasis on applications to social policy issues such as immigration, acculturation, literacy and illiteracy, poverty, war, and education. The importance of parenting styles and methods of childcare play a central role in some of this research, while demonstrations of the resiliency of children and adolescents are also emphasized. In addition, my plea for more longitudinal studies is echoed (and in many cases clearly demonstrated) in many of these studies.

Finally, as researchers begin to design their present and future cross-cultural studies of children and adolescents, they would do well to first consider Gielen's discussion of worldwide trends in childrearing environments and Aptekar and Oliver's "Ten Commandments" for conducting research with street children, which have application to other topics as well.

Perhaps an appropriate way to end this chapter is to quote the closing lines I wrote for *Lives Across Cultures* (Gardiner & Kosmitzki, 2011): "Ahead of us lie tremendous challenges and opportunities. Speculating about where our cross-cultural journey will take us next is difficult. Wherever we go, it is certain to be an interesting and exciting adventure. Perhaps some of you will be the pioneer theorists and researchers who take us to the next point on this journey" (p. 274). I eagerly look forward to that day.

Like Dorothy and her three friends (the scarecrow, tin man, and lion), all of whom landed in the magical kingdom of Oz and had many fascinating and wonderful new cultural adventures (as well as misadventures), we need to have the brains, the heart, the courage, and the sense of adventure to follow our own yellow brick road in search of new approaches that will help us understand human development in the early years of the 21st century and far beyond.

REFERENCES

Abela, A., & Walker, J. (2014). Global changes in marriage, parenting and family life: An overview. In A. Abela & J. Walker (Eds.), *Contemporary issues in family studies: Global perspectives on partnerships, parenting, and support in a changing world* (pp. 5–15). Oxford, UK: Wiley & Sons.

Arnett, J.J. (2012). *Human development: A cultural approach*. Boston, MA: Pearson. Berry, J. (1997). Cruising the world: A nomad in academe. In M.H. Bond (Ed.), *Working at the interface of cultures: Eighteen lives in social science* (pp. 138–153). London, UK: Routledge.

Berry, J.W., Poortinga, Y.H., Breugelmans, S.M., Chasiotis, A., & Sam, D. (2011). *Cross-cultural psychology: Research and applications* (3rd ed.). Cambridge, UK: Cambridge University Press.

Bronfenbrenner, U. (1975). Reality and research in the ecology of human development. *Proceedings of the American Philosophical Society, 119,* 439–469.

Bronfenbrenner, U. (1979). *The ecology of human development: Experiments by nature and design.* Cambridge, MA: Harvard University Press.

Bronfenbrenner, U. (1989). Ecological systems theory. In R. Vasta (Ed.), *Six theories of child development* (Vol. 6, pp. 187–250). Greenwich, CT: JAI Press.

Bronfenbrenner, U. (1999). Environments in developmental perspective: Theoretical and operational models. In S. L. Friedman & T. D. Wachs (Eds.), *Measuring environment across the life span* (pp. 3–28). Washington, DC: American Psychological Association.

Bushong. L. J. (2013). *Belonging everywhere and nowhere: Insights into counseling the globally mobile.* Fishers, IN: Mango Tree International Services.

Chun, K. M., Organista, P. B., & Marin. G. (2003). *Acculturation: Advances in theory, measurement, and applied research.* Washington, DC: American Psychological Association.

Coleman, J. (2014). Parenting teenagers. In A. Abela & J. Walker (Eds.), *Contemporary issues in family studies: Global perspectives on partnerships, parenting, and support in a changing world* (pp. 203–214). Oxford, UK: Wiley & Sons.

Durojaiye, M. O. (1987). Black Africa. In A. R. Gilgen & C. K. Gilgen (Eds.), *International handbook of psychology* (pp. 24–36). New York: Greenwood Press.

Durojaiye, M. O. (1993). Indigenous psychology in Africa: The search for meaning. In U. Kim & J. W. Berry (Eds.), *Indigenous psychologies: Research and experience in cultural context* (pp. 211–220). Newbury Park, CA: Sage.

Gardiner, H. W., & Kosmitzki, C. (2011). *Lives across cultures: Cross-cultural human development* (5th ed.). Boston, MA: Allyn and Bacon.

Georgas, J., Berry, J. W., van de Vijver, F. J. R., Kağitçibaşi, Ç., & Poortinga. Y. H. (2006). *Families across cultures: A 30-nation psychological study.* Cambridge, UK: Cambridge University Press.

Heine, S. J. (2011). *Cultural psychology* (2nd ed.). Boston: Norton.

Jahoda, G. (1982). *Psychology and anthropology: A psychological perspective.* London, UK: Academic Press.

Kağitçibaşi, Ç. (2013). *Family, self, and human development across cultures* (2nd ed.). New York: Routledge.

Keith, K. D. (2013). *The encyclopedia of cross-cultural psychology.* Hoboken, NJ: Wiley-Blackwell.

Mead, G. H. (1934). *Mind, self, and society.* Chicago, IL: University of Chicago Press.

Miller, G. A. (1969). Psychology as a means of promoting human welfare. *American Psychologist, 24,* 1063–1075.

Mishra, R. C., Sinha, D., & Berry, J. W. (1996). *Ecology, acculturation, and psychological adaptation.* Thousand Oaks, CA: Sage.

Mundy-Castle, A. C. (1993). Human behaviour and national development: Conceptual and theoretical perspectives. *Ife Psychologia, 1,* 1–16.

Nguyen, A-M. T. (2013). Acculturation. In K. D. Keith, *The encyclopedia of cross-cultural psychology* (pp. 7–12). Hoboken, NJ: Wiley-Blackwell.

Nsamenang, A. B. (1992). *Human development in cultural context: A third world perspective.* Newbury Park, CA: Sage.

Schwartz, T. (1981). The acquisition of culture. *Ethos, 9,* 4–17.

Segall, M.H., Lonner, W.J., & Berry, J.W. (1998). Cross-cultural psychology as a scholarly discipline: On the flowering of culture in behavioral research. *American Psychologist, 53,* 1101–1110.

Sorkhabi, N. (2012). Parenting socialization effects in different cultures: Significance of directive parenting. *Psychological Reports, 110*(3), 854–878.

Stevenson-Hinde, J. (1998). Parenting in different cultures: Time to focus. *Developmental Psychology, 34,* 698–700.

Super, C.M., & Harkness, S. (1999). The environment as culture in developmental research. In S.L. Friedman & T.D. Wachs (Eds.), *Measuring environment across the life span* (pp. 279–323). Washington, DC: American Psychological Association.

Triandis, H.C. (2000). Cross-cultural versus cultural psychology: A synthesis? In A.L. Comunian & U.P. Gielen (Eds.), *International perspectives on human development* (pp. 81–95). Lengerich, Germany: Pabst Science.

Walker, J. (2014). The transition to parenthood: Choices and responsibilities. In A. Abela & J. Walker (Eds.), *Contemporary issues in family studies: Global perspectives on partnerships, parenting, and support in a changing world* (pp. 119–135). Oxford, UK: Wiley & Sons.

Selected Bibliography

General Introductions

Arnett, J. J. (2015). *Human development: A cultural approach* (2nd ed.). Upper Saddle, NJ: Pearson.

Berry, J. W. (2013). Achieving a global psychology. *Canadian Psychology, 54,* 55–61.

Berry, J. W., Poortinga, Y. H., Breugelmans, S. M., Chasiotis, A., & Sam, D. L. (2011). *Cross-cultural psychology: Research and applications* (3rd ed.). Cambridge, UK: Cambridge University Press.

Comunian, A. L., & Gielen, U. P. (Eds.). (2000). *International approaches to the family and development.* Lengerich, Germany: Pabst Science Publishers.

Gardiner, H. W., & Kosmitzki, C. (2010). *Lives across cultures: Cross-cultural human development* (5th ed.). Upper Saddle River, NJ: Prentice Hall.

Gershoff, E. T., Mistry, R. S., & Crosby, D. A. (Eds.). (2013). *Societal contexts of child development: Pathways of influence and implications for practice and policy.* New York: Oxford University Press.

Gielen, P.M., & Roopnarine, J. L. (Eds.). (2016). *Childhood and adolescence: Cross-cultural perspectives and applications* (2nd ed.). Westport, CT: Praeger.

Keith, K. D. (2010). *Cross-cultural psychology: Contemporary themes and perspectives.* Hoboken, NJ: Wiley-Blackwell.

LeVine, R. A., & New, R. (2008). *Anthropology and child development: A cross-cultural reader.* New York: Wiley-Blackwell.

Lott, B. (2009). *Multiculturalism and diversity: A social psychological perspective.* Hoboken, NJ: Wiley-Blackwell.

Marsella, A. J. (2005). Hegemonic globalization and cultural diversity: The risks of monoculturalism. *Australian Mosaic, 13*(11), 15–19.

Rogoff, B. (2003). *The cultural nature of human development.* New York: Oxford University Press.

Saraswathi, T. S. (Ed.). (2003). *Cross-cultural perspectives in human development: Theory, research and applications.* New Delhi, India: Sage.

Stevens, M. J., & Gielen, U. P. (Eds.). (2007). *Toward a global psychology. Theory, research, intervention, and pedagogy.* Mahwah, NJ: Erlbaum.

Handbooks

Arnett, J.J. (Ed.). (2006). *International encyclopedia of adolescence* (vols. 1–2). New York : Routledge.

Bornstein, M.H. (Ed.). (2010). *Handbook of cultural developmental science.* New York: Psychology Press.

Cabrera, N., & Tamis-LeMonda, C.S. (Eds.). (2014). *Handbook of father involvement: Multi-disciplinary perspectives* (2nd ed.). Mahwah, NJ: Erlbaum Associates.

Castles, S., & Miller, M.J. (2009). *The age of migration: International population movements in the modern world* (4th ed.). New York: Guilford Press.

Damon, W., & Lerner, R.M. (Eds.). (2006). *Handbook of child psychology* (6th ed.). New York: Wiley.

Jensen, L.A. (Ed.). (2015). *The Oxford handbook of human development and culture: An interdisciplinary perspective.* New York: Oxford University Press.

Lerner, R.M., Bornstein, M.H., & Leventhal, T. (Eds.). (2015). *Handbook of child psychology and developmental science: Ecological settings and processes.* (Vol. 4, 7th ed.). New York: Wiley.

Lerner, R.M., Liben, L.S., & Mueller, U. (Eds.). (2015). *Handbook of child psychology and developmental science: Cognitive processes.* New York: Wiley.

Parillo, V.N. (2011). *Strangers to these shores, Census update* (10th ed.). Upper Saddle River, NJ: Prentice Hall.

Pellegrini, A.D. (2015). *The Oxford handbook of the development of play.* Cambridge, UK: Oxford University Press.

Robila, M. (Ed.). (2014). *Handbook of family policies across the globe.* New York: Springer.

Rohner, R.P., & Khaleque, A. (Eds.). (2005). *Handbook for the study of parental acceptance and rejection* (4th ed.). Storrs, CT: Rohner Research Publications.

Roopnarine, J. (2010). Cultural variations in beliefs about play, parent-child play, and children's play: Meaning for childhood development. In P. Nathan & A.D. Pellegrini (Eds.), *The Oxford handbook of the development of play* (pp. 19–37). New York: Oxford University Press.

Sam, D.L., & Berry, J.W. (2015). *Cambridge handbook of acculturation psychology* (2nd ed.). Cambridge, UK: Cambridge University Press.

Valsiner, J. (Ed.). (2014). *The Oxford handbook of culture and psychology.* New York: Oxford University Press.

Villarruel, F., Carlo, G., Grau, J., Asmitia, M., Cabrera, N., & Chahin, J. (2009). *Handbook of U.S. Latino psychology: Developmental and community-based perspectives.* Thousand Oaks, CA: Sage.

Waters, M.C., Ueda, R., & Marrow, H.B. (Eds.). (2007). *The new Americans: A guide to immigration since 1965.* Cambridge, MA: Harvard University Press.

Related Books

Adler, L.L., & Gielen, U.P. (2001). *Cross-cultural topics in psychology* (2nd ed.). Westport, CT: Praeger.

Bekman, S., Aksu-Koc, A., Brewster Smith, M. (Eds.). (2012). *Perspectives on human development, family, and culture.* New York: Cambridge University Press.

Brock, A. (Ed.). (2006). *Internationalizing the history of psychology.* New York: New York University Press.

Denmark, F.L., Krauss, H., Wesner, R., Midlarksky, E., & Gielen, U.P. (Eds.). (2005). *Violence in schools: Cross-national and cross-cultural perspectives.* New York: Kluwer.

Holmes, R. (1998). *Fieldwork with children.* Thousand Oaks, CA: Sage.

Jensen, L.A. (Ed.). (2015). *Moral development in a global world: Research from a cultural developmental perspective.* Cambridge, UK: Cambridge University Press.

Kağitçibaşi, Ç. (2007). *Family, self, and human development across cultures: Theory and applications* (2nd ed.). New York: Psychology Press.

Kağitçibaşi, Ç., Smith, P., & Bond, M. (2006). *Understanding social psychology across cultures: Living and working in a changing world* (3rd ed.). London, UK: Sage.

Kim, U., Yang, K.-S., & Hwang, K.-K. (Eds.). (2010). *Indigenous and cultural psychology: Understanding people in context. International and cultural psychology.* New York: Springer.

Matsumoto, D., & Juang, L. (2012). *Culture and psychology* (5th ed.). Boston: Wadsworth.

Moghaddam, F. (2007). *Multiculturalism and intergroup relations: Psychological implications for democracy in global context.* Washington, DC: American Psychological Association.

Moghaddam, F., & Lee, N. (2006). Double reification: The process of universalizing psychology in the three worlds. In A. Brock (Ed.), *Internationalizing the history of psychology* (pp. 163–182). New York: New York University Press.

Roopnarine, J.L., & Gielen, U.P. (Eds.). (2005). *Families in global perspective.* Boston, MA: Pearson/Allyn and Bacon.

Saxe, G.B. (1982). Culture and the development of numerical cognition: Studies among the Oksapmin of Papua New Guinea. In C.J. Brainerd (Ed.), *Children's logical and mathematical cognition* (pp. 157–176). New York: Springer.

Shiraev, E.B., & Levy, D.A. (2012). *Cross-cultural psychology: Critical thinking and contemporary applications* (5th ed.). London, UK: Pearson.

United Nations Children's Fund (UNICEF). (2014). *The state of the world's children 2014, in numbers: Every child counts, revealing disparities, advancing children's rights.* New York: United Nations Publications. (Published yearly.)

United Nations Development Programme (UNDP). (2014). *Human development report 2014. Sustaining human progress: Reducing vulnerabilities and building resilience.* New York: UNDP. (Published yearly.)

van de Vijver, F.J.R., Chasiotis, A., & Breugelmans, S.M. (Eds.). (2011). *Fundamental questions in cross-cultural psychology.* Cambridge, UK: Cambridge University Press.

History of Childhood and Adolescence

Ariès, P. (1965). *Centuries of childhood: A social history of family life.* New York: Vintage.

Cunningham, H. (2005). *Children and childhood in Western society since 1500* (2nd ed.). New York: Routledge.

Fass, P.S. (Ed.). (2014). *The Routledge history of childhood in the Western world.* New York: Routledge.

Klapper, M.R. (2007). *Small strangers: The experiences of immigrant children in America, 1880–1925* (American Childhoods). Lanham, MD: Ivan R. Dee.

Stearns, P.N. (2011). *Childhood in world history* (2nd ed.). Oxford, UK: Routledge.

Infancy

Adolph, K.E., Karasik, L.B., & Tamis-LeMonda, C.S. (2010). Motor skills. In M.H. Bornstein (Ed.), *Handbook of cultural developmental science* (pp. 61–88). New York: Taylor & Francis.

Chen, X., Yang, F., & Fu, R. (2012). Culture and temperament. In M. Zentner & R.L. Shiner (Eds.), *Handbook of temperament* (pp. 462–478). New York: Guilford Press.

Crittenden, P.M. (2000). *The organization of attachment relationships: Maturation, culture, and context.* Cambridge, UK: Cambridge University Press.

DeLoache, J., & Gottlieb, A. (Eds.). (2000). *A world of babies: Imagined childcare guides for seven societies.* Cambridge, UK: Cambridge University Press.

Erdman, P., & Ng, K. (Eds). (2010). *Attachment: Expanding the cultural connections.* New York: Routledge.

Karasik, L.B., Adolph, K.E., Tamis-LeMonda, C.S., & Bornstein, M.H. (2010). WEIRD walking: Cross-cultural research on motor development. *Behavioral and Brain Sciences, 33* (2–3), 95–96.

Karasik, L.B., Tamis-LeMonda, C.S., Adolph, K.E., & Dimitropoulou, K.A. (2008). How mothers encourage and discourage infants' motor actions. *Infancy, 13,* 366–392.

Keller, H. (2007). *Cultures of infancy.* New York: Taylor & Francis.

Otto, H., & Keller, H. (Eds.). (2014). *Different faces of attachment: Cultural variations on a universal human need.* Cambridge, UK: Cambridge University Press.

van Ijzendoorn, M.H., & Sagi-Schwartz, A. (2008). Cross-cultural patterns of attachment: Universal and contextual dimensions. In J. Cassidy & P.R. Shaver (Eds.), *Handbook of attachment: Theory, research, and clinical applications* (2nd ed., pp. 880–905). New York: Guilford Press.

Children around the World

Cabrera, N.J., Villarruel, F.A., & Fitzgerald, H.E. (Eds.). (2011). *Latina and Latino children's mental health: Volume 1: Development and context.* Santa Barbara, CA: Praeger/ABC-CLIO.

Chen, X., & French, D.C. (2008). Children's social competence in cultural context. *Annual Review of Psychology, 59,* 591–616.

Georgas, J., Berry, J.W., van de Vijver, F.J.R., Kağitçibaşi, Ç., & Poortinga, Y.H. (Eds.). (2006). *Families across cultures: A 30-nation psychological study.* Cambridge, UK: Cambridge University Press.

Hewlett, B.S., & Lamb, M.E. (Eds.). (2005). *Hunter-gatherer childhoods: Evolutionary, developmental and cultural perspectives.* New Brunswick, NJ: Transaction.

Holmes, R. (2013). Children's play and culture. *Scholarpedia, 8*(6), 31016.

Lancy, D.F. (2015). *The anthropology of childhood: Cherubs, chattel, changelings* (2nd ed.). Cambridge, UK: Cambridge University Press.

Lancy, D.F., Bock, J., & Gaskins, S. (Eds.). (2010). *The anthropology of learning in childhood.* Lanham, MD: AltaMira Press.

Lancy, D.F., & Grove, M.A. (2011). "Getting noticed": Middle childhood in cross-cultural perspective. *Human Nature, 22,* 281–302.

LeVine, R.A., & New, R.S. (Eds.). (2008). *Anthropology and child development: A cross-cultural reader.* Malden, MA: Blackwell.

Nsamenang, A. B. (2009). Cultures of early childhood care and education. In M. Fleer, M. Hedegaard, & J. Tudge (Eds.), *World yearbook of education 2009: Childhood studies and the impact of globalization: Policies and practices at global and local levels* (pp. 23–45). New York: Routledge.

Raffaelli, M., & Larson, R. W. (Eds.). (1999). *Homeless and working youth around the world: Exploring developmental issues.* San Francisco, CA: Jossey-Bass.

Robila, M., & Krishnakumar, A. (2006). Economic pressure and children's psychological functioning. *Journal of Child and Family Studies, 15*(4), 433–441.

Rohner, R. P. (Ed.). (2010). Perceived teacher acceptance, parental acceptance, and the adjustment, achievement, and behavior of school-going youths internationally. [Special Issue] *Cross-Cultural Research, 44*(3).

Roopnarine, J. L., Patte, M., Johnson, J. E., & Kuschner, D. (Eds.). (2015). *International perspectives on children's play.* England: Open University Press/McGraw Hill.

Immigrant and Minority Children

Alba, R., & Walters, M. (2011). *The next generation: Immigrant youth in a comparative perspective.* New York: New York University Press.

Artico, C. I. (2003). *Latino families broken by immigration: The adolescent's perceptions.* El Paso, TX: LFB Scholarly Publishing.

Berry, J. W., Phinney, J. S., Sam, D. L., & Vedder, P. (2006). Immigrant youth: Acculturation, identity and adaptation. *Applied Psychology: An International Review, 55,* 303–332.

Cabrera, N. J., Villarruel, F. A., & Fitzgerald, H. E. (Eds.). (2011). *Latina and Latino children's mental health: Volume 1: Development and context.* Santa Barbara, CA: Praeger.

Cabrera, N. J., Villarruel, F. A., & Fitzgerald, H. E. (Eds.). (2011). *Latina and Latino children's mental health: Volume 2: Prevention and treatment.* Santa Barbara, CA: ABC-CLIO.

Caldera, Y. M., & Lindsey, L. (Eds.). (2014). *Mexican American children and families: Multidisciplinary perspectives.* New York: Routledge.

Chuang, S. S., & Gielen, U. P. (2009). Understanding immigrant families from around the world: Introduction to the special issue. *Journal of Family Psychology, 23*(3), 275–279.

Davey, M., Stone Fish, L., Askew, J., & Robila, M. (2003). Parenting practices and the transmission of ethnic identity. *Journal of Marital and Family Therapy 29*(2), 195–208.

Dreby, J. (2010). *Divided by borders: Mexican migrants and their children.* Berkeley, CA: University of California Press.

Foner, N. (Ed.). (2009). *Across generations: Immigrant families in America.* New York: New York University Press.

Henke, H. (Ed.). (2005). *Crossing over: Comparing recent migration in the United States and Europe.* Lanham, MD: Lexington Books.

Kasinitz, P., Waters, M., Mollenkopf, J., & Holdway, J. (2009). *Inheriting the city: The children of immigrants come of age.* New York: Russell Sage Foundation.

Lansford, J. E., Deater-Deckard, K., & Bornstein, M. H. (Eds.). (2007). *Immigrant families in contemporary society.* New York: The Guilford Press.

Nguyen, A., & Benet-Martinez, V. (2013). Biculturalism and adjustment: A meta-analysis. *Journal of Cross-Cultural Psychology, 44,* 122–159.

Robila, M. (2014). The impact of migration on children's psychological functioning and education in the Republic of Moldova. *International Migration, 52*(3), 221–235.

Robila, M. (2010). *Eastern European immigrant families*. New York: Routledge.

Robila, M., & Akinsulure-Smith, A. (2012). Psychological ethics and immigration. In M.M. Leach, M.J. Stevens, A. Ferrero, Y. Korkut, & G. Lindsay (Eds.), *The Oxford handbook of international psychological ethics* (pp. 191–200). New York: Oxford University Press.

Spirou, S., & Christou (Eds.). (2014). *Children and borders*. Basingstoke, UK: Palgrave Macmillan.

Suárez-Orozco, C., Suárez-Orozco, M.M., & Todorova, I. (2008). *Learning a new land: Immigrant students in American society*. Cambridge, MA: Belknap/Harvard University Press.

Sung, B.L. (1987). *The adjustment experience of Chinese immigrant children in New York City*. Staten Island, NY: Center for Migration Studies.

Vaughans, K.C., & Spielberg, W. (Eds.). (2014). *The psychology of black boys and adolescents* (Vols. 1–2). Santa Barbara, CA: Praeger.

Veale, A., & Doná, G. (2014). *Child and youth migration: Mobility-in-migration in an era of globalization*. New York: Palgrave Macmillan.

Waters, M. (1999). *Black identities: West Indians immigrant dreams and American realities*. Cambridge, MA: Harvard University Press.

Wingens, M., Windzio, M., de Valk, H., & Aybek, C. (Eds.). (2014). *A life-course perspective on migration and integration*. Berlin, Germany: Springer.

Zatz, M.S., & Rodriguez, N. (2015). *Dreams and nightmares: Immigration policy, youth, and families*. Oakland, CA: University of California Press.

Intercountry Adoption

Ballard, R.L., Goodno, N.H., Cochran, R.F., & Milbrandt, J.A. (Eds.). (2015). *The intercountry adoption debate. Dialogues across disciplines*. Newcastle, UK: Cambridge Scholars Publishing.

Bowen, J. (2014). *Wish you happy forever: What China's orphans taught me about moving mountains*. New York: HarperOne.

Gibbons, J.L., & Rotabi, K.S. (Eds.). (2012). *Intercountry adoption: Policies, practices, and outcomes. Contemporary social work studies*. Burlington, VT: Ashgate.

Louie, A. (2015). *How Chinese are you? Adopted Chinese youth and their families negotiate identity and culture*. New York: New York University Press.

Parenting and Childrearing

Cabrera, N., & Tamis-LeMonda, C.S. (Eds.). (2014). *Handbook of father involvement: Multi-disciplinary perspectives* (2nd ed.). Mahwah, NJ: Erlbaum.

Greenfield, P.M., Keller, H., Fuligni, A., & Maynard, A. (2003). Cultural pathways through universal development. *Annual Review of Psychology, 54*, 461–490.

Johanson, K. (2010). Culture for or by the child? "'Children's culture" and cultural policy. *Poetics, 38*, 386–401.

Lamb, M.E. (Ed.). (2010). *The role of the father in child development* (4th ed.). Hoboken, NJ: Wiley.

Lansford, J. E., Chang, L., Dodge, K. A., Malone, P. S., Oburu, P., Palmérus, K., & Quinn, N. (2005). Physical discipline and children's adjustment: Cultural normativeness as a moderator. *Child Development, 76,* 1234–1246.

Rohner, R. P. (Ed.). (2006). Corporal punishment, parental acceptance-rejection, and youth's psychological adjustment. [Special Issue] *Cross-Cultural Research, 40,* 215–324.

Roopnarine, J. L. (Ed.). (2015). *Fathers across cultures: The importance, roles, and diverse practices of dads.* Santa Barbara, CA: Praeger.

Selin, H. (2014). *Parenting across cultures: Childrearing, motherhood and fatherhood in non-Western cultures.* Dordrecht, Netherlands: Springer.

Schlegel, A., & Barry III, H. (1991). *Adolescence: An anthropological inquiry.* New York: Free Press.

Shwalb, D. W., Shwalb, B. J., & Lamb, M. E. (Eds.). (2013). *Fathers in cultural context.* New York: Routledge.

Sorkhabi, N. (2005). Applicability of Baumrind's parent typology to collective cultures: Analysis of cultural explanations of parent socialization effects. *International Journal of Behavioral Development, 29,* 552–563.

Adolescence

Aptekar, L. (2013). *In the lion's mouth: Hope and heartbreak in humanitarian assistance.* (2nd ed). Bloomington, IN: Xeibris.

Arnett, J. J. (Ed.). (2012). *Adolescent psychology around the world.* New York: Psychology Press.

Brown, B. B., Larson, R. W., & Saraswathi, T. S. (Eds.). (2002). *The world's youth: Adolescence in eight regions of the globe.* Cambridge, UK: Cambridge University Press.

Chen, X., Chung, J., & Hsiao, C. (2011). Peer interactions and relationships from a cross-cultural perspective. In K. H. Rubin, W. M. Bukowski, & B. Laursen (Eds.), *Handbook of peer interactions, relationships, and groups* (pp. 432–451). New York: Guilford Press.

Gibbons, J. L., & Stiles, D. A. (2004). *The thoughts of youth: An international perspective on adolescents' ideal persons.* Greenwich, CT: Information Age Publishing.

Holmes, R., Liden, S., & Shin, L. (2013). Adolescent perceptions of social media in a Pacific Rim community. *Child Studies in Diverse Contexts, 3,* 81–103.

Kumar, A., & Srivastava, K. (2011). Cultural and social practices regarding menstruation among adolescent girls. *Social Work in Public Health,* 26, 594–604.

Manderson, L., & Liamputtong, P. (Eds.). (2002). *Coming of age in South and Southeast Asia: Youth, courtship and sexuality.* Nias Studies in Asian Topics, 30. Surrey, UK: Curzon Press.

Skoog, T., Stattin, H., Ruiselova, Z., & Özdemir, M. (2013). Female pubertal timing and problem behavior: The role of culture. *International Journal of Behavioral Development, 37,* 357–365.

Vulnerable Children

Batstone, D. (2010). *Not for sale: The return of the global slave trade—and how we can fight it.* New York: Harper Collins.

Child Soldiers International (2012). *Louder than words: An agenda for action to end state use of child soldiers.* http://www.child-soldiers.org/global_report_reader.php?id=562

DasGupta, S., Dasgupta, S.D., Nayak, P., Bailey, A., Madge, V., Pande, A., . . . Maisel, J. (2014). *Globalization and transnational surrogacy in India: Outsourcing life.* Lanham, MD: Lexington Books.

Grennan, C. (2011). *Little princes: One man's promise to bring home the lost children of Nepal.* New York: Harper Collins.

International Labor Organization (ILO). (2013). *Marking progress against child labour: Global estimates on child labor 2000–2012.* Geneva, Switzerland: International Labour Office. http://www.ilo.org/wcmsp5/groups/public/—-ed_norm/—-ipec/documents/publication/wcms_221513.pdf

Johnson, D.J., Agbényiga, D.L., & Hitchcock, R.K. (Eds.). (2013). *Vulnerable children: Global challenges in education, health, well-being, and child rights.* New York: Springer.

Kara, S. (2010). *Sex trafficking: Inside the business of modern slavery.* New York: Columbia University Press.

Mishra, L. (2011). *Human bondage: Tracing its roots in India.* Thousand Oaks, CA: Sage.

Sagade, J. (2012). *Child marriage in India: Socio-legal and human rights dimensions* (2nd ed.). Oxford, UK: Oxford University Press.

Shelley, L. (2010). *Human trafficking: A global perspective.* Cambridge, UK: Cambridge University Press.

Territo, L., & Kirkham, G. (2009). *International sex trafficking of women & children.* New York: Looseleaf Law Publications.

Working with Children and their Families

Aptekar, L. (2013). *In the lion's mouth: Hope and heartbreak in humanitarian assistance.* (2nd ed.). Bloomington, IN: Xeibris.

Cabrera, N.J., Villarruel, F.A., & Fitzgerald, H.E. (Eds.). (2011). *Latina and Latino children's mental health: Volume 2: Prevention and treatment.* Santa Barbara, CA: ABC-CLIO.

Chung, I., & Shibusawa, T. (2014). *Contemporary clinical practice with Asian immigrants: A relational framework with culturally responsive approaches.* New York: Routledge.

Gerstein, L.H., Heppner, P.P., Ægisdottir, S., Leung, S.M.A., & Norsworthy, K.L. (Eds.). (2009). *International handbook of cross-cultural counseling: Cultural assumptions and practices worldwide.* Thousand Oaks, CA: Sage.

Good, T.D., Jones, W., & Jackson, V. (2011). Families with African American roots. In E.W. Lynch & M.J. Hanson (Eds.), *Developing cross-cultural competence: A guide for working with children and their families* (4th ed., pp. 140–189). Baltimore, MD: Paul H. Brookes.

Joe, J.R., & Malach, R.S. (2011). Families with American Indian roots. In E.W. Lynch & M.J. Hanson (Eds.), *Developing cross-cultural competence: A guide for working with children and their families* (4th ed., pp. 110–139). Baltimore, MD: Paul H. Brookes.

Lamb, M.E., Chuang, S.S., & Cabrera, N. (2003). Promoting child adjustment by fostering positive paternal involvement. In R.M. Lerner, F. Jacobs, & D. Wertlieb (Eds.), *Handbook of applied developmental science* (Vol. 1, pp. 211–232). Thousand Oaks, CA: Sage.

Lynch, E.W., & Hanson, M.J. (Eds.). (2011). *Developing cross-cultural competence: A guide for working with children and their families* (4th ed.). Baltimore, MD: Paul H. Brookes.

Moodley, R., Gielen, U.P., & Wu, R. (2013). *Handbook of counseling and psychotherapy in an international context.* New York: Routledge.

Robila, M., & Sandberg, J. (2011). Family therapy with Eastern European immigrants: Recommendations for practice. *International Journal of Migration, Health and Social Care, 7*(4), 182–196.

Roopnarine, J. L., & Johnson, J. E. (2013). (Eds.). (2012). *Approaches to early childhood education* (6th ed.). New York: Pearson.

Wessells, M. (2006). *Child soldiers—from violence to protection.* Cambridge, MA: Harvard University Press

Zuniga, M.E. (2011). Families with Latino roots. In E.W. Lynch & M.J. Hanson (Eds.), *Developing cross-cultural competence: A guide for working with children and their families* (4th ed., pp. 190–233). Baltimore, MD: Paul H. Brookes.

Adulthood

Bouvard, M. (Ed.). (2013). *Mothers of adult children.* Lanham, MA: Lexington Books.

Cavanaugh, J.C., & Blanchard-Fields, F. (Eds.). (2014). *Adult development and aging* (7th ed.). Boston: Cengage Learning.

Cruikshank, M. (2013). *Learning to be old: Gender, culture, and aging* (3rd ed.). Lanham, MD: Rowman & Littlefield.

Eyetsemitan, F.E., & Gire, J.T. (2003). *Aging and adult development in the developing world: Applying Western theories and concepts.* Westport, CT: Greenwood.

Harper, S., & Hamblin, K. (Eds.). (2014). *International handbook on aging and public policy.* Cheltenham, UK: Edward Elgar.

Hoare, C. (Ed.). (2011). *The Oxford handbook of reciprocal adult development and learning* (2nd ed.). New York: Oxford University Press.

Klinenberg, E. (2013). *Going solo: The extraordinary rise and surprising appeal of living alone.* New York: Penguin.

Mehrotra, C.M., & Wagner, L.S. (Eds.). (2008). *Aging and diversity: An active learning experience* (2nd ed.). New York: Taylor & Francis.

Ofahengaue Vakalahi, H.F., Simpson, G.M., & Giunta, N. (Eds.). (2014). *The collective spirit of aging across cultures.* Dordrecht, Netherlands: Springer.

Parkes, C.M., Laungani, P., & Young, W. (1997). *Death and bereavement across cultures.* London, UK: Routledge.

Willis, S.L., & Martin, M. (Eds.). (2005). *Middle adulthood: A lifespan perspective.* Thousand Oaks, CA: Sage.

The Americas

Browne, K.A. (2013). *Tropic tendencies: Rhetoric, popular culture, and the Anglophone Caribbean.* Pittsburgh, PA: University of Pittsburgh Press.

Cabrera, N., & Garcia-Coll, C. (2004). Latino fathers: Uncharted territory in need of much exploration. In M.E. Lamb (Ed.), *The role of father in child development* (4th ed., pp. 98–120). Hoboken, NJ: Wiley.

Cabrera, N.J., Villarruel, F.A., & Fitzgerald, H.E. (Eds.). (2011). *Latina and Latino children's mental health: Volume 1: Development and context.* Santa Barbara, CA: Praeger.

Cabrera, N. J., Villarruel, F. A., & Fitzgerald, H. E. (Eds.). (2011). *Latina and Latino children's mental health: Volume 2: Prevention and treatment.* Santa Barbara, CA: ABC-CLIO.

Caldera, Y. M., & Lindsey, E. (Eds.). (2014). *Mexican-American children and families: Multidisciplinary perspectives.* New York: Routledge.

Ferguson, G. M., & Bornstein, M. H. (2012). Remote acculturation: The "Americanization" of Jamaican islanders. *International Journal of Behavioral Development, 36*(3), 167–177.

Good, T. D., Jones, W., & Jackson, V. (2011). Families with African American roots. In E. W. Lynch & M. J. Hanson (Eds.), *Developing cross-cultural competence: A guide for working with children and their families* (4th ed., pp. 140–189). Baltimore, MD: Paul H. Brookes.

Greenfield, P.M. (2004). *Weaving generations together: Evolving creativity in the Maya of Chiapas.* Santa Fe, NM: School of American Research (SAR).

Joe, J. R., & Malach, R. S. (2011). Families with American Indian roots. In E. W. Lynch & M. J. Hanson (Eds.), *Developing cross-cultural competence: A guide for working with children and their families* (4th ed., pp. 110–139). Baltimore, MD: Paul H. Brookes.

Kramer, K. L. (2005). *Maya children: Helpers on the farm.* Cambridge, MA: Harvard University Press.

Logie, C., & Roopnarine, J. L. (2013). *Issues and perspectives in early childhood development and education in Caribbean countries.* La Romaine, Trinidad: Caribbean Publishers.

Markstrom, C. A. (2008). *Empowerment of North American Indian girls: Ritual expressions at puberty.* Lincoln, NE: University of Nebraska Press.

Roopnarine, J. L., & Chadee, D. (Eds.). (2016). *Caribbean psychology: Indigenous contributions to a global discipline.* Washington, DC: American Psychological Association.

Scheper-Hughes, N. (1992). *Death without weeping: The violence of everyday life in Brazil.* Berkeley, CA: University of California Press.

Tsethlikai, M., & Rogoff, B. (2013). Involvement in traditional cultural practices and American Indian children's incidental recall of a folktale. *Developmental Psychology, 49,* 568–578.

Vaughans, K. C., & Spielberg, W. (Eds.). (2014). *The psychology of black boys and adolescents,* Vols. 1–2. Santa Barbara, CA: Praeger.

Villarruel, F., Carlo, G., Grau, J., Asmitia, M., Cabrera, N., & Chahin, J. (2009). *Handbook of U.S. Latino psychology: Developmental and community-based perspectives.* Thousand Oaks, CA: Sage.

Zuniga, M. E. (2011). Families with Latino roots. In E. W. Lynch & M. J. Hanson (Eds.), *Developing cross-cultural competence: A guide for working with children and their families* (4th ed., pp. 190–233). Baltimore, MD: Paul H. Brookes.

Near and Middle East, North Africa

Ahmed, R. A., & Gielen, U. P. (Eds.). (1998). *Psychology in the Arab countries.* Menoufia, Egypt: Menoufia University Press.

El-Kogali, S., & Krafft, C. (2015). *Expanding opportunities for the next generation: Early childhood development in the Middle East and North Africa* (Directions in Development). Washington, DC: World Bank Publications.

Fernea, E.W. (1995). *Children in the Muslim Middle East.* Austin, TX: University of Texas Press.

Friedl, E. (1997). *Children of Deh Koh: Young life in an Iranian village.* Syracuse, NY: Syracuse University Press.

Gregg, G.S. (2005). *The Middle East: A cultural psychology.* New York: Oxford University Press.

Gregg, G.S. (2007). *Culture and identity in a Muslim society.* New York: Oxford University Press.

Sharifzaadeh, V. (2011). Families with Middle Eastern roots. In E.W. Lynch & M.J. Hanson (Eds.), *Developing cross-cultural competence: A guide for working with children and their families* (4th ed., pp. 392–436). Baltimore, MD: Paul H. Brookes.

Wagner, D.A. (1994). *Literacy, culture and development: Becoming literate in Morocco.* Cambridge, UK: University of Cambridge Press.

Sub-Saharan Africa

Akinsulure-Smith, A.M., & Smith, H. (2014). Emerging family policies in Sierra Leone. In M. Robila (Ed.), *Family policies across the globe* (pp. 15–29). New York: Springer.

Beckwith, C., & Fisher, A. (1999). *African ceremonies.* (Vols. 1–2). New York: Abrams.

Beguy, D., Kabiru, C.W., & Ezeh, A.C. (2011). Timing and sequencing of events marking the transition to adulthood in two informal settlements in Nairobi, Kenya. *Journal of Urban Health, 88,* Suppl., S318–340.

Blum, R.W. (2007). Youth in Sub-Saharan Africa. *Journal of Adolescent Health, 41*(3), 230–238.

Holloway, K. (2007). *Monique and the mango rains: Two years with a midwife in Mali* (West Africa). Long Grove, IL: Waveland Press.

Jaramillo, A., & Mingat, A. (2008). Early childhood care and education in Sub-Saharan Africa: What would it take to meet the millennium development goals? In M. Garcia, A. Pence, & J.L. Evans (Eds.). *Africa's future, Africa's challenge: Early childhood care and development in Sub-Saharan Africa* (pp. 51–70). Washington, DC: World Bank.

Marlowe, F.W. (2010). *The Hadza: Hunter–gatherers of Tanzania.* Berkeley, CA: University of California Press.

Nduna, M., & Jewkes, R. (2012). Disempowerment and psychological distress in the lives of young people in Eastern Cape, South Africa. *Journal of Child and Family Studies, 21*(6), 1018–1027.

Nsamenang, A. B. (2008b). Agency in early childhood learning and development in Cameroon. *Contemporary Issues in Early Childhood Development, 9*(3), 211–223.

Nsamenang, A.B. (2004). *Cultures of human development and education: Challenge to growing up African.* Hauppauge, NY: Nova Science.

Saitoti, T.O. (1988). *The world of a Maasai warrior: An autobiography.* Berkeley, CA: University of California Press.

Wessells, M. (2006). *Child soldiers—from violence to protection.* Cambridge, MA: Harvard University Press.

Indian Subcontinent

Chapin, B.L. (2014). *Childhood in a Sri Lankan village: Shaping hierarchy and desire.* New Brunswick, NJ: Rutgers University Press.

Chaudhary, N. (2011). Rethinking human development research and theory in contemporary Indian society. In G. Misra (Ed.), *Contemporary Indian psychology* (pp. 165–180). New Delhi, India: Oxford University Press.

Chaudhary, N., & Pillai, P. (in press). Research and the young child in India: Shifting from alienation to adaptability. In M. Kontopodis & A.N. Perret-Clermont (Eds.), From personal to the collective and back (Special Issue). *European Journal of Psychology and Education.*

Chaudhary, N., & Shukla, S. (2014). "Children's work is to play": Beliefs and practices related to childhood among Indians. In J.L. Roopnarine, M. Patte, J.E. Johnson, & D. Kuschner (Eds.), *International perspectives on children's play.* Maidenhead, UK: Open University Press/McGraw Hill Education.

Chaudhary, N. (2012). Father's role in the Indian family: A story that must be told. In D. Shwalb, B. Shwalb, & M. Lamb (Eds.), *Fathers in cultural context* (pp. 68–94). New York: Routledge.

Jacob, N. (2011). Families with South Asian roots. In E.W. Lynch & M.J. Hanson (Eds.), *Developing cross-cultural competence: A guide for working with children and their families* (4th ed., pp. 437–462). Baltimore, MD: Paul H. Brookes.

Kakar, S. (Ed.). (1981). *The inner world—A psychoanalytic study of children and society in India.* New Delhi, India: Oxford University Press.

Mahoney, R. (2014). *For the benefits of those who see: Dispatches from the world of the blind.* New York: Little, Brown. (About schools for the blind in Tibet and India.)

Saraswathi, T.S. (Ed.). (1999). *Culture, socialization and human development: Theory, research and applications in India.* New Delhi, India: Sage.

Seymour, S. (1999). *Women, family, and childcare in India.* New York: Cambridge University Press.

Sharma, D. (Ed.). (2013). *Childhood, family and socio-cultural change in India: Reinterpreting the inner world.* New Delhi, India: Oxford Press.

South Seas and Southeast Asia

Goransson, K. (2009). *The binding tie: Chinese intergenerational relations in modern Singapore.* Honolulu, HI: University of Hawaii Press.

Herdt, G. (1994). *Guardians of the flutes: Volume 1: Idioms of masculinity.* Chicago, IL: University of Chicago Press.

Herdt, G.A. (2005). *The Sambia: Ritual, sexuality, and change in Papua New Guinea.* Independence, KY: Wadsworth.

Manderson, L., & Liamputtong, P. (Eds.). (2002). *Coming of age in South and Southeast Asia: Youth, courtship and sexuality.* Surrey, UK: Curzon Press.

Morton, H. (1996). *Becoming Tongan: An ethnography of childhood.* Honolulu, HI: University of Hawai'i Press.

Santos, R.M., & Chan, S. (2011). Families with Filipino roots. In E.W. Lynch & M.J. Hanson (Eds.), *Developing cross-cultural competence: A guide for working with children and their families* (4th ed., pp. 319–364). Baltimore, MD: Paul H. Brookes.

East Asia

Bond, M.H. (2015). *Oxford handbook of Chinese psychology.* Oxford, UK: Oxford University Press.

Chan, S., & Chen, D. (2011). Families with Asian roots. In E.W. Lynch & M.J. Hanson (Eds.), *Developing cross-cultural competence: A guide for working with children and their families* (4th ed., pp. 234–317). Baltimore, MD: Paul H. Brookes.

Chen, X. (2015). Socio-emotional development in Chinese children. In M.H. Bond (Ed.), *Oxford handbook of Chinese psychology* (pp. 37–52). Oxford, UK: Oxford University Press.

Lau, S. (Ed.). (1997). *Growing up the Chinese way: Chinese child and adolescent development.* Hong Kong: Chinese University Press.

Shek, D.T.L., Sun, R.C.F., & Ma, C.M.S. (Eds.). (2014). *Chinese adolescents in Hong Kong: Family life, psychological well-being and risk behavior.* New York: Springer.

Shwalb, B.J., Nakazawa, J., & Shwalb, D.W. (Eds.). (2005). *Developmental psychology: Theory, practice, and research from Japan.* Charlotte, NC: Information Age Publishing.

Tobin, J., Hsueh, Y., & Karasawa, M. (2009). *Preschool in three cultures revisited: China, Japan, and the United States.* Chicago, IL: University of Chicago Press.

About the Editors and Contributors

Editors

Uwe P. Gielen (PhD in social psychology, Harvard University) is professor-emeritus and executive director of the Institute for International and Cross-Cultural Psychology at St. Francis College, New York. His work centers on cross-cultural and international psychology, Chinese American immigrant children, Tibetan studies, international family psychology, and moral development. The editor, coeditor, and author of 22 volumes, he has given more than 330 scientific presentations in 34 countries. His most recent coedited books include *Handbook of Counseling and Psychotherapy in an International Context* (2013), *The Global Obama: Crossroads of Leadership in the 21st Century* (2014), and *Pathfinders in International Psychology* (2015). He has served as president of the Society for Cross-Cultural Research, the International Council of Psychologists, and the International Psychology Division of the American Psychology Association. In 2005, he received the Distinguished International Psychologist Award from APA's International Psychology Division.

Jaipaul L. Roopnarine (PhD in child development, University of Wisconsin) is Pearl Falk Professor of Child and Family Studies and director of the Jack Reilly Institute for Early Childhood and Provider Education; adjunct professor of education and senior research scientist at the Family Development and Children's Research Centre at the University of the West Indies, Trinidad and Tobago. He served as a consultant to the Roving Caregiver Program implemented in Caribbean countries, and assisted in revising the national early childhood curriculum for the government of Guyana. He has held visiting appointments at numerous universities located in India, Jamaica, Trinidad-Tobago, and the United States. His research interests include father-child relationships across cultures, Caribbean families and childhood outcomes, early childhood education in international perspective, children's play across cultures, immigrant families and schooling in the

United States. He has published extensively in the areas of developmental psychology and early childhood education and is currently the editor of the journal *Fathering*.

Contributors

Thomas M. Achenbach, PhD, is professor of psychiatry and psychology and president of the Research Center for Children, Youth, and Families at the University of Vermont. He has been a German Government Fellow at the University of Heidelberg and a senior faculty fellow at Jean Piaget's Center for Genetic Epistemology in Geneva. He authored the first book on developmental psychopathology and has given presentations on multicultural aspects of psychopathology in 40 countries.

Ramadan A. Ahmed (PhD, Leipzig University, Germany) is professor-emeritus of psychology, Menoufia University, Egypt. His research interests include cognitive and moral development, and the effects of perceived parental acceptance-rejection on children and adolescents. He has taught psychology at universities in Sudan, Egypt, and Kuwait. He edited the first handbook on Arab psychology in collaboration with Uwe P. Gielen (1998, 2006). In 1994, he received Egypt's State Incentive Award and in 2008, the Outstanding International Psychologist Award from APA's International Psychology Division.

Lewis Aptekar, PhD, is chair and professor of counselor education at San Jose State University. He is a past president of the Society of Cross-Cultural Research. He has received Fulbright scholarships, a Nehru Visiting Professorship, a Kellogg Foundation Fellowship, and a Rotarian Ambassadorship. His books include *Street Children of Cali; Environmental Disasters in Global Perspective; In the Lion's Mouth: Hope and Heartbreak in Humanitarian Assistance,* and *Street Children and Homeless Youth: A Cross-Cultural Perspective.*

Gene H. Bell-Villada, PhD, was born in Haiti and grew up in Puerto Rico, Cuba, and Venezuela. A professor of Romance languages at Williams College, he is author or editor of 12 books, among them a memoir, *Overseas American: Growing Up Gringo in the Tropics* (2005), and a collection (coedited with Nina Sichel), *Writing Out of Limbo: International Childhoods, Global Nomads and Third Culture Kids* (2010).

John W. Berry (PhD, University of Edinburgh) is professor emeritus of psychology at Queen's University, Canada, and research professor, National

Research University Higher School of Economics, Moscow, Russia. In 2001, he received Honorary Doctorates from the University of Athens and Université de Genève. He has done extensive work on acculturation and published over 30 books in the areas of cross-cultural, intercultural, social and cognitive psychology with various colleagues.

Deborah L. Best, PhD, is the William L. Poteat Professor of Psychology, Wake Forest University. She is past president of the International Association for Cross-Cultural Psychology and the Society for Cross-Cultural Research. She is editor of the *Journal of Cross-Cultural Psychology* and coedited the four-volume set, *Cross-Cultural Psychology* (2009), Sage Benchmarks in Psychology Series.

Caitlin D. Bush is a graduate student in the Department of Psychology at Wake Forest University. She received her BA in psychology from Wake Forest in 2014. Caitlin's research interests include the complexity of parent-child relationships, cultural and class differences in parenting during early childhood, and emotional development in preschoolers.

Florence L. Denmark, PhD, is an internationally recognized scholar and policy maker. She has six honorary degrees and numerous awards, including one for Outstanding Lifetime Contributions to Psychology. One of the founders of the psychology of women field, she is a past president of the APA, Eastern Psychological Association, Psi Chi and International Council of Psychologists and is involved at the United Nations. Her books include *Psychology of Women: A Handbook of Issues and Theories* and *Engendering Psychology: Women and Gender Revisited.*

Emily A.A. Dow is a doctoral candidate in developmental psychology at the Graduate Center, City University of New York. She is interested in making connections between theoretical developmental psychology and educational practices and policy implications. Specifically, her research is focused on early childhood education, with past research related to teacher-student relationships.

Harry W. Gardiner, professor emeritus at the University of Wisconsin-La Crosse, is a cross-cultural developmental psychologist with an MA (University of Hawaii) and PhD (Manchester University). He has engaged in training, teaching, and research in Europe, Asia, and the United States. He has authored *Lives Across Cultures: Cross-Cultural Human Development* (5th ed.). He is a past president of the Society for Cross-Cultural Research and a charter member of the International Association for Cross-Cultural Psychology.

Judith L. Gibbons, PhD, is professor emerita of psychology at Saint Louis University, the president of the Interamerican Society of Psychology, and the editor of the American Psychological Association journal *International Perspectives in Psychology: Research, Practice, Consultation*. Her research interests include intercountry adoption, adolescent development, gender, and cross-cultural and international psychology.

M. Annette Grove received her BS in 2007 and MS in 2010 from Utah State University. She has conducted fieldwork in Huanchaco, Trujillo, Peru and in Utah. She has coauthored several journal articles and book chapters on childhood with David Lancy.

Jennifer Ho, MA, is currently pursuing her PsyD in clinical psychology at Yeshiva University. Her interests include cross-cultural psychology, the acculturation and psychosocial adjustment of Chinese American adolescents and older adults, and integrating research into clinical practice.

Jung-Hwan Hyun, PhD, is professor in the Department of Child Care & Education at Seoul Theological University. He holds a BA from Pukyoung National University, Korea, an MS from Tokyo Gakugei University, and a PhD from Hiroshima University. His research interests focus on children's cognitive and behavioral development.

Abdul Khaleque, PhD, is working as senior scientist in the Ronald and Nancy Rohner Center for the Study of Interpersonal Acceptance and Rejection at the University of Connecticut. He also works as adjunct faculty in the Department of Human Development and Family Studies at the University of Connecticut. His current research interests include cross-cultural parenting and lifespan development, and interpersonal acceptance and psychological adjustment of children and adults.

David F. Lancy, PhD, has done fieldwork with children in Liberia, Papua New Guinea, Mormon Utah, Trinidad (Fulbright Fellow), Sweden (Fulbright Fellow), Uganda, Madagascar, and in urban schools in the United States. The *Anthropology of Childhood* draws on this previous work and also on his experience reviewing and synthesizing the work of others as reflected in a book-length survey of qualitative research methods published in 1993. Lancy has authored five and edited three books as well as over 70 articles and book chapters. In 2011, he was given Utah State University's Thorne Award as the premier scholar.

Jinsol Lee received an MEd degree from Harvard University and is currently a PhD student at the University of Pennsylvania Graduate School of

Education, studying international education and human development from a cross-cultural perspective.

Ashley E. Maynard (PhD, 1999, UCLA Psychology) is professor and chair of the Department of Psychology at the University of Hawaii. Her postdoctoral training was in anthropology and cultural psychology (UCLA Department of Neuropsychiatry and Biobehavioral Sciences). She has always used mixed methods to study culture and human development.

Jun Nakazawa is professor of developmental psychology at Chiba University. He holds BA, MA, and PhD degrees from Hiroshima University. His research interests include cognitive and emotional regulation of young children, children's socialization and fathering, and literacy of *manga* (Japanese comic) reading.

Lisa Oliver (PhD in counseling psychology, Stanford University) is the chair for the Department of Educational Leadership at San José State University (SJSU). She is currently the treasurer for the Society for Cross-Cultural Research and a faculty-in-residence for Student Academic Success Services at SJSU. Her areas of research include identity development, multicultural education, globalization in higher education, cultural psychology, student retention, and community engagement.

Carrol S. Perrino, PhD, serves on the faculty in the Department of Psychology at Morgan State University in Baltimore, Maryland. Her research reflects a commitment to developing methodological and statistical tools to enhance the investigation of real-world problems including IPV, sexual harassment, and violence against children.

Katelyn E. Poelker is a doctoral student in experimental psychology at Saint Louis University with a concentration in developmental psychology. She is interested in children and adolescents' socioemotional development, specifically the influence of culture in the social world of youth. Currently, her research focuses on Guatemalan adolescents' experiences with gratitude and envy.

Ronald P. Rohner, PhD, is director of the Ronald and Nancy Rohner Center for the Study of Interpersonal Acceptance and Rejection in the Department of Human Development and Family Studies at the University of Connecticut, Storrs. He is also professor emeritus of family studies and anthropology at the university. His research interests focus on interpersonal acceptance and rejection, major styles of parenting—especially the warmth dimension of parenting—and on their worldwide consequences for children and adults.

Barbara J. Shwalb, PhD, is retired from the Southern Utah University Psychology Department. She holds BS and MAT degrees from Southeast Missouri State University and a PhD from the University of Michigan (Combined Program in Education and Psychology). Her research interests include cross-cultural developmental and learning issues, and the development of respect and disrespect. Her books include *Japanese Childrearing: Two Generations of Scholarship* (1996), *Applied Developmental Psychology: Theory, Practice and Research from Japan* (2005), and *Fathers in Cultural Psychology* (2013).

David W. Shwalb is professor of psychology at Southern Utah University. He holds a BA degree from Oberlin College and MA and PhD degrees from the University of Michigan (developmental psychology). His research interests include socialization in school and family settings, fathering, and grandparenting. Her books include *Japanese Childrearing: Two Generations of Scholarship* (1996), *Applied Developmental Psychology: Theory, Practice and Research from Japan* (2005), and *Fathers in Cultural Psychology* (2013).

Janet A. Sigal, PhD, is professor emerita in psychology, at Fairleigh Dickinson University. Her research focuses on violence against women, and she is the coeditor of a two-volume set on international perspectives on violence against girls and women. She is a fellow in Divisions 1, 35, and 52 of the American Psychological Association. She is the past president of Division 1 of APA, currently serves as the APA Main Representative to the United Nations, and is the vice-chair of the NGO Committee on Aging.

Renata Strashnaya is a doctoral candidate in the Psychology Program at the Graduate Center, City University of New York. Her research focuses on young adults' personal and social constructions of identity across interpersonal, sociopolitical, and historical contexts. Her current project explores the transition to college from the perspective of a diverse group of first-time college students within an urban city university system as they engage in cultural practices of higher education.

Paul Vedder, PhD, is professor of clinical child and adolescent studies at Leiden University in the Netherlands. His research focuses on acculturation in youth, and he is primarily interested in inter- and intragenerational transmission processes and in the link between acculturation processes and adaptation outcomes in domains such as social competence, language proficiency, and the quality of interethnic relations.

Daniel A. Wagner (PhD, University of Michigan) is the UNESCO Chair in Learning and Literacy, and professor of education at the University of Pennsylvania and director of the International Educational Development Program. He has extensive experience in national and international educational issues, and has served as an advisor to UNESCO, UNICEF, World Bank, USAID, DFID, and others on international development issues. He is the recipient of the 2014 UNESCO Confucius International Literacy Prize. In addition to over 160 professional publications, Dr. Wagner has written/edited 23 books, including *Literacy: Developing the Future* and *Literacy: An International Handbook.*

Felicia Wright earned her BS degree in psychology from Fayetteville State University and her MA degree in experimental psychology from Towson University. She is currently a doctoral student at Morgan State University, majoring in psychometrics.

Elif Dede Yildirim is a PhD candidate in the Department of Child and Family Studies at Syracuse University. She received MS degrees in applied statistics and child and family studies from Syracuse University and a bachelor's degree in sociology from Sakarya University, Turkey. Her research interests focus on physical punishment and parenting across cultures, poverty, and children's socioemotional development.

Fatima Tuz Zahra is a doctoral research fellow at University of Pennsylvania's Graduate School of Education specializing in International Educational Development. For several years she has been serving as the International Educational Development Doctoral Concentration Coordinator.

Talia Zarbiv is currently a third year doctoral student at Pace University's School Clinical Child Psychology APA accredited program and an assistant to Dr. Florence Denmark. She graduated with honors from Rutgers University, where she wrote her honors thesis on posttraumatic stress disorder within Israeli society. She is a member of Psi Chi and Phi Beta Kappa.

Index